Natural Selection

Natural Selection

GARY GIDDINS ON COMEDY, FILM, MUSIC, AND BOOKS

GARY GIDDINS

OXFORD
UNIVERSITY PRESS
2006

OXFORD
UNIVERSITY PRESS

Oxford University Press, Inc., publishes works that further
Oxford University's objective of excellence
in research, scholarship, and education.

Oxford   New York
Auckland   Cape Town   Dar es Salaam   Hong Kong   Karachi
Kuala Lumpur   Madrid   Melbourne   Mexico City   Nairobi
New Delhi   Shanghai   Taipei   Toronto

With offices in
Argentina   Austria   Brazil   Chile   Czech Republic   France   Greece
Guatemala   Hungary   Italy   Japan   Poland   Portugal   Singapore
South Korea   Switzerland   Thailand   Turkey   Ukraine   Vietnam

Copyright © 2006 by Gary Giddins

Published by Oxford University Press, Inc.
198 Madison Avenue, New York, NY 10016
www.oup.com

Oxford is a registered trademark of Oxford University Press

Library of Congress Cataloging-in-Publication Data
Giddins, Gary.
Natural selection : Gary Giddins on comedy, film, music, and books
/ Gary Giddins.
p. cm.
Includes index.
ISBN-13: 978-0-19-517951-4
ISBN-10: 0-19-517951-X
1. Motion pictures—Reviews. 2. Music—Reviews.
3. Books—Reviews. I. Title.
PN1995.G485 2006
791.43'75—dc22
2005032469

1 3 5 7 9 8 6 4 2
Printed in the United States of America
on acid-free paper

FOR DEBORAH AND LEA

Sir Joshua Reynolds has observed, with great truth, that Johnson considered Garrick to be as it were his property. *He would allow no man either to blame or praise Garrick in his presence, without contradicting him.* —Boswell, *Life of Johnson*

"Let faith oust fact; let fancy oust memory; I look deep down and do believe." —Starbuck in Melville, *Moby Dick*

He had not lightly cast aside the disillusioning knowledge of a past which had now so strangely become the future.
—Thorne Smith, *The Glorious Pool*

DESDEMONA. *What wouldst write of me, if thou shouldst praise me?*
IAGO. *Oh, gentle lady, do not put me to't,*
For I am nothing if not critical. —Shakespeare, *Othello*

"'Tain't What You Do (It's the Way That You Do It)"
—Sy Oliver, song title

Contents

Introduction

1. Intelligent Design

My first published film reviews appeared one month before my first published concert review. It happened in a roundabout way.

I had been knocking around New York for more than a year, dutifully tying my tie and presenting my resume (four years as a recalcitrant undergraduate) at interviews that went nowhere while collecting enough rejections from newspapers and magazines to insulate a Quonset hut. For a few months I worked at a bookstore but was fired for advising a customer who had bought many books on my counsel not to buy one. Record producer John Hammond, whom I had met and corresponded with a year earlier, had promised me a position at Columbia Records upon graduation. He finally conceded, after having me visit his office almost daily for several weeks, that no such job existed. But would I like to write a liner note for an album by a *maahvelous* rock guitarist? May I do it anonymously? If you prefer. What the hell.

Columbia paid me, but happily for all concerned, decided not to use my strenuous blurb. I was more and less fortunate at RCA Victor, where a lovely woman, whose name I am ashamed to have forgotten, regularly gave me miscellaneous liner note assignments, most published pseudonymously. An inadvertent exception was *More Golden Gems from the Carter Family*. The author's credit reads, "Mr. Giddins, a free-lance writer from New York, has been a follower of the Carter Family for many years." The part regarding New York was correct in that I was born in Brooklyn—I lived on Long Island. The rest was a stretch (though I admire the Carter Family), and dissuaded me from further hackwork with or without attribution.

In this spirit, I tentatively submitted to interviews with a personnel apparatchik at *Time* who, perhaps misinterpreting my Anglicized name and rebounding from a multiple-martini lunch, volunteered that he didn't much care for Jews, and with a public relations executive who brusquely asked how I would sell his client's brand of pretzels—at which point, a discontented Cheeverian future passed before my eyes.

Earlier that year, my father had made a comment that has never failed me as unimpeachable career advice.

We were waiting on the platform for the Long Island Railroad, which headed him (playing pinochle) to his company in the garment center and me (reading) to another mislaid day on John Hammond's couch. He mentioned that a couple of my childhood friends had gone into their fathers' businesses at starting salaries that would be respectable today, 35 years later. I asked if it bothered him that I had never expressed any desire to follow in his line. He said that the trucking business had been good to him and provided him with a great life, yet he had never wanted me "to have to associate with that element." He had in mind criminals with whom he was forced to deal, not newsweeklies or pretzel flacks, but good advice is almost always flexible.

Eventually I presented myself to Dan Morgenstern, who at that time held the now nonexistent position of *Down Beat*'s New York editor and was one of the writers I most admired in the world. Dan and I chatted about jazz, and after batting around a few possibilities, he suggested I review McCoy Tyner's trio at Slug's. He called to have me placed on the guest list. That evening I was shown to a ringside table, where I asked for a Jack Daniels and laid out before me, with, I like to think, the panache of a surgeon assembling his instruments, a pen and pad. The patient arrived to enthusiastic applause. I recall nothing else except the drummer, Alphonse Mouzon, who completely drowned out Tyner and my ambition.

What I should have done, of course, is pick myself up and walk to the bar or another point in the room where the piano might have proved audible and the drummer less, shall we say, brawny. Instead, I called Dan the next morning and explained that I could not review a set I had not heard; nor did I want to make my debut with a fractious review of a musician I greatly admired. Maybe it was just a bad set. Should I go back tonight? Well, he couldn't exactly get them to comp me again. Chalk that one to experience.

Fortunately, I had also convinced Dan to allow me to pursue a different kind of story. Charles Mingus had just published a long-awaited autobiography, *Beneath the Underdog*, an extraordinary book but also a puzzlement because it in no way resembled the 1,000-page Work in Progress he had described in interviews. For one thing, it did not include any of the stimulating excerpts that had been published over the years. Moreover, it contained the prominent credit, "Edited by Nel King," with an auctorial note describing her as "probably the only white person who could have done it."

Mingus had been off the scene in the late 1960s, a difficult time for jazz, but publication of his book boosted his spirits, and he was about to bring a sextet into the Village Vanguard. Arriving early, I saw him standing alone under the awning and introduced myself. He said, or grunted, pleasantly enough, that he didn't want to talk about the book. So I listened happily to his band and wrote a review, my first, which I submitted to Dan.

I can't recall how I got Nel King's number, but she invited me to her apartment, which would have been spacious even if it had had furniture. It didn't because she was moving to California that week. There were a few chairs, a sofa on which I set a tape recorder, and, on the glossy wood floor, a portable record changer, stacked with albums by Mingus and Dave Brubeck, both of whom Nel had worked with on her one produced screenplay, *All Night Long*—a 1961 British jazz version of *Othello*, co-written with the blacklisted Paul Jarrico. She was enthusiastic, gracious, informative: everything you want in an interviewee.

There was only one problem. When I asked almost anything about *Beneath the Underdog*, she would began to answer and then motion with her hand for me to turn off the tape recorder. She did not mind telling me, but she didn't want this part to go into the article because it might upset Charles. I gave my word. After this happened half a dozen times, I threw in the towel, turned off the recorder, and listened to a score of anecdotes, none of which I could convey then or remember now. Chalk that one to experience, too.

The next morning Nel phoned to say that an old friend, Paul Sargeant Clark, had been named editor of the *Hollywood Reporter*, and asked if she would be interested in reviewing movies. She wasn't, but she knew someone who might be perfect for the job—if I was interested.

An avid film lover who had haunted movie theaters since early childhood and all but camped out at the Thalia, New Yorker, and Museum of Modern Art, I first warmed to criticism as a discipline through the movie writings of Dwight Macdonald, and for two years had programmed a film series at college. I religiously checked off titles in Andrew Sarris's *The American Cinema*, determined to see them all, and read every small, overpriced volume from The Tantivity Press. Of course I was interested! Though to be honest: At this point, if someone had offered me a post writing about wine, I would have considered all the Boone's Farm, Gallo, and checkered-tablecloth Chianti I had quaffed and thought myself perfectly suited for that job, too.

Paul Clark asked me to send three reviews—I attended a movie that afternoon and two more the next day, and mailed in my musings. He approved and put me in touch with the New York editor, who advised me of my first three screenings. That week in January, I reviewed *To Find a Man*, *XY & Zee*, and *Carry On, Henry VIII*, demonstrating a disdainful pomposity that justifiably gave Clark second thoughts. Yet he allowed me to continue. In writing for a trade paper, you review everything, including pictures that never found and did not merit a distributor or were shunted (in the ancient equivalent of straight-to-video) to triple-bills on Forty-Second Street. Watching them is torment; writing about them corrodes the soul. Still, if the devil tells you he is confiscating two hours of your life and offers you the choice between spending them sitting through *Pope Joan* or burning in hell, you'd probably be wise to choose *Pope Joan*.

Meanwhile, the February *Down Beat* arrived with my accounting of Mingus at the Vanguard. Now *that* I was proud of. Other assignments followed, and pretty soon I was raking in the dough: $5 per film review in the *Hollywood Reporter*, $7 per record review in *Down Beat*. This went on for a year.

2. Natural Selection

Did I mention that I had also acquired a day job? Ignoring my father's advice I had fallen in with a bad element and became a copyboy at *The New York Post*, sharpening pencils, fetching food and coffee, distributing AP and UPI bulletins from the wire room, and, after someone in the drama department learned that I was writing for the *Hollywood Reporter*, secretly vetting copy by a critic prone to sleeping through screenings.

A Galapagos of resentful editors and frustrated reporters, the *Post* was a kind of derelict reef where every day brought a new anecdote with which to frighten small children. At my induction, the copyboy boss gave me the tour and, pointing to the long city desk, identified each editor, finishing with the comment: "Their testicles are preserved in jars of formaldehyde in Mrs. Schiff's safe." Dorothy Schiff owned the once-liberal paper until she sold it to Rupert Murdoch a few years later. When one of her reporters was made editor, other reporters convened to ask if he could do anything to alleviate their misery. He told them, invoking union rules that shield worker bees but not management bees, "The only thing I can do today that I couldn't do yesterday is get myself fired."

For a while, I was assigned to the features department, where four disgruntled, alarmingly pale men competed for the roles of Bob Cratchit or Uriah Heep, depending on their moods or who visited their domain. When almost any woman reporter left the room, having had her copy edited, they would often unburden themselves, wittily characterizing her by her genitals. An editor sounded me out about working in the sports department. I said that the last sporting event I attended was at Ebbets Field, but that a fellow copyboy was a sports fanatic and would love that job. I was told that the department chief did not want a Negro working for him.

Affirmative action at the *Post* meant one black reporter, who had been there since the 1950s; one copyboy; a man who served in the cafeteria; and Everett, the chauffeur to Mrs. Schiff. Once when I was in the elevator, wheeling a hand-truck stacked with the latest edition, Everett and the great lady entered. I smiled as we stood in silence for several seconds, then reached over to hit Close when I noticed Everett fingering Open. I figured we were waiting for someone, until he leaned over to whisper, "Please get out." Relating this story to a reporter, I was admonished that Mrs. Schiff never shared the elevator with employees—when she enters, you exit. She may have had good reason. A veteran nightside editor was renowned for presenting women employees, though presumably not Mrs. S, with the gift of underpants.

By late 1972, I realized that I had to make a decision: music or movies. I couldn't do both without feeling like a dilettante. Not that much mulling was required. I had a fever to write about jazz and the overconfident conviction that what I had to say no one else was saying. The thought of not writing about jazz was unimaginable. Of film, I was just an eager vendor of opinions, forever obliged for the apprenticeship of writing lunch-hour reviews, but just one voice among dozens, many of them smarter, more committed, and more original than mine. Also, the decision was sort of made for me.

The way it worked at the *Reporter* was that if a film screened first on the West Coast, Arthur Knight reviewed it—on the East Coast, me. *Lady Sings the Blues* was set to screen the same day on both coasts, and I volunteered for it, explaining that I knew something about Billie Holiday, the film's putative subject, and had read the book of that name. My bid was, as they say, green-lighted, and my calm and reasoned review published. I had already come through a storm warning a couple of weeks before, when the owner's son had flown to New York and bawled me out for an intemperate review of *Cancel My Reservation*, the film that canceled Bob Hope's film career. Holding my review and shaking with anger, he sputtered, "What do you mean calling television 'the wonderful world of packaged insipidity'? Television is our family." "It isn't my family." "That's why you won't be with us much longer." "Am I fired?" No, he said, but tone it down.

The October 18 issue ran seven of my reviews (it was the time of the New York Film Festival), including notices of a few good ones—*Tout Va Bien*, *Two English Girls*, and *Images*—as well as *Lady Sings the Blues*. The way I heard it, mostly from the New York editor, Paramount threatened to withdraw advertising unless the *Reporter* ran a second review. Paul Clark asked Arthur Knight to see the film. Knight reported back that he agreed with me: The film is an abomination. No second review ran. Clark resigned or was let go. I continued to file reviews for several weeks, until the New York editor told me to desist. I wasn't fired, he consoled, but they were regrouping. Hold tight. Then he was let go. Someone would get back to me about my standing. I'm still waiting.

My music writing had picked up, however, and I began reviewing weekly for the *Village Voice*. Oddly enough, one of my first pieces was about the making of the movie *Lenny*. I had been visiting Miami, where it was shooting, and a mutual friend introduced me to the star, Dustin Hoffman, whom an editor agreed would make for a good interview. Hoffman explained that he couldn't give interviews until completion, but suggested that I take work as an extra and write about that. So I acquiesced to a haircut and an ill-fitting black jacket, and took a seat in a nightclub scene for two days. The article generated an encouraging and much appreciated letter from *Voice* columnist Arthur Bell; lunch with a book editor, who wanted me to collaborate on a biography of Lenny Bruce with Bruce's erstwhile organist (not a good fit); my first agent; and my determination to sink or swim as a critic.

On my last day at the *Post*, I was instructed to meet with an executive for a leave-taking formality. This fellow, in a three-piece pinstripe, warned me never to write about anything I had seen or experienced at the *Post*, threatening that if I did I would be blacklisted from the news-paper business for life. This, at the paper that took on Joe McCarthy! As proof of his power, he mentioned Jack Newfield, who had written an infamous piece about his time at the *Post* and now worked as a star investigative columnist for the *Voice*, not a real newspaper. Newfield, he said, would never again write for a real newspaper no matter what. (Newfield later worked as a columnist for the *Post*, the *News*, *Newsday*, and the *Sun*.) Finally, the warden said I was free to go. Breathing in South Street's fishy air, I resolved to go straight.

3. Creationism

During the next 30 years, I wrote my column, "Weather Bird," for the *Voice*, occasionally taking time to write essays and reviews of movies and books. In 1990, Jim Hoberman, the *Voice*'s luminous film critic, took a sabbatical and asked me to fill in. For a year, I returned to a regimen of screening rooms, writing a movie column every week and a music column once a month, and soon discovered that—though they were the same length—the former took me far less time to write.

One reason was purely technical. A far greater percentage of a movie review is concrete, involving the story line and the diverse contributions of director, writer, actors, photographer, and so forth. Music reviews, beyond the identification of the musicians and the tunes, are largely abstract.

Another reason was psychological. The jazz world is confined and intimate, especially in New York. It is impossible to avoid acquaintanceships and even friendships with some of the very people whose work we evaluate. That's one of the job's primary perquisites. (Have you ever hung out with Sarah Vaughan? As she so memorably sang, "They can't take that away from me.") Short of staying home and reviewing records, there is no way to avoid meeting musicians at gigs, parties, festivals, and funerals, on panels and at lectures, in classrooms and at record sessions, through journalistic assignments or purely informational queries (as in "What was the name of that third piece you played, the one that goes da-di-da-da-daaa?"). If we venture beyond criticism, as most of us have, writing album notes or producing concerts, friendships may develop into conflicts of interest.

Like it or not, in writing about jazz over a long period of time, we become a part of the jazz world. And while this connectedness doesn't necessarily mute our voices, it does call for nuance. Writing about movies, by contrast, was positively bracing, a liberating invitation to chuck fine distinctions in favor of bumptious scorn, when called for, as it often was. On the other hand, droll rejoinders proved a feckless response to a largely Hollywood diet—all those screenings of the living dead draining faith, hope, and especially charity, not to mention perspective and ordinary goodwill.

Sometimes I slipped into a syndrome described by Dwight Macdonald when trying to argue the virtue of his refusal to attend most movies. Film critics, he said, are subjected to so much junk that when they see something that keeps them awake and perhaps interested, they assume it must be a masterpiece. Macdonald, who disdained pop culture (a poor start for a film critic, which in those days meant Antonioni, yes, Hitchcock, are you kidding?), but wrote more entertainingly than most who embraced it, could not be so easily fooled. Or so he said—he left a long paper trail for all to examine. Me, I was often fooled. After a few weeks on the job, I began requesting a second screening when I liked a film too passionately; I had few doubts about passionately hating a film.

My movie year underscored for me one of the most invigorating aspects of writing about jazz, especially at the *Voice*, where I could pretty much fill my page as I pleased: the complete freedom to travel through time and write about any style or aspect of the music that appealed to me at any given moment. A newspaper critic of film, theater, dance, books, or art has to review the new work or exhibit. With music and especially jazz, the latitude is almost without limit.

Whether I felt inclined to write about mainstream, bebop, avant-garde, swing, or Dixieland jazz, instrumental or vocal, grand master or young unknown, I could scan the club listings and find something in that arena. And if there was nothing very exciting on the club scene (rarely the case), I could choose between new recordings and reissues. All of jazz constantly recycles itself, allowing the critic to choose among many destinations. The devil had little custody of my time: If I chanced upon a tiresome set, I could always check out another club or peruse the stack of discs. I could focus on what I admired—on what I wanted you to admire or at least know it existed.

Home video, to which I became instantly addicted, taping thousands of movies, then switching to laser discs, and then DVDs, increased my movie zeal. When I left the *Voice* to work on other projects, I figured I would keep my byline afloat with a monthly column in *Jazz Times* and adding a DVD column. *The New York Sun*, a politically frightening but culturally discerning daily, allowed me a chance to write essays not unlike those I wrote for "Weather Bird"—around 1,600 words, every two weeks. DVDs similarly allowed me to roam freely through time and space with one exception. I had to steer clear of the present. I couldn't review the DVD of a film that had been reviewed theatrically six months before.

Like records, which capture only one aspect of jazz and not necessarily the best part, DVDs can act as a disabling narcotic. Visits to repertory theaters continue to remind me, sometimes dramatically, that watching a film on television, regardless of print quality or tube size, is not the same as watching a movie on a flat looming screen in the company of a sympathetic audience. You not only see more, you see differently, blissfully dwarfed before the altar. A crowd veers toward laugh-lines and emotional peaks that an individual at home scarcely notices. The very tempo of the film mutates—the momentum sharpened in the absence of phone, snack, and other breaks, as individual concentration subtly shifts toward a rhythmical groupthink.

The mechanical reproduction of art proceeds apace, as collections replace canons and collectors supersede the canonically educated. The old epiphany of seeing a Vermeer and discovering that the finest prints cannot begin to reproduce its glow and affect is now routinely echoed by filmgoers viewing an old picture on a big screen. It is similarly true of many musicians and other performing artists. Life is unfair that way, coils being mortal. Didn't get to see Beethoven in concert or King Oliver at Lincoln Gardens? Too bad. Didn't get to see Louis Armstrong live? Too bad, again: The many hours of existing footage, though often magnificent, fail to capture his magic aura, a human St. Elmo's fire that was unmistakable and irreproducible. Only writing loses nothing to reproduction, though it may lose plenty to time, place, and translation.

Jazz and film have much in common, beyond parallel births, changing technologies, and competing bids as America's preeminent cultural love child, which helps to explain why so many—Vachel Lindsay, Langston Hughes, Otis Ferguson, Orson Welles, James Agee, Charlie Parker, James Baldwin, Martin Williams, and countless others—embraced them both. They are resolutely manipulative arts. Music continuously mines emotional responses; movies are structured around emotional releases, whether musical, comical, tear-jerking, shocking, pornographic, or suspenseful. Musical works and movies usually exist in concise units of time, their effectiveness dependent on tempo, rhythm, contrast, style, and interaction.

Benny Carter (a jazz god who supported himself writing film scores) once noted that the problem in playing reed and brass instruments is not the dissimilar embouchures but the necessity of giving both the same amount of time. If he practiced half an hour on alto saxophone, he did the same on trumpet. An imprecise analogy may exist for different kinds of writing, say music crit and film crit, which, similarities notwithstanding, draw on different parts of the critical sensibility—abstract and concrete, spontaneous and intellectual. They offer contrary ways to think and to sort responses, yet each exemplifies what Wallace Stevens called "a new knowledge of reality."

Which is why I was agreeably surprised to find that in choosing selections to keep company in this volume, I had faithfully practiced both embouchures—persistently if by no means equally—for some time. The essays are divided into four sections (Comedy, Film, Music, and Books), some arranged by theme, others capriciously, and many would fit as neatly in any of the four groupings: there are reviews of books about film, music, and comedy; of films about music; of music for films, and so forth. The four sections, however, do impose an arbitrary order and I prefer a foolish consistency to none at all.

Acknowledgments

Excepting the last two essays, this material was originally written for newspapers, magazines, and anthologies. Although they have all been revised, some slightly and others expansively, they are signed and dated according to their initial publication. None has appeared in my other books, with one exception: "This Guy Wouldn't Give You the Parsley off His Fish," originally commissioned by Ben Sonnenberg for his exemplary magazine *Grand Street* and subsequently included in *Faces in the Crowd*. The Comedy section seemed bereft without it, and I've taken this opportunity to append a few footnotes.

Most of this work originally appeared in either *The New York Sun* or the *Village Voice* (copyright V. V. Publishing Corporation) and is reprinted by permission. I'm grateful to the staffs at both publications, especially David Propson and Robert Messenger at the *Sun* and Robert Christgau, Howard Feinstein, and J. Hoberman at the *Voice*. Several pieces originated in the *New York Times*, for which I thank Chip McGrath, Rebecca Sinkler, Christine Kay, David Shipley, and my good friend Michael J. Anderson, a first-rate critic and brilliant editor who has vetted other pieces included here as well, always making them better.

My thanks to Chris Porter, Glenn Sabin, and Lee Mergner of *Jazz Times*; David Remnick and Leo Carey of the *New Yorker*; Robert Hilburn of the *Los Angeles Times*; Sascha Feinstein of *Brilliant Corners*; Fred Kaplan of *The Absolute Sound*; Chris Chang of *Film Comment*. Four pieces were commissioned for books, and I thank their editors and publishers, notably Mathilda Liberman for inviting me to introduce her husband's stories, *Maggot and Worm*; Jeff Salamon, who co-edited the Robert Christgau festschrift, *Don't Stop 'Til You Get Enough*; Ben Hedin, who created the Bob Dylan reader, *Studio A*; and Sean Howe, formerly of the Criterion Collection and the brains behind *Give Our Regards to the Atomsmashers*.

As ever, I'm pleased to acknowledge the staff at Oxford University Press, especially longtime editor Sheldon Meyer (this is our sixth book together), Joellyn Ausanka, Kim Robinson, Patterson Lamb, and Norm Hirschy; my agent Georges Borchardt along with Anne Borchardt and Jonathan Berman; my indispensable assistant and researcher Elora Charles and her pet muse Alexander; and members of what the splendid saxophonist Lucky Thompson (who abandoned his art and career many years ago and is dead two days as I write) called Kinfolks Corner—the Halpers, Rothchilds, Donners, and my indefatigable and inspirational mother Alice Giddins. My wife, Deborah Halper, abides as the soul, wit, and divine spark of my life and work, and my daughter, Lea Giddins (who bears no responsibility for any of my opinions, some of which she vigorously disputes), keeps me honest, focused, decently appareled, and smiling.

G. G.
August 2005

PART ONE

Comedy

People must be amuthed, Thquire, thomehow.
—Charles Dickens, *Hard Times*

1 ❖ Speechless
(Charlie Chaplin / Buster Keaton)

1.

Charles Chaplin made a crucial miscalculation late in his career when editing the climactic music hall sequence in the 1952 *Limelight*. The big number features Calvero, Chaplin's character, and his partner, played by Buster Keaton—the only occasion when the two geniuses shared the screen. In the previous scene, Calvero had performed a flea-circus bit, with inserts of an audience convulsed with laughter. For the number with Keaton, however, Chaplin decided to eliminate cutaways and the laughter. He was so confident of the material that he counted on movie audiences to supply the guffaws. They did, and Chaplin felt vindicated. The miscalculation involves us, the home video generation.

Watch that *Limelight* scene today at home, alone or in small company, and the silence is deafening. During the first minute or so, you cannot help feeling that the quiet is intrinsic to the plot: Why, you wonder, would a theater audience, so raucous a few minutes earlier, be so undemonstrative now, unless it failed to find the routine amusing? The concluding ovation tells us otherwise, but even upon seeing the film again and again, the silence is disconcerting and saddening. We care for Calvero and his partner, and we want to hear gales of laughter for them and for us. On our own we can merely chuckle. Only in a darkened room with a few hundred strangers can we guffaw.

The silence has another effect. It underscores our private bond with the characters and heightens our critical faculties. In the absence of other kinds of sensory distraction, we home in on the minutest movements of the two aging clowns and pitilessly evaluate them. The silent cinema is extraordinarily intimate in that way. Watching Keaton's *Sherlock Jr.* in a theater, preferably with those who haven't seen it before, can be a communal revelation. The non-stop invention, daring, and surprise elicit a long aggregate howl that won't be duplicated in your living room. At home, you marvel at Keaton's brilliance, chuckling in wonder. Yet no longer riding the waves of shared laughter, you take sharper notice of character, theme, and subtext. On DVD, silent pictures are a rehabilitated but altered art.

There is an apparent paradox here: the most primitive generation of films resurrected by the most sophisticated of technologies. But to buy into that, you have to accept the shibboleth that the silent cinema *is* primitive—an infant's first steps toward fulfillment through sound. If you believe that, than you may as well buy into the technocratic religion that insists color beats black and white, Cinemascope improves on 1.33:1, digital corrects analogue, computer graphics bury hand-animated drawings, and Homer is useful fodder for a miniseries. Silent cinema is one of several art forms (among them musical comedy, westerns, ragtime, tap dancing, swing bands, live radio and TV drama, popular verse) that were born and buried within the last hundred years. The modern cinema endlessly plunders its earliest stories and ideas, but the most ingenious achievements of silent films cannot be replicated because they represent a separate art with its own laws.

For one example, characters in silent comedies have a spurious relationship to sound. Very often they cannot hear others unless they speak directly to them, and even then they are likely to mime, as when Chaplin says to Virginia Cherrill in the last seconds of *City Lights*, "You can see now?" and points to his own eyes. That gesture exemplifies his gifts as a masterly actor. He probably wouldn't have done so in a sound film, nor does the narrative in *City Lights* mandate it; yet the poignancy of the moment is magnified to a tear-jerking crest by the illustration of his haplessness.

As to the relative deafness of persons in silent movies, instances abound: In *Go West*, Keaton is followed by a hundred head of cattle but doesn't know it until he turns around; in his *The Navigator*, a tribe of cannibals clambers up the side of a ship to menace Kathryn McGuire, who doesn't suspect a thing until they are on top of her; in Chaplin's two-reeler, "Police," the tramp doesn't know his girl is chatting with his rival directly behind him until she taps his shoulder; in his *The Gold Rush*, Charlie enters pursued by an apparently noiseless bear. The most famous moment in all of Keaton, the collapsing house in *Steamboat Bill*, could not have been conceived in the audible cinema. The scene requires an oblivious Buster to face forward as the front wall of a house falls on him, failing to crush him because he stands in the area of an open window. Afterward, he is genuinely bewildered, having heard no warning creaks. Silence is the great in-joke of silent comedy, allowing for the suspensions of disbelief without which you could not have that favorite gambit—*Sherlock Jr.* has the best example—in which one character shadows another, virtually on his heels.

Of course, silent movies were not really silent; they depended on music not only to soothe and manipulate audiences but also to establish the on-set mood for the actors. Even when it consisted of no more than an organist braiding stock clichés—the "Sailor's Hornpipe" for a ship at

sea, "Spring Song" for a morning jaunt—music characterized and deepened the experience of moviegoing, which is why composers are now hired
to write scores for newly restored silent pictures. The challenge is not always
well met. Modern scores are sometimes so intrusively bad you may prefer silence or recourse to records of your own choosing. (I once made three
tapes of Chaplin's "In the Park," appending three records—Joplin rags,
an Ornette Coleman improvisation, and Bach's B-minor suite for flute and
strings. The result was three different films, each score emphasizing different emotions.) When a composer as sympathetic as Robert Israel or Carl
Davis handles the score, you can sit back and relax. But Kino, which offers
an outstanding Keaton collection, stumbled badly in allowing the aptly
named Club Foot Orchestra to score *Sherlock Jr.* with self-consciously arch
music that competes with and undermines the film. Other horrid Keaton
scores are Eric Beheim's for *Go West* (a rim shot for every joke) and the
boorish effects added to the two-reeler, "My Wife's Relations."

The worst soundtrack of all is on the 1942 version of Chaplin's *The Gold
Rush*, which for decades was the only version available. Though he
called *The Gold Rush* his masterwork, Chaplin excised the inter-titles and
another 38 seconds of footage when he re-released his 1925 classic,
reducing the running time by 10 minutes; he added a talky narration that
congeals with patronizing superiority, referring to his finest creation as
The Little Fellow. Happily, he shuts up during the dance of the bread
rolls. Yet the elemental story is so expertly told it requires no narrative
aid. [In 2003, Chaplin's estate released vastly improved DVD masters
of his feature films, distributed by Warner Brothers and including a restoration of the original version of *The Gold Rush* along with the sound
version.]

You see the pitfalls: Chaplin erred by deleting sound from *Limelight*
and by adding it to *The Gold Rush*. Of all people he should have known
that sound movies and silent movies are entirely different animals.
Which does not mean that new technology cannot improve the experience of a vanished art. On the DVD of *City Lights*, you get to watch a
window-boxed image, taller than it is wide, with greater clarity than any
theatrical revival boasted in decades. For the same edition, Carl Davis
reproduced Chaplin's score, which is offered in addition to the old
monaural version. (I like both tracks, though I enjoyed them more on laser,
which allows you to toggle from one to the other. The lasers also have
useful notes, with timings and annotations.) The chance to own nearly
all of Chaplin—only his dreary swan song, *A Countess in Hong Kong*, and
the wonderful Mack Sennett Keynotes are missing—and Keaton is a gift
that not long ago seemed almost unimaginable.

2.

If you woke me in the middle of the night and insisted I name my favorite picture, I would probably blurt *City Lights*. Shot in 1930 and premiered early the following year, it was an act of defiance: a silent movie that partakes of sound only on Chaplin's coquettish terms. The famous score employs essential sound effects, including gibberish spoken by politicians in the first scene and an all-important timer bell during the hilarious boxing match. Chaplin's gift extended to the conjuring of dreamy bittersweet melodies, which he hired real composers (like David Raksin) to orchestrate, usually giving them little if any credit. The *City Lights* score creates an ardent, claustrophobic melodic world as indicative of Chaplinland as the tramp, who is first glimpsed asleep in the arms of a statue.

The film's flawlessness derives from its infallible balancing act between pathos and comedy. Chaplin displays an unerring sense of when to shift gears. Before we have a chance to tire of the tramp's adoring glances at the blind flower girl, the mode switches to comedy, and before we have fully recovered from belly laughs, the mood turns serious. The harmony between burlesque and sobriety is played out in the film's shrewdest conceit—Charlie's relationship with a millionaire who is magnanimous when smashed and brutal when dry. In the years when the critical pendulum swung away from Charlie to Buster (as if one had to make a choice), Chaplin was targeted for sentimentality and directorial ineptness.

There is a difference between sentimentality, which is almost always crass and phony, and pathos, the comedian's acknowledgment of tragedy. Chaplin has ruined numerous comedians who wanted our tears but didn't possess his equilibrium (Jerry Lewis, Jackie Gleason, Steve Martin, Robin Williams, and Billy Crystal for starters). At his best Chaplin's sentiments are felt and profound. Movies always try to manipulate emotions. We are pleased to admit that a filmmaker can make us laugh or keep us in suspense, but we are reluctant to credit one who makes us cry. Yet the latter effect requires as much precision and perhaps even more taste. In *City Lights*, Chaplin pulls out that particular stop only once, in the last scene, when Cherrill feels the tramp's sleeve and realizes he is the mysterious benefactor who has restored her sight. With perfect pitch, Chaplin fades not on her recognition, but on the tramp's acceptance of how absurd he must look in her eyes. The director spares them further embarrassment and us the affront of a happy (truly sentimental) ending. As a picture about the senses, *City Lights* embodies the cinematic conundrum of sight and sound. When blind, Cherrill recognizes Charlie as a kind and heroic gentleman (a conceit previously used to great effect by

Harry Langdon in *The Strong Man*); yet her eyes reduce his infatuation to a clown's vanity.

Pathos was not Chaplin's original perspective. A graduate of the English music hall and the Mack Sennett slapstick mill, the tramp was at first a not-infrequently hostile character who gave as good as he got. The 14 two-reelers that cinched his place as an international sensation in the years 1915–16 were made at Essanay and for decades could be seen only in worn and butchered prints. They have been restored by David Shepard for Image's Blackstone Films, augmented by two bonuses: a Bronco Billy short, "His Regeneration," to which Chaplin contributed, and the 1918 Essanay patch-up of unused footage, "Triple Trouble." The three-volume set corrects several distortions. I parenthetically mentioned "In the Park," which I transferred to tape from a 16mm print my father bought in the early 1950s. Not until I watched these DVDs did I realize that what I knew as "In the Park" was merely a hodgepodge of scenes taken from two or three Essanays.

Here is the legendary Charlie, said in those years to be the most famous man on earth, perfecting the pigeon-toed hobble, the skidding around corners, the balletic grace, and the kick in the rump. In "The Tramp," he walks off, for the first time, into the horizon, shaking his leg like a dog. As Darn Hosiery, in his burlesque of *Carmen*, he closes with a stunning, completely serious murder-suicide, only to wiggle back to life and demonstrate the phony dagger—a conceit Tod Browning lifted for *The Mark of the Vampire*. In "A Night Out," he recreates the obnoxious drunk that brought him to Sennett's attention. In the remarkable "Police," he begins by satirizing the piety of phony zealots and closes by walking off Christlike, until a grinning, fist-shaking cop chases him back toward the camera and into our lap.

It is preposterous to criticize Chaplin for directing his films around himself: He *is* the show, surrounded by grotesques. Occasionally, he allows a sloppy edit, but his midrange visual style, as opposed to Keaton's more polished lay-of-the-land long shots, is almost always arresting. And he is capable of inspired directorial moments, as in his long neglected 1923 drama, *A Woman of Paris*, which continues to pack a punch by daringly undermining a thrice-told story. A good girl (bovine Edna Purviance) goes bad because of the malevolent influence of a wealthy playboy (a perfectly unctuous Adolph Menjou), except that she isn't so good, he isn't so bad, and the pure-hearted artist she loves is a prig. Chaplin added his own urgency to the technique of starting with a wide shot and then cutting into a scene, and was much imitated for it. One of his finest touches is the illusion of a departing train, achieved by shadows superimposed over the heroine's face. His motive was economic (no train), but the effect is more emotionally acute than if he had had the railroad at his disposal. Chaplin's equally economic manner in revealing character should have led to other dramatic films, but while critics loved *A Woman of Paris*, audiences had no desire to see a Chaplin film without Charlie (he appears unrecognizably for a few seconds as a train porter). The film remains compelling and entertaining, and the DVD is made irresistible by coupling it with his last major performance in the equally neglected and unjustly reviled *A King in New York* (1957)—a bitter rejoinder to the McCarthy red scare and postwar America that is nonetheless filled with moments of comic inspiration, not least his responses to Dawn Adams's dinner-time advertisements.

I do not mean to neglect Chaplin's other landmarks, all superbly rendered on disc, including his early (1921) harmonizing of pathos and comedy, *The Kid*; his 1936 leave-taking of silent pictures, *Modern Times* (another gut-wrenching ending and the definitive enactment of what it means to be a cog in industry's wheel); and the 1928 tour de force, *The Circus*, which offers a template for Orson Welles's hall of mirrors in *Lady of Shanghai*, as well as one of the most serenely timed edits in movie history (when Charlie and a pickpocket suddenly race toward the camera) and the virtuoso display of an actor obliged to be unfunny when he's trying to get laughs and uproarious when he isn't.

Recent currents in criticism are often more content with Keaton's architectural construction of gags and refusal to indulge tears than with Chaplin's outbursts of grief, yet the passing of time increasingly unites them as immigrant and native-born versions of outsiders knocking at the constraints of the new world. Is there a more delectable moment in all movie romance than the one in *The General* when Buster, frantically flinging wood into the locomotive furnace, notices his girl Marian Mark devotedly carrying a toothpick, and briefly strangles her?

Keaton's masterpieces were embargoed for many years by Henri Langlois's Cinemathèque Française, during which we rarely got to see them in movie theaters and never at home, except on faded multi-generational bootlegs. Kino's 10-volume set, combining feature films with shorts, is a staggering endowment, as essential to an educated home as a complete Shakespeare and Louis Armstrong's Hot Fives and Sevens. Still, Kino could have done more. While the Chaplin extras are mostly confined to memos and scripts (the 2003 release adds the very considerable bonus of a penetrating documentary written and directed by Richard Schickel), Kino provides nothing at all—no commentary tracks or liner essays, and I have mentioned the peculiar musical scores. Ultimately, who cares? The chance to watch *The General*, *The Navigator*, *Sherlock Jr.*, *Steamboat Bill*, and the rest, all made between 1920 and 1928, induces in me a paroxysm of gratitude. Not only can we savor them repeatedly; we can also pry into his secrets through still-frame, and surmise, in ways earlier generations could not, how he pulled off some of the most astonishing stunts on film.

For Keaton is not only a nonpareil actor-director, whose oddly beautiful visage is far too expressive to satisfy the Great Stone Face cliché, but is likely the equal of Yakima Canutt as a stunt man and of Harold Lloyd and Douglas Fairbanks as an athlete. Keaton makes it all so funny, you don't always notice. Still-frame some of those falls and leaps and you cannot help realizing you are watching an Olympics-level master at work. Some of his stunts—like leaping from one skyscraper to another and missing (*Three Ages*) or posing while the house falls on him in *Steamboat Bill* could no longer be achieved because no actor could get the insurance to risk his life. Special effects experts are on record saying they have never figured out how he jumped through a window and into a dress or into an old lady's abdomen in *Sherlock Jr.* Yet still-frame reveals much, while taking nothing from the magic. The first time you watch almost any Keaton picture, you become a slack-jawed kid at your first circus. Chaplin has the dust of Edwardian England on his shoulders, but Keaton and the vistas he must conquer are defiantly modern.

Another quality about silent films, exemplified by the 46 minutes of *Sherlock Jr.*, still the most astute film ever made about film, or the 38 minutes of Chaplin's *Shoulder Arms*, the most durable of World War I travesties, is the discrimination regarding length. Within a decade after the introduction of sound, double bills dictated a picture's running time—90 minutes to two hours for the top feature, and 60 to 75 minutes for the B feature. With the passing of twin features in the 1960s, the average length froze in the area of 95 minutes to two hours, longer in the case of spectacles, but rarely shorter—as if book publishers elected to bring out only novels, not short novels or stories (okay, many have done precisely that, but writers find ways to circumvent demands of the market). *Sherlock Jr.* is a film novella, its length mandated by its content and not the reverse.

The essential difference between Keaton and Chaplin, beyond the obvious distinctions in personal style and approach, is that Keaton is unmistakably American. That is, he puts American tableaux at the center of his work. Chaplin's films could be set in any municipality, any park, or countryside. His supporting players, with their beetle brows, old-world beards, and indifferent dress, would be at home in Ruritania. Keaton exults in the particulars of locations. His rivers, mountains, towns, shops, homes, and picket fences could be located only in Prohibition America. His costumes, including his straw porkpie, are no less indicative, while Chaplin's derby and tattered tux might have been found in any European capitol. Except for *The Navigator*, which is set almost entirely at sea, Keaton's films poeticize the great territories. His epic masterwork, *The General*, as flawless as *City Lights*, translates a factual Civil War story (Disney told it straight in *The Great Locomotive Race*, 1956) into the ultimate comedy of man and machine while relinquishing most standard elements of burlesque or satire. The emotions of heroism, patriotism, romance, enmity, and despair are played for real as well as for laughs; as an evocation of American history, it is the equal of Griffith or Ford.

Viewing the whole body of his work illuminates his repeated use of motifs and his development of gags. His fop in *The Navigator*, for example, is cousin to the rich stooge in *The Sap Head*, though in the later film he matures and takes control. The theme of the ineffectual rich kid who becomes a man through adversity is explored in *Battling Butler* (with a boxing parody that may have spurred Chaplin), reaching an apotheosis in *Steamboat Bill*. The mechanized meal in *The Navigator* elaborates a gag introduced in the two-reeler, "The Scarecrow," and his surreal wrestling with a boat in 1924 anticipates his escapade of 1927 on *The General*. Another Keaton theme is comedy in great numbers, seen twice in 1925— *Go West* (cattle overwhelm Los Angeles) and *Seven Chances* (he is pursued up hill and down dale by dozens and then eventually hundreds of women wearing bridal gowns). *Three Ages* was conceived as a parody of D. W. Griffith's *Intolerance*, but today's filmgoers may recognize it as a precursor of Mel Brooks's *History of the World, Part One*—much as admirers of *Run Lola Run* will find plenty of precedent in Buster's many sprints in *Go West* and other films.

I began by remarking on Chaplin's miscalculation regarding his scene with Keaton in *Limelight*. By all accounts, he made another in cutting out much of Buster's best shtick. Call it narcissism if you will. I prefer to think of it as one comic god remembering that he had long ago met his only match and continued to bristle with anxiety. They ought to have bonded: In 1952, Keaton was largely forgotten and Chaplin no longer welcome. In posterity, they are inseparable.

[*The Perfect Vision*, August 2000]

2 ❖ *Hanging Tough* *(Harold Lloyd)*

Harold Lloyd remains the least known of the great silent comedians, little more than an ineffaceable image—the man dangling from the sprung clock of a skyscraper—surrounded by clichés about those beloved American vanities, innocence and gumption. The blame for public and critical neglect can be placed at the Lloyd doorstep. A savvy businessman who, like Charlie Chaplin and Irving Berlin, maintained ownership of his major works, Lloyd doled out his films in clip shows and infrequent screenings for the better part of four decades, until his death, at 77, in 1971. In recent years, his estate, administered by his grand-daughter, Suzanne Lloyd, has marketed his legacy in theatrical retro-spectives, broadcasts on Turner Classic Movies, and even the publication of his 3-D nude photography—the hobby of a wealthy middle-aged man with lots of time on his hands. Home video, however, did not lure her to the trough until 2005, and so his films have nothing like the currency of Chaplin's and Keaton's—though that will change with the release of the magnanimous *Harold Lloyd Comedy Collection* (New Line), offering 28 films and hours of extras.

Maybe she was right to hold out. DVDs have permanently altered our experience of movies, but that doesn't mean a great deal hasn't been sacrificed along with the audience. Lloyd does as well by the audience as any filmmaker who ever lived, better than all but a handful—which is why infrequent Lloyd festivals at Film Forum and other repertory theaters are so rewarding: Even if you can watch *Safety Last* and *The Fresh-man* to your heart's content at home, that experience cannot replicate the tribal harmony of laughs and gasps, the collective heart-thumping pleasure of discovering or rediscovering Lloyd as a theatrical tradition fueled with roller-coaster dynamics.

Vestiges of critical ambiguity emanate from Lloyd's humility in not claiming co-directorial credit. Surrounded by a loyal and like-minded crew, he was undoubtedly as responsible for setting up shots and constructing gags as Keaton, who, in claiming partial credit, satisfied the dictates of historians blinded by auteurist simplification. Lloyd is not listed in any directory of directors, not even John Wakeman's 2,400-page *World Film Directors*. The pattern of unavailability and auctorial confusion has re-legated Lloyd to the second tier, although it is common wisdom that he was "the third genius," more popular than his rivals, and at times funnier. It has also led to assumptions that require revision.

As a character, Harold (Harold Lloyd in *Safety Last*, Harold something-else in the other films) is justly recalled as an indefatigable go-getter, whose modest attributes are pushed to the breaking point by his vast ambitions. Beyond that, he is encrusted in a few myths—regarding his methods and characterizations—that the work itself invalidates. Despite Tom Dardis's 1983 biography, *Harold Lloyd: The Man on the Clock*, which recounts a few of Lloyd's conflicting explanations of how the 18-minute skyscraper

scramble in *Safety Last* was accomplished, several observers hold to
Walter Kerr's insistence that it was all real, as evidenced by an abiding
view of the street below. Kerr, in his exceptionally astute (but in this instance credulous) 1975 classic, *The Silent Clowns*, went so far as to argue
that the scene works *because* the audience can trust the veracity of the
camera. While it is true that process shots were not in use, Lloyd—though
loathe to undo a legend that so many wanted to believe—ultimately came
clean about his construction of various smaller three- and four-story
buildings on hills. Ingenious camera placement and scrupulous editing
did the rest.

What fascinates today is Kerr's need to cling to that myth every bit as
tenaciously as Harold clings to the clock, a double metaphor: Harold frantically grasps time and Walter desperately searches for times lost. Lloyd
was undoubtedly an athlete of immense skill, rivaled among comedians
only by Keaton, who once felt challenged enough to dismiss him as
an acrobat. He takes real spills in every picture and climbs trees, fences,
and all kinds of vehicles and animals with reckless confidence. Where
Chaplin will gracefully avoid an open manhole, Harold will always
plummet. Where Keaton usually runs from something, Harold almost
always runs after something and catches it. He looks like Clark Kent, but
his powers are inevitably exposed as superhuman. The idea that he put
his life at risk, grabbing for a clock's minute hand or a rope that slips
through his fingers, dancing on a precipice with a mouse in his pants, is
quaint and irrelevant. Modern audiences assume that he is somehow safe,
without giving it much thought, and they gasp and cheer and laugh all
the same. You haven't seen *Safety Last* until you've seen it in a crowd.

Another myth is that Lloyd is never personally funny—only the gags
are. He is a not especially sympathetic everyman to whom funny things
happen. Yet no one played chagrin better than Lloyd, and some of the
brightest moments in his peak years, between 1924 and 1928, are inserts
of Harold registering everything-happens-to-me mortification, as when
he mistakes a doughboy's helmet for a traffic button in *Hot Water* or loses
his suit, thread by thread, in *The Freshman*. His burlesque of a desperate
criminal, in *Hot Water*, when he thinks he has murdered his mother-in-
law, exemplifies the Hal Roach tradition of exaggeration wed to clueless
resolve. Perhaps the misguided arrogance he displays in his once widely
televised talkies robbed memories of the poetical expressiveness embodied in his silent self, much as Keaton's barking voice despoiled the
beauty of the Great Plains face. Lloyd's most appealing quality is the
modesty of his acting, as opposed to the crashing immodesty of his characters. He suffers no pity—I can't think of a single tear-jerking moment
in his films (spurts of pathos are whacked away by resolve). In life, he

similarly refused to call attention to the fact that he lost his right thumb and index finger to an explosive; watch closely and you can see he wears a form-fitted glove and does most physical business with his left hand.

The most intriguing received wisdom regarding Harold is his putative niceness, when in fact his serious flaws, in nearly every picture, primed audiences with points of identification. It's a stretch to compare him with Macbeth, though not so much if one remembers Mary McCarthy's description of the Scottish golfer, the murderous Babbitt, prey to over-imagination and delusion. To impress his girl, Harold acts like an over-bearing bureaucrat, and she, no paragon of small town values, likes him for it. "Function is / Smothered in surmise, and nothing is / But what is not" can stand as a motto for either man. Lloyd's favorite gag, which appears multiple times in each of his films, involves the pitfalls of surmise. Harold is forever confusing one object for another, one person for another, one sound for another, and forever paying the cost. Sometimes he plays the joke on the audience, as in the opening scene of *Safety Last*, when a prison and noose turn out to be a railway station and mail hook, or during the climactic fight of *The Kid Brother*, as his iron head turns out to be an iron bar. He enters *Girl Shy* with his posterior, as a customer mistakes him for a pair of trousers. But usually the joke is on Harold. He runs two false touchdowns in *The Freshman* because he mistakes a hat for a football and a steam whistle for the referee's.

Nothing is but what is not. In *Girl Shy*, he pretends to be a great lover; in *The Kid Brother*, a sheriff; in *The Freshman*, the big-man-on-campus football star. In the end, he will become all of those things, but getting there requires the conscience of a narcissist. To get what and where he wants, Harold steals more cars that one can count, lies, boasts, and leaves other people's lives and property in shambles. In *Girl Shy*, his pride is so great that when he thinks his book won't be published, he cruelly wounds the woman he loves rather than confess his failure. His innocence is no match for his vanity. A title card informs us that the town bully hates the innocent he plays in *The Kid Brother* because Harold had once sold him doorknobs as eggs. Yet we identify with him so completely that we usually support the liberties he takes with law and civility. And if we don't, those fantastic climaxes would close the sale: He rings one variation after another on the big football game or the big fight or the big chase, leaving us all but breathless and very pleased at the outcome.

The climaxes are the most evident examples of Lloyd's genius at building gags; he wastes and wants not. One of his most underrated films, the hour-long *Hot Water*, includes three two-reel situations concerning Harold, his wife (played by the best and most frequent of his leading ladies, the pixielike and, when necessary, gimlet-eyed Jobyna Ralston), and her unbearable family. In the first episode, he wins a live turkey and must manipulate it and an armful of packages on a trolley shared with a spider and short-fused riders. The turkey disappears during the second part, which concerns a new car that is soon demolished, but makes a brief and unforgettable reappearance in the third, when Harold mistakes its claw for the long arm of the law. If this last section, with its ghosts and constantly misinterpreted dialogue had been released as a short, it might have become a classic. It is a virtuoso compilation of old and new bits played with relentless speed and savoir-faire—and the priceless help of Canadian native Josephine Crowell, the barnstormer said to be born in 1849. She doesn't look nearly that old, though she is clearly too old to have such young children; she required much stunt doubling. But Lloyd was willing to let his supporting players have a few laughs and Crowell gets plenty, not least when she rises from bed at the hip, like Boris Karloff in *The Black Cat*—a laugh the first time she does it, a solid payoff guffaw the second time.

Lloyd approaches perfection in *The Freshman* and *The Kid Brother*. The first is his most spiritually autobiographical film in that it addresses head-on the obstinacy with which he approached film comedy. As Kerr takes pains to elaborate, Lloyd lacked the cosmic gifts of Keaton and Chaplin, and spent seven years figuring out how to win popularity equal to theirs through ardent study and hit-and-miss variations. *The Freshman* was released in 1925, the same year Fitzgerald published *The Great Gatsby*, and the similarities are unmistakable. At the end of the novel, Gatsby's father shows Nick his son's copy of *Hopalong Cassidy*, with a flyleaf on which the young Gatsby had written a schedule for self-improvement: rise from bed, exercise, work, play sports, master elocution, learn to attain poise, "read one improving book or magazine per week." *The Freshman* begins with the delusional Harold, crowned with a beanie, studying movies, novels, magazines, and old yearbooks on how to succeed in college. He plans to win friends with a jig and a handshake that, as performed by Lloyd, is at once pathetic and funny. Harold learns that he has become the campus joke only after he acts like himself and slugs a bully pawing at his girl. Even then, however, he dreams of making his comeback on the football field—and succeeds. Gatsby gets killed, but Harold has no reason to doubt the efficacy of delusion, ambition, and never-say-die spirit.

The Kid Bother has its parallel in Keaton's *The General*, also released the same year (1927); they share a rural pictorialism of great beauty; an economy that underscores characters and relationships; an unruffled tempo from which comedy eloquently emerges—and both films were reviewed disparagingly. Sound was on the horizon and reviewers were nodding.

This time the nominal director, Ted Wilde—who also co-wrote *Girl Shy* and directed the excellent *Speedy* (Lloyd's last silent film and the last for Wilde, who completed two talkies and died suddenly at 36, in 1929)— may have had a more than nominal responsibility. *The Kid Bother* looks like nothing else among Lloyd's films. It opens with a twilight pastoral shot (you can see the dust motes) that incorporates an abandoned barge, where the film will conclude, and the medicine show wagon, where it begins. Usually, Harold leaves the sticks and makes his way to the city; here, he stays put, at one with the environment—as indicated when he climbs a tree to watch the leading lady ride into the sunset, each higher branch disclosing a further bend in the road.

Many of Lloyd's gags were imitated in sound comedies, from *Bringing Up Baby* (Harold loses the back of his trousers) to *Road to Utopia* (genial pickpocketing). Others cannot fail to remind filmgoers of *The Birds* (Harold assaulted by pigeons) or *The French Connection* (a motor chase that narrowly misses a woman and her baby carriage) or literally dozens of other films. I am not suggesting that these moments were copied, only that Lloyd's films are so copiously imagined that they endure as a lexicon of indispensable movie bits. Lloyd copied himself, specifically *The Kid Brother* fight, in his 1932 talkie, *Movie Crazy*, inadvertently illustrating what he lost when he gained dialogue. Though the scene is played almost entirely without speech, the very possibility of speech weighs him down physically and imaginatively. In the earlier film, he imprisons a villain in a dozen life preservers and then rows him to shore (not unlike Keaton and the diving suit in *The Navigator*), a fine piece of business—impossible, yet believable in a silent picture. With sound, time is altered and Lloyd settles for one preserver, this time used to pin down his own arms. Sound ties up the audience, too, telling us more than we want to know about Harold—who, speechless, is whatever we choose to make of him.

[*The New York Sun*, 22 April 2005]

3 ❖ *There Ain't No Sanity Claus* *(Groucho Marx and Brothers)*

1. We've Grown Accustomed to His Face

The 20th century's most durable masks—having taken their place alongside Comedy and Tragedy or Pulcinella and Pierrot—are Frankenstein's monster, as incarnated by Boris Karloff, and Groucho Marx. Groucho's is pure caricature: spectacles, heavy moustache and eyebrows, cigar. "Groucho glasses," marketed as early as the 1940s, turn up today in children's goody bags. The film critic Otis Ferguson wrote in 1935 that Groucho Marx "would be funny in still photographs," and he was right. Never did a mask carry so much attitude. Put Groucho glasses on anyone who has ever seen the Marx Brothers and that person will fall into a crouch, raise his hand to flick imaginary ashes and crack wise with a velvety, back-of-the-throat, quasi-Jewish inflection.

In the early years of the last century, the Marx Brothers, sons of a German-Jewish family living in Manhattan's Yorkville section, were pressured by their mother Minnie to quit school and sing in vaudeville. Oddly, Minnie initially forbade their attempts at comedy. As Stefan Kanfer writes in *Groucho*, his smart, briskly appealing but indifferently researched biography, "She once watched horrified as all three of her sons interrupted their own number to follow the progress of a large bug crossing the stage." When they went on the road with a school-days act, the brothers adapted the most commonplace stock characters of the era: Leonard put on a pointy hat and polished his stage Italian, Adolphe wore a red fright wig to play an Irish loon, and Julius impersonated a beady-eyed, whiskered German professor in a black swallow-tail coat and cravat.

Their uncle, the vaudeville star Al Shean, told Adolphe his Irish nut would be a lot funnier without dialogue. Adolphe was offended, but when a newspaper critic expressed the same opinion, he resolved to be mute; he added "an old automobile horn to honk his replies," along with "a raincoat to stow his props." Julius, the canniest of the brothers, came up with the routine in which Adolphe denies stealing silverware, which proceeds to drop from his sleeves. According to legend—on which Simon Louvish casts some doubt in his new book, *Monkey Business*—the brothers were renamed during a poker game in Galesburg, Illinois, when a monologist compared the Marxes to figures in the funny papers. Taking the comic strip "Sherlocko, the Monk" as his cue, he dealt them names ending in "O." Leonard, who chased women and affected an Italian accent, became Chico; Adolphe, who played the harp and an Irishman, became Harpo; Julius, who was acerbic and hid his money in a grouch bag, became Groucho. Their two younger brothers, Milton and Herbert, were called Gummo and Zeppo, but they never developed grotesque masks and had no place in the act; Zeppo seems as out of place in his five pictures as Chico would have in *The Godfather*.

After the Lusitania was sunk in 1915, Groucho and many of his compatriots stopped playing Germans. He modulated his accent to a distinctive Jewish singsong. (Decades later, Charlie Chaplin told him, "I wish I could speak on the screen as well as you.") One evening he walked funny, got a big laugh, and made slouched scurrying part of his shtick. Over time, the ethnic parodies became surreal and blurred, a collection of crazy masks that demolished the original stereotypes. As Al Shean used to sing to his largely immigrant audience, "It Isn't What You Used to Be, It's What You Are Today."

Groucho's eureka moment occurred when his son was born and he was late getting from the maternity ward to a theater in Queens. Having no time to glue on whiskers, he painted a mustache with greasepaint. It got laughs, but the theater manager fumed, insisting customers had paid to see real false hair. Groucho knew a good thing, however, and defied the manager (and his despotic boss, E. F. Albee). When the brothers made their first movie, *The Cocoanuts*, in 1929, the director, Robert Florey, demanded a genuine mustache, maintaining that the audience would never believe a painted one. Groucho explained, patiently one presumes, "The audience doesn't believe us anyhow." Working on *Monkey Business*, the writers Arthur Sheekman and S. J. Perelman asked the associate producer Herman Mankiewicz to clarify the psychology of the Marxes. Mankiewicz, their peer in acerbity, replied, "One of them is a guinea, another a mute who picks up spit, and the third an old Hebe with a cigar. Is that all clear, Beaumont and Fletcher?"

The greasepaint was the necessary touch to finish and perfect the mask. That big rectangular block of black represented the clown's assertion of amiable fantasy, not a difficult concept for a nation raised on circuses, minstrel shows, and vaudeville. In their often sublimely mad films for Paramount—*The Cocoanuts*, *Animal Crackers* (1930) *Monkey Business* (1931), *Horse Feathers* (1932), and *Duck Soup* (1933)—the Marx Brothers, in their childlike anarchy, are far more appealing, sane, and believable than the slippery lovers, inviolate dowagers, and assorted con men who surround them. As Chico later observed (in 1935 in MGM's *A Night at the Opera*), "There ain't no Sanity Claus."

With the masks in place, despite the accent on fast verbal humor, the Marx Brothers' faces took on a reality independent of their characters and became curiously interchangeable. Kanfer's narrative overflows with instances of doppelgangery. Director Leo McCarey toyed with the idea in the brilliant (silent) mirror sequence in *Duck Soup*, in which Harpo and Chico are disguised as Groucho and even Groucho is not sure if he sees his reflection or a double. Yet the brothers impersonated one another long before then. Back when Leonard and Adolphe played Willie the Wop and Silent Sam, they exchanged wigs and took each other's roles and no one could tell the difference. They brought others into the charade. When Walter

Winchell was banned from a theater, they dressed him as Harpo and convinced security guards that since the real Harpo was prone to seizures they carried a spare.

During the Broadway run of the play *Animal Crackers*, the eternal dowager Margaret Dumont once opened Captain Spaulding's trunk and a fleet of Grouchos emerged—all stagehands and musicians with greasepaint mustaches and cigars. After movies made the brothers nationally famous, Marx masks turned up everywhere; people gave parties at which guests were obliged to come as the Marx of their choice. By the late 1930s, Kanfer writes, "The image of Groucho was now so manufactured" that when he did not appear for a publicity photograph, a writer put on the makeup and posed with Harpo and Chico: It was the writer's face and body, not Groucho's, that looked out from a poster for the film *Go West* (1940). Without their masks, the brothers went unrecognized. Traveling with the Victory Caravan during World War II, Groucho was the only celebrity ignored by fans when the stars stepped off a train. He sneaked back on board to put on greasepaint, glasses, and cigar, and then disembarked with bent knees to much applause.

Given the ubiquity of the Marx masks, especially Groucho's, one is startled to realize how briefly the Marx Brothers held the attention of their contemporaries. They did not achieve permanent cultural acceptance until after 1967, when Groucho received the imprimatur of the Museum of Modern Art. Before that, they had enjoyed two three-year stints of Hollywood glory, 1930–32 and 1935–37. As Kanfer notes, Graham Greene put his finger on the moment when the riotous satirists became as toothless as the stereotypes they burlesqued: In an enthusiastic review of *A Day at the Races* (1937), he expressed his dismay at a scene in which "a real person," Maureen O'Sullivan, said they were "silly." "Silly," Greene continued: "Good God, we cannot help exclaiming since we are real people too, have we been deceived all along?"

Two years later, in the troubling but vastly underrated *At the Circus*, no one could fail to mistake how much of the Marx Brothers' once infallible intuition had been sacrificed to Hollywood journeymen. It was one thing for Chico to tutsi-frutsi Groucho out of money, another thing entirely for him to push him into the mud or for Eve Arden to leave him dangling helplessly in pantaloons. We will accept Groucho deceived, but humiliated? Never.

Kanfer is onto something when he describes the Marxes as "boys dressed up as men in funny faces and outlandish costumes, like celebrants en route to a costume party." Many of their contemporaries adapted bizarre faces and costumes to play children—among them Ed Wynn, Fanny Brice, Joe Penner, the Three Stooges. But the Marxes were grown-ups pretending to be children pretending to be grown-ups; we may laugh at adults playing children, but we don't want to be them. We do, however, wish to retain a little of the childhood anarchy that defies the Margaret Dumonts breathing down our necks. That was a hard act to sustain for actors in middle age. Groucho once said he envied Jack Benny, who could get laughs without a mask.

Then came the wilderness years. Chico, a compulsive gambler and womanizer (when his wife caught him kissing a chorus girl, he protested he was merely whispering in her mouth), survived by leading a band and playing piano, aiming his right hand like a gun and "shooting" the keys—an irresistible bit because he made it look so easy when, in fact, it requires the timing of a master comedian. Harpo married late in life, adopted children, and enjoyed his family. He sagely remarked that Groucho "is an imaginary character who needs the other three characters to give him substance." Groucho looked lost in the movies he made on his own. He tried to make it as a writer; when a book of his did not sell, he told a reporter, "I only write first editions." Yet he was eventually born again as the brazenly disparaging quizmaster of *You Bet Your Life*, during its 14-year stint on radio and television. He grew a real moustache, but by then his face had taken on all the attributes of caricature. If Jack Benny could get laughs with a stare, Groucho did as well wagging his eyebrows.

Unhappily for his wives and children, the mask had calcified. He could no more turn off the spigot of wisecracks and casual cruelty than he could his insecurity and fear. He drove two of his three wives and one of his three children to drink and estranged them all. Groucho earned his misogyny the hard way. When he lost his virginity, he contracted gonorrhea. His mother encouraged him to see "fast women," to avoid commitments that might hurt the act. A married woman lured him into a situation that later inspired a line in *The Cocoanuts*: "You know, a yes like that was once responsible for me jumping out a window."

He was a devoted father as long as his children were small and defenseless. He rushed home from the studio to change diapers and feed the infants, usurping his wives, until the kids were old enough to talk back—at which point they could no longer win his approval. He spent his last years with a woman Kanfer portrays as greedy, bullying, and sexually taunting: Minnie squared. Groucho preferred her to his often cowering and resentful children. When Groucho died in 1977, at 86, you can't help feeling he lasted a few years too long.

Kanfer, the author of *Serious Business*, about animation, and *A Summer World*, about the Catskills, has written a biography with many virtues. He describes the supporting players splendidly, from the little-remembered gag writer Al Boasberg to the deservedly forgotten critic Alexander Woollcott. He stays away from facile psychology and moves his story along at a clip. Those attributes, however, are undermined by missteps, like a section in the present tense, pointless Gallicisms ("au fond," "poitrine"), chronology problems, and an almost arrogant lack of scholarship. The absence of a filmography and of information like Groucho's birth date is strange, but the absence of source notes is inexcusable, especially when he alters familiar stories, accepts apocrypha as fact, offers unattributed conversation, and appears to know what people are thinking. He is weak on the movies, recycling standard tales and reprinting dialogue, much of it also included in his amusing anthology, *The Essential Groucho* (Knopf).

Kanfer relies chiefly on previous books, including those by Groucho himself, which he takes a mite too seriously, and Hecter Arce's superior *Groucho* (1979), which is out of print and in need of revision but remains the best general biography. Kanfer's attacks on Richard J. Anobile are unseemly, since he has taken much from Anobile's *The Marx Brothers Scrapbook*, including mistakes (like the assertion that *The Cocoanuts* was the first film musical or screenwriter Arthur Sheekman's account of a bridge-playing incident, since amended by his widow, Gloria Stewart, in interviews and her memoir, *I Just Kept Hoping*).

The accretion of small errors in Kanfer's biography and anthology undermines his authority. Bert Granet and Sheekman did not write *The Big Broadcast* (Louvish makes the same mistake, but blames Arce, who started the rumor); Kitty Carlisle was not "an untried singer" when she made *A Night at the Opera*, the fourth and last of her 1930s musicals; Humphrey Bogart married Mayo Methot, not Virginia Mayo; NBC paid Groucho $4,800 per episode of *You Bet Your Life*, not $48,000; Louis Untermeyer annotated an album Groucho made for Decca not out of intellectual solidarity, but because he was Decca's house annotator; Morrie Ryskind is, in fact, credited as a writer on *The Cocoanuts*; the bazooka was named after an instrument invented by the comic Bob Burns, not vice versa; and on and on.

Louvish is a more committed researcher and has come up with new material. He has elected, however, to publish his research rather than write a book. His occasional error (like crediting Brenden Behan with Thornton Wilder's uncovering of "Grouchin" in *Finnegans Wake*) is nothing compared to howlers like tagging an unknown girl who may have grown up with the Marx brothers as an "embryonic Maggie Dumont." His relentlessly jokey, cliché-ridden, pointlessly data-packed prose will repel all but the most ardent fans. The Louvish who published *The Man on the Flying Trapeze*, a sober biography of W. C. Fields, in 1997, is unrecognizable in

Monkey Business. A pity, because he has interesting things to say about scripts versus finished films and fills in details Kanfer omits—like when and how Harpo started playing the harp.

Louvish consistently and Kanfer occasionally fall into an obvious trap: When writing about a comedian do not compete for laughs. You cannot top the man who said of the heinous tenor in *A Night at the Opera*, "You're willing to pay him a thousand dollars a night just for singing? Why, you can get a phonograph record of 'Minnie the Moocher' for 75 cents. For a buck and a quarter, you can get Minnie."

2. This Means War!

The Marx Brothers, a Broadway phenomenon of the 1920s, triumphed briefly as film stars: first in the early 1930s, peaking with the mediocre *Monkey Business*; then in the mid-1930s, with *A Night at the Opera*, the audience having ignored their intervening masterpiece, *Duck Soup*. Their true peak, however, occurred posthumously, in the 1960s and 1970s, when a generation raised on televised movies adapted the Marxes as simpatico anarchists and took them off to college. The long-surviving Groucho crowned their revival with his 1972 Carnegie Hall show, his first appearance on a New York stage since 1929. Countless books and screenings followed, but 30 years later, it must be conceded that the best chance an undergraduate has of encountering the Marxes is in a film studies course.

That dreary thought is made harder to bear by a suspicion that classroom showings are encumbered by as many footnotes as Dryden and Pope—equally sly comics of an earlier day. The "strange interlude" joke parodies the title and technique of a Eugene O'Neill play. "Monkey-Doodle-Doo" is Irving Berlin's take on the rejuvenating powers of monkey glands. "The Trial of Mary Dugan" was a 1929 Norma Shearer flick. "Ten cents a dunce" refers to a Rodgers and Hart song. And so on and so forth, line for line, pun for pun. Yet the Marxes transcend the details; they are funny men who grow funnier as the topicality of the writing recedes in importance. I confess that after a lifetime of Marxist contemplation, I have no idea what the following speech from *Horse Feathers* means: "Scientists make these deductions by examining a rat or your landlord who won't cut the rent. And what do they find? Asparagus." One learns to live with these things.

The two jokes central to their work do not date and have never been emulated successfully. No one in Marx Brothers movies knows the brothers for the lunatics they are; at the same time, the brothers themselves fail to comprehend the futility of the chaos they beget. The first joke requires supporting casts to stand around like mannequins as the occasionally sadistic clowns disport themselves. It obliges allegedly sane characters to hire Chico and Harpo as spies, managers, or football players, and to appoint Groucho college president, sanitarium director, or hotel manager. It inclines wealthy dowagers—played by the imperturbable Margaret Dumont, who responds to each dig with a recyclable look of mild umbrage—to woo the lustily impotent Groucho. The second joke nails their isolation, adding a touch of mordant pathos as they age. The chase and a leering remark are as intimate as they can get—with one impromptu exception. Toward the end of *Duck Soup*, Harpo actually grabs Dumont's buttocks. She turns, aghast, only to end as the object of greater abuse in what may be the funniest closing shot ever.

In the five pre-production code films made for Paramount between 1929 and 1933 and collected in Universal's new DVD set, they insult everyone, including stiff romantic leads, whose awkwardness heightens the comedy. In their eight post-code films, of which seven are collected in a Warner Bros. DVD set, they become enablers for young lovers, who in turn treat them like amusing children or strange uncles. An insensible cliché in film criticism downgrades the first two films, *The Cocoanuts* and *Animal Crackers*, as photographed stage plays, but that is their strength. The corny dancing; the hapless actors (in a movie theater, Oscar Shaw gets a laugh each time he reveals his prissy smile in *The Cocoanuts*); the stationary shots, which force actors to turn around so we can see who they are and catch the dancers up-skirt; and the many flubs and consequent ad-libs contribute to an unparalleled spontaneity. The scenes had been endlessly rehearsed on stage, yet the films feel like middle-school theatrics in which only the Marx Brothers wield real power, thus enhancing their roles while reducing every one else to bland caricatures (the impish Lillian Roth in *Animal Crackers* is an exception). *Monkey Business*, directed by Norman McLeod, was their first Hollywood movie and introduced the judicious idea of upgrading Zeppo from hapless gofer to romantic lead, but notwithstanding 50 minutes of shipboard mayhem, climaxing in a delightful quartet of Maurice Chevalier impersonations, the liberated camera inclines them to wearying action scenes.

The drawback with *The Cocoanuts* is Berlin's "When My Dreams Come True," which is reprised relentlessly, like bad operetta—as happens with the similarly monotonous "Alone" in *A Night at the Opera*. To paraphrase Groucho, he has to stay but we can fast-forward. While much credit has been given several writers recruited for the Marxes (the eminent names are George Kaufman, Morrie Ryskind, and S. J. Perelman), insufficient respect is accorded the songwriting team of Harry Ruby and Bert Kalmar, who not only protected them from operetta but allowed them to lampoon it with unequaled ferocity, beginning with "Hooray for Captain

Spaulding" in *Animal Crackers*, rising to greater Gilbert and Sullivanian heights with "I'm Against It" in *Horse Feathers*, and leaping the moon with the magnificently hitless score of *Duck Soup*, including "Freedonia Hymn" and "The Country's Going to War," which turns into a full-bore minstrel show complete with xylophoned helmets, "All God's Chillun Got Guns," and "Turkey in the Straw." Director Leo McCarey packed so many visual and verbal gags into 68 minutes that the film plays like a sustained inspiration. McCarey sets up gags so adroitly, he can go directly to the punch line, as when, after showing Harpo cutting everything in sight with scissors, he has Zeppo enter with half a hat. The most celebrated moment is rendered in silence—the broken mirror mimicry, a bit McCarey originally worked out for a Charley Chase silent short (available on Kino's *The Charley Chase Collection*). *Duck Soup* is peerless.

But *A Night at the Opera* and *A Day at the Races*—the first films they made for MGM with big budgets and the humorless director Sam Wood (who concentrated on romantic ballads and a grueling peasant dance), but without Zeppo—come close enough to win a crate of Cohibas. Here are the stateroom scene, the contract dispute, the tutsi-frutsie racing manuals, the ultimate burlesques of *Il Trovatore* and every racetrack film ever made, and much more, including the only great musical number in a Marx Brothers film not involving the brothers: "All God's Chillun Got Rhythm," in *A Day at the Races*, sung by the incomparable Ivie Anderson, accompanied by the Crinoline Choir and (physically if not musically) members of the Duke Ellington Orchestra. This scene was cut from TV for years and decried as racist by sensitive white liberals. They are free to skip it; the rest of us can head straight for DVD chapter 22 to see Anderson in clover. Racism manifested itself less in Catfish Row stereotypes than in the failure to cast her in other movies.

The later films are increasingly uneven, yet often savory. The stage play *Room Service* and *The Big Store* are generally tiresome, but *At the Circus* merits closer inspection (despite "Two Blind Loves," a song so awful it is perversely fascinating) for comic bits, including an inspired closer, and its reverse sadism aimed at Groucho. *Go West* takes a long time breaking loose but eventually does, and the underrated *A Night in Casablanca*, free of songs, has more memorable lines (including Groucho's riposte to Chico, "I don't mind being killed but I resent hearing about it from a man whose head comes to a point") than their previous four films combined. It begins as straight drama for three minutes until the first and much-anthologized sight gag (Harpo "holding up" a wall). If only it did not dissipate in an endless airplane chase.

The few extras in the Universal box are negligible, but the prints are mostly excellent, except for the restored "lost" scenes long ago excised from *Animal Crackers* and the boudoir episode in *Horse Feathers*, which is unaccountably pocked by a dozen splices—hard to believe they couldn't find better sources for that one. The Warner Bros. box is fat with worthwhile extras, including Robert Benchley shorts and rare cartoons, though one wonders why they omitted the brothers' last film, *Love Happy*, which is admittedly dire but no more so than *The Big Store*. The Warner Bros. prints are superb—even the lesser films are enhanced by the refurbished glow, especially *A Night in Casablanca*. Both are perfect gifts for matriculating freshmen.

[*New York Times Book Review*, 18 June 2000 / *The New York Sun*, 7 December 2004]

4 ❖ This Guy Wouldn't Give You the Parsley off His Fish (Jack Benny)

I became interested in Jack Benny in the early 1970s, when I saw him live. The occasion was a New York concert appearance by George Burns, who, after several years of relative inactivity, was embarking on his highly successful comeback. Benny came along to introduce him. It took him about 10 minutes, and I don't remember a word he said. But I have never forgotten that as soon as he walked out—body flouncing, arms swinging to breast-pocket level, eyes glazed with stoic chagrin—I was convulsed with laughter, an effect his TV appearances had never had on me.[1] If Burns was good, Benny was bewitching. During the past year my impressions of that evening have been confirmed almost nightly, thanks to the Christian Broadcasting Network. CBN harvests souls by day, but by night lures prospective recruits with back-to-back reruns of old programs by those same wily Jewish comedians, Burns and Benny. After a year of late-night viewing, often of shows that I recalled from childhood

---

[1] This seems incredible to me now, as I gratefully absorb his TV appearances (usually on DVDs exchanged with fellow antiquarians), laughing with not a little awe at the kind of humor that springs intrinsically from Benny—a clown disguised as a perfectly ordinary middle-aged man. When I wrote this piece, 20 years ago, I could still recall my childhood indifference, one reason that his appearance with Burns was so epiphanic. Growing up, I probably saw him as one of many 1950s funny men and women, including some who spoke more directly to me. Yet few speak to me now, while Benny glides through time like a renaissance poet.

with a rather indifferent fondness, I've become a Jack Benny zealot, recounting bits and anecdotes, hoarding pregnant pauses and martyred stares, and even composing this tract about a radiantly funny man whose humor stands up against all odds.

The fact that I can't recall anything Benny said in concert is germane, since he may be the only great comedian in history who isn't associated with a single witticism. He got his biggest laughs with two exclamations— "Now cut that out!" and "Well!"—and impeccably timed silences. When he died in 1974, I watched the news stories for samples of his jokes. There weren't any. The one bit they frequently played came from radio: Benny, out for a stroll, hears footsteps behind him. A holdup man says, "Your money or your life." Benny says . . . nothing, for a very long time. That's the joke. But it isn't the topper. The holdup man repeats his threat and Benny shouts, "I'm thinking it over!" On the original radio broadcast, he followed through with yet a third variation on the theme: The holdup man gets abusive and Benny, a model of agitated innocence, responds, "If you wanted money, why didn't you just ask for it?" Needless to say, none of this is funny if you don't know the character of Jack Benny. What an arduous exercise it would be to try to explain Benny's unprecedented and unequaled success in American comedy to an audience unfamiliar with the sound of his voice or his deadpan face. Happily, that task is not yet necessary.[2]

Everyone I know knows Benny, though the degree of knowledge depends on age. Those under 40 remember him from TV; those over 40 remember him chiefly from radio (specifically, a Sunday-night-at-seven ritual so widespread that in 1943 NBC declared the time slot his no

---

[2] Two decades later, that may no longer be the case. Does the CBN still exist? Not on my cable provider, and I'm unaware of Benny broadcasts on other available stations, though many of his TV broadcasts are available on public domain DVDs. Yet I'm told by several young people who adore Benny that they know his radio shows from NPR broadcasts, Garrison Keillor homages, and the kind of word-of-mouth that leads to MP3 compilations. One young man offered to copy me a collection of 500 Benny radio shows. Benny's films are far more difficult to find, beyond the brilliantly cast Lubitsch gem, *To Be or Not to Be*. Yet *Artists and Models Abroad*, *Buck Benny Rides Again* (ranked as the third top-grossing film of 1940), *The Meanest Man in the World*, and *It's in the Bag* are among his essential works, long overdue for rediscovery. He redeems the more dated if prestigious property, *George Washington Slept Here*, which provided him with a fine anecdote. Benny browbeat Jack Warner into hiring the eccentric character actor Percy Kilbride for the movie adaptation of the Kaufman and Hart play. Benny had seen Kilbride—later famous as Pa Kettle—in the Broadway production and found him hilarious. Warner couldn't understand why Benny, the star of the picture, would wage a fight to bring in an unknown who would undoubtedly steal it from him. The mogul finally agreed to a Kilbride screen test when Benny offered to pay for it. It was a disaster: Benny couldn't stop laughing. Even after Kilbride was hired, Benny kept cracking up on the set. Warner threatened to fire Benny for holding up production.

matter what sponsor bought it). Benny was a comic institution for four decades and apparently had no detractors—though Benny wouldn't have been too sure. In his later years, an insurance group eager to use him in its newspaper ads, hired a marketing researcher to measure his popularity. The company was elated by the results: He was loved by 97 percent of the American public—a higher number than for anyone else. "What did I do to that 3 percent?" Benny wanted to know.

Yet the character he created and developed with inspired tenacity all those years—certainly one of the longest runs ever by an actor in the same role—was that of a mean, vainglorious skinflint: a pompous ass at best, a tiresome bore at near best. To find his equal, you have to leave the realm of monologists and delve into the novel for a recipe that combines Micawber and Scrooge, with perhaps a dash of Lady Catherine De Bourgh, and a soupçon of Chichikov; or, better still, a serial character like Sherlock Holmes, who proved so resilient that not even Conan Doyle could knock him off. The Benny character was no less fully rounded—an obsessed fan, armed with hundreds of broadcasts, might construct a reasonably detailed biography of him. On the other hand, no one believed Doyle was Holmes, while many people believed Benny was "Benny," a phenomenon that amazed the actor as much as a literary parallel would later distress Philip Roth. A lawyer once dunned him with outraged letters for refusing to pay Rochester his piddling back wages (a plot contrivance on radio); the exasperated Benny finally wrote him, "I only hope you're making in one year what Rochester makes in one month."

Many veteran entertainers who pioneered on radio, exchanging a string of vaudeville theaters for millions of living rooms, were surprised by the new audience's credulity and its implications. A fan once asked Gracie Allen if Benny was really cheap; she responded, "Am I stupid?" Yet Benny, like Roth, courted trouble by injecting just enough reality into his work to confuse the issue, and by sustaining his conceit—this, perhaps, was his greatest achievement—through all the fashions that attended the Depression, the Second World War, the affluent society, and the switch to television. Once he established his image, he remained intransigently loyal to it. No but-seriously-folks closers or nice-guy apologias for him. Unlike every other comedian you can name, he never stepped out of character. He seems to have sensed early on the new medium's potential as a mirror for the more commonplace foibles of a mass audience. In any case, he emerged over the decades as a comic staple who could bind the sensibilities of several generations.

Meredith wrote of Molière that he "did not paint in raw realism [but] seized his characters firmly for the purpose of the play, stamped them in the idea, and, by slightly raising and softening the object of his study

... generalized upon it so as to make it permanently human." Benny's fictions evolved so humanly that the actors who incarnated them ended up adopting the names of their roles. Eddie Anderson had many credits before he joined the Benny crew, but was thereafter known in private life as Rochester.[3] Owen Patrick McNulty legally changed his name to Dennis Day after his first four years with Benny; his family convinced him to change it back, but he performed exclusively as Day. Sadye Marks, Benny's wife, legally assumed the name of the dumb gentile shopgirl she played and remained Mary Livingstone Benny even after retirement. Benny also underwent a name change, though not to suit a script. During his apprentice years in vaudeville, his real name, Benjamin Kubelsky, prompted two lawsuits—the first from a violinist named Kubelik who thought a violin-playing Kubelsky would confuse people; the second from Ben Bernie, who complained that the resulting pseudonym, Benny K. Benny, was a deception designed to cash in on Bernie's fame. ("Now Jack Osterman is suing me," Benny used to tell friends, referring to a comic of the day.)

If the Benny character looms as a kind of metafiction, it isn't in Victorian novels that its genesis is to be found. Benny virtually invented situation comedy, and like most significant innovations, his was a natural outgrowth of local traditions: the American stereotypes and modes of entertainment predominant at the turn of the century. When Benny came along, minstrelsy's ritualistic subordination of individual performers to a faceless (or blackfaceless) group was on the wane, but the idiom's conventions had a lasting influence. The minstrel olio was the first American variety show, typifying theatrical fragmentation and creating such enduring specialties as the Irish tenor (who traditionally sang the first solo), the stout announcer and buffoon (Mr. Interlocutor), sketch dialogues (Mr. Tambo and Mr. Bones), and grotesque caricatures of every racial and ethnic group.

Vaudeville, its immediate heir, freed the specialty acts from an oppressive scheme, not to mention blackface, and forced the performers to assume more individual identities. Still, nostalgia for the old minstrel troupes lingered. The first variety show ever broadcast was a 1924 performance by Dailey Paskman's Radio Minstrels, and tributes to minstrel stars regularly turned up on radio and in movies through the mid-1940s.

---

[3] In *Sunday Nights at Seven: The Jack Benny Story*, by Jack Benny and his daughter Joan Benny, he explains why Rochester was a good name for a butler: It sounds "kind of English and it was incongruous for me to have an English butler. Also the word has a good hard texture. It's a name you can bite into. If I was mad at him, I could yell, 'RAH-chester.' It was an ideal name when I lost my temper."

During the broadcast premiere for the 1940 film, *Love Thy Neighbor*, the banter between Benny and Fred Allen turned into a kind of minstrel badinage, which prompted Benny to ad-lib (and fluff!) a reference to Mr. Tambo: "We'll go right into a black routine," he says, imitating the endmen laugh, "Yuk, yuk, yuk." He had a right to patronize the old style. The best of the untethered, unmasked comics on the vaudeville circuit had long since originated more precise and inventive personae, often working in pairs—a straight man with a laugh getter. Sketch humor had come into its own.

Into that world, enter Benjamin Kubelsky, a very young and eager violinist manqué. He was born on Saint Valentine's Day, 1894, in Waukegan, Illinois, the son of Russian immigrants who were Orthodox Jews. At six he began violin lessons and at eight was acclaimed a local prodigy; at 12 he persuaded a friend to get him a job in a theater and worked his way up from ticket taker to usher to musician in the pit orchestra. He must have been pretty good, because Minnie Marx tried to hire him as music director when her sons played the theater, an offer his parents made him decline. In 1912 Benny was expelled from high school and went on the road with a flashy pianist and veteran performer named Cora Salisbury. When she retired after the season, he teamed with another pianist, Lyman Woods, and in 1916 "Benny and Woods: From Grand Opera to Ragtime" played the Palace Theater at $250 a week. They did 11 minutes of musical parody, and although *Variety* called it a "pleasing turn for an early spot," they flopped. Yet they toured for nearly five years, until Benny learned his mother was dying and returned home. A year later he joined the Navy, where he devised a routine with the famous novelty composer and pianist Zez Confrey. More significantly, he also did his first monologue in a Navy show that eventually toured the Midwest. By the time he returned to the civilian circuit, Benny was concentrating on getting laughs while holding on to the violin as a prop. He was billed as "Ben K. Benny: Fiddle Funology," then "Jack Benny: Fun with a Fiddle," then "Jack Benny: Aristocrat of Humor," and finally "A Few Minutes with Jack Benny."

Robert Benchley praised his cool bravado and subtlety when Benny returned to the Palace in 1924, but others panned him for what they construed as egotism and aloofness. Benny was studying other comics to learn how to sustain narratives and raiding joke books for one-liners, including occasional "cheap jokes"—for example, "I took my girl to dinner, and she laughed so hard at one of my jokes that she dropped her tray." Nevertheless, he was regularly employed. Nora Bayes hired and romanced him, and the Shuberts installed him in the revue *Great Temptations*, on which tour he courted and married 18-year-old Sadye Marks. Never a major vaudeville star, Benny appeared in three unsuccessful movies and worked mostly as an emcee during the next few years. Yet he was making good money in 1930—$1,500 a week—as the comic in *Earl Carroll's Vanities,* when he faced up to the fact that vaudeville was through and began looking beyond it.

Ed Sullivan gave Benny his first radio shot in 1932; he opened with, "Ladies and gentlemen, this is Jack Benny talking. There will be a slight pause while you say, 'Who cares?'" No one did, but the following summer his agent got him a job as emcee on a show featuring George Olson's band. Benny experimented with topical humor, and began kidding movies and the sponsor ("I was driving across the Sahara desert when I came across a party of people . . . ready to perish from lack of liquid. I gave them each a glass of Canada Dry Ginger Ale, and not one of them said it was a bad drink"). By summer's end, he had made a terrifying discovery. Radio consumed material faster than he could get it. A joke that might have worked for a whole season in vaud was good for only one night on radio.

In 1934, at age 40, Benny saw the promised land. His guide was a writer George Burns had introduced him to named Harry Conn, who seems to have played Herman Mankiewicz to Benny's Orson Welles. Accounts differ about Conn's contribution, since Benny and Conn parted bitterly a few years later, but there is no doubt—Benny himself was emphatic about it —that Conn was instrumental in conceiving the brainstorm that revolutionized radio: situation comedy based on the lives of the performers, complete with sophisticated sound effects. Instead of revue skits and strings of jokes, each show would be a variation on a constant theme: life with Jack Benny. It was Conn's misfortune to underestimate the importance of Benny's delivery, timing, personality, and script editing in making the initial concept work. Once the idea was established, writers could be replaced, as Conn was when his demands grew unreasonable. But before that happened, he and Benny came up with many of the motifs that would become the star's trademarks: the scenes set in his home, the Irish tenor, the jovial announcer, the dumb girlfriend, the obnoxious bandleader, and the reductio ad absurdum of shows that depicted only a mock rehearsal for the show on the air. It was not an immediate hit; in 1934, the *New York World Telegram* named Benny the most popular comedian on radio, but two sponsors dropped him. Not until 1936 and 1937, when Rochester and Phil Harris joined the cast, did the Benny magic take hold.

When Benny surpassed Eddie Cantor in the ratings in 1937 as the most popular star on radio—a position he maintained for most of the next 15 years—he rang the death knell, symbolic and real, for vaudeville. Cantor later remarked, "He made all the other comics throw away their joke files." His popularity had no equal in radio, then or ever. Utterly stymied by

Benny's success on NBC, CBS produced an ambitious series of topical dramas for the Sunday-at-seven slot, because no sponsor would buy the time. (The notion of combating popularity with quality seems rather quaint today: CBS, which bought Benny's radio show in 1948 and made a fortune with it, canceled him on TV in 1964, when *Gomer Pyle* beat him in the ratings.) As Fred Allen told Maurice Zolotow in 1950, "Practically all comedy shows on the radio today owe their structure to Benny's conceptions. He was the first to realize that the listener is not in a theater with a thousand other people but is in a small circle at home. . . . Benny also was the first comedian in radio to realize that you could get big laughs by ridiculing yourself instead of your stooges. Benny became a fall guy for everybody else on the show." Or as Benny put it, "The whole humor of Jack Benny is— here's a guy with plenty of money, he's got a valet, he's always traveling around, and yet he's strictly a jerk."

Some jerk. Everyone knows a few things about radio's Jack Benny: he was eternally 39, cheap, bald, self-admiring, drove a dilapidated Maxwell (is there any other kind?), lived alone with a valet named Rochester, and had irresistibly blue eyes. With the possible exception of the last, none of this was true of the real Jack Benny; in fact, he had to eliminate the bald jokes when he moved to television. Henri Bergson wrote, "The comic comes into being just when society and the individual, freed from the worry of self-preservation, begin to regard themselves as works of art." Benny honed that generalization to a lunatic specificity, making himself a clown by acting the part of an artwork. No matter the humiliations he had to endure, his self-esteem remained untouched; like cartoon characters who fall off cliffs, are momentarily flattened, and quickly recover, Benny and his vanity were emboldened by adversity. The better the audience knew that, the less he had to do for a laugh. *He* was the laugh. A carnival pitchman bets him a quarter that he can correctly guess Benny's age, and guesses 39. Benny simply gazes helplessly, and the audience is right with him, agonizing over his impossible choice between the quarter and his vanity.

He opened one television show by striding center stage and calmly announcing, "Well, here I am again, standing in front of millions of viewers, completely relaxed, and not a worry in the world. Now, some critics will attribute this to my years of experience; others will say it's the temperament of a true artist. Personally, I feel that it's nauseating confidence." Right away, the audience likes him. Yet he continues in a mode of fake candor, as though he were stepping out of character: "My psychology in starting out with a remark like that is to get you people to dislike me immediately. Then when you realize you're disliking a nice, harmless, elderly man, this gives you a guilt complex. Guilt leads to sympathy, sympathy leads to laughter, and laughter leads to applause. And then when the applause is over, you go home and I go to the bank. That's when I laugh."

Money, and Benny's affection for it, was his most successful leitmotif, one that required some courage to pursue, since it underscored the most persistent of negative Jewish stereotypes (and yet another convention of minstrelsy). Of course, by carrying it off so well, Benny helped to dispel penuriousness as an anti-Jewish barb. Still, this was a matter of concern to him. In 1945, at the height of the fad for radio contests, his show offered a prize to listeners who could best complete the phrase, "I Can't Stand Jack Benny Because..." in 50 words or less. Benny approved the idea, but worried about anti-Semitic responses and asked that they be pulled. Of 270,000 entries, only three were offensive. Benny's Jewishness, in the context of his comedy, is a rather complicated issue, and the manner in which he broached it suggests the degree to which the Jews of his generation felt, in Bergson's phrase, "freed from the worry of self-preservation."

Before 1900, Jewish grotesquerie was a familiar ingredient in the entertainment world, but Jewish humor that wasn't self-deflating simply didn't exist on the American stage. "There were plenty of excellent Jewish performers," according to vaudeville's chronicler Douglas Gilbert, "but they were doing Dutch, blackface, or singing and dancing acts. Some of them were good Irish comedians. Indeed, Weber and Fields at one time did a neat Irish act." Gilbert traces the emergence of Jewish humor to the Mauve Decade success of one Frank Bush, whose doggerel included:

> Oh, my name is Solomon Moses I'm a bully Sheeny man,
> I always treat my customers the very best what I can.
> I keep a clothing store 'way down on Baxter Street,
> Where you can get your clothing I sell so awful cheap.

But no single performer can liberate a people's pragmatic instinct to keep their ethnicity under cover. Something more, a confident sense of assimilation, is necessary. Years later, Al Jolson seemed to personify and answer that need: first he Anglicized his name and hid behind blackface, then he wiped it off to emerge as a celebrity whose renown in the Jazz Age was rivaled only by that of Babe Ruth and Charles Lindbergh. As Jack Robin (in *The Jazz Singer*), he was the Augie March of his time—a fast-talking all-American hustler who could discard or employ his Jewish roots with equal facility. Which isn't to say that Jewish entertainers weren't apprehensive about their gradual acceptance as Jews; even in the Hollywood of the '30s and '40s, Jewish producers avoided Jewish subjects, and Jewish actors played Italians.

Benny's ambivalence about Jewish humor runs throughout his program. Mary Livingstone, who variously turned up as his wife, girlfriend, or just another prickly opponent, had no Jewish characteristics. Benny drew directly on his own Jewishness only rarely. In a TV episode, he auditions actors to play his father in a movie to be based on his life. One actor identifies himself, with a thick burr, as Kevin O'Houlihan. Benny stares haplessly into the camera, before blurting, "NEXT!" On a radio show, guest star Bing Crosby told of how he'd been rejected by a country club for being an actor. Benny ad-libbed, "How would you like to be an actor *and* a Jew?" To his friends, he was the quintessential Jewish monologist. The harmonica virtuoso Larry Adler, who toured with him and considered himself a disciple, told me that Benny "not only epitomized Jewish storytelling and intonation, but showed everyone else how to do it." That intonation comes across more clearly in off-camera interviews and, oddly enough, his highly amusing letters—some of which are collected in Irving A. Fein's *Jack Benny: An Intimate Biography*—than on the air. Nevertheless, the Benny cast included two Jewish dialecticians—Sam Hearn in the early years, and later the more enduring Mr. Kitzel (played by Artie Auerbach).[4]

A harmless, middle-aged man who speaks with a chirpy Ellis Island twang and wears a glassy-eyed smile, Mr. Kitzel is the *only* recurring character who doesn't treat Benny like a jerk. No matter how harassed he is, Benny is always delighted to hear Mr. Kitzel's "Hallo, Mr. Benny," and to play straight man for his corny jokes. Mr. Kitzel isn't nearly as funny as the other cast members (especially Frank Nelson as a maddening repertory character with prim mustache and uniquely chromatic way of saying "Ye-e-e-e-s?"), but for Benny he represents one bright moment amid a regimen of humiliations. On an early TV show, Benny takes the Beverly Hills Beavers, a boys club, to the carnival. Mr. Kitzel plays a utility man, who keeps turning up in different guises—first selling hot dogs, then in a gorilla suit, and so forth. The show ends when the boys want to see the belly dancer, and Benny says he doesn't think it would be right. We zoom in on the dancer's face, and hear Mr. Kitzel's voice as she lip-synchs, "It's all right, Mr. Benny, it's only me." Benny turns an amazed smile to the camera, shrugs his shoulders, and leads the pack into her tent.

---

[4] Benny on ethnic humor, in *Sunday Nights at Seven*: "Bad as you may think this kind of humor was, I think it was a way that America heated up the national groups and the ethnic groups in a melting pot and made one people of us—or tried to do so. . . . I do not feel today that Rochester and Mr. Kitzel were socially harmful. You don't hate a race when you're laughing with it. You couldn't hate Rochester. You loved Kitzel. You loved Rochester."

Benny was probably wise not to make too many direct Jewish allusions. After all, his alter ego embodied enough standard Jewish stereotypes to effect not only the anti-Semitic backlash he feared but to intimate the self-denigrating humor of early vaudeville. He toted a violin, postured with the vanity of a young girl, mistreated the help, and hid his money in a dungeon surrounded by a moat. Yet he played the role with such originality and brio that his failings seemed at once too particularized and too broad to represent an ethnic group. His moot sexuality is a good example of his restraint. In a TV episode, he explains to Rochester why the studio wants to film his life: "I wasn't exactly the first choice, but they found out mine was the only life they wouldn't have to censor. [Intent pause.] Darn it!" Though he was eternally youthful (else the age jokes wouldn't have seemed quite so crafty), and, at least in his early years, a great success with women, Benny so convincingly embodied the ineffectual fop that he became a professional neuter—sexless even when playing opposite Carole Lombard in his best film, *To Be or Not to Be.*

On radio, Benny was sexually anchored by Mary; on TV, he became slightly hysterical (Barbara Nichols, in her usual floozy role, played his occasional date). He was surrounded by sexuality that was vulgar (Phil Harris), sly (Rochester), and placid (guest couples such as the Ronald Colmans on radio or the Jimmy Stewarts on TV). But Benny remained a naif, a mama's boy without a mama, or, more precisely and oddly, a mama's boy with a black male servant for a mama. Yet unlike Johnny Carson, who, for all Benny's obvious influence on him, is sexually cold and untouchable, Benny was warm and intensely physical—constantly patting the hands of his female guests and wrapping his arms around the shoulders of his male friends. (Benny prefigured the *Tonight* show host in his movie *The Big Broadcast of 1937.* He played a radio host named Jack Carson, who boosts his ratings by having a couple get married on the air, a la Tiny Tim.)

Most of Benny's character traits evolved accidentally. If a certain joke worked one week, he played a variation on it the next. The age jokes, for example, didn't start until he was 55, and a nurse in a sketch asked him his age; he paused and said 36. It got a big laugh, so he remained 36 for the rest of the season. The following year, he was 37; in the next, 38. He decided to freeze at 39, because it's a funnier number than 40. His most fertile subject was his stinginess, an angle that produced countless variants. Here is a small garland of them:

He pays his agent 9 percent.

He keeps Mary's fur in his refrigerator: it's "a better deal than the storage company."

He plays a one-hundred-dollar Stradivarius—"one of the few *ever* made in Japan."

For 15 years, he drives a 1927 Maxwell—sound effects by Mel Blanc—that he reluctantly sacrificed to the wartime need for scrap metal. Reborn as a bomber, it makes the same sputtering noises.

When traveling, he pawns his parrot rather than leave it at the pet shop at 75 cents a day.

He stays at the Acme Plaza in New York—the basement suite, which "underlooks the park."

The act of pulling a dime out of his pocket produces suction.

He discovers his tux is stained. Rochester: "That's what you get when you rent a dress suit." Benny: "Well, let's be careful who we rent it out to."

When Fred Allen visits him in the 1945 movie *It's in the Bag*, Allen finds a hatcheck girl in the closet and a cigarette machine in the living room. "This guy wouldn't give you the parsley off his fish," Allen mutters.

Benny's secretary calls a cab for him, and is told it'll take two hours. "Are they that busy?" he asks. "No, they say they'd like time to think it over."

A terrorist throws a rock through Benny's window with a note that warns, "Get out of town before it's too late." "Hmmm," Benny muses, "just a note, no ticket."

At the race track, Benny says, "I hope I win, I can sure use the money." Mary: "Why? You've never used any before."

On TV, Benny lives in characteristic middle-class, sit-com modesty —his house and those of his movie star neighbors could easily be exchanged for the dwellings on *Father Knows Best* or *Leave It to Beaver*. On radio, however, his vault is somehow located in a subterranean passage, protected by a drawbridge, a moat, a creaking door, a guard who hasn't seen daylight since the Civil War, and finally a combination safe. "You must have a million dollars in the vault," Mary assures him when he worries about money. "I know," he says, "but I hate to break up the serial numbers."

Benny's cast of characters was fine-tuned by the same hit-and-miss system that produced his most enduring conceits. Some performers remained with him for decades. The most celebrated was Eddie Anderson, a vaudeville star whose appearance as a Pullman porter in a 1937 episode was so successful that he was brought back as Benny's valet. He continued as Benny's long-suffering but shrewd and frequently impertinent sidekick until he retired 21 years later. As Rochester Van Jones, Anderson delivered a brazenly hoarse counterpoint to Benny's spry chatter and usually got the best lines. On his day off, Rochester might don an outrageously gaudy smoking jacket and sprawl on a chaise, sipping a mint julep and smoking a cigar, refusing even to answer the phone. But he earned those days. Rochester had to dip his typewriter ribbon in grape juice because Benny wouldn't replace it. When Benny tried to talk him out of installing his own phone, assuring him he could use his, Rochester said, "I know, boss, but look at it this way. Suppose the house is burning down and I haven't got any change?" They didn't quite love each other; but they were perfectly at home in each other's company. One Christmas, Rochester asked a department store clerk to help him choose a gift.

CLERK: What kind of man is your boss? Is he the athletic type?
ROCHESTER: No.
C: The intellectual type?
R: Well, no.
C: The executive type?
R: Hmmm, no.
C: Perhaps the outdoor type?
R: NO!
C: Well, perhaps he's the playboy type.
R: (Laughs.)
C: I'm afraid there isn't very much left.
R: That's him!

It was a source of pride to Benny and his staff that when the NAACP and other groups condemned the portrayal of blacks in the media in the 1950s, there was no protest about Rochester. Nor could anyone doubt Benny's personal feelings. In 1940 he refused to perform or board in segregated establishments, and in 1968 he returned $17,000 rather than fulfill a touring contract that would have taken him to South Africa. Yet his public image was utterly nonpolitical. Indeed, his refusal to link his comedy to serious issues made him especially valuable in the 1960s, when everyone else made a show of taking sides. Benny continued to fulfill the comedian's contract to focus on manners rather than morals. I've been able to find only one instance of his making a political statement: "I am neither a Democrat nor a Republican. I'm a registered Whig. If it was good enough for President Fillmore, it's good enough for me. Now don't laugh about President Fillmore. After all, he kept us out of Vietnam."

I don't imagine there will ever be another generation of entertainers who can sustain the loyalties of successive generations as Benny and a handful of his contemporaries did. President Kennedy is said to have been eager to meet Benny because he recalled the Sunday evening ritual in the 1930s when his father[5] made the whole family sit around the radio. The tempo of life, the dissolution of family entertainment, and the increasing disposability of popular culture have imposed new imperatives and standards. Does this mean that Benny himself will simply fade away? Will the very character-induced economy that enabled him to get laughs simply by staring into the camera undermine the effectiveness of his programs when the character is no longer widely known? One innovative cultural critic, John A. Kouwenhoven, has suggested that the strengths of American art lie in its open-endedness, in its fulfillment of Emerson's dictum that man is great "not in his goals but in his transitions." Situation comedies, like other American variations in high and low culture—including skyscrapers, jazz, *Leaves of Grass*, comic strips, the Constitution, and soap operas (to use some of Kouwenhoven's examples)—derive their integrity not from a notion of finalization, but from process and continuity. They are designed with interchangeable parts, to be altered and disposed. What survives is the motivating idea, the germinal core.

Benny himself was a remarkably adaptable figure in the entertainment world, taking every technological twist and popular fashion in stride and refusing to wallow in sentimentality and nostalgia. Yet his radio shows are largely inaccessible to contemporary tastes,[6] as are virtually all radio shows from the pre-TV era—except to satisfy those same maudlin longings Benny rejected. The TV shows are another story, primarily because we still live in a television age. Ironically, despite the visual humor and the irresistible physical presence of Benny, they are not as richly made as the radio series. But they will suffice to keep Benny from becoming primarily a show-business metaphor—much as films kept Will Rogers and W. C. Fields from becoming mere metaphors, respectively, of cracker-barrel wisdom and inebriated impudence. In the relaxed ambience of Benny's TV skits, a singular clown holds his ground—"completely relaxed, and not a worry in the world." The viewer who hasn't been primed on the fine points of Benny's world will pick up on them soon enough; though even a naïve viewer may find Benny's preposterous carriage and delivery sufficient to evoke a deeply, perhaps unexpectedly, satisfied smile. It's not the situations in Benny's comedy that compel attention; it's

---

[5] Given the anti-Semitism of Joseph Kennedy, the bootlegger and Hitler apologist, I treasure this image as an instance of popular culture undermining social prejudice. It reminds me of an early morning phone call from writer Albert Murray in the mid-1970s, urging me to turn on a talk show because Vice President Spiro Agnew was sitting at the piano playing "Sophisticated Lady."

[6] As noted in a previous footnote, this may no longer be the case, though if you give proper due to the adverb *largely*, it probably is.

Benny himself—or, more accurately, Benny qua "Benny"—a peculiarly durable character.

[*Grand Street*, October 1985]

5 ❖ *Cowardly Custard (Bob Hope)*

1. *The Tribute Collection*

When Bob Hope turned 99 in May 2002, he was in poor health and uncharacteristically did not appear on a TV special made up of once-censurable outtakes, which were no more amusing than most of his TV work. Oddly, the show never mentioned his birthday; we were getting little of the centennial buildup that attended the final two-digit birthdays of Irving Berlin, Eubie Blake, and George Burns. Yet the TV ratings were better than respectable. Hope remained a princely figure to many Americans, and not just those once designated members of the silent majority. Even erstwhile Vietnam War protesters are likely to respect Hope's untiring devotion to entertaining the troops. Some years ago, he was the subject of a hatchet job by Arthur Marx, concerned almost exclusively with Hope's miserliness and sexual drive. Yet Marx expressed awe regarding the comedian's courageous tours, staged on hastily assembled planks as deep into the jungle and as far to the front as the army would permit. Does anyone care if he also nailed his co-stars or entire chorus lines?

Hope's parsimony, given his titanic personal fortune, hurt himself more than anyone else. Comedy writers like to joke that Hope stopped being funny because good writers refused to work for him; he had fired them all, some repeatedly, usually when a raise was at issue. On the other hand, he had started many important comedy careers, including those of Melville Shavelson, the team of Norman Panama and Melvin Frank, and Mort Lachman—writers who began with him on radio and contributed more telling work to his movies. The irony of Hope's longevity is that it was fueled by six decades of broadcasting, very little of which is likely to endure. He first became nationally famous on radio (he had already established himself as a Broadway leading man) and increased his standing on TV, in part with many years of hosting the Academy Awards. But the fast, cheeky topicality of his political cracks, often girded with double entendres, dated irrevocably, and—increasingly sanctified as the rich, conformist, golfing buddy of every White House duffer—he eventually allowed the gags to turn soft and predictable.

In movies, however, Hope remains a figure to reckon with. It is the one arena, other than U.S.O. history, in which he is assured of ongoing respect. During little more than two decades, from *Road to Singapore*, in 1940, to *The Facts of Life*, in 1960, he was a formidable attraction—one of the country's top-10 box office stars for 13 consecutive years (1941 to 1953), peaking in 1949. Initially, his popularity leeched Bing Crosby's: His numbers were always highest in the years when a *Road* picture was released, and he fell off the list after the series' penultimate entry (*Road to Bali*). But Hope soon became a phenomenon in his own right, and Crosby—although his solo pictures in the 1940s were more successful than Hope's—owed him plenty, including a radical loosening of his own comic inclinations. They linger as a unique if much imitated team, with Hope's double takes and loose-goose improvisations engendering most of the laughs.

Until James Bond arrived in 1962 (the year after the disappointing but profitable *The Road to Hong Kong*, which boded *Dr. No*'s sci-fi tangents and set design), the *Road* pictures constituted the highest grossing, longest running movie franchise ever. Avoiding the stooge-and-straight-man formula of Abbott and Costello or Martin and Lewis, Bing and Bob functioned as competitive equals, each eternally bent on getting the upper hand. Hope also played straight roles that were sentimental (*Sorrowful Jones*), biographical (*The Seven Little Foys*), and situational (*The Facts of Life*), and did them well. But his principal characterization was perfected on the road with Crosby.

Along with Charlie Chaplin, Buster Keaton, Harold Lloyd, Laurel and Hardy, Joe E. Brown, W. C. Fields, Jack Benny, Mantan Moreland, Danny Kaye, Jerry Lewis, Richard Pryor, Steve Martin, Bill Murray, and Eddie Murphy, Hope created a clownish identity that transcended specific roles. He was always the lovable, wisecracking coward—a decisive influence on Woody Allen's approach. His self-referential one-liners seemed to take filmgoers into his confidence, encouraging their suspension of disbelief in an unbelievable personality. Jokes about his movie studio, his radio sponsor, and especially his sometimes partner, Crosby, who made half a dozen cameo appearances in Hope's films (never the reverse), underscored continuity as he turned up in ever more unlikely situations—genres ranging from swashbucklers to westerns, settings encompassing 18th-century Paris and Venice and 20th-century vaudeville and politics. No matter the costume, Hope was Hope, a large and graceful man with strong features centered on a ski-slope nose; a lively voice amplified by a complement of growls and giggles; an innate gift for timing; and a congenial physicality that made his interactions with men and women intimate, surprising, and seemingly spontaneous. If most of his "ad-libs" were spoon-fed by writers, his body truly had a mind of its own.

Hope was already 35 when he first arrived in Hollywood, ambitious yet skeptical about a town that had ignored his work in vaudeville and on Broadway and radio; he had, in fact, made a couple of one-reelers in New York, but they indicated little potential for movies. One of his early coups came about when he was hired as the emcee for a week at the Capitol Theater, in December 1932; Crosby was the headliner, and after a routine opening night, the two men began talking up comedy ideas at a bar and trying them out on stage—"imitations," Hope called them. One, involving two conductors who meet on a street and end up dueling with their batons, was resurrected for *Road to Zanzibar*. Hollywood lured Hope to introduce a new song in *The Big Broadcast of 1938*; overcoming his disappointment at learning that his number would be a duet (with Shirley Ross), he listened to an audition of "Thanks for the Memory" and knew it would be a hit. The film, a minor variety revue in the Paramount series that had introduced Crosby to feature films in 1932 (*The Big Broadcast*, a wildly surreal comedy that demands resurrection), also stars W. C. Fields, Martha Raye, and Dorothy Lamour. Yet only Hope's song made a lasting impression. Paramount rushed him into a tiresome Burns and Allen vehicle, *College Swing*, as the studio began to doubt his long-term value.

Hope had another ace to play. As soon as he and his wife had arrived in Los Angeles, knowing hardly anyone, he called Crosby to renew a friendship that had lain dormant for five years. Although they were almost exactly the same age (born May 1903), Crosby was king at Paramount and one of the most powerful figures in the entertainment world—with topgrossing movies, the hugely popular *Kraft Music Hall* radio hour, and dozens of hit records. They got together for golf, and Bing invited the Hopes to the season opening of the new race track he had helped to build in Del Mar. At the main evening show, Crosby invited Hope onto the stage and they went through some of the old Capitol Theater routines. When Paramount executives got a load of these two guys, they ran back to the studio determined to team them in a picture. Knowing nothing about the Capitol, they thought Crosby and Hope had made up the routines on the spot.

Their fervor waned with their hangovers, but Bing's did not. His resolve coupled with Hope's surprise success as a cowardly leading man opposite Paulette Goddard in the horror spoof *The Cat and the Canary*, guaranteed the development of a project. And so an outmoded adventure-in-the-East script was retailored by writers Frank Butler and

Don Hartman, rigged with songs by Johnny Burke and James Monaco, and handed to director Victor Schertzinger, who had a big surprise in store. During the first day's shooting, he was stunned to find his stars, egged on by rival gagmen, trying to outfox each other with lines not in the script. Paramount hedged its bets by billing Hope third, after Crosby and Dorothy Lamour, who makes her first appearance 30 minutes into the film.

Road to Singapore opened in early 1940 and out-grossed every other picture that year. Never intended to ignite a series, *Singapore* is the most straightforward of the seven *Road* trips—the only one with a trace of misguided pathos. When Bob realizes that Dorothy loves Bing and not him, he has to play one of those aw-go-ahead-ya-big-lug scenes. They never made that mistake again, nor did they ever again bill Hope third. Most of the essential components are here: romantic crooner and comic fool are girl crazy yet swear off girls and head into the wilds with nothing more than vaudeville savvy and good old American gumption. Crosby and Hope anticipate each other's every move. No other male team had ever combined the natural camaraderie of Laurel and Hardy with virility and (a purely relative) realism. If the gags pale in comparison with those to come, the interaction remains fresh and absorbing. We know they are reciting lines, but, like the Paramount executives at Del Mar, we suspect they are making at least some of them up.

The illusion of ad-libbing has less to do with humor than that imponderable thing called chemistry. In fact, and despite references to Paramount and current events that delighted audiences at the time, the funniest bit belongs to Jerry Colonna singing "Carry Me Back to Old Virginny." Crosby and Hope emote a far subtler magic, unmistakable in their first song together. They have already shown off their patty-cake teamwork, when Hope entertains a party of wealthy snobs with "Captain Custard," miming a uniformed movie usher who suffers delusions of military grandeur. Bing joins him in an expression of us-against-the-squares solidarity, demonstrating how game they were. The irreverence was mild but innovative; this wasn't an ordinary movie comedy-adventure, but an extended inside-joke to which everyone was privy.

Hope went back into harness to team with Goddard for another horror comedy, *The Ghost Breakers*, an admirable entertainment if you can get past the politically correct shibboleths that have kept it off TV for years. The controversy stems from a performance by Willie Best as valet to Hope's radio gossip, Lawrence Lawrence (an inside reference to Crosby's radio writer, Carroll Carroll). Best, a lanky rail-thin actor in his early 20s, had developed a slow-witted, puttering character that came to embody—along with Mantan Moreland's bug-eyed chauffeur or Louise Beavers's beaming maid—racial stereotyping. Yet they were gifted entertainers who beat the system while catering to its restrictions. Best had begun perfecting the part at 14 and worked in more than 80 pictures between 1930 and 1951, though this was his only important role. His timing and control are on a par with Hope's, and the give and take between the fast-talking spieler and the cautioning dawdler is very funny. Their camaraderie, including much physical interaction, is nervy and way ahead of its time. Best's roles were often saddled with silly names (Drowsy, Sleep 'n Eat, Exodus), and, according to the trailer, this part was originally named Syracuse. Somebody thought better of that idea, however, because he appears as Alex.

The Walter Deleon script seems seriously compromised; a subplot involving Lloyd Corrigan is never explained and the final 20 minutes bog down in haunted house nonsense that lacks the verbal zing of the preceding hour. But Charles Lang's dead-of-night photography is impressive, especially the long scenes that are supposedly lit only by candles and moonlight; fans of EC horror comics will experience a shock of recognition at the way Richard Carlson is lit from below in his final scene. George Marshall directed a first-rate cast (Paul Lukas, Anthony Quinn), making two films in one; all except Hope and Best play it straight, as if they don't know they're in a comedy. Hope's signature character was not yet fully formed: In his best scenes, he is a coward, in others a conventional leading man.

A year later he ceded the coward priority and license. *Road to Zanzibar*, a send-up of Tarzan movies, is played strictly for laughs. The friendship between the honestly dishonest crooner and the deceptively clueless clown, two bosom buddies who repeatedly sell each other out, is now stable, as is the vaudeville subtext. For the first and last time, Lamour is introduced as a swindler, along with Una Merkel, rather than as a distressed damsel—they are female equivalents of Hope and Crosby, on the run and on the make. A memorable scene (some of it genuinely ad-libbed) involves Hope and Crosby and a cave filled with drums. Cannibals, played by such estimable actors as Noble Johnson, Ernie Whitman, and a delightful Leigh Whipper (as the witch doctor), translate their drum solos into something that gives umbrage and prepare them for dinner. Crosby: "That's life. Here today and just a burp tomorrow." I'd bet that Orson Welles saw *Zanzibar* and remembered the look and use of its cockatoo.

Many regard *Road to Morocco* as the best in the series—it has a fine Burke and Jimmy Van Heusen score (including "Moonlight Becomes You"). But *Road to Utopia*, written by Panama and Frank, is the funniest. One line from the latter that convulses today's audiences more than those of 1946 concerns a talent contest in which the two men compete with a monkey.

Bing assures the nervous Hope, "You could beat the monkey by your-self." Much was made in the '40s of crazy gags like a talking camel or bear. Yet that kind of thing dates quickly, as does much of Robert Benchley's narration in *Utopia*. The banter between the principals, how-ever, abides, including *Morocco*'s colloquies between Bing and Bob's Aunt Lucy who, played by Bob, mocks Bing's jazzy singing, "Ho-hum, zoot!" *Morocco* opens with a fabled ad-lib: a camel spit in Hope's eye (blinded, he tottered into the frame) and, before director David Butler could shout, "Cut!" Bing patted the camel's flank, muttering "Good girl, good girl." Butler kept it in the picture. *Utopia* has one of the best closing lines of any comedy before the *Road*-inspired *Some Like It Hot*. The line ("We adopted him"), which Hope speaks to the theater audience by way of explaining why his son is a Bing look-alike, was thought up by studio chief B. G. DeSylva, who alone believed it would elude the censors. *Utopia*, completed in 1944, was canned for two years so as not to crowd the 1943 *Morocco* and to put some distance between its release and hushed-up reports of a tragedy: The film's bear killed its trainer—a day after it had lum-bered over a genuinely terrified Crosby and Hope.

Hope's increasing confidence as an actor can be traced by comparing *My Favorite Blonde* (1942), which he once declared his favorite role (in later years, he justifiably gave *Monsieur Beaucaire* pride of place), and *The Paleface* (1948). The former came about as a result of Hope's radio gags about how he pined for the gorgeous Madeleine Carroll. She called to thank him and suggested they make a movie together. Panama and Frank *and* Hartman and Butler were put on the case, devising a parody of her best-known picture, *The 39 Steps*. Once again, the villains —including Gale Sondergaard and George Zucco—play straight (not so much as a chuckle during the first eight minutes); and Hope, as a vaudevillian with a penguin act, chews the scenery, verbally dueling with Carroll and registering a plethora of facial expressions to demon-strate fear. The film is briskly paced, except for a protracted scene of Irish fisticuffs. Crosby appears for a cameo, as does Dooley Wilson, though in his case it wasn't thought of that way. In the year of *Casablanca*, they gave him one line as a porter.

Hope had not completely adapted the cowardly persona for *My Favorite Blonde* and is recognizably human in several scenes. That cannot be said of *The Paleface*, with buxom and buckskinned Jane Russell play-ing her part as though starring in a Saturday matinee western. Hope appears as a dentist, briefly convinced of his eminence as an Indian fighter and gunman, while Russell secretly does the shooting. With Looney Tunes grad-uate Frank Tashlin working on the script, Hope is more cartoonish than ever before. A scene in which Russell motions for a rifle to intervene in Bob's big gunfight augurs the same scene played seriously in *The Man Who Killed Liberty Valence*. Indeed, screening them back to back underscores the dramatic absurdity at the center of John Ford's autumnal film. The best-known sequence precedes the gunfight, as Hope wanders through the town computing the shooting advice he's been given—an exercise in confused wordplay that anticipates Panama and Frank's incomparable vessel-with-the-pestle episode in *The Court Jester*. *The Paleface* is otherwise mildly diverting at best (*Son of Paleface* is better), but Ray Rennehan's Technicolor is eye-popping, a show in its own right.

Universal has done a splendid job releasing these films on DVD as "The Tribute Collection." The prints are stunning, especially the ominous photography of *The Ghost Breakers* and the saturated primary colors of *The Paleface*. No less impressive is the clarity of the four *Road* films; they've never looked better: The detail—the texture of clothing, the play of light, the very artificiality of the studio sets and props—greatly adds to their plenary joys. All the *Road* discs have an original but unenlightening 14-minute low-budget promo called "Bob Hope and the Road to Success," with three talking heads and familiar footage. *Singapore*'s six-minute featurette, "Entertaining the Troops," is more of the same. *Zanzibar* and *Morocco* respectively offer five-minute excerpts from Command Performance shorts made in 1944 (also on *The Ghost Breakers*) and 1945 (also on *The Paleface*), with no explanation as to why they are incomplete.

The jewel among the old shorts is found on *Utopia* and *The Ghost Breakers*: the complete 19-minute "Hollywood Victory Caravan," a 1945 star-studded backstage Treasury Department film with Crosby singing "We've Got Another Bond to Buy," and appearances by Hope, Humphrey Bogart (thumbs under belt as though he were doing a Bogart impression), Barbara Stanwyck, Alan Ladd, Franklin Pangborn, Betty Hutton, and many others. The best extra, if you can call it that, is the co-feature included with *My Favorite Blonde*. *Star Spangled Rhythm* (1942), the finest of the all-star wartime studio revues and an extra only in that Hope is one of dozens of Paramount contract stars who appear in sketches leading to the big flag-waving, Mount Rushmore-glowering finale in which Crosby sings "Old Glory" (by Johnny Mercer and Harold Arlen, who also contributed "That Old Black Magic," sung not by Crosby, but by one Johnnie Johnston and danced by Vera Zorina). What makes it stand out from similar efforts by MGM, Warners, and Fox is the presence of a plot (Eddie Bracken, Betty Hutton, and Victor Moore are the leads) and a mischievous edge—Walter Abel plays a studio boss named B. G. DeSota.

2. Here and Gone

Heading for the elevator to see Rosemary Clooney perform at Rainbow and Stars, we ran into Bob Hope. My nine-year-old daughter's eyes widened; she had grown up watching his movies while Daddy worked on a biography of Bing Crosby, and though Hope little resembled the athletically robust jester of the 1940s, she had no trouble seeing past the red-rimmed eyes, jowls, and bent 95-year-old frame. It was May of 1998. I had interviewed him a few years before, and so took this opportunity to introduce her. "Look at her!" he said, laughing, as he shook her hand; he could not have been more charming. Lea was thrilled. Yet when I asked her the next day if she had told anyone at school, she said, "No, my friends never heard of Bob Hope and they would have ruined it for me."

When network television shut the door to black and white movies, it disenfranchised the culture of a giant swath of history. The baby boomers saw Hope coming and going. He once cracked that he could switch channels and watch his hairline recede, which was not far from true. There were endless showings of movies in which he perfected the cowardly inno-cent abroad—trekking through the jungle with Crosby, fighting Indians with Jane Russell, outwitting a stream of ghosts, pirates, spies, psychos, vaudevillians, swordsmen, and pneumatic women, generating more pleasure than not. And there was the present-day Hope, the indefatiga-ble U.S.O. warrior and pitchman: "This is Bob [fill in sponsor] Hope," he began his TV monologues, which were no more amusing than the skits in which he and other middle-aged men wore dresses and wigs and puck-ered their lips, and elicited gales of laughter, mostly from laugh tracks.

It would be dishonest to pretend that the latter-day Hope, with his poor choice of playmates (politicians and generals who craved his company), did not distort our judgment of the often brilliant comic who had been a top-ten box office attraction every year from 1941 to 1953. You would not know it from the eulogies that greeted his death last week, but by the early 1970s, Hope was a profoundly divisive figure. The *New York Times* ran a devastating reassessment in 1970, by J. Anthony Lukas, that went so far as to suggest that films like *Road to Zanzibar* "may have contributed to many middle-aged Americans' naïve image of Asia and Africa," a notion that bleeds naiveté. At a Madison Square Garden appearance a couple of years later, Hope did a hippie joke and was raucously booed. To many Americans, though, he was well on the road to secular sainthood as the patriotic entertainer who in his seventh decade continued to visit the troops.

So which Hope are we to remember and honor? Not, I suspect, the broadcast Hope, although the longevity of his career owed more to the ether than any other medium. He had started out as a vaudeville hoofer, and like many vaudevillians, learned to do everything: he could dance, carry a tune, tell jokes, ad-lib, read lines, and contort his handsome rubbery face into a broad array of clownish responses. He was a natural who, before long, triumphed on Broadway and radio. Hope was already 35 when Hollywood recruited him to sing "Thanks for the Memories" in *The Big Broadcast of 1938*. A friendship with Crosby led to the "Road" pictures that made him a force at Paramount, but *The Pepsodent Show Starring Bob Hope*, broadcast Tuesdays at 10, from 1938 to 1948, made him an institution. Two years later, he turned to TV, and when his movies began to sag, it was TV that sustained him; for several years, he even emceed a dramatic series.

Little of that wears well. Political jokes that seemed brave and innovative in the 1940s are dated by their very topicality. The bigger Hope became, the softer his jokes. The best monologists are outsiders who thrive on skewering the status quo. Hope was an inveterate insider who treasured his access to the powerful. Unlike Crosby, who declined to be photographed with politicians (except Shirley Temple Black), Hope lined his office with shots of himself and a long line of White House duffers. Mark Twain's barbs sting even now; Hope's never really did. He was a game sketch artist, but savory moments in his TV clip-shows are few and far between.

The Hope I admire and would like my daughter's generation to respect is found elsewhere. From a purely historical perspective, his U.S.O. work is a valiant achievement. He didn't prolong or encourage war, as was said during Vietnam; he brought succor to the soldiers in the dirt and consoled countless families of those who didn't make it back. During World War II, he didn't limit himself to training camps and safe territories, but inched as close to the front as he could, never giving himself or his staff a break. His standard opening on entering a hospital filled with paraplegics was, "Don't get up." A man has to have a special kind of empathy to get away with that.

Hope's U.S.O. work is lasting for another reason. At his best, he was an irresistible performer, fast on his feet and relentless in his energy; choice moments are captured in film shorts and newsreels shot at golf benefits and on plank stages of World War II. Still, the best part of his artistry survives in his films. Hope was the great comic actor of the 1940s, an original whose persona often transcended lame scripts. He can still get you with his gangly physicality; his many shades of discomfort, fear, or lechery; the trademark gurgle; the off-handed badinage with Crosby; and the luckless romancing with any number of sham femme fatales. In *My Favorite Blonde*, Madeleine Carroll puts his life in jeopardy, confessing, "I'm a British agent." Hope says: "Well, you're too late, I've already got an agent." The line is pure Hope—snappy, ridiculous, cool. Some argue that his comedies lack emotion. I think his bluff refusal to indulge facile sentimentality makes them, despite the period references, timeless and absurdly modern.

[*The Perfect Vision*, 2002; *New York Times* 3 August 2003]

6 ❖ *Idiot Semi-Savant*
(Jerry Lewis)

Aldous Huxley argued that the reason French poets venerated Edgar Allan Poe, while English-speaking nations relegated him to the children's corner, was that the Mallarmé translations retained Poe's themes and images but lifted the "curtain of verbal and rhythmic vulgarity." Huxley thought that foreign readers "were endowed with a fortunate deafness and blindness" to Poe's "rather painfully popular harmonies." His insight offers a possible explanation for the Gallic adoration of Jerry Lewis; once again, the foreigners benefit from sensory deprivation. They get to marvel at Lewis's physicality along with his agile camera movements, hallucinogenic color schemes, and dexterous command of pictorial space while remaining blind to the sanctimonious talking head who sapped the affection of a generation with horrific television appearances, and enjoying a liberating kind of deafness, as dubbing and subtitles spare or distract them from the jarring excesses of his voice.

One intriguing extra on Paramount's new set of 10 DVDs (along with outtakes, bloopers, and auditions) is a French-dubbed soundtrack for many of the films. A spot-check comparison shows that the French actor not only mutes the manic yelps and grueling self-pity but, more important, reduces the gap between them. On the other hand, the commentary tracks offered on several discs trigger memories of why many of us turned from Jerry-love to jeez-what-a-putz. Steve Lawrence, in the Paul Schaeffer role of obsequious giggler, repeatedly asks Lewis to describe his invention of the Video Assist, a TV monitor system that allows the director to see what the camera sees. Unsatisfied with taking credit where credit is due, however, Lewis also takes bows for the performances of other actors, musical scores, scripts he co-wrote, and Edith Head's costumes. The price one pays to laugh at Jerry is more Jerry. But it is a price we must live with. These discs provide the first opportunity in decades for fair reassessment. Previous home-video editions were cropped or faded and—love, hate, or admire them with reservations, as I do—his films demand to be seen as he envisioned them.

Lewis's bipolar voices underscore his reluctance to create a stable character. Unlike the personae of other great film comedians, Lewis's "idiot," as he calls his screen double, is consistent in his lack of consistency. He enters with a bang, a model of arrested development pleading not to be hit or yelled at, then discloses himself as a wounded soul with fragile feelings, then alternates idiocy and sentimentality, and often ends up with a young beauty who has inexplicably fallen for him. Only in *The Nutty Professor* did he solve the problem by playing two solid personalities that melt into each other at comically opportune moments.

The classic Lewis character sports a costume—white sox, pegged trousers, greased hair, and a tuxedo when in lounge lizard mode—and relies on familiar gags. These include backbreaking spills, cartoon-like visuals, gratuitous destruction, prop-driven improvisation, a score of funny faces, and verbal riffs that combine Catskills intonation with Las Vegas slang. Yet he remains a dolt in transition, striving to learn life's lessons, so it's no surprise that Lewis rewired three key archetypes of transformation: *Cinderella, Dr. Jekyll and Mr. Hyde,* and *Pygmalion.*

Within and without those tales, Lewis's film persona flourished with eruptions of his childlike inner anarchist, an effect once loved by children and despised by critics as vulgar. Lewis lost the children not because he no longer generated laughs but because his dreaded inner adult demanded equal time. In his book, *Who the Hell's in It,* Peter Bogdanovich complains that Lewis made former fans squirm because they were taught to keep their "deepest feelings always in check." Having once been dragged up a theater aisle by my mother, who worried that I might hurt myself laughing at *The Delicate Delinquent,* I beg to differ.

We turned away from Lewis for two good reasons. After *The Patsy* and *The Disorderly Orderly,* his films rapidly declined, contaminating memories of the earlier films. And Lewis manifested his feelings in a way that suggested a frighteningly ominous narcissism. He tells Bogdanovich, "When I wake up in the morning, I think of me first and then my wife and then my children. I'd like to meet the guy that can honestly admit he does differently." This suggests not only a lack of empathy but of imagination, and helps to explain why none of the supporting characters in his films are fleshed out.

Lewis's disinclination to see the world as anything but a reflection of himself explains his ambition, well into his fourth decade, to play Holden Caulfield. Come to think of it, why not? Both contributed in equal measure to the infantilization of a culture that produces film stars like Tom Cruise, Leonardo DiCaprio, and Tobey McGuire, none of whom could have succeeded in the box office polls of the 1930s and 1940s, any more than Tracy, Bogart, and Robinson could today. Rat-pack locker room bravado now seems more dated than Jerry's rampaging id. The inner child has even made it to the Oval Office, twice: first as a lecherous wonk, second as a petulant clown.

The earliest film in the current release, *The Stooge* (1952), is the only one with Dean Martin, and it has no interest beyond an autobiographical plotline in which an arrogant vaudevillian flops until he hooks up with an inadvertently funny twit. Lewis's bout with a bathroom sink is as stillborn as the intentionally bad audition his character would later undergo in *The Patsy*. Froglike Percy Helton, in an uncredited bit as a songplugger, gets the biggest laugh—unless you count Dean playing the accordion. *The Delicate Delinquent* (1957), written and directed by Don McGuire and produced by Lewis, was his first solo flyer. You can't go home again: This time, my own inner child marched me out of the room when Jerry started to sing "By Myself" ("Oil face the unknoooown"). Still, before he reverts from nitwit to whiner, Lewis has terrific moments mugging and miming with a theremin.

Cinderfella (1960) is one of eight films Lewis made with his mentor, director Frank Tashlin, whose occasionally sadistic sight gags counter Lewis's instinctive masochism. It's a minor effort, yet Lewis's performance was his most nuanced to date, and the first half is rife with inspired bits— combing his hair, orgasmically squeezing oranges, reading an endlessly inscribed ring, an equally endless pullback on a dining room table (and the routine that follows), and best of all, Lewis's trademark mime to Count Basie's record, "Cute," especially the Frank Wess flute solo. Basie later appears, but by then the film has gone off the rails. For his big transformation, he enters the ball in Buddy Love finger-snapping drag, and then abruptly resumes his yucky voice of humility.

He has no voice at all in *The Bellboy*, which he directed after completing *Cinderfella* but released first to fulfill Paramount's demand for a summer comedy. (Paramount nonetheless forced Lewis to finance it himself, a windfall for the novice director and an enduring sore-point for the studio.) The first in an informal trilogy of plotless movies in which Jerry and crew move into a playpen and perform a discontinuous series of gags, it was a tremendous hit. The setting is a Miami hotel and most of the punch lines are telegraphed a mile off. Yet they unwind with unaffected whimsy as dozens of second-string comics do walk-ons. Lewis's next four films, all self-directed, are the heart of his oeuvre, and though only *The Nutty Professor* (1963) is completely satisfying, albeit in a deeply disturbing way, each has masterly episodes.

If Lewis had hired a real writer to provide a plot and a payoff, *The Ladies Man* (1961) might have been his masterpiece. It is definitely something to see—perhaps the most lavishly colorful Technicolor film since *Meet Me in St. Louis*, for which much credit goes to cinematographer W. Wallace Kelley. Nothing is left to chance, from fiery reds on the sidewalks and mailbox to a virtuoso tour of the famous dollhouse set (choreographed by Bobby Van to the trombone playing of sexy Lillian Briggs) to the expert timing of the gags. Helen Traubel and Kathleen Freeman are splendid, but they have no real parts, and the film goes nowhere, petering out in the last third in an overextended parody of *Person to Person*. No matter: This is the movie with Buddy Lester's hat, undead butterflies, the smudged painting, broken glassworks, and a non sequitur Bluebeard angle that brings in Harry James and a spider woman.

With *The Errand Boy* (1961) Lewis returned for the last time to black and white. Nothing is made of the plot, which involves him spying on the employees of the film studio, but the visual gags make good use of the Paramount lot. Many are effective, including another jazz record mime. (Veteran comic Benny Rubin, who has uncredited bits in a few of Lewis's films, does his ancient routine about the pronunciation of his name, which Robert De Niro borrowed for *The King of Comedy*.) As the sentiment kicks in, Lewis muses over the meaning of comedy—unfortunately, in a conversation with a puppet—reviving a theme definitively explored by Chaplin in *The Circus*, insinuated by Harold Lloyd in *Movie Crazy*, and alluded to in *The Stooge*, regarding the difference between the inadvertently funny and the deliberately funny, a theme he later dissected in *The Patsy*.

But first he proved he could combine sight and sound gags with a plot and developed characters in *The Nutty Professor*. In the key scene, he burlesques the point-of-view tracking shot from Fredric March's version of Jekyll and Hyde, building up expectations of the monster's hideousness only to show him as Buddy Love, his poster boy for masochistic self-revelation. Buddy isn't funny, but he is compellingly revolting—his verbal seduction of Stella Stevens is as nervy as Richard III—and for once Lewis came up with a perfectly ambiguous ending that prefigures the ensuing drug culture, which along with the film's acceptance of student-faculty intercourse seems very 20th century.

The Patsy (1963) has an atrocious it's-only-a-movie closer, previously used in *The Road to Morocco*, subsequently used in *Blazing Saddles*, and undermined here by Lewis's ego. The point he wants to make is not that showbiz is pretense, but that Mr. Lewis—as Ina Balin addresses him —controls the pretense. He sadly undermines his ingeniously original story line: A famous entertainer dies and his entourage decides it can mold any idiot into his heir. Two set pieces are justly celebrated: the demolition job the idiot does on his music teacher's home, after balletically *not* allowing any vases to break, and a left-field pantomime introduced by Ed Sullivan doing an impression of Ed Sullivan.

Though highly regarded now, *The Patsy* flopped, forcing Lewis back into the arms of Frank Tashlin for what turned out to be one of their funniest films, *The Disorderly Orderly* (1964). Lewis says that Peter Lorre, whose last performance was in *The Patsy*, referred to him condescendingly as "the face-maker"; in this film, he breaks the face-making bank, miming sympathy pains with patients and driving Kathleen Freeman into a clenched-teeth breakdown. Despite a peculiar subplot about a suicidal cheerleader stalked by Lewis, Tashlin's cruelty is the perfect antidote to the orderly's egocentric torments. The closing ambulance chase is a classic in its own right.

With *The Family Jewels*, the rot had congealed. Lewis became addicted to Percodan around this time, and some observers have blamed it for his bad decisions. Maybe it was also responsible for his bad timing. Old jokes and characters (Kelp, Buddy) return as Lewis plays half a dozen uncles, including a Terry-Thomas pilot, but only the opening bit with spastic Jerry, and his turn as a buck-toothed gangster who sounds like Slapsie Maxie Rosenbloom, have much bite. His great years as a filmmaker were over and it had become fashionable to cringe at the mention of his name, a punch line in jokes about France. Has enough time passed? Can we now look at the films as films? Can we keep from laughing? Yes, yes, and no.

[*The New York Sun*, 26 October 2004]

PART TWO

Film

Recently I saw a moving picture so much worth talking about that I am still unable to review it.

—James Agee, *On Film*

7 ❖ Best Picture, 1889
(Edison: The Invention of the Movies)

If the idea of watching 140 silent movies ranging in duration from three seconds ("Record of a Sneeze," 1894) to 85 minutes ("The Unbeliever," 1918), totaling 12.5 hours and supplemented by two hours of scholarly chat and hundreds of documents and photographs, conveys all the allure of a sadistic high school homework assignment, you may find *Edison: The Invention of the Movies* a revelation. True, it is fraught with educational value. But once you learn to pilot the four discs in this handsomely packaged collaboration between Kino Video and the Museum of Modern Art, you can filter all that and watch in rapture as the infant art learns to mewl, dribble, crawl, rise to its feet, and take over the house.

Purely as a moviegoing experience, this is exciting stuff—one of the most impressive DVD projects to date. The deceptively slim carton encompasses a cinematic museum and provides a portal into a past not yet blanketed in self-consciousness. Audiences who saw these films in nickelodeon peep shows or at Vitascope screenings were daunted by their clarity and realism. At the 1896 debut of seashore footage, a reporter observed that people feared getting wet; at later offerings, onlookers gasped at a kiss and ducked before a raised gun. Over a century later, our awe is tempered by analysis, yet there remains an irreducible level of astonishment as the scrapbook of another age morphs into life and the occasional ancestor looks back at us (note the fellow on the Hudson River dock in "European Rest Cure"), bridging the chasm with near-mystical amity. The locations alone are stimulating, not least in bad films, which in the absence of such distractions as art and entertainment disclose themselves all the more clearly as historical peepholes. We look beyond the skills of the filmmakers, their themes, techniques, and conceits, to examine the clothes, cars, settings, and manners. The films become anthropological texts. Predilections invisible to one audience are exposed to audiences twice removed.

The earliest image, an 1889 test, presents an unfocused amoebalike humanoid that seems to channel a universe out of electricity; the second image is slightly more distinct. The third, shot three years later, is of a fully corporeal man waving his hat in welcome. Soon the images are configured to document sites and tell stories. They form a parade of dancers, snuggling couples, firemen, boxers, historical tableaux, scenic pans, performers in Wild West shows, and vaudevillians. The 1902 "Trapeze

Disrobing Act" is a sexy circus stunt that still looks pretty impressive. Some images are famous: the May Irwin kiss, Annabelle's hand-tinted butterfly and serpentine dances, two dancing men accompanied by a violinist. Practically all were staged and filmed in the Black Mariah, a tarpaper-covered shack in New Jersey that served as the first film studio. It isn't hard to imagine the enthusiasm of patrons choosing among peep shows, or of Edison's delight in counting the nickels—the clinking of which briefly deafened him to the idea that movies might do better if projected on a wall.

Edison was an inventor first, a businessman second, and never an artist. He did not direct the films made by his company. Nor did he appreciate their potential. His studio began to decline in part because while others dreamed of longer and better films, he devoted his energies to patenting a home-video projection system that resembled a modern plasma screen. Edison was ahead of his time, not quite of it. To gauge the contribution of his studio to cinema, these films ought to be looked at in the context of work done by the Lumière brothers and Georges Méliès in France, and the Biograph and Vitagraph studios in New York, all of them working by 1896—all represented in Kino's earlier anthology, *The Movies Begin: A Treasury of Early Cinema 1894–1914*. Taken on its own, the Edison story traverses the rise of film from isolated peeks to the still-dominant menu of generic themes. The films from Edison's peak years, 1894 to 1910, freely engage in voyeuristic delight, violent aggression, cultural stereotypes, and comic irreverence. Far from dating, they increase their reach into our own world.

In 1934, art historian Erwin Panofsky wrote that "the films produced between 1900 and 1910 pre-establish the subject matter and methods of the moving picture as we know it." He hadn't seen nothin' yet. The 30-second "Burglar on the Roof" (1898) augurs the crime film as clearly as "Old Maid Having Her Portrait Taken" and "College Chums" (1901, 1907) prefigure the transgender comedy. The latter is also a benchmark in animation, as a telephone conversation is rendered in letters traveling over long-distance wires. A firing squad shooting Cuban rebels in the back combines early propaganda with wish fulfillment. A 23rd Street subway grate blows a woman's skirts, albeit not as revealingly as Marilyn's; the tinted coat of the little girl in "The Great Train Robbery" adumbrates the similarly tinted little girl in *Schindler's List*. Buster Keaton adapted the plot of "How a French Nobleman Got a Wife from the New York Personal Columns" (itself a remake of a Biograph film) for his bachelor-chasing epic, *Seven Chances*. "The Strenuous Life," a burlesque of Roosevelt's advice to multiply, portends *The Miracle of Morgan's Creek*, not to mention the Dionnes; while "Getting Evidence," in which an inept detective uses various disguises, including blackface, to collect compromising information on the wrong woman, could serve as a Jerry Lewis script.

Edwin S. Porter, who is little remembered beyond the 12-minute blockbuster "The Great Train Robbery," directed most of these films and this set ought to generate increased interest in his achievement. He proved innovative in blocking time (an incident shown sequentially from different views in "Life of an American Fireman"), virtuoso pans ("Coney Island at Night"), trick photography (his effects replicate nausea and dizziness in "Dream of a Rarebit Fiend" and the stop-motion bears in "The Teddy Bears" lose nothing in droll esprit when compared to King Kong or Ray Harryhausen), comic timing ("A Suburbanite's Alarm" and several others), and comic schematics (the Mutt and Jeff casting in "The Rivals"). He displays social consciousness that, by today's barometers, leans left and right. The former tends toward O. Henry-style sentimentality, savoring the plight of a good-hearted ex-con ("The Ex-Convict") and the unbalanced scales of justice for rich and poor ("The Klepto-Maniac"). He leans the other way in suborning racial stereotypes, but as Michele Wallace, the most thoughtful and original of the commentators, observes, he does so with singular nuance. "Cohen's Fire Sale" involves a Jew as an arsonist wearing a fright wig and Fagin nose (he cannot kiss his wife without poking her eye), but the comedy is relatively good-natured. Blacks depicted as childish watermelon thieves come off as innocents compared to punitive whites willing to burn their home over it.

Three of Porter's most remarkable films from 1905–07 are "The Train Wreckers," "The White Caps," and "Laughing Gas." The first uses melodramatic conventions that would later become the stock and trade of Pearl White for a study in gratuitous violence; the gang is out to destroy a train just to watch the havoc—like the guy in California a few weeks ago who parked his car on the tracks and destroyed three trains. Thwarted by the heroine, they lay her unconscious body on the tracks. Spoiler alert: She is saved, and in a manner that directly anticipates one of the best-known gags in Keaton's *The General*. "The White Caps" is a surprisingly ambivalent view of vigilante justice. The villain is a brutal wife-beater. But the actions of a hooded clan of terror-inducing enforcers—they tar and feather him, an activity I've never seen recreated in such detail—quickly undermine our initial anger at their victim. "Laughing Gas," which prefigures by 15 years the best-selling "OKeh Laughing Record," is about a big, beautiful, and charming black woman whose contagious laughter surmounts every obstacle, from getting a seat on the subway to triumphing in court to undermining the piety of a black church service. Vitagraph had made a similar film, but apparently without a black lead; if there is any racism here, it is in the eye of the beholder, not the film.

Porter was fired in 1909, and the quality of Edison films immediately declined. (The most generously reviewed Edison films of this period, "The Prince and the Pauper" and "Frankenstein," are not included, presumably because the former no longer exists and the latter is in the hands of a private collector.) Filmmaking had become more sophisticated, favoring middle-range shots that allowed actors to communicate subtly, but Edison had succumbed to a fit of family values. The sensuality and violence that spurred Porter's imagination gave way to generic conventions—"House of Cards" is a laughably bathetic western, a screed against gambling; "The Unsullied Shield" (directed by Charles Brabin, who redeemed himself in 1932 with *The Mask of Fu Manchu*) is a temperance lecture. The fourth disc begins with a series of routine genre pieces (including a John Buchan-type spy story, "The Ambassador's Daughter"); significantly, these films credit the writers, not the directors. Yet the disc recovers with the feature-length World War I film *The Unbeliever*, directed by Alan Crosland (who later pioneered the introduction of sound in *Don Juan* and *The Jazz Singer*), one of the first films in which Erich Von Stroheim introduced his bestial hun. It is also worth watching for deft recreations of trench warfare.

The presentation is imperfect. A scripted history would have been more efficient and informative than casual interviews ("and uh they see it uh this is a big uh exciting moment uh and then the press comes out and sort of Edison's motion picture device uh you know has entered the public realm"). No one addresses a basic issue: What percentage of existing Edison films does this anthology represent? An alphabetical index of the collection would have made more sense as a printed insert than as a feature on one disc, and the absence of chapter titles in the main menu is annoying. The advisable way to watch is either to play the films alone (without commentary) or through the notes option, which provides brief written introductions by Charles Musser and includes relevant documents and optional commentary excerpts.

An extraordinary bonus on the first disc is a presentation of 20 films synched to Edison recordings. This music is far superior to the uneven new scores—piano and organ solos commissioned for each film. The music for "Uncle Tom's Cabin," a virtual dance fest, is fine, but elsewhere the buoyant joys of ragtime are sacrificed to dull diatonic clichés. There are a few errors: The 1896 "Watermelon Eating Contest" is repeated twice (you can see a later version in the notes section); and the key scene in "Life of an American Policeman" is unaccountably missing. These are quibbles. *Edison* is an infinitely involving and illuminating collection, a slate of old dreams that foretell the future with the tenacity and accuracy of "The Great Train Robbery"'s gunman, aiming at the heads of all who dare look.

[*The New York Sun*, 1 March 2005]

8 ❖ *Who Was That Masked Man?*
(Lon Chaney)

If the original 1925 film of *The Phantom of the Opera* isn't the best bad movie ever made, it may be the most reverberant—endlessly imitated and packed with haunting visual conceits that eclipse the unintentional comedy of its melodramatic style. The most stunning image, of course, is the phantom himself, a movie emblem as durable as Chaplin's tramp, Garbo's stare, Karloff's monster, or Monroe's body. More than the others, he is almost completely unmoored from his movie origin, which is not often seen today. But an excellent print and the high spot of Kino's eight-volume series, *Lon Chaney: Behind the Mask*, puts the old boy back where he belongs, not on a poster or Halloween mask, but in his grotto, five levels below the Paris Opera. Seventy years after his unmasking provoked movie patrons to shriek, the phantom remains an implacable memento mori.

Pause buttons were invented to freeze the phantom's hideous death's-head so that we may peer at length at Lon Chaney's disguise in hope of finding some semblance of the actor, or an understanding of how the makeup was achieved. But the mask is impervious and Chaney nowhere to be found. While filming *Frankenstein*, Karloff reportedly reassured a nervous Mae Clarke by wriggling his up-camera little finger to remind her that it was only Boris coming at her. What could Chaney have wriggled for the benefit of ingénue Mary Philbin, who seems genuinely distressed every time she has to look at him? Chaney achieved the opposite of conventional makeup—not a prodigious showcase for the application of Max Factor, but rather a stripping away of his own face, leaving behind the visage described by Buquet, the character at the outset of the film who has seen him: eyes "like holes in a grinning skull," face "like leprous parchment," "there is no nose."

Chaney died in 1930, at 47, but reemerged nearly 30 years later, when James Cagney, at 58, played him in *Man of a Thousand Faces*—a disconsolate yet oddly enchanting biographical tribute. At the same time, television stations all over the country began broadcasting Universal horror films; Hammer in England and AIP in the United States began manufacturing new ones; and the magazine *Famous Monsters* fetishized the classic ghouls, with Chaney serving as pater familias. Articles appeared that purported to explain Chaney's secrets, as if he were the Houdini of greasepaint. And like Houdini, he was depicted as a noble masochist, suffering horrible physical contortions for his art. It was said that he wore a 70-pound hump in *The Hunchback of Notre Dame* and inserted celluloid discs inside his cheekbones and dulled fishhooks in his nose and mouth.

Well, of course, he didn't do anything of the kind—not according to Michael F. Blake's *Lon Chaney: The Man Behind the Thousand Faces*. According to him, Chaney's hump weighed 20 pounds and celluloid discs and fishhooks are no more credible than werewolves and vampires. Blake details the elaborate and innovative ways Chaney (who wrote the makeup entry for *Encyclopedia Britannica*) turned one face into another, while emphasizing the hardships he did endure: walking on his knees, working without arms, four-hour daily makeups. Yet the nonsense about fishhooks underscores the popular assumption that he worked from the inside of his head out, which is the impression several of his makeups give.

With *Phantom*, Chaney practically reinvented medieval grotesquerie in the monster film, going far beyond John Barrymore's transition into Mr. Hyde to achieve an irreducible equation of ugliness and evil. His Erik the phantom had particular resonance for those who had seen similarly disfigured victims of the First World War's artillery and mustard gas. The Phantom is living death, a walking warning whose background is dimly suggested in references to political upheavals, torture chambers, and a Devil's Island for the insane. We learn that he was a self-educated musician and master of the black arts, but are given no explanation for his "accursed ugliness." When *Phantom* was remade by Universal in 1943 and Hammer in 1962, Erik was provided with a conventional backstory in which he is scarred by acid, a good man driven mad by injustice. Chaney's film is more durable because it eludes explanation at the base level of anxiety. Its mystery is focused in Erik's atrophied face. In *Man of a Thousand Faces*, even Cagney, who composed the film's gloomy waltzes and out-Chaneyed Chaney in his recreation of *The Miracle Man*, was stymied by the phantom. All makeup guru Bud Westmore could come up with was an oversized rubber mask: Cagney looks like the creature from the black lagoon.

Phantom had a troubled production. Its weird blend of serial chills and flagging tempos are equally the fault of a despotic director, Rupert Julian, whom Chaney effectively replaced in his own major scenes, and an indecisive studio that jumbled multiple scripts and endings. Yet at times it has the elegance of a fairy tale, as when the phantom steers his gondola through concentric underground archways or his beneficiary/ victim, Christine, comes to him through her own looking glass. The unmasking echoes the Bluebeard legend: He provides Christine with fairy-tale clothes, a sensuous bedchamber, and the warning, "You will not be in peril as long as you don't touch my mask." Naturally, she's gotta have it. By then we are 43 minutes into the film, and all we have seen of Erik or Chaney is a man with large ears, in a mask and skull cap, acting with imploring eyes and long expressive hands. Though virtually invisible, he is physically and emotionally riveting, bringing a different posture to his every guise—a slinking shadow on the wall, a disembodied arm delivering a letter, a stately Red Death sauntering at the *bal masque*.

Those scenes, along with most of the other films in the Kino series, illuminate Chaney's virtues as a stylized, disciplined, vital actor beyond the makeup box. Everything about him suggests intense commitment. He is not as manic as Cagney, but he portends Cagney's coiled energy. As a pantomimist who at times seems only a step removed from the kind of stage player who tied the ingénue to the railroad tracks and twirled his mustache, he heightens the barnstorming tradition of overemphatic melodrama. His face, au natural, is a mask, with its sad triangular eyes, vertical creases, crooked mouth, slicked hair. Oddly, he is most likely to go over the top when least disguised. Hidden in makeup as Fagin, Quasimodo, or Erik, he is controlled and inspired. Just as blackface liberated music hall performers, gargoyle disguises sharpened Chaney's power.

Within a few years of *The Phantom of the Opera*, Chaney would emerge with Clara Bow as Hollywood's top box office attraction, dominating the transitional years before sound took over. In his sole talkie, *The Unholy Three* (1930), the man of a thousand faces speaks in five voices, proving himself a divertingly modern performer. But in the silent pictures, he is more than that—a live wire, and one of few non-comic actors from that world who still speak to us.

The Kino selections cover the years 1920–25, stopping short of the more contemporary-looking MGM films. Most of these pictures have not been seen in decades. *The Hunchback of Notre Dame* was Universal's first big-budget blowout and Chaney's first star-turn as a physically repulsive freak with a sensitive soul—but only the spectacle and Chaney's acrobatics keep it alive. Frank Lloyd's *Oliver Twist* probably hasn't looked this good since 1922. Chaney's excessively grizzled Fagin boosts the film's drive, and Jackie Coogan, a year after *The Kid*, is impressively impish as Oliver. Rarer gems include Tod Browning's *Outside the Law*, a Chinatown crime vignette in which Chaney plays two roles: the villainous Black Mike, whose seedy clothes, white face, and red lips strongly suggest Olivier's Archie Rice, and Ah Wing, who kills Black Mike in split-screen. Mike devours the air with his obscene smile and oily hair, but Ah Wing has a more resonantly modern bit of business—shucking and jiving for the white folks, then privately registering the intelligence that will save them. The last 15 minutes are badly damaged, but the deterioration actually complements the climactic battle. For a moment, I thought it was a special effect suggesting the flames of hell. *Nomads of the North* is an unaffected 19th-century melodrama about a Disney-like maiden (she communes with birds and squirrels), her dying father, a vile suitor and would-be rapist ("love is impulsive," a priest explains), and Chaney as a visibly uncomfortable hero with a bad wig and a pet bear whose mother he ate.

Shadows finds a somewhat cloying Chaney once again playing a servile Chinaman and once again saving white folks while appealing for racial tolerance. Set in Maine, this fast-moving parable has a curious subtext about a priest's determination to convert the heathen. He succeeds, after a fashion. But the true religious payload comes with *The Shock*, directed by the ruthlessly prolific Lambert Hillyer (*Dracula's Daughter*), in which Chaney's crippled gangster finds redemption in the arms of the woman who gives him a Bible; is then saved from forces of evil by "the cleansing hand of providence" (the San Francisco earthquake to you and me); and finally learns that, like Dr. Strangelove, he can walk! *The Shock* is teamed with a 30-minute abridgement of *The Light in the Dark*, the first film Clarence Brown directed on his own, in which Chaney is a thief who steals and is redeemed by the Holy Grail. Nice work if you can get it.

The sum experience of these films—including an original documentary by Bret Wood, *Lon Chaney: Behind the Mask*, which employs footage from other films as well—succeeds in Kino's stated purpose of getting behind the putty, wigs, and spirit gum, but also instills a hunger for the masks and the empowerment they represent. Near the climax of *Phantom*, when Erik challenges Christine to turn the lever that will blow the place up (a plot device that became a Universal trademark, e.g., *The Black Cat* and *The Bride of Frankenstein*), he stands away from her, registering by turns malice, fear, pique, relief. But he doesn't go over the top, as in his long redemption in *The Shock*. Rather he exhibits the strength of a great stock character, artful yet credible—a remnant of *dei maschere*, and a peep-show pleasure. Unlike Christine, we eagerly take up his dare to glut our souls on his accursed ugliness. The movies invite that kind of bravery; in reality, we'd hide him away with the hopelessly deformed WWI casualties, and contemplate social engineering.

[*Village Voice*, 23 January 1996]

9 ❖ *Reviving Ghosts*
(Olive Thomas / Hindle Wakes*)*

Two kinds of cinematic antiquarianism are on view in new releases from the admirable Milestone Collection, a catalogue that has revived several obscure films from the silent era. In the first, the rather grandly titled *Olive Thomas Collection*, an amusing Frances Marion comedy, *The Flapper* (1920), directed with more flash than usual by Alan Crosland, is paired with a lame documentary. Together they reclaim from anonymity a captivating brunette whose once-fabled beauty, despite ringlets and cupid lips, maintains a curiously timeless candor. In the second, *Hindle Wakes* (1927), the object of adoration is a forgotten near-masterpiece, a startling adaptation of a once-famous play, directed by a prolific hack, Maurice Elvey, whose entire corpus—said to be the largest by any director in British film history—will now likely be sifted in search of additional treasure.[1] Finding Olive is fun; finding *Hindle Wakes* is an event.

Thomas won't rouse embers to the degree of the lately resurrected Anna May Wong, not least because the latter's rehabilitated vehicle, *Piccadilly* (1929, also distributed by Milestone), is an exceptional movie, perhaps the high point in the career of its transplanted German director, E. A. Dupont. Nor is Thomas as sexy as Wong. Famous in her day as a Zeigfeld girl and early Selznick star, she rapidly faded into oblivion after the furor over her death, at 25, in a Paris hotel—the victim of an accident, a suicide, or murder: The jury is still out. Few of her films survive, and many buffs remember her only as the first Hollywood scandal, a kick-off chapter in Kenneth Anger's *Hollywood Babylon*, which, as usual, gets all the details wrong.

The Flapper is a deft diversion about an innocent 16-year-old girl, Ginger, who is dispatched from her insular resort home, where thrills are confined to church and soda fountain, to Mrs. Paddle's boarding school in Lake Placid, New York. Free of her father, a senator who has his own priest in attendance, and a martinet housekeeper, she pretends to be older to attract a mysterious gentleman who proves to be just that and not a pederast. (Obviously, you could not make this film today.) Trading

---

[1] His silent films include adaptations of *Bleak House, Don Quixote, Adam Bede, The Wandering Jew*, and two Sherlock Holmes novels and an omnibus of Holmes stores, and his 1920s films about World War I (at least half a dozen) garnered much admiration for their realism and attention to detail.

in her "Peter Thompson" school uniform for flapper clothing, makeup, and headband, she pretends to a torrid past, but ultimately turns her misadventures into triumph, retaining her virginity: the looks of horror when the community fears otherwise are about as ripe as the satire gets.

Thomas's brightest moment is her brief shimmy with a ukulele, and the film's peak is its location shooting in Manhattan. Marion's wit is expended in alternately clever and arch title cards, and what promises to be a subtext about class evaporates when "the moth among the butter-flies"—Hortense, the boarding school's charity case—turns out to be a vamp and a thief. Class will out, no doubt. A cliché-ridden piano score supports the film, barely, but the excellent print reflects the high level of the original production.

Thomas suggests a transitional force between Mary Pickford's eternal child and Clara Bow's ravenous sprite, and you can imagine her grow-ing into Norma Shearer or Kay Frances roles—if, that is, she had a voice, which is an issue unexplored in the documentary by Andi Hicks. The pur-ple script, narrated by Rosanna Arquette as if she were waking from a coma, leaves no platitude behind: she was "a beauty who loved life and lived it to the fullest," who had a "bi-coastal life style" and a "high-flying life style," and "set the tone for a new generation." (The level of research is characterized by the actor who reads a passage from cameraman Billy Bitzer's memoir in a thick German accent—Bitzer hailed from Roxbury, Massachusetts.) Married at 16, and then again at 20, to irresponsible Jack Pickford (his sister Mary apparently disapproved), Thomas slept with Zeigfeld and either one or two Selznicks, all of whom kept her on a skyward trajectory. Yet the same year she completed *The Flapper*, she ingested bichloride of mercury, used externally for syphilis symptoms, and lingered four torturous days—a front-page story soon displaced by the travails of Fatty Arbuckle, William Desmond Taylor, Thomas Ince, and others in that fun-loving tribe.

The notion that Olive augured the modern woman is as frayed as Ginger's attempt to embody the romantic excesses of cheesy fiction. Fanny Hawthorne, of *Hindle Wakes*, is the real thing, the English version of Ibsen's Nora, unwilling to trade a satisfying fling for a lifetime's mar-ital obligation. She pensively participates in her own deflowering, and is emboldened by it. Stanley Houghton's play is no longer much per-formed, but it caused a storm in 1912, moving him to the head of the Manchester School of realistic drama; he died of meningitis a year later, at 32. The near-simultaneous DVD releases of *Piccadilly* and *Hindle Wakes* add two titles to the exceedingly small list of distinguished British silents, a field little celebrated beyond the apprentice work of Alfred Hitchcock. Both films illustrate the liberation enjoyed by the camera in the final years of that era. With the introduction of sound, the camera would once again lose its mobility, as filmmakers waited four years for technology to catch up to the creative juices that gushed in the mid-1920s.

Elvey had filmed an adaptation of the play in 1918, but in returning to the subject, he came up with the ingenious idea of showing the events that generate the play's drawing room debate. As a result, *Hindle Wakes* is one of the least stagy of theatrical adaptations. It's as if a director filmed *A Streetcar Named Desire* with an hour of footage dramatizing Blanche's mishaps before she turns up shattered on her sister's doorstep. The title refers to the vacation period (wakes) enjoyed by the mill workers in Hindle, a community in Lancashire, spent at the still-thriving working-class amusement park at Blackpool. The 14-minute Blackpool sequence is one of surpassing inventiveness, as the camera mounts a tower, rides a roller coaster, scans the neon vistas, and looks down, with documentary authority, at swirling couples (including same-sexers) on a dance floor. Of the two musical tracks offered, choose the one by the duo that calls itself In the Nursery. It excels especially in the dance hall scene, replicating the sounds of a jazz band with an added edge of brittle dissonance, then departing entirely from the dance band orchestra, as a beaming light shines on the floor and confetti rains on the dancers, underscoring the episode with dreamlike foreboding.

Elvey's eye is no less judicious in footage of the mill, which suggests the kind of industrial films Joris Ivens was just beginning to master. The entire first hour is a skilled montage of varied shots, including close-ups that serve no purpose but to fill in the social milieu, and parallel symbols: the whistles, both corporate and railroad, that govern everyone's time; details that distinguish rich and poor, conventional and idiosyncratic—the sentimental "master" of the mill prefers to drink his coffee from the saucer, like a cat. A constant motif consists of ground-level shots: wheels, legs, feet and, especially shoes, from the massed legs of women changing their shoes at end of day to Fanny's exit, feet first, descending the stairway of her now stifling home.

The shocker that scandalized critics in 1912 and won the support of Emma Goldman (whose essay can be accessed through a DVD-ROM feature) concerns Fanny's refusal to marry the son of the master, following their escapade. She asks the dim and vacillating Allan, "I'm a woman, and I was your little fancy—you're a man and you were my little fancy. Don't you understand?" He does not, but is happy to make a beeline back to his fiancée, the Mayor's daughter, while Fanny, anticipating her mother's determination to humiliate and exile her, packs her bags and goes off, Nora-like, to live on her own, still working in the mill, unfazed by the scandal. This last part is fantasy—she probably would have had to board a train for distant parts. The film loses inspiration, but not tempo (this is a two-hour silent film without a dreary frame) when it is obliged to come inside for the theatrical working out of the plot. Elvey deepens the conflict by focusing on the awkward relationship between Fanny's father, a middle-level mill worker, and the master, former school chums; the master likes to have his old friend around to remind him of his lack of success, but he also wants to rekindle the virtues of their boyhood camaraderie—and consequently is determined to do right by him and have his son marry the compromised Fanny.

Fanny, photographed with evident affection and played by Estelle Brody with a smirk of patient superiority, represents a measure of independence no one else can comprehend. Two other standouts in the generally excellent cast are Humberstone Wright as her father and Peggy Carlisle as her best friend, Mary. With her bobbed hair and Harry Langdon clown face, Carlisle makes so powerful an impression that her disappearance midway is more unsettling for the viewer than for the other characters. Her off-screen and insufficiently explained death leaves an emotional hole that can be filled only by screening the film from the top. If the last third of *Hindle Wakes* is prophetic social consciousness, the first part is filmmaking magic—epical, intelligent, and credible. Elvey died in 1967, at 79, remembered, if at all, as a journeyman who turned out low-budget quickies that defined the mediocrity of the British film industry. In 1927, at least, he was in its vanguard.

[*The New York Sun*, 17 May 2005]

10 ❖ The Pulse of the World
(Fritz Lang)

Spies, Fritz Lang's 1928 tour de force of serial thrills, megalomania, and oppressive but thoroughly justified paranoia, opens with a rifled safe, a motorcyclist speeding off the screen, and a diplomat murdered in broad daylight. The center cannot hold and there is no time to catch your breath. Terrorists strike at will, yet no one knows who they are or what they want. Meanwhile, the public mocks the hapless government, as does an exposed spy who blithely warns the head of the secret service that he will regret learning who is behind the terror. He's not far wrong, because the underworld autocrat pulling the strings, a Lenin look-alike named Haghi, has (like his Langian predecessor, Dr. Mabuse) other identities with which he hides in plain sight. By definition, espionage obliterates the line between friend and foe: Everyone in *Spies* is a spy of one kind or another.

Lang was the most prophetic of 20th-century filmmakers. The comprehensiveness of his futuristic vision puts him on par with Wells, Huxley, and Orwell, the trinity of British Jeremiahs, who subjected human nature to science and politics, while his anatomy of chaos anticipates, no less than Kafka and Canetti, a world of ceaseless fear, moral dubiety, organized lunacy, fascist ambition, and implacable revenge. We describe everyday frustrations as Kafkaesque, but immersion in Lang is likely to produce a similar sense of Langian parallels: Nothing is what it seems, crime and social order are indistinguishable, and technology is our salvation and ruin. As Kafka uses literary techniques and tropes to set up deterministic parables, Lang relies on the fundamental resources of film: the pulp fiction of serial thrillers, from Louis Feuillade to *The Perils of Pauline*; the visual effects of Lumière; the interweaving plot strands of Griffith; the stark documentation of newsreels. In addition to inventing the rocket countdown in *Woman on the Moon*, instant messaging in *Spies*, and urban castles in *Metropolis*, Lang foretells our obsession with serial killers in *M* while exploring the rise of fascism and pathology of crowds (with a clarity that adumbrates Canetti's 1960 *Crowds and Power*). Lang also created stick figures without which modern popular culture is unimaginable, including 007 and his nemeses.

The hero of *Spies* is 326, an improbably wealthy government agent who wears a tuxedo when at home with his servant, but goes undercover as a derelict. Played by the engaging and mostly understated Willy Fritsch, he resembles a cross between the young Rutger Hauer and Dwight Frye. Unlike James Bond, he is a one-woman man, but the woman is Haghi's most effective agent, a Russian émigré whose family was destroyed by Tsarist supporters (the film's politics are confusing and besides the point), played by the soulful Aryan goddess Gerda Maurus; her many crimes are forgiven when she betrays the fiend in favor of 326. Lang's favorite archcriminal, Rudolph Klein-Rogge, who also created Dr. Mabuse, brings Haghi to life. He is part Blofeld and part Dr. No, with aspects of Strangelove and Mr. Memory, the music hall performer Hitchcock devised for his version of *The 39 Steps*.

Spies is a variation on *Dr. Mabuse the Gambler* (1922), but sprints with far more authority. After a smashing opener, there is an adagio movement of about 20 minutes as the threads of the narrative are established (the score, which might have helped here, slips into an unaccompanied piano coma). The payoff is the last hour (as the score explodes into orchestral fireworks), a carnival of astonishing sequences comprising a wicked seduction, hara-kiri, a train wreck, a car chase, an assassin who looks like

Hitler and goes completely crazy, shooting indiscriminately while shouting into a microphone and then taking cyanide (how prophetic is that?), and a finale so startling—a contender for the most haunting finish ever filmed—that, even 76 years later, it would be an injustice to disclose it to anyone approaching *Spies* for the first time.

Kino's DVD has no extras to speak of, but the splendid print, which restores 50 essential minutes, requires none. The same is true of *Woman in the Moon*, for which Lang reunited Fritsch and Maurus; from the first moment Fritch looks longingly at her, you know her husband is not long for the world—which, in this flipped cosmos, turns out to be the moon. Widely regarded as minor Lang, chiefly because it was long available only in mutilated versions, it commands attention for nearly three hours and the primary set-piece, the launching of the rocket (Lang invented the countdown because he thought it more suspenseful than counting up), remains impressive. The crowd scenes, surely inspired by the Lindbergh landing, prefigure the opening of Renoir's *Rules of the Game*, and the accuracy of the science—Lang's advisers were physicists Willy Ley and Hermann Oberth—caused the Nazis to ban it for fear it would give away their plans for the V1 and V2 rockets. Once again the villain, played by the chillingly unctuous Fritz Rasp, suggests Hitler, complete with Little Colonel military fatigues and a greased comb-down (*Mein Kempf* appeared four years earlier), and the plot is riddled with spies, greed, blackmail, and fanaticism. The hero declares, "I do not intend to colonize the moon with criminals," but a world without crime would leave Lang empty-handed.

By 1929, film directors were coming to grips with sound, and the best of them were determined to use it in ways unique to cinema—Clair in France, Hitchcock in England, Mamoulian in Hollywood. Lang's producers had tried to force him to add sound to *Woman on the Moon*, but he refused and consequently remained silent for the next 18 months. His return, with *M* in 1931, innovatively used offstage and overlapping dialogue, yet much of its enduring power resides in extended silent passages, where even a musical score would be intrusive. This virtually flawless work, which made Peter Lorre an international sensation, is so compelling that Irving Thalberg once castigated the MGM team for not making films as good. Imagine his reaction had one of his employees suggested a film about a child murderer who trades accusations with a Brechtian union of criminals depicted as interchangeable with the police.

The Criterion Collection released what seemed a perfectly acceptable version of *M* in 1997, despite a gray bar running across the top of the image, but the new two-disc edition is far more than a collector's enhancement. For the first time, the film is presented in the original aspect ratio (taller than it is wide), which removes the gray bar and adds information to the top of the screen. It also restores the original ending. The previous version ends with the mother of a dead child wailing, "We too should keep a closer watch on our children." The corrected line is "One has to keep closer watch . . . over the children! [fade to black] All of you!" More impressive than any of that is the dazzling restoration of the print —the blacks, whites, and grays far more sharply delineated.

The extras include a 50-minute interview with Lang, in which he describes in detail the circumstances in which he left Germany after meeting with Goebbels—a tale now thought to be, in part, a fabrication, and Claude Chabrol's 10-minute version of *M*, plus a too-brief interview in which he marvels at Lang's technique, mentioning shots that can only work if timed exactly as he did them. One of the most remarkable shots in Lang's film, which Chabrol refrained from attempting, is a two-and-a-half minute tracking pan (it begins at 42:17) that explores the beggars in their lair, similar to the way Martin Scorsese would later trail his camera through a social club in *Goodfellas*. Midway, the shot closes in on a sandwich board and you expect an edit, but the camera rises toward a window grating and goes right through.

In 1936, Lang himself would wriggle through the grating of Hollywood and make films there for 20 years: an unparalleled study of lynching, *Fury*, for MGM, which had no further use for his services; a template for *Bonnie and Clyde*, *You Only Live Once*; and his American masterpieces, *The Woman in the Window*, *Scarlet Street*, *Ministry of Fear*, *Rancho Notorious*, *The Big Heat*, and *While the City Sleeps* (a serial-killer film told from the vantage of a corrupt press). Great as those films are, Lang could never recapture the diffuse and gargantuan vision of his German period when he seemed to have the pulse of the world pumping in his veins.

[*The New York Sun*, 21 December 2004]

11 ❖ Ways We Weren't (Vitaphone Shorts)

The demonization of jazz in the 1920s and—in a verbatim replay of rhetorical hyperbole—rock and roll in the 1950s is a familiar tale of American cultural ambivalence. In both eras, the guardians of morality warned that the young were being corrupted. They meant sex, though they often referred to drugs and Communism, and of course they were right. But fear of sexual havoc masked the more intense fear of race, of sex between the races: *The Ladies Home Journal* of 1921 blamed jazz for the increase in rape; 30 years later a Lait and Mortimer best seller, *U.S.A. Confidential*, blamed black and integrated music for the warping of white womanhood.[1] Well, they were right about one thing: vernacular music did more to promote integration and tolerance than the combined efforts of politicians, athletes, and high-art pundits.

The forces of repression were widely ridiculed but they enjoyed short-term victories as the neater codifications of swing sublimated the jazz hounds of the '20s, and teenage travesties supplanted the white trash and black holy rollers of '50s pop. Eddie Condon once described himself and his compatriots as outlaws playing black music to defy the Republicans; Glenn Miller and Frankie Avalon were the Republicans. The repression sponsored by the movies, however, was more lasting and insidious. For more than seven decades, blacks were presented with implacable conde-scension, resulting in the socially condoned fabrication in which Negroes were invisible other than as happy or addled servants—of which one sub-set included entertainers.

In recent years, as dozens of music videos from the '20s and '30s have been made available, the details of that fabrication became clearer. In the 1933 two-reeler "Rufus Jones for President," Ethel Waters appeared with the amazingly precocious seven-year-old Sammy Davis Jr., who falls asleep in her lap and dreams he is president. The black Senate, recall-ing Reconstruction as depicted in *Birth of a Nation*, has a "check your razors" sign in the cloakroom and a gambling obsession that leads to the appointment of Senator Bones as "Dice-President." The insults disappear whenever Waters and Davis perform, but remained the price they were obliged to pay to offer their wares.

At one point, Waters sings "Am I Blue," a signature song she had intro-duced four years earlier, with a bale of cotton, in the otherwise soporific feature film revue, *On with the Show*. Untalented white chorines marvel at her from the wings, unaware that the timelessness of her performance will underscore the direness of theirs. In "Rufus Jones," she has traded in her bandanna for a svelte gown, but she follows "Am I Blue" with

[1] A passage excerpted in Glenn C. Altschuler's *All Shook Up* (2005) offers a taste of right-wing "reporters" Jack Lait and Lee Mortimer. They blame juvenile delinquency on the "tom-toms and hot jive and ritualistic orgies of erotic dancing, weed-smoking and mass mania, with African jungle background." They note that "Many music shops purvey dope; assignations are made in them. White girls are recruited for colored lovers. . . . We know that many platter-spinners are hopheads. Many others are Reds, left-wingers, or hecklers of social convention. . . . Through disc jockeys, kids get to know colored and other musicians; they frequent places the radio oracles plug, which is done with design . . . to hook juves and guarantee a new generation subservient to the Mafia."

"Underneath the Harlem Moon," which exults, "Once we wore bandannas, now we wear Parisian hats. . . . Once we were Republicans, but now we're Democrats," to sustain the myth of happy Negroes: "We just live for dancing / We're never blue and forlorn / Cause it ain't no sin to laugh and grin / That's why we schvartzes were born." Substituting "schvartzes" for "darkies" is supposed to salve the wound by turning it back on the songwriters.

The Waters film is one of 45 Vitaphone shorts—made between 1932 and 1946—collected on MGM/UA's laser disc set *Swing, Swing, Swing!*, produced by George Feltenstein and Will Friedwald. (The promising subtitle Volume 1 was unfulfilled, and most of the material has yet to appear on DVD.) The eight-and-a-half hours of music videos are rich in historical glimmerings: physical evidence of the period; the long cultural arm of minstrelsy, which is everywhere; styles in music, dance, dress, and comedy; fleshy chorines, whose taste in lingerie presages the T&A of MTV; the evolution of moviemaking itself. But the big governing lie is segregation: At a time when black and white musicians routinely socialized and performed together, these films never cross the color line. With one exception—the black harmonica player in "Borrah Minevitch & His Harmonica School"—they're either all white or all black. When a black performer appears in a white film, he is really a white performer in blackface or a figure of sadistic fun, like the bug-eyed caricature in George Hall's "Skeleton Dance."

The selection is limited to the Vitaphone catalogue—there is no Ellington, Basie, or Goodman, but plenty of Ozzie Nelson (who, along with Desi Arnaz and Artie Shaw's leggy dancer, adorns the segregated cover) and Larry Clinton. Nor is sufficient information provided—tunes are identified, but not musicians. Part of the fun, though, is scouting stars in the making, hidden here as sidemen, frequently deprived of solos while inferiors get the spotlight. The surprises include a 16-bar solo by Bunny Berigan on "China Boy," the first tune in Freddie Rich's "Mirrors"; Roy Eldridge's trumpet break as Sid Catlett pirouettes behind the traps in Elmer Snowden's "Smash Your Baggage"; glimpses of Doc Cheatham, Ben Webster, and Milt Hinton in Cab Calloway's "Hi-De-Ho"; Eddie Miller's tenor solo and the unexpected sight of section man Glenn Miller in the Ben Pollack short; Edmond Hall playing section saxophone with Claude Hopkins; and Benny Morton soloing with Don Redman, whose "Tall Man" was a premature riposte to Randy Newman. Bobby Hackett appears in "Saturday Night Swing Club," emceed by Mel Allen with a teenage Les Lieber (the future jazz impresario) playing pennywhistle, and a band led by Leith Stevens, long before he became known for scoring *Destination Moon* and *The Wild One*, among many other feature films.

Expected pleasures are provided by Artie Shaw, the Boswell Sisters, and Helen Forrest (who never gets a close-up), as well as the underrated singers Nina Mae McKinney and Nan Wynn, best known for dubbing Rita Hayworth movies. Skinnay Ennis performs a 1940 Gil Evans arrangement of "Birth of the Blues." Joe Thomas, Willie Smith, and Eddie Tompkins (who tosses his trumpet in the air) are featured in the only Jimmie Lunceford short ever made, which begins with the devil calling for the return of rhythm. "And rhythm is our business," Lunceford says, a rather prim front for the slickest band of them all. The Vitaphones give a good sense of what swing was like in the years before the Swing Era, and how quickly the Ozzies and Larrys took it somewhere else. Of several copycats on display, the most amusingly desperate is singer Johnny Marvin, who mimics Ukulele Ike in one clip and Jimmie Rodgers in another. The most popular songs represented—four times each—are "St. Louis Blues," "Begin the Beguine," and "Nagasaki."

Dancers are copiously featured: How else can you make music vids watchable? The style here is tap, either acrobatic or contortionist, with much ballroom jitterbugging and some jump rope added to the mix. Watching the impeccably outfitted and assured Bill Robinson in "King for a Day," you can see why he inspired Louis Armstrong, whose vocal style is echoed in film after film after film. Betty Hutton is 18 in her first important gig, with Vincent Lopez, and as manic as she would ever be. The incomparable Nicholas Brothers, seen in three films made between 1932 and 1936, have the panache as kids that they would bring to feature films as adults; and they have unshakable dignity—no eye-rolling or raggedy costumes for them.

Two especially prolific directors worked at Vitaphone. Roy Mack was strictly a journeyman, often content to do little more than turn the camera on. Yet the black shorts, with which he was most often associated, inspired him in a way the white ones never did; he took to the offensive stereotyping as much as to the comic narratives and vaudeville diversity. At the end of "Mills Blue Rhythm Band," an observer of the dancing remarks, "Boy, don't that remind you of the old days in the jungle." "It sure do." And behold! Harlemites dissolve into natives of the Skull Island variety, in fright wigs and sarongs. The other key director was Joseph Henabery, a D. W. Griffith protégé (he played Lincoln in *Birth of a Nation*), who left Hollywood when sound arrived and went to work at Vitaphone's Brooklyn-based studios. The Edgar Ulmer of the one-reeler, his shorts are consistently sharper, with more attention to props, elaborate settings, imaginative staging, harsh lighting, dissolves, wipes, a mobile camera, and Griffith-like sentimentality—e.g., an insert of gramps smoking his corncob on the porch while Bea Wain sings "Old Folks."

But the director who really dazzles is Jean Negulesco, exiled to Vitaphone during the three years before he achieved acceptance as a serious filmmaker with the 1944 *Mask of Dimitrios*. He made six of the shorts in this collection, and they are instantly recognizable in the use of shadows, mirrors, huge art deco sets, ceiling views, ornate camera pans, reaction shots, and title cards that announce tunes but not performers. He probably saw *Citizen Kane* before filming the Casa Loma Orchestra: He multiplies his one dance couple into infinity with mirrors. Still, the Oscar goes to Gjon Mili for "Jammin' the Blues," presented here in an immaculate print. From the concentric circles of Lester Young's porkpie hat to the sparkle of Jo Jones's teeth, each shot compels attention. Barney Kessel, playing guitar in the shadows, is said to have darkened his hands so as not to look white—this in 1944.

For a reality check, compare period photographs by such great jazz photographers as Herman Leonard, Charles Peterson, and Milt Hinton. They show a different world in which races and genders are usually mixed, suggesting an unfussy integration that was an important part of the jazz life in the 1930s. Hollywood pickled jazz in the conventions of reactionary kitsch; the still photographers, not worried about southern distribution, capture the reality of a paradise lost.

[*Village Voice*, 28 February 1995]

12 ❖ *Naked Truth* (Children of Paradise)

"There is no essential incongruity between crime and culture."
—*Oscar Wilde*

1.

Shortly before fulfilling his "calling" as a murderer in *Children of Paradise* (*Les Enfants du paradis*), the fop and would-be dramatist Lacenaire tells his beautiful "guardian angel," Garance, "Never look back at the past, my angel. It leaps at your throat like a mad dog." Yet neither he, Garance, nor other principals in Marcel Carné and Jacques Prévert's masterpiece have much choice. Childhood, fate, and character are intertwined and inescapable. Life and love, as more than one character insists, can be beautiful and simple, but no one evades time's lunging beast.

We are who we were. We become what we are. The film's very structure —two 90-minute episodes, the second working out aspirations of the first—underscores a reckoning with the past, much as the gleaming DVD restoration by Criterion opens a window on cinema's past.

Lacenaire may have anticipated Satchel Paige, but he does not speak entirely for Carné, the director, and Prévert, the screenwriter. Their sixth collaboration revisited Paris in the 1820s and depicted it with a romantic diligence that attains a realm beyond time, like Shakespeare's Nile. *Children of Paradise* has been called, with familiar hyperbole, the greatest picture ever made. Let us say, rather, that it abides as a contender—a perfect balance between writer and director, like *Citizen Kane* or *Vertigo*, or *Rules of the Game*, for which Jean Renoir was both. The script is a roundelay of past and present, artifice and realism, life as theater, theater as life, maskings, unmaskings, duels at dawn, an ace up the sleeve, a shiv in the waistcoat—all of it ornamented with symbols, signature phrases, and some of the cleverest dialogue ever conceived for the screen. The direction is invisible when it wants to be and graphic when necessary; Carné infallibly underscores every emotion while choreographing incandescent performances as well as hundreds of reveling extras, a glorious score, and a fantastic, encompassing set. Not a single prosaic scene is to be found in the film's epical running time.

Midway in the shoot, realizing that the picture would exceed two hours, Carné consulted with his original producer, who suggested he extend the story another hour and release it in two parts. Ultimately, it was shown exclusively as a single film; but part two, "The Man in White," was prepared with the same credit roll as the first part, "The Boulevard of Crime," along with a summary of the latter. Length was the least of Carné's problems, for the film was shot, mostly in Nice, between August 1943 and June 1944, under the eyes of German film unions and Vichy collaborators. Imagine filming *Gone with the Wind* during the siege of Atlanta. He had to contend with work stoppages and spies who sneaked in as extras, though he managed to expel most of them before the cameras began to roll. The political winds shifted only when an Allied victory appeared inevitable. The actor initially cast as Jericho, an informer, was, in fact, a real-life informer, who fled the country and was sentenced to death *in absentia*; he was replaced by Pierre Renoir, Jean's elder brother. Carné began stalling completion so that his film—the most expensive in the history of French cinema to that point—would be the first major work of the Liberation and not a triumph for the Occupation. This created an embarrassment. At the time of the premiere, his Garance, the exquisite Arletty, was under house arrest: She had had an affair with a German officer. Only her capture and imprisonment saved her from snipers and an outraged mob. Arletty famously remarked, "My heart is French, but my body is international," a line Prévert might have written for Garance.

2.

When *Les Enfants* was about to open in New York as *Children of Paradise*, it was touted by a trailer (included on the DVD) that borrowed a suggestive extract from *Newsweek*: "Arletty represents sex appeal as it is recognized everywhere in the United States except in Hollywood!"—a good line reduced to Hollywood bally by shrill punctuation. Arletty was 46 when the picture was made, an age when Hollywood glamour queens are more likely to play mothers, maiden aunts, or axe murderers than objects of desire or even *objets d'art*, which is how Garance describes herself to a clumsy policeman. Her mature beauty serves as the film's center of gravity.

Garance is an all-knowing if oddly innocent chameleon who does not actually change, yet is seen differently by each of her suitors: as guardian angel, goddess of love, sexual conquest, expensive possession. They all experience her as a manifestation of the way she is introduced to us, as a sideshow attraction, seated nude in a well of murky water up to her shoulders, gazing into a mirror and billed as "the Naked Truth." She is the muse who will enable each man to fulfill his destiny—inspiring a self-pitying mime to reinvent Pierrot as a figure of soaring romanticism; instilling in a rising actor a jealousy that empowers him to master *Othello*; validating a scoundrel's need to bring about his own apocalypse; and generating death and despair, respectively, for two drearier souls— a stiff-backed aristocrat and a devoted wife—who are the casualties of her adultery.

Children of Paradise offers many analogical interpretations involving the Occupation. But unlike American films of the '50s, with broad subtexts involving racism or McCarthyism, its political message never overwhelms its respect for character. The supremely human story was not crafted as agitprop. Still, a key symbol develops from the idea of France as a great whore—desired, loved, abused, betrayed, exploited, and independent. The film suggests that France's fate will rest with Garance, the autonomous, insightful, life-affirming courtesan with a 14k heart. Though she is a fiction, her most sympathetic lovers are artfully drawn from history. The comic actor Frederick Lemaître, played with seductive wiles by Pierre Brasseur, and the pioneer pantomimist Baptiste Deburau, played by the no less innovative mime, actor, and director Jean-Louis Barrault, were vital figures in the development of French theater. The rogue who unknowingly forces Garance into a gilded cage and then liberates her with a *coup de theatre* is also taken from life: The murderer Pierre-François Lacenaire, played by Marcel Herrand, inspired Dostoevski's Raskolnikov and Baudelaire's admiring nihilism. In a memoir written in the shadow of the guillotine, Lacenaire gave voice to the serial killer's credo: "Society will have my blood, but I in turn shall have the blood of Society."

3.

Children of Paradise is beguiling the first time one sees it, yet reveals itself only through subsequent encounters. While the same can be said of every work of art, this is a film packed with parallels and echoes that first-time visitors are not intended to see or hear. It begins with a charcoal drawing of an old-fashioned billowy stage curtain. Before the credits appear, we hear an insistent knocking on the floorboards—a theatrically tradi-tional device that will resound in the final scene, in the unheeded knock-ing of Baptiste's wife, Nathalie. The first heraldic chords of the score prepare us for a festive time. Joseph Kosma's melodies combine yearning, almost Mozartian jubilation with march-like snare drums and a lush, romantic theme that might have served Puccini or Tchaikovsky. His music elabor-ates what Criterion's DVD commentator, Brian Stonehill, refers to as the "deep vein of euphoria running beneath the film's surface, as if to sug-gest in keeping with its title that even the poorest among us are already in paradise." Kosma's screen credit comes last, on a card with that of set designer Alexandre Trauner, revealing their "clandestine" participation. As Jews they worked in hiding, through front men.

The charcoal drawing rises on one of the most eye-popping scenes and sets ever devised: Trauner's magnificent Boulevard of Crime. It seems to extend to far horizons, but is in part a cinematic *trompe l'oeil*. The distant buildings were constructed on a declining scale and populated with chil-dren and dwarves. A street fair in progress, choked with performers and gawkers, instantly draws us in as gawkers of 1820s France, an era when assimilated romanticism is about to liberate her performing arts. First we see the tightrope walkers, a visual pun anticipating the Funambules (lit-erally: tightrope walkers), the theater of mime that gives the film its title; its obstreperous fans in the upper balcony are called "children of paradise." (During a performance, a bourgeois patron down below shouts at them, "Shut up! We can't hear the mime!") A first-time viewer won't notice the ratlike ragman crossing the lower part of the screen or hear his twice-played call on a tin-horn—a furtive introduction to the snitch, Jericho. The camera pans with him, and cuts to a weightlifter, then to a trained monkey, a carousel, and finally the booth featuring "Naked Truth." We follow the marks in for a quick peek.

Outside the camera picks up a stage-door argument—Frederick Lemaître attempting to talk his way into the Grand Theater. When the stage-door manager mocks his actorly ambitions, Lemaître assumes a dynamic theatrical pose as he conjures up his name on a marquee. But rather than argue the point, he is distracted by the beautiful Garance, who has just quit her job as Truth. This is the first of several scenes set in the street and handled so deftly that the principals never get lost in the crush of extras. They gaily flirt before she drolly puts him in his place ("Paris is small for those who share so great a passion as ours"). Lemaître quickly turns his attention to another pretty lady, while Garance continues to the storefront of the Public Scribe, Lacenaire, a legal copyist who writes for the unlettered and deals in stolen goods. He is a sight: Medea curls pasted to his forehead in large rings; a drooping mustache that he ominously fingers; a gleaming, frilly white shirt. He regards books as "so much dust in a child's head," yet fancies himself a dramatist. His real ambition, however, is to pull off a crime worthy of his Ubermensch egoism. Apparently impotent, he flaunts his lovelessness to Garance; she shrugs and insists the only reason she visits is for his amusing theatricality. He has a horror of humiliation and a need to humiliate.

Garance and Lacenaire join a small crowd at the Theatre Des Funambules, where the tout publicly ridicules his son, Baptiste, a woeful, whitefaced, bone-thin mime who is permitted to perform outside as a come-on but not with the performers on stage. Here is another intersection between art and life. Barrault, who had launched the film by suggesting that Carné film Deburau's story, had once studied mime with Etienne Decroux and then feuded with him; Carné cast Decroux as Deburau's arrogant father. Lacenaire disappears after stealing a watch from a bourgeois who accuses Garance. Baptiste saves her. Having witnessed the sleight-of-hand from the stage, he now reenacts the theft in mime— a two-minute improvisation that elicits cheers in movie theaters and instant replays at home. She gratefully tosses him a rose. He is hopelessly smitten.

4.

At this point, after 20 minutes, all the primary characters have been introduced, except Nathalie, the Funambule actress who is desperately in love with Baptiste, and Montray, the smug nobleman who tries vainly to buy Garance, leaving her his card in case she should require his influence.

They are the most pitilessly treated figures in the film, and the closest to representative types—she of the middle class, he of the aristocracy. Nathalie, played by Maria Casares, who created a more stirring role months later (1945 marked the rebirth of French cinema) as the spurned, vengeful mistress in Robert Bresson's *Les Dames du Bois Boulogne*, is often referred to with contempt (not least in Charles Affron's DVD commentary). She is disparaged for trying to keep Baptiste, the poetic dreamer, from his true love, a view that interprets the picture as a repudiation of bourgeois responsibility and a mandate for love and freedom at any cost.

Yet audiences of today are bound to be more sympathetic to Nathalie and her son, twice ignored by Baptiste in his desire to find Garance. Her final confrontational speech is eloquently written, and her possessive cluelessness not without a poetic yearning of its own. She, after all, loves Baptiste as deeply as he loves Garance, and it was his lunatic behavior (Garance invited him into her bed and he rejected her for failing to embody his ideal of romantic purity) that led to estrangement from Garance and marriage to Nathalie. Similarly, the boy, once insensibly described by Pauline Kael as "an abominable offspring," exerts a far more empathic claim in our child-centric universe. But then, *Children of Paradise* always encourages us to draw our own conclusions.

"The Boulevard of Crime" concludes as Garance, falsely accused of a second crime, flashes her winning smile and Montray's card, stopping the prosecution cold for an ingeniously pleasing denouement. When the curtain rises on "The Man in White," several years have passed. Lemaître and Baptiste are now luminaries, the former acclaimed for his irreverent improvisations, the latter as Pierrot, the crown prince of mime. Garance, however, now caged as Montray's mistress, has lost her laugh and the gleam in her eye—a gleam radiantly captured by cinematographer Roger Hubert in virtually all of her scenes with Baptiste. She now shows up anonymously every night, a mysterious society lady, to watch the great mime perform.

5.

Early in the film, Lacenaire ridiculed tragedy as "an inferior genre" (the characters "kill one another, yet never get hurt"), and near the end, he will conflate tragedy with farce. But *Children of Paradise* is suffused with hurt, and much of it is played for laughs on stage, including one of the film's two murders. In part one, we saw the Funambule show in which Baptiste created his Pierrot. Garance appeared as the goddess Phoebe, and Lemaître, forced to put aside his ambitions to work in an idiom he loathes, played Harlequin. ("Joan of Arc was lucky," he complains, "She heard voices.") In a scene that parallels the actors' lives, Harlequin effortlessly seduces the goddess and they float away on a barge to alluring Spanish music. Pierrot prepares to hang himself, an effort undone by a little girl who borrows his rope to skip and a woman (played by Nathalie) who uses it to hang laundry. At a subsequent show, in part two, the now celebrated Pierrot brutally murders a ragman—the audience's laughter freezes—to obtain a suit of clothes that will allow him to pursue his lover at a ball. Consider the reverberations: Baptiste is played by his real-life heir, Barrault; he kills a ragman costumed to resemble the informer Jericho, who unknowingly provided the costume as part of his rag-trade; the ragman is played by Baptiste's father who is played by Decroux, Barrault's disaffected tutor.

The real murder—the one that takes place off-stage—occurs in the film's most flamboyant interior setting, a Turkish bath, and involves the historical Lacenaire and the fictional Count Eduoard de Montray, played by Louis Salou. During Lemaître's debut as Othello, Lacenaire, who prefers slitting throats to taking up a quill, draws his inspiration from honest Iago. After baiting Montray as a cuckold, he dramatically pulls aside a curtain to reveal Garance in Baptiste's embrace. This, Lacenaire is proud to note, is a far more satisfying spur to action than a stolen handkerchief; besides, Garance is no Desdemona. Montray makes a fatal error in attempting to humiliate Lacenaire by having him ejected from the theater (what else can he do?), after challenging the innocent but intervening Lemaître to a duel. We know that Montray, a marksman, has already killed one man who returned Garance's smile. Lacenaire, for his part, abhors dueling ("absolutely not")—an aristocrat's sport in which you can never be sure of the outcome. Instead, he and his sidekick, Avril, attend to Montray at the bath, where, naked but for a robe, he appears resigned to his fate. Lacenaire draws his dagger and glides forward.

Here we have one of Carné's most ingenious feints. Lacenaire approaches the camera, Avril standing to the side, the Count off-screen with us. Instead of cutting to the action, the camera slowly dollies toward the only figure in the frame, Avril, whose sudden tic of revulsion is accompanied on the soundtrack by a groan and splash of water—a ghastly moment. Lacenaire, rather magnanimously, sends Avril away, choosing to wait alone for the police, anticipating his fifth act: a fashionable trial and what he hopes will be a sensational climax with his head in a basket. (In 1942, Camus's Mersault strode to his death craving the mob's "howls of execration.") Lacenaire told Garance in their first scene together that his father had always told him he would end up on the guillotine. Replied Garance: "Always obey your parents."

6.

With his "masterpiece," Lacenaire, in one stroke, kills the symbol of a craving he can never satisfy, membership in the aristocracy; saves Lemaître from a duel he could not win; and liberates Garance to an uncertain future, presumably on the Boulevard of Crime, with no hope of regaining Baptiste, whom she has abandoned to his wife and son. The director has no interest in showing just how successful Lacenaire's trial really was. It caused so great a stir in 1835 that intellectuals paid homage and a publisher brought out his early poetry; courtroom seats were harder to get than at the simultaneous trial of Deburau, arrested for an accidental death. Even his beheading caused an uproar—they had to do it twice as the blade got stuck on the first descent. Neither does Carné tell us that the real Lacenaire ratted out Avril, also executed, or that they had murdered and mutilated a widow and her son. Carné doesn't absolve Lacenaire, whose villainy is never in doubt, but he recognizes a kinship between artists, like himself, who create, manipulate, and destroy history and life, and criminals, whose actions unsettle the very fabric of social complacency. Othello solves problems of the state, but Iago generates the drama that topples the hero. If Garance is a muse, Lacenaire is her most decisive artist, resolving her fate with his own.

Before Carné abandons Lacenaire, coolly awaiting his arrest, he shows the arm of Montray hanging over the side of the bath into which his corpse has been tossed—an image emphatically suggestive of Marat. In this fleeting shot, Montray, the philistine aristocrat, is tied to the bloodthirsty "friend of the people," Marat, and Lacenaire to the Girondist and descendant of Corneille, Charlotte Corday, who similarly used a blade and did not attempt to escape. The consequent ambiguity inclines us to see the deadly rogue as a rationalist buying the freedom of another with his own life, and the reactionary Count as a mad radical who sends people to death on a whim.

As for Garance and Baptiste, the lovers with whom the film is most in accord, she disappears in her carriage, expecting to return to her cage with Montray, hoping to dissuade him from the duel with Lemaître. Baptiste, unrecognized in his street clothes, vainly chases after her, shouting her name but hindered by Jericho, now proffering himself as a moral man, restraining him on behalf of Nathalie, and by dozens of Pierrots: carnival celebrants costumed in homage to the revered mime—the first Elvis impersonators. The ending is stirring, romantic, untidy, bleak, and thrilling, and the final descent of the final charcoal curtain is an intrusion, cutting us off from a world we are in no hurry to leave.

7.

Children of Paradise is superbly acted—the highwater mark in the film careers of Arletty, Barrault, Brasseur, and Herrand, all perfectly wedded to their roles. We hear a great deal about the childhoods of their characters, and never doubt that they lived them, that they live them still—especially Garance ("a girl who grows up too fast doesn't stay alone for very long") and Baptiste, who was beaten for dreaming and obliged to learn to fight. During his initial courtship of Garance, he tells her, "You're beautiful." "No," she says, "I'm just alive." When he expounds an impossibly ideal-ist love, she tells him, "You talk like a child. People love that way in books and in dreams, not in real life." "Dreams, life," he replies, "they're the same." In their final scene, after their only night together, Carné photographs them as Madonna and child. Baptiste, the poetical soul, is in many ways the audience's point of identification, and the figure with whom Carné most empathized. Pierrot, of course, is "The Man in White." Yet he often behaves worse than we would—spurning Garance's sexual-ity, refusing to assuage Nathalie's anguish—except as an artist or under threat, when he is better, braver, and quicker than we can imagine.

Brasseur is magnetic as the indefatigable charmer Lemaître, an archetypal French lover who thinks he is immune to jealousy. A telling scene involves his and Garance's seduction across windowsills. When she admits that her door is unlocked, he puckers his lips and suavely retracts his body from the ledge, reappearing in her room a moment later. The episode would have been as unthinkable in a Hollywood picture of the period as her frankness, weeks later, concerning the attenuated returns on their romance: "We're not happy or unhappy. It's no one's fault. Still, it's nothing to be proud of." (In *Les Dames du Bois Boulogne*, a suitor observes, "There is no love, only proofs of love.") Herrand's Lacenaire is an unfor-gettably silky villain: a lethal peacock, prim moralist, and laughably inept criminal, fueled by a bottomless well of gall. His consuming hatred is in constant search of a deserving target. The leads are backed by a sideshow gallery of character actors, from Casares, Renoir, and Salou to Pierre Palau as the riotously overheated manager of the Funambules; Fabien Loris as the goon, Avril; Jeanne Marken as the bovine landlady, Mme. Hermine; and Gaston Modot as Silk Thread, the "blind" beggar with 20/20. When Silk Thread meets Baptiste in a moment of egalitarian esprit (and furtive reminder that the film was made by outsiders: liberationists, homo-sexuals, Jews), he declares, "Oh, I love mime." "Vous?" asks the startled Baptiste. Catching himself, Silk Thread explains, "I have a friend who describes it all."

As does the Criterion DVD. In fact, it has two describers: the late Brian Stonehill, whose laser disc commentary accompanies "The Boulevard of Crime," and Charles Affron, who offers new commentary for "The Man in White." Stonehill is particularly good at pointing out subtleties of lighting, decor, sets, shots, symbols, themes, and specific references to the Occupation. Affron offers a perspective on 19th-century French theater and the story's historical figures as well as interpretive insights. The DVD also has an introduction by Terry Gilliam, the American trailer, improved subtitles, an English translation of Prévert's treatment, production designs by Trauner and Leon Bardacq, Carné and Prévert filmographies, examples of the restoration, and a gallery of about 70 stills. It does not, however, replicate all the extras from Criterion's 1991 laser disc, which has a superior stills gallery, Stonehill's 1990 Carné interview plus a reenactment of it in English (the DVD booklet reprints excerpts), his commentary on "The Man in White," and his visual essay on the film's mimetic use of great paintings. The important picture here, *Children of Paradise*, has never looked more alluring.

[*The Perfect Vision*, 25 June 2002]

13 ❖ *Things That Go Bump (Horror Films)*

1. Freaks of a Feather
(Freaks / Village of the Damned / Children of the Damned)

Freaks is back. Actually, since the 1960s, it has enjoyed a state of perpetual return, showing up periodically at art houses and campus screenings and on video and laser disc. Not many television airings, though—a tribute to its undated ability to cause distress. After Todd Browning's 1932 sideshow thriller was pulled from release by a chagrined MGM, it was butchered and suppressed for nearly 30 years. Yet *Freaks* provides the same voyeuristic kick for which millions of Americans happily shelled out money in carnival tents around the country—only more so and with a twist. It survives as a pulp tour de force.

The censors and critics initially trounced it not for the bizarre sexual trysts and rude remarks (a brazen pun about prophylactics skipped merrily past their radar), but for exploiting "nature's mistakes." What did they care that Hollywood provided Browning's performers better pay and accommodations per day than an average week on the midway? They were probably more disturbed that Browning's vignette (running little more than an hour) presents its armless, legless, limbless, mindless, bound-at-the-hip, skeletal, and double-gendered wonders in the light of day. Watching them all—more 10-in-1 attractions than any real circus could afford—romp at a picnic in the French countryside makes the psychological hat trick of feeling pity while recoiling in horror more difficult.

A penitent introductory scroll, tacked on when *Freaks* was first revived (and included as a DVD extra along with a commentary and talking-heads documentary), has the unintended effect of increasing the dread. It promotes the film as a last chance to observe these special people, because modern medical practice has succeeded where Hitler failed. Browning, whose career flourished in the silent era as Lon Chaney's collaborator and fizzled after *Dracula* and *Freaks*, begins the film by admiringly introducing his cast for the better part of half an hour. In one scene, the limbless Prince Randian strikes a match and lights a cigarette with his face, then dares a boastful and physically complete performer, "Hey, can you do anything with your eyebrow?" The line is baffling (and unintelligible without the subtitles), but the point is clear: These people use what they've got.

When the plot finally kicks in, the film turns dark and stormy. A German midget, Hans (Harry Earles), is engaged to someone his own size, Frieda (Daisy Earles), but falls head-over-heels for Cleo (Olga Baclanova), the blond, Amazonian, bitch-goddess of the trapeze. When Cleo learns that Hans is heir to a great fortune, she contrives to marry and murder him, a scheme that she rather foolishly publicizes at the wedding banquet. This is one of the unforgettable episodes in world cinema. As the director's camera slyly circles the congregants, Angelo Rossetti (another little guy, who went on to appear in many low-rent movies) leaps onto the table and wiggles toward Cleo bearing a huge loving cup, as they chant, "Gooble gobble, one of us"—an invitation she frantically declines.

To avenge the attempted murder of Hans, the freaks gang up on her in a torrential downpour and, with a surgical skill you won't find at Beth Israel (it's done off camera, so their secrets are safe), they turn her into a human duck or chicken or fowl of some sort. Apparently, the moral is that when one of theirs is threatened, freaks can get supernaturally freaky. Which raises a problem of interpretation, however, and here the producers of this otherwise admirable DVD have made a serious miscalculation. Browning, harried by censors and forced to cut nearly a third of the film, was ultimately compelled to respond to front-office concerns that audiences would feel uncomfortable seeing sweet little Hans turned into a vengeful sawbones. So he filmed an epilogue, which showed Hans as a reclusive guilt-ridden millionaire, reunited with Frieda. A wiser head—presumably that of Irving Thalberg—prevailed; the epilogue was cut, and the film as released ended with the revelation of a quacking, clucking Cleo.

It is a perfect ending. The picture begins with a carny guide who leads the marks into a tent, showing them but not us the revolting creature, and spins a tall tale to explain how she got that way. As the entire film is a flashback, *Freaks* begs the question of whether any of it happened. The spiel does double-duty, playing on ancient fears in caricaturing the misbegotten while cunningly recognizing that sideshows revel in creative fraud. Not content to include the discarded epilogue as an added feature, the DVD tacks it onto the film, sabotaging one of the cinema's great visual punch lines with a badly staged and acted happy fade-out, complete with a patronizing wink from the (relatively) normal clown who reunites the midgets. Foul!

The restored *Freaks* debuted at the 1960 Venice Film Festival, in retrospect an instance of cosmic timing. That was a banner year for horror, as *Psycho, Peeping Tom, Black Sunday, Terror of the Tongs, The Fall of the House of Usher,* and other bellwether shockers subverted various movie taboos. One, *Village of the Damned,* was short on gore and lust, but introduced a memorable special effect (whited-out eyes) and a prophetic idea: The most terrifying aliens are our children, especially little Aryan ones with bangs.

Based on John Wyndham's lively novel, *The Midwich Cuckoos,* Wolf Rilla's film portrays a pastoral English village (the opening shot is of a flock of sheep) happily caught in a cultural time-warp—there are no televisions, and the phonographs play 78s. One morning the population blacks out for a few hours, after which a dozen women awake, soon to bear immaculate conceptions. As the censors prohibited the use of words like "pregnant" or "virginity," there's a lot of euphemistic hemming and hawing. But the real subject, left over (like those 78s) from World War II, is the male fear of returning from war to find one's mate claimed by another. George Sanders is unusually sober in the lead role. Misty silent black-and-white pans augment the growing claustrophobia.

The 1964 *Children of the Damned* is a sequel in name only, though it begins with the closing image of its predecessor, a clock. John Briley, who contributes a commentary track, wrote an overtly political and religious variation on the theme. This time the children are a virtual United Nations of Darwinian freaks whom the powers want to kill out of sheer raging paranoia. The story plays out in a dilapidated church that could double as Castle Dracula—for that matter, London's oddly abandoned alleyways are distinctly Caligarish—and the children confess that their hallowed purpose in life is to, well, die. As in the first film, dynamite is the species-cleanser of choice.

Children makes little sense but has more wit and twists than the original. It also boasts the unctuous, lizard-eyed, scenery-chewing Alan Badel, an English stage star who, despite several attempts, never proved exportable to the international film market—not because he disappeared into the strenuous makeups of his diverse roles, but because the roles disappeared into the maw of his actor's ego. In this film, the insinuation of a homosexual liaison between his character and his roommate, though eventually undercut by the script, is writ large in his performance. He is compulsively watchable, like a cat.

2. *Creeps by Night*
(*Val Lewton*)

A fondness for freaks and monsters is not a requirement for relishing the nine B-pictures Val Lewton produced for RKO between 1942 and 1946, now boxed by Warner Bros. as *Val Lewton Horror Collection*—five DVDs, complete with a rote but informative talking-heads documentary. A protégé of David O. Selznick and prolific pulp fiction writer who immersed himself in the higher frequencies of the arts, Lewton was given a free hand as long as he accepted a few stipulations: small budgets, abbreviated running times, horrific subjects, and titles mandated by the studio before the films were made or even conceived.

So put yourself in his place. You've been given your own unit and have just completed an as-yet-unreleased first film (*Cat People*), when the bosses order you to begin work immediately on a second, to be called *I Walked with a Zombie*. What to do? You adapt *Jane Eyre*, of course, and begin with a voice-over by the Jane-substitute, Betsy (a fetching, intelligent performance by little-noted Frances Dee), who recalls with a modest giggle, "I *walked* with a zombie. It does seem an odd thing to say."

As directed by the inspired Jacques Tourneur from a Curt Siodmack-Ardel Wray script that Lewton vetted, revised, and punched up with elaborate details, the result is an oddly poetic meditation on identity, race, religion, and moral ambiguity—more than two decades before Jean Rhys adapted the same source, setting, and themes in her acclaimed novel, *Wide Sargasso Sea*. When a doctor refers to Betsy's catatonic patient as a zombie and she asks him to define the term, he tells her about Voodoo and adds that it's also the name of a drink. Lewton's oeuvre is nothing if not of this world.

Lewton could not ignore the horror component. But he did three things that distinguish his films from the Universal staples RKO wanted him to emulate. The monsters are entirely human; violence is almost always suggested rather than portrayed; and the viewpoint is usually that of a woman. His trademark scare tactic, a high point in practically all his films, is a long, dark, nightmarish walk, where every sound is magnified and every object threatening. In *The Ghost Ship*, that "walk" is transferred to the cabin of the victimized third officer; in *Bedlam*, to the corridor of the insane asylum. It's a ploy that never fails.

In the early 1930s, the sexual fantasies and fears of male adolescents were dramatized in the immaculate conception of *Frankenstein*, the neck-hickeys of *Dracula*, and the smirking invincibility of *The Invisible Man*. Lewton's films are keyed to mother-daughter disorders, sisterhood crises, sexual assertion and repression, lesbianism, romance, loneliness, vulnerability, and suicide. Even in those dominated by men, women serve as beacons of sanity. In *The Body Snatcher*, directed by Robert Wise, the Robert Louis Stevenson story is sharpened and enhanced as a fatal match between a surgeon and a body snatcher, each morally compromised and therefore lost (all nine films are haunted by variations on the walking dead). The one character who can see the ignominy and predict the endgame is the "secret" wife of the surgeon, whose fall is set in motion by a little girl's need for an operation. In *The Ghost Ship*, which is entirely concerned with male conflict (Richard Dix's lunatic captain is a prototype for Queeg), a woman shown only in shadow appears in the final shot as the possibility of salvation.

Men are little more than optional accessories in *The Seventh Victim*, directed by Mark Robson. An innocent young woman, Mary (Kim Hunter's film debut), quits the Lowood girls' school (*Jane Eyre* again) in search of her missing sister, a Greenwich Village free spirit who has left her dull husband to take up with Satanists and an apparently libidinous psychiatrist—Lewton's films wallow in appearances as relationships are rarely spelled out. Mary's vulnerability and strength are emphasized in a famous shower scene, photographed from the rear, her defenselessness heightened by a shower cap, as an older woman threatens her through the curtain, the shadows turning her hat into hornlike extensions of her head. In Hitchcock's shower, water changes from a soul-cleanser to an agent of perversity, as voyeurism leads to murder and the shower to a flushing toilet. In Lewton, water affords protection—a magic circle, as in the swimming pool in *Cat People* or the ocean in *I Walked with a Zombie*. The closing shot of *The Seventh Victim*, involving a chair and a consumptive, oblivious neighbor (named Mimi, what else?) is still devastating after 60 years.

Lewton's films, like certain books, ought to be experienced in child-hood so that they can be returned to later in life, the indelible moments now cast amid subtler evocations and themes. Only on a second viewing is one likely to realize that the first shot of *I Walked with a Zombie* shows

Betsy strolling by the sunlit sea with the film's (apparently) genuine zombie, and appreciate its explicit post-story rapprochement between Christianity and Voodoo, whites and blacks, real and imagined. A second look is especially warranted by Tourneur's *The Leopard Man*, which has turned out to be Lewton's most influential film, though both men dismissed it at the time as cheaply violent.

In the 1940s, Lewton was admired for his understatement—the use of light and sound that forces the viewer's imagination to supply the fear. In *The Bad and the Beautiful*, Vincente Minnelli pays homage to the *Cat People* as a low-budget solution to the absence of a monster suit. *The Leopard Man* similarly keeps violence off-screen, but cruelly focuses on the plight of its victims. In effect, it is the first slasher film, though we never see any slashing. Yet the murders are more disturbing than those in *Halloween* and its imitators, in which death is reserved for the sexually aggressive: *The Leopard Man* dispatches two virgins and one (apparent) hooker, and not when we expect. Twice we follow the wonderfully haughty dancer Clo-Clo (played by Margo), whose castanets augment Roy Webb's pulsing score, on menacing walks. Each time she escapes while we are sidelined to young women she passes in the street. No one who has seen the puddle beneath the door can forget it.

The Leopard Man concerns shared guilt—the putative hero and heroine who solve the crime are responsible for the chain of terror, while the audience is made complicit in the voyeurism. The police are impotent bystanders; indeed, their presence is unusual for a Lewton film. As with dreams, his stories are largely devoid of police and other social guardians. He prefers the horrors of daily life, which must be battled by frontline civilians, usually without success. Nothing can save Simone Simon's cat woman, who confuses Eros with death, and yet her ghost frees the troubled little girl and her uncomprehending father in *Curse of the Cat People*, an ingenious children's fantasy that deepens the meaning of the earlier film. A ghost's help is about the best you can expect.

Lewton's brief autonomy, which ended with the war, depended on a first-class team and his knack for finding actors memorable in their ordinariness. He had at his disposal elaborate RKO sets, including the archway from *The Hunchback of Notre Dame* and the grand staircase from *The Magnificent Ambersons*; composer Roy Webb; photographers Nicholas Musuraca and Robert de Grasse; superior dialogue writers; and three directors, two of them novices, who shone for him—the stylish Tourneur, the wily Wise, and the more conventional but clearly stimulated Robson.

Among the actors, his most important collaborator was Boris Karloff, whose participation Lewton initially fought, not wanting to echo the boogie men at Universal. But Karloff, one of the most inventive and stereo-typed actors of the studio era, was desperate for respectable work, and he raised three of Lewton's films to levels they could not otherwise have attained. His very presence, looming and tragic, rescues *Isle of the Dead* from talky incoherence. He brings a comical undercurrent to the sadistic poetaster Sims in the marvelous *Bedlam*, waddling on bowed legs while readjusting his wig, obsequiously taking the measure of his masters, accom-modating the idiocies of a slatternly niece, putting the screws to the film's moral and heroic center, as played by Anna Lee, before ending up like the fool in "The Cask of Amontillado."

Karloff's pinnacle, however, is *The Body Snatcher*, a masterly film heightened by his curiously modern performance, the character completely subsuming the actor. Like Brando at his peak, he charges his every scene with coiled energy and watchful wit. His face-offs with the equally engaged Henry Daniell may constitute the best acting ever in an American horror film. Daniell's surgeon is by turns haughty, fervent, desperate, and self-involved; his barroom analysis of an apparently unsuccessful operation has the flavor of distracted candor. By contrast, Karloff's Cabman Gray, the grave robber and murderer whose only plea-sure lies in making Daniell hop to his whims, is always in control. With no inner life left to explore, he survives as a malevolent if unmistakably human observer.

Lewton worked on a few other projects after RKO dismissed him, but he never regained the magic of those five years. He died of a heart attack in 1951, at 46, nearly a decade before *Psycho* and Italian *giallos* replaced his trademark shadows, literary epigrams, Hogarth etchings, Chopin etudes, Calypso commentaries, and nightmarish atmospherics with jets of blood and heaving silicone.

3. They've Got You Under Their Skin
(Eyes Without a Face / Videodrome)

Beauty is skin deep, but then so is ugliness. Eros and Vanity build their temples on a paper-thin epidermal layer that masks a bloody, deteriorating mechanism most of us regard with fear and revulsion. Indeed, the soci-ety of the squeamish excludes only doctors, butchers, serial killers, and certain filmmakers for whom the other three are nearly interchangeable. The horror field has always been consumed with flesh and its conceal-ments, producing medical men who double as ghouls, megalomaniacs, and shape-shifting scoundrels. And this least respected of movie genres remains the most enduring and prophetic. Basic fears do not abate.

Better examples than Georges Franju's *Eyes Without a Face* (1959) and David Cronenberg's *Videodrome* (1983) would be hard to find. Initially greeted with derision and censorship, they have now received the Criterion Collection's A+ imprimatur: classy restorations, film-school extras, and the companionship of weirdly complementary short films. Franju's grisly-lyrical documentary of Paris's abattoir, the 22-minute "Blood of the Beasts" (1949), is an ideal prologue to his main feature, just as Cronenberg's meditation on cinema's theft of youth, the six-minute "Camera" (2000), is a suitable epilogue to his. Both films explore the corruption of flesh, the madness that is a by-product, and the gore beneath the surface.

Still, the differences are more illuminating than the thematic parallels. Franju's film unfolds as a dream, a poetical thriller pitched in the land where Jean Cocteau and Walt Disney nod. Cronenberg's is an addled hallucination, a black comedy with a political soul that crosses Andy Warhol and George Orwell. Franju shunned color because, he said, it would make the subject of facial surgery repulsive. Cronenberg, fortified by Rick Baker's special effects, *loves* the repulsive. If you think the 44 years of graphic slashing unleashed by *Psycho* has inured you to bloodletting, you may be surprised by incisions in both films. But it isn't the blood and guts that makes them frightening; it's the prognoses.

Eyes Without a Face begins with a lengthy traveling shot, as Alida Valli races through the night with a crumpled corpse in the backseat, enclosed by an endless line of skeletal trees and accompanied by Maurice Jarre's funhouse score—imagine Philip Glass programming a carousel. Daylight exteriors are no more comforting; everything is cold, gray, and remote, like the crazed trio of protagonists and the reliably ineffectual police. The basic plot is old-time Universal/Monogram: An arrogant doctor (Pierre Brasseur) accidentally caused his daughter Christiane's disfigurement and, aided by a devoted mistress whose face he has successfully remade (Valli), kidnaps young women and attempts to graft their faces to what is left of his daughter's. In Franju's documentary "Blood of the Beasts" we learn that butchers decapitate live cattle so that the veal stays white. The doctor similarly operates on living—though not for long—women. Yet the grafts fail.

The Boileau-Narcejac screenplay (they also wrote stories on which *Diabolique* and *Vertigo* were based), as photographed by Eugen Schüfftan and directed by Franju with studied deliberation and a mesmerizing mixture of horrific and innocent images, explores issues of morality, patriarchy, vanity, guilt, beauty, and fixation that take the film beyond the realm of, say, Bela Lugosi's insane plastic surgeon in *The Raven*. This film has little patience with kitsch or comedy and only begrudging tolerance for melodrama. Instead, it offers the indelible figure of Christiane, played by Edith Scob—a lean, blonde, elegant, and improbably expressive actress, considering that she wears a white mask with cutouts for her eyes.

Scob is reason enough to cherish this film. Everyone remembers the unmasking of Lon Chaney in *Phantom of the Opera*, but his most affecting scenes were played with the mask in place; this is also true of Claude Rains in *The Invisible Man* and Peter Lorre in *The Face behind the Mask*. Scob's mask is different: It is so form-fitted to her face that at times it's like watching a botox experiment gone awry. Morally complicit, she haunts her every scene, an often mutely accusing wraith. Only when she realizes that her father won't succeed and that his motives have little to do with her does she take action, loosing his mistreated dogs (shades of *The Island of Dr. Moreau*) and her pet doves, which alight on her as she finally leaves the castle: Snow White in the enchanted forest—a fairy-tale finale, except that the price of restored innocence is madness.

David Cronenberg's script for *Videodrome* seems to have metastasized from an urban myth of the 1950s: If you sit too close to the TV, kids, the radiation will stunt your growth (like smoking) or kill you (like smoking). The Videodrome signal, broadcast underground in Pittsburgh and devoted to torture and murder, causes cancerous tumors that drive you crazy and then kill you. It's all part of a right-wing conspiracy to destroy eraserheads who watch such drivel—an effort to make America tougher. *Videodrome* depicts a world in which the dependence on television morphs into sexual union, producing new high-definition flesh. For the climactic scene in which a television literally spills its guts, Cronenberg visited the local abattoir to stock up on pig entrails.

For all its undeniable originality, *Videodrome* is pitched on familiar territory. The fascist control of TV is central to *1984* and Elia Kazan's post-McCarthy exercise in pop paranoia, *A Face in the Crowd*. Nor is reality TV anything new. It derived from radio and was built into the video schedule from the beginning, in Senate hearings, quiz shows, and sports; *Queen for a Day* was the 1950s' *Survivor*. The idea that terror can cause physiological growths generated the spinal parasite in William Castle's *The Tingler*—violence broadcast by Videodrome similarly triggers spinal receptors for its deadly signal. Even Cronenberg's sexual metaphors derive in part from Marshall McLuhan's notion of television's "tactility" and Stanley Kubrick's astronaut crawling into HAL's womb.

But Cronenberg's radical visual style and storytelling ambiguities completely reshuffle the deck. He presages the apparent inextricability of man and monitor. Millions of people now spend more time staring at a screen—television, computer, cellphone—than they do sleeping, making love, bathing, and eating combined. If *Videodrome* initially reflected the druggy humor of the '70s (and a Warholian immersion in gore as reflected in *Flesh for Frankenstein*), it now mirrors a technological addiction that has yet to be fully understood or cinematically explored. In that sense, his 1983 film is about as contemporary a film as you will see this year.

Videodrome is rife with urban-ugly colors and visual jokes (the Cathode Ray Mission is represented by a heart wrapped in thorns with a cross sticking out of a central ventricle). Its most disquieting images range from James Wood's abdomen turning into a vaginal cavern, roomy enough to house a Betamax, and a television screen that billows forth in the shape of a gun, to torture scenes that can't help but remind one of Abu Ghraib and an assassin recruited with promises of a better world to come. The best visual joke, however, was almost certainly accidental, though I was sure it had to be intentional when I first saw the film in a theater: James Woods gives one of the strongest performances of his career, but the more deranged his character gets—cheeks sunken, hair parted in the middle—the more uncanny is his resemblance to Zacherley, the host of late-night horror-movie broadcasts back in the day. Such is the way of all flesh.

[*The New York Sun*, August 2004–October 2005]

14 ❖ A Few Stops on the Way
to the Grave
(Films Noir)

W. R. Burnett has gone the way of many best-selling novelists: into the pit of obscurity reserved for those who were treated well by the movies. He wrote some 35 novels, none of them presently in print, though films made from them live on, and he worked on as many screenplays, from *Scarface* to *The Great Escape*. But who in an auteur-driven culture thinks of those films in terms of the writers? Along with Dashiell Hammett and James M. Cain, Burnett invented modern American crime fiction. Hammett gave us the detective, Cain the toxins of mad love, and Burnett the professional criminal—organized (*Little Caesar*) and plebian (*High Sierra*), working out a heist (*The Asphalt Jungle*) and corrupting munici-palities (*King Cole, Little Men, Big World, Vanity Row*). He also turned out two comedies of errors about the dark side of jazz, the atmospheric *The Giant Swing* and *It's Always Four O'Clock*.

Hammett stuck with the whodunit as his formal motif, and with the arrival of a princely if curmudgeonly heir in Raymond Chandler, it looked as if he had patented the genre's future: lonely knights of the night, cleaning up other people's messes. Then came Elmore Leonard and his legion of imitators, who cast a retrospective glory on the Cain-Burnett tradition in which detection is passé and the only mystery is: how will it all work out? If Burnett has proven to be the odd-man-out, it's because he lacks the literary flair of Hammett and Cain: memorable dialogue, fast pace, and vivid portraiture are not enough to sustain a long-term interest in books, in part because movies can sponge and improve on those attributes.

Hammett and Cain are nearly adaptation-proof; it's never just the story but the telling we keep returning to. John Huston indelibly captured the caper and characters of *The Maltese Falcon*, but Hammett's prose, sensibility, and thematic asides (the Flitcraft story) remain untouchable. After Huston's luminous film of *The Asphalt Jungle*, on the other hand, Burnett's text reads like a novelization rather than source material. Huston took everything good in it and added enhancements, generating performances so true to Burnett's descriptions that it's impossible to read about the crooked lawyer Emmerich without visualizing Louis Calhern in what may have been the best performance of his long career; or the master criminal Riedenschneider without hearing the quizzical inflections of Sam Jaffe, though he looks nothing like the corpulent original; or Dix, the scowling hooligan of uncertain age played by Sterling Hayden with a chilling lack of vanity. The same goes for minor characters, especially the "ferret"-like Cobby, brought to prodigiously sweating life by Marc Lawrence, and the washed-out whore Doll, played on the edge of hysteria by Jean Hagan, who two years later would score the biggest laughs in *Singin' in the Rain*.

Huston was an ideal director for Burnett; God doesn't exist in the novels or in his films. Huston's constant theme is that it all ends in the grave, pal, so the only question is how you behave on the way. As Huston tells it, Dix discovers a measure of his own humanity while leaking blood from a bullet hole and thus is allowed a semi-rapturous passing on the bluegrass of his old Kentucky home. No one else gets to leave the asphalt. He opens the film with a parody of John Ford—the horizon, shot from below. Only instead of cavalry marching across the perimeter, we see a police car coasting a junkyard's rim.

The Asphalt Jungle (1950) is the most respectable of five films collected in the DVD bargain of the year, *Film Noir* (Warner Bros.); it's also the print most in need of refurbishing, although its graininess is a minor annoyance. The other four are as bright and welcoming as Venus flytraps, the masterly black and white cinematography primed to accentuate every stylized shadow. The only extras are optional English titles and uneven commentary tracks (the ones for *Gun Crazy* and *Murder, My Sweet* are quite good). The movies are enough of a draw on their own.

Postwar French film critics coined the term "film noir" to denote similarities between Hollywood's new wave of brutal crime films and the pulp fiction that had appeared in France under the rubric, "Serie Noire." Most were B-pictures, the bottom halves of double features made by an underclass of filmmakers who played catch-me-if-you-can with the Hays office and received little critical attention. No surprise there. The surprise was the tenor of the films. We had just emerged triumphant from an unparalleled slaughter—the boys came home, the Depression was cured, affluence to follow. So why were movies so glum? Bing Crosby was the top box office attraction from 1946 through 1949, but even his films were turning dark (notably the all-singing, all-dancing, all existential desperation Technicolor extravaganza, *Blue Skies*). Film noir candidly took on the discontents bubbling under the surface—a cauldron stirred by chance, change, bad luck, betrayal (especially by women), murder, corruption, and the not-so-friendly police, whom one character in *The Asphalt Jungle* repeatedly refers to as "the happiness boys."

Is it coincidence that many if not most major noir films had someone in the cast or crew who would later come a cropper during the Red Scare? Huston joined the march on Washington; Marc Lawrence and Sterling Hayden named names and then wrote books about it. Edward Dmytryk and Adrian Scott, the director and producer of the meticulous, mannered Chandler adaptation, *Murder, My Sweet* (1944), were among Hollywood's unfriendly 10, as was Dalton Trumbo, who wrote the astonishing *Gun Crazy* (1950), though credit went to his "front," Millard Kaufman. Their films express social concerns but are rarely political. Looking at them today you get the sense that these filmmakers had more fun tweaking the censors than the status quo; for them, the censors *were* the status quo.

Burnett's earliest contribution to the noir canon was his work on *This Gun for Hire* (1942, Universal), which helped define the genre's look and themes a year after the way had been paved by *The Maltese Falcon* and *Citizen Kane*—a noir prognosticator, with its angular shots, claustrophobic sets, and exaggerated lighting. Based on Graham Greene's *A Gun for Sale*, it transferred the story to San Francisco, turned the hired gun's harelip into a broken wrist, and bathed the action in patriotic twaddle. The film remains fascinating as the mutant love child of two warring instincts—Paramount, the studio of Crosby and Hope, looking for new stars in Veronica Lake and Alan Ladd (his blond hair dyed black), and the subversive instincts of writers Burnett and Albert Maltz (also of the Hollywood 10) and director Frank Tuttle (a Communist who named names). Perhaps the shrewdest participant, though, was the influential cinematographer John P. Seitz, who with Tuttle managed to configure one scene as a send-up of old-dark-house thrillers. Seitz was then in the process of working out the dynamic chiaroscuro lighting he soon brought to fruition in Billy Wilder's *Double Indemnity* and *Sunset Boulevard*.

This Gun for Hire begins with a vicious double murder, making it a hard sell to garner sympathy for Ladd no matter how many dreamy close-ups he gets (plenty). The problem is resolved by having him victimized by scum even lower on the food chain: a sexually ambiguous sybarite addicted to peppermints (the incomparable Laird Cregar) and an industrialist manufacturing poison gas for the Japanese, played by a wheelchair-bound Tully Marshall, groomed to resemble a crazed John D. Rockefeller. A more damning critique, however, seems almost unintentional; the honest cop (Robert Preston) is a deadly bore and Lake, a singing magician doubling as government spy (really), leaves everyone but the cop dead.

If *This Gun for Hire* is half-hearted noir, Joseph H. Lewis's *Gun Crazy* and Jacques Tourneur's *Out of the Past* spin happily beyond the pale, though the problem of empathy remains. Forget empathy. Movie lovers will be content to revel in filmmaking that is, shot for shot, as stylish as anything from that period. Those less aesthetically inclined may want to throttle Robert Mitchum and John Dall for not seeing through, respectively, the magnificently rapacious femmes fatale, Jane Greer and Peggy Cummins. *Gun Crazy* begins with the tedious remonstrations of a judge (played by the blacklisted Morris Carnovsky), sentencing gun-crazy Bart to reform school. Yet from the moment Bart sees Cummins's Annie—emerging from the lower screen with six-guns blazing, firing at targets in profile to show off her luscious figure—the picture veers off into a new direction. Dall's ear-to-ear grin may have mirrored the audience's recognition that the days of Andy Hardy were over. Lewis's film posits a split between the gun-crazy/crazy-in-love couple and the cheerless life of small-town America. Tourneur's film creates a different kind of split, between urban decay and small-town decency, as the hero—Mitchum's erstwhile detective turned gas-jockey—vainly tries to escape his past.

A similar optimism upends Robert Wise's otherwise lightning-fast and hard as nails fight movie, *The Set Up* (1949), filmed in real time with frequent shots of clocks (a device imitated three years later in *High Noon*). The always-compelling Robert Ryan is a noble loser who wins a match he's expected to throw. Wise's contempt for the riff-raff in attendance is relentless, establishing a noirish tension between the fighter—admirable if deluded—and the blood-lusting audience. Unfortunately, Ryan has to contend not only with gangsters who cripple him in revenge, but also the awkward line readings of Audrey Totter, who spouts tears of joy when she realizes her man won't have to fight any more.

Every one of these films has censor-mandated add-ons. In *This Gun for Hire*, it's the dirty traitors; in *Murder, My Sweet*, it's a cute ending chaperoned by paternal cops; in *Gun Crazy*, it's a tacked-on scene in which Bart and Annie commiserate about how rotten they are; in *Out of the Past*, it's a liberating lie that allows Mitchum's hometown girl to marry the town sheriff; and, most risibly, in *The Asphalt Jungle*, it's a speech by the chief of police assuring everyone that most cops are not as dishonest as the one in the story. To be fair, Burnett had written that speech in his novel.

[*The New York Sun*, 14 September 2004]

15 ❖ *Hokum Became Him (William Wyler)*

William Wyler never made a film noir, but his postwar oeuvre began with a quartet of films as relentlessly grim as any dark-alley second feature, particularly the 1952 box office disaster *Carrie*, derived from Theodore Dreiser's *Sister Carrie*. (The appellative was dropped for fear that Americans and Brits, respectively, would think it about a nun or a nurse.) A decade earlier, Wyler had triumphed with *Mrs. Miniver*, a picture admired by Churchill and Goebbels for its value as propaganda. It quickly went the way of most propaganda, and Wyler later dismissed it as "synthetic." During the war, he lost his hearing in one ear while flying on high-altitude bombers to shoot Air Force documentaries. He returned to Hollywood determined to avoid banal uplift and to challenge the Production Code.

Wyler was much honored for *The Best Years of Our Lives* (1946), *The Heiress* (1949), and *Detective Story* (1951), which furthered his reputation for long takes, diagrammatic staging made possible by deep-focus photography, and ensemble acting. The gloominess of those films was offset by stylistic bravura and reasonably positive codas. No such coda lightens *Carrie*, shot in 1950 as a fin de siècle companion to *The Heiress*, but suppressed by Paramount for two years, then released after anxious pruning (a process that replicated the initial treatment of Dreiser's novel). Today's viewers will find such pussyfooting inconceivable: The DVD restores a two-and-a-half-minute sequence set in a Bowery shelter, its prior omission now mysteriously explicated as "due to the political state of affairs in our nation."

Audiences didn't shun the picture because of its politics, however, but because it dealt, despairingly, with a subject the studios rarely broached: male menopause. Wyler had been there before, with *Dodsworth*, filmed in 1936, when he was 34—first coming into his own and with good reason to believe in second acts. Pushing 50, he was less sanguine. Despite the title (he couldn't very well call it *George*), his treatment of *Sister Carrie*, adapted by Ruth and Augustus Goetz, reworks the emphasis from Carrie Meeber to George Hurstwood. Though he toys, as Dreiser does not, with the possibility of a happy ending, he closes with Hurstwood shuffling off to a rented room and a gas jet, not with Carrie's oblivious success.

The film follows Carrie to the big city, where she is hustled by Eddie Albert's Drouet and victimized by evil labor practices (the censors driven by the House Un-American Activities Committee accepted this but not the disclosure of homeless men and poverty). Yet from the moment we see Laurence Olivier's Hurstwood, framed in middle-distance by the appurtenances of his pricey restaurant-saloon, the story belongs to him. The last act isn't about Carrie leaving him; it's about Hurstwood being left, descending into hell accompanied only by the viscous orchestrations of David Raksin's music. The audience is allowed emotional release in the tear-jerking finale—Hurstwood asking for a handout, insensible to her love-filled eyes; Carrie offering resuscitation, insensible to the weight of his despair (we are a long way from Dreiser). But Wyler offers no comfort. The movie is a series of missed connections. Every character lies to every other character or misinterprets motives. Wyler not only rejects the softening of Dreiser's more maudlin offspring, as in *Showboat* (though his Carrie shows symptoms of Magnolia's magnanimity) or *A Star Is Born* (she would never sign off as "Mrs. George Hurstwood"), he refuses Dreiser's piety about innocent versus thoughtful people. Wyler has leeched out all hope.

Yet there is much to enjoy. Olivier is magnificent, under-acting with rueful suspicion; he never once laughs, and checks each smile at the gate, as though afraid to divulge too much. Jennifer Jones is surprisingly effective, once you accept that she's a bit long in the tooth to play Dreiser's maiden. She is, at times, awkward with Olivier—after several viewings of one scene, I'm not certain if she withholds kisses from him because Carrie is conniving or Jones is clumsy. She is at her best in the Goetzes' exceptionally well-written "I ruined him" scene with Eddie Albert, when she can focus on her forte: obedient tear ducts. Given the ending, the film had no choice but to elevate her with a bit of sainthood.

Dreiser was the master of hotel lobbies and restaurants, and Wyler's chamber piece honors that with scrupulously art-directed interiors. There is a lovely moment at the saloon when Hurstwood and Carrie are shown walking in deep-focus parallel paths. The exteriors, however, are undermined by sanitary sound stages. The illusion of urban decay and clamor is never captured. Chicago seems grossly underpopulated and lower Manhattan—meant to show us how far George has fallen—is busy but antiseptic. (As is Jones's makeup. The print is so sharp you can see her lip-gloss and eyeliner as she recovers from a miscarriage; her perfectly manicured nails do not indicate a great deal of dishwashing.) The director's heart is not in the streets. It's in the drawing rooms with his actors, and in those environs the film is convincing.

Where Dreiser sought tragedy and hit verismo, Somerset Maugham reached for irony and rang melodrama—a better fit for commercial cinema, which is partly why he remains among the most frequently adapted of writers (*Being Julia* is the latest entry). Wyler's 1940 film, *The Letter*—taken from the Maugham play, which was taken from a Maugham short story, which was closely based on a 1911 murder in Singapore—is one of Wyler's most durable achievements. Hokum became him, allowing him to concentrate on style for style's sake. As the DVD release proves, time has been very kind to this film.

From the opening nighttime pan of a rubber plantation, interrupted by a gunshot and fluttering cockatoo, and finished with an inexorable closing in on Bette Davis, who has followed her victim onto the verandah and pumped five more bullets into him, you know you are in the hands of ardent filmmakers and can only hope that they sustain the inspiration for another 90 minutes. They do. The set design by Carl Jules Weyl and Tony Gaudio's photography belie the constrictions of the sound stage. Max Steiner's music, as arranged by Hugo Friedhofer, is more nudging than pronounced (never a staccato blast). And the key actors are beyond cavil: Davis never gave a more measured or original performance, alternately frigid and feverish, and Herbert Marshall, his voice a great bassoon, has the effect of a damp cloth on her brow. James Stephenson's lawyer binds them—he holds whole episodes together by his very stillness.

There is a moment in *Carrie*, when Olivier twirls his mustache in imitation of a stage roué; the material he parodies is not far removed from that of *The Letter*. To the 1911 murder Maugham had added the hoariest of 19th-century conventions, an incriminating letter, and an acquittal (the real murderess was sentenced to hang but was later pardoned to die in an English asylum—not much irony there). Wyler's version is reminiscent of D. W. Griffith's transformation of the antiquated barnstormer *Way Down East*. It is at once a critique of and an embodiment of the gaslight thriller, so knowing in its design that it remains a vital feat of lighting, staging, acting, and cinematic invention.

Wyler toys with the clichés of melodrama, as in his use of consecutive reaction shots to punctuate disclosures. He contrasts the strengths of theater and cinema, as when he shoots Davis's recounting of the crime from the rear, as if she were performing for an invisible audience, and then tracks away from her altogether, as only the camera can. He shoots Davis's swelling eyes in opposition to the moon, which—call it astronomic license—is always full. He introduces Gale Sondergaard as an apparition in a car's headlights. He draws attention to reflections in hair and on foreheads, to dislocated shadows. He portrays Davis's attempt at corrupting her lawyer from behind the sofa on which she lies, stressing her raised left arm as the lure. Shot for shot, Wyler's film is an elaborate feast of controlled abstractions countered by vividly grounded performances.

It is not, however, flawless. Howard Koch's smart screenplay had to contend with the Production Code, which mandated retribution (happiness is a dead adulterer). Worse, a cop steps out of nowhere so that we may surmise that the killer's killers will also pay the piper. The original discarded ending, included on the DVD, shows that the filmmakers were concerned that the audience might not go along with the killing of Davis unless reminded of her remorseless infidelity, forcing Koch to add the scene with the famously campy line (bannered on the DVD box), "With all my heart I still love the man I killed." He was also obliged to change Maugham's Chinese mistress to a "Eurasian" widow, played by Sondergaard with the rigidity of a dressmaker's mannequin and looking a lot more Asian than Euro. Wyler slightly overdoes the alluring moon shots and the Madame Defarge routine of Davis constantly knitting pillow lace.

No matter. Wyler followed his bleak postwar quartet with a return to uplift, spectacle, and family values, regaining his audience and his Hollywood ranking with *Roman Holiday, Friendly Persuasion, Ben Hur*, and *Funny Girl* (he did return to form and the dark side with *The Collector*, in 1965). *The Letter* is a grander entertainment than any of them, and though—or because—it doesn't add up to much in the way of social relevance, it seems a lot more meaningful as well.

[*The New York Sun*, 18 January 2005]

16 ❖ *Primal Fear*
(Nightmare Alley)

The 1947 film *Nightmare Alley* is not as compelling, convincing, or original as William Lindsay Gresham's novel, a best seller of the previous year, but its own virtues cannot be denied. Considering the material—degradation, adultery, alcoholism, murder, larceny, spiritualism, high-stakes cons, and child abuse, set against the Depression scrim of anarchy, racism, desperation, and top-down corruption—we may marvel that the film was made at all. We may also assume that the film was made 25 years too soon, in an era when the motion picture code and a nervous studio chief (Daryl F. Zanuck) mandated a softer focus, a softened protagonist, and, if you don't look too closely, what passes for a happy ending.

Yet had the film been made postcode, it would have lost everything that makes it worthwhile: the almost palpably textured black-and-white shadowplay of cameraman Lee Garmes, the blanketing symphonic dissonance of composer Cyril Mockridge, the casual verisimilitude in conveying carny life and high society (on a back lot), the shrewd discretion in portraying the unspeakable, and its masterstroke of counterintuitive casting. Tyrone Power's performance is the picture's raison d'être, for us as it was for the actor, who spent all his star power to realize the project. Power had been Fox's top leading man in the late 1930s and early 1940s, until he was drafted. His only box-office peers at the studio were musical moppet Shirley Temple, language-mangling ice-skater Sonia Henie, and his leading lady in three films, the glorious but too-independent-for-studio-life Alice Faye (during the war, they were all displaced by Betty Grable). None were as pretty as he, a fact he had begun to resent.

After the war, Power demanded deeper roles and scored a hit with his first picture in three years, as Maugham's secular saint in *The Razor's Edge*, directed by the veteran king of women's weepies, Edmund Goulding. Zanuck feared moviegoers would not accept Power as the devil—which, at times, Stanton Carlisle in *Nightmare Alley* all but embodies. At one point Fox, which has released a bright DVD print of the film, announced that the film would star Mark Stevens and Anne Baxter. But with the reliable Goulding in tow and the skilled screenwriter Jules Furthman, whose stock had been lately restored by a couple of collaborations with Howard Hawks (including *To Have and Have Not*) on board, Zanuck gave Power and the unlikely producer George Jessel (he had made money with *The Dolly Sisters*) a green light.

The film flopped and Zanuck did not have to bother with "I told you so" in subsequently assigning Power to vehicles like *Captain from Castile* and *The Luck of the Irish*. But Power gave the performance of his life: a 34-year-old with a head of shiny black hair essaying the part of a 21-year-old blond sociopath—a role that retrospectively imparted depth to much of what he did before and after. A better Stanton is hard to imagine. What is more, Power surrounded himself with an ideal cast to share Goulding's and Garmes's claustrophobic close-ups: Joan Blondell, Colleen Gray, and Helen Walker as the women who successively hand him his fate, and Ian Keith, who shows it to him reflected in his own face— that of a vaudeville luminary gone to seed.

Gresham frames his novel with a *Death in Venice* conceit. Like Aschenbach, the esteemed historian who shudders at the sight of a decadent old man, rouged and dyed to look young, Carlisle is obsessed with the geek, the lowest attraction in carnival life, who bites the heads off live chickens and snakes to secure a daily bottle. Each novelist has to convince us his hero will fall into a pool of primal fear. Gresham's carny boss explains to Stan that you don't find a geek, you make one. Furthman, perhaps forced by censors to avoid laying out the immorality of the film's more amiable carny folk, settles for Stan's meditation, "I don't understand how anybody can get so low," and an elliptical response from Zeena, a mentalist sensibly embodied by Blondell: "It can happen." This exchange has a peculiarly Fox-like rhythm: "How can you live without hope?" a wide-eyed Betty Grable asks psycho-cop Laird Cregar in *I Wake Up Screaming* (1941). "It can be done," he says.

Gresham knew about falling low and losing hope. Born of an old Baltimore family, he was a roustabout, working at various jobs, devoting himself to serial fixes—a rich wife, communism, philandering, religion, spiritualism, drink. Fascinated by carnival life, he learned the word *geek* as an epithet for lowlifes and with his novel popularized it as a particular kind of performer, the lowest ever on the scale of paid entertainers. (In the only earlier literary work on geeking, "Keela the Outcast Indian Maiden," Eudora Welty never used the term.) He then wrote an equally bizarre but jumbled novel, *Limbo Tower* (1949), a schematic Grand Hotel about anguished misfits confined to the ninth-floor tubercular ward of a hospital, prefiguring *One Flew over the Cuckoo's Nest* and *Cancer Ward*. With its failure, he turned to nonfiction—a biography of Houdini and an engaging, personal tour of the *Nightmare Alley* milieu, *Monster Midway*. Suffering from tongue cancer, he checked into a hotel using the name of the main character in *Limbo Tower* and took his life in 1962, at 53.

The film of *Nightmare Alley* is riveting during the first 48 minutes, when confined to the carnival and a seedy hotel. Stan learns the ropes as a utility man and finds his forte in "cold readings," convincing the chumps he can see into their pasts. An utter narcissist, Stan readily concedes that he has no concern for other people. But his real failing is that he cannot distinguish between his gift for manipulation in a carny act and in his life. His lovers and co-workers tell him that he can't con them, but he knows better and he is usually right. When he falls prey to a better huckster, he has nothing left.

Power lets us see the emptiness and malice behind the pretty façade. When Zeena tells him he can't have her act because the Tarot warns against it, he nuzzles her and says it's okay with him. She breaks away from a kiss, looking down, insisting she has to think; he pushes her head back to get at her lips, not with his hands, but with his nose and brow, nudging her back like an animal, a gesture you don't see in golden-age movies. Absent a conscience, he is all flashing eyes and self-infatuated grin. Forced to marry the innocent Molly (Gray), he realizes he can get his revenge on the world by working up an act with her, making lemonade out of lemons after all. She avows her love and promises fidelity, but he's no longer paying attention to her. Grinning giddily at his own future, he turns the famous Power beauty on itself and the view is fearsome.

He plays one of his best scenes with Ian Keith as Zeena's rumdum husband Pete, once a headliner, now a drunk. When Stan gives him a badly needed drink, Pete revives his old charm as if out of a hat, and the actor's own former status as a theatrical matinee idol is a mirror of Power at his peak. One of Goulding's best moves is an exterior tracking shot in which we see Stan walk Pete into his tent and emerge from the other side, before turning down the midway, strolling toward his fate. But it's also here that the film begins to compromise. Stan gives Pete the wood alcohol that kills him accidentally—not intentionally as in the novel—and from then on, he is just noble enough to merit deliverance in a Hollywood finale.

This in itself is not displeasing. The force of Power's characterization requires our identification. Nor is the film's ending an egregious betrayal of the novel. Gresham's finale, in which the degenerate Stan, forced to sell himself with a childlike politeness we haven't seen before, is offered the geek job, is faithfully shot and then some. In the book, we don't get his response—here, his face distorted by drink, his eyes ringed and droopy, the pupils swimming in soup, he rears back and agrees to the offer. The film's coda, in which he goes on a rampage and discovers that Molly has been hired on to the same carnival and is going to save him, is happy only to the degree that we believe he can take a cure for drink and safely evade the powerful industrialist he bamboozled.

What is troubling about the last half of the film is the absence of detail that animates the carny scenes. All the great set pieces of the novel, including the house he embezzles and rigs with mentalist contraptions, his ability to outwit a hermetically sealed scale (the most suspenseful and amusing episode in the book), his willingness to prostitute Molly, his railroad encounter with a mysterious black man who is making his way to the industrialist he set out to scam, are gone, along with the social awareness that gives the novel a multidimensional richness. They are replaced with by-the-numbers scenes hurriedly designed to bring Stan back to where he began.

The script improves on the novel in one incident—introducing the shifty psychologist Lilith (played by an ominously still and half-smiling Helen Walker, the thin lines beneath her eyes belying her 28 years) as a skeptical member of Stan's nightclub audience, rather than the shrink he sees to cure his dreams of running down a nightmare alley. On the other hand, the filmmakers could not resist adding an up-to-date technological wrinkle—a home device for recording transcription discs, which Lilith uses to blackmail Stan. The mechanism provides a shrewd visual touch while reflecting the menacing qualities then associated with hidden recording devices of any kind, but it stretches credulity for Stan, who immediately discovers the device, to then almost immediately forget its existence when he lies down on her couch to tell all.

Not that it matters much. The fascination of *Nightmare Alley* does not reside in logic but in qualities beyond the powers of a novelist. In the expressive chiaroscuro of the lighting—even Lilith's office is a model of German expressionism, with inexplicable bar-like shadows turning the walls into a cage—and in Power's vanity-free dissection of Stan (he has blackened gums and sagging cheeks in the final scenes), this picture turns conventional Hollywood starlight upside down and inside out. Had he lived long enough to see *Nightmare Alley* earn its long-standing cult status (it was televised frequently from the 1960s through the 1980s), Power might have had the chance to tell Zanuck, "I told you so."

[*The New York Sun*, 14 June 2005]

17 ❖ *Tales of Treachery and Loyalty* (*Jules Dassin / Jacques Becker*)

Two modes of gangster film have predominated since the silent era: thugs at war with the law and thugs at war with one another. The first restages the morality plays of the old West with spats, machine guns, and electric chair. The second recapitulates Western sentimentality, portraying the urban underworld as a social microcosm, an alternate landscape of proto-capitalists, tragic misfits, and thieves with honor. A culture that resurrects Jesse James as Tyrone Power will venerate the Corleones for having better manners and looks than their enemies. Gangster films liberate themes of loyalty and heroism (and stratagems of warfare and revenge) from the repressive details of logic while guaranteeing shoot-outs, chases, and other kinetic denouements. They are our fairy tales.

The Criterion Collection has now released elaborate DVD restorations of four crime films made between 1949 and 1954, two each by the American director Jules Dassin and the French director Jacques Becker. They reflect a Brechtian (or Langian) immersion in underworld self-sufficiency—the appearance of cops in each suggests an almost comic irrelevancy. Like all good genre films, they restate complicated issues in terms a child can understand. A filmmaker working in that period and concerned with themes of loyalty and moral quandary might have looked at the choices facing colleagues asked either to accuse friends of faux-treason or face a blacklist. But as that was impossible, Dassin, a Communist Party member between 1937 and 1939, was dispatched to London to make what would be his last American film: *Night and the City* (1950), a character study of a remorseless weasel, an "artist without an art," who discovers his calling in duplicity. Harry Fabian (a gritty, luminous, career-high performance by Richard Widmark) betrays everyone including, after he runs out of dupes, himself. Betrayal is an addiction for him, a back-alley puppeteer intoxicated with pulling strings.

Becker also knew something about treachery and loyalty. A former assistant to Jean Renoir, he served a year in a German POW camp yet managed to direct films during the Occupation. He might have found his subject in the deadly spying all around him. But that, too, was impossible. So he achieved his creative breakthrough with the incomparable *Casque d'Or* (1952), a romantic tragedy set at the turn of the century, concerning former inmates who sacrifice themselves for friendship—a theme revisited in his contemporary crime thriller, *Touchez pas au grisbi* (1954).

Each of these pictures is posted with the label film noir, and labels can hide as much as they clarify. American critics ignored the subtleties of 1950s westerns by Anthony Mann, Budd Boetticher, and even John Ford because they were westerns. *Night and the City* may be, as DVD commentator Glenn Erickson argues, the ultimate example of film noir, but it seems discourteous to pigeonhole so exceptional a work—as if Dassin, writer Jo Eisinger (working with the title and central character but not the plot of Gerald Kersh's still-potent novel), and cinematographer Max Greene consciously strove to join a fashionable club of postwar despair.

Night and the City, which was largely dismissed in the United States and London in its initial release, is like no other film. The picture has antecedents, not least a Dickensian or Wellesian cast of supporting grotesques. Dassin surely recalled Orson Welles racing through the sewers in Carol Reed's *The Third Man*, but he prefigures Welles's *Mr. Arkadin* with his close-up gargoyles and insistence that character is fate. Fabian has no backstory and no connection to any other world beyond the rat maze in which he spins his wheels. Everyone in this film is a manipulator, though most speak like conservative merchants, and no one gets what he or she wants—not even the coiled-to-strike crime-boss (swarthy, glassy-eyed Herbert Lom), who nonetheless walks away unmolested by the useless police.

Nor does the film look like any other. Shot on location in London, Dassin turned the city into a soundstage, going so far as to include a drive through Trafalgar Square in which crowds gawk at the camera evidently mounted on his car. Those crowds become de facto members of the sucker class, perpetual outsiders to the men (criminals or filmmakers) going about their insulated business. Except for a few grainy day shots, the film stock seems to glisten, exteriors and interiors alike fashioned into patterns of pitch and light. In the nightclub office, Phil (the truly Dickensian Francis L. Sullivan, thrust into 20th-century chicanery), hovers on one side, his back to the camera, while a parallel space discloses Fabian's girlfriend (the miscast Gene Tierney); the screen is thus broken into Mondrianesque squares, parts of the maze in which they are stuck. When Harry sidles up to a bar lit by candles, the light shines in his eyes, on his tie and carnation and wrist, all made opalescent in contrast to swatches of absolute blackness. Dassin stylized every shot with thematic purpose. Before Phil's desperate wife Helen (implacable Googie Withers) kisses Fabian, dragon smoke issues from her nostrils.

Richard Widmark's suppressed energy turns boyish when released, and sullen or hysterical when opposed. His pas de deux with Helen is perfectly gauged—each is certain that the other is buying a bill of goods (he's right)—as is his forlorn meditation in the riverside shack of Anna (Maureen Delaney, inadvertently grooming him for a parallel setting and character in *Pickup on South Street*). One of his most appealing moments is entirely visual. Thinking he has it made, Harry hurdles a stair railing into Phil's club, affecting a Chaplinesque stance, his feet splayed (the light picking up what appear to be white spats) and arms outstretched, before beating out his briefly enjoyed elation in a drum solo. He is a bystander, however, in one of the film's peak sequences: a four-minute wrestling match between Stanislaus Zbyszko (a former champ, unforgettable in his only picture) and Mike Mazurki (also a former wrestler), a set piece that fully draws on Dassin's ingenuity.

One of the DVD's supplements argues for the validity of a different cut of *Night and the City* released in England with an understated score and alternative scenes (a few are excerpted in a short featurette). Criterion elected not to include that version in deference to Dassin, who, at 93, is said to abominate it. One can understand his disgust with its revoltingly romantic conclusion, but the British score by Benjamin Frankel seems much superior to the one by Franz Waxman, which telegraphs every emotion—a kind of composing often mandated by producer Daryl Zanuck.

Thieves' Highway is a misfire, albeit a fascinating one that works better on subsequent viewings, when you are prepared for the utter idiocy of the hero played by Richard Conte. Here, for a change, there is no musical score beyond the credits, and the ordinary sounds of location shooting in groves and markets worked by truckers hauling fruit intensifies many scenes. Conte is a Greek son, home from the sea and out to avenge his father, who was robbed and crippled by Lee J. Cobb's ruthless wholesaler. But Conte turns out to be more Candide than Odysseus, instantly diverted by Valentina Cortese's whore with a heart of you-know-what. "You look like chipped glass," he tells her. "Took me a long time to get that way," she says. Yes, and it took many men to name Shanghai Lily.

When the film sticks to corruption, betrayal, and revenge, it stays on target. But there is more than a touch of sadism running through it, especially at the conclusion of a spectacular truck crash, when two pointless inserts underscore the fact that the driver is burned alive. When Conte falls for Cortese, the movie is not about to force him to choose between her and his fiancée, so presto change-o his fiancée turns into a rabid golddigger, while Cortese (who provides her character an earthiness the script strenuously tries to undermine) takes a symbol-laden shower from which she emerges with the film's best line: "Aren't women wonderful?" According to an interview with Dassin, the studio tacked on the ghastly ending—involving deus ex machina police and Conte's marriage proposal to Cortese, which today's audience will greet with howls of derision—without the director's agreement or knowledge.

Although Becker's *Casque d'Or* was initially panned in France, it soon earned an international reputation as a lapidary masterpiece, and it remains agelessly and compulsively absorbing, drawing energy from one of the cinema's great star turns. Simone Signoret, whose blond hair is the title's "helmet of gold," has few lines, and her all-purpose smile and hypnotic eyes make most of them superfluous. A guillotine sequence suggests the law's blind but brutal efficiency, and the film never softens or romanticizes the killers (chief among them the double-crossing Leca, played by Claude Dauphin in his most unlikely and wiliest performance) and thieves of la belle époque beyond extreme male bonding. Yet there is a lyricism at the core, beyond the painterly evocations of lakeside picnics and lovemaking.

This is no less true of *Touchez pas au grisbi*, a modern-day saga of under-world rivalry that takes place after a heist—the heist itself is of no consequence, only the titular imperative, "Don't touch the loot." (Dassin's heist classic, *Rififi*, which reestablished him as a filmmaker, debuted in France months later.) The pacing is as confident and disarmingly easy as Jean Gabin's masterly performance or the persistently reiterated harmonica tune, which augurs musical scores by Ennio Morricone and the specific melody of *The Godfather*. Maybe Becker's films are more human and balanced because of their easiness with sex. Casual couplings, whatever complications may ensue, give the characters and milieu enduring credibility, a feeling of life lived. In the absence of sexual release, the gangsters and settings of Dassin's films grow gnarled with frustration and cruelty—even the stylishness is stark and ominous. *Night and the City* never stops moving. *Touchez pas au grisbi* has time for wine and pâté.

[*The New York Sun*, 1 February 2005]

18 ❖ *Incomparable*
(Greta Garbo)

Back in 1965, 24 years after Greta Garbo, at 36, walked away from the most fabled Hollywood career of her era, the historian A. J. P. Taylor judged her the dominant figure in film in the 1930s, but one whose allure had vanished—"a sex symbol who now appears in retrospect astonishingly sexless." At the time, that assessment seemed astonishingly clueless, yet it always comes to mind when I watch her movies. Taylor was not far wrong, beyond his assumption that sex symbolism and sexiness invariably go hand in hand, as they did for, say, Rita Hayworth and Marilyn Monroe. Ingrid Bergman and Simone Signoret were sexy without being sex symbols; Garbo epitomizes sexual conflict without the desire to seduce her audience. She was too remote and self-involved to exude salacious promise—the planes of her face too perfect, the angularity of her slope-shouldered body too concealing. Yet as a sex symbol, who can compare? The prolific film chronicler James Robert Parish came closer to the mark when he referred to her "carnal spirituality."

"All my life I've been a symbol," Garbo's Queen Christina laments. During the long afterlife of her career, between 1941—when the disastrous "Two-Faced Woman" suggested that her future in movies might be too ordinary or competitive to suit her own mythology—and 1990, when she died, her very presence furthered the saga of the Swedish sphinx who surmounted Hollywood on her own terms. Hidden among mortals but for rare sightings, she required no public relations to sustain the suspicion that she might be the finest actress the movies ever produced, unimaginable in any other medium.

Garbo reminds us that cinema is the ultimate expression of voyeurism: Her close-ups are her money shots. She rewards scrutiny with actorly gestures and looks of overwhelming candor and acuity, but the primary pleasure she affords is simply that of watching. We feel we are seeing something we shouldn't, something intimate, because after all she would rather be alone. Yet, as her best directors knew, Garbo existed to be gazed at, and never more so than when she was caught gazing. Her keeper, MGM, sobered by the Garbo mystique, swaddled her in costume dramas, as though only history and elaborate gowns could contain her. Graham Greene wrote (twice) "A dreadful inertia always falls on me before a new Garbo film. It is rather like reading *Sartor Resartus.*"

What contemporary audiences make of her we may soon learn. September 18 marks her centenary, an occasion commemorated by her imminent appearance on a postage stamp, showings throughout the month of her complete works on Turner Classic Movies, and the release of *Garbo: The Signature Collection* (Warner Bros.), an exceptional 10-disc set, involving nearly half her output—three silent pictures, eight talkies (including the English and German versions of *Anna Christie*), and an illuminating documentary. The selection is admirable (though *Love,* her silent version of *Anna Karenina,* ought to have been included with the talkie) and the prints sharply focused, if occasionally showing scratches and other signs of age.

With one exception these are not great films. We look to them for Garbo, anticipating her every appearance and marveling at her subtle turns—the look of knowing gratitude when she realizes Gaston has filled her purse in *Camille,* or the one-eyed (the other is shadowed) look of sexual daring as she takes communion in *Flesh and the Devil.* Every film is a passion play in which sex rehabilitates her abiding androgyny and love is denied. After the silent triumph of *Flesh and the Devil,* where she is so hot that the film cools her off by drowning her in an ice floe (as two men dueling over her put down their pistols and embrace, oblivious to her fate), she became a goddess of transcendent one-nighters. Camille asks, "How can one change one's entire life and build a new one in a moment of love?" Ninotchka believes so much happiness must be punished. Garbo's characters are constantly changing their lives and paying for it in spades. Queen

Christina abdicates her throne, Karenina throws herself under a train, Ninotchka loses country and principles—all for Camille's one moment.

The Annas are no better than they ever were, but the others remain entertaining, and *Camille* is more than that, an inspired reworking of 19th-century kitsch as likely to last, in this 1936 film, as long as *La Traviata*. In *Camille*, the Mona Lisa of impending doom reaches beyond MGM's museum glamor. It's an amazing thing: Directed by George Cukor, this warhorse fabricated in cliché and sentimentality is in the playing-out a credible, insightful fairy tale of obstinate youth, money, and a courtesan with a 14k pumper and TB. The sets are sumptuously dressed, especially the Parisian salons, though even rusticity is brocaded with enchanting details. Cukor, employing the style he had used in *David Copperfield*, shoots tight so that the frame is full and bustling, implying an equally busy world beyond it. Garbo plays Camille as a whore who chose her occupation as a means of staying aloof and in control. "Too much wine has made you sentimental," she admonishes Robert Taylor's Duval, before sipping from the same vine. He's a pain, but Camille is in charge, whether she is soothing or eviscerating him.

Other than phony-looking rear projection, the film has a fussed-over perfection: from the watery reflections of Camille and Duval as they happily cross a bridge to the precision editing (Margaret Booth wielded the razor) in Garbo's three great encounters, each a lesson in film acting. Her meeting with Duvall's father (Lionel Barrymore, underplaying for once, at least by his grumpy standards) is a play unto itself, and Cukor's impeccably timed close-up when she says, "Make no mistake, monsieur," is studio filmmaking at its best—melodrama cracked on the spine of her realism. Her death scene is too famous to belabor, but perhaps not as gripping as the duet with scoundrel Henry Daniel. He plays piano, the two speaking at loggerheads but somehow rising to the same crescendo. Daniel, a gifted scene-stealer, limited by his chiseled voice and his bearing of ominous contempt, was never more textured than here. His laughter is chilling.

After *Camille*, Garbo made only three more films—the stuffy Napoleonic *Conquest*; the modern-day comedy *Two-Faced Woman*, where she is out-screwballed by Constance Bennett (neither film is included in this set), and, inbetween, the Ernst Lubitsch comedy *Ninotchka*, which was advertised with the tag, "Garbo Laughs!" As she had already laughed uproariously in *Queen Christina* and for exactly the same reason (her future lover's mishap), and laughs throughout *Camille*, the catchphrase might be interpreted as shorthand for, "Garbo allows others to laugh at her." She had had comedic moments before, playing in drag in *Queen Christina* and parodying herself in *Grand Hotel*, but as the deadpan Soviet envoy who says of Stalin's show trials, "There will be fewer and better Russians," she discloses novel subtleties of timing and timbre. Ninotchka succumbs to Melvin Douglas, stands up to Ina Claire (who, before they meet, says, "I guess one gets the face one deserves"), and then ceases to be funny as she loosens up and the film trades Lubitsch's temperate farce for screenwriter Billy Wilder's heavy-handed satire—*Ninotchka* has the director's touch, but is neither as moving as *The Shop Around the Corner* nor as funny as *To Be or Not to Be*.

The gem of Garbo's pre-*Camille* talkies is Rouben Mamoulian's *Queen Christina*. If Lubitsch is the poet of seduction and foreplay, Mamoulian, in this 1933 film, has the last word on post-coital afterglow: His camera trails Christina as she walks around her and her lover's room in an inn, committing it to a memory she expects to kindle the rest of her life. The three-minute scene, silent but for music, closes with a 15-second close-up, a harbinger of the celebrated unblinking divinity with which the film ends, and a cinematic oil painting in its own right. John Gilbert, her silent-screen lover resurrected for one last go, can only stare at her, as we do. Curiously, they part on the morning-after with a handshake. The film is predicated on the preposterous idea that when Garbo puts on britches everyone thinks she is a boy (a conceit made worthwhile by her demure, patient expression as she removes her doublet and waits for Gilbert to notice her breasts), and is burdened with rabble. But Garbo was never more mesmerizing, and the superbly baroque opening scenes anticipate the claustrophobic interiors of Eisenstein's *Ivan the Terrible*, much as the awesome closing shot of Christina at the ship's prow presages her abdication from the movies.

The individual DVDs are not big on extras, though the stand-alone documentary obviates the need. Two significant additions greatly augment this collection. *Camille* includes the 1921 silent version starring Alla Nazimova, whose initial appearance suggests an emaciated clown with seriously bad hair. She subsequently achieves subtler dimensions and, though *Camille* does not rank among her better films, the chance to see Nazimova in her prime is irresistible, as is the very affecting performance by a pre-*Sheik* Rudolf Valentino.

Far more rewarding is the German version of *Anna Christie*, shot on the same sets and on the same days as the Hollywood version, but directed by Jacques Feyder instead of Clarence Brown. The 1930 American film, Garbo's belated entrance into talking pictures, is a bore, her performance as uninteresting as the nailed-to-the-ground camera shots. Garbo preferred the German film, and now we can see why. There is no comparison—from the moving camera in the opening shot through the rhythmically edited dialogue and expressionistic lighting to the romance with a young, handsome Burke, who generates genuinely sexy eye contact with Anna, something not possible with crusty Charles Bickford in the Hollywood film. For her entrance in the U.S. film, Anna is outfitted in waterfront chic; in the German film, her clothes are precisely what Eugene O'Neill described as "the tawdry finery of peasant stock turned prostitute." In the U.S. film, when Anna recalls her rape, Garbo looks down at her cigarette, tossing off the lines; in the German version, she stares at the camera, seething with fury. It's still *Anna Christie*, a bad play with Swedish dialect ("Dot vhisky gat kick, by yingo!") and folksy musings about the sea—*Camille* with a happy ending—but Feyder's film gives it life and adds another telling character to Garbo's luminous if abbreviated gallery.

[*The New York Sun*, 13 September 2005]

19 ❖ *Awash in Ambiguity (Marlon Brando)*

In 1943, Marlon Brando—born in Omaha in 1924, raised in a farmhouse 35 miles outside of Chicago, and recently expelled from the Shattuck Military Academy in Minnesota—traveled to New York and signed up to take classes at the New School's Dramatic Workshop. The renowned acting teacher Stella Adler, who within six years would found her Conservatory of Acting, instantly recognized his genius and practically adopted him, encouraging him to focus his plenary gifts. She was determined to prove to him that "artists can change the world," as Patricia Bosworth relates in *Marlon Brando*, one of the more illuminating volumes in the increasingly uneven Penguin Lives series of short biographies. He was skeptical then, and he remained so. But he did change the world as well as his profession.

Brando gave American actors new modes of being racked with ambiguities. By turns wounding and wounded, charming and terrifying, manly and boyish and feminine, Brando brought an unpredictable verisimilitude to his characters and a matchless mastery of space and tempo. You can't take your eyes off him, even when his performance is absurdly misguided—for example, his contemplative Nazi in *The Young Lions* (1958), quietly issuing commands while bullets blaze around him. His greatest film performances—in *A Streetcar Named Desire* (1951), *Julius Caesar* (1953), *On the Waterfront* (1954), *Reflections in a Golden Eye* (1967), *The*

Godfather (1972), *Last Tango in Paris* (1972)—are so minutely detailed and intimately imagined that they almost capsize the films that contain them. In many instances, his lesser performances salvage films that we would not otherwise remember.

Adler insisted, "Don't act. Behave," and Elia Kazan claimed the job of directing was to turn "psychology into behavior." In Brando, they found an actor whose behavior on- and off-stage mirrored a pervasive anxiety that combined the familiar ingredients in the postwar generation's drift toward self-immolation: a deep-seated fear of change and a seething impatience with the status quo. Brando was never a rebel without a cause. He knew the causes very well, and he was especially attuned to issues of racial discrimination. But as an artist, he also knew that the need to rebel is a cause in itself. If the insurgent impulses of World War I's lost generation were drowned in a feckless squabble with Prohibition, the impulses of Brando's era could not be so easily quelled. In the years before rock and roll rent the culture, a period during which, as Bosworth comments, "adolescents were becoming like aliens," he symbolized the tentative young American coming of age in a spasm of distrust, anger, self-pity, and audacity. To his chagrin, a generation of filmgoers hoped to emulate him, no matter how reprehensible the characters he played.

Even today audiences tend to experience his Stanley Kowalski one way while *A Streetcar Named Desire* is unspooling, and another in recollection. Brando refused to soften the edges in his depiction of a narcissistic bully who weeps copiously when he fails to get his way through brute force. His attitude toward Blanche is made ominous with his initial greeting, a ghastly yet maddeningly coy meow, and turns savage when he clears the dinner table—an eruption that makes James Cagney and his grapefruit seem almost benign in comparison. The censors prevented him from speaking the play's crucial line, "We've had this date with each other from the beginning," prior to raping Blanche, but they could do nothing about the sadistic flash in his eye. (A member of National Theater of the Deaf told Bosworth that Brando is their favorite actor because "even though we can't hear what he's saying, we know exactly what he means.") Yet days after seeing the film, one's revulsion is strangely vitiated. We are charmed in spite of ourselves and in spite of what Tennessee Williams originally intended. Has Brando tilted the play? Or has he added an essential component, revealing better than Williams why—the movie censors notwithstanding—Stella will never leave Stanley?

After touring with Katherine Cornell in *Candida*, Brando expressed his disdain for her imperious theatrical style. "Acting with her," he remarked, "is like trying to bite down on a tomato seed." The line, typical of his wit, would seem to apply to the whole school of bewigged, studied acting that predominated when he came along. Yet, as Bosworth shows, Brando's approach was entrenched in the tradition of externals, as opposed to the Method's emphasis on "internal abilities—sensory, psychological, and emotional." His favorite actor was Paul Muni, who disappeared into makeup, accent, costume, and gestures. Brando's most obvious triumph in that vein was as Don Corleone, but he had always gravitated toward disguises. Adler, unlike her rival Lee Strasberg, believed that, combined with the actor's imagination, "the art, architecture, and clothes of an era were crucial to shaping a role." According to Bosworth, it was Stanley's costume—a torn T-shirt, tight jeans, dyed hair—that released Brando emotionally.

Not that he needed much urging. Brando's emotions were always simmering, which is perhaps one reason his dramatic rages—the table-clearing in *A Streetcar Named Desire* or the "No!" he shouts at his mother-in-law in *Last Tango in Paris*—are so explosive. His childhood bruises never quite hardened into scabs, and their freshness remained a ready source of inspiration. His father was a drunk who brutalized and humiliated him and later squandered much of his fortune. His mother, also a drunk, adored him, hoping he would achieve the dramatic success she coveted. Brando worshipped her, though on one occasion he had to escort her home naked from a bar—one of several memories he drew upon for his improvised monologues in *Last Tango*.

Brando received his first notice in the military academy's paper: "The new boy shows enormous talent." His primary talent lay in mimicry and pantomime. He had the kids "squirming in their seat," Bosworth says, with his Dillinger impersonation, and was so popular that the cadets went on strike to protest his expulsion. In New York, his mimetic talents were widely admired by friends. He would ride the subway and adapt the physical posture of each person in the car, men and women alike; he had no fear of indulging the androgynous sexuality that deepened in his mature work. Bosworth makes much of the extensive research and improvisation that went into his acting; some of his finest ideas solved logistical problems. Neither the director nor the writer of *On the Waterfront* could come up with a reason for Eva Marie Saint to walk with the man who has inadvertently killed her brother. So before the cameras rolled, Brando asked her to drop her glove. Instead of handing it back to her, he put it on his own hand, forcing her to stand shivering in the cold, hearing him out. As Corleone, he devised the orange-peel fangs to hold the attention of the little boy playing his grandson.

But Brando's doubts about acting and himself, along with his draining emotionalism and troublesome finances, combined to blunt his art and, for a long time, his box office clout. In his memoir of 1963, *Stage*

Directions, John Gielgud described him as "a thrilling artist," but complained of a public that encouraged him to "over-cultivate a kind of mannered technique" that stultified his imagination. By 1971, a year before *The Godfather*, Brando was considered unemployable. Yet a year after the successes of that film and *Last Tango in Paris*, he again allowed his career to fizzle into decades of glorified—and extravagantly paid for—cameos and hackwork, desiring only to escape to Tahiti where the people have "happy, unmanaged faces." He apparently despised not only his profession but his own beauty. Excepting Orson Welles, has any other actor cloistered himself in so much fat? And yet even now, in films utterly beneath him, he can mesmerize—revealing, most recently, comic aplomb and the occasional epiphany in such misdirected junk as *Free Money* and *The Score*.

Patricia Bosworth, a superb biographer, has written lives of Montgomery Clift, Diane Arbus, and most impressively, her father, Bartley C. Crumm, in the brave, candid memoir, *Anything Your Little Heart Desires*. A former actress, she is an ardent but critical Brandophile, who quickly puts life and work into context (though she does slightly skew the plot of *Last Tango in Paris*), paying necessary attention to Brando's politics and extremely complicated marital life. *Marlon Brando* disappoints only in its brevity. When she writes that the nasty 1966 potboiler, *The Chase*, is being reevaluated, one is eager to learn how and by whom. Indeed, one would like to hear her discourse at length on all of Brando's films, good and bad, almost as much as one would like to see King Marlon, at 77, assay a role that requires him to survey his empire, fatally misinterpret those who love him best, and rail against God and nature.

[*New York Times Book Review*, 9 September 2001]

20 ❖ *Going His Way* *(Bing Crosby)*

The Film Society of Lincoln Center's weeklong retrospective of Bing Crosby ("What a Swell Party This Is! A Salute to Bing Crosby")—13 movies and one teleplay—will surprise those who recall only his road trips with Bob Hope or have never seen him on the big screen. Crosby is the most conspicuously neglected of the Golden Age Hollywood stars, given his then-unexampled popularity. He ranked in the top 10 of box-office attractions for all but five years between 1934 and 1954, and he was the only actor of his time to crown the polls for five consecutive years (from 1944 to 1948). He was nominated for three best-actor Oscars (winning for *Going My Way*), and introduced more prizewinning and nominated songs than any other performer—all this while sustaining the most successful recording and radio careers in the 20th century's first half, in addition to building a racetrack and launching the first celebrity pro-am golf tournament.

Yet his persona, on and off screen, was that of an incorrigibly lazy man: self-sufficient, unperturbed, shrewd, cool—a grown-up Tom Sawyer, complete with pipe, battered hat, mismatched clothes, and jivey lingo. Crosby invented a screen character so resonant that even people who knew him had a hard time separating it from the real Bing, though obviously he was the least lazy man in town. The public perception of Bing (he was always Bing) as an easygoing all-American Joe probably contributed to his posthumous decline in popularity. The casual, laid-back attitude that proved so engaging during decades of Depression and war seemed remote and grandfatherly in the 1950s, when atomic cocktails, rock 'n' roll, and jet travel boiled the national tempo. Bing had grown older while the country grew younger.

Many of the qualities that worked against him posthumously were no different from those that briefly stymied him when he first sought a Hollywood career. He certainly didn't look like a movie star, with his wingy ears, receding hairline, and expanding waistline. Nor did he behave like one, when success came, refusing publicity, disdaining love scenes, populating his pictures with musician-friends, and refusing to be billed alone or above the title. That last directive, which inclined David O. Selznick to pronounce him the smartest man in Hollywood, was entirely pragmatic. If a film succeeded, he'd get the credit; if it failed, he'd share the blame with co-stars. The failures were few. As a result, he helped launch the film careers of several leading ladies (including Carole Lombard, Joan Bennett, Frances Farmer, Kitty Carlisle, Mary Martin, Joan Caulfield, and Rhonda Fleming) and men, notably the young Donald O'Connor. Bing's idol, Louis Armstrong, was the first black artist to receive—at Crosby's insistence—top billing in a white film, though he had only a cameo role.

From the first, Bing proved himself an inventive comedian (he apprenticed in Mack Sennett shorts), using the same impeccable timing that characterized his singing. His ability to ad-lib business or exude tranquil charm made his vocal interludes the pinnacles of his movies, and encouraged Frank Capra to declare Crosby one of the best actors in the business—a remark echoed by actors and directors as varied as Leo McCarey, Miriam Hopkins, Jane Wyman, Raoul Walsh, Robert Mitchum, Blythe Danner, Ray Walston, William Holden, and George C. Scott.

Lincoln Center's selection, curated by Martin McQuade with the participation of Kathryn Crosby omits a few of Crosby's best films, but covers much ground and more than 30 years.

A lively comedy could be made about the making of 1933s *Going Hollywood*. William Randolph Hearst financed it as a vehicle for Marion Davies, who held up shooting with lavish meals, rivers of wine, and an inability to memorize lines—yet, in the end, director Raoul Walsh and Crosby were banished from the MGM lot for 20 years. Davies is grand (note the erotic 90-second close-up when she hears Crosby's voice on the radio), but Bing steals this pre-Production Code satire with over-the-top musical numbers, demonstrating his gift for shtick on "Beautiful Girl"; swinging for the bleachers on the brief title song; emoting ("very Russian Art Theater," he called it) "Temptation" while bingeing in a Mexican brothel; and guiding Marion through nauseating giant daisies (they were both high) during "We'll Make Hay while the Sun Shines."

Pennies from Heaven (1936) and the rarely seen *Sing You Sinners* (1938) are quintessential Depression films, utopian visions of community that nonetheless mask corruption at the core—the former begins on death row; the latter applauds gambling as an alternative to labor. Crosby is a street-smart troubadour, envying no one and thoroughly independent. The Burke-Johnston score for *Pennies from Heaven* is a classic, but is upstaged by Louis Armstrong's stunning performance of "Skeleton in the Closet," which established his Tinseltown credentials. *Sing You Sinners* hasn't been shown in decades. Director Wesley Ruggles conceived it for the purpose of portraying Crosby as the appealing scapegrace his friends knew him to be. Upon reading the script, Bing said, "I guess I can play myself." It's not really a musical and Bing doesn't get the girl, though he tries to seduce his brother's fiancée. Twelve-year-old Donald O'Connor wins a horse race.

Anything Goes (1936) is a fascinating mess that turns out to be a lot more fun in a theater than it was in butchered television prints. Lewis Milestone was hardly the ideal director for Cole Porter's early masterpiece, and by the time the censors got through with the song lyrics and libretto, all any director could do was sit back and pray. Yet a steady diet of laughs (Charlie Ruggles has aged especially well) and fast pacing compensate for the omissions. Ethel Merman preserves some measure of her Reno Sweeney; Ida Lupino wafts by, blond and striking; Bing swings the few Porter tunes that made the cut as well as Hoagy Carmichael's first movie song, "Moonburn"; and if "The Shanghai-de-ho" by Robin and Hollander doesn't drop your jaw, nothing will.

Victor Schertzinger's 1940 *Rhythm on the River* increases its cult standing with each screening. For one thing, the Billy Wilder–Jacques Thery story (scripted by Dwight Taylor) involves an ingenious deconstruction of popular songwriting. A burned-out tunesmith (Basil Rathbone) hires, unbeknown to each other, Bing and Mary Martin to write songs with him. Rathbone weds Crosby's music to Martin's words, and writes nothing, while collecting royalties and public adoration. Bing is perfectly splendid, especially rendering James Monaco's best melodies and drumming his way through a jazz piece that features Wingy Manone and Bing's Rhythm Boys partner Harry Barris (pretending to play saxophone). Oscar Levant is a bonus.

Schertzinger also directed 1941's *Road to Zanzibar*, though to hear observers tell it, he merely called for action and then sat back to see what Crosby and Hope would say and do—they had rival writers feeding them material not in the script. The second of the road movies hasn't got a sentimental bone in its anarchic body and mandated a stream of outcries from the censors. Production Code chief Joseph I. Breen advised, "There must be no evidence of the slave trader pointing up the breasts of the slave girl when he says, 'Sambo wocky-dockies,' and Hope's reply, 'I'll say she has.'" This is the one in which Bing and Bob find tribal drums in a cavern and send the wrong message; in which Dorothy Lamour pretends to be a slave and the victim of lions; in which accomplished black actors Noble Johnson, Leigh Whipper, and Ernest Whitman play cannibals.

Leo McCarey's 1944 *Going My Way*, once the most lucrative film in the history of Paramount Pictures, is now a neglected masterpiece, often dismissed as sentimental and simplistic. It is neither—the tears it elicits are as hard-won as those in, say, Robert Bresson's *Au Hassard Balthazar*. In this film, the world is reduced to one Irish Catholic parish in New York—with one ghostly church (Bing's Father O'Malley cannot initially find it), one cop on the beat, one realtor, one troublemaker, one loving couple (other than Crosby and the irreplaceable Barry Fitzgerald), and one opera singer, who conspicuously displays her crucifix. James Agee praised its verisimilitude, which may seem incomprehensible now, but McCarey and Crosby set out to re-create their own childhood experiences in Catholic gangs that never committed crimes more threatening than stealing pies or turkeys. It encompasses four generations: the kids, Crosby, Fitzgerald, and Fitzgerald's mother, whose surprise arrival unfailingly moistens audiences. The Crosby-Fitzgerald relationship has lost nothing to time, and Bing's performance is astonishing—convincing, appealing, and original. Don't miss Risë Stevens's reaction shot when she sees Crosby's white collar. Who but Crosby would have had the nerve to sit beside another man's bed and sing him a lullaby? This great film, which generates much empathic laughter in a theater, is overdue for reconsideration.

The second teaming of Crosby and Fred Astaire, one of the most popular releases of 1946, was the Technicolor extravaganza *Blue Skies*, directed by Stuart Heisler and featuring Joan Caulfield, one of those blue-eyed, rosy-cheeked, alabaster blonds seemingly born for saturated color schemes. The film is wall-to-wall Irving Berlin (about 20 songs), and the plot one of the strangest in any Hollywood musical, involving Crosby as an obsessive-compulsive creator of nightclubs who loses interest in them as soon as they open, as he loses interest in his wife and daughter. The finale strives to be straight out of Happy Ending 101, yet one of the principals has lost his career to a boozy accident and all three have wasted years at cross-purposes. Crosby steals "A Couple of Song and Dance Men," because he's funny, but Fred brings down the house with "Puttin' On the Ritz," one of his all-time showstoppers. At bottom, this film is as dark as the Martin Scorsese film it influenced, *New York, New York*.

Billy Wilder made his name with the script for Ernst Lubitsch's *Ninotchka*, but his own quartet of films about Americans abroad never quite jelled, perhaps because he usually made the Americans brashly unsympathetic. He hated *The Emperor Waltz*, a huge hit when it was released in 1948, but he was too hard on it. Beautifully filmed in Canada, the picture is perhaps too fond of its doggy-romance jokes (the plot pivots on dog genetics) and Crosby demonstrates little chemistry with Joan Fontaine, who for once gets to be imperious instead of whimpering. Yet his performance perfectly realizes the character of the arrogant, bumbling American (he plays a phonograph salesman in the court of Franz Joseph, perpetually whistling "The Whistler and His Dog") who is certain that he and his country will inherit the world. His opening scene is startling, and if the romance and music (some of it treated as parody, some not) are less than riveting, the underlying conceit sustains its own heat.

George Seaton directed two of Crosby's greatest dramatic performances, in *Little Boy Lost* (not in the series) and 1954's *The Country Girl*. Crosby's wife, Dixie Lee, had just died after years of alcohol abuse, and Crosby himself had been known as a binge drinker in his early years, so Seaton hesitated in sending him the script for the latter. But Crosby agreed instantly to play his most daring role. The film, vastly improving the Clifford Odets play, makes Frank Elgin a musical-comedy star rather than a dramatic actor. To make the part work, Crosby must create opposing characters: the irresistible entertainer who radiates goodwill on stage and the guilt-ridden boozer and liar who makes everyone else's life miserable. Grace Kelly (in her best dramatic role) and William Holden are first-rate, but like the characters they play, they end up supporting Crosby, who holds nothing back in the many silent and extended close-ups Seaton gives him. An unforgettable interlude is Bing's barroom duet with chanteuse Jackie Fontaine, his parting shot a choice ad-lib.

High Tor is a find—a New York theatrical debut, in fact—originally broadcast in 1956 on the CBS series *Ford Star Jubilee* and little seen thereafter. Directed by James Nielsen and based on Maxwell Anderson's play, to which Arthur Schwartz added mostly undistinguished melodies, it is remembered for the American debut of Julie Andrews—airing just five days before she opened in *My Fair Lady*. For fans of high camp, however, it may linger in the memory for the croaky singing of Everett Sloane. Oddly, Julie sings to Bing and Bing sings to Julie, but they have no duet. Shot in 12 days, this Hudson Valley fantasy is a peculiar time capsule, as sleepy as Rip Van Winkle. The pristine print, provided by Kathryn Crosby, is of a version prepared for but soon withdrawn from theaters; it includes a prologue song by Andrews not shown on TV.

High Society, from 1956: Crosby, Frank Sinatra, Louis Armstrong, Grace Kelly, Celeste Holm, Cole Porter songs, arrangements by Nelson Riddle and Conrad Salinger. It is damned near perfect, despite the smug source material (*The Philadelphia Story*), and then some—for example, the trumpet obbligato as Bing sings "Little One."

Blake Edwards's 1960 *High Time* gets the biggest boost when shown in a theater—partly because expectations are low. Broadcast in a truncated pan-and-scan version, it is tedious and old, working overtime at snappy visuals and succumbing to the charisma vacuum created by Fabian, Richard Beymer, and leading lady Nicole Maurey. Yet Edwards used every inch of the Cinemascope canvas, emphasizing rectangular activities, like canoeing and football. Seen as intended, the pace picks up and the original old-guy-returns-to-college flick generates a surprisingly agreeable sense of community (Tuesday Weld helps, as always). Not to say there aren't longueurs, as well as misguided slapstick by Gavin McLeod, a Fabian vocal chorus, and a laborious ending in which nimble Bing is obliged to deliver a sentimental speech, fly around the room, and look noble. Crosby plays his drag scene (the film was initially advertised, "He's the campus queen!") without self-consciousness and is in great voice for "The Second Time Around" (though Sinatra scored the hit). Too bad they didn't give him an upbeat song to take advantage of Henry Mancini's robust jazz score.

Finally, Gordon Douglas's *Robin and the Seven Hoods*, from 1964, marked the end of the Rat Pack: Indeed, it was because Sinatra quarreled with Peter Lawford that he was forced to pay Crosby a king's ransom to portray Alan A. Dale. He shows up past the midway point and—guess what?—commits total larceny. Crosby comes across as the only unruffled pro in a sea of over-exerting scene hogs; he sings "Style" in tandem with Sinatra and Dean Martin and all but renders them invisible. Edward G. Robinson parodies himself, Frank sings "My Kind of Town," Sammy Davis Jr. dances a tribute to armaments: a truly bad movie truly worth seeing once.

As the movie musical went into terminal decline, Crosby became harder to cast. The television detective Columbo was initially offered to him—he wisely declined. He unwisely returned to the priesthood in *Say One for Me*, but proved quite effective as two contrary doctors: the philosophical alcoholic in *Stagecoach* (a futile effort, made savory by his performance) and the eponymous serial killer in *Dr. Cook's Garden*, an early made-for-television film.

By then, he preferred to be on the golf course or at the track. Mostly, he preferred to be with his family: his young wife, the former Kathryn Grant, and their three children. He had made a botch of his first family, though his marriage to Dixie Lee and their four boys had been publicly perceived as a template for America's domestic life. Good Catholic that he was—classically educated by the Jesuits at Spokane's Gonzaga University (he dropped out before graduation to sing professionally)—he saw the second family as his second chance, and he grabbed onto it with both hands.

A generation came of age knowing him only for the Crosbys' annual Christmas telecasts and his ubiquitous orange juice ads. Aside from narrating a section of MGM's self-celebration, *That's Entertainment*, Bing disappeared from the screen. He planned to return, however: the script for his eighth jaunt with Hope neared completion at the time of his death, in 1977, at 74.

[*The New York Sun*, 20 July 2005]

21 ❖ *Blond and Beaming (Doris Day)*

Oscar Levant's much-repeated crack about knowing Doris Day before she was a virgin has grown stale. But it had bite four decades ago, when a new generation was discovering its sexuality and Day was shielding her middle-age chastity with the tenacity of the Viet Minh in Hanoi. In truth, the only thing virginal about her was her insuperable blond and beaming independence, fortified by confidence, notwithstanding the occasional "Ooooh, he makes me so mad" episode. In a blond and beaming era, she went her own way, never parodying sexuality, a la Marilyn, or bottling it up the better to smolder, a la Princess Grace. Yet she ended happily in bed more than either of them, almost always on her own terms. Over the course of 25 years, she survived more than three dozen leading men, representing three generations of style and/or beefcake; most of them quickly faded while she marched cheerfully onward.

The coolest and sexiest female singer of slow-ballads in movie history; the only female band singer to achieve movie-musical superstardom; and the only major star of movie musicals, female or otherwise, to survive their passing and win even greater popularity in comedies, Day had been around. She had toured as a dancer at 12, signed as a band singer at 16 (a car accident had forced her to change priorities), married and had a son at 18, and had the number one record in the country at 20— "Sentimental Journey," with Les Brown and His Band of Renown, in 1944. Maybe she looked like the girl next door, but her voice, with its impeccable intonation and uncanny lilt (taking her time, she turned vowels into sighs), promised sultry nights in the Casbah. Seek out her Christmas CD and see what she does with "Winter Wonderland." Or stick with the movies, and notice how she halts that misguided epic, *Jumbo*, to emote a full-bore "My Romance"—candid and captivating, and never a trace of sentimentality.

Michael Curtiz attempted to interview her while she wept copiously over an impending divorce (number two) in 1948, and he not only gave her the lead in his cruise-ship farce, *Romance on the High Seas* (introducing "It's Magic," her first solo number one hit under her own name), but also signed her to a personal contract. He must have been elated. The Hungarian-born director—best known for reinventing the swashbuckler in the sound era while establishing the career of Errol Flynn (the recent "Erroll Flynn Signature Collection" has the best of them, *Captain Blood* and *The Sea Hawk*), and for the definitive wartime melodrama, *Casablanca* —adored American showbiz. He directed more backstage musicals than anyone else, with the possible exception of David Butler, including the genre's all-time tour de force, *Yankee Doodle Dandy*. With Day, he glanced at nightclub singing in her debut, the trials of radio in *My Dream Is Yours*, and passed her off to Butler for the Hollywood spoof, *It's a Great Feeling*.

The eight-film "Doris Day Collection" begins with her fourth film, Curtiz's stylish jazz melodrama, *Young Man with a Horn* (1950). Though long ridiculed for its obsession with high notes and for betraying the theme of racial identity that animates Dorothy Baker's admirable novel, the picture has aged well, thanks in part to the brilliant location photography by Ted McCord, Curtiz's preferred cameraman from then on. One of Curtiz's most decisively composed movies, it is nonetheless paced with his trademark speed.

In the novel, the white orphan Rick Martin discovers who he is through a deep friendship with a black drummer, Smoke (at one point, he calls him "honey"), whose sister, Josephine, is a Florence Mills-type singer; in the movie, Smoke and Jo, no longer siblings, are played by Hoagy Carmichael and Doris Day. The screenplay substitutes a more conventional relationship between white boy and black mentor, but in so doing creates a powerful moral figure in the expanded character of Art Hazzard, played with urgent finesse by Juano Hernandez. His hold on Rick ultimately overwhelms the good girl/bad girl quandary represented by Day and Lauren Bacall, who makes a classic mid-film entrance in a mirror. Kirk Douglas is convincing, Bacall is scary, and Day looks worried (despite star billing, she is, for the first and last time, a supporting player with no romantic involvement) but sings like a lark. The end is sappy—the film has earned something better—and Harry James's often schmaltzy trumpeting for Douglas undermines the argument of good versus commercial music: He plays with a Bixian poise in the jam sessions and lays on the suds when Rick is emoting. But listen to the playing of Art Hazzard, as dubbed by Jimmy Zito, a studio pro who had worked with Day in Les Brown's band and later recorded with Frank Zappa. He always swings, even in the scene where Art is supposed to be failing.

A year later, David Butler directed Day in *Lullaby of Broadway*, negligible despite a marvelous selection of songs (and a neat specialty number by the "dancing dolls," a number you will want to instantly replay to see how the illusion is managed); the book is a coat hanger of clichés to support the numbers—an effort to which leading man Gene Nelson lends little. Too showy and slick to strike any sparks, he does his thing in a vacuum, intruding on her, as does the unstoppable mugging of S. Z. Sakall. Day brightens the picture whenever she is left alone.

In 1953, Butler did right by her, cementing her box-office cachet with the western musical *Calamity Jane*, perhaps the only film in which Howard Keel is reduced to an onlooker as Day steals every scene, singing in peak voice, dancing with spirited athleticism, taking Keystone spills, and mining every line for comic emphasis (she gets a laugh with "Whar's the varmint?"). The gender switching and cross-dressing is nonstop, and Day sets the tone in her very tight britches and masculine open-legged postures (a close-up of her perfectly manicured nails contradicts the image). You have to wait till the final 10 minutes for "Secret Love," but the whole Sammy Fain–Paul Francis Webster score is seasoned, and Butler's control of the material is consistently impressive.

Among biopic musicals, now undergoing a shaky renaissance, Charles Vidor's *Love Me or Leave Me* (1955) is one of the hallmarks, certainly in the top five circling beneath *Yankee Doodle Dandy*, partly for the same reason—James Cagney, now older and squatter, but absolutely riveting. That Day holds her ground, manipulating him with arias of integrity while conveying the bitter calculating ambition that keeps her going, makes this a central film in her canon. Based freely on Ruth Etting's conflict with her thug husband and manager, Marty Snyder (a relationship not entirely unlike that between Day and her husband, Marty Melcher, whom she married in 1951), and his nonfatal shooting of her lover, pianist Myrl Alderman (Johnny in the film), the script is mostly fiction. Alderman is part of the story 15 years before Etting actually met him, and the first scene finds her working a dime-a-dance joint, something she did only in the 1930 one-reeler, "Roseland" (included on the DVD, along with an inferior 1932 two-reeler, "A Modern Cinderella"). All three were alive when the film was made, and fixes were undoubtedly necessitated. It doesn't matter. The film leavens the crude flamboyance of speakeasy entertainment with backstage drollery (Harry Bellaver helps as Cagney's Runyonesque sidekick), but the stench of desperation is there in Day's multifaceted performance, except when she sings and lights up. Etting's sleepy-eyed sexiness and mournful nasality are no match for Day, whose interpretations of her 1920s songs all but wipe the originals from memory.

The Day persona—independent, clear-eyed—was now fairly fixed. (In Hitchcock's 1956 *The Man Who Knew Too Much*, husband James Stewart patronizes her with a sedative, but it is Day who saves the day, twice.) In 1958, she made a transitional picture for Paramount, George Seaton's *Teacher's Pet*, a prelude to the series of sexual innuendo charades to follow. One of the first movies sent out to test theaters trying to get by on single features instead of double-bills, it is a smart city desk comedy in which Day once again holds her ground against old Hollywood. Clark Gable was a quarter of a century older than she was and looked it, but he clearly enjoyed reusing his comedic chops, despite a few too many goggle-eyed double takes—occasionally sending up attitudes he made famous in *It Happened One Night* or learned first-hand from Captain Bligh. The film goes unaccountably soggy in the last half-hour, as niceness spreads like pollen, but the first three-quarters, despite a lack of credibility, sustain it as an enduring standby in the newspaper comedy sweepstakes; no *Nothing Sacred*, but pretty funny all the same. Day's journalism teacher, who enters breasts first, brings Gable's misogynistic, egghead-hating editor to heel while losing her own officiousness—in effect, trading in one daddy for another. Gig Young got a lot of mileage as a know-it-all professor, and Mamie Van Doren, "the gal who invented rock 'n' roll" (a number Day parodies—shades of Irene Dunne in *The Awful Truth*), tells Gable that Young is "dreamy" and "must be from Hollywood," a line that won't reverberate for a generation that doesn't know who or what Gable was.

The remaining Warner titles have moments, many moments. From the opening tracking shot of a determined John Raitt, you can see that director Stanley Donen is set on undermining the staginess of *Pajama Game* (1957); he no more succeeds than do the screenwriters in injecting a plot. Carol Haney and Eddie Foy Jr. are fun, and Day sings "Hey There," but the stitching is strictly pro forma, Barbara Nichols is stuck playing a character named Poopsie, and Bob Fosse's fey, hunched-over, quasi-beatnik numbers, once the toast of the town, have dated no better than coonskin caps, also popular at the time. Charles Walters's *Please Don't Eat the Daisies* (1960), a not entirely glowing view of the marriage of Walter and Jean Kerr, might also have been called "Mortimer Brewster Builds His Dream House"; it opens with fine comic business by Day and her four sons, but as the story kicks in, humor is leeched out, though she stays the course—well backed by David Niven and Janis Paige. *Jumbo* (1962) gets bogged down in widescreen circus vistas and Stephen Boyd's anti-charisma (his singing was dubbed by one James Joyce), but Day has a glorious Rodgers and Hart score to celebrate, and Jimmy Durante and especially Martha Raye to play off. A worthy highlight is Day's duet with Raye, herself a gifted vocalist of the 1930s, on "Why Can't I." The Busby Berkeley finale is more outrageous than clever, and very long. Frank Tashlin's unjustly forgotten *The Glass Bottom Boat* loses itself in slapstick at the end and it's weird to see Dom DeLuise imitating Jerry Lewis, but the gags are built ground up, and Day times them out with the precision of a silent clown.

[*The New York Sun*, 3 May 2005]

22 ❖ *The Two Leons*
(Animal Farm / Looney Tunes Golden Collection, Volume Two)

Most of the world was feeling pretty relieved in 1945, when George Orwell detonated the little bomb he called *Animal Farm: A Fairy Story*. Conceived in 1943 and rejected by several publishers as prematurely anti-Stalinist, the book was initially scheduled for publication in May, which would have coincided with VE day. But a paper shortage postponed printing until August, just in time for VJ day—and seven months before Churchill warned undergraduates in Missouri of an iron curtain. Orwell's 1949 prophecy of *1984* may have been skewed (or, once again, premature), but he captured the looming fear and trembling in the wake of peace with diagnostic accur-acy. *Animal Farm*, which had made him famous, was celebrated as a renouncement of totalitarianism everywhere, though its farm life echoed that of one particular farm run by Uncle Joe.

Shortly after Orwell's death and two years before Stalin's, an American film producer and newsreel pioneer, Louis De Rochemont, hired Britain's husband and wife animation team, John Halas and Joy Batchelor, to adapt the book into a cartoon feature—the first ever made in England. In notes to HVE's DVD, it is suggested that De Rochemont outsourced the project to save on costs and because he questioned the loyalties of American animators: Who better to exploit paranoia than a paranoiac? The film, released in 1955, was a hit, despite criticisms of Disneyfication (mostly vented on a comical duckling) and a happy if unconstitutional ending: The pig government is violently overthrown by other animals. The United States Information Agency helped with distribution.

What was not known then—even by the animators, according to their daughter—was that the novel's screen rights had been procured by the CIA, whose agent, the future Watergate burglar Howard Hunt, hired De Rochemont. This disclosure has now been offered as an explanation for the film's comic relief, which in any case does little harm, and rousing climax, which is happy only in a thematic sense that would have pleased Lenin as much as Jefferson: The cure for revolution is more revolution. Yet the CIA's heavy hand does seem to explain two more troubling alterations.

Orwell abominated Stalin and those who made excuses for his show trials and purges. These are the subjects of some of his novel's most powerful pages—which, not unexpectedly, are weakly marked in the film. He remained, however, a committed socialist ("Nothing has contributed so much to the corruption of the original idea of Socialism as the belief that Russia is a Socialist country") and harbored—which of us do not?—a soft spot for Leon Trotsky. If there is a tragic figure in *Animal Farm*, it is the old Bolshie's stand-in: the warrior trotter, utopian orator, and prince of blueprints, Snowball. Only when the malefic boar Napoleon sics the dogs on Snowball, forcing him into exile, and his achievements are obliterated by slander, does the fable turn into a Gulag nightmare and the pigs into loathsome humans.

In the film *Animal Farm*, a pig is a pig and you can hardly tell Snowball from Napoleon; they enter together with rude condescension and matching sneers. The ensuing ouster and probable murder of Snowball registers little feeling. His heroism in battle is glossed over and his speech is delivered with blustery self-importance, distorted by snorts and squeals. Napoleon's speech, by strange contrast, is rendered in more intelligible English. (Maurice Denham did all the voices other than Gordon Heath's narration, an impressive feat.) Clearly the filmmakers could not bear to depict Snowball as a martyr, let alone as a leader among pigs. They do, however, underscore the Russia-centricity of the fable with a second transformation. Orwell's anthem, "Beasts of England," which is described in the novel as a melodic fusion of "Clementine" and "La Cucaracha," is replaced by a wordless variation on "The Internationale" —sort of an "Animationale," with quacking and bleating, effective in its own right, though "Beasts" would have been funnier and a lot more international.

For all that, and in spite of a dreary narration that supplants Orwell's prose and dialogue, *Animal Farm* retains much of the book's power thanks to inventive animation and a sharp pace. The most memorable images are bleak and ominous, often involving shadows and overhead shots, and the few attempts at humor suggest a woebegone whistling in the dark. If Napoleon's ferocity is softened, the addition of barbed wire fences and a portrayal of humans even more pitiless than in the book help to balance accounts. The film's ending—complete with a reprise of the "Animationale"—is, in fact, more radicalizing than Orwell's, probably not the CIA's intention.

For a steadier mixture of laughs and anarchy, we can thank another Leon, the penurious and humorless head of Warner Brothers' cartoon division. Leon Schlesinger initially wanted to follow the Disney lead, but instead he hired a fabled group of ingenious animators and writers— among them, Bob Clampett, Friz Freleng, Tex Avery, Robert McKimson, and Chuck Jones—and gave them permission to break the mold. As censors curbed the sexy surrealism of the Fleischer Studios (Betty Boop, Koko, Popeye) and Walt Disney suburbanized his transgressive mouse, Warner's Looney Tunes and Merrie Melodies leapt into the ring with a company of immortals—Bugs, Porky, Daffy, Elmer, their respective species known to all.

Looney Tunes Golden Collection Volume Two offers 60 cartoons—most in eye-popping prints—plus commentaries, featurettes, and other bonuses (though not "Sinkin' in the Bathtub," the first Looney Tune, dropped after the package promising it went to press), and is a more impressive selection than its predecessor. Warner is still chary with its black-and-white cartoons (who do they think will invest in these elaborate boxes if not the very fanatics who want *them* most of all?) and shows no sign of breaching the political correctness that proffers amnesia as a cure for history.[1]

We get a generous portion of Bugs and the relentless theme-and-variation chases of Sylvester and Tweety (the latter foils the former) and Wile E. Coyote and Road Runner (the former foils himself). But the real treat is the assortment of anomalies, comprising a mini-dictionary of pop culture references from the 1890s through the 1950s, including "The Dover Boys" (Rover Boys melodrama that introduced a new style in animated concision), "Porky in Wackyland" (like mom said, they didn't need drugs to get high on life), and the entire fourth disc, which combines caricatures of famous books ("Have You Got Any Castles?" is introduced by a parody of the long unread Alexander Woollcott); Hollywood stars (tactfully spoofed with visual and verbal puns); crooners ("I Love to Singa," featuring Owl Jolson, is a more astute analysis of the incipient jazz culture than *The Jazz Singer*); the white mainstreaming of swing ("Katnip Kollege" employs Hollywood's favorite paleface jazz mimic, Johnny "Scat" Davis, for the sound track and spoofs the insufficiently forgotten Kay Kyser); the crossroads between cool jazz and rhythm and blues ("The Three Little Bops"); and insolent slaps at the classics, including the Wagnerian "What's Opera, Doc" (kill the wabbit!) and the equally wondrous "Rhapsody Rabbit," a take on the Hungarian Rhapsody No. 2 and a tour de force centered entirely at the piano, cutting anything in *Fantasia*. When the animals do take over, this is what they will be watching.

[*The New York Sun*, 23 November 2004]

---

[1] The third volume of *Looney Tunes*, released late in 2005, does acknowledge the tip of racist caricature, reasonably introduced by Whoopi Goldberg.

23 ❖ *Kong Has Crazed His Mind (Ray Harryhausen)*

The cinema of Ray Harryhausen, the rare special-effects wizard of whom it may be said that a cinema—an unmatched body of work—exists, is a tribute to obsession: his and ours, at least those of us whose adolescence he marked. At my age (I shall never see 14 again), I confess a vague guilt in accounting the hours spent watching his movies on screen, videotape, laser disc, and now DVD. They do not improve over time; the dismal acting and gauche scripts aren't reckless enough to qualify as camp, and the main appeal, stop-time animation, is as dated as Ben Turpin's eyes. On the other hand, Turpin is still pretty funny and Harryhausen's creatures continue to evoke a sense of the marvelous. If the fish-faced Venutian, cyclopean centaur, homunculus, seven-headed hydra, swooping harpies, sword-fighting skeletons, massive bees, dancing kali, giant crab, and seductive tentacles are no longer frightening, they have taken on a creaky mythological familiarity that transcends childhood nostalgia.

In this, I suspect Harryhausen has succeeded beyond his wildest dreams: Surely, mythmaking was his ultimate goal. To those of us who grew up with his pictures in the 1950s, 1960s, or 1970s, they shepherded us through three stages, from "wow!" to "how did they do that?" to "oh, that's how it's done." The payoff is that the third stage is the most profound. Somehow, seeing the tricks deepens their appeal. The incredible manual labor involved in making tiny sculptures with copious armature sockets come to life, one frame at a time, and then projecting them in such a way as to allow them to interact with flesh-and-blood actors, imbues them with a curiously tactile humanity beyond the capability of computer-generated images.

The best special effects don't require special pleading. The most tiresome moment in *Jurassic Park* comes before the introduction of the dinosaurs, when the camera focuses on actors with glazed eyes and dropped jaws. With that kind of set-up, whatever they are looking at better impress us as well. Yet all we (finally) get to see are computer-drawn dinosaurs and there is nothing wonderful about them. Harryhausen never treated his audience cheaply, never told us how to respond; he sprang his creatures in the most dramatic ways he could think of (can anyone who saw *Jason and the Argonauts* in youth forget the first movement of Talos's bronze head?), trusting the audience's eyes and jaws to register wonder—as Buster Keaton did in the best special-effects film ever, *Sherlock Jr.*; after 70 years, Keaton's trickery continues to provoke concurrent laughter and incomprehension.

For Harryhausen, the transforming film was *King Kong* (1933), which he saw at 13 and determined to ape in the family garage. After years of experimentation and subsequent work on George Pal's Puppetoon shorts, he made his feature debut alongside the stop-motion pioneer who animated Kong, Willis O'Brien, on the comic children's matinee fare, *Mighty Joe Young* (1949), in which a gigantic gorilla in trouble with the New York police redeems itself by saving orphans from a fire, to the strains of "Beautiful Dreamer." Harryhausen shunned sentimentality after that—no easy feat as he was forced to tailor most of his work to children. Indeed, for all his devotion to Kong, he never animated creatures that were quite as sympathetic or anthropomorphic (beyond his penchant for manly musculature) as Kong.

That might have manifested a failing, especially as so many of his actors are less anthropomorphic than his sculptures, but I think the sobriety of his imagination redounds as a plus. The absence of emotional empathy (do we really give a damn about any of the three woodenly acted Sinbads?) heightens the schematic precision of his best work: *Earth vs. the Flying Saucers*, *Mysterious Island*, *The Golden Voyage of Sinbad*, and his undeniable masterpiece, *Jason and the Argonauts*, in which the effects are ingeniously woven into an exceptionally smart script (far more Homeric in its integration of men and gods than the unspeakable *Troy*), enlivened by a largely excellent cast.

Most Harryhausen films have the structural logic of MGM musicals or pornography: long bouts of trite dialogue interrupted by "big numbers"; instead of tapping feet or sexual hydraulics, these consist of animation scenes often cut so deftly that every glimpse of a particularly ingenious creation—the homunculus, the leering skeletons—has a visual frisson. The fact that Harryhausen is the focus of these DVDs, implying his auctorial control, indicates the upside and downside of his role. For the most part, the films were shot on European locations with actors staring at or fighting ghosts. When live shooting was completed, Harryhausen went to work, animating his sculptures and inserting them into the live-action footage. He was master of his domain, but the rest of the picture was often in the hands of second-raters and the loyal but frugal producer, Charles H. Schneer, who was determined to remember his adolescent base.

As a result, we get tiresome leads (William Hopper in *20 Million Miles to Earth* wins the cake), stock military figures (the ubiquitous Thomas Brown Henry, the spit and image of Major Hoople), Aryan Arabs, and curvaceous doe-eyed femmes. We get Richard Eyer as a chubby boy-genie in need of Ritalin, in *Seventh Voyage of Sinbad*, living in a lamp unfurnished but for a bucket of dry ice. We get Arabian Nights dialogue lacking contractions and stiff as steel: "Perhaps hunger has crazed his mind"; "The wind screams like ten thousand fiends." We get *First Men in the Moon* as a Victorian flubber comedy with little dramatic relief, though farceur Lionel Jeffries tries his best to save it—his rendering of the line, "Hello moon," is almost worth the trip. And we get Gulliver, in *The 3 Worlds of Gulliver*, as a nice guy and the subject of an appalling song, while the Brobdingnagian king (who, according to Swift, creams Gulliver in a *Crossfire*-like debate over Parliamentary rule) emerges as a dolt under the influence of a malefic magician. We also get much repetition: The Sinbad films, of which the last, *Sinbad and the Eye of the Tiger*, may be avoided, have the same plot (sorcerer up to no good, Sinbad sails to remote island to undo his evil). What is the easiest way to defeat a Harryhausen monster? Lure it to a high place and push it over.

Stop-motion photography was only part of Harryhausen's art; he also mastered rear-view and foreground projection to heighten the illusion of seamless interaction. The seamlessness was never completely successful, however, because of the graininess of the rear-view mattes, more evident than ever on DVD: As soon as the color turns slightly gray and soft, you know that a Harryhausen toy is about to race out of a cave or descend from the sky. Still, he knew how to design a scene. The shadowy, erect profile of the freshly hatched alien as Joan Taylor enters the trailer in *20 Million Miles to Earth* is genuinely eerie; his introduction of Gulliver on Lilliput and of the Brobdingnagians is menacing in a way Swift never had to worry about—never has a 12-year-old girl looked so terrifying as the giantess looming over Gulliver. And he kept testing himself with the kind of technicians' wit that translates into turning the screw one notch after another. In *The Golden Voyage of Sinbad* he shows an ailing homunculus with two humans, switching angles to heighten the illusion of their being in the same scene, though the actors were on a screen and the homunculus in Harryhausen's lab. Then he has the human and homunculus touch. Then he has the human carry the homunculus on his arm (a solid sculpture with fluttery wings). Then the homunculus flies out the window, at which point the sorcerer, played to the gills by Tom Baker, observes, "Magic purges the soul, Achmed." Right on, Ray.

Four of these films have achieved additional immortality thanks to the participation of another obsessive, composer Bernard Herrmann, whose work was so little noted at the time (despite his contemporaneous Hitchcock films) that his name did not appear in the ads and does not appear on the DVD boxes. His combination of horse-galloping triplets and three Rachmaninoff chords drives the balloon sequence in *Mysterious Island* (a high-action film directed by the accomplished Cy Endfield, with a too small role assigned Joan Greenwood, who makes her own bagatelle out of the line, "Are you English?"), and his bam! bam! bam! d'deedle-deedle-dum opens the sesame of *The Seventh Voyage*. His score for *Jason*, a film that is also expertly directed (by Don Chafee, including a great opening shot), ranks with Herrmann's work on *Vertigo* and *Psycho*.

Music and effects aside, subtexts are worth contemplating—for example, the unrequited sexuality in the early pictures ("You're starting something you won't be able to finish," the scientist's wife warns just before the flying saucers attack, and those tentacles in *It Came from Beneath the Sea* are after more than food) and the vicious colonialist undercurrent of *First Men in the Moon*. But they are sidebars, intrusions of reality in worlds of fantasy. A more unwarranted intrusion is the sloppy job

Columbia has done with this series, which is available boxed and separately. The same extras are repeated on most of the discs, and though these include the fine Richard Schickel documentary, *The Harryhausen Chronicles*, there are no commentaries. The prints are uneven: some are excellent (*The Golden Voyage* looks refurbished and is presented widescreen and in the more accurate full screen, which has far more information above and below while losing only a smidgen at the sides) and others are matted in the wrong aspect ratio—most egregiously, *The 3 Worlds of Gulliver* and *The Seventh Voyage of Sinbad*—or suffer from excessive darkness (*Mysterious Island*) and grain. The early black and white films have the more radiant transfers. The others deserve better. Considering their mythic longevity, they will probably get it someday.

[*The New York Sun*, 15 February 2005]

24 ❖ *All the Screen's a Stage* *(Jean Renoir)*

Shakespeare shows us the world as a stage, Pirandello the stage as the world, and Renoir the cinema as subverter of the two, standing apart and inextricably mingling one with the other. It is an old theme, this business of conflating truth and appearance, as Renoir readily acknowledged. "Plagiarism should be encouraged!" he thunders in one of the several on-screen interview excerpts included in Criterion's vibrant presentation of his de facto trilogy. He meant that artists spend too much energy contriving originality, when art requires style and sincerity. He certified his point with saturated colors and not a few surprising twists in *The Golden Coach* (1953), *French Cancan* (1955), and *Elena and Her Men* (1956)—boxed as *Stage & Spectacle: Three Films by Jean Renoir*.

Having grown up with two identities, one real and the other represented by his father's paintings of him, Renoir was perhaps destined to see frames or prosceniums everywhere. In these films, the director of *Grand Illusion* and *Rules of the Game* conjured limelight with the wily confidence of Prospero, fusing realism and fantasy in a way that generated much controversy and continues to startle. Initially shown in the United States in dubbed, mutilated prints (Criterion presents gleaming restored editions, with only the last minute of *The Golden Coach* badly damaged), they eventually won champions without achieving widespread acceptance. It's not hard to see why. Renoir's films need to be lived with: The first viewing is like a first date, particularly for a foreign (that is, American) audience so busy reading subtitles it misses unobtrusive comic details that sharpen every scene.

When Renoir went to Italy to make *The Golden Coach*, he was not quite the internationally lionized figure he became. His masterwork, *Rules of the Game*, had yet to be restored, and the debacle of its 1939 premiere (it was banned as immoral and unpatriotic) had led to frustrating decade-long exile in Hollywood. *The River*, filmed in India in 1951, reawakened his career and introduced him to the possibilities of color as manipulated by his brother, the innovative cinematographer Claude Renoir. Color had never been used in quite as painterly a manner as in *The Golden Coach*, in which scenes modulate from one tonic shade to another—a kind of Technicolor variation on the tinting process created for silent pictures. Each color complements a hue in Columbine's dress, worn by Camilla as played by Anna Magnani in her first English-language film (optional English subtitles are useful for unraveling a few of her pronunciations). Her barking laughter and abrupt mood swings keep the audience and her fellow actors attentive—especially a bemused Duncan Lamont as the viceroy.

A Vivaldi score establishes the cheery tone of this Italian romance, set in the early 1700s and involving a commedia dell'arte troupe that has traveled to a Spanish colony in Peru. The film's curtain opens on a stage play, yet with the first edit the stage disappears and we are tossed in among the characters. When Laurence Olivier employed this gambit in *Henry V*, his point was to turn theater into film; Renoir cuts from theater to the illusion of life—a fine but crucial distinction. In this "reality," Camilla's suitors are as costumed as the actors: the viceroy in a preposterous silver wig, the bullfighter in his cape, and the troupe's manager-turned-soldier decked out in a crimson uniform.

Renoir, who began his 1974 memoir (*My Life and My Films*) with a tribute to Mack Sennett, packed his "theater" films with unembarrassed slapstick. In *The Golden Coach* it takes the form of backstage knockabout that mimics and halts the on-stage production, and of clandestine entrances and exits. First the viceroy vainly tries to keep two competing women apart; then Camilla has no more luck compartmentalizing three lovers, all of whom she ultimately saves and loses as she and the film return to the secure yet liberating custody of the proscenium arch.

The Golden Coach is a pleasure to watch, but it is overly schematized and too conscious of its themes. The almost flawless *French Cancan*, however, is as disarmingly unaffected and disciplined as a Fred Astaire dance solo. Reunited with Jean Gabin, playing a fictional version of the showman who created the Moulin Rouge, Renoir portrays le belle époque in plush pastels. One reason the film was misperceived for so long is that, superficially, it is the standard backstage musical, the plot a series of predictable stations made familiar in *42nd Street*, *The Great Ziegfeld*, and countless other American films, not least *The Producers*. One could parse it into chapter headings: Humble Beginnings, The Big Idea, Auditions, Romances, Spite, The Money Men and the Chorus Girls, The Disaster, Rescue at the Last Minute, A Trouper Is Born.

Yet Renoir makes it all new, oddly real, and very adult—not merely because his characters slip in and out of one another's beds (this when married couples in Hollywood movies had single beds separated by a nightstand), but because we immediately recognize them as human. No one ever behaved like Astaire in *Top Hat* or Gene Kelly in *An American in Paris*; their characters have no reality beyond the screen. Renoir's do, however sentimentalized his approach to the demimonde. His knowing affection for an unruly crew (the one near-saintly figure is a foreigner who attempts suicide, pays the bills, and leaves Paris) suffuses it with a spirit that finds its corollary in an exhilarating can-can. Significantly, the climactic dance never ends. Instead, Renoir cuts to a long shot of the Moulin Rouge, where a drunk, stumbling across the pavement, turns to us and bows in farewell.

The can-can exerted a curious fascination in the 1950s, as witness Cole Porter's musical *Can-Can* and John Huston's impressive film *Moulin Rouge*, itself a benchmark in color photography. Huston had taken the opposite tack from Renoir, beginning rather than closing with a luminous abstraction of the dance—a whirl of primary colors and rhythmic editing—before settling in on an insistently glum portrait of Toulouse Lautrec (who, true to Hollywood form, is shown spending his first night with a whore in separate beds). A defining point for comparison are the treatments of a former can-can dancer (inspired by La Goulou), fallen on hard times. Huston depicts her as an alcoholic hag bellowing for attention, Renoir as an aged, Shavian flower girl, content to accept occasional coins from Gabin. Yet Huston's censorious realism verges on melodrama (a Cyrano subplot doesn't help), while Renoir's picture-postcard fantasy seems genuine, the product of a comprehensive vision in which benevolent but hardly naïve conceits (the story is animated by sex, infidelity, jealousy, and commerce) trump theatrical clichés.

One of Gabin's backers tells him he doesn't mind if he carries on with his (the backer's) mistress as long as the two keep up appearances, a premise Renoir elaborates in the more rarely seen *Elena and Her Men*. A businessman who compromises his own betrothed to gain control over tariffs, orders his doltish son, "Love all you like, but not in public and not in front of your fiancée!" Renoir conceived the picture as a comedy for Ingrid Bergman, and unaccountably thought the travails of General Boulanger (a rightist who in the 1880s nearly declared himself dictator of France but lost heart and committed suicide on his mistress's grave) would fit the bill. Renoir ultimately decided to fictionalize the general and improvised a different approach—to the film's detriment, he later conceded. Indeed, the tacked-on ending is borderline offensive: A mob is seduced into an orgy of public romance while an observer offers the comforting thought that France could never succumb to dictatorship because it is a nation of lovers. Yet a second viewing reveals how artfully the bricks and mortar have been structured, lending deeper credibility to a finish that is in any case quite entertaining. Imagine *Rules of the Game* produced by Sennett.

Once again, the color is stunning, the camerawork invisible, and the humor vintage: The first scene, in which Bergman and a pompous composer play a piano duet that is rhythmically derailed by a brass band marching outside the window, is a variation on the old Bugs Bunny cartoon, "Long-Haired Hare." That's the relatively subtle part. For the rest, there are chases and couplings, in and out of doorways, above and below stairs, two duels, and an indulgence in physical postures from the dawn of silent comedy, most notably a Chaplinesque skidding around corners. *Elena and Her Men* was meant for theaters, in which laughter waxes contagiously (though in 1956, not many were laughing), and not a solitary viewer. Still, familiarity breeds contentment, especially when aided by undeniable charm, sumptuous décor, and political, sexual, and financial subversions.

Bergman's Elena is a Polish aristocrat on her uppers ("I've nothing to sell but myself"), ready to marry for security, yet always willing to help an ambitious man achieve his dream, even unto dictatorship. A running gag explains her assertiveness by noting that she is, after all, Polish. The film is divided in thirds, the first set in Paris, the second at a chateau like the one in *Rules of the Game* (it includes a sequence of military maneuvers to parody the stalking hunters in that film), and the last and best in a brothel where most of the principals end up disguised. A convenient troupe of Gypsy players along with the playacting Elena and the most determined of her suitors enables the general (who, fortunately for France, finds the idea of breaking the law repugnant) to sneak off with his mistress. Prospero is unmasked in the closing dialogue: "Tonight's full of trickery." "Simply the end of a dream." William Faulkner once mischievously observed, "Art is simpler than people think." Renoir would have understood.

[*The New York Sun*, 3 August 2004]

25 ❖ *Eternal Times Square* (Shadows)

As a film star John Cassavetes embodied the kinetic, wild-eyed, insanely grinning villain. He seemed born to the role, with his volatile energy and dynamic outbursts, luminous yet curiously deadened eyes, wide gaping mouth (David Thompson likened it to a shark's). From the moment he shows up, he suggests a loose screw: Think *Saddle the Wind* (1958), *The Dirty Dozen* (1967), *Rosemary's Baby* (1968), and *The Fury* (1978), in which a lifetime of pent-up malevolence is released in a quaking detonation— a Roman candle of rage. Of course, he also played good guys, like the pianist-detective on the 1959 TV series *Johnny Staccato*, a short-lived *Peter Gunn* imitation that enabled him to pay off debts from *Shadows*, which cost all of $40,000. But even as a hero, he was too unpredictable to inspire confidence. Thus it may come as a surprise to learn that the Cassavetes *behind* the camera, the one who launched America's independent cinema of the 1960s and ultimately made a dozen films (most of them completely under his control), considered himself and was considered by associates as a missionary of love. "I have a need for characters to really analyze love," he once said. "That's all I'm interested in—love and the lack of it."

Shadows exemplifies the obsession, which is perhaps the main reason it remains as fascinating and gripping as it does. A work of its time that honestly captures its time, it is consequently a work of our time as well. It has no hero, no villain, no linear plotline, no gerrymandered suspense, no practiced comedy, and only as much sex and violence as just about all of us have encountered. An honest work of art, *Shadows* shows that life's costumes, settings, and slang change, but human situations remain relentlessly constant.

Like Orson Welles, Cassavetes played the Hollywood game as an actor to defy the Hollywood industry as a director. Yet unlike Welles, Cassavetes triggered no consensus; even now, a critical middle-road is hard to find. Loved or loathed, his work is therefore perfect for a DVD reappraisal, which allows us closer examination of those ensemble moments that are undeniably exceptional, and an occasional intermission, if needed. On one score, there is general agreement: His films do not look, play, or sound like anyone else's. He has been called the American Godard, but a double-bill of *Shadows* and *Breathless*, each of them shot mostly in 1959, reveals the latter to be almost glossy by comparison. Cassavetes has called *Shadows* "the film I love the best," because it was the first, the result of a two-year improvisation that produced successive debuts, two years apart, of two dramatically different versions. Only the second one met the director's ultimate criteria.

Before going further, we need to scrutinize two land mines: "improvisation" and "approved version." *Shadows* closes with a credit line that identifies the film as a collective improvisation. Cassavetes and his cast have acknowledged that the final work was, in fact, almost entirely scripted. Nevertheless, if ever a film evolved as an improv, *Shadows* did. Most films, including Cassavetes's, begin with an idea that generates a script, which is then brought to life by cast and crew. *Shadows* came about in reverse fashion. It began in workshop classes conducted by Cassavetes, largely with inexperienced actors who developed situations and relationships that inspired him to make a radio plea (on the popular *Jean Shepherd's Night People*) for contributions to finance an independent film about contemporary life. An hour-long version of the film debuted in 1958—disastrously, according to most witnesses, though critic and filmmaker Jonas Mekas hailed it as a masterwork. For Cassavetes, however, the screening was just another station in a process, convincing him to write new scenes to make a stronger and more coherent film. In other words, the improvisational route led him to realize the limits of improvisation. Mekas detested the second version for its more conventional plotting. Yet to his accusations that Cassavetes had sold out, no less radical a scold than Dwight Macdonald—who admired the film's "lyrical realism" and compared the dialogue to O'Neill's *Long Day's Journey into Night*—responded, "Although obscurity is now equated with purity, I have a reactionary prejudice in favor of communication and I therefore favor a reasonable amount of selling out."

Cassavetes himself characterized the first version as a "totally intellectual movie and therefore less than human." Few would say that of the completed *Shadows*, the thoroughly affecting depiction of three siblings, two passing for white and a third attempting to succeed as a Billy Eckstine-style blues crooner. Cinematically, *Shadows* belongs to a period when young iconoclasts like Stan Brakhage, Jack Smith, Kenneth Anger, Myra Deren, Shirley Clarke, and others reclaimed film as the right of any artist with a camera. Socially, it belongs to the era of beat panic, introverted jazz, existentialist blather, chic alienation, and especially racial rapprochement—as witness plays and films like *A Raisin in the Sun* (1961), *Edge of the City* (1957), in which Cassavetes starred opposite Sidney Poitier, the remake of *Imitation of Life* (1959), *The Connection* (1961), and *The Defiant Ones* (1958). Of these, *Shadows* is conspicuously devoid of didactic messaging. Indeed, racial discomfort produces one of the film's casually funny scenes, when Lelia's white lover apologizes for his bad behavior on first learning that she is black, and her brother Ben solemnly promises to convey his contrition. Cassavetes is less concerned with miscegenation than with Lelia's cheerless sexual initiation—an astonishing scene in the year that Doris Day safeguarded chastity in *Pillow Talk* (1959).

Shadows documents a New York that could afford the luxury of nihilistic posing. We get a taste of it during the credits, which roll over a party where the visual and audio don't fit (rock and roll on the sound-track, a lone trumpeter on the screen, an anonymous soul contributing "Whooos"), while Ben sidles in with his beatnik accoutrements (bongos and cigarettes), settles into a corner, and affects a James Dean façade—lonely in a crowd. The film begins and ends with Ben, who cavorts with his friends Tom and Dennis, picking up faded women (one mockingly calls Dennis, "good boy, big boy"), racing through the Museum of Modern Art, losing a lopsided rumble. But the heart of the story resides in the relationships between his brother Hugh, a mediocre singer hum-bled (as Cassavetes once was) into introducing a chorus line, and his manager Rupert; and between his teenage sister Lelia and her spineless seducer Tony. Never have siblings looked so unalike, yet they are strangely convincing, especially in the morning-after sequence when Ben, toying with his trumpet (not unlike Ernie and his saxophone strap in Jack Gelber's *The Connection*, shortly to be filmed by Shirley Clarke), tells Lelia a story about the jazz god Charlie Parker.

Language was important to Cassavetes, and he mines a broad range, from Dennis's "You couldn't be wronger" (in the MOMA scene) to the literary partygoer discussing existentialism and determined not to end a sentence with a preposition: "I know the article to which you refer," she says. Lelia hunts girlishly for suitable metaphors while Rupert and Hugh pump themselves up with faithful camaraderie. Music was also important. Jazz scores were in vogue in the late '50s: Miles Davis improvised in Louis Malle's debut, *Frantic* (1957) and Art Blakey revved Roger Vadim's *Les Liaisons Dangereuses* (1959), while David Amram and Freddie Redd created famous scores for *Pull My Daisy* (1959) and *The Connection*, respectively. Cassavetes signed the matchless Charles Mingus, who insisted on written arrangements. The irony of a world-class improviser notating the score for a film (purportedly) afloat in improvi-sation may have been lost on Cassavetes, who tired of Mingus's delays. In the end, the director settled for a few minutes of Mingus's solo bass and several more minutes of Mingus's alto saxophonist, Shafi Hadi. Mingus never completed a single arrangement for the film, but his sketches were later extended into such jazz classics as "Nostalgia in Times Square," "Diane" (or "Alice's Wonderland"), and "Strollin'."

The actors also left strong impressions, not least on young directors like Philip Kaufman, who cast Ben Carruthers in his first two pictures

(*Goldstein* [1964], *Fearless Frank* [1967]) and Lelia Goldoni in *Invasion of the Body Snatchers* (1978). Goldoni, who claimed to lose roles because casting directors assumed she was black after *Shadows*, also worked with Martin Scorsese in *Alice Doesn't Live Here Anymore* (1979) and with John Schlesinger in *Day of the Locust* (1975). The wonderfully charismatic Rupert Crosse died young, having played the second lead in Mark Rydell's *The Reivers* (1969). They and the rest of the cast (look for walk-ons by Gena Rowlands and Bobby Darin in the chorus-line scene; Cassavetes protecting Lelia from a 42nd Street masher, and Seymour Cassel getting gut-punched by Ben) are indelibly associated with *Shadows*, where they seem as real as the preserved cityscapes that are a key plea-sure of the movie.

Cassavetes was never big on symbols, but he seems to have had a lot of fun with Times Square theater marquees (clues, incidentally, to which shots were made in 1957 or 1959). *The Most Happy Fella* introduces Ben, flush with 20 dollars. Lelia wanders in a movie neverland consisting of double features made up of 1940s Errol Flynn war films, *Naked Paradise* and *Naked Africa*, and a Bardot sex farce teamed with *Man or Gun*, before she disappears under the shadows of *Girls Inc. Ten Thousand Bedrooms* plays down the street from *The Ten Commandments*, and Tony makes his plead-ing phone call under a banner for *Top Secret Affair*. You couldn't ask for a better illustration of Nelson Algren's *The Neon Wilderness* than the last image of Ben, alone and wearing shades at night, fading into the dull blare of Times Square—a graveyard for the kinds of movies Cassavetes hoped to annihilate.

[*John Cassavetes: Five Films*, Criterion Collection, 2004]

26 ❖ *Once upon a Time on the Via Veneto* (La Dolce Vita / Divorce Italian Style)

Federico Fellini's breakthrough film, *La Dolce Vita*, was a seminal event in 1960, when it debuted in Europe, and in 1961, when it traveled to the United States. The distribution rights went for a reported million bucks —unparalleled for a movie with subtitles. I recall it as a movie that banned children, making it an instant object of desire. The Catholic Church tried to ban adults as well. Most Americans never got past the title and a series of widely publicized stills, most famously one of bosomy Anita Ekberg in a black gown wading in Trevi Fountain, but also a promotional shot of grandmaster Fellini wearing a dark fedora with the brim turned up, a long white scarf around his neck, and a matching kitten on his shoulder. Oh, those crazy Italians.

The title was assimilated into international discourse—"la dolce vita" conveyed far more oomph than "the sweet life"—and so was a neologism formed from the name of the protagonist's friend, the predatory tabloid photographer Paparazzo. The picture made an international star of Marcello Mastroianni, who played the affectless Marcello. Yearning, disillusioned, emotionally impotent, he was a new kind of star, representative of the encroaching adultness of European cinema at a time when we first heard names like Godard, Truffaut, Antonioni, Wajda, Resnais, Chabrol, Olmi, and others. Here was *Daisy Miller* in reverse: the world-weary old country putting on a show of chic ennui for the babes in toyland—just two years after we were legally allowed to read *Lady Chatterley's Lover*.

Fellini had already established himself with a deceptive slant on neorealism that might be farcical (*The White Sheik*), affecting (*I vitelloni*), poetical (*La Strada*), or triumphant (*The Nights of Cabiria*), but was always trenchant. *La Dolce Vita* marked a leap in ambition, an epic of nearly three hours that revels in moral decay—it's a fun movie about sad people trapped on a carousel, doomed to libidinal boredom. The church ought to have nodded in solemn approval: Fellini's Via Veneto is a recruiting station for the inferno.

His autobiographical 1963 masterpiece, $8^{1}/_{2}$, did more to bury *La Dolce Vita* than its detractors could. Fellini followed it with more fanciful, elaborate, sometimes gaseous productions that made his once-notorious landmark seem a transitional and dated anomaly, neither as poignant as its predecessors nor as creative as its successors. I doubt that teenagers encountering it today could begin to fathom the original controversy; compared to reality TV, the film is totally chaste.

Well, surprise, surprise: *La Dolce Vita* is finally available on DVD, and it still has a kick. The vivid DVD print is accompanied by many extras (including an enlightening commentary by Richard Schickel, an hour of fake "commercials" that Fellini created for but didn't use in *Ginger and Fred*, and 1980s interviews with Mastroianni and Ekberg). More rewarding, Fellini's sardonic moralism remains unwavering. His episodic structure, which encouraged diverse moods, seems more canny and effective now than when first shown.

The episodic method became Fellini's standard procedure; he had used it in *The Nights of Cabiria*—the accretion of incidents building toward a definition of character—and it dominated his later films. Yet there is a classicism to *La Dolce Vita* that sets it apart, not merely in symbols borrowed from Dante and Catholicism, but in the way the sequences are mapped out. They suggest a collection of interrelated short stories in their parallel configurations and ellipses: We learn all we need to know and nothing more. I'm reminded of Hemingway's *In Our Time*, made up of stories mostly concerning one character, plus a theme-setting preface, ancillary chapters, and "L'envoi." *La Dolce Vita* is a series of seven stories, between 17 and 30 minutes in length, plus an introduction, three interludes (three or four minutes each), and a farewell. A breakdown might go like this:

1. Introduction: Christ borne by a helicopter over an Italy that is half ancient ruins and half antiseptic housing projects.

2. First story: Marcello, the faux-writer whoring as a gossip columnist, rebounds between the rich, beautiful, willful Maddalena (Anouk Aimée) and his earthy, possessive, suicidal mistress Emma (Yvonne Furneaux).

3. Second story: Marcello's misguided romancing of the Hollywood movie star, Sylvia (Ekberg), the longest and best remembered sequence, is played with heavy-handed satire and several deft comic moments, notably a Trevi Fountain kiss that never happens and a proto bar mitzvah band that switches from "Arrivederci, Roma" to rock and roll to Perez Prado's "Patricia"—a recurring theme in Nina Rota's marvelous score.

4. Interlude: The introduction of the philosopher Steiner, playing Bach in an empty church.

5. Third story: The big religious carnival generated when two children claim to see the Madonna—a genuine Fellini spectacle that, by the sheer number of extras alone, can't help but comment on Hollywood's religious spectacles of the era; Emma knows it's a fraud, but prays fervently all the same for Marcello's love.

6. Fourth story, part one: The Steiner salon, which Marcello idealizes as the perfect home, is actually an occasion for bad poetry and sententious epigrams. Through the windows we see klieg lights revolving like windmills.

7. Interlude: Marcello is inspired to try serious writing and is distracted by an angelic young woman from Perugia.

8. Fifth story: Marcello's estranged father (Annibale Ninchi) turns up, looking for entertainment, and Marcello introduces him to a game chorus girl (Magali Noël); but he suffers impotence or another ailment and vanishes as suddenly as he appeared. The first of two references to 1922, the year Mussolini took power, indicates a political reason for his absence during Marcello's childhood.

9. Sixth story: Fellini's answer to Lampedusa's *The Leopard* is a wicked send-up of the aristocracy, which is portrayed searching for ghosts in an old castle, chattering in high-flown accents. Marcello and Maddalena declare their love for each other, then succumb to quickies with strangers.

10. Interlude: Marcello sadistically abandons Emma on a road at night, following his only emotional outburst in the film, but takes her to bed in the morning.

11. Fourth story, part two: Steiner commits an unspeakable crime, made worse by the paparazzi pursuing his unknowing wife, while Marcello stands bewildered in the heat (a dry run for his performance in Visconti's *The Stranger*).

12. Seventh story: Time has passed, Marcello's hair is flecked with gray, and he has descended from gossip columnist to press agent; he attempts to preside over a sexless orgy in which a striptease generates yawns. "I've never seen such boring people," he observes, defeated amid a shower of pillow feathers.

13. L'envoi: A giant stingray is beached, and the angelic young woman from Perugia offers salvation, but Marcello can't hear her and turns away. In the last frame, her eyes make contact with the camera.

La Dolce Vita isn't as beautiful or powerful as Michelangelo Antonioni's similarly themed *L'Avventura*, also released in 1960, or as exhilarating as $8^1/_2$, but it retains a unique charm as well as great performances and music and shots that genuinely merit that ludicrously overused adjective "iconic"—not least the existential wanderer, Mastroianni, who countered his image a year later in Pietro Germi's ingenious comedy, *Divorce Italian Style*, one of the funniest films ever to cross the Atlantic with no apparent loss in connotation.

It unwinds with a clockwork precision, antithetical to Fellini's operatic episodes, which Germi had the brass to lampoon. Everything fits: the intricacy of the script, the meticulousness of the camera work and editing, the uniform excellence of the performances—excepting that of Mastroianni, who exceeds mere excellence, launching himself into the realm of comic originality where Keaton and Chaplin dwell. Intended initially as a drama (Germi had been previously associated with Italian neorealism), *Divorce Italian Style*—a huge international success in 1962—burlesques a loophole in Italian law mandating mercy for killings that avenge marital dishonor.

Mastroianni plays the baron of an old and fading Sicilian family. Married to a plump, cloying woman with one m-shaped eyebrow and the whisper of a mustache, he wants to kill her so that he can marry his teenage first cousin. His plan is to find her a lover, catch them in the act, and execute her to clean the dreaded imputation of cuckoldry from his family's escutcheon. Mastroianni plays the role with his nose in the air, droopy eyes, the walk of an oiled dandy, and a deadpan expression broken by a twitchy clicking of the teeth. His hair has a role of its own —variously slicked back or matted with a net or unruly as a mop or half and half. The structure involves a flashback so slick you hardly see it coming, as Mastroianni, emerging from a toilet on a train, ruminates on Sicily, introduces characters, and guns the plot, which stays gunned, returning to the train only for the penultimate scene.

The shrewd musical score includes a piano waltz, Donizetti, and the rock and roll sequence from *La Dolce Vita*, the recent premiere of which is extensively satirized. The comic techniques include fast-motion, zooms, fantasy murders, interior monologues, and the hero's recurring stumbling upon his sister and her fiancée, forever jumping out of the dark, straightening their clothes, and protesting their innocence. If early Preston Sturges had collaborated with middle-period Tolstoy, they might have conceived something as fiendishly immoral (*The Kreutzer Sonata* meets *Unfaithfully Yours*)—if, that is, they did not have to worry about the Hays office, which even as late as 1962 would have seethed with apoplectic rage at the unapologetic decadence of *Divorce Italian Style*. Apparently, not even Germi (whose next film was the similarly sub-versive international hit, *Seduced and Abandoned*) could quite repeat its inspired lunacy, although we can't be sure until his later films are re-issued. The exemplary Criterion DVD comes with extras—documentary, interviews, screen tests—that whet the appetite for more Germi, who, unlike Fellini, remains under-exported and under-appreciated.

[*The New York Sun*, 12 October 2004 / 12 April 2005]

27 ❖ *Charming Imagination* (*L'eclisse*)

Symbolism habitually troubles filmgoers and especially film critics. If the symbol—a visual or aural metaphor—is vague, it generates complaints of muddled obscurity, and if it is obvious, as all good symbols are, it offends the sensibility of the intellectual. What use is a symbol that anyone can understand at first blush? Schoolteachers often like symbols for the wrong reason: the presumed necessity of explaining them. But the most effective symbols withstand and even flout explanations. They are in-extricable pleasure-giving components that augment a work and convey meaning through correlation. In the final shot of John Huston's *The Maltese Falcon*, Sam Spade descends a staircase as the shadow of an elevator signals the more final descent of wicked Brigit. One may praise the design of the image (a filmmaker's conceit not available to the novelist), but any attempt at explanation trivializes a moment best reflected in the satisfied laughter that accompanies it whenever the film is screened in a theater.

Michelangelo Antonioni, reportedly still active at 92, heralded the arrival of a new symbolist cinema in the early 1960s with films that embodied a declaration of cinematic independence: *L'avventura* (1960), *La notte* (1961), and *L'eclisse* (1962). Nearing 50 and with a dozen years of filmmaking behind him, including short documentaries and increasingly personal features, he suddenly became an international celebrity and a magnet for controversy. At the 1960 Cannes Festival, he was raucously booed and then awarded the Grand Jury Prize. In the United States, highbrow critics rose to defend *L'avventura* and then lost interest in what followed. One critic complained that the symbols were too obvious; another coined the term "Antoniennui"; another decided that "the impersonal life of modern man" wasn't much of a theme anyway. If you've seen one western, thriller, or existential thumbsucker, you've seen them all. After Antonioni brought his own paint box to explore color in *Il derserto rosso* (1964), he went Anglo and landed one hit, *Blow Up* (1966), and was hit back by pundits for the vastly underrated *Zabriskie Point* (1970).

A measure of Antonioni's accomplishment is that, four decades later, one can still appreciate all the fuss. He had turned away from conventional narrative logic, from genres, from denouements, even from characters, who in his pictures prematurely disappear. The startling beauty of his images, matched by an unimpressed sense of tempo, seemed indulgent and long-winded to some. He filmed ordinary upper-middle-class people who have little recourse to guns, espionage, screwball hi-jinx, and other plot-drivers; who are unhappy and don't know why; who look for satisfaction in money, sex, romance, and art while vaguely noting the threat of a nuclear holocaust. His films of the early 1960s predict the world he depicted in the middle and late 1960s, and are so eye-catching that the decline in popular interest, directly corresponding to a rise in critical acclimation, is surprising. I suspect one reason is the search for meaning—not on the part of his characters, but as a requirement of his audience. It is an obligation that ought to be resisted.

I don't mean to suggest that Antonioni's themes and his means of telling stories don't merit and reward interpretation. But so do those of Hitchcock. Yet too often, in the case of Antonioni, the worrisome business of finding answers, of figuring it out, deflects the sheer pleasure he affords as one of the most sensual and pictorially discriminating artists the cinema has ever known. As a conceptualist consumed with settings and objects and architecture, he invariably creates surfaces that, partly through the use of symbols, are self-explanatory and at times transparent. He generates suspense as much by the discontinuity of his presentation as by his concern for people and the stories in which they are embedded. He transmits their feelings not through blather and close-ups (he is notorious for shooting the backs of heads), but rather through behavioral detail and a lexicon of metaphors that communicate as immediately and clearly as Huston's elevator.

Criterion has released an impeccable DVD rendering of the masterpiece, *L'eclisse* (*The Eclipse*), though it has unwisely and, I think, wrongly bannered it as "the conclusion" to Antonioni's "trilogy on modern malaise." I am not sure where the notion of a trilogy originated—with the director or with critics—but the suggestion that it must be seen as the third part of a triptych is misleading. Beyond the consistency of his unmistakable style and the appearance of the Roman goddess Monica Vitti (she made five films with Antonioni and *L'eclisse* represents her pinnacle in their collaboration), the films are profoundly dissimilar. One can find points of continuity: *L'avventura*, set in Sicily, ends with an insecure young couple; *La notte*, set in Milan, portrays the futile lovelessness of an older couple; and *L'eclisse* begins (optimistically in the Antonioni scheme of things) with the breakup of a long relationship. Yet each stands alone, except as a development in Antonioni's art.

Having contributed to the rise of Italian neorealism, Antonioni's penchant for a symbolist approach is not much different from the response of 19th-century French poets to naturalism. Edmund Wilson's extract from Mallarmé (*Axel's Castle*) might have been voiced by Antonioni: "To name an object is to do away with three-quarters of the enjoyment of the poem which is derived from the satisfaction of guessing little by little: to suggest it, to evoke it—that is what charms the imagination." *L'eclisse* opens with a still life involving books and what may be a white cloth lying over them; only as the camera pans do we realize that the cloth is a man's elbow. The first shot of Vitti finds her arranging objects in an empty frame, creating her own three-dimensional still life. From that point on, the film is a museum of frames and frames within frames: picture frames, doorframes, window frames, gates, bars, and grills. Naming them, as Mallarmé says, detracts from their pleasure. Meaning is intimated: The erotic luster of visual poetry explicates invisible emotions as clearly as music.

Vittoria and Riccardo have been up all night, arguing over her decision to leave him. ("I wanted to make you happy," he protests, rather dutifully. "When we first met I was 20 years old. I was happy then," she says.) It's a virtuoso set piece in which every shot redefines space from a different angle. Vittoria steps back, toward the camera, then sidles left to stand before a mirror, where she is transformed into a still life. Her hair—a blond globe when shot from behind, eclipsing her lover and much of the screen—flutters like wings before we see a small table fan responsible for the draft. She leaves the house, gliding through divided rectangular gates.

Antonioni's technical genius is apparent throughout the film, most obviously in the long breakup and in the scenes in the Borsa, in which we see the vitality and frenzy of the stock market from so many perspectives and with such evident interest on the part of the director that we can only guess at the number of cameras or how the crew was marshaled to stay out of the way. He introduces Vittoria's home at night from a distance, her body passing through lighted windows like M. Hulot (another homage to Jacque Tati follows when a passel of dogs race by). A distant shot of Vittoria leaving her apartment cuts to an African woman as though we were seeing her point of view; but after a second, we realize that the woman is a photograph, as a real woman, Marta, recently relocated from Kenya, opens the door to admit Vittoria and another friend. The apartment becomes their mental picture of Africa as Vittoria appears in blackface for a startling dance that degenerates into a racist, colonialist rant. The irony that Vittoria never appears more herself—playful, engaged, transported—than when "playing Negro" requires no interpretation.

Nor does Antonioni's inspired decision to trace the courtship between Vittoria and the callous stockbroker Piero (Alain Delon) by having them avoid their own constricting apartments in favor of their parents' homes, complete with their preserved childhood bedrooms—hers displaying a bed much too small for her, and his a pen that, when turned upside down, unclothes its imprisoned woman. Back in 1962, one critic sneered at the obviousness of Vittoria watching two nuns pass beneath the window of Piero's childhood home; in a theater, though, that shot invariably gets a laugh. In the extras included with the film (a documentary, commentary, interview with Italian critics), no mention is ever made of humor, yet Antonioni was never more playful than in *L'eclisse*—the very piling on of parallel symbols provides levity.

The ending (spoiler alert) is now so famous that it may no longer be possible to experience the sense of wonder that audiences felt when the film was first shown. After a timer goes off, interrupting an afternoon idyll, Vittoria and Piero avow loyalty, hug each other like frightened rabbits, plan a rendezvous for that evening, and part. He replaces his many phones (another laugh) on their hooks and returns to work, as she slowly descends an old, angular, wooden staircase from his office. She stares up at the trees, then turns to the camera—never in her career did Vitti look more exquisite than in that shot—and exits the frame and film. The next seven minutes recapitulate their romance in a breathtaking montage of places they have been, now devoid of their presence. Several shots show water seeping into the ground or a sewer, and sprinklers, which are abruptly turned off. For a while, it looks like a premature depiction of the work of a neutron bomb—the buildings stand, people are gone. But there *are* people—a blond who looks like Vittoria from the back, an older man who suggests what Piero might look like a few decades later. It's as if Antonioni contemplated one of those *An Affair to Remember* stories in which *neither* of the lovers shows up at the appointed rendezvous, yet the place remains—a character in its own right. There are many ways to read the title, but good symbolist that he is, Antonioni moots the issue by closing in on a streetlight, a blaring oval light that looks like a flying saucer, suddenly eclipsed with the appearance of "Fin."

[*The New York Sun*, 29 March 2005]

28 ❖ *I Spy*
(The Counterfeit Traitor)

George Seaton, one of Hollywood's forgotten men, made his initial reputation as a comedy writer in the 1930s (he worked on *A Day at the Races* for the Marxes and a version of *Charlie's Aunt* for Jack Benny), but found his true métier in the postwar era, building sand castles of humor, drama, sentiment, and social observation on the mud of personal anguish intensified by moral quandary. In his best films—*Miracle on 34th Street, Apartment for Peggy, The Big Lift, Little Boy Lost, The Country Girl, Teacher's Pet, The Pleasure of His Company, The Counterfeit Traitor, Airport* —a moment invariably arrives when the protagonist slumps under the world's weight or realizes that everything he believes is wrong.

As a writer-director, Seaton enjoyed a long association with producer William Perlberg that allowed him an unusual degree of control in choosing and carrying out his projects. They made about 20 films together (not counting those they co-produced and assigned to other directors), and nearly half were successful financially and critically. Yet their work is rarely considered as an oeuvre, despite Seaton's consistent themes of personal disorder and growth. His contemporaries considered him a clever writer (four Oscar nominations, two wins) and journeyman director with a knack for eliciting defining work from diverse actors, among them Edmund Gwenn, Bing Crosby, Montgomery Clift, William Holden, Lilli Palmer, Clark Gable, Gig Young, Doris Day, Helen Hayes, and two remarkable nine-year-olds, Natalie Wood and Christian Fourcade. He even won an Oscar for Grace Kelly—but then, the Academy always crowns a glamorous woman willing to wear ratty clothes and underplay the Max Factor.

Seaton's talents far outweigh his shortcomings in *The Counterfeit Traitor* (1962). A popular film in its day, it improves with age, partly because the passing of time underscores the honest treatment of its reluctant hero, World War II's industrialist-spy, Eric Erickson. Seaton's telling is reasonably accurate, and the liberties he took underscore the ambiguities of espionage, a world in which a Nazi may behave more decently than a democrat. The subject isn't good and evil but the necessity of ruthlessness in war. By the time Erickson, played with wary authority by William Holden, says that a Jew whose life he tried to save "choked to death rather than cough," we cannot be certain Eric didn't suffocate him. The film ends on that note of uncertainty.

Erickson's story, first reported in 1945 but little known until Alexander Klein fleshed it out in his stiff, novelistic book, *The Counterfeit Traitor* (1958), was that of an American businessman who gave up his citizenship to build an oil-importing business in Stockholm. Recruited by America's ambassador to Russia two years before Pearl Harbor, he eagerly accepted the challenge of creating a cover to give him access to German oil refineries; his information triggered numerous Allied bombing raids but required him to stalk and murder an acquaintance he thought would turn him in, and cost him friends and family until the truth was revealed. Only his wife and Sweden's Prince Carl Bernadotte knew of the deception, which concluded with a safe return to Stockholm under the protection of no less a protector than Himmler.

In the film, Erickson is blackmailed into spying; his unknowing wife leaves him (how, one wonders, did the real Mrs. Erickson feel about that?); he evolves from a business-obsessed opportunist to a willing freedom fighter; and he undergoes a long, grueling escape from Germany—a curtsy to movie conventions. Seaton, though no master of suspense (the episode is overlong and clumsy), tricks up the finale with such memorable touches as a dominatrix-spy, Gestapo dogs befuddled by cocaine, and the Hitchcockian intervention of hundreds of Danish bicyclists. His real interest lies with Erickson's character: the ease with which a blackmail victim becomes an accomplished blackmailer, and the disparity between his avowed doubts and his evident relish as he outsmarts everyone, friends and enemies alike.

The first quintessential Seaton moment is the depiction in long shot of a slow hanging that changes Erickson and his German confederate into activists, a scene played with no visible emotion. Seaton delays the outbursts of horror for two episodes that made lasting impressions on film audiences: one in which Erickson's lover, Marianne von Mollendorf, realizes that she has confessed her activities to a Gestapo agent, not a priest, and another in which he witnesses her execution. In life, Erickson was made to stand on the prison grounds, remaining impassive. The film is more dramatic. He awakes alone in a cell, sees her in the courtyard, and cries out her name as she is shot. They both reach their arms out at the climactic moment. It may sound like melodrama, but it plays as harrowing, because the scenes are edited with meticulous economy and because the never-better Lilli Palmer plays Marianne. The Holden-Palmer romance is smartly constructed to progress from playacting to chaste descriptions of each other's private parts (in case anyone should ask) to erotic longing stirred by the proximity of death. In the era of James Bond, *The Counterfeit Traitor* recalled Ambler and prefigured Le Carré.

Seaton's film has another precedent in Fritz Lang's *Cloak and Dagger* (1946), also based, much more loosely, on a true story involving an American scientist sent undercover and aided by an Italian agent—Palmer in her Hollywood debut. Elements of *The Counterfeit Traitor* later showed up in Hitchcock's botched *Torn Curtain*, particularly the idea that spying requires callousness verging on sadism. Holden communicates this very well, aided by such disarming dialogue as, "I've lost all my friends and been dropped by every club except the Book of the Month," and "[Goebbels] was oily and over-polite and so was I," and "My conscience has always been like a well-trained dog." In unleashing Erickson's conscience, the film doesn't dilute (as Steven Spielberg's tempered portrayal of Oskar Schindler does) the depiction of an entrepreneur as a heroic and quick but nonetheless self-serving bastard. When told that Nazism preaches sacrifice and not profit, he replies, "And business must profit, not sacrifice. Amazing how they get along." After arguing over the side effects of their intelligence—the phrase, "collateral damage," was not yet coined, and no attempt is made to jerk tears to memorialize the 120 children incinerated in a raid—Erickson haplessly suggests that Marianne see a priest, inadvertently triggering her destruction.

Except for a brief distortion near the two-hour mark, Paramount's no-frills DVD ably captures the splendid location photography of Jean Bourgoin (he also shot *Mon Oncle* and *Black Orpheus*), which is at once sumptuous and believable—you can almost inhale the air and varied light of Stockholm, Berlin, and Copenhagen. The audio track does full justice to Alfred Newman's score—percussion-and-brass fanfares, spiraling strings—and Holden's narration, a reminder that, along with Orson Welles and James Earl Jones, he possessed one of the most decisive voices in American movies.

[*The New York Sun*, 17 August 2004]

29 ❖ *McCarey Nods* (Satan Never Sleeps)

Fox recently and quietly released Leo McCarey's 1962 swan song, *Satan Never Sleeps*, a universally loathed romantic comedy involving priests, Communism, rape, and familial dysfunction at a Chinese mission in 1949. The very clash of generic conventions indicates that the film is misbegotten in a way unique to its oddly divisive director.

I am not about to defend the indefensible: *Satan Never Sleeps* is a bad film. One of its most obdurate detractors was Leo McCarey. Here is an excerpt from his last interview, with Peter Bogdanovich, recorded shortly before his death in 1969:

> "You didn't get along well with [William] Holden.
> "No."
> "Did you like Clifton Webb?"
> "No."
> "How about France Nuyen?"
> "No."
> "You really didn't like that picture."
> "No—it was a nightmare. I finally let the picture go and my assistant shot the last five days."

McCarey's primary gripe was that William Holden vetoed his original story, in which a young priest is tempted by a Chinese beauty, whose brutal rape he is forced to witness, and resolves his dilemma by sacrificing his life. Holden did not want to die. The astonishing and quite risible ending edited in McCarey's absence has the older priest (Clifton Webb) making the sacrifice, while Holden marries the woman to her rapist and exchanges a golly-gee sitcom grin when she announces that she will name their baby after him. One would cringe if one's jaw hadn't already hit the canvas.

So why dredge it up? Because if ever a stubbornly individual film-maker rewarded the not infrequently tested patience of admirers it was McCarey, and *Satan Never Sleeps* is not without its McCarey moments. Jean Renoir famously observed, "McCarey understands people better perhaps than anyone else in Hollywood." Yet it is virtually impossible to find a critic who will take him whole. Even the impassioned defenders Leland Poague and Robin Wood (who champions *Rally 'Round the Flag, Boys*, of all things) are mum on *Satan Never Sleeps*. The more conventional critics celebrate McCarey for having introduced Laurel to Hardy and super-vising much of their best work; or directing the best Marx Brothers film (*Duck Soup*), the best screwball comedy (*The Awful Truth*), the best movie about growing old in the United States (*Make Room for Tomorrow*, which AARP might consider reviving as propaganda for social security); or the hugely popular Father O'Malley films (*Going My Way* and *The Bells of St. Mary's*); or such anomalies as *Ruggles of Red Gap*, and the much remade *Love Affair* and his story for *My Favorite Wife* (illness required him to delegate direction), not to mention vehicles for Eddie Cantor, Mae West, W. C. Fields, and Harold Lloyd. But hardly anyone champions them all, least of all that misapprehended cudgel, *My Son, John*, a film that in 1951 reeked of anti-Communist hysteria, yet now ranks as a devastating critique of generational fault lines and the battle between unthinking conservatism and cultist rebellion.

Renoir's observation defines the problem. McCarey is invariably too humane to paint his characters as good and evil, and his approach neces-sitates a nimble tread over a tightrope tautly pulled by comedy and drama, the one gaining on the other with scarcely a warning. Robert Warshow's attack on *My Son, John* ("Father and Son—and the FBI") enumerated instances that show the American Legionnaire father as, in fact, loonier than his Communist son—as though McCarey had not intentionally developed that situation. Watching that film and *Satan Never Sleeps* today, you can hardly avoid the conclusion that Communism didn't much interest him except as a device to illuminate relationships in crisis —no more than Nazism did in his even more bizarre romantic comedy set against the Holocaust, *Once upon a Honeymoon*, which introduced some of the plot contrivances extended in *Satan Never Sleeps*.

The provenance of the film is confusing; it is credited as a script by McCarey and Claude Binyon based on a Pearl Buck novel, yet Buck's only novel of that name is a novelization of the script, published as a paper-back tie-in. According to letters from her agent and publisher (in the Nora Stirling Collection at Randolph-Macon Woman's College, for which I am grateful to librarian Frances Webb), Buck had submitted an original script to 20th Century Fox, called *China Story*; McCarey and Binyon rewrote it. When the picture was nearing completion, the Fox publicity department asked Buck to expand the story as a novel. She complied, but— regarding the result as "a relatively minor effort"—refused to have it published in a "trade" (hardcover) edition. It is unclear who came up with the basic conflict between young and old priests, an idea McCarey had popularized in *Going My Way*. At the time when *Satan Never Sleeps* was slogging through production, priests and nuns were everywhere: Bing Crosby and Spencer Tracy had taken their collars out of mothballs; Audrey Hepburn had taken her vows as Deborah Kerr returned to her habit for John Huston, who himself would receive holy orders for Otto Preminger's *The Cardinal*; and Norah Lofts's story of Chinese warlords who invade a women's mission, *7 Women*, had been televised and would soon be remade as the last film of John Ford.

Satan Never Sleeps instantly mutes political urgency with a loopy theme song, sung by Timi Yuro in the manner of Nancy Wilson and co-authored by McCarey: "And in the ember of the flame / you'll have your foolish heart to blame." This is followed by a shot of Holden leading France Nuyen in front of a traveling matte shot and arriving at a mission where he explains his tardiness in a scene conceived entirely for laughs (Nuyen mugs amusingly), until it breaks into hysteria as he abandons her. From that point on, the picture runs like a plane with a wobbly gyroscope, veering between funny, sentimental, dramatic, and melodramatic. There are misunderstandings, changed loyalties, late-night comings and goings, and the rape, which the production attempts to soften—though the final scene of victim and tormentor reciting nuptials is as unsettling as any in the movies of that era.

McCarey might have called the film, *My Son, Ho San*, as the story is ultimately animated by a former protégé of Webb's priest who becomes a rabid demagogue until a ham-handedly evil Russian threatens Ho San's future, murdering his Christian-convert parents before his eyes. That event and the birth of his son moves him abruptly into the older generational slot, where he resolves to live in a country that allows parents to speak freely to their children, a gift he did not permit his own parents. The commandment that troubles McCarey in several films is recited in this one: Honor thy father and mother.

Ho San (Weaver Lee) triggers several McCarey moments, including his response, after Webb tells him to go to hell: "I cannot roast in your hell. I'm no longer a member." The more Ho San asserts himself, the more the nuns persist in treating him like a juvenile delinquent—his violence seems as aimed at them and Webb as his victim. After he seizes Webb's cognac as a symbol of Western exploitation, Holden says, "Be sure to divide that equally among the poor. [Pause] If you can't think of a clever answer, just go." Whereupon Webb pours half his glass into Holden's and observes, "As the saying goes, share and share alike." After Ho San opts to save them, he shoots a soldier in the back and explains, "That was my last act as a non-Christian." Realizing an enemy jeep is in pursuit, he kills all the passengers and exults, "So now I have performed my first act as a reconverted Christian." Passages like these, a slap-fest reminiscent of the boxing scene in *The Bells of St. Mary's,* and Nuyen's logical argument that Holden become Protestant, testify to the peculiar charm of an irreplaceable filmmaker. The DVD, incidentally, has no extras except for a sexy photo of Nuyen in a sheath dress on the back of the box—it's from another movie, of course.

[*The New York Sun,* 12 April 2005]

30 ❖ *Across the Pacific*
(Zero Focus / The Demon)

Postwar Japanese cinema is as powerful and influential as any in the world, yet its standing in this country remains tenuous. Excepting Akira Kurosawa, whose films enjoy a singular international pipeline, the most celebrated Japanese filmmakers are known here for isolated breakthroughs, which rarely beget a comprehensive importation. New DVD releases are addressing the drought, but not always as one might expect.

Zero Focus (1961) and *The Demon* (1978) should stimulate interest in director Yoshitaro Nomura and novelist Seicho Matsumoto, whose work he faithfully adapted. Both were hugely popular in Japan between the 1950s and the 1980s, without achieving traction in other time zones. Few of Matsumoto's best-selling police procedurals, which are admired in Japan for their social scrutiny, have made it into English; the one that has achieved some success here, *Inspector Imanishi Investigates* was filmed by Nomura as *The Castle of Sand* (1974), a film touted on the packaging of the current DVDs, though it isn't available here. These two films are enough to warrant a serious look at Nomura, who is listed in no standard reference works about international directors.

The cover of *Zero Focus* classifies the film as Hitchcockian—standard shorthand to promote every sort of suspense thriller. In this instance, the comparison cheats no one but is superficial all the same. Hitchcock rarely made mysteries and the stylistic connections are too general to mean much: the thrashing waters against a rocky cliff, as in *Suspicion*; the deadly fall, as in *Vertigo*; a mini-*North by Northwest* trek from Tokyo to the Noto Peninsula; plus such Hitchcock constants as the brilliantly descriptive musical score (by Yasushi Akutagawa), lots of train scenes, sexual shame, buried secrets, odd point-of-view shots, and much suspense. There is even a deceptive flashback, as in *Stage Fright*, but where Hitchcock's was a deliberate lie, Nomura's is misguided speculation—leading to a bravura flashback within a flashback that, being truthful, is far crueler.

Nomura's genre borrowings in *Zero Focus* greatly exceed the smatterings of Hitchcock. Among them: Raymond Chandler's whore who marries money and kills to keep her secret, Cornell Woolrich's isolated woman forced to investigate a crime the police have bungled, and Daphne DuMaurier's mousy young wife and assorted doppelgangers. In the specifics, however, the film is purely Japanese, from Takashi Kawabata's stimulating black-and-white location photography to such details as absurdly oversized telephones. More significant are two endemic societal issues that animate the story: women who turned to streetwalking during the American occupation and men who resorted to bigamy in the years that followed.

No less quintessentially Japanese is the acting. Nearly every character is obliged to pretend to be something other than what he or she is, so that a peculiar stiffness pervades the first half. When the masks finally fall away, the performances turn volatile. On a second viewing, nothing is more accomplished than the actors' control, which parallels the director's infallible tempo in unraveling the narrative's secrets. The main performers are women, and though the stars Yoshiko Kuga and Hizuru Takachino are compelling as the wife and her nemesis, the exquisite Ineko Arima as the "other woman" steals the picture from under their noses.

The Demon similarly cuts through the veneer of the communal fabric and is a more startling and original film, but not one as easily recommended. It isn't a horror film in any conventional sense—no monster, nothing supernatural, not much violence—yet its subject is so horrific that some people (say, parents) will quail at the thought of it. Once again, the story involves the dangerous cliffs of western Japan, bigamous men, and murder (cyanide figures in both pictures). This time the intended victims are small trusting children and the demon is their loving dad. Needless to say, *The Demon* could never have been made in the United States. Yet Matsumoto's novel was based on a widely reported incident that took place during a time of pervasive child abandonment.

No less grueling than the material is Nomura's radical shift in tone. An abandoned mistress tracks down the married father of her three children, dumps them on him and his furious wife, and disappears. For the next half-hour, you think you're watching situation comedy in which a likable, clueless father learns to take responsibility. Weaned on Hollywood, we expect his irate wife to eventually cool down and reveal her maternal instinct. Instead, she grows increasingly malevolent and, after a heated bout of lovemaking, convinces her husband that the offspring must die. What follows is terrifying, right through to a conclusion that is as satisfying as it is utterly unexpected.

Nomura's deliberate pacing, the exceptional performances by his cast, the saturated color photography of Kawabata, and the lush music of Akutagawa conspire to disarm you, until the veil falls away. Paradoxically, the most dreadful moment is an elegant long shot in profile of the cliff's edge, also used in *Zero Focus* but to different effect—as an aesthetic breather at a moment when you need one.

The Demon bears comparison to Shohei Imamura's true-crime study, *Vengeance Is Mine*, made a few months earlier. Both films dispassionately observe unspeakable evil and feature the great Ken Ogata as a sociopath who destroys, with shockingly impulsive malevolence, those he professes to love—and wins sympathy in spite of himself. The roles are radically different (in the first, a slick con-man and serial killer; in the second, a desperately poor printer enslaved to some kind of insane logic) and Ogata so thoroughly personifies each that one can scarcely believe it's the same actor. Mayumi Ogawa is also in both films, a desperate mistress twice over, but the actor who most impressively withstands Ogata's demonic power is a six-year-old Hiroki Iwase.

(*The New York Sun*, 28 September 2004)

31 ❖ "My Life Makes Me Cry" (The Insect Woman)

Shohei Imamura's gripping, emphatic sixth film, *The Insect Woman*, was briefly released here in 1963, after winning several prizes in Japan, and though admired, was faulted for its poorly translated subtitles. The new print on view at the Public Theater is newly translated (though a laser disc release uses the old print), so there is no excuse not to give it its due.

In the early '60s, distribution beyond the art house circuit depended on what were called "graphic sex scenes" or at least flashes of female flesh. Imamura obliged, and those scenes, which are neither erotic nor, by contemporary standards, particularly graphic, remain powerful. The film's subject is exploitation, and sexual manipulation is the coin that keeps the carousel turning. Imamura was not concerned with satisfying voyeurs. Now that home video has replaced the art house, chances for theatrical distribution beyond rare and isolated screenings are even less sanguine —a bare bosom doesn't go as far as it once did, alas: *The Insect Woman* is the best film I've seen this year.

Imamura is so confident a storyteller that he can make brutish squalor electrifying. In tracing the drudging, disappointed life of a farmer's daughter from a mountain village to a Tokyo brothel, he explores 45 years of largely unfamiliar Japanese terrain, beginning in 1918. His episodic script, written with Keiji Hasebe, is imbued with novelistic detail. Some episodes are fleeting and others distended—most are introduced with dates, like chapter headings; epiphanies are punched up with photographic montages that objectify the "insect woman's" hard-scrabbling amorality. The war, the surrender, the Mayday riots, and the rise of labor, industry, and religious cults are present as reactive forces, but the foreground is occupied exclusively by the protagonist, Tome Matsuyki. Nearly every sexual encounter undermines the fabric of community, as Imamura sees it, and tears another veil from Tome's innocence, her sense of romance, her illusions. In her poverty-stricken mountain region, open complicity acknowledges and winks encouragingly at nymphomania, incest, and rape; in the city, sex is merchandise.

On two occasions, Tome thinks she has found a worthy lover. The first is a labor organizer who gets her to help form a union and then abandons her when management offers him a better position. The second is a married businessman who sets her up with her own brothel and asks her to entertain his associates. "Don't you mind?" she asks, flabbergasted but resigned to the request. "Of course!" he blusters, then storms away. He subsequently bribe's Tome's illegitimate daughter into becoming his mistress; when she escapes, pregnant, back to her farm and boyfriend, he begs Tome to bring her back. The film ends with Tome plodding through the dust on that vile and presumably unsuccessful mission.

Tome's plight and Imamura's anthropological designs indicate a relentless pall of cyclical despondency; yet, remarkably, his film avoids a didactic heavy-handedness—notwithstanding the conceit of the title. He opens with an extended shot of an ant making its way in the sand, and closes with Tome grubbing just as doggedly. True, the vicious cycles are schematically plotted. Tome is recruited as a maid for a brothel at a Jodo Buddhist meeting ("Madame met her at God's place," a whore observes) and is manipulated into taking customers. Eventually, she informs on Madame, takes her place, and is informed on in turn. Yet the copious images and multitude of memorable characters keep the film on course. Plots and subplots unravel as in a Victorian page-turner, with a kindred Brechtian detachment—destiny hovers, details disarm.

Among the particulars are Tome's ambiguously incestuous relationship with her addlebrained stepfather (he sucks the milk from her breasts to ease the pain after her daughter is born, and she later offers him her nipple as he dies asking for milk); the cynical, grizzly women in the family who try to force her into marriage with a landowner (he rapes and impregnates her instead, and when they midwife a girl—another useless mouth—ask her to let the baby die); the minutiae of the brothel ("Men are such fools—what's so good about virgins?" one whore asks another, while a third injects a vial of cat blood into her vagina because the customer is always right); various religious cults (Tome combines worship of the mountain God and Jodo sect); and Tome's righteous devotion to her stepfather and her equally desperate daughter, Nabuko, for whose welfare she justifies her own descent into a calculating stoniness. Shortly before Madame takes her on, Tome confesses, "My life makes me cry."

Yet the film has an exultant quality, illustrating Imamura's love of the medium and command of his materials—reflected in the vigorous camera movements and editing, the harsh black-and-white photography, the absence of mawkishness, the enormous compassion and respect for all the characters, even the villains, and the incisive performances. Sachiko Hidari's Tome is the film's soul; as she gradually loses her illusions and youth, her eyes deaden and her once seductive mouth thins —in two hours, she lets us see what it means to be 24 and 31 and 45. Also outstanding are Kazuo Kitamura as her unswerving stepfather; Seizaburo Kawazu as her malevolent patron, Karasawa; Jitsuko Yoshimura as her disarmingly perky daughter; Tanie Kitabayashi as Madame; and Masumi Harukawa as Midori, a woman who hires Tome as her maid and eventually becomes one of her whores. As a maid, Tome stands in the kitchen, quietly weeping, listening to Midori make love to an American serviceman; as a Madame, Tome cheats Midori and scalds the hand of her own maid in a rage of frustration. The miracle of *The Insect Woman* is that you follow Tome from one plane to the next and, despite the distancing intrinsic to Imamura's expeditious narrative, you bleed for her at every step.

[*Village Voice*, 3 April 1990]

32 ❖ The Holland Line
(Dutch Movies)

Dutch culture is most appealing in its unswerving consistency. How reassuring it is to find all the clichés that have accrued to America's midwife played over and over again in its books, music, and films. The Euclidean dreamscape, wrested from the sea with dykes and landfills; the mixed population of stodgy rationalists and urban water-rats, bankers and whores; a countryside of windmills and wooden shoes; and a city of concentric circles (Camus's stand-in for hell in *The Fall*) that lead from Rembrandt and Vermeer on the outer rim to an international drug market at the nub. Holland was made for art and metaphor. Yet paintings, Anne Frank, and red lights aside, Dutch cinema and literature have not been widely exported, in part because only the Dutch speak Dutch.

Dutch movies have launched a successful incursion in the United States lately, thanks to Paul Verhoeven, whose films (*Spetters*, *The Fourth Man*, *Robocop*) helped launch the careers of Rutger Hauer, Jeroene Krabbe, and the less widely recognized Renee Soutendijk. The veteran director Fons Rademakers has also enjoyed some success here with *The Assault*. Yet the only Dutch filmmaker of international reputation is the innovative documentarian Joris Ivens, who did propaganda work for the United States in the 1940s and was then run off by HUAC. "NetherLandscapes: 85 Years of Dutch Filmmaking," eight bills presented by Anthology Film Archives, is a welcome corrective to the widespread neglect of Holland's film industry, ranging from a largely improvised comedy made in 1905 ("The Adventure of a French Gentleman Without His Trousers") to the 1987 feature, *Return to Oegstgeest*, by Theo Van Gogh, thought by many to be the most talented of Holland's younger directors.[1] A few observations hold true for virtually all the selections chosen by Wendy Lidell of the International Film Circuit and Rudy Engelander of Amsterdam's Foundation for Cultural Exchange: they are sumptuously photographed, often sardonic, pitched on the boundary line between illusion and reality, and abundant with jarring juxtapositions.

It's Me, an erotic 70-minute fantasy by Frans Zwatjes, was shown along with his shorter, more frankly experimental *Anemnesis* (1969) in a program called "Cinema Unraveled." Zwatjes has his cake and eats it, too:

---

[1] Van Gogh, a descendant of the painter, was murdered in 2004, at the age of 47, the victim of a fanatic seeking retaliation for his television film, *Submission*, which explores violence against women in Islamic societies.

He provides enough narrative information to hang a rational explanation while lingering over images that are their own justification. For nearly a minute, the stationary camera shows the rim of a bath and the wall behind it. Soapy hands and legs rise in a Beckettian ballet of dislocated limbs. More Beckettian still is a funny piece of business in which a phone rings and the bather tries, obsessively, to make her sponge sit on the bath rim before rising Venuslike to answer it. Willeke van Ammelrooy, who appears to be in her mid-thirties and is the film's only performer, is striking: the finely chiseled planes of her face set off sensuous lips and glowing eyes.

What follows can be read in one way or in many. The one way might be subtitled "An Actor Prepares": The caller inquires about a role for Ammelrooy (all dialogue is electrically distorted beyond comprehension). The script is on the floor. She fastidiously makes up her face, disguising her beauty with rouge and lipstick, tries on a series of dresses and attitudes, stares and smokes and cries, makes her opulent body look puffy and hunched, slobbers over food, changes her clothes, cleans up, makes a phone call, and addresses the camera smiling the smile of Mrs. Bloom's yes. The many ways lead to the deeper terrain of a woman alone; the implications of a woman as actor or actor as woman in the intimate setting of her dressing room are buoyed by the fluent camerawork, confident legato editing, and masking and unmasking of Ammelrooy. Are the masks roles or alter egos and does it matter?

Rationalism is given a more conventional drubbing in Fons Rademakers's psychological thriller, *The Spitting Image* (1963), dreamily photographed by Raoul Coutard with the muted shadings he'd introduced in *Breathless* and *Jules and Jim*. Why it was not distributed here at the time of its release, when it might have brought some New Wave glory to Dutch films, is a mystery; the "NetherLanders" catalogue alludes to a controversy over the subject matter and a disinclination on the part of its sponsor, Heineken, to have it widely shown. It's a doppelganger story set during the war. A timid young merchant, the cuckolded Ducker, observes the descent of a parachutist named Dorbeck in the dead of night. A fearless member of the resistance, Dorbeck is Ducker's spitting image, except that his hair is black instead of blond. He enlists the aid of Ducker, who himself becomes a resourceful assassin and impulsive lover. After the Liberation, Ducker is arrested as a traitor: he is astonished to learn that his actions caused more damage to the resistance than the Nazis, and he is unable to prove Dorbeck ever existed.

The film's intrigue is magnified by its divergence from the genre's familiar gimmicks: The evil twin drives the protagonist to his doom, but as there is no need for one to impersonate the other, the resemblance is fortuitous. Did Dorbeck exist? In the series catalogue, Hans Beerekamp argues that Rademakers (unlike W. F. Hermans in the original novel) resolved the question in an epilogue that shows Dorbeck and Ducker's girlfriend years later on a beach, she telling him she knew someone who looked like him during the war. I see no reason to read that epilogue as anything more concrete than the final illusion of the dying Ducker, a scene that confirms his darkest fears about his manhood and recapitulates the film's motifs of sexual confusion—the hairlessness of Ducker/Dorbeck's chest, Ducker's belief that his lover loves only the Dorbeck in him, Dorbeck stealing Ducker's clothes and forcing him to parade around Holland in a dress. Whether or not Dorbeck is real, the story has the logical consistency of paranoia, which may help explain why it caused a stir in Holland in 1963. *The Spitting Image* is Walter Mitty's version of the resistance, the fantasy of a desperate soul dislocated by war, driven toward an irresponsible heroism. Lex Schoorel, with his baby face, cheerless eyes, and dimpled chin, is memorable as the driven Ducker and the Machiavellian Dorbeck. The movie is paced to keep you guessing and loiters in the mind like a nightmare—it is a lost classic.

The official lost classic of the series is Max Ophuls's *Comedy of Money* (1936), a characteristically lyrical but unusually mordant parable about *das kapital*. A costly and heralded film in its day, it has all but disappeared from accounts of Ophuls's career, which at that time was centered in France except for isolated forays into Italy and Holland. Not surprisingly, as a tourist, Ophuls set out to show the landscape, and his exteriors of the canals provide charming counterpoint to the fantastic sets meant to depict the fearsome International Finance Institution. A meek bank clerk loses a great sum of money and is disgraced; while he contemplates suicide, the shady IFI, which assumes he's stolen the money and can save the corporation from ruin, makes him director. Much of the comedy is whimsical, but the finale is inspired: a Brechtian explanation in which youth saves the day and the clerk's jail sentence is reduced, through the magic of film editing, to a matter of seconds. As a trial run for Ophuls's mature work, *Comedy of Money* is an irresistible text, complete with a singing ringmaster to explain everything and elaborate tracking shots that are sometimes less poetic than audacious, including a delirious 360-degree whirl around the director's office. Herman Bouber as the clerk, Rini Otte as his daughter, and Cor Ruys as the monocle-eyed capitalist you love to hate are splendid; the officious bank clerk who shares the hero's office could be Sig Ruman's evil twin.

The series' one acknowledged classic is Joris Ivens's 1931 hymn to the workforce, *Philips Radio*, commissioned by the Philips company and also known as *Industrial Symphony*. Nearly 60 years later, it remains a remarkable exercise in montage. The static camera peers from odd angles in tribute to assembly line efficiency, stressing the glorification rather than the dehumanization of organized—though not necessarily unionized—labor. From the glassblowers to the shippers, everyone at Philips is exalted, and the free-floating radio speakers at the end are a perky addendum. No less impressive is a little-known Ivens masterpiece from 1963, *A Valparaiso*, set in a part of Chile where there are "42 hills, 42 villages." Chris Marker's eloquent text and Georges Strouve's sun-drenched photography —black and white but for a red-tinted insert on the area's piratical past (including Uncle Sam driving a wedge through Panama)—are splendid, and Ivens's generosity to his subjects, whose lives are dictated by endless climbs and whose racehorses end up in Buffalo Bill's butcher shop, is exemplary and disturbing.

A Valparaiso contrasts interestingly with Johan van der Keuken's feature-length documentary on Kerala, India, *The Eye Above the Well* (1988), exquisitely shot by the director in color as lavish as fresh dyes, and at a tempo that dawdles around the countryside and switches to fast montage in the city. Although most of the episodes through which van der Keuken realizes Kerala are evocative, he weighs down the film with a portentous anecdote about man's desperation to suck the last drop of honey from a desperate life. In truth, the Keralans seem neither desperate nor unduly concerned about the future. The best passages show various gurus instilling traditions in young people—notably a dancing class for young girls who are instructed to "sway like an elephant, move like water." In the country, van der Keuken follows the rounds of a polite loan shark who is hated and feared and invariably asks, "Shall I go?" as he leaves. The absence of narration is typical of the current vogue in documentaries, and though it isn't missed much in van der Keuken's film, Ivens's *A Valparaiso* shows how a fiercely committed narration can swell a movie's temperature.

Mention should be made of *A Strange Love Affair* (1985), the third feature by the experimental gay filmmaker Erik de Kuyper and his first in collaboration with Paul Verstraeten, who seems to have brought a conventional veneer to de Kuyper's work. A film professor has an affair with a male bisexual student and travels with him to his hometown, where he learns that the boy's father was his lover 16 years earlier. The professor and the father leave together, abandoning the boy. This is set against a steady discourse about love as found in movies, particularly *Johnny Guitar* (the controlling metaphor for the entire story), *Now, Voyager*, and *Senso*. On the plus side, the score is an amusing combination of Korngold and opera (the professor used to be an opera critic); the black-and-white photography by the legendary Henri Alekan (who did *Beauty and the Beast* with Cocteau four decades earlier) is ravishing. On the down side, the English-language acting is so amateurish that you never trust the actors to convey appropriate emotions, or believe that anyone loves anyone else, or care. In the end, the father leaves the prof, the boy pleads for the prof's love and is rejected, and the father does or does not return to the prof—you choose. The movie is framed by the same scene played first without, and later with, a reunion. Which, I suppose, proves that even marginalized Dutch filmmakers cannot get away from that illusion/reality thing.

[*Village Voice*, 16 January 1990]

33 ❖ Still Curious
(I Am Curious)

When Philip Roth's *Portnoy's Complaint* appeared in 1969, sending the intelligentsia into exegetical panic over masturbation and self-loathing, Roth remarked that his book was at present an event, but in time would be a novel. It did not take long; the author of the far more subversive *Sabbath's Theater* is or ought to be on track for the Nobel. Yet it has taken 35 years for the other cultural-sexual sensation of 1969 (one that originated in Sweden two years earlier) to achieve even the possibility of reassessment. Perhaps no film in cinema history sparked as much critical and popular mayhem as Vilgot Sjoman's *I Am Curious (Yellow)*, only to be consigned to nearly instantaneous oblivion.

After its initial, highly lucrative, court-delayed release, the 1967 film was rarely screened, and the video revolution passed it by. The only available prints were washed out, with frequently unreadable and censored pale-white subtitles. The title alone retained a lasting fame, often parodied by headline writers. Hardly anyone, including reviewers, bothered to see its companion piece, *I Am Curious (Blue)* during its momentary stateside appearance. *Blue* lacked the publicity bonanza of bluenose interference. *Yellow* had been seized by U.S. Customs, guaranteeing not only a trial (could a film widely admired in Europe bring about moral collapse in the United States?), but also enthusiastic highbrow support and palpitating pietistic outrage. Thus Norman Mailer proclaimed *Yellow* "one of the most important pictures I have ever seen in my life," while Rex Reed called it "vile and disgusting," "a dirty movie," "crud," and "as good for you as drinking furniture polish." He derided Sjoman as "a very sick Swede with an overwhelming ego and a fondness for photographing pubic hair."

Well, which do you think sold more tickets—Mailer's endorsement or the remark about pubic hair? When the crowds actually saw the picture, however, they felt cheated; pubic hair was in short supply, the sex was unerotic, and the running time mostly given over to a droll, Brechtian-Pirandellian, mock-verité exploration of the chasm between the political and the personal. Not that it wasn't shocking in its day. I was 21 when I saw it with my father, who took it in stride until that notorious moment when Lena kisses her lover's flaccid penis, at which point he observed with dismayed awe, "They used to arrest you if you had something like that in your home." (In some states, they arrested you for doing it in your home, but that's another story.) Since male genitals are still banned from Hollywood movies, you can imagine the anxiety raised by actor Borje Ahlstedt's member, the only appendage of its kind seen on America's big screens as of 1969.

Yet within a year or two, suburban theaters routinely programmed nudity-filled potboilers about nurses and stewardesses, soon to be followed by *Deep Throat*. Never again would audiences have to put up with socially redeeming values in the pursuit of pornography. *Yellow* triggered the sea change that resulted, ironically, in the subsequent indifference toward *Blue*. It altered the American moviegoing experience, pointing the way to a postcode cinema.

In that sense, it served as a fitting finale for a decade that began with *Psycho*, which opened the portals to slasher violence while crossing a new frontier of intimacy—the opening shot of half-dressed Janet Leigh at a seedy midday tryst, the flushing toilet, the voyeurism. Thanks to Hitchcock, movie theaters were no longer safe or, for that matter, informal; by insisting that audiences not be allowed entry once the picture started, he ended the walk-in-any-time habits of a generation. *Psycho* was the first Hollywood film in decades that parents forbade their children to see. If Dashiell Hammett "took murder out of the Venetian vase and dropped it into the alley" (as Raymond Chandler observed), Hitchcock relocated horror from Transylvania to the mind of mother's little helper. The major taboo he left in place concerned casual sex and nudity. Hitchcock later told Truffaut that he wished he had had Leigh play her first scene topless—as if he could have gotten away with it. After *Yellow*, he could and did, removing Barbara Leigh-Hunt's bra (or rather that of her body double) in 1972s *Frenzy*.

Yellow had changed everything. If its distributors were the first to bring nudity and coupling to middle America, they were the last to get away with charging premium prices. Female nudity and the occasional male rear end became so much a custom of modern cinema that it is difficult to name more than a handful of American actresses who achieved stardom in the '70s without undressing for the camera. But *Yellow*'s influence was not exclusively sexual. In his use of documentary techniques, hand-held cameras, and the interpolated footage of "real" events—involving Martin Luther King Jr., Soviet poet Yevgeny Yevtushenko, Swedish politician Olof Palme, and nameless citizens—Sjoman, a protégé of Ingmar Bergman (he assisted him on *Winter Light* and acted in *Shame*), let loose a welter of films that blurred reality, surreality, and unreality. Haskell Wexler's *Medium Cool*, which also opened in 1969, incorporated footage of the 1968 Chicago riots, a blending that John Simon noted "does not jell so smoothly as in *I Am Curious*." In Belgrade, Dusan Makavejev, who had begun directing two years after Sjoman first fell afoul of Swedish censors with *491* (1964), worked along similar lines. Only after *Yellow* did he examine liberated (explicit) sexuality as a basis for politics in *WR: Mysteries of the Organism* (1971).

Influence aside, *Yellow* and *Blue*—named for the colors of the Swedish flag, and mostly filmed together (a few scenes in *Blue* postdate completion of *Yellow*)—merit reconsideration. To paraphrase Roth, they are now merely movies, and as such hold particular interest for what they say about the 1960s. Along with Antonioni's much-reviled *Zabriskie Point* and Peter Watkins's suppressed *Punishment Park*, they offer a more honest and re-cognizable depiction of that era than the glossily sentimentalized *Alice's Restaurant* or the indulgently romanticized *Easy Rider*. The protagonist's curiosity is exercised in questions that young people asked in major cities throughout the world in the mid-'60s—questions that revealed passive indifference on the part of their elders; questions that fanned anger, dis-satisfaction, and rage; questions that activated short-term political move-ments and long-term sexual insurrections regarding gender, power, education.

Much of *I Am Curious*'s strength and charm derive from Lena Ny-man's brave performance. Nyman is now known to American film audi-ences, if at all, for her poignant performance as Liv Ullman's debilitated sister in Bergman's *Autumn Sonata* (1978)—a role in which Sjoman's heroine is virtually unrecognizable. Her Lena was so convincing that "fan mail," as sampled in *Blue*, consisted of death threats and insults. By engag-ing in the faux-sex of *I Am Curious*, Nyman had crossed a line, and was perceived not as an actress but as a "whore" (a dilemma familiar to Philip Roth's admirers). Yet her Lena is funny, touching, and genuine, never more vulnerable than in the couplings she engages in or—as with *Blue*'s remarkably non-neurotic lesbian episode—witnesses.

The press was hardly gallant. "She seems to me porky and stolid and only sulkily interesting from time to time," wrote Stanley Kauffmann. Yet her ordinariness is clearly the point; Lena is no movie goddess, not a suit-able role for Catherine Deneuve or Faye Dunaway. She is the girl we all remember from college: sincere, self-absorbed, naïve, secretive, bold, and confused. Her sex scenes have not dated because they lacked self-consciousness in the first place. Neither she nor Sjoman are out to seduce the viewer. Simon, who along with Kauffmann and Mailer, testified on the film's behalf, noted that the sex is never erotic because Lena and Borje are not "particularly attractive," but recognized that Lena's "liveliness is almost as good as loveliness." He also observed that the potential for eroticism is undermined by the profusion of "humorous or unglamorous details." Those details heighten a reality that exists in opposition to Lena's imagined interviews with famous persons, not to mention her fantasy of performing a Lorena Bobbitt on her faithless lover.

With her short round body and pendulous breasts, Lena Nyman the character is a young woman whose looks are yet another obstacle (she faces many) to happiness, one that Lena Nyman the actress was willing to amplify by playing some of the nude scenes comically. Sjoman, who appears as a semblance of himself as Lena's director and soon-to-be-cashiered lover, bullies her about her weight, an issue that helps set up the marvelous episode at the health retreat—a harbinger of New Age charlatanism. The entire cast is convincing. Sjoman spares himself little as he grows increasingly crabby and dictatorial; Ahlstedt is unctuous and violent as Lena's lover and imperious as the actor playing Lena's lover (and stealing her from Sjoman); Bim Warne, Gunnel Brostrum, and Sonja Lindgren represent women Lena encounters during *Blue*, which, unlike *Yellow*, is structured as an odyssey. Most haunting is Peter Lindgren as Lena's hapless father, Rune, who retreated from the Spanish Civil War, to his and Lena's shame. In 1968, when *Blue* debuted, Scandinavian audiences recognized the woman Lena greets in the last scene as Gudrun Ostbe, the actress Sjoman says he has hired to portray Lena's absentee mother—an important point, lost to American audiences then and today.

Sjoman himself was lost to American audiences, his subsequent films never distributed here; now 78 (he was born in 1924), he is at work on a novel. During his 15 minutes in the crosshairs of international furor, he explained his intertwining films as studies of violence, as attempts to depict candid sexuality. Yet today's audiences are bound to view his work differently. Lena's sexual adventures are depicted with refreshing, often droll bluntness, but the paradoxical structure now seems far more significant than it did when *Yellow* was on trial. *I Am Curious* belongs to the genre of films about filming—it's a benign answer to Michael Powell's *Peeping Tom* and makes its own circuitous claims. Vilgot Sjoman and crew follow Lena around Stockholm as she asks people about politics. Yet whenever the story reaches dramatic pitch, he interrupts with a direction, usually captious, reminding us that his performers perform for him. But who is filming Vilgot? And who is filming Lena and Borje when they go off together, leaving Vilgot to mope in frustration?

The two films begin and end with self-advertisements as well as clichéd slogans, most of them tacked on walls by Lena, all of which suggests a filmmaker's lark. Yet the narrative also suggests a core of dread; *Yellow* begins with Lena and Vilgot in an elevator and ends with Lena and Borje in an elevator. The director—ostensibly in charge—directs himself out of the picture and out of Lena's life. His portrait of honest sexuality is played in a setting of distrust: Every sexual relationship we see involves betrayal. Nowhere is the frustration experienced by the principals more acute than in *Yellow*'s startling climax—a scene that was largely ignored in 1969. When Lena sees that her room has been violated, she tears it apart with the fury of Charles Foster Kane. Then, like a picador, she thrusts knives into the eyes of the despised Franco, whose poster dominates her bedroom. Like the dead eye on the bathroom floor in *Psycho*, the blinded Franco incarnates an assault on vision in a film that explores the kind of curiosity that looks but doesn't see—a failing that may explain its total neglect for more than three decades.

[*I Am Curious*, Criterion Collection, November 2002]

34 ❖ *Broken Promises* (The Honeymoon Killers)

Rarely has schizophrenia been closer to the surface of American cinema than in the transitional period of 1969–71. Hollywood had just abandoned its censorship code after nearly 35 years, and the behemoth studios were heaving and rattling into oblivion or an afterlife of distribution and free-agentry. Tectonic cultural shifts atomized the audience as illustrious directors faltered, stars faded, and producers hustled t&a for art's sake. The public was subjected to a diet of historical pageants, John Wayne, and elephantine musicals, occasionally spiced with thumbsuckers about wayward youth, corrupt cops, bygone wars as substitutes for the one in progress, and a hallucinogenic future ruled by monoliths or apes. From the audience's perspective, choosing a movie was like joining a political party: *Paint Your Wagon* or *The Wild Bunch*, *Love Story* or *Midnight Cowboy*, *The Green Berets* or *Five Easy Pieces*?

At the same time, a bonanza of eccentric independent films—photographed, significantly, in the soon-to-be-obsolete shadowplay of black and white—boldly rivaled Europe, Asia, and Mexico in the dominions of realism, violence, horror, and sex. Most successful was John Cassavetes's *Faces*, a triumph of the autonomous glamor-free cinema. Less respectable but more influential were George Romero's *The Night of the Living Dead*, which resuscitated an anemic genre; John Waters's *Multiple Maniacs*, made to "glorify carnage and mayhem for laughs"; Melvin Van Peeples's *Sweet Sweetback's Baad Asssss Song*, the launch pad for blaxploitation; and, most mysteriously and perhaps most durably, Leonard Kastle's *The Honeymoon Killers*—an anti-*Bonnie and Clyde* true crime tabloid shocker. Here you will find no glitz, sex appeal, fiddle music, or Aesopian moral about the dehumanization of violence. Instead, we have a display of irate humor and voyeuristic mischief as two sociopaths and their deluded victims live and die by the axiom: He (or she) who cons last cons best.

Based rather closely on the yearlong bilk-and-murder spree of Martha Beck and Raymond Fernandez, the Maggie and Jiggs of serial killers, this is one angry film, derisive of its characters and audience. It depicts a tawdry America floundering in subterfuge amid flag-waving songs and holidays. Consider the matchless grotesquerie of the first lonely hearts captive, Doris (Ann Harris), pitifully middle-aged and naked in her bath, bellowing "America" and waving her sponge with patriotic fervor—while the groom and his accomplice rifle her belongings. Doris, at least, is spared her life; the film spares her nothing else. Janet Fay (an unconventional characterization by the radio veteran Mary Jane Higby) succumbs to one of the longest and most grisly movie deaths this side of *Torn Curtain*. But by then, the film has already disposed of her humanity and mined for laughter her penny-pinching deceits and Jesus icons, defying the most saintly among us to forswear thoughts of homicide every time she chirps, "Innat cuuuute?"

Of course, Martha and Ray aren't among the most saintly. Yet in the seedy moral tableau of *The Honeymoon Killers*, we are encouraged to roll our eyes in solidarity with them—until, that is, Martha raises the hammer or, drawing on her nursing background, helpfully offers a tourniquet, by which time we (like Janet) are begging for a mercy that the filmmakers (like Martha and Ray) have no intention of providing.

Watching and re-watching *The Honeymoon Killers* (originally titled *Dear Martha*) is like boarding a roller coaster; it rouses and deflates you in the same way every time. You're not sure you really want to do it again, but who can resist the thrill of confronting one's own moral ambivalence? Compulsively diverting, it is a movie that taunts you for having a good time. But that's the way it is in this peculiar territory. *The Honeymoon Killers* is frequently placed in a lineage of films about criminal couples, from the romanticized *They Live by Night* to the overwrought *Natural Born Killers*.

But it has far closer ties to films about a particular finicky breed of serial killers who prey upon women in order to fleece them.

Filmmakers almost always treat these predators with humor, as though rich elderly women who search for love deserve a sorrier fate—the very argument Joseph Cotton, as the Merry Widow killer, makes in Hitchcock's often droll *Shadow of a Doubt*. While no one (except perhaps John Waters) could find giggles in say, the Boston strangler, the 20th-century Bluebeard, Landru, generates slapstick in Chaplin's *Monsieur Verdoux* and wry amusement in Chabrol's *Landru*. True to form, Kastle offers one-liners that Tony Lo Bianco's meticulously imagined Ray plays like a violin: grandly informing Martha that he could never live off a woman or complaining of a victim, "Christ almighty, I'm earning my four thousand tonight!" He makes a sonata of "I remind her of the late and lamented Mr. Fay when they were married. She doesn't seem to realize how long ago that must have been," and manages to get a laugh every time he says the magic words, "Valley Stream." The high-pitched mommy voice he uses to calm his besotted wives, however, is downright chilling.

Much of the humor is visual, notably Ray's pretend seduction of Martha's mom, his ass wriggling across the screen, or Martha—played by Shirley Stoler with a wily mixture of infinite hurt and infinite disdain—eating. There is lots of sex or near-sex, but the real eroticism occurs between Martha and a pretzel (she sighs with contentment), Martha and a box of chocolates (she is recumbent, as if battered by orgasms), Martha and a cookie (she snaps into it as a reward for getting Janet to admit she's got the dough). Other shots stay in the mind because they are terrifying, none more so than the sequence ending with the murder of Delphine Dowling (Kip McArdle) and her little girl, Rainelle (Mary Breen): the ruthlessly close focus on the mother's drugged eyes; the off-camera scream after Martha takes the daughter to the cellar; the camera panning back as Ray cringes at the ghastly sounds.

So who is Leonard Kastle and how did he come to make so accomplished a first and only feature? The idea began with TV producer Warren Steibel (*Firing Line*), who remembered the extensive newspaper coverage accorded the "lonely hearts killers." Martha and Ray had freely roamed the land from around February 1948 through February 1949, and ended up in Sing Sing's electric chair in 1951. He asked Kastle to research the story and devise a treatment. Neither man had ever worked in film. Kastle, a 39-year-old composer known for his opera about the Mormons, *Deseret*, which had debuted on NBC in 1961, later wrote *Pariah*, an opera about the sinking of the whale ship *Essex*. Hiring Stoler and Lo Bianco was, obviously, a masterstroke, and so, one would have thought, was their initial choice to direct: a young, eager Martin Scorsese. Yet Kastle and Steibel decided that Scorsese was wasting time and money on irrelevant shots, and in the stormy environment that developed, he was dismissed after 10 days.

Shirley Stoler has said that Scorsese filmed the two set-ups for the opening hospital scene, something Kastle has disputed. Whoever shot them, it is interesting to note how utterly characteristic they are of Scorsese's mature style. Each is a long master without inserts, the first a receding pan that picks up Martha with a slight zoom and follows her toward the room of an unexplained explosion, the second a mobile survey of the room, as Martha dresses down the staff. That shot ends with a splendid cut, presumably by Kastle—who soon took command of the film—to Martha's foot as she kicks a child's wagon from her path. No one questions Scorsese's participation in the lakeshore scene in which Stoler nearly drowns; it marked the start of the shoot and Stoler insisted that the fear she displayed was genuine.

Kastle was greatly aided by cameraman Oliver Wood, who helped him to realize his ideas and figured out how to work with available light; after a long hiatus, Wood went on to photograph several big-budget Hollywood potboilers. One of the most widely noted of the visual conceits they devised resulted from Kastle's idea for surprise blackouts as Martha and Ray turn off the lights in their respective rooms. Kastle credits Wood for the film's semi-newsreel look. Between the naturalistic gray light and the director's claustrophobic interiors, the picture resembles the approach of late-'60s documentaries such as the Maysles and Charlotte Zwerin's *Salesman* and Frederick Wiseman's *Titicut Follies*. The uneven echoey sound adds to the effect, although the bad dubbing in a few scenes detracts from it.

That a filmmaker with no previous experience could bring all the pieces together qualifies as a minor miracle. Yet everything gels, from the performances to the realistically bare set design to a score made up entirely of excerpts from Mahler (the First, Fifth, Sixth, and Ninth Symphonies) that regularly punctuate the film with gloomy alarums. At the heart of a work that includes Antonioni and Truffaut among its admirers is Kastle's clever script. The film is a convincing, inventive, economically contrived (note the montage of letters that bring Martha and Ray together) telling of a story that, in most respects, happened just this way. It deviates from the facts in eliminating Martha's children, whom she abandoned to go off with Ray, and the police, who caught the couple after a neighbor of the Dowlings tipped them off. Kastle preferred a more

classical, symmetrical ending with the couple doing what comes naturally
—trying one last con, this time on each other. *The Honeymoon Killers*
doesn't give a damn about crime and punishment. It has its sights on loving and lying. Its cri de coeur is provoked when insanely jealous Martha
finds Ray canoodling with a mark and bawls, "You promised!"

[*The Honeymoon Killers*, Criterion Collection, 2003]

35 ❖ Calm, Cool, and Now Collected (Steve McQueen)

Steve McQueen exemplified film acting as a force of will. Born in 1930,
a product of reform school who drifted through the navy, oil fields, and
carnivals, he may have lived the life Brando played, but he came of age
before Brando's generation rewrote the book on cinematic stature. He usually avoided elaborate makeups, palpable anxiety, and verbal suppleness,
preferring a quiet, pent-up steadfastness that crossed Bogart's wariness
with Mitchum's reticence. A self-conscious specialist in screen-walking,
screen-posing, and screen-tumbling, he bet everything on presence, and
won the bet. Robert Mitchum is said to have described McQueen's acting as boring, perhaps sensing a poacher in his own backyard. They have
in common animal naturalness, often characterized as cool. In their best
roles, they act as though acting were beneath them.

McQueen also has a steely boyishness. Not the kind that attracts
coddling of any kind—he is rarely effective with or even interested in
women—but instead finds release in toys: motorbikes, fast cars, playing
cards, guns, games, hats, horses, objects that focus his attention without
distracting from his intense narcissism. His authority is remarkable. He
wore his sandy hair in the same, short, artfully artless style in films set
in every decade from the 1930s through the 1970s, as well as in the
antiseptic Old West, and he rarely modulated his voice, preferring
Garboesque close-ups to speeches of any length. But he is almost always
credible, and his line readings are frequently canny.

His career, which barely exceeded two decades, began and ended as
a bounty hunter. In 1958, after three years of minor parts on television
and in movies, he landed the lead in *The Blob*, a bargain-basement science-
fiction film about teenagers battling alien gloop, and a television western, *Wanted: Dead or Alive*. This was a period in which the faltering
studios were desperate for new stars, and McQueen was one of three—

James Garner and Clint Eastwood were the others—launched by small-screen cowboy shows, of which his was the most bizarre.

Outfitted with a ludicrous sawed-off carbine that seems to clip onto his holster (he never actually raises his elbow to draw it), McQueen plays Josh Randall, a bounty hunter with a heart of mush—he tithes rewards to the unfortunate, including survivors of people he inadvertently gets killed. A sampling of the first season's 36 episodes (the show ran three seasons) proves that his bungling was more chronic than occasional, as was his propensity for being knocked unconscious. Restored to a gleaming black-and-white, the series is fast, violent, trite, pious, and clever enough to open with a bang but not thoughtful enough to avoid gaping wounds of illogic. The casts mostly combine aging movie actors with young comers, from George Macready and Victor Jory to James Coburn and Charles Bronson (one episode involves Richard Arlen, Sidney Blackmer, Robert Strauss, and Daryl Hickman). The opening credit closes with a freeze-frame of McQueen looking adenoidal. His immaculately pressed saddle tramp is never real, but always watchable.

John Sturges put him on the Hollywood track with a small role—little more than a cameo brawl—in *Never So Few* (1959), an affront to veterans, non-veterans, and filmgoers of every stripe, which Warner Bros. has included in the mostly pleasing *The Essential Steve McQueen Collection*. Frank Sinatra, who enters with a goatee to match the wave in his toupee (when he sits down with Brian Donlevy, they look like delegates at a wigmakers' convention), romances Gina Lollobrigida into a stupor when he isn't busy with mercy killing and massacres on the China-Burma front. For this, he is threatened with hanging, but receives congratulations instead.

Sturges saw that McQueen's insouciance eclipsed the wattage around him and gave him a major role in the immensely popular *The Magnificent Seven*, which along with their subsequent collaboration, *The Great Escape*, established his Hollywood bona fides. Both films (available on MGM DVDs) are very much of their day and hardly representative of the actor's best work. In the first, he indulged in shameless scene-stealing that almost brought him to blows with Yul Brynner; it may have seemed nervy then, but now his constant playing with his hat looks neurotic. His motorcycle fence-leap in *The Great Escape* continues to spark the dreams of adolescent boys, but the picture, with its inanely cheerful score and blushing rectitude in the face of Nazi violence is, at best, distastefully entertaining.

Amid several unmemorable attempts at comedy, romance, and period melodrama, McQueen seemed taller, leaner, and altogether more prepossessing in Norman Jewison's *The Cincinnati Kid* (1965, included in the

Warner Bros. set), a knock-off of *The Hustler* with poker replacing pool. If the latter was about character, the former is about reading character, an ideal metaphor for acting, in this case a duel of old and young Hollywood. McQueen challenges the matchless Edward G. Robinson, who is introduced in the finest Mephistophelean entrance (emerging from the smoke of a train) since he entered knees-up in steam in *Key Largo*. Robinson wins all around, but McQueen holds his own and their mutual appraisals make up for the schematic character-is-fate plot, as does an exceptional supporting cast and close-ups of a card shark's hands (sitting in for Karl Malden and Joan Blondell), which mystify even in slow motion. (Jewison's commentary track is informative, except when he says, twice, that jazz was born at Preservation Hall, which opened in 1961.)

The Warner Bros. box includes three other worthy films. The most durable is probably Peter Yates's *Bullitt* (1968), which makes shrewder use of its San Francisco locale than *The Cincinnati Kid* does of New Orleans. Remembered for its vertiginous car chase, it captures the cynicism of the day and ultimately regenerated the police drama as the new western: A lone cop battles official lassitude and creeping corruption. The picture doesn't make much sense. In addition to an eye-popping continuity flub (a hospital search in the middle of the night moves outdoors where the sun is shining), it has professional hit men who not only fail to make certain that their mark is dead but wait around for the ambulance in case he pulls through; they generate the big car chase for no particular reason. It doesn't matter though, because this is star-driven stuff and McQueen is thoroughly in charge. Robert Vaughan is perfect as a smarmy D.A. while Jacqueline Bisset is strictly decorative, obliged to say lines like, "What will happen to us in time?" No wonder Steve looks fed-up.

The Getaway (1972) is second-draw Sam Peckinpah, mired, after an excellent credit sequence, in dawdling scenes between McQueen and the pitiful Ali MacGraw, who is truly impenetrable—by comparison McQueen looks like a fount of emotion. When he finally starts knocking her around, you can't be certain if it's his character or the actor, trying to wake her up. Once the chase kicks in, however, the director begins to hit on all cylinders, and the film has some of the best set-pieces he ever shot, especially those involving a con man in a train station (the editing is ingenious), a sadistic subplot centering on Al Lettieri, an actor who exudes pure evil (which, of course, makes you wonder why no one in the film can see it), and a slam-bang shoot-out. The last is a feel-good massacre that leads to a sentimental ending in which the good thieves and killers get away from the bad ones, not to mention the law. A "virtual" commentary track has McQueen mumbling (small wonder he found dialogue a chore) about the virtues of killing someone for a reason.

If the finale of *The Getaway* disinfects Jim Thompson's source novel, Franklin J. Schaffner's *Papillon* (1973), billed as "The Greatest Adventure of Escape," ignores the escape that made the source memoir an international sensation. The film focuses instead on prison conditions on French Guyana's Devil's Island and the camaraderie between McQueen's Papillon and Dustin Hoffman's counterfeiter Louis Dega. Hoffman's broken smile, cracking voice, and inch-thick glasses scream ACTOR, and not ineffectively, yet McQueen's stillness controls the mise-en-scène. Though not his best film (slow-mo falls and an ambiguous paradise don't help), this may be his most intricate performance, especially during a 30-minute episode in solitary, when he does a Renfield bit ("I eat bugs!") and still retains unflinching dignity. It should have opened him up; instead (not unlike Brando's *Last Tango in Paris*) it shut him down, leading to the consummate payday of *The Towering Inferno* and a long retreat, interrupted only by a tiresome hirsute adaptation of Ibsen and two bounty hunter films—the Warner box includes the incompetent botch, *Tom Horn*, which substitutes postcard vistas for plot and action—that document indifference and illness in the months before he died, in 1980 at 50.

A livelier McQueen, game for anything, is captured in the neglected Mark Rydell version of *The Reivers* (1969, from Paramount), an often funny, engrossing film that ultimately fails because it fails Faulkner, despite reasonably faithful adherence to the plot. The novel takes great pains to establish 11-year-old Lucius as leader and instigator of much of the action, and lacking in the presumed innocence of boyhood. So the filmmakers Opie-fy him and belabor his innocence. The film is additionally injured by the narration read by Burgess Meredith, licking his chops and turning each line into porridge, and an atrocious John Williams score that telegraphs every emotion. McQueen's presence demands an increased role for and more syrupy interpretation of Boon Hogganbeck, which he handles well enough, notwithstanding a few too many "dumb" looks—pursed lips and wide eyes, as though he could not count to three backward. But Rupert Crosse is an unforgettable Ned, cleaned up yet vital, witting, and sure, and McQueen gives him leave to walk away with the picture (as Ned does the novel). There are also memorable appearances by Will Geer, Juano Hernandez, and Dub Taylor, expert set design, and excellent staging of the mudhole incident. *The Reivers* isn't a true McQueen picture, but one measure of his talent is that he knew it and acted accordingly.

[*The New York Sun*, 2 August 2005]

36 ❖ Rock Heads
(Martin Scorsese)

Vladimir Nabokov attributed his "initial shiver of inspiration" for *Lolita* to the newspaper account of an ape, who, when induced to make a charcoal drawing, sketched the bars of its cage. Humbert's narration paints in minute detail the mental confinement of his prison, and Nabokov's ventriloquial genius is such that he obliges us to acknowledge that even monsters have their reasons. In his middle-period gangster films, *Goodfellas* and *Casino*, Martin Scorsese employed a first-person narration, and the unexpected result was that it launched us headlong into the story yet distanced us from the speakers. It is not hard to see why: If Jimmy Doyle, of *New York, New York,* or Jake La Motta, of *Raging Bull,* spoke to us as they do to other individuals in those movies, we would like them even less than we do.

How we feel about Scorsese's heroes governs our experiences of his films, and I think the more we live with his best work the better we understand and accept all but the most criminally psychotic of them. His characters have no choice; they are who they are, like Humbert, and behavioral modification is never really an option. La Motta begins and ends with the mantra "I'm the boss," having tried out interim mantras including "dummy dummy dummy" and "I'm not an animal." Doyle admiringly observes of Liza Minnelli's Francine, "You haven't changed," but the warranty of their undoing is that neither has he. Scorsese's compassion for lost souls is central to his achievement.

The diverse worlds he creates are so complete in every detail that each one exists only as a specific setting for the people it enfolds. His New York is never the same place twice: It is distinctly different in *Mean Streets, Taxi Driver, New York, New York, Raging Bull, The King of Comedy, After Hours,* and *Goodfellas,* not to mention his 19th-century evocations (*The Age of Innocence, Gangs of New York*), as if reflecting discrete geographies of the mind in accordance with the exclusive cages of the protagonists. Though always confined and feverish, the city is remade in look, feeling, and tempo—not true of other New York filmmakers, like Sidney Lumet or Woody Allen. But, then, their characters are obsessed with moral choices and not with obsession itself. They favor Hamlet, Brutus, and Moses. Scorsese is more intrigued by Othello, Macbeth, and Jesus.

In *Raging Bull,* the mobster Tommy Como complains of Jake, "This man's got a head of rock." One could argue that most Scorsese heroes are rock heads; they have no idea of who they are or how they strike others. Blinded by talent, desire, and fury, they resist social engineering. The ideal ornament of isolation is a mirror, the window of nothingness, and Scorsese's alter egos often examine their own reflections in lieu of seeing outward or inward: Travis Bickle, in *Taxi Driver*, daring, "I'm the only one here"; Francine gazing, doe-eyed, a cipher even to herself; Jake reciting "I coulda been a contender" in a monotone to his bloated self.

Jimmy Doyle's persistent obnoxiousness suggests an illness. In the bravura 20-minute opening scene of *New York, New York*, Francine has no doubts about keeping him at bay until she sees an old friend, an ordinary schmo, and suddenly Jimmy's kinetic unpredictability seems appealing. Scorsese knows the feeling: Johnny Boy, in *Mean Streets*, can no more master civil behavior than fly; Rupert Pupkin is as much a prisoner of his *King of Comedy* fantasies as he is of his bad suits and haircut; La Motta wants to catch Vicki being unfaithful, if only to justify his paranoia; Bill the Butcher, in *Gangs of New York*, is as hard-wired to his fate as Jesus is in *The Last Temptation of Christ*, or Howard Hughes, with his urine-filled milk bottles, is in *The Aviator*. Their abilities, profound or meager, are inseparable from their fixations. They can be killed, but not easily broken.

MGM has released an odd quartet of early Scorsese films, separately and in a carton called *The Martin Scorsese Film Collection*. *Boxcar Bertha* (1972) is strictly an apprenticeship work turned out for the Roger Corman factory—a Depression Era crime-and-fiddles exercise with requisite nudity from the always-game Barbara Hershey and an unfortunate crucifixion climax. Based on a hoax-memoir (no, there never was a Boxcar Bertha), it smacks of prodigal self-consciousness, complete with collegiate in-jokes and a showy overhead shot. Yet it is mildly entertaining, not least for a bit part by John Carradine as an evil tycoon named Sartoris.

Scorsese's two musicals, filmed simultaneously, are perfectly suited to DVD, because though you want to savor them, you do not necessarily want to watch them in one sitting. *The Last Waltz* (1978) documents and stylizes the 1976 leave-taking concert by The Band, playing in peak form by itself and in collusion with such guests as Bob Dylan, Paul Butterfield, Emmy Lou Harris, the Staple Singers, Eric Clapton, Joni Mitchell, Dr. John, and Muddy Waters—the elder statesman in the bunch and the only performer who acts out and articulates the lyric. Scorsese, looking rather Rasputinish, conducts intervening interviews ("What about women?") with producer and charismatic screen-hog Robbie Robertson and other members of The Band. Though hardly verité (Scorsese staged a few numbers after the fact), it remains one of the best musical documentaries ever made.

And *New York, New York* (1977), though doomed to neglect and misapprehension, remains one of the best MGM musicals and the last. A flop when first released in mutilated form (a key number, "Happy Endings," the film's rejoinder to *Singin' in the Rain*'s "The Broadway Melody," was cut to kindling), it is either adored with scruples or despised with relish. Shot on a soundstage New York, marginally more realistic than the ones in *Guys and Dolls* or *The Bandwagon*, and set in 1945–55, Scorsese's picture is a fantasia employing state-of-the-art Hollywood décor, design, costume, and music. At the same time, it avoids the musical conventions of rehabilitated characters, pat endings, and maudlin adieus. In one of the films that inspired Scorsese, Michael Curtiz's *My Dream Is Yours* (1949), Doris Day realizes the man she loves is a heel and surrenders to the dreary conformist who loves her—the type from whom Scorsese rescues his heroine. Instead, the perpetually surprised Francine gets talented saxophonist Jimmy Doyle (dubbed by Georgie Auld, who also appears as a bandleader and consequently gets to audition himself). Jimmy marries Francine to own her; failing that, he abandons her after she gives birth to their son, using her hospital bed sheet to wipe his nose so as not to soil his handkerchief.

The film feels long—a few scenes are stretched beyond the point of peak effectiveness—but the talky energetic rhythms have an intoxicating humor that blunts the apparent mismatch of De Niro, who is always convincing, especially on the bandstand, and Minnelli, who regains her sparkle only after they part. Jimmy doesn't require a backstory; we know everything we need to from De Niro's posture, inflections, and broken smile (he has the V-shaped Satan smile Dashiell Hammett ascribed to Sam Spade). The neglect of Francine's private life, however, undermines the equation. How does she handle being a single mom? Does she have boyfriends? Parents? She does have a voice, we learn two-thirds into the film: Minnelli's rendition of "The World Goes Round," a Garland-worthy showpiece, is her finest moment on film, not excluding *Cabaret*. Scorsese's camera respectfully keeps still, merely pulling back a bit to give her air, and when she finishes she looks as if she had just experienced life-changing sex. The "Happy Ending" sequence, which recapitulates the plot, and the debut of the title song, previously fragmented in the score, sustain the energy. Perhaps she was asked to sing less well (too much vibrato, no swing) in her earlier numbers with Jimmy, to underscore the size of her accomplishment after he is out of her life.

Although the film looks and sounds fine, MGM's "Special Edition" of *New York, New York* is a letdown. It incorporates the same commentary as on the 1992 laser disc, but offers only a third of the laser's outtakes (which included Minnelli's impersonation of Jo Stafford) and a fraction of its hundreds of photographs; it omits press interviews with Scorsese and Minnelli and the illuminating shooting script. MGM should have made this disc a contender—as it did with the genuinely special "Special Edition" of *Raging Bull*. The black-and-white 1980 film is impeccably transferred and supported by more commentary and interviews than anyone but Scorsese's biographer will care to explore.

Raging Bull, a hothouse masterpiece in which every component defines its unique vision, almost qualifies as a subliminal musical. The Mascagni themes link an extraordinary assemblage of jazz and pop records wafting into scenes, as if from a passerby's radio. About 15 minutes into the picture, the story shifts from Jake's apartment—as a big band tune comes on the soundtrack—to a gym, where the band tune is completed by four punches, each a quarter-note *bam* calibrated to the tempo of the music. For all the attention to detail, Scorsese allowed himself and us a privileged moment toward the end, when De Niro accidentally upsets some dishes and Cathy Moriarty, as Vicki, starts to laugh and turns her head; De Niro saves the take with an ad-lib and she instantly resumes character. Her millisecond of unfeigned reaction adds another level to the intersection between cinema and reality in a film that is emotionally balanced between observation and reproach.

Raging Bull finds boxing barbaric and details a homophobic undercurrent that carries over from the ring to the vicious treatment of women. In a neighborhood where the worst imprecations are insults to manhood, Jake can't see the connection between his worry about having "girl's hands," his sexual denial ("I got to fight Robinson," he tells a rejected Vicki, "I can't fool around"), his outrage when Vicki describes another fighter as good-looking, his destruction of his own body, and prolonged kissing and hugging with his brother. Scorsese sees everything, and forgives him his blindness. He may even love him for it.

[*The New York Sun*, 15 March 2005]

37 ❖ *Real Reality TV* (The UP Series)

On the one occasion I mustered the courage and curiosity to attend a high school reunion, I had the impression (never experienced when looking in the mirror) that my classmates had retained their childhood faces, and that all the changes wrought by excessive or diminished hair, makeup,

and furrows were masks, vainly disguising the impervious looks and personalities of those who had long ago played with, tormented, or ignored
me. Sartre was half-right: Hell is other people one knew in grade school.
Better to stay home and watch Michael Apted's *The UP Series*, a virtual
reunion for everyone but the 14 souls sucked into its endless vortex of
seven-year checkups.

Apted's serial documentary (in England, each installment is greeted as
a holiday) began in 1963, when the independent Granada Television
decided to confront the British class system. The producers of *World in
Action*, chose 14 seven-year-olds from the upper, lower, and middle
classes to suggest the rigid boundaries that would circumscribe their lives
and, by extension, the nation's. Today, Granada is well known for such
dramatic adaptations as *Brideshead Revisited*, *Prime Suspect*, and Jeremy
Brett's outstanding Sherlock Holmes, but in the early 1960s, its license was
limited mostly to working-class areas like Yorkshire and Liverpool,
which approved of its activist blue-collar politics. The 40-minute "Seven
Up" aired in 1964, with no thought of a sequel. It ends with the avun-
cular narrator describing the children at play (the poorer kids build a
house, he notes approvingly), followed by orchestral chords of a sort that
in movies usually signify an approaching shark.

The show was fascinating and grim. One of the rich kids reads the *Times*
because he owns shares in it and speaks with convoluted flourishes.
"And so do I think so," he interpolates by way of explaining why schools
should charge high tariffs, not unlike Miss Jellyby in *Bleak House*: "Very
well, so am I shocked too; so we are both shocked, and there's an end
of it!" Another, brought up on an immense but lonely Scottish estate,
has never met a colored person and doesn't care to, "thank you very
much." Their educations have been mapped out. By contrast, a boy in
a children's home hesitantly asks, "What's a university?" Others like him
have little ambition; they would like to become astronauts or, barring that,
coach drivers. These twain shall never meet.

And then something remarkable happened. Apted, a 22-year-old
assistant on the program, chose to revisit Granada's petrie dish seven years
later to make "7 Plus Seven," and every subsequent seven years for "21
Up," "28 Up," "35 Up," and "42 Up"—"49 Up" goes before the cameras
later this year. What happened is that the vagaries of life trumped the
political equation, not rubbing it out entirely, but reducing it—as art will—
to insignificance in the face of marriage, divorce, work, children, and death.
You may want to throttle Tony, the failed jockey-turned-taxi-driver,
when he says he has no interest in trade unions, since of all the participants he most needs to develop an interest. All he cares about is family,
he boasts—a sentimental avowal not lost on conservative party leaders

everywhere. But Tony's inner strength surprised even Apted (who thought he would end in jail), and he grows increasingly self-sufficient and sure, while two rich kids, including the self-styled reactionary John, leave the show in fits of self-importance.

By collecting all six programs in one DVD package, First Run provides an experience beyond that of any of the individual films, not only because so much is left out with each successive installment, but because as Apted (a prolific filmmaker whose pictures include *Agatha, Coal Miner's Daughter, Thunderheart, Me & Isaac Newton*) turns each stage into a transitional moment, it loses the urgency of the present one. The project thus approximates, as no fictional film could, the sequential vignettes of Virginia Woolf's *The Waves*. The amount of repetition can be numbing (poor Paul is forever invoked as the seven-year-old who fears marriage because his wife might force him to eat greens), but the characters are so strong and the quotidian details of their lives so inexorably normal—economics aside, they all shed tears over lost parents—one cannot help but analyze, identify with, worry over, critique, and admire them by turns.

The children had no say in participating in the first program, but as adults they are coddled, cajoled, and paid to reappear. As Apted makes clear in his commentary track to "42 Up" (the only DVD extra, but an essential one), they now function as equals with the director. At least one, the solicitor Andrew, insists on previewing his footage, and I can't help wonder how their influence shapes the films. Apted does not explain why he spends so much time on certain spouses while ignoring others (Lynn's is most conspicuous in his absence, given their successful marriage of 20-plus years); I assume he has little choice. He acknowledges mistakes in the original selection of children—only one "ethnic," the illegitimate child of a mixed couple; only four women; only two products of the middle-class; and, surprisingly, no gays, at least so far as we are told. For that matter, no felons, no celebrities, no early deaths.

Each segment has dramatic high-points—in "42 Up," the selfless Bruce, whose privileged background led him to an East End teaching post and educational work in Bangladesh, takes a wife (Apted was about to ask if he were gay), and Tony, who gets bit parts in movies, spills the beans about his infidelity (the wife never bats an eye). But the program's great fascination is in the way individuals bloom and fade at different points in their lives. Suzi, tossed into boarding school at seven, reeling from her parents' divorce at 14 (sitting on the grass, resenting every question, she doesn't notice her dog killing a rabbit just behind her), appears at 20 as a cynical, gaunt, defensive, chain-smoking dropout; seven years later, she has blossomed, the very picture of maternal rectitude. Andrew, an increasingly charming and thoughtful figure in prior segments, turns nervously cautious at 42. The nuclear physicist Nick, the only child in the Yorkshire farming community in which he was raised, reinvents himself at an American university. Neil, the most adorable and loquacious of seven-year-olds, turns taut as a bowstring at 14, and is homeless after that—shaking compulsively and fearing for his sanity. In "35 Up," he sees his future as a London beggar; seven years later, though still unemployed, he is twice elected to a political council and shows once again something of the glow that distinguished him at seven.

Apted lets down his project and audience when he fails to explain why someone leaves a particular segment, a failing compensated for in his commentary track. He explains that Symon, the introverted, unmotivated black child who became a contented father of five, disappeared from "35 Up" because of his shame over a divorce; Symon returns triumphantly at 42, newly married. No less intriguing is Peter, the apparent slacker whose last appearance, in "28 Up," presented him as a bitter, unfulfilled teacher. Apted discloses that Peter's mild rebuke, in that show, of the Thatcher government's withdrawal of educational funds provoked such vitriolic attacks against him in the British press that he retired from the series, but not—I am relieved to learn—from life; he returned to the university and now practices public law. Another absentee is Charles, a successful producer of television documentaries who won't participate in the most celebrated documentary ever to emerge from British television. What Charles, Peter, and John fail to realize is that they have no more right to take flight than if characters in a novel informed their author they were leaving the page. The terrible truth is that we want to watch them enjoy and endure each of life's pleasures and hardships, unto the grave. Better them than us.

[*The New York Sun*, 4 January 2005]

38 ❖ *Roll Out the Sixties and We'll Have a Wonderful Time*

1. Berkeley in the Sixties

In Mark Kitchell's documentary, a Berkeley radical named Frank Bardacke recalls first hearing of the campus while attending Harvard and watching a government propaganda film about alleged Communist dupes behind Berkeley's Free Speech Movement. It inclined him to travel west, where he found that most of the other radicals also had been drawn there by what they heard in the media. Berkeley in the '60s held the allure of a Disney theme park for the disaffected. Long before the clown princes of the antiwar movement found a national platform, the tall, earnest, and enigmatic figure of Mario Savio engaged the imagination—not least, perhaps, because his old-country name seemed to place him squarely in the tradition of anarchists and martyrs. I recall a visiting philosophy professor who spoke to an extracurricular group at my Long Island high school about the existentialists, connecting Sartre and company to Savio and instilling in many of us the promise of life after 3 P.M. But Savio proved an elusive hero. Within a few years, Berkeley was more widely associated with the Summer of Love, People's Park, and Oakland's Black Panthers. Kitchell's absorbing *Berkeley in the Sixties* attempts to put events of that decade in perspective.

The year's third documentary on the sixties is the best of the lot if for no other reason than that it isn't about the filmmaker and thus stands as a refutation of the idea that the '60s was merely a narcissistic bender, a proposition personified by Jim Klein's *Letter to the Next Generation* (see below). Kitchell is sharper than documentarians who know what they want to say and ferret out material to support it. His film narrates a complicated series of events, yet one gets the feeling that he allowed the material to shape his understanding of them. Instead of trimming the talking heads with cutaways to excise stuttering and equivocations, he gives them plenty of space, humanizing them at the expense of propaganda. The same Frank Bardacke who, in 1969, crowed to reporters, "We got the kids, we can't lose," now takes credit for toppling LBJ—a true believer in rabbit holes and, in light of all that has passed, faintly absurd.

Kitchell's film goes beyond the simplistic terms of revolutionary youth versus corrupt establishment to explore breaks in the ranks of the counterculture. At first, the sides were clear. The picture opens buoyantly with people protesting the HUAC hearings, getting bounced down the steps of a municipal building to the soundtrack wailing of Little Richard's "Keep a Knockin' but You Can't Come In." The usual congressional louts, dripping with sanctimony, repudiate them as the victims of commie infiltrators. So far, so good—anyone can see who is right and who is wrong and feel a bit sanctimonious for being on the side of the angels. When Berkeley attempts to banish the Free Speech Movement (FSM), its rolls are increased a thousandfold. How incredibly uncomprehending are the rhetorical responses of Clark Kerr, president of the University of California and once an effective reformer and labor negotiator, and others in response to Savio's artless urgency. The administration is determined to gush gasoline on a brushfire.

One former student, Jentri Anders, looking back a quarter century, captures perfectly the moment when the FSM emerged triumphant and Savio's audience began to disperse: Savio stops her dead by exhorting everyone to turn their attention to stopping the war. "What war?" she wondered. The moral challenge of Vietnam was murkier than the prior restraints of HUAC or the holy war against segregation. Not too long after May 1965, when Berkeley declared a Vietnam Day, leaders of the antiwar movement felt the ground shake. Political tacticians suddenly found themselves confronting a matriculating groundswell of the turned on and dropped out. One faction tries to end the war; another chants peace slogans while toking up. Barry Melton, then of Country Joe and the Fish and now a lawyer, recalls, "We just weren't going to deal with straight people"—a consortium that included members of the FSM. Meanwhile, the lizardlike governor of California expressed outrage that Berkeley permitted students to hold a dance at which no fewer than three rock bands performed while weird colored lights bounced off the walls; and a bus tour of the Haight included remarks on the strange habits of hippies.

By decade's end, increasingly insulated by its own naiveté, the movement resorted to violence. Remembering a Stop the Draft debacle, in which leaflets were handed out to draftees in the hope that they would actually break ranks, one Suzi Nelson seems genuinely surprised that she and her compatriots failed to convert a single draftee. The romance with guns and the Black Panthers ultimately sapped the strength and even the convictions of many members. Bobby Seale tells how he and Huey Newton raised money for weapons by buying copies of Mao's Red Book in Chinatown and marking them up for sale to white sympathizers—"we hadn't even read the thing." The decline in revolutionary fervor is telegraphed by a change in musical accompaniment, from the collective bravura of the Student Nonviolent Coordinating Committee (SNCC) Freedom Singers to the farcical sight of the Panther army, dressed in black leather and berets, chanting, "Off the pig." At the same time, another genuinely new revolution was breeding in the ranks of Berkeley radicals. Women, who had been involved from the beginning, suddenly realized they were expected to be there for "our brothers," to keep the coffee hot and distribute leaflets, and maintain respectful feminine silence.

The most appalling footage in Kitchell's film, now largely forgotten, is of the peaceful protest that followed the university's disingenuous actions involving People's Park. A concrete plot of land had been assiduously turned into a park, which was then taken back by the state guard, subjugating the city for a month. In a notorious confrontation, students were illegally imprisoned on campus during a nonviolent demonstration. They realized why when a helicopter hove into sight, spraying a gas that induces nausea. One student was killed. It was enough: The Berkeley radicals began to disperse. By then, Seale points out, there was no longer a coherent vision, just a series of "emotional moments."

I assume that Savio, now a graduate student in physics, refused to be interviewed, which is unfortunate. But the talking heads Kitchell assembled are good ones, and though they all speak as former members of the counterculture, they make it possible to track a complicated arc in civilization and its discontents, underscoring the era's unequivocal triumphs as well as its befuddled fade-out. One inexplicable failing mars his film: Many speakers, witnesses, and performers in the archival footage are unidentified. I can recognize Joan Baez, but could use a refresher on some others.

2. Letter to the Next Generation

Kent State was our Tiananmen Square and the 1960s came to an end there on May 4, 1970, when four students were shot down without reason during a protest against the Nixon-Kissinger incursion into Cambodia— a war crime that ranks high among the perfidies of a perfidious century, though Americans have never been forced to accept nor have we volunteered responsibility for the resulting holocaust. The impact of the Kent State killings, for which no one was brought to trial, was decisive: Those of us in school can recall the moment we heard about it as clearly as the news of the Kennedy and King assassinations. My alma mater shut down entirely, requesting students to vacate the campus in 48 hours. Student response was less emphatic: After an assault on the ROTC building, we got high and dispersed—unrequited prophets doomed to lives of smug disapproval of the generations to come. Nothing new there, except the speed and efficiency with which the transition took place. It took the lives of only four students to send Jerry Rubin to Wall Street, Bob Dylan to Christianity, and everyone else to parapsychology and alfalfa sprouts.

The images of what happened at Kent State are so powerful that *Letter to the Next Generation*, a nervously didactic documentary, comes to brimming life despite a superficial recounting of the events of May 4. But Jim Klein, a talented filmmaker whose previous work includes *Union Maids* and *Seeing Red*, is less interested in exploring the tragedy or its aftermath than in berating the present student body at Kent State for not having a social conscience as rarefied as his. The result is preachy, self-important, and inattentive. "What about the inner soul?" he earnestly asks a student who typifies the ideology of party hearty. As Paul Lynde used to sing, "Why can't they be like we were / Perfect in every way / Oh, what's the matter with kids today?"

Much of the film is given over to interviews with students who are no more or less callous than the conventional, frightened kids of the '50s and '60s who grew up to be Morton Kondracke, Mona Charen, and Ted Bundy. They are easy targets, and by the fifth or sixth time Klein cuts to the student who applied to Kent State because the drinking age is lower in Ohio than in his home state of Pennsylvania, you wish he'd pick on somebody his own size. But Klein boxed his film when he made the crucial miscalculation of interposing himself on the material. Lacking the most rudimentary sense of showmanship, he never confronts the camera, preferring to represent himself as a patiently sincere man ("The beard is me," he says by way of introduction), always seen by himself, making notes or thinking sincere thoughts. His narration occasionally betrays recognition that he isn't sure what he wants to say—a confusion underscored by the credits, which begin, "A film by Jim Klein" and end, "A film by James Klein." Maybe Jim is a regular guy who wants to know what these kids are up to, and James is the type who orders all students who don't show a better attitude toward social ills to report to the dean by 3 P.M.

One thing *Letter to the Next Generation* makes clear is how obsessed Kent State is with the events of 20 years ago. One professor, who was present at the invasion, teaches a course on it and there are annual ceremonies (an affecting candlelight vigil) on the site of the killings. Klein doesn't seem to appreciate the significance of Kent State assuming the burden for keeping alive the memory of an incident that might have taken place at any number of universities. When a teacher asks her class if anyone can name the fallen students, Klein seems disturbed that most cannot. I was astounded that one student could. Klein shows us the preoccupation with tanning and drinking and material goods. A few students cheerfully admit that they never read or think, and you can see they mean it. He also portrays dismayed faculty members who recall the May 4 horror and bemoan the values of current students while predicting that the '90s will witness a return to activism.

Among the most astute witnesses are Dr. Edward Crosby, of the Pan African Studies Department, who addresses the rise in racism (Klein found a few white students who prove Crosby's point), and Captain Roger Richardson, an ROTC instructor who seems mildly nostalgic for the days when students believed "dope will get you through times of no money better than money will get you through times of no dope." Crosby is an obviously admirable man, and so in his guarded way is Richardson. *Letter to the Next Generation* has a radicalizing impulse, which works when demonstrating the administration's collusion with fast-food chains or student abasement before a Chrysler executive. But it is muted by the director's competitiveness with people to whom he all too obviously feels superior.

These kids grew up with MTV; they have no attention spans; they all know the theme to *The Brady Bunch*. He never asks the most obvious question raised by exercises like this: Why do disaffected liberals and radicals of the '60s always reserve their concern for students and not adults? A less portentous and more relevant film might have been *A Letter to My Generation*. What the hell kind of role models are we anyway?

[*Village Voice*, May–October, 1990]

39 ❖ 'Round and Around and Around (Twist)

"I have been caught in, in, in, twisting, yes, with other people, not even realizing it."

—Marshall McLuhan in *Twist*

Every generation enjoys a spate of fads and fancies that are sure to embarrass the generation to follow. Baby boomers missed out on hip flasks, bobbed hair, Mah Jong, and the counsel of Emil Coue, but they had in store a lifetime of their own balmy leisure pursuits, beginning with coonskin caps and hula hoops. Indeed, they were guinea pigs in the sales strategy that ultimately zeroed in on their own toddlers, proving that not even the first of man's seven ages is immune from merchandising. In *Twist*, an illuminating and frequently hilarious 1992 film, Ron Mann focuses on one fad that many of us recall with queasiness: a dance requiring a semi-squat posture, hula hips, and arm motions that prefigure exercise on an elliptical machine—another boomer artifact.

Yet Mann reclaims the twist as a cultural crossroads, a mid-century phenomenon that embodies racial theft and rapprochement, generational reversals, shameless commercialism, and that landmark moment when lindy-hopping, which paired generations of dancers, gave way to free-standing solo gyrations. As a white woman in one of Mann's priceless clips approvingly observes: Keeping one's partner "at arm's length" reduced the danger of romance. On the other hand, President Eisenhower thought that the twist signified the end of decency and morality. Naughtiness is in the eye of the beholder; silliness is more cosmic. For all its cultural reverberations, twisting morphed into an incredibly silly diversion.

Mann, the gifted Canadian filmmaker whose documentaries include memorable stylized portraits of avant-garde jazz (*Imagine the Sound*), comics (*Comic Book Confidential*), beat poetry (*Poetry in Motion*), and reefer madness (his masterpiece, *Grass*), touches on every aspect. Just when you might be inclined to cringe at a talking head's earnest reference to parents who thought their children were out of control, he edits in a clip in which someone tosses a shoe on a dinner table—the film's best non sequitur. For the most part, *Twist* is fastidious in its design. It opens and closes with a voiceover by Joey Dee offering instructions for the dance that was popular because, as Chubby Checker remarks, anyone could do it. Yet it produced legions of unctuous instructors. Atlantic Records issued a collection of Ray Charles hits with a twist chart showing where to place one's feet: on the floor, one in front of the other.

The film, fittingly, is divided into a series of seven lessons. The talking heads are uniformly introduced by brief shots of them dancing against a black background, each with a different abstract design and pastel color. This detail is characteristic; in *Imagine the Sound*, Mann devised a different color-coordinated set for each of his four jazz artists. With *Twist*, he has also mastered the period montage, and there are two good ones: one on '50s TV and another on the waxing of the '60s. He allows nothing to get in the way of his story, which unfolds with stark clarity and remarkable comprehensiveness—despite the absence of a narrator—while introducing us to several engaging people. Most notable is rhythm and blues star Hank Ballard, who created the twist only to see it taken over by Checker. If Ballard failed to emerge as the star of twist history, his drollness and acumen make him the undeniable star of *Twist*.

In 1959, as white suburban parents indulged in funny barbecue aprons, the cha-cha-cha, and fallout shelters, their children traded in their bubble gum cards for dances that proliferated like mayflies, but with a shorter life span. Mann eases his way into the story with a not entirely fair comparison between white nerds (Gale Storm doing the polka) and virtuoso black jitterbugs whirling each other through the air. He shows how black bands began to choreograph their acts, inspiring the audience to dance, and how white kids rather subversively brought that black influence onto largely segregated TV dance shows, most famously Dick Clark's *American Bandstand*. One couple speaks of introducing a dance they learned from blacks and being forced by the program to claim it as their own invention. The climate was so sulfurously, idiotically racist that one is inclined to feel pity rather than contempt for the gentleman posing with his whites-only bumper sign, pledging to rid the country of "vulgar animalistic nigger rock and roll bop." After all, he feared that rock would liberate libidos and encourage race mixing—and he was right. Consider the evangelist who speaks against the sins of rock; he is himself coiffed for rock stardom, his moves closer to those of Elvis than of Oral Roberts.

Twist is no advertisement for melanin. How is one to explain the spectacle of Arthur Murray teaching TV audiences the mambo? Or the intonation of Frankie Avalon, who seems determined to do away with the tempered scale? Or the socialites who stole the twist from their kids and made it an upper-class rite of the New Frontier? Enter Joey Dee, who is to dancing what Avalon was to singing. It is now 1961, and, as one woman says, "It really is the in-thing to do . . . if you don't do it, you're just considered out. . . . I don't know anyone who doesn't do it at the moment." When one twistocrat insists that sex is the last thing she thinks of while doing it, we sympathize, knowing she has not seen the footage of Harlem nighteries where sex was not the last thing on every twister's mind.

Inevitably, the merchandisers took over. Ozzie and Harriet twisted to sell milk. After that, the deluge: the monkey; the fly; the frug; the limbo; the mashed potato; the hully gully; the loco-motion, which looks like a bunny hop; the watusi, which appears to have been taken from *King Solomon's Mines*; and the incomparable elephant, which suggests the "Prehistoric Man" number in *On the Town*. More than 40 years later, despite the exceptions afforded by Latin music and retro-swing, we are still flailing away separately on dance floors. One might say that we have become, in the words of one of Mann's oddball ghosts from the past, the epitome of "molecules-a-go-go."

[Twist, HVE, 2002]

40 ❖ *Color Him Purple*
(Listen Up: The Lives of Quincy Jones)

Quincy Jones's genius for self-promotion has reached such empyrean heights in the past decade that I wasn't surprised to hear that he was the subject of an industrial film, directed by Ellen Weissbrod and produced by Courtney Sale Ross, whose husband is chief of Time Warner. According to the press release, the company has placed "virtually every division of the company" at her disposal, while supplementing the film with the publication of a book and poster and the release of an album. Jones, who is a partner with Time Warner in a new company, is an ideal trumpet to herald various commercial ventures involving such as Michael Jackson, Steven Spielberg, and even Barbra Streisand (who never says what it was she did with Jones). He even wears a Batman T-shirt in one episode. He's black, he's appealing, he's enormously well liked, he's worked in just about every aspect of the music industry during the past 40 years, and he's crossed the Rubicon from bebop to hip-hop.

Weissbrod's interminable documentary (nearly two hours in reel time, though it feels longer than *Shoah*) convinces me that a good film could be made about him. *Listen Up: The Lives of Quincy Jones* is a trailer for that film—a slice-and-dice assemblage of overlapping dialogue, sampled music, fancy-dan camera moves, and absolutely no narrative drive at all. Worse, it fails to answer the foremost question raised by the effort: Who is Quincy Jones? I thought I knew, but am less certain now. For nearly 15 years, Jones was known as a trumpet player, composer, arranger, and bandleader; he achieved relatively marginal distinction in each of those areas, except trumpet playing, in which he achieved no distinction at all. In the early '60s, after his very promising big band folded, he became a full-time record executive for Mercury. He had previously served as producer for Barclay in Paris and later spent more than a decade in the offices of A&M, but it was at Mercury that he became the first black appointed to a vice-presidency, after producing hits for singers as diverse as Dinah Washington and Leslie Gore.

In 1965, he composed a powerful score for *The Pawnbroker*, which led to nearly 40 other films, notably *In Cold Blood* and *In the Heat of the Night*. He returned to performing in 1969 with the lightweight pop-jazz album, *Walking in Space*. His name became associated with compromise—e.g., a television tribute to Duke Ellington for people with no patience for the music of Duke Ellington. Which is the kind of film *Listen Up* is. It's a film about a composer and arranger, yet none of his music is played through—not one piece. The musical work that gets the most sustained hearing is "We Are the World," the song that gave charity a bad name. With money enough to produce a conventional feature squandered on a mere documentary, Weissbrod has come up with a kaleidoscopic fury of grunts, pregnant looks, and famous people testifying as to what a nice fellow "Q" is. In the absence of style or a point of view, the constant flash cutting suggests a fear of settling down, as though the development of an idea would allow the emptiness to peak through. Indeed, for all the lip service given his early years as a musician and composer, the picture was bankrolled because of the enormous profits he has generated for the company, and it's hard to make a heart-warming movie about an energetic businessman.

The vagueness with which musical subjects are broached takes many forms, from bite-sized clips of James Moody and Sarah Vaughan (seconds' worth) to a disinclination to reveal in what ways Jones served the musical careers of Ella Fitzgerald, Ray Charles, and Streisand. Many of these performers were conveniently gathered for his *Back on the Block* recording sessions, which Weissbrod filmed, but the brief comments suggest a far more comprehensive professional relationship than exists. One of Jones's most fruitful associations was with Count Basie: Dutifully, a bite is included in which he calls Basie his mentor and a lot of other nice things. So much for Basie. More attention is given the unlamented convicted felon Morris Levy, who was interviewed about Birdland: Levy says it was named after Charlie Parker, who was called "the Bird," but doesn't mention that he had Parker eighty-sixed from the club.

In order to beef up Jones's importance as a historical jazz figure, implicit credit is given him for the work of others. On a couple of occasions, the camera pans over a page of music, on which many famous jazz titles, doodles, and a "by Quincy Jones" legend can be seen. Why show it if not to suggest that he wrote that music, including Dizzy Gillespie's "Manteca" and "Shaw Nuff"? On another occasion, we hear an excerpt from Jones's recording of "Killer Joe," a Benny Golson piece written about a pimp. The film not only credits the tune to Jones but also says it was his tribute to Joe Louis! Most of the footage is not concerned with jazz, however. Various rappers take the stage throughout, rhyming tributes to Jones and other musical legends. The filmmakers clearly have more feeling for them than the older guys, and this is not surprising. They are young and spunky and fun to watch, and they underscore the film's self-congratulatory theme of a black man who made it against all odds helping black kids to do the same—a laudable life's work.

Yet the reduction of Jones's enormous success to a triumph over victimhood reeks of calculation. The film ignores all the interesting issues of his artistry, including his rare ability to reconcile three generations of black music. At one point he says, "The times are always contained in the rhythms." It's the most provocative statement in the film, yet goes entirely unexplored. The director seems to think that if anyone, even the star, spoke more than two sentences at a time, the audience would reach for the remote control. Instead, the film settles on a theme readily understood at cocktail parties in the valley. The usual stories of racism are trotted out—the restaurants that would not serve black bands, the physical assaults, Dizzy's inability to get a haircut from a white barber in his hometown only two years ago. And, of course, they are as chilling as ever. The film's whizbang cutting even slows down some to get them across. Combined with the cherubic faces of young musical discoveries and the proud declarations of the rappers, they add up to a banquet of feel-good moralism. "Allow yourself to have joy," Quincy benevolently advises. We are the world. You can do anything. Yes I can. Not a word is said of the racism that presently besets the movie and record industries, other than a cutting remark from Miles Davis ("When you say pop, that's white, right?"), which in this context is simply a hip justification for selling out.

The tone of moral superiority is so contagious that some people, including the only one of Jones's several children who agreed to an interview (none of his wives did), cheerfully excuse him for his horrible treatment of his families. It's not his fault if his career ruined his marriages and estranged his children—they believe that in Hollywood. Besides, they were able to close with a birthday party in which all the children surround him with loving devotion, and even Jesse Jackson shows up for a benediction—he seems almost as starry-eyed as Spielberg, who says, "Quincy is like a spray gun of love." Yes: a spray gun of love. Perhaps that's why the director elected to make a spray gun of a movie. "I can't put it all together," Jones says at one point, trying to recall something from his childhood. Neither can we. Amid the eulogies and hosannas, the clips of Grammy ceremonies, stories told by three voices simultaneously (a technique played into the ground), the charismatic hero slips clean away. I doubt if anyone drawing exclusively on these two hours for information could say for certain what Quincy Jones does or why this tribute was mounted.

[*Village Voice*, 9 October 1990]

41 ❖ *Call It Anything*
(Miles Electric)

In 1975 I wrote an irate, dismissive review of what turned out to be Miles Davis's last recording for six years, *Agharta*. A few days after it appeared, I was told that a suspicious-looking package had arrived for me at the *Village Voice*; it had been dropped off at night—a foot-square carton that rattled. A lobby guard sliced through the masking tape to reveal a handful of large Q-tips, half a dozen industrial-strength scouring pads, and a card that read: "The next time you review Miles Davis clean out your head." I was impressed by the trouble someone had taken (I'd been writing a jazz column for only two years), but my main response was a sniffy "harrumph." What did this clown know? For that matter, what did Miles know? When you fail to understand an artist's new directions, the easiest thing to attack is his motive: Miles sold out, and the evidence was how poorly his trumpet playing sounded on the latest release.

Agharta became, much later, one of my favorite albums from Davis's electric period—it may be the most sheerly exciting of them all. True, Davis's embouchure failed him and his playing is spotty and pained. It doesn't matter: He drives the ensemble with a few well-placed organ chords; alto saxophonist Sonny Fortune and guitarist Pete Cosey attain career peaks; the themes are dramatic and the tension unremitting; and there really is not a moment when the music fails to reflect the ministrations of the sorcerer himself. By the time I had come to my senses, Davis had overcome a long night of life-threatening ailments, depression, drugs, and reclusiveness bordering on agoraphobia. I was so happy to see him again I probably over-praised a few comeback concerts and recordings, which grew stronger during his last decade as he made peace with all facets of what had become a 46-year quick-change act. Toward the end, he conceded that he had been pressured to sell out: 40-minute modal jam sessions—some sellout.

Davis's transitions, especially the one from acoustic to electric with all its genre-busting sociological implications, offer material for a great film that Murray Lerner has almost made. His *Miles Electric* belongs to the waste-not-want-not school of documentaries. Lerner filmed the 1970 Isle of Wight Festival, producing an overall record, *Message to Love: The Isle of Wight Festival*, as well as detailed accounts of performances by Jimi Hendrix and the Who. He still had a captivating 37-minute set by Davis, skillfully and comprehensively shot, and the long-awaited theatrical release of it guarantees *Miles Electric* a respectable place in the roll of music films. He prefaces the musical set with some 40-minutes of talking heads and brutally curtailed snippets of earlier Davis performances, and follows it with another five minutes of talking heads and musical tribute—including a voice and percussion interpretation of electric Miles by Airto, which hits the nail on the head while robbing the film of a more poetic ending: Miles's reserved goodbye wave to an audience estimated at over half a million. The new material is fine—I especially like the way Lerner brought Davis's album cover art to life.

The history, however, is potted, a deserved tribute to Miles that doesn't explore, let alone resolve, the questions raised. Lerner lines up a dozen musicians to extol Davis's courage and genius in crossing the divide from jazz to pop, inventing his own no-man's-land in the process. Against them, he places critic Stanley Crouch as a kind of fall-guy devil's advocate, attacking Davis as a money-hungry fraud. The fine points of the controversy aren't really broached. Lerner interviewed Dave Holland and Chick Corea, who are all smiley and nostalgic, but neglected to ask them about their quitting the band after the festival, complaining at that time of feeling stifled by Davis's music. Nor does the film acknowledge the strange fact that the music press ignored Davis's appearance at the festival. Most of the musicians Lerner interviewed in 2003 returned to acoustic music—Holland, Jack DeJohnette, Gary Bartz, Keith Jarrett, Dave Liebman, as well as Corea and Herbie Hancock, who are posed at electric pianos but are just as likely to lead straight-ahead jazz bands.

The Isle of Wight performance, despite a few longueurs and stagnant rhythms, speaks for itself and captures an historic moment. Davis was in fighting shape and the music attains exhilaration. When asked what the band had played, Davis said, "Call it anything," but in fact he played a loose-limbed medley built on a few familiar themes, notably "It's About That Time" (from *In a Silent Way*), "Spanish Key," and his bop-era closer, "The Theme." The question remains: Did this kind of playing disappear or has it been absorbed into subsequent funk, hip-hop, and jazz forms? Another film can deal with that. Meanwhile, what is Pete Cosey up to and when do we get to hear him again?

[*Film Comment*, November 2004]

42 ❖ *Savage Servility* (Glory)

From the moment Colonel Robert Gould Shaw and much of his Massachusetts 54th regiment were wiped out in the charge, in 1863, on an impregnable sand dune called Fort Wagner, he took pride of place among abolitionist martyrs. Generations of Brahmin poets, from Emerson to Robert Lowell, made of him a resonant metaphor; Saint-Gaudens bronzed him for the Boston Common. (Lowell: "Their monument sticks like a fishbone / in the city's throat.") Shaw's futile assault was historic because the 54th was the Civil War's first Negro regiment, and it fought valiantly; as a result, more than 180,000 blacks were inducted as Union soldiers. Lincoln called their participation decisive and a journalist predicted that Fort Wagner would come to represent to blacks what Bunker Hill meant to whites. It didn't turn out that way, perhaps for the same reason that the Japanese do not celebrate their kamikazes. The 54th didn't have a chance: The white regiments they were ostensibly advancing did not show up in time.

In many respects, Edward Zwick's *Glory*, a blemished but often stirring account of the 54th, does justice to an incident that encapsulates not only the barbarism of the war but also the politics that elevates dead saints over live victors. Kevin Jarre's screenplay orders the basic facts into single file, beginning with Shaw's survival at Antietam, and the homecoming party where a mute Frederick Douglass (the actor isn't even listed in the credits) and philanthropist Francis Shaw stand by as Shaw's son is offered the command of the first black troops. Most of the film is taken up with training them, and as usual in army movies, the regiment is deconstructed into one tentful of representative blacks (in truth, the 54th recruited some white soldiers as well, including the younger brother of Henry and William James). We have Trip, the escaped slave who hates whites and just about everyone else; Rawlins, the wise middle-aged volunteer; Thomas, the educated free black who was a childhood friend of Shaw; and Sharts, the field hand who stutters for comic relief. You don't need a weathervane to tell you that Trip will come around and distinguish himself as a martyr for all seasons.

The clichés might be deadly if the actors didn't transcend them. Zwick doesn't allow his passion for the surfaces of historical accuracy (the Boston parade in celebration of the 54th's impending glory and the assault on Fort Wagner are especially convincing) to impede the development of his characters. When Denzel Washington, whose Trip is the film's most hair-raising performance, intimidates Thomas (Andre Braughner, all glasses and teeth) by moving in on his space, nose to nose, the tension is fairly electrifying. One of the most tautly executed scenes is also among the most elemental—a ritualistic campfire round of prayerful testimony before battle. Sharts (Jihmi Kennedy is funny as the stuttering innocent), Trip, and Rawlins take turns as soldiers clap in time to a spiritual, and the power and glory are made almost palpable.

Rawlins is played by Morgan Freeman, who, having pimped in *Street Smart* and inspired inner-city students in *Lean on Me*, now chauffeurs a white lady in *Driving Miss Daisy* and surmounts slavery in *Glory*, rapidly exhausting the panoply of Negro film roles (though he has yet to turn up as a police chief). That he is an astonishing actor who disappears into each role can be lost on no one, but it remains to be seen whether he will get to play parts that aren't earmarked for the hot black actor of the moment. The range suggested by the knife-menacing scene in *Street Smart* and the solemn dignity of his handclapping by the campfire in *Glory* is bound to secure his stardom: You may want to see *Glory* if only to watch Freeman's face light up with spiritual composure.

With Washington setting off firecrackers and Freeman holding the emotional fort, Matthew Broderick's effectiveness as Shaw comes as something of a surprise. But it's one of the film's more touching conceits to recall that Shaw was an innocent himself, though his age is needlessly fudged: Shaw was 25 or 26, not 23 as he says in *Glory*. When Thomas, who's been having a rough time, stops Shaw to say "Merry Christmas," Broderick's relief at the avoidance of a confrontation is that of a lost adolescent trying dauntlessly to be a martinet and grateful for a few seconds to remember who he is and where he comes from. At times, Broderick chews over his line readings, eyes limpid, self-conscious soulfulness spreading like a stain, but on balance he humanizes Shaw more than the poets did.

The battle scenes are among the best ever filmed. These are not the soldiers of Griffith or Huston, swarming over hills and ducking behind trees, but nakedly vulnerable opposing flanks, armed with one-shot rifles and backed by mortars. The assault on Fort Wagner faithfully reproduces a famous print, but it is the apprentice skirmish at James Island that curls one's hair, a scrimmage fought over a few yards, men on both sides dutifully trying to reload without cover while bodies drop up and down the lines. *Glory* is good at depicting the racism on the Union side (the refusal of the quartermaster to give Shaw's men shoes) and doesn't fudge the burning of Darien by Colonel James Montgomery, in which Shaw was forced to participate. But the rebels don't exist in *Glory*, except as a faceless evil. Hollywood abolitionists have come a long way since *Santa Fe Trail*, in which Raymond Massey played John Brown as though he were a mad doctor from the Universal horror cycle; still, the dehumanization of Confederate soldiers rather mutes the issue of barbarism.

For that matter, *Glory* has little to say about the politics of martyrdom. Shaw is shown volunteering his regiment to lead the attack on Fort Wagner, and in fact his troops were hungry to prove their mettle when the offer was made; the question as to whether they were set up by white commanders is ignored. The smarmy expression worn by Peter Michael Goetz as Shaw's father ably suggests the presumed superiority of a man who, rather than demand the return of his son's body, manufactured propaganda out of his interment in a ditch with his men. That's another issue the film avoids.

A movie can do only so much, and *Glory* does quite a lot, though its effectiveness is undermined by Zwick's tendency to telegraph key events, as though he feared the audience wouldn't get them if the music didn't swell to signify significance. James Horner's Dvorak-flavored score is atrocious: The juice is pumped to the max when Shaw discovers his men haven't deserted, yet the audience knows full well they won't; when Shaw falls in battle, the voices (the Boys Choir of Harlem, no less) and strings sound like emissaries from *The Omen*. Sounds of explosives and screams of dying men are all that the soundtrack needed for the final assault. No less distressing is a centrally placed confrontation between Shaw and Trip, who, expounding 1989 politics, argues that the war is pointless. It's as though a slave in *The Ten Commandments* asked, "What's the point, Moses? Even if we do get out of Egypt, we'll never get into their country clubs." Probably not what Robert Lowell had in mind when he wrote of the Saint-Gaudens relief, "a savage servility slides by on grease."

[*Village Voice*, 19 December 1989]

43 ❖ *Simplicity Itself (Robert Bresson)*

The first time I attempted *The Red and the Black*, in high school, I had a paperback with a Clifton Fadiman introduction, warning that the novel could not be understood in one reading. Knowing that my effort would amount to no more than a dry run put me off Stendahl for years. (Thanks, Clifton.) What he might have written is that *every* Great Work of Art rewards revisits, but that every GWA also offers initial frissons that can be had only once, in the course of virginal submission.

I mention this with regard to Robert Bresson's films (only 13, made between 1943 and 1983—an earlier film, from 1934, is lost) for two reasons. First, his work is ideally suited to DVD, on Fadimanian grounds. His films offer emotional experiences that bring you back repeatedly to peer deeper into the work and yourself. Second, people who venerate Bresson often find naked emotions embarrassing and tend to validate them with intricate exegeses. This helps to explain why most Bresson films were greeted first with ambivalence and upgraded to masterpiece on second thought, and why he is reputed to be a difficult filmmaker when his best work offers first-timers the almost frightening pleasure of simplicity itself.

Au Hasard Balthazar (1966) and *L'Argent* (1983), recently released by Criterion and New Yorker, respectively (each now has three Bressons in its catalogue; collect them all), complement each other, underscoring a Bressonian paradox. He paints a world of unrelenting sadness, malice, cruelty, and corruption—so why do we emerge into the daylight feeling elated, stronger, better? The answer lies not in the redemption he holds out for his characters (some, not all, and fewer as he grew older), but in a pact he makes with his audience, neither to compromise nor condescend.

Au Hasard Balthazar is one of the most elegant, calculated, and strikingly textured films ever made. Ghislain Cloquet's black-and-white photography bleakly reflects the grim, disenchanted lives in Bresson's rural

French village. At the center of the story is Balthazar, a donkey baptized by children; whipped and burned by a chain of brutal owners; briefly honored as a circus "genius" (he can do multiplication); declared a saint by a woman who loses her daughter and husband but not her moorings; exploited by bungling criminals, and killed by a stray bullet. The donkey is the central character, a mute witness (braying aside), the one with whom we ultimately—incredibly—identify.

If this sounds like a hee-haw version of *Black Beauty*, albeit with an unhappy ending, it may be because a précis cannot convey the effect of the telling, so economical and graceful that each frame, line of dialogue, and off-screen sound adds essential information. The ending, especially, defies storytelling logic; it isn't really unhappy, though fans boast of how copiously they weep. Bresson, a Catholic whose work resounds with harsh religiosity, crafts Balthazar's death as deliverance—a scene that believers and nonbelievers alike not only accept (for that matter, we accept vampires and Looney Tunes) but feel in our bones. Call it devastating, apocalyptic, inspiring, redemptive, beautiful—"unhappy" doesn't cut it.

Bresson found his stimulus in a remark Myshkin makes about the delightfulness of a braying donkey in *The Idiot* (Dostoevsky provided much of his source material, though he also accessed Bernanos, Diderot, Mallory, and Tolstoy, among others), but the closest he comes to suggesting Myshkin's crazy benignity is in the character of the alcoholic Arnold (Jean-Claude Guilbert), who may or may not be a serial killer: He is falsely accused of informing on local thugs, inherits unwanted money, and accepts punishment and death with a bemused indifference. Arnold is a relatively minor yet essential figure, who saves Balthazar's life, then tries to brain him, and terminates his idyll in the circus. Ah yes, the circus— in which Balthazar exchanges meaningful looks with other animals, a stunning episode that probably can't be described (QED) without making the film and the describer sound foolish.

The central human character is a girl, Marie—played unforgettably by Anne Wiazemsky, an amateur (with few exceptions, Bresson rejected professional actors for his films)—whose life parallels that of Balthazar. A heartbreaker, Marie is brutalized in a masochistic relationship with Gerard (François Lafarge), the tormentor of Balthazar, whom she loves and neglects. By the time Gerard is finished with her, her capacity for love is extinguished. Bresson believes in motiveless malignancy; he is less interested in why people behave than in the unintended consequences of their behavior. For one example, Marie's fatally proud father chases off the bland yet faithful Jacques, who might deliver her from drudgery and himself from debt, setting her up for the fall that will destroy them all.

Ultimately, they all accept their fate, which Bresson seems to admire—his actors typically lower their eyes in desolate humility. Balthazar runs away twice, but cannot escape his burdens. Marie runs from the thug Gerard but only gets a few yards, then waits to see what will happen. People pray and their prayers are unanswered or renounced. God is inactive, yet present—not least in the remarkable soundtrack. The score mixes pop records blaring on Gerard's radio, Balthazar's braying, and in rare instances a passage from Schubert's Piano Sonata No. 20—godly music oddly dispensed. We hear it during opening credits, in the final moments of the donkey's ascension, and, incongruously, when Gerald threatens Balthazar with fire and the donkey acquiesces.

Balthazar is an object, a useful tool to most of his owners. He may, as the title suggests, represent a random soul, but his life is blessed and a blessing. *L'Argent* is a darker film, shot in cold, metallic colors, also concerned with a relayed object. The tool here is a forged banknote that brings ruin to most of those who pawn it off on unsuspecting dupes, defining a world so devious that petty crime leads to wholesale slaughter. Except for a prison prayer group, spiritual comfort is nowhere to be found. The central character, Yvon, loses his job, freedom, child, wife, moral compass, and sanity, retaining only his spooky tranquility—he attempts suicide with Valium, which his body seems to naturally manufacture—as he delivers himself to the police, having axed an entire family, including a crippled child.

In this film, redemption is no longer an episode to observe, but something for us, Bresson's collaborators, to experience. As the murderer is taken into custody, the crowd gawks in shadows with a there-but-for-fortune curiosity, emphasizing a randomness that might have fastened on any of those faceless souls, luring him or her into madness. Bresson's choice is especially severe, given his source material—Tolstoy's last novella, published posthumously, *The Forged Coupon*. Tolstoy tells his story in two parts, the first an ethical thriller in which the coupon poisons the souls of all who handle it; the second a didactic reverie on contagious Christianity—the murderer achieves sainthood, and infects everyone else with goodness and desire to help the peasantry.

Bresson adapted the first half with discerning fidelity, but beyond the confession and an anecdote concerning a Robin Hood thief, he skips the second part. Tolstoy's tutorial is ridiculous, a pipe dream—yet Bresson doesn't reject it entirely. Malignancy is everywhere: a transition from city to country suggests at first a contamination of the natural order, but it is already polluted with exploitation and despair—the doomed widow with whom Yvon shares one exquisitely erotic moment (eating hazelnuts) courts her own destruction. As do we all: The crimes that instigate the mounting atrocities are nothing special—just paltry lies and selfish connivances. Rather than dramatize a relay of saintliness, Bresson takes a far more radical approach, extending the spiral of madness directly from the screen to the audience, as Yvon walks toward the camera, forcing us back on our own resources.

[*The New York Sun*, 5 July 2005]

44 ❖ *Pretty Boy*
(Alain Delon)

The French cinema has produced many stars that Hollywood producers sought to borrow and bottle, almost always with abysmal results—if not career suicide, then career stasis or diminishment. Blame Maurice Chevalier, whose enormous popularity at the outset of the sound era briefly buoyed the fortunes of Paramount until the Production Code put the kibosh on charming impropriety. His dire 1950s revival (*Gigi* excepted) proved no less seductive and illusory. Almost every other Gallic import came a cropper, settling for studio crumbs (Marcel Dalio) or acceding to hilarious miscasting (Yves Montand as Faulkner's corncob rapist Popeye). The women, from Michele Morgan to Jeanne Moreau, fared no better. Most returned home and flourished, though many of the pictures that sustained and enriched their Continental standing never crossed the pond.

Consider Alain Delon, the prettiest of 1960s pretty boys, the yang to Jean-Paul Belmondo's yin. His career soared with a quartet of French and Italian triumphs: *Purple Noon* (as the most convincing of Patricia Highsmith's Ripleys), *Rocco and His Brothers*, *L'eclisse*, and *The Leopard*—then motored past several Anglo distractions and into a steady cruise of crime pictures, including two middling international blockbusters (*The Sicilian Clan* and *Borsalino*) and two neglected, butchered Jean-Pierre Melville epics, *Le Samourai* and *Le Cercle Rouge*. In the 1970s, Delon began producing films, often working with *Borsalino* director Jacques Deray. Kino has released three of them, which prove strangely complementary: *Two Men in Town* (1973), *Borsalino and Co.* (1974), and *Flic Story* (1975).

All involve cops and robbers, but they take place in three different decades and allow Delon to straddle the divide, playing, respectively, a rehabilitated criminal martyred by his past, a ruthless gang chief who is less ruthless than his rival, and a preening detective tracking down an escaped psychopath. There are no lost masterpieces here, nothing on the level of *Le Samourai*, but each film is worthy and interesting in a different way. They all register Delon's peculiarly vacant yet insinuating understatement.

Two Men in Town is a loaded brief against capital punishment, specifically the guillotine, which is depicted in the same grueling detail as the gas chamber is in Robert Wise's *I Want to Live!* (1958)—it's barbaric but a whole lot faster. Indeed, this film is something of a companion piece to Camus's "Reflections on the Guillotine," complete with existentialist postmortem. Chance is the real culprit, the rumpled Jean Gabin concludes: "Some pray, but that's no solution." The film was written and directed by José Giovanni, a Resistance fighter who later fell in with criminal gangs, was himself scheduled for the headsman, and upon reprieve wrote several notable films (including Jacques Becker's *Le Trou*) before turning to directing; he died last year at 80. Anecdotal details, including an alarming jailhouse suicide, are presumably drawn from life, but the story is drawn from Victor Hugo. A hardened criminal, brought to salvation by parole advisor Gabin (who is as understated as Delon yet projects a lot more of the mental gears) is persecuted, tricked, and framed by a Javert who provokes him to murder. Designed as tragedy, it plays as irony.

Borsalino and Co., directed by Deray, is the commercially disappointing but superior sequel to *Borsalino*. The sequel part—avenging the murder of the Belmondo character in the 1970 film—is achieved in the first few minutes with a murder that triggers a grotesquely violent and giddily stylish gang war that at times suggests the sadistic pleasures of *The Abominable Dr. Phibes*. That comparison is underscored by the fastidious 1930s setting, though plot points owe more to Dashiell Hammett (gang war as in *Red Harvest*), Raymond Chandler (forced addiction as in *Farewell My Lovely* and *The Blue Dahlia*), and especially Fritz Lang (Nazi sympathizers, sponsored by capitalists, plan to conquer major cities by getting the liberal or decadent elements addicted to heroin). In order to make Delon's gangster—who, left to his own designs, is on good terms with the police and is content to run a brothel and a musical theater—sympathetic, he is confronted with an enemy from hell: an Italian fascist-gangster named Volpone who, as played by Riccardo Cucciolla, is a dead ringer for Lucky Luciano. He gets his just deserts, following a wonderful minute-long silent pan of a train, in a scene worthy of Dr. Phibes.

The most interesting and resonant of the films is Deray's *Flic Story*, based on the memoirs of the egomaniacal police detective Roger Borniche. It concerns the 1947 hunt for Emile Buisson, played with a sneering malevolence by Jean-Louis Trintignant, whose hair-trigger keeps the film pulsing despite the director's often too deliberate pacing. It opens with a touch of Hollywood parody: We hear Borniche's cynical voiceover and see his lower legs climbing several stories to his office, where he is shown as the perfectly trench-coated and coiffed Delon, who is made visibly uncomfortable by his partner's rough interrogation technique. The film ends with a longer voiceover, by which time we half expect another explosion from Buisson, despite the calm narration—no anti-capital punishment argument here. Instead, we get a late-arriving doppelganger connection between cop and killer. For all his cool demeanor and ultimate success, Borniche rocks the film's stability with several instances of incompetence and his willingness to put others, including his fiancée, at risk. The details and supporting characters are richly observed, as is the underworld milieu. Delon's best line comes near the end, when the apprehended Buisson says he would like to take a hacksaw to an informer's throat and stop every once in a while to hear his screams. Borniche listens blankly and responds almost consolingly, "You won't get the chance."

[*The New York Sun*, 16 August 2005]

45 ❖ *French Doubt*
(Too Beautiful for You / May Fools)

After seeing Bertrand Blier's subtly ingratiating *Too Beautiful for You*, you may never be able to hear Schubert's G-flat impromptu again without smirking. It steals into the life of Bernard—a philandering but good-hearted husband with a head of tin—like an elusive memory, underscoring his constant sense of impending perplexity. What organ chords are to soap opera, Schubert is to Bernard's tangled existence. Wherever he turns, he is badgered by one of a dozen of the composer's most romantic themes, creeping in on cat's feet. Eventually, he submits. Pasqual, a friend of Bernard's to whom the injured wife has turned in retaliation, asks him during a patch of commiseration, "Shall I put on some Schubert?" Bernard: "You got some?" Like Schubert, the movie grows on you.

Putting a whammy on Schubert is a characteristic predilection for Blier in this abundantly whimsical variation on the standard triangle. Bernard, played by Gerard Depardieu—looking more than ever like a heavily sedated Karl Malden—is married to the primly beautiful Florence, played or at least modeled by Carole Bouquet. Impossibly, it would seem, he hungers for his secretary, the plain and frumpy Colette, a role attacked by Josiane Balasko with a sexy bravado that will gratify similarly distressed "other women." After she sees Florence, who visits the office to make sure her husband's new assistant poses no threat (Florence takes one look and leaves reassured), Colette admits to Bernard, "Beauty clobbers you. It hurts."

Yet Colette has an unmistakable moxie of her own, and she knows the way to a man's testosterone. The perpetually dazed Bernard is so smitten, he tells Florence of his affair without identifying the obscure object of his desire. It isn't that he wants to protect Colette. His conventional side knows that adultery, like business, has its pecking order, and that giving up Florence for Colette would be like abandoning the boardroom for the mailroom. Florence's pain, too, would be aggravated by the inscrutable nature of his lust. And then there are the two small kids, one of whom has suddenly developed a baffling taste for Schubert.

She finds out, of course, as do their friends, in the movie's most comical and elaborate set piece, a surreal dinner that reverts between pure fantasy (Florence dressed in white) and impure reality (Florence in black). In the former realm, one of their frequent dinner guests casually remarks—to a chorus of napkin folding and eye rolling—that he has always had a ravenous yen for Bernard's neglected wife: Specifically, he would like to wake up to find her sitting on his face. The exquisite Florence takes charge as the table turns into a lavish banquet. She apologizes for being too beautiful (applause), announces with great resolve, "Now I intend to be probed more violently," kisses Bernard passionately, and asks, "Any more questions?" They all wake up to the presence of Colette and the hermetic strains of Schubert.

Blier is heir to the Bunuellian sensibility, which locates political insinuations in domestic mores. His humor is quiet and cumulative, building through an accretion of peculiar remarks, glances, pauses, and actions. *Too Beautiful for You* brings to mind the appearance, tempo, and feeling of late Bunuel, *The Discreet Charm of the Bourgeoisie* and especially *That Obscure Object of Desire*, in which the teenage Bouquet, one of two actresses alternating as the Object, made her film debut. Blier's style has a stimulating clarity, given the befogged story: Virtually every scene is shot straight on—the camera rarely if ever looks up or down. The sets are polished as chrome, and movements of the agreeable cast are as carefully blocked as a dance. Depardieu's congenital resignation provides much of the humor. But Blier's cleverly discursive script allows all three points of view to emerge, Colette's with the most sympathy. When Florence confronts her after a tryst, she pulls the covers up, looking overweight and vulnerable. Florence is the princess coming to grips, remarking, "An ice cold hand has me pinned to the wall." None of them get what they want. In the last line of the film, Bernard concludes, "Your Schubert is a pain in the ass"—followed by Schubert's full-screen credit. It's all *his* fault, or may as well be.

American filmmakers cannot quite divest themselves of the '60s, but neither can they capture what Louis Malle calls "the Utopian dream, the gaiety, the constant improvisation." Hollywood's comic recollections of long hair, dope, and bellbottoms; its penitential big-chill reckonings; and its somber rehearsals of Vietnam never evoke the era's essential exhilaration—its messianic capriciousness. Malle's nostalgia for utopian joy complements the American experience but wasn't inspired by it. He was 35 during the May 1968 student demonstrations in France, and when he returned to Paris for the 20th anniversary celebration, he grieved to find the observances dominated by bourgeois sentimentalists. *May Fools*, his most discerning and sustained comic romp since *Murmur of the Heart*, in 1971, is set in the days but not in the location of the demonstrations. A family congregating on an old estate in southwestern France (wine country) follows the turmoil on radio. Malle had had the bizarre inspiration to dramatize the threat and appeal of social upheaval as a country house farce—a variation on Renoir's *Rules of the Game*.

The opening sequence establishes the consistently skewed tone. The matriarch is in the kitchen, fighting back tears. The camera pulls back to show her chopping onions. She promptly has a heart attack, and, singing to keep herself calm, climbs the stairs to die on a bed of childhood dolls. The woman, played by Paulette Dubost, who also played the maid in *Rules of the Game*, is laid out in the parlor—an object of respect, scorn, greed, and, ultimately, a fetish for collusive irreverence. Poor Dubost, lying there scene after scene, her jaw pummeled by a child concerned that dirt will get in her open mouth, never twitches a muscle.

The role of her son, Milou, is yet another opportunity for Michel Piccoli to confirm his place as the most casually authoritative presence in French movies since Jean Gabin. Milou gathers the family together for the funeral, which, since the gravediggers are on strike like everyone else, must be improvised. As the relatives arrive and the radio continues to blare news of the revolution, a flirtatious minuet gets under way. Everyone is sufficiently infected by the political mood to consider a partner-swapping orgy. They are saved by the bell: A neighborhood couple arrives—capitalists, tweedy and bearing arms, running from the imagined horde of students. In a reenactment of the Orson Welles *War of the*

Worlds scare, they and others like them flee into the woods, chased by the hobgoblins of radio, guilt, and perhaps a bit of wish fulfillment.

The family could use a good revolution. Milou's censorious, self-centered, 40-something daughter, Camille (Miou-Miou) would like to see a few students killed just to teach them a lesson. Neglected by her husband, she is also inclined to rekindle an affair with the family's slimy lawyer, Daniel. Her daughter, Françoise (Miou-Miou's real-life daughter, Jeane Herry-LeClerc), is a 10-year-old Greek chorus, crowned in a Beatles do, observing and questioning everything: "Grampa, what's a dyke?"

The dyke is Claire, Milou's orphaned niece, an impassioned but failed pianist, who is accompanied by Marie-Laure, an impetuous but failed ballerina, whom Claire ties to the bedpost at night. Milou's brother, Georges (Michel Duchaussoy), a writer for *Le Monde*, arrives with his sexy young wife, Lily (Harriet Walter), who takes a reciprocated interest in Milou. Georges's son, Pierre-Alain, a student and witness to the joy of the demonstrations—people holding hands, free love—makes the trip home by hitchhiking a ride with a sex-obsessed truck driver named Grimaldi (Bruno Carette, whose last film this is). Pierre-Alain likes Marie-Laure. Claire settles for Grimaldi, who proclaims, "The breeze, the sun, May!—makes me want to feel a woman's breasts." Claire is fully supplied.

So . . . they all pair off, but Malle yokes the strings and the debauchery never quite gets under way. The participants are too distracted by the business of dividing the spoils, carving up the estate. Only Milou wants to keep the house, which holds the family together. The others would just as soon fly out of orbit. Complicating the competition for jewels and dishes is the final codicil to the matriarch's will, which gives a fourth of everything to her trusted servant, Adele.

For all the diversity in subjects and settings that has distinguished his career, Malle is never stronger than when plotting the feints, deceits, attractions, revulsions, losing battles, and gallows humor of family life. In Milou, who is at home with nature and himself, Malle finds a solid focus for the familial madness. Milou is as willing to test the anarchic spirit as his nephew, and when he discovers that his shotgun-toting neighbor is a polluter whose chemical plant has killed all the fish in the estate's stream, he is the best bet for radicalization. Like Renoir's masterpiece, *May Fools* shimmers and reverberates with insight and much pleasure. The ghostly finale, in which Milou dances with his resurrected mother in the abandoned house, furnishings piled into salable lots all around them, embodies in one lovely gesture Malle's ambivalent generosity and the disarming mastery of his execution. Enhancing every step by the engaging ensemble, which includes Dominique Blanc, Rozenn Le Tallec, François Berleand, Martine Gautier, and Renaud Danner, is a sprightly score by violinist Stephane Grappelli, not the least reason to embrace this enchanting film.

[*Village Voice*, March–June, 1990]

46 ❖ *Blown Away*

1. *A Shock to the System*

Hollywood moviemakers have been telling us for a while (*Wall Street* style) that greed is bad, which is a bit like having to endure lectures on self-control from your neighborhood crack dealer. A haven is provided by *A Shock to the System*, a brackish comedy in which propriety is renounced and Reaganomic commandments—Thou Shalt Covet, Thou Shalt Have No Other God Before Number One—are taken to their logical extremes: murder as a means of solving dilemmas in business and marriage. It opens with the tranquil voiceover of Michael Caine's character, Graham ("It all began . . ."), boosted by a musical score of chirpy pizzicato strings, so you surmise right off—though increasingly you can't quite believe it— that whatever happens, he will come out of it all right. After his fourth homicide, though, with a persistent policeman closing in, you prepare yourself for a Production Code finish. You don't get it. What's more, the film refuses to sustain the conceit that Graham is an irresistible charmer or that his killings are of cartoonish inconsequence.

Graham learns how to succeed in business and emanate power ("magic," he calls it), and lives to contemplate his achievements in ghoulish serenity. Yet the movie has an uncertain tone that may keep audiences away. Caine and the director, Jan Egleson, could have made Graham an object of identification. To be sure, most of the victims are plainly disposable. You may find yourself regretting the instantaneous demise of Benham (Peter Riegert), an insufferably smug bastard whose primary offense is getting the promotion Graham wanted—death by inches would be more fun. Yet Graham enjoys playing the game too well, and as he becomes the perfect corporate cutthroat (this is the point of the whole exercise), you regret his corruption more than his crimes. Can't a homicidal maniac have ethics, too?

The point is somewhat muted by the director's giddy determination to prove himself a stylist. His camera is never still: Bring a Dramamine to combat motion sickness. Every setup is a complicated tracking shot or pan. Egleson, whose first theatrical feature this is, never shoots an actor straight on when he can peer through blinds, over beams, and around corners. He trails people walking through crowds, or has them stroll in and out of the frame. You find yourself distracted from dialogue, wondering why the camera is circling the speakers instead of simply photographing them. When the plot becomes as heady as his ambitions, he settles down and proves himself an efficient director. Some of the pans are properly ominous, and the editing between parallel images (for example, from the blown lightbulb that fries Graham's wife to the light in Graham's hotel room) is nastily effective.

The tonal control is intermittently successful, switching from suburban comedy to competent suspense. You string along with the killing of Graham's nagging wife (Swoozie Kurtz)—"Honey, I forgive you for failing"—until you see the horror of it registered in the eyes of Graham's colleague, lover, and alibi, Stella (Elizabeth McGovern). Yet as the voice-over switches from first to third person, Caine becomes a tad too creepy: Andrew Klavan's script has him say "bibbity bobbity boo" several times too often. And subversive satire played as realism has a few obligations to reality, which is sorely tested when the police lieutenant (Will Patton) breaks into Graham's apartment, or when Graham's colleague and fellow commuter, Brewster (John McMartin), having been forced out of the corporation by the foul Benham, continues to commute to Grand Central Station to spend his days tippling with the derelicts. *A Shock to the System* doesn't have enough madness to be really satisfying. But it is coolly unnerving, and that counts for something.

2. Pretty Woman

How is one to explain the preponderance of prostitutes as Hollywood heroines? Do the moguls spend all their time whoring in the hope of molding a Galatea into star or wife, or do they simply think all women are whores anyway, so why not reduce them to their streetwalking fundamentals? In the insidious *Pretty Woman*, all women who aren't explicitly identified as tramps are gold-digging wives or snooty shopkeepers. It's the kind of working-class fantasy that wants the men in the audience to identify with a ruthless corporate pirate (Richard Gere) and the woman to identify with a simple but grandhearted streetwalker (Julia Roberts), who, given a chance, could be a lady's lady. The manager (Hector Elizondo) of Hollywood's ritziest hotel doubles as her fairy godfather.

The attempted laughs (few succeed) are at her expense. She's so stupid she doesn't know how to eat pâté, so stupid she doesn't know that opera involves music. Yet she wins the heart of her zillionaire client after

six days of baths and blowjobs, revealing to one and all her essentially
girlish decency: (a) She stopped taking drugs at 14 (note the implicit equation between drugs and masturbation); (b) she sheds tears like a snake
sheds skin; (c) as a girl, she dreamed of a knight on a white charger; and,
this above all, (d) she passes the opera test—those who truly love it,
Siddhartha Gere instructs, are a blessed few. She really loves it: Her eyebrows flutter and her nostrils quiver. Needless to say (this whole review
is needless, but it's my job), Roberts turns Gere into a decent fellow who
abandons his corporate raider ways. (Greed is BAD, BAD!) She even cures
his vertigo. They go to the park to read Shakespeare. He becomes so decent,
he spends his nights in the hotel lounge playing New Age piano for the
janitors. He's so decent that in the final clinch, no one ever mentions the
words: Prenuptial Contract.

Decent, perhaps; an actor, perhaps not. Richard Gere has become
the Sonny Tufts of his day. His every line is spoken in a flat monotone—
including when he slugs his lawyer and shouts at him to leave (it's a quiet
shout). He has no timing, and he never focuses his beady little eyes on
another actor. When Roberts wanders into the lounge and discovers him
at the piano, they grab each other (e.g., *The Fabulous Baker Boys*), yet the
scene, for all the humping, is so chaste, it is laughable, and the director
(Gary Marshall) cuts away as if embarrassed. This is a movie in which
Roberts retains her modesty, while Gere's nipples are the subjects of two
full-screen close-ups—at first you think they're his eyes. The theme song
is tremendous.

3. The Hot Spot

If the character Dennis Hopper played in *Blue Velvet* had set out for
Hollywood and persuaded a major studio to let him direct a movie (not
an altogether implausible scenario), *The Hot Spot* might be the result.
In the age of weird, Hopper out-Lynches Lynch. Having given his social
conscience a tug with *Colors*, he now returns to the Hollywood of old,
reviving the lost art of soft-core porn in the context of by-the-numbers
noir. Both genres are essentially adolescent male fantasies, and *The Hot
Spot* is about as close to a high-budget stag film as we are likely to see
this year. Not because of the nudity and simulated sex (other current films
have more of each), but because the fantasies that trigger them are so
claustrophobically those of a 15-year-old boy rocked by his hormones
that women and, for that matter, adults may experience intense alienation.
Me, I sort of liked it.

The movie, maddeningly baroque and 20 minutes too long, plays
like a hash of James M. Cain, Jacques Tourneur, and Russ Meyer, and

doesn't make a bit of sense, except perhaps as a wet dream. In the production notes, Hopper sounds very sober about the film: His orthodox plot synopsis has little relationship to the hysteria played out on screen, and his observations—"I think noir is every director's favorite genre . . . a great depiction of human frailties and perversities . . . the decadence and hidden corruptions of small town life"—hit all the right buttons without suggesting the obsessive flamboyance that topples his ambition along with his apparent sincerity. The film itself is more reassuring. It is insane, but crafted; you scoff, but you don't look away. Hopper may have intended to make a grand guignol B-movie, but he has devised something more like an opera without music. Of course, music is all that makes a deranged libretto tolerable, and Hopper knows that well enough to secure a terrific soundtrack, supervised by Jack Nitzsche, with Miles Davis improvising against the elliptical guitars of John Lee Hooker and Taj Mahal. The score's sustained blues wail (the Antilles album is worth searching out) nearly balances the riotous action.

The Hot Spot is based on a 1953 paperback, *Hell Hath No Fury*, by Charles Williams, whose *Dead Calm* was filmed more conventionally last year. Williams co-scripted with Nona Tyson, but since they died, respectively, in 1975 and 1982, it's safe to assume that the diabolical excesses are Hopper's. The elements of adolescent fantasy are in place from the start. Harry Madox (Don Johnson, of course) wanders into a nondescript town called Landers—no telltale accents—and finds immediate employment with a used car dealership run by George Harshaw (Jerry Hardin). Before the sun sets, he learns that the local bank is left unattended during fires, and is enticed by two of the sexiest women in the Western hemisphere. One is a leggy, vaguely innocent brunette named Gloria (Jennifer Connelly), with a secret. The other is Harshaw's southern trash wife, Dolly (Virginia Madsen), a hot blond with glistening lips and the largest collection of lingerie since Jean Harlow.

Madox spends the next two hours alternating between the two women. He has more fun with Dolly, but doesn't respect her afterward until he gets hard again. It's Gloria he wants to spirit away to the Caribbean with the money he steals from the unattended bank. But as always happens in these situations, the spurned wife causes havoc. Naturally, she requires him to kill her husband, who has the requisite weak heart. Madox is every boy's idea of manhood: unconquerable in a fight, handy with a firebomb, quick on his feet, irresistible to women. If you thought about it, you might wonder what he's doing wandering around tank towns selling used cars. He's also got courage and the rudiments of a conscience. When a drunk is imperiled in the fire he sets, he risks his life to rescue him. When Gloria is imperiled by a blackmailer, he kills the cad and makes it look like suicide (at least to the local police, credulous morons all). He draws the line at killing husbands.

The characters are pasteboard figures made lively by the cast. Style is everything here, and Hopper's is audacious enough to compensate for the lack of credibility. What more perfect metaphor could one want for the fusion of film noir and film blue than Madox's first boudoir encounter with Dolly? He wanders into her unlocked house at night and steals up to the bedroom, where she awaits him gleaming in black satin. As he steps forward, she springs from the bed with a small revolver; while pressing it hard against his neck, she gives him a blowjob—an effective one, judging from Madox's instant grimace. The silliness must have gotten to Hopper, because instead of bringing the film back to earth, he revs it up, and the sex gets increasingly comic book. Soon the audience is grimacing. The scene that elicited the loudest hissing has no sex: Gloria confesses her secret, via a flashback, in which she and her sister sit naked by a creek. Hopper shoots them breast-on, with an ostentatious impertinence that you will find either offensive or amusing.

The first hour of *The Hot Spot* moves with a knowing legato tempo that speeds up as the plot coagulates. The opening shots, taken from Madox's point of view, are leisurely and cautious, and the introduction of the main characters is crazily efficient. Practically the first people he sees are Gloria, along with fellow car salesman Lon (played by Hume Cronyn look-alike Charles Martin Smith in a big cowboy hat that seems to push him into the ground), and the evil blackmailer, Sutton (William Sadler), who has a Playboy Club token dangling from the rearview mirror of his car. All of the performers are convincing, as is Ueli Steiger's realistic photography. Johnson is acceptable because he's kept on a low flame and when he does anything overt—like smile or grunt—you are relieved that he is about to come alive.

But the actor who should get the biggest boost from *The Hot Spot* is Madsen, as the kinkiest femme fatale since Ann Savage in Edgar Ulmer's *Detour*. Her preferred method of birth control is to hurl herself off a high railing: "It's not the fall that does it, but the climb up," she explains. From her first scene, toying with her skirt, deciding how high to raise it to bait Madox, she has him and the film between her knees. "Only two things to do around here," she tells him. "You gotta TV?" He says no. "Well, now you're down to one," she says, trailing the scent of magnolia, then adds with an edge, "Lots of luck." She's a spider, like Maerose in *Prizzi's Honor*, except that her web is furnished with stuffed animals (bears and lions) and Hawaiian music plays on the stereo. Dolly is the adolescent fantasy come to petrifying life and, unlike her husband, whom she dispatches as best she can ("I'm fucking you to death," she tells him and does), is invincible. Madsen isn't too beautiful to be spooky; but her Dolly thinks she is—and her iron-maiden heedlessness makes the role memorable.

Jennifer Connelly, on the other hand, is so appealing, you half hope she and Madox will have their happy ending, an event that would fulfill the film's promo line, "Film noir like you've never seen it." The unhappy ending, with the femme fatale holding the upper hand, is noir as we always see it, though there is something of a twist in Madox's acceptance of his fate: We last see him in the passenger seat, wearing an outsized cowboy hat, as Dolly drives them down the highway. "Yes, indeed, I found my level and I'm living it," he says. A simpler ending would have had the advantage of shortening the movie, which climaxes in an extended bottleneck of revelations and reversals. You have to give Hopper credit for taking the fantasy down the pike, but Madox's defeat is no more convincing than his fistfight with Sutton, in which every bone-cruncher is loudly amplified on the soundtrack yet never does any damage. Hopper's saving grace is that he knows he's off the reservation. When you know he knows it, you don't mind following him.

4. White Palace

What's with all these blowjobs? They represent Hollywood's latest code for breaking the ice, for reaching out and touching someone, for initiating a sincere and meaningful relationship. No more kissing on the mouth, no more "What was your major?"—just cut to the fly, followed by a shot of an actor faking instantaneous ecstasy. TV shills are accustomed to labeling such scenes "steamy," but on the basis of recent cinematic blowjobs, I doubt it's possible—outside the realm of pornography, which boasts the respectable goal of honest titillation—to film one in a style that fails to provoke giggles. Putting aside issues of motivation and verism, how many ways can you photograph the back of an actress's head in a push me/pull you bob? How many ways can an actor clench his face and say, "Ahhhhhhh"? Since the point is made as soon as the former falls to crotch latitude, which muses does the director serve in repeatedly cutting from bobbing head to gritted teeth. And what are we to make of the fact that blowjobs are rated R (*Pretty Woman, The Hot Spot, White Palace*), while genital sex along with bathing (*Tie Me Up, Tie Me Down*) and wilted penises (*Scandal*) threaten to undermine the empire, and in fact instigated a revision in the ratings code?

Even when a blowjob is depicted graphically, as in the 1986 *Devil in the Flesh*, the effect is to stop the action rather than propel it. The problem with pornography as art is that it changes the narrative mode from fiction to documentary. The effect is more surprising than shocking —the deed demystified, flesh reduced to flesh. The lingering eroticism of the great Hollywood romances of the '30s and '40s is inseparable from a grown-up attitude toward privacy, where the suspense pivots on whether the protagonists will get into bed, not what they do once they get there. Do we want to see what Bogart and Bergman were up to while her husband attended the underground meeting?

I confess some embarrassment in watching Susan Sarandon and James Spader put through their paces in *White Palace*, in part because they are so good when plying the more conventional aspects of their trade, like interpreting dialogue, and in part because the movie almost succeeds as an agreeable love story. The now hoary twist of teaming a young man (27) with an older woman (43) is handled with sensitivity to both. When they resolve their differences, as you hope they will, you are willing to take a leap in faith for the sake of requited love. But if the film begins to curdle in the mind an hour later, the problem may be the simulated sex. In their adaptation of a novel by Glenn Savan, scenarists Ted Tally and Alvin Sargent have constructed a script that pins the story to two fronts: We either watch the principals, Nora and Max, enjoying a perfect marriage of the flesh or arguing over the differences likely to pull them apart.

That might be enough if *White Palace* were simply about a sublime erotic encounter. People kill each other for less, and the film might have found a way to take that story in either direction—the death of eros or its affirmation. But this movie aims for something more didactic: a portrait of how people are changed when passion turns to love, and the responsibilities they are willing to embrace. In the end, Max gives up his job, his home, his family, and friends (all in St. Louis) to follow Nora to New York (he rents a tenement in Hell's Kitchen, no less). To justify his obsession, the film is obliged to include at least one scene in which we get to see them do something other than fuck or fight. Clever screenwriting of the '30s and '40s excelled at conveying pre- and post-coital pleasure. During the past 20 years, verbal contrivances were replaced by montages (happy couple trots along the beach as soundtrack swells). *White Palace* dutifully includes such a montage, which ends with him giving her head—and it isn't enough.

Evading the substance of their love, the film relentlessly details all the differences between them: He's Jewish, rich, anal compulsive, celibate, a nonsmoker, and listens to Mozart; she's a lapsed Catholic, poor (she works in the eponymous burger joint, modeled after White Castle), slovenly, promiscuous, a chain-smoker, and listens to the Oak Ridge Boys. He's ashamed to show her to family and friends, which leads to much squabbling, all handsomely written and played—the film is never more alive than in those episodes. He thinks he's terrifically clever to buy her a dust-buster, wrapped like a birthday present. "You bought me cleaning equipment?" she asks with disbelief, before kicking him out. He returns sheepishly with flowers.

In a standout scene, the Thanksgiving dinner at which Max finally introduces Nora to his mother and friends, Nora hot-headedly faces off with another woman on the relative efficacy of their blowjobs, then redeems herself by asserting her working-class credentials against the facile pontifications of the host's father. Back at Nora's place, you expect the longed-for moment when Max and Nora can take some mutual pleasure in the debacle of the party. Instead we get a replay of an earlier scene, in which Nora calls Max a liar and Max once again can't think of anything to say. The contrivance of having her leave town in the dead of night, so Max can make his sacrifice and track her down—unless I misread the scene, he takes a taxicab from St. Louis to New York—puts more weight on the pleasures of the flesh than flesh can withstand. There is something chilling about a movie that gives you the blowjob but shies away from the small talk.

Director Luis Mandoki shines when he has Max and Nora in the grip of their compulsions. His tempo is sure, and he respects most of his characters. The secondary roles tend toward stereotype without quite falling into caricature, excepting Eileen Brennan as Nora's overbearing, clownishly made-up psychic sister; if I thought anyone like that lived in New York, I would move to St. Louis. Sarandon is superb, as usual. She seems able to act without the intercession of vanity. In the toilet confrontation at the Thanksgiving dinner, Mandoki shoots her from a distance and she affects a posture that suggests cocky resolve and gross awkwardness at the same time. Her close-up after the blowjob is the most erotic moment in the film. If the character of Nora isn't fleshed out enough to serve the conceit of the story, Sarandon isn't to blame.

Spader does his best to make Max credible, playing the early scenes smug and cold but with enough vulnerability to attract Nora. Another curious note on the sexual frontier: Nora's sister asks Max and Nora how they met. Max becomes gallant, explaining that he seduced her instead of the other way around. Nora kisses him in gratitude and the sister is practically vaporized by Max's lovely sentiment. Except for that scene, the film admires Nora's independence—it treats sexual warfare as an issue of class, not gender. Yet in one egregious moment, we are reminded that even in this shameless age, it is considered chivalrous to shield a woman's promiscuity.

[*Village Voice*, March–October, 1990]

47 ❖ *WWII and the Whole Truth* (The Big Red One / Devils on the Doorstep / British War Collection)

In celebrating Homer as the paradigm of writers who tell the whole truth, Aldous Huxley singled out the episode in which Odysseus and his men, having watched six of their companions devoured by Scylla, weep and then prepare a masterly meal before succumbing to a gentle sleep. Other poets, Huxley argued, would have ended the canto with tears. I find myself thinking of Huxley (and of Homer) when watching Sam Fuller's *The Big Red One*. A baby-face recruit named Kaiser, whom we have come to enjoy, is abruptly killed in battle, his last words: "Did I kill the guy that killed me?" The film cuts to a raucously funny dinner, where Kaiser's division plans an orgy to stage the fallen virgin's sexual fantasy.

This is the Fuller touch—an almost unbearably tense or tragic moment capped by an aphoristically comic one-liner or a scene of utterly contrary dimensions—and it is felt throughout *The Big Red One*. His odyssey tracks the progress of an old sergeant, played by Lee Marvin in the most resonant performance of his career, and four young recruits, from the Algerian coast in 1942 to the liberation of a Czech concentration camp three years later. One recruit, Griff, is brave enough when lobbing grenades, but cannot shoot a man face to face. After experiencing numbing horror at the Czech camp, however, he encounters a Nazi who is out of ammunition, and in a moment of transfixed madness kills him, firing bullet after bullet into the corpse. The sergeant cautiously approaches Griff, pats him on the back, and drawls, with a casual let's-move-on camaraderie, "I think you got him."

Tellingly, the orgy talk disappeared from the film when Warner released a butchered but brawny two-hour cut in 1980. Fuller, a decorated veteran who died in 1997 at 85, had spent most of his career writing and directing idiosyncratic B-budget films in which sex, violence, survival, miscegenation, and madness are habitual themes. He hoped his original vision might be patched together, but after more than two decades, that dream seemed no more likely than restorations of *Greed* and *The Magnificent Ambersons*. Yet a couple of years ago, cans of missing footage were found warehoused in the Midwest, and Richard Schickel, the critic and documentary filmmaker (his "The Men Who Made the Movies" segment on Fuller is included on the DVD), was hired to supervise the recreation. Using Fuller's shooting script and some conjecture, Schickel reinstated nearly

50 minutes of new material, producing a deeper, faster, more coherent, and more truthful work—a candidate for the best film ever made about World War II, which is saying a lot.

More movies have been made about World War II than any other subject. If the tally includes films about prewar Nazism, home fronts, service comedies, musicals, and postwar resettlement, the total is in the area of 2000—the kind of number we associate with whole genres (war films, westerns), not a specific subset. The reason goes beyond the historical magnitude of a conflict that remade the world. Successful genres promote audience identification and dichotomies between good and evil. The reality of a citizen army is now remote, but the appeal—at least in the realm of fantasy—of battles in which any of us might have been thrust is not. The war film allows us to weigh ourselves in the balance, and World War II remains near enough to supersede the alienating effects of antiquated uniforms, jargon, and armaments.

Morally, World War II is the safest of military harbors. In assessing the Northern temper after the Civil War, Robert Penn Warren said it had assumed a monopoly on the Treasury of Virtue, a not undeserved stance, he conceded, but one that blinded the victors to their own ethical failings. Every national cinema can feel virtuous about World War II—even those of Germany and Japan, for overcoming and surviving temporary bouts of insanity. Antiwar films focus on the insanity of battle, but truth tellers are obliged to recognize that sometimes the only cure for insanity is more insanity. Not even Homer could have invented a better kicker than the liberation of the camps, which justified the agonies of war after the fact, at least for the survivors.

Fuller sees battle as a socially condoned madness in which killing (or murder: his soldiers debate the semantics) is approved, but he is nonetheless mindful of the stakes. In a film that has almost as much eating and drinking as battleground engagements, he does not condone the madness. He laughs uproariously at it, and turns his attention to the immediate problem: survival. *The Big Red One* is unapologetically schematic, beginning and ending with precisely parallel events; it depends on the premise that his recruits (they call themselves the Four Horsemen) and their sergeant are invincible, while dogface replacements fall all around them. Fuller's vision is epical: The scheme is fantastic, the details realistic.

The same may be said for Jiang Wen's *Devils on the Doorstep* (2000), which won the Grand Prix at Cannes in a longer version, later cut by Jiang, a writer and director who also plays the lead role. Questions have been raised about the cuts, because Jiang's career was put on hold by disgruntled Chinese officials, but the 139-minute version feels complete and right, and we can only take his word, stated on the DVD, that the cuts were aesthetic and not political. The picture opens with a black screen and the order, "Attention!" From the first shot of Japanese soldiers waddling through the village to an absurdly upbeat march, Jiang commands attention and holds it.

In a small Northern area of the Great Wall, called Rack-Armor Terrace, a peasant named Ma Dasan is interrupted during lovemaking by a rifle-wielding intruder who identifies himself as "Me" and leaves two Japanese prisoners wrapped in sacks, demanding that Dasan protect and, "in his spare time," interrogate them until "Me" retrieves them in five days. What follows is an improbably funny nightmare, part Kafka (six months pass as the community hides, feeds, and cleans up after its prisoners, never learning why or for whom), part Abbott and Costello ("Who is 'Me?'" "How do I know who you are?"). One captive is a translator who keeps himself and his suicidal commander alive through mistranslation. When the soldier wants to curse out the Chinese, the translator teaches him to say "Happy New Year." That's nice, says Dasan, but why does he sound so angry? When the soldier later discovers he has been tricked, he says, "Educated people are so evil."

As played by Jiang, with his jug-ears, bedroom eyes, and permanent state of fearful confusion, Dasan is naturally comic, yet also resourceful and determined to hold onto his sense of decency. "We can't kill and we won't," his pregnant girlfriend insists, and he concurs, though he does search out a swordsman who doesn't live up to his reputation as One-Strike Liu. When the captives convince the Chinese to trade them back to their army in exchange for grain, the tone of the film changes from comedy to outright horror. The full brutality of the Japanese occupiers emerges at a banquet that we know will end in disaster, though the warning signs don't mitigate the shock.

Just as Fuller's sergeant (whose career began in World War I) killed a surrendering Hun not knowing that the Armistice has been signed, the Japanese launch their massacre after Japan has surrendered. The difference is this: The Japanese commander knows. After the devastation, the Chinese army, supported by gum-chewing U.S. troops, replaces Japan's army. Dasan, shaken to the core, realizes that revenge and death are preferable to acceptance. He goes on an ax-wielding rampage against the imprisoned slaughterers, and is publicly executed, welcoming death as the film turns from black-and-white to color and his decapitated head winks at the viewer with satisfaction. Insanity has its privileges.

The powers in China resented Jiang's depiction of the coldly supercilious, young Chinese leader who spouts empty rhetoric, ordering the death of Dasan for killing "Japanese devils": He asks, "Are they not human, too?" Presumably, Chinese leaders do share Dasan's outrage at a barbarous invasion. (In an interview included with the DVD, Jiang points out that he cast Japanese friends in key roles and had to convince them that their countrymen really did perpetrate atrocities.) Even so, China has been relatively taciturn about the eight-year occupation, which is one reason *Devils on the Doorstep* is so novel. They, too, were searching for power through the barrel of a gun, while the West's Treasury of Virtue covered a multitude of imperialist sins.

After the Battle of Britain, the English—or at least Vera Lynn—knew that the old music hall favorite, "A Nightingale Sang in Berkeley Square," or the more recent "We'll Meet Again," would replace "Rule Britannia" as their theme song. As early as 1942, the British film industry could see the future. An amiable guide (Mervyn Johns) welcomes us to a churchyard in scenic Bramley End, where the defeated Nazi invaders were buried: "They wanted England, the Jerries did, and this is the only bit they got."

This is the opening of a remarkable film with the ungainly title, *Went the Day Well?*—the earliest of five, mostly made at Ealing Studios and collected in *British War Films*. (A complete absence of supplementary material represents a tremendous opportunity missed, but the feature Americans will most long for is the option of English subtitles; these films make no allowances for local accents and period slang.) Briskly piloted by Alberto Cavalcanti from a Graham Greene story, *Went the Day Well?* presumes to look back at the war as a rousing break in quaint village life, while pointing a finger at traitors among the neighbors—most nefariously, Leslie Banks, whose actual war-scarred face never looked more ominous. After a series of suspenseful episodes, including the shooting of a young boy, that portend a Nazi victory, the residents rouse themselves in one of the most violent episodes in any English film before Hammer unleashed its monsters—one elderly woman buttons a German with an axe. That bit of church ground was not bought cheaply.

Within a couple of years of the war, the British film industry went full throttle in honoring its heroes on land and sea and in the air and in POW camps. In 1952, Charles Frend directed Eric Ambler's efficient script of the Nicholas Monserrat bestseller, *The Cruel Sea*, a landmark film not least for establishing actor Jack Hawkins as the British lion for the next decade. A compelling heavy, Hawkins later gave a memorable performance as the bitter ex-army officer organizing a heist in *The League of Gentlemen*, but here he personifies the paternal side of the stiff upper lip, the commander everyone would like to serve—a man, who, having killed sailors expecting to be rescued from the sea, because a German U-boat lurks beneath them, weeps copiously, doubting himself and the whole bloody war. John Wayne must have blanched; Homer would have understood.

This was the same year as *High Noon*, a western criticized by Howard Hawks because the marshal asks civilians to help him out of a jam—something he said could not happen. Yet the template for *High Noon* was the citizen army that Hawks himself had sentimentalized in *Sergeant York*. *The Cruel Sea* draws its moral edge from the sacrifices of amateurs. Filmed with documentary precision (including a helpful explanation of sonar), here was a film made for those who had served, a justification and historical finale. The battles at sea are excellent, but the real drama accrues with personal issues, now considered war film clichés: the good commander versus the self-important martinet (in this instance, Stanley Baker, who is dispatched faster than you can say duodenal ulcer), uncertainty at home, the madness of impersonal killing. Upon destroying a German sub and bringing survivors aboard, Hawkins says, "This is quite a moment. We've never seen the enemy before."

The Dam Busters, the nickname for Squadron 647, is never used in the film of that name. The mission it details achieved little of military value and is largely forgotten, but the story is so good that Michael Anderson's pedestrian direction cannot derail its interest. Told in four sections, the picture shows how Barnes Wallace (Michael Redgrave) worked up the apparently preposterous idea of dropping 5,000-pound cylindrical bombs that would skim over lakes like flat stones (but only if dropped from a height of exactly 60 feet at 240 miles per hour) until reaching German dams; how Wing Commander Guy Gibson (Richard Todd) trained the squadron in secrecy and led the attack; how the last hours were spent; and how the attack did and did not succeed on May 16, 1943—at the cost of 19 planes and 56 British flyers.

When shown in American theaters, the 1954 film was cut by 20 minutes and Gibson's black dog was renamed Trigger (to rhyme with the actual name); the DVD restores it to its original form, which builds at a leisurely tempo to a fiercely fought mission. The special effects are dated but effective, and though it honors the flyers, the film refuses to patronize them or the audience with inserts of doomed pilots or overstated claims for what they did. It ends not on a note of victory, but with bone-weary exhaustion, a job of work done, as Gibson walks off to write letters to the families of the dead and missing.

The remaining two films, both made in 1955, are less imposing. Guy Hamilton's *The Colditz Story*, a hugely influential film in its day, remains one of the better POW pictures, playing down the comical German officer of *Stalag 17*, and sustaining tension as escape attempts mount and various prisoner armies come to an accord. Although the film wisely keeps to Colditz castle, emphasizing the claustrophobia and ignorance of the outside world, the summer camp quality that pervades most POW films undermines interest in the characters—a failing that John Mills and Eric Portman do nothing to reverse, though it is fun to see Lionel Jeffries, too briefly, in a straight dramatic role.

The Ship that Died of Shame (1955), based on a Monserrat story, directed by the undervalued Basil Dearden (assisted by producer Michael Relph), and photographed superbly by Gordon Dines, deploys much talent on a kind of EC-comics mystical anecdote about a ship that rebels against its postwar repatriation by smugglers. Richard Attenborough is a repellant villain, never more rat-faced than as a Brighton Rock sharpie whom the ship ultimately tosses overboard. The ship didn't mind killing Nazis, but transporting a German child molester (right out of *M*) is more than it can abide.

There is a serious theme here: the difficulty that demobilized servicemen had in finding work in a country salving its wounds with black-market balms. The early battle scenes and a romance involving George Baker and Virginia McKenna are convincing, as is the knowing split established between those living in the past (getting together to sing "We'll Meet Again") and would-be entrepreneurs, encouraged like Prohibition bootleggers to engage in the putatively harmless crime of giving people what they want. The smugglers, who come in two classes, murderous and good-hearted, disturb the filmmakers because they waste whatever is left in the Treasury of Virtue. If the filmmakers had allowed the characters and not the ship to mete out justice, it wouldn't have been the whole truth, but it would have been plausible.

[*The New York Sun*, 7 June 2005]

Do you remember the Christmas before Bird died, when we were in somebody's loft in the Village with Bird and Hank Mobley? Bird said, "Hear with your eyes and see with your ears." I never forgot that.
—Art Blakey, *Notes and Tones*

48 ❖ Mixing Hot Licks with Vanilla (Fats Waller / Glenn Miller)

Centennials make for strange bedfellows. Glenn Miller and Fats Waller were born in the same year, 1904, and died on the same date, December 15. In 1943, on the return lap of a West Coast tour, Waller died of pneumonia at the age of 39. A year later, Major Glenn Miller's plane disappeared over the English Channel en route to a victory concert in Paris. He is now thought by some—the issue is much disputed—to have been the victim of Allied bombers dropping payload from a higher altitude. (I'd like to think fighter-pilot Jimmy Stewart was the culprit, but that's me.) The works of both are sampled on rather chintzy anniversary collections that illuminate the enduring appeal of mush and mockery at the hotly contested border between jazz and pop.

Few pop idols survive changing fashions unscathed, but Miller and Waller seem to have done just that. One might have expected the renown of Miller, a hard-nosed martinet who devised the big-band sound most associated with reveries of the 1940s, to fade with recollections of the war in which he lost his life. Instead, critics who once denigrated him as a humorless purveyor of diluted swing, banal novelties, and saccharine vocals are reassessing a sound that clings relentlessly to the collective memory. The unimpeded preeminence of Thomas (Fats) Waller is perhaps less of a surprise, given the dazzle of his pianism, the thumping pleasures of his small band, and the frequent hilarity of his satire. Still, considering how much of his popularity derived from vocal parodies of Tin Pan Alley detritus, one is inclined to echo his sighing meditation: "One never knows, do one?" Waller's comedy has grown in stature; critics no longer write of it defensively (spare us your guilty pleasures) or reproach RCA-Victor, his record label (and Miller's), for forcing him into the role of jester. In short, as with Miller, the public was right and the critics are playing catch-up.

We do better to consider the overlooked similarities between Miller and Waller than to belabor their obvious differences. Too much has been made of a racial divide that turned them into emblems of black cool and white corn—stereotypes typified by, say, Waller's serenade to marijuana, "If You're a Viper," and Miller's plea for home-front fidelity, "Don't Sit Under the Apple Tree." It is true that Miller reached millions of whites for whom the names Ellington, Basie, and Lunceford meant little and that Waller was characterized as (in the words of one radio announcer) "that hot man of Harlem" trafficking in "rhythmic hot-cha." But everyone danced to Miller, and more whites than blacks bought Waller records.

They had much in common. Waller recorded his share of unadulter-
ated corn while Miller's resourceful swing arrangements mitigated his many
soggy vocal numbers. They also shared a penchant for hiring capable but
humdrum musicians, including their tenor saxophonists—Miller's Tex
Beneke (who also sang) and Waller's Gene Sedric, two B-list versions of
Coleman Hawkins, whose centenary also falls this year. The era inspired
similar goals: Waller encouraged people to laugh through the privations
of the 1930s and Miller induced them to romanticize American values
during wartime. Both men kept the nation's feet tapping and bodies
swaying with a steady beat, and both used jazz as a conduit to reach a
larger public than jazz per se could command—witness their summonses
to Hollywood, where they provided window dressing for middling
musicals. They were defined by the times. Now they define those times
for us.

Waller's pinnacle as a recording artist, from 1934 to 1939, directly preceded Miller's (which began in 1939, with "Moonlight Serenade"). But
Waller had been a force in New York from the beginning of his career,
achieving widespread recognition for the stream of popular songs—
including "Ain't Misbehavin'," "Black and Blue," and "Honeysuckle
Rose"—he wrote for the 1929 revues *Hot Chocolates* and *Load of Coal*. Among
musicians, he won greater acclaim for an astonishing body of piano
music, which brought a Mendelssohnian composure to the charged
Harlem stride style of James P. Johnson. His serene touch, rhythmic tact,
and treasury of melodic ideas established him in New York's jazz and
theatrical vanguards long before he crossed into the mainstream, in the
mid-'30s, with a six-piece band called Fats Waller and His Rhythm.

From then on, Waller's regimen in the studios was unparalleled. He
recorded some 500 sides, working with little or no time for rehearsal
and often with material that few others would touch ("Nero," "Floating
Down to Cotton Town," "The Curse of an Aching Heart," "You're Not
the Only Oyster in the Stew"). He proved himself able to alchemize the
dreariest of songs into nuggets of pure swing, transforming himself in
the process into an irrepressible and, even now, instantly recognizable
derby-crowned dandy. This was hardly a sellout. Waller's technical ease
and emotional undercurrent are no less apparent on his popular records
than in his formal solos. The feathery detachment and weighty bravura
juxtaposed in "Then I'll Be Tired of You" is, in its way, as impressive
as the dense compositional cunning of "African Ripples" or the blues-
driven ease of "Numb Fumblin'." His nimble vocals, whether droll or
moving ("I'm Gonna Sit Right Down and Write Myself a Letter" is an
incomparable instance of the latter), reflect a knack for instantly sizing
up which notes or lyrics are best served straight up, mixed with bitters,

or injected with spritzer. Thus he bestows a kind of immortality on songs never intended to transcend their provenance.

Many of the numbers mentioned above are included on Bluebird's *Centennial Collection*, selected by Mike Lipskin, a skillful stride pianist who has daringly ignored obvious hits like "Honeysuckle Rose" in favor of a fresh montage. (The one misstep is the inclusion three times of "Your Feet's Too Big," twice on a short accompanying DVD.) By contrast, Miller's *Centennial Collection* is a predictable assemblage, which means too many Ray Eberle vocals and an obligatory dose of wartime infantilism —"The Boogie Wooglie Piggy," with Miller's rather creepy vocal group, the Modernaires, harmonizing the oinks. This is too bad, because Miller is overdue for a compilation of his finest work, including his inventive Army Air Force Band performances, not least "Mission to Moscow" (arranged for Miller by its composer, Mel Powell, who later made his career as an avant-gardist combining 12-tone rows with electronics). Instead, we get a mood-killing electronica remix of "Pennsylvania 6-5000" and a DVD with home movies in which no one is identified.

Miller's stardom helped revive a flagging record industry, inadvertently launching the gold record tradition as a publicity stunt in 1942, when RCA presented him with a gold-lacquered disc of "Chattanooga Choo Choo," to celebrate sales of more than a million copies. By the time Miller achieved success, at the age of 35, he had endured more than a decade of freelance arranging and whatever sideman gigs his limited abilities as a trombonist allowed, and it seems likely that this left him somewhat bitter. He once told the critic John Hammond, who had reviewed him disdainfully, that he ought not be criticized, because his only interest was in making money. Though he affected strained folksiness on the air, Miller exuded little warmth on or off the bandstand. Yet once the band struck up its theme, audiences were done for: throats clutched and eyes softened. Can any other record match "Moonlight Serenade" for its ability to induce a Pavlovian slaver in so many for so long?

James Stewart created a suitable posthumous personality for Miller in *The Glenn Miller Story*, the 1954 film that inaugurated a short-lived genre of musicals about white bandleaders. These pictures, though basted in conformity, flattered the taste of the 1950s audience by recasting Miller, Benny Goodman, Eddie Duchin, Red Nichols, and Gene Krupa as young radicals braving ridicule. Miller was depicted as an innovator hunting for an elusive sound, and Stewart had to recite breathtaking inanities like "To me, music is more than just one instrument. It's a whole orchestra playing together." Miller offered a more credible precept in the lyric to his 1942 hit "Juke Box Saturday Night": "Mixin' hot licks with vanilla."

That modest recipe gave him his identity. It remains unmistakable: a clarinet playing lead, supported by closely harmonized saxophones, with responses from a large brass section (often muted to minimize vibrato) and a politely clumping four-man rhythm section. Less widely noted were Miller's affinity for dissonance and his tendency to combine 12-bar blues with 32-bar song form—hardly characteristic of a musical cynic. Yet once he found a winning combination, he did not waver and soon delegated "the Miller sound" to superior arrangers like Jerry Gray and Bill Finegan, who in effect out-Millered Miller.

The formula reached perfection in three masterpieces of jazz-influenced pop. "Moonlight Serenade" began life as an exercise that Miller worked on for an arranging course. It failed as a conventional song with lyrics and might have disappeared had he not dressed it in what would become his trademark sound. The clarinet lead, handsomely intoned by Wilbur Schwartz, and the swaying melody pinned to the first beat of each measure evoke a vanished age, even for those who never knew the age. The listener hardly notices the unusual 44-bar format, which flirts with but avoids blues harmonies in its key 12-bar melody. "In the Mood," which all but defines swing for those who grew up with it in the '40s and'50s (or '90s, when it became the refrain of retro-swing), is a blues punctuated by a 16-bar middle section. Miller's recording is patched together from jazz's spare parts. The main phrase had previously served Wingy Manone in "Tar Paper Stomp" and Fletcher Henderson in "Hot and Anxious," and was later organized into a theme by Joe Garland, who sold his arrangement to Miller. The famous episode in which the orchestra fades down had been similarly used by Goodman to soup up "Don't Be That Way." The genteel saxophone exchanges wink at the genuine saxophone duels popular at the time, and the startling ascending coda by the brasses suggests an inversion of the legendary Louis Armstrong cadenza that opens "West End Blues." Yet the resulting performance is unmistakably Milleresque in every measure.

More affecting is "A String of Pearls," a quintessential Miller piece that Miller didn't write (it was the work of Jerry Gray). A 4-bar introduction meshes hot brasses, a bass walk, and a guitar break, and the undulating theme combines 8- and 12-measure formats. The contrast between the high reeds and the bass-clef responses is palpable, the saxophone exchanges are substantive, and Bobby Hackett's lyrical trumpet solo—played over a neat trombone figure introduced in the preceding passage—draws the blues as far from its roots as anyone could until Miles Davis explored related harmonies after the war.

Miller and Waller embody the A side and B side of a time when melodic tranquility and robust rhythms found common cause. Listeners who come of age in such a period think it will last forever—ask any veteran of Sgt. Pepper's Lonely Hearts Club Band. But the Swing Era expired in short order; hip-hop is already twice its age. The end of the war meant the end of the big bands, as the music that followed—bebop, rhythm and blues, pop novelties—moved away from gentle lyricism and foxtrot rhythms. Yet the Swing Era has much to teach us. Beyond the pleasures of their performances, Waller and Miller provide another service: They humble critical stereotypes and show ways that jazz and pop once enriched each other, and might still.

(The New Yorker, 31 May 2004)

49 ❖ *Brush Up Your Porter (Cole Porter)*

Among connoisseurs of the Hollywood musical, a special ring in hell is reserved for songwriter biopics of the 1940s, which followed two inviolable rules—tone down the Jewishness (imagine the brainstorming that cast Tom Drake and Mickey Rooney as Rodgers and Hart in *Words and Music*), and avoid any indication of polymorphous sexuality: hence the straight or straightened Cary Grant as Cole Porter in the largely fictitious *Night and Day*. In the marginally less fictitious *De-Lovely*, Kevin Kline's Cole Porter, says of the earlier film, "If I can survive this movie, I can survive anything." Porter did survive it for 18 pain-ridden but often-creative years. *De-Lovely* might have proved fatal.

Night and Day ignored Porter's partiality for men. Big deal. *De-Lovely* degrades his genius for song writing—a far graver dereliction. *Night and Day*'s wall-to-wall music was ably performed by singers who, excepting Mary Martin and Ginny Simms, were not well known then and are entirely forgotten now. Yet they imbued the songs with a glowing conviction. *De-Lovely* gives Porter's music plenty of screen time, but here the interpretations denude it of all its wonders: melodic distinction, harmonic ingenuity, rhythmic élan, erotic subversion, debonair wit, unconstrained gaiety.

The producers slipped on the oldest banana peel in show business, recruiting inappropriate performers in the hope of making a historic work look au courant. Most of these singers handle Porter's lyrics as though they were learned phonetically; they mangle his expressive melodies like melisma-addled amateurs who, unable to hit a note on the button, slither into it—usually with a groan to let you know how involved they are. Many contemporaries can do or might have done justice to Porter's art (among them: Dee Dee Bridgewater, Dianne Reeves, Michael Feinstein, Karrin Allyson, Cassandra Wilson, Mary Cleere Haran, Rebecca Luker, Sting, Allan Harris, and Madonna, not to mention a certain Mr. Bennett), including two who are in the picture—Diana Krall and Natalie Cole. The former is undermined by a lifeless arrangement and relegated to background ambience, leaving only the latter to shine with her rendition of "Ev'ry Time We Say Good-bye," which, significantly, recalls classic renditions by Ella Fitzgerald and Betty Carter.

Porter will survive this, too—he survives everything. No songwriter is more frequently rediscovered, decade after decade, always with a renewed surprise at the depth and breadth of his work. In the years after his crippling 1937 equestrian accident (which *De-Lovely* stages as cosmic punishment for sexual indulgences it pretends to absolve), he scattered some of his finest songs in uneven stage shows, until the 1948 master-piece, *Kiss Me, Kate* ("Too Darn Hot," "Why Can't You Behave?" "So in Love," "Always True to You in My Fashion," "Brush Up Your Shake-speare"), spurred the first of several Porter renaissances.

The second occurred only eight years later, when in quick succession a woefully expurgated film version (the second) of *Anything Goes* was off-set by the smash double-LP *Ella Fitzgerald Sings the Cole Porter Songbook* (one of the best-selling jazz albums of all time) and the MGM film *High Society*, in which Bing Crosby and Grace Kelly introduced Porter's last million-seller, "True Love." In *De-Lovely*, Porter composes "True Love" in the 1920s, and disparages it as froufrou designed to please his wife; in truth, he took much pride in its waltzing simplicity, its subtle diminished chords, and, above all, its immense popularity. He hoped in vain that it would win him an Oscar.

Although his songs sparked a dozen films, Porter had never been an easy fit for Hollywood. His 1932 stage show *Gay Divorce* was adapted as a 1934 vehicle for Fred Astaire and Ginger Rogers, *The Gay Divorcee*, with all but one of his songs ("Night and Day") cut. A couple of years later, Ethel Merman joined with Bing Crosby to bring Broadway au-thenticity to the first film of *Anything Goes*, and the censors went nuclear. "All Through the Night" was killed because of the line "You and your love bring me ecstasy" and "Blow, Gabriel, Blow" because it might have offended religious propriety. A hack lyricist was hired to rewrite the title number, which was nonetheless nervously relegated to background music for the credits. Also cleaned up: "I Get a Kick Out of You" and "You're the Top." In three decades only four of Porter's songs were nominated for Academy Awards (eligible songs that weren't nominated include "In the Still of the Night," "I Concentrate on You," "Don't Fence Me In," "Be a Clown," and "Who Wants to Be a Millionaire?")—he never won.

After Porter's death, in 1964, the cabaret singers Bobby Short and Mabel Mercer generated another revival, which continued to wax in 1971 with the publication of Robert Kimball's anthology of lyrics, *Cole*. Kimball's more comprehensive collection, in 1983, also triggered a renewed interest, generating recordings and shows, culminating in *Kiss Me Kate*'s 1999 return to Broadway. It's easy to see why Porter keeps coming back. Like Irving Berlin, he wrote words and music, but unlike the autodidactic Berlin, Porter was a trained and erudite composer. His lyrics, with their irreverent topical references, work as superior light verse (Library of America is contemplating a Porter anthology), while his melodies are structurally complicated yet listener friendly.

The current revival is attested to by three Porter compilations on *Billboard*'s jazz chart, in addition to the film soundtrack's high ranking on the pop chart. Notwithstanding Natalie Cole, the last can safely be ignored except as a how-not-to—the prime offenders being Sheryl Crow, whose "Begin the Beguine" is morbidly tenuous, and Alanis Morissette, whose whirring vibrato on "Let's Do It" recalls Alvin the chipmunk, except that Alvin sang in tune. There is a correct way to sing Porter, much as there is a correct way to act Shakespeare—and they are not dissimilar. In both instances, the first order of business is mastery of, though not obeisance to, the text.

The recent compilations are quite good, especially *It's De-Lovely: The Authentic Cole Porter Collection* (Bluebird), a shrewd melding of vocal and instrumental performances, including Artie Shaw's sublime 1938 big band recording of "Begin the Beguine," arranged by Jerry Gray as a concerto for clarinet. Here is the ultimate example of a song so daunting in length (it broke the song-form bank with 104 measures parsed in an AABACCD structure, all but one section 16 bars long) that the record label attempted to discourage Shaw from recording it at all. Yet the combination of a firmly percussive grounding and Shaw's dramatically elated interpretation made it the best-selling disc of its day. In a more recent style, Sonny Rollins's 1962 "You Do Something for Me" shows the saxophonist's distinctive embellishments elaborating the original melody. Vocalists in the set include such accomplished Porterphiles as Fred Astaire, Frank Sinatra, and Rosemary Clooney. Also notable is the spooky 1930 version of "What Is This Thing Called Love?" by the Leo Reisman Orchestra and featuring an uncanny Bubber Miley trumpet solo.

The other new collections, *Ultra-Lounge: Cocktails with Cole Porter* (Capitol) and *The Very Best of Cole Porter* (Hip-O), are built almost entirely around singers from jazz and pop who breathed the air in which the songs were written. They thrive on minor key melodies and exult in the impertinence of the lyrics. The delights include Kay Starr's charged "C'est Magnifique," Sarah Vaughan's affecting "Ev'ry Time We Say Goodbye," Nat Cole's suave "Just One of Those Things," and Ella Fitzgerald's and Duke Ellington's intoxicating "Let's Do It" on *Ultra-Lounge*; and Fitzgerald's scalding "Too Darn Hot," Peggy Lee's dynamic "My Heart Belongs to Daddy," Jeri Southern's sweetly declarative "It's De-Lovely," Anita O'Day's knowing "Just One of Those Things," and Dinah Washington's blistering "I Get a Kick Out of You" on the more adventurous *The Very Best of Cole Porter*.

But don't stop there. Two older Verve collections worth looking for are *I Get a Kick Out of You: The Cole Porter Songbook Volume II* (the usual suspects plus Louis Armstrong, Shirley Horn, Blossom Dearie, Betty Carter) and *Cole Porter in Concert: Just One of Those Live Things* (concert performances by Ella and Sarah as well as Dee Dee Bridgewater, Charlie Parker, Clifford Brown, Art Tatum). Any list of definitive Porter records would have to include Sinatra's rambunctious "I've Got You Under My Skin" (*Songs for Swingin' Lovers*, Capitol), Crosby and the Andrews Sisters' playful "Don't Fence Me In" (*Bing's Gold Records*, MCA), and Clooney's daring "Why Shouldn't I?" (*Love*, Reprise), as well as such full-bore explorations as Fitzgerald's 1956 Verve album, in which her insights into Porter surprised even her most ardent fans, and 1982s *Rosemary Clooney Sings the Music of Cole Porter* (Concord Jazz). No one could invest a lyric with more layers of meaning than Clooney. Listen to the way she changed the pronouns on "I Concentrate on You" to underscore the erotic tension:

> Your smile so sweet, so tender
> When at first your kiss I decline,
> The light in your eyes when I surrender
> And once again our arms intertwine.

Like the other great Porter interpreters, she knows this is music for grown-ups and that desire, with or without consummation, aces self-pity every time. In *De-Lovely*, clueless singers reduce everything to dress-up and pretense. Porter's music is too rich, droll, provocative, and serious for pretense of any kind.

[*The Los Angeles Times*, 8 August 2004]

50 ❖ Long-Playing
(Duke Ellington)

Always when writing about Duke Ellington there is the temptation to become a list maker. Because once you get past the generalities and charge joyfully into the specifics, you find yourself in a Borgesian labyrinth no less alluring to an Ellingtonian than a cloister is to a medievalist. The inclination to get lost in Ellington and write about nothing else was never greater than in the middle and late 1970s, when his posthumous works appeared almost weekly—many of them important, all encouraging revisionist speculation and, oh, maybe, hyperbole. Ellington copyrighted between 1500 and 2000 works (his estate has added to the total) and at least five times as many recordings, either intentionally or fortuitously, thanks to legions of tapers and pirates, whom he blithely encouraged. Due to this plethora of versions and discrete interpretations, the labyrinth grows more intricate the deeper you wade.

Put aside the masterpieces and you find more masterpieces, or at least works of undeniable enchantment and satisfaction. A favorite record of mine is a version of "In a Jam," performed—according to discographers—in New York, at an unknown location (presumably for a radio broadcast) sometime late in 1944. Ellington recorded the piece flawlessly in 1936, abandoned it for eight years, dug it out briefly, and then shed it once and for all. The AABA tune is oddly ancillary to a dramatic 8-bar introduction that recurs throughout—for example, extending the 6-bar finish of the first chorus to 14 bars. Trombonist Tricky Sam Nanton plays that chorus, as on the original, using two different mutes. But the G-spot of this particular performance is a chase episode—two choruses—by Johnny Hodges and Ray Nance. In 1936, Hodges and Cootie Williams traded impeccable two-bar phrases. In 1944, Hodges and Nance roll out a riotous conversation in which phrases are two, three, and four measures, including a mimicked glissando that always makes me laugh. After that, tenor saxophonist Al Sears plays a chorus, the sagacious Rex Stewart leaps in with a break and half-chorus, and the band goes out with that killer intro.

My point, beyond the one about God and details, is that this delightful find exists by accident; it is more fun than the original; it radiates a wholly distinctive charm within the immense Ellington canon; and there are hundreds more where it came from. Ellington wrote so much music he lost track of a few potential hits. The other night at the Firebird, I heard Daryl Sherman sing an evocative melody—unknown to me—called "It's

Kinda Lonesome Out Tonight." A little research shows that Ellington introduced it in 1947 on Armed Forces Radio, with a vocal by one Chester Crumpley, and never played it again—until 1973, when he recovered it for a Teresa Brewer album. Well, who listens to Teresa Brewer? As Daryl's rendition gets around, it ought to become a new Ellington standard. Then there are the pieces he abandoned and re-configured. The shapely "Black Butterfly" was a not particularly exciting 1938 vehicle for Lawrence Brown. Ellington jilted it for 30 years, only to revamp it for a 1969 European tour as an exquisitely dynamic concerto for Johnny Hodges.

People often describe their first time with Duke Ellington in terms of losing their virginity, and for me it seemed like the next best thing. I began at 15, with *Masterpieces by Ellington*, which I selected from the bewildering bin because the title promised a logical entrance point for a musician about whom I knew nothing. The album was recorded midway through the remarkable and often neglected 1947–52 period that produced *Liberian Suite*, *A Tone Parallel to Harlem*, "The Clothed Woman," the Betty Roche vocal on "Take the A Train," "The Tattooed Bride," and the so-called "concert" arrangements of Ellington songs that he conceived to exploit the new long-playing album. The first of the four long tracks on *Masterpieces by Ellington*, a vividly languorous version of "Mood Indigo," struck me as serenely erotic. All those strange, weaving instrumental voices spoke like personalities, and what they said seemed privileged, like the Varga pinups in *Esquires* stacked behind my father's hatboxes or the adult conversations that dried up as soon as I appeared.

Treating the familiar theme as a 48-bar reverie, the performance undulates in a sustained voluptuous yawn, primed to a subtle swinging pulse (much credit to bassist Wendell Marshall), achieving diverse epiphanies in the bright lyricism of Hodges (his last major Ellington session for nearly four years); the languid high-notes of the obscure vocalist Yvonne Lanauze (just "Yvonne" on the original LP), with her lazy phrasing and lax intonation; and the animal-metaphor plunger-mute of trombonist Tyree Glenn, who makes every phrase a mewing vocalized "ya ya." Indeed, I could not tell back then if the latter episode was the work of a weird instrumentalist or another weird singer.

I soon learned that the private, gossipy, moaning, declaratory, seductive, angry, dreamy, and exultant expressions of the individual characters assembled in this greatest of all bands were the essence of Ellington's music. "My aim is and always has been to mold the music around the man. I've found out that it doesn't matter so much what you have available, but rather what you make of what you do have." Ellington crafted a score as though casting roles in a drama—he wrote a "Concerto for Cootie," never a concerto for trumpet. He could not have assessed the idiosyncrasies of his players so completely had he not maintained their loyalties for so long. This became especially important during the LP era, when his populist instincts as a songwriter took a backseat to his growing aspirations as a composer. Ongoing royalties from his mostly prewar hits paid the bills as he took on commissions to write concert works, and the fidelity of his magnificent if sometimes unruly ensemble sustained his inspiration.

What the musicians got from Ellington was the chance to play great music fashioned specifically for them. Consider all the Ellington stars whose work outside the band was largely negligible. The incomparable Hodges, a member for 37 years, scored a major rhythm and blues hit in 1951, during his five-year sabbatical, but accomplished little else; when he returned to the fold, he reached even greater heights than before he left. What Ellington got from them was the chance to hear everything he wrote as soon as copyists prepared the scores. Whether he was battling the deadline for a suite or amusing himself with a bauble, he was able to audition and revise it immediately. The bond between Ellington and his men encouraged him to try everything. Intuitive and pragmatic, he fashioned cryptic orchestrations that sound dreamy to listeners and dancers, yet befuddle musicians attempting to emulate them. Today, 100 years after his birth and a quarter-century after his death, Ellington's genius is more widely recognized than ever. Though he had passionate admirers in and out of the academy as early as 1927, the verdict was mixed for a long, long time. When I was an undergraduate, a member of the music faculty said he would concede Ellington's importance if his music were still being played in the next century. The clock is ticking, pal. And when were you last requested to play your Concerto for Dental Drill?

A constant problem in comprehending Ellington is the uneven documentation by record companies. Ellington's most acclaimed period is the early 1940s, the years Billy Strayhorn, Ben Webster, Jimmy Blanton, and Ray Nance joined up. Given carte blanche at Victor, Ellington enjoyed enormous record sales in those years, and he produced one benchmark after another. A record consumer in the '50s and '60s could buy anthologies on the order of *In a Mellow Tone*, *At His Very Best*, or *Things Ain't What They Used to Be*, and know that in each instance he or she was getting 16 superb tracks. In the age of completism, you are asked to invest in the triple-disc *Blanton-Webster Band* with the admittedly small amount of chaff restored (including the first cut!) and no creativity or logic in the sequencing of 66 tracks. The consumer is now expected to do the work of the producer. I exultantly purchased the complete works when, in the

'70s, French RCA issued 24 LPs covering 1927–1952 and French CBS released 16 LPs covering 1925–1937. But I don't play them as much as the crafty anthologies and I suspect that the absence of those anthologies explains why the Ellington labyrinth daunts many potential listeners. He has become received wisdom and homework, like Shakespeare, certain to make you a better person if you take the trouble. Trouble? Go play "Sepia Panorama" and see if the opening passage fails to make you glow; listen to "Conga Brava" and consider how he might have flourished in hip-hop America. This music is so enlightened you can scarcely believe the recording dates. "Rockin' in Rhythm": 1928. "It Don't Mean a Thing if It Ain't Got That Swing": 1932. *The Far East Suite*: 1966.

BMG has just released a $400 limited edition 24-disc box, containing all of RCA Victor's Ellington, 1927–1973, with uneven but generally acceptable fidelity, in chronological order. Ellingtonians will gratefully gorge themselves. But it will be a poor centenary if, when breaking the box into individual volumes, the label sticks to the madness of chronology. Once again, BMG messed with the resplendent *And His Mother Called Him Bill*, though not as badly as on the 1987 CD. This time it's properly sequenced except for an inexplicable alternate take of "Raincheck," but is spread over two discs. With sensible sequencing, the entire original LP would have fit on one disc, ending with the unforgettable heartbreaker "Lotus Blossom," as intended. Columbia, which has more to answer for because it keeps more out of print, is starting to make up for lost time, with mixed results. *Such Sweet Thunder* is unaccountably missing a few measures, and *Ellington at Newport* (for which Ellington and George Avakian originally combined studio recordings with live material to recreate on vinyl the excitement of the concert) is now a petulant two-disc set. Live and recorded music are not the same thing: *Ellington at Newport* sold millions and made history; the *Complete Ellington at Newport* will sell thousands and make research.

The irony is that Ellington loved records and proved prescient in writing for the new technology. Just as early radio producers sought baritones rather than tenors, Ellington recognized the virtues and limits of early recording techniques and wrote accordingly. His bottom-note voicings and ingenious figure-and-ground orchestrations for ensemble and soloist make his records sound more vibrant today than those of his contemporaries, especially the records he made for Victor, which had the best engineers. He began chafing at the three-minute limit as early as 1931, when he released the two-sided "Creole Rhapsody." (Decca's president, Jack Kapp, was appalled and declined to renew his contract.) A year later, at Victor, he was one of the first to make a true stereo recording, with discrete mike placements. In 1935, he recorded for Columbia the four-sided

"Reminiscing in Tempo," eliciting critical derision that sent him into a brief, embittered seclusion. The 1940s concert works, beginning with *Black, Brown and Beige*, were documented in excerpted form or not at all until the advent of the LP.

When tape was introduced in American studios in 1947, followed within a year by microgroove, Ellington was ready. Tastes in jazz and pop music had radically changed and many stars of the '30s and '40s were no longer climbing the charts. Victor's doughnut-hole 45s sustained the jukebox trade, but the tape-engendered high fidelity and long-playing discs that held 20 minutes per side were made to order for affluent grown-ups in postwar America. Performers like Ellington, Count Basie, Ella Fitzgerald, and Frank Sinatra could no longer compete on AM radio; the LP proved ideal for them and their audience. At the same time, Ellington revised his rhythmic attack, hiring virtuoso drummer Louis Bellson to help drive the increasingly daring propulsion of his music, now punchier and less ornate than during the war. This new attack complemented the liberation he experienced at being able to record extended works.

Many artists failed to see the LP as anything more than a compilation of 78s—a dozen three-minute tracks instead of two, a symphony on one disc instead of six. Others instantly recognized two ways of using the LP to distinguish it from 45s: live recordings, which retained the real-time ambience of a concert; and thematic recordings, which explored moods or catchall subjects such as songwriters and particular eras. Jazz musicians availed themselves of extended playing time to record longer solos or longer versions of pieces that could be expanded or contracted at will. But few addressed the issue of form and function the way, for instance, Miles Davis and Gil Evans (and later the Beatles) did, creating works that required the roominess of the LP while taking advantage of advanced sonics and tape trickery. Ellington was way ahead of them.

A key transitional work was 1947's *Liberian Suite*, commissioned for that nation's centenary and made up of a heraldic opening and five diverse dances. Ellington used the new technology to overdub Al Hibbler's vocal in the first movement, and Columbia released the completed work as a pioneer 10-inch LP. Two years later, Ellington began documenting his extended tone poems. In late 1950, he recorded *Masterpieces by Ellington*, which, eros aside, was one of the first genuinely innovative 12-inch LPs, combining the "concert" arrangements of three of his '30s hits and a genial slice of postwar modernism that tips its hat to the Swing Era, "The Tattooed Bride." A year later came the most stirring of his long-form works: *A Tone Parallel to Harlem*, commissioned for but never performed by Toscanini and the NBC Orchestra. With this series of works, averaging 12 to 15 minutes, Ellington ignored the suite format in favor of extended pieces that reflected the inspiration of the LP. The audience and the critics, however, lagged behind. Even the glorious *Harlem*, a triple-theme rhapsody that begins with the plaintive wail of cornetist Ray Nance, continues with the entwined romance of Harry Carney's baritone and Jimmy Hamilton's clarinet, pulses with Louis Bellson's rumbling drums, and attains resolution in the eight-bar hymn introduced by trombonist Britt Woodman, received little fanfare. Ellington went on to record it several times, but he got it right the first time.

Harlem raises questions about the nature of jazz. Excepting one blues chorus, midway, that appears to be extemporized by Nance, it allows for no improvisation. Nor does it have a role for the pianist. Yet it undoubtedly belongs to jazz, unlike Gershwin's *Rhapsody in Blue*, which it resembles in length and structure (each begins with a cadenza and blossoms at the two-thirds mark into divine melody). Unlike Gershwin's piece, it is ingeniously harmonized with inimitable Ellington voicings, and it swings. The structure consists exclusively of basic jazz forms—two eight-bar themes with a blues in the middle. The lovely third theme, superbly evoked by Woodman, is a hymn without words.

Ellington did an injustice to this work when he described the many elements of Harlem life he tried to portray—a long list that led impressionable listeners on a fruitless search to identify each programmatic detail. In fact, *Harlem* is efficiently and sparingly wrought, with each theme allotted 10 choruses, plus several artful transitions, notably the interlude that sets up the hymn. It begins with a two-note wake-up call, a rise-and-shine Ray Nance call that builds to a frisky whinnying at the new dawn. Throughout the work, each instrumental voice is deployed decisively—Carney, Hamilton, Paul Gonsalves, and others are as vital as Nance, Woodman, Marshall, and Bellson, whose drums announce the blues section at 4:39: a series of bracing ensemble choruses (note the turnback at the close of the fourth blues chorus) that build with counterpoint, sundry tempos, and a reprise of the wake-up call, before yielding to the piquant cortege (clarinet with commiserating trombones). A four-measure passage by Carney's bass clarinet sets up the trombone sermon, which carries the piece to a high-note climax, capping an American masterpiece still largely unknown to America.

The next year, Ellington, like Sinatra, left Columbia for Capitol, which for him was a mistake. He began his new association with a bang, "Satin Doll"—his last hit single and, for many, the quintessential hi-fi big-band track. But this was not a happy affiliation. With Hodges and Lawrence Brown gone and Bellson compelled to leave to accompany his wife, Pearl Bailey, Ellington appeared to be second-guessing his direction and his past triumphs. The best of the Capitols are his deeply moving piano trios; his attempts at revision or modernization occasionally border on parody, if not blasphemy. He sprang back, unfettered and undaunted, with the shot heard around the world: his electrifying set at the 1956 Newport Jazz Festival. Hodges and Brown had returned along with his confidence. One result of the Newport appearance was *Time*'s belated cover story, which, if nothing else, symbolized a renaissance in his creative powers that he sustained without letup over the next 28 years. After the relatively brief period, 1943 to 1952, when he concentrated on extended forms, Ellington realized that the LP and his talent were best suited to the suite: a long form consisting of short forms, the miniatures at which he excelled.

So let me yield to temptation and offer a short list after all—a 12-step program through the often undervalued labyrinth within the labyrinth: the mature Ellington, the wise Ellington, the all-encompassing Ellington, the long-playing Ellington. 1. *Ellington Masterpieces* (Columbia), with the concert version of "Mood Indigo" and his affirmation of times gone and coming, "The Tattooed Bride." 2. *Uptown Ellington* (Columbia), Bellson's finest hour, with the original *Harlem* and *Liberian Suite*. 3. *Ellington at Newport* (Columbia), with the heroic Paul Gonsalves tenor saxophone solo on "Diminuendo and Crescendo in Blue." 4. *Such Sweet Thunder* (Columbia), the Shakespearean suite, flush with musical and numerical analogies to the plays and sonnets. 5. *Ellington Jazz Party* (Columbia), with guest appearances by Jimmy Rushing and Dizzy Gillespie and a melody written for percussion, "Maletoba Spank," that will rattle in your memory until you die. 6. *The Ellington Suites* (Pablo), including *The Queen's Suite*. 7. *The Great Paris Concert* (Atlantic), an exceptional live performance that begins with an authoritative "Rockin' in Rhythm" and closes with a bracing *Harlem*. 8. *The Popular Duke Ellington* (RCA), exemplary chestnuts (excepting a throwaway "Do Nothin' Till You Hear from Me") superbly executed and recorded. 9. *The Far East Suite* (RCA), the pinnacle of his last decade, a riot of melody, rhythm, and racy dissonance, and a feat of assimilation. 10. *And His Mother Called Him Bill* (RCA), perhaps the most sumptuous and moving of Ellington LPs. 11. *Latin American Suite* (Fantasy), with Ellington and Gonsalves in clover, recycling suggestions of 1940s south of the border melodies. 12. *The Afro Eurasian Eclipse* (Fantasy), focused on the reeds and rhythm (no brass solos), accessing chants, modes, rock rhythms, and one-world conceits that were just then coming into play.

My list is a worthy introduction to Ellington in the LP era, and only that. (I hear murmurs and feel your pain: How could he not mention the remake of *Black, Brown and Beige*, *Nutcracker Suite*, *Anatomy of a Murder*, *Money Jungle*, *Piano in the Foreground*, albums with Armstrong, Hawkins, Basie, and Coltrane, the Sacred Concerts, and so on?) Ellington is the whole world at play. Wander down this corridor and you may never come out.

Fervent, original, and self-reflective, his music echoes its own echoes, world without end, amen. Plus, you can dance to it. And one way or another, you will.

[*Village Voice*, 28 April 1999 / 2005]

51 ❖ *Jazz for the Eyes* (The Sound of Jazz / Jazz on a Summer's Day)

1. TV Press Conference

Never having seen a transcription of Lester Young's single-chorus, 39-second blues solo on the 1957 *Sound of Jazz* TV version of "Fine and Mellow," I am speculating when I suggest that it consists of no more than 50 notes. Those who recall the solo's impeccable efficiency may think he plays even fewer notes than that. Perfection beguiles even the vigilant. The solo is so sublimely constructed that after you've heard it a couple of times it becomes part of your nervous system, like the motor skills required to ride a bicycle. Young, who achieved perfection in more solos than perhaps any other jazz improviser, was not expected to achieve much at all on that live December 8 broadcast. He had appeared, ailing and remote, in the CBS studios three days earlier to perform on the album that would be issued early the following year as a memento of the program. At that session, only his backing of Jimmy Rushing on "I Left My Baby" sparkled. His "Fine and Mellow" solo, while presaging ideas in the TV version, was flat and weary; on "Dickie's Dream," one of his perfect inventions back in 1939, he sounded almost asthmatic.

Nat Hentoff, who with Whitney Balliett selected the musicians for *The Sound of Jazz*, has recalled that Young was told he could play his sole TV solo seated if he preferred. When Young leapt from his chair, as Ben Webster completed his own chorus, the cameraman was clearly unprepared. He had to pull back to get him in. Altogether, Young was seen from three camera angles, the third descending from his face down the expanse of his tenor saxophone before the director cut away midway into the chorus. You saw Young a total of 20 seconds during the entire hour, all he needed to steal the show with a whispered solo, securing the program's reputation as the best hour of jazz ever broadcast on American television.

Either director Jack Smight or producer Robert Herridge (whom Hentoff credits with keeping the show *"Partisan Review*-pure") further immortalized the moment by cutting from Young to the only person who could justify the abrupt discontinuity.

Billie Holiday, the primary performer on "Fine and Mellow" and the singer with whom Young had shared many perfect moments in the 1930s, responded to the solo with a mosaic of facial expressions—swinging her head, moistening her lips, arching her brow, aggressively nodding her final accord—that seemed to illustrate and even anticipate Young's every note. If it is possible for two people to make love while one partner is playing the tenor saxophone 10 feet away from the other, that is what Young and Holiday were doing Sunday afternoon on TV. Which is what made the solo not merely a great performance or a potentially great record, but great television. In those few seconds, the audience—which had no way of knowing the two had not spoken to each other in many years—heard a musician improvise a solo of shimmering beauty and got to see or at least surmise the deep waters of a personal relationship that had not quite become the legend it became after 1959, the year each of them died.

Like the murder of Oswald or the final game of the 1986 World Series, it was unexpected and very real. Holiday's pantomime of pure pleasure embodied a sensual appreciation of the music in a way no actor has ever succeeded in doing. Duke Ellington used to conclude concerts with a "finger-snapping routine," set to "Dancers in Love," in which he parodied the affectations of the wannabe hip with a lesson on how to look acceptably cool when listening. Throughout the show, and not just during Young's solo, whenever the director cuts to a Holiday reaction shot, she delivers a lesson in authenticity. But then reaction shots are so much a part of why *The Sound of Jazz* continues to enthrall, and why the recordings are less satisfying—Columbia's December 5 studio date is now available on CD; the much superior TV soundtrack has been issued as a "bootleg." CBS, which, incredibly, never rebroadcast the show (though it was a success in its premiere), allowed the copyright to run out, encouraging legally dubious home video releases.

The Sound of Jazz, unlike other CBS-TV jazz landmarks from the late-1950s (including Edward R. Murrow's *See It Now* segment on Louis Armstrong and the Leonard Bernstein lecture, "What Is Jazz?" on *Omnibus*), got a second life in the early '70s, after the late film collector Dave Chertok showed it at a midtown jazz club one afternoon. During the next 15 years, it was repeatedly pillaged for jazz documentaries and traded by collectors. Bits and pieces came out on video, but not the whole hour, until 1991.

Most of the assembled players were veterans with long interrelated histories. The show was resolutely casual (several musicians wore hats; Holiday, in slacks and ponytail, was initially furious at not being able to wear a gown she'd bought for the occasion) and it was live. They could have called it *The Faces of Jazz*; you don't see many such faces now: Henry Red Allen, with his bulldog features concentrated at the center of a Mr. Potato Head; dapper Coleman Hawkins, his sentient eyes betraying an intriguingly suave virility; starved Pee Wee Russell, his putty nose jutting in three directions from a face frozen in an attitude of bemused pain ("Pee Wee's gaining weight," Eddie Condon once remarked, "under each eye"); Rex Stewart, the satanic glint in his eye underscored by a trimmed mustache and curled goatee; the wonderfully transparent Roy Eldridge, who had the opposite of a poker face—you always knew what he was thinking.

The ringers were Gerry Mulligan, who fit snugly among the swingers and double-timed his way through a memorable "Fine and Mellow" chorus, and Thelonious Monk, whose trio was on hand to represent the cutting edge, as bop per se had been banished. Just how spacey Monk was considered in 1957 can be construed by two cornball touches that attend his performance: Basie was asked to sit behind Monk's piano and, though a compliant model, he conveys chiefly a touch of noblesse oblige (unlike Hawkins, who candidly snaps his fingers in delight); and John Crosby, the slightly confused host with fortunately little to say, affects a listening pose right out of the Ellington school of hip posturing. The one misfire was the Jimmy Giuffre Trio (an unsurprising choice for the day, though hindsight would have favored more enduring modernists such as Sonny Rollins, Charles Mingus, Miles Davis, and George Russell): "The Train and the River," which received quite a bit of radio play at the time, sounds dated and pallid in comparison to all that precedes it.

The main bands—those led by Count Basie, Red Allen, Monk, and Holiday—provide virtually nonstop highlights, the soloing an unbroken strain of excellence. Hawkins swaggers, Dicky Wells constructs, Vic Dickenson winks, Joe Wilder belies the intensity of his ideas with his executive aplomb. Red Allen's unique method of stomping off tempos was a barking, "Whamp-whamp"—a medium whamp-whamp for "Wild Man Blues," faster for "Rosetta." Jimmy Rushing is captured in all his rotund glory (the voice still robust, dewy) on an extended "I Left My Baby," shorn of the original record's dramatic out-choruses (though one was inserted midway to set up the string of solos), but extended by two extra vocal choruses. You expect to miss Young behind the singer but Webster moves in with momentous authority. Basie's witty chorus includes a bass rumble he might have employed as a youth accompanying silent movies.

Elsewhere, especially on the stirring "Dickie's Dream" (Eldridge plays an entire eight bars in the Albert Ayler register, and Hawk positively stomps out his arpeggios), Basie delivers the wicked stride he played in Kansas City before he became famous and famously laconic. At one point, Holiday leans over to tell him something; he laughs, his left hand never missing a stroke. The program begins and ends with Jo Jones, who not only plays like the wind but looks like a man who plays like the wind.

2. For All Seasons

The late 1950s were exceptional years for jazz on television and, as it happened, on film, because the chic photographer Bert Stern got it into his head to shoot the fashionable crowd at the 1958 Newport Jazz Festival. The result, *Jazz on a Summer's Day*, more than compensates for its shortcomings. The first of the musical festival films was actually shot over three summer days at the 1958 Newport Jazz Festival, and released two years later. Though enthralling and frustrating in equal measure, it grows in stature as its era recedes. One is no longer inclined to gnash one's teeth as the camera abandons Thelonious Monk in favor of fashion-mag photography of a boating contest, or roll one's eyes at the staged episodes, or the interpolated Bach, or the patronization of audience members, who tend to appear bored or stoned. Because that, too, was part of a long-ago scene, as was the mediocre Dixieland band, the beer blast, the sexy dancer, the crew cuts, and the officious introductions from the Voice of America himself, Willis Conover.

The movie created several indelible jazz images: Anita O'Day, in a feathered sun hat and black sheath dress with white fringe, thrusting her glottis at "Sweet Georgia Brown"; Dinah Washington sailing through "All of Me" in a baggy dress fitted below the hips with a large bow bumping to the rhythm, her face a radiant pond of brown and red hues; Jack Teagarden grinning as though he'd crashed an unexpected party while Chuck Berry rocks "Sweet Little Sixteen"; Gerry Mulligan personifying cool; Eric Dolphy playing meditative flute; Louis Armstrong recounting his unlikely answer to the Pope, who asked if he had children ("No, daddy, but we're still wailing"), then playing an autobiographical set with a supersonic "Tiger Rag" (Stern cuts to the audience right before he plays the glissando on "Lazy River"). Above all, there is a justly acclaimed performance by Mahalia Jackson. Conover intones, "It is Sunday, and it is time for the world's greatest gospel singer," by which he means it was just past midnight at the Saturday concert. She swings harder than anyone else in the film. "You make me feel like a star," she tells a thundering crowd, and then sings the Twenty-third Psalm with penetrating intensity. Aw shucks, indeed.

Fans of *Jazz on a Summer's Day* forget that the 1958 festival presented Sonny Rollins, Miles Davis, Duke Ellington, Benny Goodman, Horace Silver, Randy Weston, Joe Turner, Ray Charles, and Lee Konitz—none of whom were filmed, though many of their performances were issued on records. For that matter, the filmmakers neglect to mention producer George Wein, preferring to celebrate the gentry (Newport's Lorillard family), who paid the bills. Then there is the auteurist issue. The film is credited to the director, whose radiant photography has been spiffed up in a vivid new DVD print, but it was assembled by the editor Aram Avakian, whose work landed him such Hollywood assignments as *The Miracle Worker* and *Mickey One*. (He later directed *End of the Road*.) According to Avakian's brother, George, who served as musical consultant, Stern botched the first night's filming (which, among the musical acts, caught only a woodenly shot segment of Jimmy Giuffre's trio), and Avakian took over for the next two days. Ego clashes aside, the film remains a marvel of its kind.

[*Village Voice*, 22 January 1991 / 27 July 1997]

52 ❖ *Regrets, They've Had a Few* (Sinatra)

How blunter than a serpent's tooth is the ambivalent child of a neglectful yet powerful parent. Tina Sinatra's Executive Producer credit appears on the screen at the close of both halves of her five-hour CBS miniseries, *Sinatra*—a punch line that may or may not explain the preceding spectacle. Her portrait is a defense of her father's honor and an unmitigated assault on his style; that is, she absolves dad of the more damning accusations concerning mob involvement and physical intimidation, but she revels in depicting him as a lout—a compulsive adulterer and bully who lost his charm almost immediately after he sank his teeth into Hollywood, or vice versa. He should have spent more time with his kids. By the lights of Tina, his youngest of three, they barely existed for him, and so they barely exist in her dramatization. They are background props, remote and forlorn. Frank Jr.'s kidnapping is never mentioned; neither are Nancy's boots.

Directed with little inspiration by James Sadwith from a sincere yet equivocal teleplay by William Mastrosimone, *Sinatra* is offered in lieu of an autobiography. The singer cooperated by giving lengthy interviews, and many scenes are staged anecdotes. Yet the show does little to resolve the central enigma of an important artist, adored and reviled, whose public posture seems often in direct contradiction to the generous, vulnerable impulses of his genius. Perhaps only a novelist, working a quarter into the next century, will succeed in adjudicating our feelings about an often-inarticulate entertainer who so acutely embodied the vagaries of American life for more than half a century. Still, if his daughter can't do it, we don't have to consult Kitty Kelly to infer this much: Frankie's mother, Dolly (Olympia Dukakis), pegged her son from the start when she called him, repeatedly, "you little sonofabitch." The Sinatra in *Sinatra* is deeply disagreeable.

Philip Casnoff is effective in the lead role; shot in profile in the shadows of stage lights, he looks remarkably like the young singer. In early scenes, his oleaginous smile is not unappealing, and you hope he'll get a grip on this singing thing as he wends his way through one movie musical cliché after another. They—the clichés—are *all* here, ticked off like a shopping list: the neighborhood kids who ridicule him because he carries sheet music; the father (Joe Santos) who calls him a bum; the prospective father-in-law who calls him a bum; the envious gaze at the city across the river; the vocal coach who tells him he doesn't understand lyrics. If you've seen only a few of Hollywood's depictions of entertainers, you could probably have scripted the first hour of *Sinatra* on your own and come within hailing distance of Mastrosimone's effort.

But a remarkable sea change in Casnoff's performance and in the show occurs after Sinatra makes it and falls out of love with big Nancy (Gina Gershon), his wife and the mother of his children. The charm disappears and the smile turns grim. You never root for him again. His suffering is cold, distant, and deserved. The little sonofabitch becomes so remote that even his triumphs are trivialized; his '50s comeback is depicted as a montage of album jackets and film slates. The most damning sequence of all is filmed with a single sustained medium-distance shot. It's the Rat Pack on stage in Vegas, enacting one of the routines that were considered hip and spontaneous and emblematic of the much-coveted inside track in the days of Camelot. It is bloody awful: The actors who play Dino and Sammy are merely inept, and the static staging suggests that even the Chairman of the Board's daughter could no more empathize with those middle-aged delinquents than the rest of us who turned to rock and roll in self-defense. Could they really have been as bad as all that? Rent *Ocean's Eleven* and see for yourself.

Is the dramatization accurate? In terms of the big picture, yes—surprisingly so. It's easy to nitpick. Sinatra's mother compares her son with

Rudy Vallee in 1925, when Vallee was little known beyond Yale. Tommy Dorsey is unfairly depicted as the heavy in his contract dispute with Sinatra: He had demanded a third of Sinatra's earnings over 10 years (not "life," as the teleplay insists) in return for a loan made when the singer left his band and not as a precondition for hiring him. The Hoboken Four episode is skewed, with Major Bowes organizing them (Dolly had pressured The Three Flashes into adding Frank to the group). Left out is their blackface routine, though they are shown performing, horribly and frequently, their audition number, "Shine," in the arrangement made famous by Bing Crosby and the Mills Brothers. The lyric, however, has been revised to omit racist references—an offensive instance of retroactive pc.

Most of the show's running time concerns the avid love affair and tempestuous marriage of Sinatra and Ava Gardner (Marcia Gay Harden), which differs in the details from Ava's memoir (one big diff: She says he faked suicide twice to lure her back; the teleplay depicts an actual attempt), but squarely highlights the more notorious, publicized moments. Much of this long episode is unaccountably dull and embarrassing. Great passions don't work on TV. Must we watch them groping at each other? Do these scenes ring chimes for Tina, whose mother is reduced to a dejected, spurned woman? "Gawd, Frank, you don't know when to stop," Ava gasps as he crawls on top, once again. They traipse around the globe, he punching out photographers, she smoldering then flouncing away as his temper explodes, once again. The drama is fair to Ava, all things considered; the same cannot be said of Sinatra's other allies in adultery, including a married Hoboken woman who brought him up on a morals charge and entertainer Marilyn Maxwell, both of whom practically have *slut* emblazoned on their foreheads.

So the drama follows with a fair degree of faithfulness the vicissitudes of Sinatra's rise and fall and rise, parading many members of his entourage (not Jilly, though; not the goons), his disputes with journalists (credit Sinatra for making enemies of the vocation's scum, mainly Westbrook Pegler and Lee Mortimer); his reawakening in *From Here to Eternity* (no dead horse, in fact no effort at all in getting the audition or the part—Harry Cohn calls him personally with the good news, according to *Sinatra*); and so forth. Elsewhere, the program dissembles by omission. Mafia connections? That was all the fault of Joe Kennedy. He asked Frank to speak to Sam Giancana (Rod Steiger) about getting the unions to swing the election. Sinatra was simply loyal to friends, even if they were pols or gangsters, which is more than could be said of the Kennedys when it came to Sinatra. Indeed, when Jimmy Roselli suggests to Giancana that he waste Frank and his "nigger" friend, and Sinatra refuses to be pressured into asking Robert Kennedy to cease his investigation of the mob, you get the idea that he's a stand-up guy. No mention is made of Judith Campbell Exner. Nor do we see the Sinatra who pushed a woman through plate glass and roughed-up a customer at the Polo Lounge.

Sinatra is less offended by corruption and violence than by the man's rudeness. Casnoff never ages, never loses his hair, and never puts on weight. The sameness eerily underscores the portrait of a man who had courage and charm during the years of youthful struggle but became a vulgar parody of himself when he abandoned the Eden of big Nancy and the children. Abusive, petulant, whiny, demanding, he betrays his muse and his manager as well as his family. All of Hollywood, especially his friends, is treated with benign contempt. The actors who play Bogart, Dean, Sammy, JFK (presented as just another ratpacker), and Mia Farrow (a moonfaced hippie) are hilariously wide-of-the-mark cartoons. And so, finally, is Ol' Blue Eyes: the closing scene of him strutting at Madison Square Garden in 1974 ("That's Life"), suddenly gray but still bean-thin and unjowly, after a brief retirement, is tinged with pathos but not triumph. His voice wavers, the crowd cheers, lights shade him from scrutiny. He seems less the returning champ than the ghost of palookas past. Who is this guy and why should we care?

The answer lies in the music, of course, and that's where *Sinatra* is most disappointing. The great years of his 1950s comeback are bereft of a single scene in the studio or with arrangers and musicians. Neither Axel Stordahl nor Nelson Riddle, who was as instrumental in forging Sinatra's transcendent second career as the Academy Award, is mentioned. Riddle doesn't even appear in the LP montage, unlike Billy May and Gordon Jenkins. Sinatra's leftish politics are hinted at, but not the musical consequence: Earl Robinson's Oscar-winning "The House I Live In." Nothing is made of Frank's craftsmanship beyond his penchant for imitating Dorsey's breathless phrases. He does get to insult a few rivals, though, including Morton Downey, Buddy Clark, Frankie Laine, and Bo Diddley ("that's crap," declares the Chairman of the Board).

Technically, the music is efficiently done: added vocal performances by Tom Burlinson and Frank Jr. are imperceptibly woven in with Sinatra's recordings. Casnoff is fine at lip-synching, but the distinct difference in the timbre of his speaking voice tends to kill the illusion. The songs merely comment on the narrative—"I'm a Fool to Want You" for Ava, "You Make Me Feel So Young" (way out of its real time frame) for Mia—when they ought to be at its heart. The show is less compelling than interesting, marking familiar stages in a career we are all presumed to have faithfully followed. You never get emotionally caught up the way you do with Sinatra's records. Despite many rationalizations it offers about diverse controversies, the show undermines him in a way his enemies never could: *Sinatra* makes Sinatra seem smaller than life.

[*Village Voice*, 10 November 1992]

53 ❖ *Ambassadors*
(A Great Day in Harlem / The Real Ambassadors)

Though she worked as a radio producer for many years, Jean Bach is best known as Greenwich Village's great jazz hostess. So it is fitting and not at all surprising that her first work as a film producer is itself a party, an open house. *A Great Day in Harlem* is a wonderful documentary that manages to evoke deep feelings with a resolutely light hand. Bach doesn't appear on screen and asks only a few questions off, and yet she and her editor and director convey not merely her own affection for the music and its musicians, but a kind of meta-affection, a universal jazz camaraderie that reduces audiences to tears, although nothing in the film is mournful except for the passing of time. Indeed, it is a very funny picture.

In jazz, laughter and tears are often contiguous—musicians and the times they represent are fleeting. When jazz musicians reminisce, they hardly ever speak of records. Coleman Hawkins records are what we have in the absence of Coleman Hawkins; his accumulated masterpieces add up to less than the man himself. This is a sentimental position, and one area where jazz resembles the pop art it sometimes longs to be: Its stars are venerated for who we think they are no less than for the music they create. Hawkins and Lester Young are the be-all and end-all of far more than the range of timbre on a tenor saxophone. Rex Stewart is the most ingratiatingly satanic grin ever painted on a human face, no less than a scorching cornetist and an elegiac memoirist. Film is the best way to make this case.

The subject of Bach's film is the celebrated Art Kane photograph, shot for *Esquire* in the summer of 1958, in which 57 musicians—all but one (who was Bill Crump?) renowned in jazz—and 12 neighborhood children posed on and around the stoop of a 125th Street brownstone. Kane, an art director who went on to become a well-known photographer, had never done a professional shoot, and when he put out the call for musicians, he had no idea who would show up or what he would get. He got a religious emblem: a symbolic, strangely flat, sunlit mural in which in-novators and journeymen, soloists and singers and section men, look at posterity (or, in the cases of Mary Lou Williams and Marian McPartland and Roy Eldridge and Dizzy Gillespie, at each other) and mark a distant moment. I've seen people touch the faces on a large blow-up of the photograph as though it were the Viet Nam Memorial.

Bach began interviewing various survivors in 1989. Talking heads advance the narrative in standard ways but also give the film its humor and heart, because Bach favors bits that are more idiosyncratic than informational: sometimes an extended joke—Hank Jones addressing the weight gain of every one in the picture, or Horace Silver on vegetarian-ism and steak love—and sometimes just a beady eye, a groan, a smile, an exhalation. Gillespie, who has the hilarious tag line, is thrown in at times simply because he is so much fun to watch. One story that threads through the film tells how Bob Altschuler, of Riverside Records, escorted Thelonious Monk, who kept the cab waiting as he rummaged through his wardrobe before choosing a light jacket on the assumption that everyone else would dress dark.

No less remarkable is the secondary photographic material Bach located. Kane was not the only shutterbug present. Willie the Lion Smith brought his protégé Mike Lipskin, who brought his Brownie; Milt Hinton, who was there to pose, carried with him a still camera and an eight-millimeter movie camera, operated by his wife, Mona. In addition to their shots, Kane had kept his rejects. Working with this trove, editor Susan Peehl and director Matthew Seig have made Kane's original pic-ture leap to life—the first few times a frozen black-and-white image turns to color movement, or to another frozen image taken seconds later, you can hardly believe your eyes.

The narrative is necessarily a maze, but the primary construction is a series of brief vignettes of 15 or so musicians no longer living—includ-ing the Lion, Luckey Roberts, Stewart, Hawkins, Young, Stuff Smith (wearing a tuxedo at 10 A.M., he looks like Harvey Keitel in *Pulp Fiction*), Mary Lou Williams, Basie (seated, of course), Vic Dickenson, Henry Red Allen, Mingus, Oscar Pettiford, Roy Eldridge, and Pee Wee Russell. Sonny Rollins tells of waiting on Hawkins's stoop for an autograph, Milt Hinton observes how musicians who played the same instrument con-gregated together ("water finds its own level"), Nat Hentoff speaks of the "protean" Mingus, who is also glimpsed in footage from the 1961 U.K. howler, *All Night Long*. A particularly fine sequence involves Maxine Sullivan, who is radiant singing "Some of These Days" in a '40s clip, and Jimmy Rushing crooning "I Left My Baby" from *The Sound of Jazz*, the CBS-TV show that provided much video for this film. At 59 minutes, *A*

Great Day in Harlem can hardly do justice to all the musicians who went to Harlem that day, nor can it explicate the history and significance of those singled out. Happily, it doesn't really try, preferring to suggest by subtle gesture or anecdote what they represented to those who knew them. Younger musicians refer to older ones with reverence; older ones refer to each other with delight. The easy, contagious intimacy makes the film affecting and real.

Still, the movie is cut too fine, and that may be one reason it's having trouble finding distribution despite universal acclaim. (It was the hit of the Playboy Jazz Film Festival last month in Los Angeles, won top prize for documentaries at the Chicago International Film Festival, and is scheduled for several European competitions, though the New York Film Festival turned it down.)[1] When Rushing is faded out so that Kane's assistant can tell a trite story about how he misloaded the film, you experience a rare shudder of disappointment, and when the film ends before a word has been said of Lawrence Brown, Dickie Wells, Miff Mole, and J. C. Higginbotham, just to mention the unacknowledged trombonists (Vic Dickenson gets his due from Hentoff), you feel bereft. Nor has its brevity helped get an American TV airing thus far; that PBS turned it down would be appalling if PBS had any credibility left. The best resting place may be a home video disc that will allow you to freeze the film long enough to roam that distant world with your eyes and your mind's eye.

Esquire's World of Jazz reprinted Kane's photograph, in 1962, as an illustration for an indignant essay by Gillespie ("Jazz Is Too Good for Americans") that the editors introduced with the reassurance that Gillespie was "a remarkably able ambassador of goodwill abroad." Jazz's ambassadorial uses were much discussed between 1957, when Louis Armstrong canceled his Russian tour to protest Eisenhower's dithering over Little Rock (there's a reason they dithered over putting Satchmo on an American stamp for almost 25 years), and 1962, when Dave and Iola Brubeck adapted cold war politics as the theme for one of the best Broadway shows never to reach Broadway—*The Real Ambassadors* was performed just once, at the Monterey Jazz Festival. Perhaps the problem was that the material was too well tailored to its lead, Armstrong. Except for Roy Eldridge, I can't imagine anyone else in the role of a cultural figure-

---

[1] It was also nominated for a 1995 Academy Award, and generated Bach's short subject, "The Spitball Story," edited from material gathered for the original film (concerning the real culprit who threw the spitball at bandleader Cab Calloway, for which Dizzy Gillespie was famously blamed), as well as a book, edited by Charles Graham, *The Great Jazz Day*. In 2006, a double-disc DVD was released, with four hours of additional material.

head who casually sings, "I represent the human race and don't pretend no more." Well, maybe James Brown.

Columbia/Legacy recently reissued the 1962 recording, adding five selections left off the original album. I look forward to reading a review by a critic under the age of 40, to see what someone with no recollection of Camelot will make of it. In 1962, a gag that depended on confusing the first lady with Jackie Robinson was dim, but possible, as were coy lines about "Khrushchev pounding both his shoes" and "'specially the Russians can't claim jazz." So were more deeply felt attitudes like, "though I represent the government, the government don't represent some policies I'm for." *The Real Ambassadors* is a time capsule, grown in stature, with a brassy vitality that reflects the Broadway glitter of the early '60s, when the classic prerock musical made its last stand, and that fast-fading moment when jazz was still too popular to be weighed down with academic respectability.

As with the original release, there is no libretto, no inkling of a plotline. But the politics are clear, and while they are obviously aimed at the gallery, they are more specific than angrier works of the same period by Abbey Lincoln and Max Roach. The cover may be red, white, and blue, but the mood is more sorrow than uplift, especially with the restoration of the lost pieces; these are of little interest musically, but they do give greater depth to the characterizations, notably Armstrong's recitation, "Lonesome." Brubeck has told of writing "They Say I Look Like God" for an easy laugh, and how Armstrong's interpretation turned it into a cry of anguish, but listen also to "Remember Who You Are" in light of what we know of the FBI's harassment of Armstrong or Jack Valenti's inquiry into his patriotism. And note how Carmen McRae, who has rarely sung better than on "Good Review" and "My One Bad Habit," can do nothing with the Armstrong triumph "Summer Song." And listen to the first cracked note of Armstrong's solo on "Cultural Exchange," and try to imagine anyone else stepping into his shoes.

The melodies include some of Brubeck's freshest work, and I can only attribute the failure of the best ballads to win acceptance to the perfection of these recorded performances. Iola Brubeck's lyrics are inventively spry, if occasionally verbose. As brilliant as *Esquire*'s constellation of musicians was, one can easily imagine an equally impressive photo of *another* 57 contemporaries—think Ellington and his constellation, Los Angeles and Chicago, Billie, Sarah, Miles, Coltrane. None of the artists responsible for *The Real Ambassadors* (all signed to Columbia Records at the time) were in the picture, yet I find the boisterous conviction of this recording an emotional companion to the staunch authority of the morning convention in Harlem. Armstrong, Brubeck, Carmen McRae,

Lambert, Hendricks, and Ross, and Trummy Young similarly represented a marriage of the old and new, of the down home and the sophisticated, and their overriding outlook here is that the great day may, at
least, be dawning.

[*Village Voice*, 25 October 1994]

54 ❖ *Explosive*
(Count Basie)

In 1957, Roulette Records made Count Basie an offer he could not refuse,
and inaugurated his new contract with an album that had one of the most
memorable covers of the era: a red-tinted atomic explosion, with the title,
Basie, in blue and dancing on the crest of a mushroom cloud, and a white
caption that reads: "E=MC2=COUNT BASIE ORCHESTRA+NEAL
HEFTI ARRANGEMENTS." Inevitably, fans often referred to the album
as the atomic Basie, and it has even been released on a Blue Note CD as
The Complete Atomic Basie, with the addition of three tunes and two alternate takes that are not by Hefti and obviously have nothing to do with
the stated concept. The producer Teddy Reig conceived the original
monophonic album as a showcase for the Basie band's different sections,
luxurious textures, and rattling dynamics. The sound was superior for its
day and the Blue Note CD captures it well enough.

Classic Records has now worked its abracadabra on a vinyl edition of
Basie and has come up with a disc that could serve as a demo to test audio
equipment. The whole band—from Basie's punctilious piano and its
reverberant overtones to the baritone saxophone's cavernous grumble
and the bass's clipped resonance—is made so luminous that even my
middle-end rig snaps to attention to take it all in, or give it all out. More
than that, this disc recaptures the elusive chimera of musical warmth:
Turn up the volume and you feel you are hearing Basie, not an electrical
reproduction of Basie. The freedom from digital harshness is liberating.
Classic Records could do nothing to offset the one flaw in the original,
the underrecording of Freddie Green's guitar, but it has produced a
definitive version. *Basie* has never sounded more atomic. Unfortunately,
the same conscientiousness that generated exemplary sound led to the
annoying decision not to correct typographical errors or include—on the
cover or as an insert—a personnel listing and other relevant information.
(*Basie* was recorded at two sessions in October 1957, with trumpeters

Wendell Culley, Thad Jones, Joe Newman, Snooky Young; trombonists Henry Coker, Al Gray, Benny Powell; saxophonists Marshall Royal, Frank Wess, Eddie "Lockjaw" Davis, Frank Foster, Charlie Fowlkes; pianist Count Basie, guitarist Freddie Green, bassist Eddie Jones, and drummer Sonny Payne.)

This was the first of many albums in which Basie explored the work of a single arranger. Having lost several of his most celebrated soloists over the years, he resolutely refused to be dependent on the personalities of stars like Lester Young or Illinois Jacquet when he reorganized in 1951. He set about creating a writers' band, a virtuoso orchestra with a unique attack and matchless precision. Several hit records in the mid-50s, including "Every Day" and "April in Paris," increased his popularity, but *Basie* commenced a new era of instrumental excitement and copious sensations. Hefti, who had already provided Basie with superior pieces, surpassed himself with this showcase, creating a capering piano concerto in "The Kid from Red Bank," recalling Basie's pedigree in Fats Waller and showing off the technical agility he usually understated; a show-stopper, "Whirly-Bird," that evoked a thrilling three-chorus solo from tenor saxophonist Eddie "Lockjaw" Davis; and a famous blue-ballad, "Li'l Darlin'," which comes alive only at one very specific and very slow signature tempo.

Considering the variety and sequencing of the album, one marvels at the limited palette Hefti used. Seven out of 11 selections are blues, including the first three, but the album is neither repetitious nor predictable. "The Kid from Red Bank" (Basie was born in Red Bank, N.J.) starts smashingly on the first beat of the tune—no intro—and is a riveting example of how he could dislocate rhythm, a feat made easier by the unwavering support of the rhythm section: Green, bassist Eddie Jones, and drummer Sonny Payne (also slightly underrecorded). One of the key reasons for the album's ongoing celebrity is the amplitude of Basie's piano throughout. "Duet" is a medium-slow blues, centered on an exchange of four-bar passages between trumpeters Joe Newman and Thad Jones. "After Supper" establishes a more dilatory groove, with Jones playing an obbligato to the theme, followed by Davis's tenor coasting over brass punctuations and a customarily oblique rhythm-section interlude.

The four-man rhythm team was recorded quite well on "Flight of the Foo Birds," as was the creamy writing for the reeds; one chorus is split between Frank Wess's alto saxophone and Jones's trumpet, and a full chorus is claimed by Jaws, who earns his nickname with a carnivorous entrance. "Double-O" is built for speed and set in motion by Basie's crushed chords; after the ensemble states the 32-bar head, the arrangement does a fake-out—what promises to be a Joe Newman trumpet solo lasts two bars, a transitional passage leading to three choruses by Jaws and the ensemble, for a de facto tenor sax concerto. "Teddy to Toad" is an unusual Basie blues because other than the Basie interlude, it permits no improvisation, featuring instead a written two-chorus episode by the trombone choir. "Whirly-Bird" is a definite highpoint, with its splendid Lockjaw solo followed by a chorus of ensemble glissandi and another that opposes brass punctuations to saxophone half notes.

"Midnite Blue" (incorrectly listed on the jacket as "Midnite"), another feature for the leader, is slow as molasses, the better to appreciate Charlie Fowlkes's unbelievable first-beat baritone sax accents and the band's blasting dynamics during the penultimate chorus. "Splanky" also builds to a vibrant finish, after discrete section work—reeds against brasses—and a suave tenor solo by Frank Foster; it's the only piece on the album that ends with Basie's patented three-note trademark closer. Frank Wess comes to the fore on "Fantail," playing two choruses on his own and sharing two with Payne's drums. Finally, on the incomparable "Li'l Darlin" (incorrectly punctuated on the jacket), we get to hear Freddie Green loud and clear—his fleeting arpeggio is the switch that puts the ensemble into motion, indulging textural finesse and commiserating with trumpeter Wendell Culley, whose principal moment this was. It's a brandy chaser, the perfect finish for a quintessential Basie album.

Because of sessions like this, Frank Sinatra soon claimed solidarity with Basie in a series of albums and nightclub appearances. And no less than Sinatra, Basie—the formerly scrappy scion of Kansas City swing—had come to represent high-stakes adult rhythm music, not so much a bulwark against rock and roll as a brief oasis for those who grew up with big bands and figured the affluent society ought to be able to afford a few. Time, which no one calculated more scrupulously than the kid from Red Bank, was running out or at least a-changing. *Basie* was part of the cultural blowout, very atomic and now very distant, yet miraculously undated.

[*The Absolute Sound*, 21 March 2002]

55 ❖ *"I'm Supposed to Deliver"* (B. B. King)

This interview with B. B. King has been gathering dust for 35 years, though I have periodically shown it to people who were writing about him or the blues and who ask why I don't publish it. I've often thought of including it in an essay collection or cannibalizing it for a retrospective on King, but it never fit anywhere and it resists intrusions, perhaps because the circumstances of the interview and the great man's voice remain so vivid to me. Yet it deserves to be rescued from oblivion: Here is King at a pivotal moment, in the process of crossing over from inner-city venues to a level of mainstream acceptance unparalleled in blues history. Listen to him speak in 1969, and imagine his response if someone had told him then that in the near future he would be so famous as to be routinely courted for TV ads. We live in a different country; this conversation reflects the one we came from.

As the student concerts chairman at Grinnell College, I arranged for King to perform in the school gymnasium on September 13, 1969. At the time, Riley B. King had been recording for 20 years (starting at Bullet in 1949, with a studio band including Phineas Newborn Jr. on piano)—about 225 singles and 30 LPs altogether—and had a deep and loyal following among urban black audiences. Thanks to the British and Southern white blues bands that venerated him (and to Charles Keil's groundbreaking study, *Urban Blues*, which apotheosized him), he had only recently begun to reap national recognition.

King's performance at Grinnell was exceptional. When it was over, instead of packing up and heading for his hotel, he sat down on the stage steps, in his tuxedo, surrounded by several fans (and a tape recorder), toweled his face and neck, and talked for 90 minutes, until a buildings and grounds custodian cleared us out. His voice and forthrightness, as represented here, will be familiar to readers of his excellent 1996 autobiography, *Blues All Around Me*. Just as that memoir ultimately disproves his opening lines—"I struggle with words. Never could express myself the way I wanted"—this interview is a candid, articulate, and finally spellbinding rumination on music, race, class, geography, and business.

Born in Ita Bena, Mississippi, in 1925, King is cousin to country blues singer Bukka White. He began to teach himself guitar in 1943, and later studied the Schillinger System. In 1948 he moved to Memphis and worked as a radio disc jockey. Three years later, with a style all his own, he released his first hit single, "Three O'Clock Blues." From then on his career became a series of one-night stands and record sessions, mostly for Crown and Kent. He signed with ABC in 1962, a lasting affiliation despite or because of the numberless, often successful attempts to increase his drawing power through the imposition of unsympathetic rhythm sections, vocal choruses, and strings—an issue he addresses here. Through it all, he retained his equilibrium and the power of his art, as his concert tours have proved well into the new century. His influence on singers and guitarists is incalculable, in and out of blues.

This transcription appears as it did in a Grinnell College one-shot magazine, *Montage*, in 1970.

How do you feel about the young white blues musicians like Elvin Bishop and Michael Bloomfield?
BBK: I think they're great, not only as musicians but as people. Those cats opened doors for guys like me, and not only that but they are tremendous musicians. I don't think there's anybody alive who hasn't gotten an idea from somebody, cause I used to listen to cats and learn from them and I still do. But the trouble with some of us is—I may listen to you, listen to somebody else. But I'll tell you the truth. I was thickheaded, kind of stupid when it came to learning, and I'd hear a cat play something and I'd try to play it, but I could never play it like him. So I would try to convince myself that I *wouldn't* play like that when the reason was I *couldn't*. Therefore I would take that idea and add my own thing to it and I usually came out with a thing of my own. I guess that's how I got the style that I have, because my style is a mixture of many, many people.
Who were some of your strongest influences?
BBK: Blind Lemon Jefferson, Lonnie Johnson, and then T-Bone Walker just did it—that was the first time I heard blues on the guitar.
Some of your lines have a kind of jazz fluency to them.
BBK: Well yes, I listened to jazz too. I'm coming into that. Then I heard Charlie Christian and then at last I heard a guy called Django Reinhart and that really did it! I'm still crazy for him. All those people—Elmore James, Kenny Burrell's a good friend. Wes Montgomery was, too. But I could never play like these cats. I guess I was somewhat influenced by them because I like them.
Have you ever played with a jazz rhythm section?
BBK: I have been in jam sessions with people who play like that and it's nice, but I can't be me when I play like that. To me, I'm more B. B. King when I'm doing the blues like I'm doing.
Have you read Charles Keil's book?
BBK: *Urban Blues*, yeah.
How do you feel about his distinction between urban and city blues?
BBK: If you were going to classify the different types of blues, I would be lost. It's a funny thing, like I'm from Mississippi, but very few of the guys I used to listen to were from Mississippi. Like Blind Lemon and T-Bone Walker were from Texas, Lowell Fulson's from Oklahoma. I would hear these people in the delta of Mississippi, and I guess the same thing was true with Muddy Waters and John Lee Hooker, cause we were all from Mississippi. So it's kind of hard, and there wasn't any big city

around there. You know, now when you get to England everyone thinks that everybody playing blues is from Chicago. Are there any blues singers really from Chicago?

Buddy Guy? Butterfield?

BBK: Buddy's from Louisiana. Well, Paul, but he's the only one. Maybe today, right now, there's a couple.

Why is Chicago the center place?

BBK: Things were so bad down south that anybody that was in Alabama around through Arkansas wanted to go where he thought things would be better for him and the nearest place was Chicago. People farther east like the Carolinas, Georgia, they would go to New York. And the people farther west would go on to California. But Chicago was the kind of place where you would come to make a living. There were always many little joints, beer joints that stayed open late. Every time I was there, I was there to work, but I remember, I'd go around many places and if you showed up the proprietor would maybe give you a drink. Everybody was pretty nice with you. In other words, you were sort of recognized, they gave you a chance. And most other places, unless you played jazz you didn't get a chance. And then you had more of the, I would say, lower-class people, construction workers or whatever, the kind of people you feel comfortable being with. And they were there to support you.

Where do you live now?

BBK: No place really. I was living in California till almost four years ago. I was married then. My wife and I were divorced and I left. I guess I'd have to say my home is Memphis because my personal office is there and I have a little farm there—my dad is there. So if I were going to say home, I really would have to call that home. But really, I live in hotels across the country.

You've been playing how long?

BBK: Twenty-one years traveling.

It's only been in the last four or five years that you've had large white audiences.

BBK: It hasn't been that long.

Do you think the same thing's going to happen to people like Bobby Bland and Junior Parker, because they're still not well known outside the South?

BBK: I don't know. I hope so.

You started Bland recording, didn't you?

BBK: I wouldn't say that I actually started him, but I would say that I was a big influence. I would say I influenced most of the guys my age or younger because, well, Bobby Bland used to ride around with me—like we're together now, he'd be around with me. Junior Parker was the same way. I knew Magic Sam. I knew most of the guys that have been recording long before they were recording. Let's put it that way.

Many musicians, jazz or pop, when they get a big hit have to play the same stuff night after night because that's what the audience wants. Do you ever get tired of playing the same things?

BBK: Not if people really dig it.

Do you feel it every time? You've convinced me that you do.

BBK: I feel what I'm doing. Let's put it that way: I'm pretty lucky. When I first started, sure I was doing like most guys do. I was playing anybody's number that was on the jukebox. But after about a year of recording, I made so many records, I came to find out people are this way: They're sure they want to hear what they want to hear. Like, if you've got a big number out, they want to hear it. But you've got to think a little bit, too, for your public, because that number that's big—had you played it before it was recorded, they wouldn't like that one either. So I'll try to sneak in a new song every now and then. I won't mention it, I won't say it's a new song, but I'll try to work hard and get everybody to really jumping and moving and then I'll slide in a new one. This keeps it from being one of those things, you know, night after night after night.

I would assume that you're most comfortable with a small group.

BBK: I carried a large group from '55 to '63 and of course I have nothing against a large group, but wanting to eat. So I worked those years for the band. Oh, I love a big band but I'm happy playing with the group I have right now, because they let it all hang out.

With a big band you have to worry about charts.

BBK: Yeah and that definitely can get to be a thing unless you've got some really good writers. I'd probably write some but my musical knowledge is, ah, sad.

What precipitated your transition from spirituals to the blues?

BBK: Most of the people where I was brought up were very religious or hypocritical. If they weren't religious they were hypocritical, because they pretended to be. So I was brought up with the spiritual deal. But this is actually what started to get me more interested in the blues. I would work real hard and we would sing spirituals on the weekend and during the week and nobody would pay us. They'd look at us, you know. But if you played blues you could put an admission on the door. It was funny. I would work a whole week and I think I was making about $21 a week. And before that, I was picking cotton for 35 cents a hundred and chopping cotton for 75 cents a day and driving tractors for two-and-a-half a day but I dug it. Don't misunderstand me, I dug it because I wasn't used to anything else and I believed in walking through the field. Chopping cotton and the tractor—that was an advance, a promotion. But, that was Monday throughout Saturday most times, or Monday through Saturday noon. So that evening I'd get paid off and I'd buy a ticket and sometimes get a hundred miles from home and just play around the streets. Man, I'd be standing around on the streets like a blind man. And I would make more bread that evening—from people I wasn't asking anything from. They'd just ask me to play tunes and I would play them and they would tip quarters, half-dollars—and I would make more money that evening than I made the whole week on the farm. I'm serious. So they gave me some ideas—hey, something's happening. Then I was drafted into the army, in '43, and that's when I started singing blues, baby! So that's how it came about. But actually that spiritual thing is still there when I'm on the stage now. And I think that any guy who is singing blues, real blues, has some kind of spiritual background. And that don't have to be his color either, believe me.

Is the current so-called re-awakening of the blues a re-awakening of the performers or of the public?

BBK: It's the public. Because one thing I'm grateful for is that I haven't changed at all. I'm now doing the thing I've been doing all my life. And the people have become aware of it now and dig me for being myself. Some people appreciate those years that I ate sardines mixed with pork and beans. They're glad of that because all of that helped me to keep going and to help me to be where I am now. In other words, here in Grinnell or in some other place, people can hear us and then use their own opinion; it's either good or it's not good. Whereas, other times, you didn't have the chance because you could never hear it—we weren't played on the radio, you couldn't see us on television—so you wouldn't have had a chance to know about it had it not been for guys like Bloomfield.

Yeah, but isn't there a little dissatisfaction at the fact that those guys have come up recently, haven't paid the dues that people like you and Bland have, and yet they're asking for prices far higher than yours and getting it?

BBK: Well, I say it like this. I've had many people asking me, "Am I bitter?" No, I've never been bitter. The world's changing and the world needs to change. People need to be people, people need to respect people for what they are and they don't need to fight about it. You know, if I had my way, there would be no wars: if a cat's an 'a', he's an 'a', if he's not, he's not. But I was hurt for a long time—not bitter but hurt—because I felt that a lot of the cats that were making it I was happy for them. I believe anybody who can make it deserves it, but I was hurt because everybody seemed to be accepted and a lot of the people were doing the same thing that I was, so why was I omitted? I don't think that anything should be given to me, but if I merit it I can have it. And so if these cats are able to do it, that's great.

How many one-night stands do you do in a year?

BBK: On the average of 300, but one year I did 342. And that doesn't mean I wasn't working those other days.

Do you play many club dates?

BBK: We're beginning to do more. Now we're beginning to play places where everyone can come. It used to be we'd play across the track south: all black. We'd play across the track north: all white. Now we're beginning to play *on* the track. Everyone can come. You see, we—most of the blues guys—don't think in terms of black blues and white blues. We think in terms of the music that we're producing. Either we like it or we don't like it.

How much control do you have in a recording session?

BBK: Not too much. Not too much. But if I can manage to get a little, I will. I'll tell you this, all my life I have felt this way: If a person owed me two dollars and I can get a dollar-eighty, I'd be happy. My reason for saying it like that is that there are so many people around that can sing, can play, and a lot of them are much more talented than I am. So a person could have—just like you and me here tonight, you could have had T-Bone Walker, you could have had Bobby Bland, people like that, you could have anybody of your choice. You didn't have to have B. B. King. I always remember that so I'm grateful.

Well we had to have you if we wanted your sound.

BBK: Well, thank you. But what I'm talking about—you had your choice. So I don't ever want to be one of those guys that you can't touch, that you can't talk with. Because I feel there's always somebody that you can touch, that you can talk with. And I think the same thing when I'm in a recording studio. They don't have to record me.

Are you going to stay with ABC?

BBK: Well, I have a contract with ABC until '75. This one I signed about two years ago, but I was with them before. One thing about the major companies that really excites the average blues singer that never had anything is that they are this way: They're cold after the contract, but they will live up to what they say they are going to do. So you go to them and ask for 10 dollars, and if they agreed to give you 10 dollars, you're going to get that! But it's no more buddy-buddy after that. Now with the average independent company, you can go to them and say, "Hey, 10 dollars." They say, "Yeah baby, 10 dollars, but 10 is a little high, can you settle for seven-fifty?" And in a lot of cases, you say yes. Later on, things may be bad, and then you will sidle up to him and say, "Man, I sure could use five," and you'll get it. I'm just talking in terms of money. So when I went to ABC, finally, after I'd been with the other company for a long time, I asked them for a sum of money and they gave it to me. And this is when you win a cat's heart. Myself and most of the guys, we never had anything. And maybe the cat wants a home, you know, a place to live. If you've never had a place—like I never had a home until I was 20 years old because my dad wasn't able to buy a house. When I got to be 20, well, I worked and we bought one. So like maybe you have five or six payments that need to be paid off; you go to ABC, Atlantic, one of these big companies, and they pay it off for you. And these people will let you have a few bucks—maybe you want to get some clothes or a payment on a car that you never had before.

If your producer at ABC said, "We're going to get you a bigger audience" in the manner that was done for Howlin' Wolf and Muddy Waters, and they gave you country and western or pop songs to do, music and musicians that you didn't dig at all, would you have to record it?

BBK: Yes. I may not dig it, but like I said, they're the boss.

How would you compare the situation of the older blues singers, country blues singers like Blind Lemon and Lightnin' Hopkins, with the blues singers of your generation?

BBK: I think of it this way: Blind Lemon was one of the forerunners. I don't classify him with myself or any of the guys I hear today. He was one of the forerunners who didn't have a guideline so I set him up there by himself. Lightnin' and a lot of other cats came along with me—of course, Lightnin' is older than I am, but he still had Blind Lemon and many other cats that he could listen to. That's the difference. It's like: Suppose there's no colleges, no universities, no schoolteachers where you can learn. Let's say you come out to be a genius. Where'd you get it? You dig what I'm talking about? So everyone would have to look up to you cause here's the cat that made it and didn't have none of these facilities. He had nothing but himself. So that's the way I look at Blind Lemon. Here's a man that couldn't see and everybody rejected him. In most societies, until lately —you know, people have just begun to recognize people for being people. At that time, it was bad, man. The black people in his area, even his own people, I'm talking about his relatives . . . Like, I remember when people had tuberculosis in the area where I was born. When they found out a cat had tuberculosis they'd build him a little house out behind the main house and they'd have two or three people who would feed him and he would stay out there until he died. I also remember what they did to the deranged people. Like somebody would be born that wasn't quite together? They'd put them in a back room and anytime you came to visit them, that door was always closed. I'm not lying to you. Everything I've told you is the truth. So then, after telling you this, think in terms of a cat like Blind Lemon and you can see the difference yourself.

Have black 15- and 16-year-olds accepted you and blues performers like you in the way that they have, for example, the Motown groups?

BBK: No. They haven't accepted us like that. And I don't really hate them for being that way. I feel sorry for them. It hurts. It's another time I get hurt. And the reason for that is, over the years, the last few years, with this rock and roll, you had a lot of younger disc jockeys, black disc jockeys, and the black people, especially in the areas I come from, have tried to elevate themselves so hard—some the right way, some the way that I wouldn't. But all in all, everybody has been trying to elevate themselves. Now, I put it this way: they had heard about blues like B. B. King and Muddy Waters and many other people like that. But a lot of middle-class people, like the doctors and the lawyers, people from the black race— when they started having an influence in the schools, like the first cat you're going to hear about is Beethoven or Leonard Bernstein, and if they happen to mention a black artist, it may be Duke Ellington, and it's a heck of a ways from Duke down to B. B. King. You understand what I'm talking about? So you got the Temptations and the Supremes and everybody else all between them. So the black kids figure, this is what Dr. James says is OK and Lawyer Bird says is fine, well then I'm going to listen to them. So they bypass me and a lot of the other guys, and they're not played on the radio. They're not on the radio, they're not seen on television, they're not in movies. So the kids think, "This must not be what's happening. You know, that's just funky blues. That ain't it." So really I can't blame them because it's just like those mentally deranged kids that I mentioned being in the room with the door closed. Those young disc jockeys, the black disc jockeys on the black-operated stations, or the ones that are supposed to be black-directed stations, they play the thing they thought would elevate the kids and that excluded B. B. King and a lot of other cats. So we didn't get any records played until recently. But there's something I've got to explain to you. You know, when I was a kid, even in Mississippi, I had white friends. A lot of times I would want them to come and visit me but I wouldn't know if my mother and father would like it. And I know that they wanted me to come and visit them, but they didn't know if their mothers and fathers would like it. So we didn't ever go. We'd meet up on the creek bank and that's where we would play, you know, on neutral ground. And we had a ball. I'm trying to say this: It's just starting to happen. Not too long ago, man, people began to realize who they are and what they are and began to be proud of who and what they are. But for a long time, if a cat called me a black boy it was almost like an insult, especially if it was a white cat. But I started thinking about it. All my life, in my area, we called the white people white people. So why can't I be called black people and why should I be insulted by it, because that's what I am? And it took a long time for this to get into me. And it's taken a long time for each race to be proud of its heritage, to be proud of being what you are. And to remember and believe the reason we are all here—it's a job for everybody. We were put here for a reason. So heck, I may not be a schoolteacher but I'm a blues singer. There's a job for everybody. And this is what the people are now beginning to realize—and the time is coming soon. So now, trying to answer your question, young blacks are starting to realize that regardless of what he may do or how he may look, he's still black and he's a person and he or she can make his or her own way in society if given the chance, and the chances are coming. When people like you will help them to have their chance. So now a lot of times kids come to me and say, "Hey, my mother and dad got your records. I don't dig blues but I dig you, you're alright." So they've come that far. After a while they'll dig it, they'll dig the other guys because we all influenced each other. Learned from each other. See, here's one thing. Now I don't want to pat myself on the back, but through the rugged life I've lived I've always been constantly gaining just a little ground all the time. I've never been in trouble. I've never had any bad publicity. It's not because I was so good—cause I was mischievous as any other cat coming up. I was just lucky enough to have the door closed. So all these cats respect me as a gentleman—not that I really am, but they think I am—and I can be on a show and all those cats can come to me and talk. This includes a lot of the soul singers. I don't know why—I know I don't look intelligent—but I guess they figure I've been around so long that I should know something about it. So they'll come to me and talk. And when I hear them perform, I'll listen and learn from them because no one can know it all. You know, according to a book I read, Einstein, for all his greatness in mathematics, didn't know how to eat. So nobody can know it all. So I learn from them—many new chord changes, rhythm patterns. And they influence me, too.

You made a record recently with Pharoah Sanders. What kind of thing did that turn out to be?

BBK: It was more like a jazz session—jazz mixed up with blues and a little rock.

Who did you record it for?

BBK: We just put it on tape but I believe it'll have to be released on ABC because most of the people jamming were connected with the label.

Do you have to have lived the blues in order to play the blues?

BBK: I think that anything you practice, if you have talent, can become superior. But I do think that with anything you do, any experience you can get helps. So a lot of times, I sing about what I know about, and a lot of people sing about what they've heard about.

Is there any particular key you like to play in?

BBK: No, I play in all of them.

When was Live at the Regal *recorded?*

BBK: I think it was about '58.

Many critics think that's your best record, that if you want to hear B. B. King that's the record to get.

BBK: Well, I'm glad. I don't want to cut off my nose to spite my face. Let's see. A lot of times that I've recorded, man, and a lot of sets that I've played, well, I didn't think they were what a lot of people thought they were. I hope that answers your question.[1]

Do you have any preference among your own albums?

BBK: Yes. I have three records that I really dig; one a long time ago called *My Kind of Blues* on the Crown and Kent label, then a spiritual album that I liked very much, and the thing that's called *Live and Well*. Those are my three albums. You know, over the years, you try and you do many things—a lot of things you want to do, a lot of things you're forced to do, a lot of things because somebody says you ought to do them. And you never know, because you're trying to make your own way. And sometimes these things turn out good. And a lot of them you think stink. So that's the way it is. Like, when we did *Live at the Regal* parts of it I dug, yes. And parts of it I didn't. Because we were playing for a live audience of kids, black kids, and a lot of them listened to . . . There's one thing I have to say about Chicago: In Chicago people haven't been ashamed of the blues. They've played it on the radio stations—especially WVON, Chess's station. So Chicago has been a little hip all the time. Until the underground stations started, most of the country wasn't hip to blues. But God bless FM stations. Those AM people, well, you know, want to make a buck. In the industry everybody's got to live. But I sure hope they don't have to live for the buck exclusively.

Are there any places you particularly like working?

BBK: Well, you've got to think in terms of Fillmore East and West. And then the Cellar Door in Washington and the Village Gate. You can't exclude those, because that's where people come that want to hear you. Those places, and the colleges we're beginning to play now, are where people come to listen, to hear what you've got to say. So if you say it and they

---

[1] This business about *Live at the Regal* set us back on our heels. Actually, it was recorded in 1964. King's ambivalence about it has remained unchanged. In *Blues All Around Me*, he writes, "Even though the *Live* album was cool, I've probably played hundreds of better concerts than the one taped at the Regal. But who am I to argue with critics?"

dig it, they let you know. And if you don't say it and they don't dig it, at least they're still courteous. And this is one of the things that makes you work. If I didn't do what I thought was my best tonight or any night, man, it would worry me. I'd go home and almost cry about it. If anything went wrong this would really disturb me. Because the people came to hear me and I'm supposed to deliver. And if I'm short in delivering, it worries me, bothers me. That don't happen too often, quite frankly, but it has happened.

Do you have any specific ideas about what you would like to record that you haven't yet?

BBK: Yes.

What are they?

BBK: I haven't pulled it out of the sky yet. I didn't mean that to be a corny answer but, you know, I hear things but I don't have a name for it. Or I don't know how to set it to music. But I do want to get . . . Well, I have one thing that I'll mention to you. It's a thing called "Ghetto Woman." Now this story tells about a broad and doesn't have anything to do with what color she is, but she's a chick that digs her man so much. Now they're fighting in Vietnam and everything is happening—rats running across the floor, roaches running up the walls—and none of this bothers her because all she is is a ghetto woman and she's waiting for her man to come home. In other words, the idea that I'm trying to get over is, she don't care about all the other things happening, people rioting and everything—she don't give a darn about none of it, she's so in love with her man. She's so in love with her man she wants to be where he is. And so he's left her—this cat's a hustler—he's trying to get things going and she's sitting there and the only thing that bugs her is he's not there. Do you dig what I mean? The whole change in the world don't mean nothing to her. Cause her world is that cat. . . .

Do you use many head arrangements?

BBK: No, they're all written out. Most of the things we do are written out. But I don't like people on the stage, especially with a small group, so we get together and we rehearse them, we write out. All the cats write. I'm the most limited cat in the band—everybody else is far advanced over me. We get together and we rehearse what we're going to do. Then after the cats learn the guidelines, whatever the charts may be, I like the cats to play free. For instance, you have a guy speaking: He's got a subject he's going to talk about. He may talk around it and say anything, but everything's going to lead back to that one thing. But later on, man, it gets to be a drag playing the same thing every night. I don't dig it. Let's change it. Like Louie Jordan used to say, "Let's move it up a little bit."

At Newport last summer, you played and then Johnny Winter came on and you played with him. Was that rehearsed?

BBK: No, that was a first. It's a thing, man—they tricked me into that. Johnny's a good friend of mine and they tricked me. He had George Wein come and get me cause they thought it would be good for the festival, which I didn't mind, but if I'd known what was going to happen I would have gotten ahead, I would have said, "Well, let's do so and so." But they tricked me into that, which was bad in a way. You see, Johnny and I are dear friends, we've been close, very good friends, but when we get on the stage we're enemies. In other words, we're like two fighters in the ring. And usually some good things come out of it. We had the same thing happen in Dallas, which was a beautiful festival, man. And the last night there, when we got off, there were a lot of kids at another park that didn't have any bread to come to the festival and Johnny and I went over there and we jammed for them for about three hours. There were about 10 to 15 thousand people over there, man, and we had a ball. Because the people were for real. They weren't there because they had to be there. And we went over there and had a good time.

Constructing guitar solos night after night, do you ever surprise yourself anymore?

BBK: Yes, I did tonight. Yeah, certain times I hit certain things that I didn't think was going to come out as well as they did. Other times I hit things that I didn't think were going to be as sour as they were. Yeah, it happens. I learn things daily.

What kinds of records do you listen to?

BBK: If I tell you this you won't believe it. I'm very moody—sometimes I want to hear blues, sometimes rock, sometimes jazz, but most times when I'm working and, like, I want to relax, I like the kind of music that you hear in stores. That's the truth.

That's like Louis Armstrong saying he likes to listen to Guy Lombardo.

BBK: Yeah, it's true. This is the type of sound that it would be. You know, you hear strings and the cats playing the raw materials like "Star Dust" and you hear cats playing saxophones like they got molasses in 'em. But they know what they're doing, though. They're real good musicians. And that's what I really listen to. Now I listen to that more than I do anything else.

How did the talking routines—like on "How Blue Can You Get?"—come about?

BBK: It just happened. It was never written out or anything. It's some-what experience. Like when I talk about a jealous cat, I was pretty jeal-ous myself—now I know a lot of cats who were much worse. I mean this is actually the truth. And I've known about cats fighting broads and broads fighting cats, you know. This is the life. It's really life. I've known cats that lived that way, that didn't want people to visit their homes and things like that. So I started talking and it looked like people were digging me saying it so I said it again the next night. It was never written out, never suggested, or nothing like that. I guess it started 10 or 15 years ago when I was playing one night and the drummer's foot pedal had broken. He was trying to fix his foot pedal and I was just talking to the people, trying to keep them calm till we could go into another thing. That's how I got it. And each night, what I'm talking about is the truth—I'm really not lying. And a lot of people think I am and they have to think about it three or four times.

How do you get yourself together when you're in a cold studio and there's nobody there but the producer?

BBK: I play on his sympathy. I've learned over the years that you can get many things done much better by asking a person, being a little meek and a little humble and straight and truthful if you can. In other words, I'll get up to a cat and, like if we don't have charts and we're doing a head thing, I'll tell the musicians first—maybe they're cats I've never met, like if we're doing it with studio musicians—and I'll say, "Fellas, I've got three or four. I don't know what I'm gonna do. I don't know nothing of my own and I don't have no special way I'm going do it. But here's my lines. This is the idea that I had."

[A building-and-grounds man blinks the gym lights on and off.]

BBK: [Shouting to the b&g man] Okay. We got it. We got the message. So anyway I tell the cats, I don't know what I'm gonna do so any help I get, I appreciate.

[The lights blink off and on again.]

BBK: [To the b&g man] Okay, okay, we're coming!

[Montage, February 1970]

56 ❖ *Brother Al*
(Al Cohn)

Charlie Parker and his comrades generated the modernist revolution in jazz, but Lester Young primed the troops, though most of them didn't know it at the time. Dexter Gordon once remarked that Coleman Hawkins played everything you could play on tenor saxophone whereas Young told a story. The story he told was terse, and therefore cryptic; fleet, therefore intrepid; personal, therefore erotic; daring, therefore dangerous. A generation of saxophonists found themselves in Young's music—in its clarity and confidentiality—as an earlier generation had in Hawkins's rococo virtuosity. Young's influence was unique in its capacity to probe and elicit racial distinctions at the core of jazz.

Hawkins's impact, like that of Louis Armstrong, was monolithic. Young was the Pied Piper whose tune was heard differently by blacks and whites. As Gordon recalled, "We used to jam together—Zoot, Al Cohn, Allen Eager. Zoot and I worked in a club in Hollywood for Norman Granz. He was playing Lester and I was playing Lester, but there was always a difference." The difference became more pronounced with the years. Black tenors modified Young's legato phrasing into a more forthright attack, emphasizing the muscularity and expressiveness of his style, to the extreme of rhythm and blues honking. White tenors focused on Young's airy lyricism, to the extreme of supercool preciosity.

Black Lester reached its first generic apex in the dueling tenors of West Coasters Gordon and Wardell Gray, while White Lester achieved its first generic peak as the orchestrated tenors in the East Coast bands of Gene Roland and, more famously, Woody Herman. After Herman recorded Jimmy Giuffre's "Four Brothers," that title came to represent every white tenor who worked in what Stan Getz, the most accomplished of the brothers, called "the Lestorian mode." White Lester remained popular throughout the '50s, but amid the fury of '60s New Music, it was often dismissed as flaccid and derivative. Allen Eager and Brew Moore dropped out for decades, Warne Marsh took day jobs when his music was mocked as too intellectual, Al Cohn put his energies into arranging, and even the prolific Zoot Sims took a six-year sabbatical from recording. Getz recharged himself with Bossa Nova and rode out the night. One often heard fatuous references to "all those white tenors," "all those Lester Young imitators."

"I'm always hearing about all these white tenors. Who are they?" a record producer challenged me, when I casually made precisely that comment during a long evening spent listening to obscure bebop records. "Well, Al Cohn . . ." "Leave my home! Are you out of your mind?" Instead of pursuing the subject, he bided his time for a few hours and then craftily blindfold-tested me with a new record. I made a few haphazard guesses, not having any idea who it was, though confident that it wasn't Al Cohn. There was nothing pale or prim about this music: He had a sound so enfolding you could paste fur on it and wear it as a coat; he lagged behind the beat and then punished it for getting ahead; and he moaned and sighed and swelled with an emotional complexity that made his melodies momentous. Of course, it was Al Cohn. The producer was Don Schlitten, who two years later invited me to an Al and Zoot record session (their first in 12 years), which he produced on March 23, 1973, a month before I started writing for the *Village Voice*. By that time, I had bought the two Cohn records still in print and taped several others, but they were small beer in the light of that luminescent afternoon. The rhythm section consisted of Jaki Byard, George Duvivier, and Mel Lewis, and the music was a revelation. You could, as they say, look it up: *Body and Soul*.

The date began with a swing riff called "Doodle Oodle," which gave me a chance to observe the different temperaments of the two tenor saxophonists. Cohn stood before one mike and Sims sat before the other. Cohn sprang into a vital, knockdown chorus, but when Zoot took his turn, he puttered around. The same thing happened on the next take, and a third, and maybe more. Finally, they played a take for which Zoot, just before his solo, rose to his feet and rode herd over the piece. "Too bad he didn't stand up sooner," someone said. And someone else, probably Schlitten, explained that Al plays his best on the first take and then starts to fade, while Zoot starts slow and builds—the trick was to catch them on equal footing in the middle ground. This, incidentally, was the session at which Zoot uttered a line much repeated over the years and sometimes attributed to other musicians. A player broke a Dexedrine tablet in two, popped half, and was about to discard the other. "Don't throw that away," Sims said. "Don't you know there are kids in India who are sleeping?"

Body and Soul was widely greeted as a long overdue reunion by the duo Leonard Feather called the Damon and Pythias of jazz. But the producer had another agenda, revealed in the album's title. "Body and Soul," the acid test for tenors ever since Coleman Hawkins's 1939 recording, featured Cohn alone, a showcase at a time when Sims's reputation was far more secure. The keystone of the record, it shows how sinewy and authoritative Cohn's style had become during those years in the wilderness. Just as Sims's adoration of Young had been tempered and individualized by his reassessment of Ben Webster's approach, so Cohn's had been radically altered by a grounding in Sonny Rollins's phrasing and sonority. Each had been toughened, and "Body and Soul" was Cohn's quietly masterful declaration—a mature and sturdy solo that marked his independence from the mossy genres that had grown over his tracks. Pretty soon he began to jettison the tag of musician's musician and win an appreciative audience, though for a time he remained a cult figure. One night after closing time at Buddy's Place, the club Buddy Rich owned on Second Avenue in 1974, Rich remarked that he got his biggest satisfaction from introducing great players. He started to count them off on his fingers, beginning with Cohn, at which point I lamented, "Nobody knows about Al Cohn." "Yeah," he leaned in with a glint, "but isn't it a gas for those of us who do?"

When Al Cohn passed away on February 15, 1988, of liver cancer, jazz lost a consistent and imaginative performer, a relentless swinger who could shake you up—especially at a jam session, where he always excelled. Although he achieved his finest work on tenor during the last 15 years, there's no doubt that he exerted a powerful spell on musicians as long as 40 years ago. The emotional directness of his playing made his melodies and the way he phrased them sound not only right but paradigmatic. As a result, players on the bandstand with him often aped his sound and attack. What he borrowed from Young or Rollins or anyone else he invested with his own plaintiveness, his own rolling logic, and—always—his enveloping sound with its cantorial echo. You can hear him setting the pace for the tenors on Woody Herman broadcasts from the '40s, and in recorded jams from the '80s. The last time he played in New York was in December 1987, at a tribute to Herman by the American Jazz Orchestra. No one thought he would want to sit in a section again (it had been a long time), but he agreed without hesitation, and though he looked ill, his commitment and that broadsword tone were inspiring. Another tenor in the band remarked that sitting next to him was like being in someone's glove; you could hardly hear yourself think for trying to blend into his sound. He arrived early at every rehearsal—a sideman, no big deal, whatever you want, impervious to the fact that most of the musicians were in awe of him.

Cohn's eyes, magnified by glasses, were a bit crossed, the right larger than the left, giving him an earnest, quizzical expression. When he smiled, all the features came into place in a disarming and rather dashing configuration. He was, in my experience, a tough interview—laconic and all too direct. An easy subject embellishes questions with anecdotes and other elaborations. Cohn would smile and say, "You're right about that," or stare owlishly and say, "I don't think so." But since he lived music, he was great to talk music with, and his facial shorthand said a lot, especially when he recalled the major musicians in his life, like Jimmy Rushing ("I loved him and I still miss him. To me he was the greatest blues singer of all time") and Charlie Parker ("He even paid for the cab," he said in amazement, recalling the time Bird, whose tabs were routinely picked up by others, brought him home for a visit). I remember him speaking warmly of Ella Fitzgerald, the Basie band, Nelson Riddle, Sinatra, Nat Cole, Herman, Sims, and especially Billie Holiday. His wife, the former Flo Handy and subject of his tune "Mama Flossie," is a fine Holiday-influenced singer, and his son Joe a gifted guitarist—practically a musician's musician.

Alvin Gilbert Cohn was born in Brooklyn in 1925, and studied clarinet and piano, but not tenor. He joined Joe Marsala's band at 18, and began to draw attention four years later in Buddy Rich's band. He wasn't one of the original Four Brothers, but 16 months with Woody Herman—he arranged for the band before he joined it—placed him forever in their company and in later years he orchestrated several Brothers-style recordings. His friendship with Sims began then as well, though nine years passed before they formed a band. In the interim he played briefly with Artie Shaw, then retired from music, coming back in 1952 with a stint in Elliot Lawrence's big band. In those early years, he recorded a few times for Savoy and Progressive (the most durable session had Horace Silver and Max Roach); wrote a Prestige session for Miles Davis (the 58-bar "Willie the Weeper," which features both men in alternate choruses, is a standout), and came into his own during a busy period at RCA, when producer Jack Lewis exploited his talents as saxophonist and arranger on a great variety of discs. Six were issued under Cohn's name, the last of which (*From A to Z*) reunited him with Sims. At the same time, he established himself as a TV orchestrator, turning out charts for Sid Caesar, Steve Allen, Pat Boone, Andy Williams, the Tony Awards show, Gershwin specials, and many others.

In 1957, the Al Cohn-Zoot Sims Quintet appeared, unofficially heralded by a Cohn album on Coral ("featuring Zoot Sims"). The quintet didn't record with proper billing until 1960 (the intoxicating *You 'n' Me*, beloved by all who know it), by which time the band had become a fixture at the Half Note, on Hudson and Spring. They continued to play there intermittently until the club moved uptown in the mid-'70s—together or alone, one or the other or both accompanying Jimmy Rushing on weekends. Cohn made records for Epic, Dawn, Mercury, and RCA through 1961, and then dropped out for 12 years, as far as LPs went. He prospered as an orchestrator, though one of his peak collaborations as a writer remains little known even now: the jubilant 1962 Rushing album, *Five Feet of Soul*, on Colpix. He played in clubs and had his share of studio sessions, but there were no Al Cohn records until Schlitten set about refurbishing his career as a tenor saxophonist, recording him on Rushing's nostalgic swan song, *The Me and You That Used to Be*, half an MPS album with James Moody, and *Body and Soul*. Then the deluge: the Xanadu albums with Barry Harris, *Play It Now*, *Al Cohn's America*, and *No Problem*; the magniloquent duets with Jimmy Rowles, *Heavy Love*, also on Xanadu, as well as the encounters with Dexter Gordon, Billy Mitchell, and Earl Coleman; the Concord Jazz sessions, *Nonpareil*, *Overtures*, *Four Others* (with

Woody, the nominal leader, cheerleading Cohn, Flip Phillips, Sal Nistico, and Bill Perkins), *Tour De Force* (with Buddy Tate and Scott Hamilton), and concert jam sessions.

Shortly after Al's death, East Stroudsburg University in Pennsylvania established the Al Cohn Memorial Jazz Collection. Numerous musicians and friends donated photos and mementos to the archive, and a series of picture albums was published, along with a regular and ongoing newsletter, "The Note," for which Phil Woods writes an acerbic and amusing lead article. Yet you don't hear much about Cohn now—many young jazz lovers know little if anything about his recordings. Listening to his crafty wail on "Them There Eyes" on *Heavy Love* or "The Note" on *You 'n' Me* or "Raincheck" on *Nonpareil*, I think of Buddy Rich confiding, "Isn't it a gas for those of us who do?"

[*Village Voice*, 8 March 1988 / 2005]

57 ❖ The Arranger
(Gil Evans)

According to Goethe's formulation, Providence sees that extraordinary persons accomplish their missions on earth, and then passes them to a higher plane "so that others might still have something left to do in a world created to last a long while." Maybe so: We can't know if Mozart (at 35) and Charlie Parker (at 34) finished their missions. Jazz lovers used to argue with fierce indecision about what worlds were left for a Beiderbecke or a Coltrane to explore, and they usually concluded that they departed at a fated zenith. No one could bear to imagine them scuffling into middle-age bloat, indifference, fusion, or worse—retrenching with the rest of the world to formulae they had helped to demolish. The youthful dead gain in aura what they lose in work time. Never mind that the Armstrongs and Ellingtons and Gillespies and Rollinses and Taylors (not that there are more than one of each) prove that the creative life may wax long after the initial peak of inspiration. For the long-lived and still fighting, the end is expected, but the sting is no less acute, our desire for more no less ravenous.

Gil Evans, who had the waist of an anorexic, the mien of a country boy, and the face of a shaman, and who liked to conduct his band in cut-off jeans, waving his branchlike arms or playing what he called "cheer-leading piano," was 75 when he died of peritonitis, on March 20, 1988, in Mexico. His career, like his life, followed no rules and made few if any compromises. He was invariably the old man in the group, beginning in the 1940s with the Miles Davis nonet sessions, yet he always seemed the youngest in manner, temperament, spirit, and energy. There were many, here and especially in England and Japan, who thought he was the greatest living American composer—quite a testament, because in the strict sense of the word, Evans composed very little. He was primarily an arranger, someone who took the melodic and harmonic nuggets of other composers and transformed them—though as Davis told *Newsday*, "What he did with pop songs was like writing an original piece." In this, he was rivaled by very few: Ellington, of course, though most of his arrangements were of his own compositions; Nelson Riddle in the pop world; . . . I've run out of rivals. John Lewis recently observed that Evans's version of "Django" led him to a new understanding of his own composition.

No arranger in musical history worked with such diverse sources: Delibes, Cyril Scott, Mussorgsky, Ravel, Tchaikovsky, Parker, Ellington, Monk, Morton, Lewis, Jamal, J. J. Johnson, Clifford Brown, George Russell, Weill, Lead Belly, W. C. Handy, Willie Dixon, Jimi Hendrix, Gershwin, Rodrigo, De Falla, and dozens of Tin Pan Alley songsmiths. He interpolated Kreisler's "Caprice Viennois" into Jacquet's "Robbin's Nest," and Ellington's "Ko-Ko" into Tchaikovsky's "Arab Dance." He had a fearless and pandemic love of music, and showed no signs of slowing down or going rote. His performances last summer at the Umbria Jazz Festival, which reunited him with George Lewis and other fiercely loyal stalwarts was as exhilarating as any I've heard. He never looked back; indeed, he refused to accept any of his accomplishments as definitive, and often found it difficult to listen to them. This makes not only his career a perilous subject for the wholesale evaluation it has yet to receive, but his music as well. Whenever he had the chance to control the reissue of his records, he reedited them—sometimes to the extent that they became new works: He did this with sessions made for Ampex, RCA, Verve, and others.

Evans was established, if hardly in great demand, as an orchestrator when he began playing piano at age 40, an accomplishment that liberated him, inclining him toward an ever-increasing appetite for improvisation. Though written passages usually remained the highlights of his recorded work, he became fascinated with ways in which he, as a bandleader and composer, could spur and spontaneously organize free-form episodes. In this, he stands as the transitional figure between conventional conducting and the "conductioning" innovated by Butch Morris, whose work with big bands involves an impulsive kind of composition, unplanned yet coherent. Evans required only a vamp to get the motor charged; sometimes he provided nothing more, except signals to begin or stop solos or for sections to enter or desist, depending on the mood and the moment. He did not require a large repertory for his orchestra, though he had an extensive one, because each piece was reborn with each performance.

Gil loved his musicians and believed in them, and though he proved repeatedly to have little patience for business (no royalties for the albums with Davis, but then Riddle fared just as badly with Sinatra—arrangers need a union of their own), he fought to get them top dollar. They, of course, reciprocated, often turning down better-paying gigs to make his tours and concerts and to sit in Monday nights at Sweet Basil, where, on a good night, the line between composition and improvisation disappeared. (I'm assuming there were not-so-good nights, but I missed them.) You couldn't mistake the lusty themes, often etched in brass over festive rhythms, but gray areas proliferated. For example, Evans sometimes employed notated solos in the rhythm section, around which the ensemble would cohere, and episodes for the winds that were so elliptically sketched they could be approached in diverse ways. He favored great massed chords (they were often compared to clouds in the 1950s) and long phrases, requiring tremendous lung power, disguising rests—as the composed segues on *Miles Ahead* disguised the separate tracks. Anything could happen, everything was grist, and accidents counted. His preferred instrumentation included a division of rhythm players—acoustic and electric—that outnumbered the other musicians; gentility was no more his thing than geriatrics. His sets were musical parties, a joyous clatter that fused mainstream jazz, avant-garde jazz, rock, and rhythm and blues, *really* fusing them so that the elements were indivisible. It took sound engineers a decade to figure out how to balance the band. Evans proceeded undeterred.

He taught himself largely through records and he never hesitated to say that his key influence was Louis Armstrong. The first record he ever bought was Armstrong's "No One Else But You," and he would readily demonstrate his ability to sing several Armstrong solos. One day he called when my answering machine was configured to play only an excerpt from "Blue Again." He sang the rest of the solo and then remarked how important that record was. "I learned how to handle and appreciate a song from Louis, that's where I got the feeling," he said. In 1960, he met Armstrong, who surprised him by saying he had bought *Porgy and Bess,* the highpoint of the Evans-Davis collaboration, and suggesting they do a record together. "You're not gonna hand me none of them funny chords," he said jokingly. When Gil went to the office of Armstrong's manager, Joe Glaser, he was turned away, and later worried that Louis might have thought he wasn't interested. Other dream sessions got away, too. Evans was set to work with Lester Young and Jimi Hendrix at the time of each man's death.

The first time I heard about Gil's *Out of the Cool* was in a record store, when I asked a seemingly knowledgeable clerk about it. His eyes widened, he clasped his face with both hands, and proceeded to narrate a bar by bar breakdown of "La Nevada." Since I bought it just to get away from him, I will resist the temptation to do the same. Something is always happening on this record, and some passages have a hallucinatory vividness that nonetheless conceals vital evidence, so you listen again and again trying to discover how Evans works his magic. "La Nevada" is built on a 4-bar melodic fragment and a design for the rhythm section, yet builds relentlessly for 15 minutes, especially after tenor saxophonist Budd Johnson enters loaded for bear. Jimmy Knepper shines on the enchanting "Where Flamingos Fly," and the orchestrations of "Bilbao Song" and "Stratusphunk" are dreams. Ray Crawford and Johnny Coles play exceptionally well, as does Ron Carter (especially when accompanying soloists), and the final piece, "Sunken Treasure," is a brilliant joke: a reverie on the scores to every underwater movie you've ever seen. Coming on the heels of *Sketches of Spain* and released in the same year, 1961, as *Miles Davis at Carnegie Hall* (for which Evans conducted a 21-piece orchestra), *Out of the Cool* received sensational notices and promised to bring Gil out of the background. In effect, that's what happened, but not in a conventional way.

At the time Impulse printed the covers for *Out of the Cool*, it also printed covers for a sequel, *Into the Hot*. By the time the latter album was due to be recorded, Evans's producer, Creed Taylor, had left Impulse for Verve and Gil elected to turn over the sessions to two composers he admired who could not get recording contracts: John Carisi, one of the Miles Davis nonet writers, and Cecil Taylor, who debuted three pieces that dramatically advanced his standing in jazz's advance guard. The album was released under Gil's name, but he had no involvement with any of the music beyond being the sponsor. A reunion with Davis the next year, *Quiet Nights*, was a disaster, little more than half an album's music, including a couple of undeveloped sketches, released without Davis's or Evans's approval. Evans would later contribute to Davis's work (he wrote, uncredited, most of *Filles de Kilimanjaro*), but despite an ongoing friendship and many plans (*Tosca*, for one), they never again shared a marquee.

Not until 1963 did Evans record a suitable follow-up to *Out of the Cool*: *The Individualism of Gil Evans*, which along with the arrangements he wrote the following year for Kenny Burrell's *Guitar Forms*, both on Verve, represent the pinnacle of what, in retrospect, might be considered the first half of his career. Evidence of a new direction was apparent in pieces like "Hotel Me," which remained in his repertoire, and "The Barbara Song," but the musical world was changing, and the Verves led to a prolonged absence, nearly five years (hardly anyone knew of his involvement with the 1968 *Filles de Kilimanjaro*). The 1969 release of *Gil Evans*, on the short-lived Ampex label, surprised the few people who knew of its existence. It marked his entry into the same orbit that Tony Williams and Davis were charting at that time, and is probably the first jazz album to exhibit an awareness of Jimi Hendrix. Evans's career as a work-for-hire arranger had ended. For the next two decades, he worked as a bandleader, taking on other projects only when they represented a challenge or an outstanding payday. He maintained a large and largely faithful ensemble through parlous times—a band whose regulars included Howard Johnson, Hannibal Peterson, Billy Harper, Sue Evans, Arthur Blythe, David Sanborn, Trevor Koehler, Lew Soloff, John Stubblefield, Warren Smith, Bob Stewart, Pete Levin, George Adams, George Lewis, Mark Egan, Hiram Bullock, Chris Hunter, Tom Malone, Dave Bargeron, and his son, Miles Evans, who kept the band going after Gil's passing.

I was nervous the first time we met, partly because I was in awe, but also because an element in his music that seemed icily intellectual (a misperception) led me to expect an intimidating man. He was, to the contrary, as natural and unpretentious as Armstrong, with whom he had more than music and temperament in common. In 1983, I organized a concert retrospective of his music for the Kool Jazz Festival, fronted by Lee Konitz and directed by Don Sickler. The idea was for an orchestra of Evans alumni (including Budd Johnson, Johnny Coles, Bill Barber, and, in the Miles Davis role, Jon Faddis), to play an opening set of his classic pieces, from "Moon Dreams" to "Saeta" to "La Nevada," and for the current Evans band to play the second half. Gil was a bit unnerved by the prospect of hearing the old stuff, and he spent the first hour alone in a dressing room, listening to the performance through speakers. He was so pleased that he bounded out at intermission to shake every musician's hand. He and Konitz made an impromptu decision to open the second set with a duet. When I announced them, only Lee appeared. As the audience tittered, I shrugged and returned to the wings, where I saw Gil standing, casually smoking an old-fashioned corncob pipe. As I reached him, a stage manager ran over, gesturing frantically, and shouted, "What the hell are you doing?" Gil removed the pipe, smiled broadly, and said, "Sinsemilla." He played the duet, then turned up the amps and kicked out the jams for 90 minutes.

[*Village Voice*, 5 April 1988 / 1997]

58 ❖ *A New Kind of Virtuosity (Christopher Earl)*

Christopher Earl, a 23-year-old alto saxophonist and orchestrator, graduated from Texas State a year ago and, with remarkably little effort, managed to secure enough work in the gruelingly competitive Los Angeles studios to finance his recent leap to New York. "It was luck more than anything else," he says. "I had met Marshall Royal at a clinic at school and when I got to the coast and called him he suggested me as his sub at a record date. Then Billy Watrous, who was on the session, recommended me when the lead took ill at a soundtrack dub, and before I knew it contractors were calling me for other gigs." At a recent memorial concert for Trummy Young, he played a medley of three Bud Powell compositions in duet with Ray Brown, which elicited a rave from Leonard Feather in the *Los Angeles Times* and led to a record date (to be released this fall on Muggles Jazz). "Things were going so unbelievably great that I was hesitant to leave, but I always meant to get to New York as soon as possible, to absorb all that energy and hear the bands."

He hadn't even unpacked when Stanley Crouch introduced us one evening at the Vanguard in early spring. "Chris is the next alto king," Stanley assured me, and since he knows such things six months before everyone else, and since no less an alto king than Benny Carter had expressed his own enthusiasm when he passed through town a week before, I was eager to hear Earl play. "Right now, I just want to listen," he said, adding with a gusty laugh that he didn't yet have anything resembling a job . . . but if I wanted to hear a cassette of the forthcoming album, he just happened to have one in his pocket. It kept me up most of the night. Christopher has a tart, glancing sound, which he manipulates for timbre, employing a wide vibrato and plum notes in dramatic cadences, and a lean vocalistic edge for the eighth-note arpeggios that decorate his stately, baroque style. He is fearless in his use of quartertone pitch, one measure of his admiration for Ornette Coleman, and he slips in and out of off-pitch sequences with a startling equilibrium, invariably staying in tune with himself.

His surprisingly diverse program includes—in addition to a blue balled and an unaccompanied solo based on a cycle of sixths—pieces from the jazz repertoire that have been so little played as to seem brand new, especially in his brightly irreverent arrangements. They include a funny hard bop treatment of Fletcher Henderson's "Dirty Blues" and a jumping contrapuntal treatment of Cecil Taylor's "Bulbs." Perhaps the most fanciful and successful numbers are his riotously energetic and angular reading of Powell's "Bouncing with Bud," and "Variations on Rosetta," which unfolds, amid key and tempo changes, into readings of Ellington's "Gypsy without a Song" and Parker's "Yardbird Suite," as if to underscore the melodic and harmonic similarities among them. On the Powell piece, he dissects the chord changes as though they constituted a Schoenbergian row: His first chorus after the head is an orthodox improvisation, the second chorus treats the chords backward, the third reduces them to four scales, the fourth discards them entirely, and the next five choruses reverse the process so as to conclude symmetrically.

A few weeks later we spent an afternoon talking in his nearly bare apartment near Prospect Park. Tall and wiry, he speaks mostly with careful deliberation in soft midwestern cadences redolent of his native St. Louis. "My father, Jackson Earl, played trombone with dance bands and was always buying records, so I was surrounded by music from the time I was born. I started on alto at 10, playing in the school band and with friends in a rock band that knew one jazz tune, Horace Silver's 'Song for My Father'—I don't know how it got in the book. Then someone showed me an old issue of *Down Beat* where various musicians were asked what the first step was in mastering jazz. Buddy Tate said the first thing was to get your own sound, and reading that was like a bomb going off. Here I'd been trying to learn the saxophone as though there was one perfect sound you could get if you practiced hard enough, and Tate's talking about *starting* with your own sound. So I worked on timbre, and things you could do with embouchure effects—especially after I heard Ben Webster and Albert Ayler. But I learned that you don't find your sound through regimented search. You find it by coming to grips with who you are. Your sound is already there. The work comes in learning how to let it flow naturally and uninhibited. The funny thing is it wasn't until I felt my playing had matured some that I realized that wasn't the answer for me."

What other answer could there be, I asked.

"The price of knowing who you are is acknowledging your limitations, and it soon became obvious to me that I'm no genius and that what really excites me about the music is the whole idea of interpretation, which has been largely unexplored in jazz."

But isn't the act of improvising, of exuding a personal authority, the essence of a jazz performance?

"To a certain degree, yes. But that's like saying that Schnabel failed his inspiration because he played Schubert instead of writing imitation Schubert sonatas. I found that my own sound, if I have one, is a montage of what I know about the production of sound, and what fascinated me was how different musicians mastered entirely different approaches to timbre. I wanted to know what Johnny Hodges did to make those kinds of notes, and the same for Pete Brown or Benny Carter or Charlie Parker or Lee Konitz. I thought if I could figure that out then maybe I could make a contribution in interpreting classic jazz."

I confess I was beginning to feel edgy. Although greatly in favor of jazz repertory as a means of maintaining and presenting jazz masterpieces of the past, I explained, I am ambivalent about the prospect of musicians neglecting the existential bravura of spontaneous composition in favor of what may prove to be mere academic exercises in musical mimesis—especially when a musician is as gifted as Earl's album proved him to be.

"That's because you're blinded by the romance of jazz, the myth. Existential *what*? Did you ever hear what Toscanini and Horowitz did to Tchaikovsky's piano concerto? Listen, critics are afraid of jazz repertory because of records, which they think represent some kind of unimpeachable authority. The classical people never had to labor under that prejudice. There are no recordings of Beethoven conducting, so Toscanini and Bruno Walter could battle each other for years about who was closer to the composer's intentions. But if I were to conduct Ellington's *Harlem* or Mingus's *Half-Mast Inhibition*, neither of which has much if anything in the way of improvisation, I would have to put up with you guys and your records saying, ah, but that's not the way Ellington and Mingus did it. Either the music is good enough to perform or it isn't and if it is, then it's good enough to merit interpretation. Ellington himself interpreted *Harlem* in different ways."

Yes, but precisely because of the idea you gleaned from Buddy Tate, about the primacy of personal sound, jazz lends itself less readily to interpretation. Notes on a score only hint at the final work—you can't separate what Johnny Hodges plays from the way he plays it.

"Exactly. That's why I'm trying to prepare myself to be able to play Hodges-style or any other style. What I want to see is a repertory orchestra in which the musicians are able not only to sight-read a complex score, which has always been a commonplace skill in jazz, but to read it with an approach to sound and time that makes an interpretation true to the intention of the composer—remembering that in jazz a composer often composes spontaneously. There's no reason a trumpet player can't be responsible to the music of Rex Stewart in one selection and to Fats Navarro in the next. We're talking about a new kind of virtuosity, perhaps, but a more valuable kind than that which encourages studio lions to lose themselves in jingles and dubs. Still, even when you have such an orchestra, you can't be rigid—you have to be able to distinguish between imitation and interpretation. The distinction is absolutely paramount and the choices are profound. Every piece raises different possibilities. That's why you need a conductor. I know how well made *Harlem* is and I can always hear the Ellington performances on record. But I'd like to be able to hear it conducted by Muhal Richard Abrams or Benny Carter or Butch Morris or Maurice Peress or anyone else who cares enough about the piece to mount a serious interpretation. Wouldn't you?"

I would, but the obstacles seem insurmountable, and I worry about the implications for a music grounded in improvisation.

"God save us from enthusiastic conservatives. Look, I'll say it one more time—one does not exclude the other. Got that? It seems to me that a musical culture worthy of the name has to be innovative on three planes —the musical or physical level; the social or metaphysical level; and the philosophical or procedural level.

What does that mean?

"Be quiet, I'm rolling here. The main musical innovation of jazz is the introduction of a harmonic system based on blues scales. The metaphysical innovation of jazz is swing, which can't be notated. The philosophical innovation is the raising of improvisation to a plateau equal to that of composition. Louis Armstrong did it all: He proved the emotional weight of blues, the inspiration of swing, and the durability of great improvisation. He created a new way to think about and play music, and nothing can change that. But after a century of such improvisations, do we really want to say that all that work—not just the big compositions and the swing-band arrangements, but the accomplishments in individual tonal production by geniuses like Hawkins, Young, Rollins, and a hundred others—do we really want that legacy filed away on record shelves, with no hope of renewed life in the concert hall?"

Gosh, no, but . . .

"Now the first thing we need to do is get a hall for jazz, a hall built to satisfy the acoustic demands of this music. The second thing is to organize an institutional orchestra of the highest quality, supported in the public and private sectors like a philharmonic orchestra. We will offer a series of concerts to subscribers and serve as an umbrella to guest soloists, conductors, and composers, whose work we will commission."

But . . .

"The possibilities are intoxicating. As somebody once said, there are three rules for creating great music—unfortunately, no one knows what they are. We'll find out as we go. Compromise is for politicians and record executives, not for artists."

But . . .

"BUT WHAT!"

Nothing, it's just that you're almost too good to be true.

"Well, that could be a problem if I'm no more than the product of your zealous imagination."

More a composite, I'd like to think.

"Think what you like, but to paraphrase Gertrude Stein, there's no here here. And you bear some responsibility for the void. You critics want musicians not only to bear the fruit of innovation but your own historio-graphical evaluations and prejudices as well."

But . . .

"What you really want is what we already had, another Duke Ellington, and if he comes along you'll carp him to death, too."

But . . .

"You critics have to strive for generosity and perspective, much as I have to strive for technique and originality, not to mention corporeality. It's a tough job, but it has to be done. Questions?"

I had many, but my floppy disc was full and I needed a break. We agreed to talk again when he found work.

[*Village Voice*, 25 June 1985]

59 ❖ *Beale Street Talks*
(Harold Mabern)

Is there a Memphis style in jazz, a Memphis sound or school? The city is so steeped in the genealogy of blues, from publisher-patriarch W. C. Handy to the postwar Beale Streeters (B. B. King, Bobby Bland, Johnny Ace, Junior Parker) to Sam Phillips and the sons of Sun to the rhythmic ministrations of Muscle Shoals, that it is difficult to think of any Memphis-related music as anything but bluesy. The major Memphis-born or -bred jazz musicians generally fit the bill and, not unexpectedly, many of them attained a foothold in Chicago, another town famous for the blues, before moving on to New York. Yet Memphis blues is different.

The only member of King Oliver's Creole Jazz Band and Louis Armstrong's Hot Five who was not from New Orleans was Memphian Lil Hardin, the least prepossessing blues player in either ensemble. But of those musicians, only Lil could turn out the durable blue ballad "Just for a Thrill," which suggests a kind of urbanity far removed from the basic 12- or 16-bar form. Indeed, bona fide Memphian bluesmen tend to mitigate the raw expressiveness of blues with compositional finesse, creating a kind of localized African-American Tin Pan Alley strain, exemplified by Handy's melodic compositions, Johnny Ace's throbbing ballads, and Al Green's tempered soul. Most of their jazz brethren share a collective dark-night-of-the-soul memory eased by harmonic and technical sophistication.

It may be mere coincidence that Memphis produced Alberta Hunter, the singer who wrote a classic blues for Bessie Smith and then played *Showboat* in London; Buster Bailey, the clarinetist who became one of the first jazz stars to accrue extensive classical training (which compromised his blues); Jimmy Crawford, the drummer who brought a cocksure backbeat to bear on the most wittily genteel of swing orchestras, Jimmie Lunceford's; and Sonny Criss, the alto saxophonist who amplified Charlie Parker's amalgamation of blues, bop, and pop. But a profusion of coincidences generally adds up to something very like a tradition. The central figure in Memphis's postwar jazz scene was virtuoso pianist Phineas Newborn Jr., whose career was blighted by illness but whose activities in the late 1940s, before he earned national recognition, seem to have touched everyone who followed him out of Beale Street, including his brother, guitarist Calvin Newborn, trumpeter Booker Little, saxophonists George Coleman and Frank Strozier, bassist Jamil Nasser, and pianist Harold Mabern. From the time he arrived in New York, Newborn generated controversy—acclaimed for captivating technique, attacked for glibness. His uneven recordings support both of those strenuously contested opinions. Yet at his best Newborn was an original and inventive stylist whose facility suggested Tatum and whose disposition was best served on medium-tempo blue ballads.

His truest heir, Harold Mabern, got a very different response when he traveled, by way of Chicago and the MJT+3 (a way-station for Memphians, led by drummer Walter Perkins, who recruited locals Muhal Richard Abrams and Bob Cranshaw as well as Little, Coleman, Strozier, and Mabern) to New York in 1959. He was instantly welcomed into the fold, and within a decade could add to his resume work with Lionel Hampton, the Art Farmer–Benny Golson Jazztet, Donald Byrd, Miles Davis, Sonny Rollins, J. J. Johnson, Freddie Hubbard, Lee Morgan, Hank Mobley, Stanley Turrentine, and a cluster of singers, markedly Joe Williams, Sarah Vaughan, Arthur Prysock, and Dakota Staton. Critics were respectful in a half-attentive way—undoubtedly a solid player, he lacked the originality of, say, McCoy Tyner or Bill Evans. So he didn't get many recording sessions of his own and seemed to resign himself to the increasingly scarce role of eminent sideman, not least as a dominant figure in Stanley Cowell's Piano Choir. He never lacked for work.

Recently Mabern has achieved a smattering of renown in his own right, abetted by his fellow Memphians. His affiliations over some 40 years with

Coleman, Strozier, and Nasser have failed to produce an adequate documentation on records but have earned lasting and grateful recognition among New York fans—a perquisite for keeping at it so long. Fashions come and go, but you can bet the ranch on the rhythmic intertwining of Mabern and Nasser, especially in their work with Coleman, which has grown downright tenacious. In December, they appeared at the Jazz Standard with the George Coleman Quartet, ably supported by George Coleman Jr. on drums, and made time jump through hoops. Coleman welded his short, nudging phrases into rangy sinuous payoffs while the rhythm trio rumbled like a dynamo—Mabern pumping chords and tremolo fills, heavily percussive yet nimbly airborne, alternating teeming blues-drenched voicings with modal harmonies that drove the ensemble to the wide-open spaces. Mabern often builds his solos in the manner of Wes Montgomery, from single-note hammering in the octave left of middle C to double-barreled deep-pocket chords. With the wind at his back, he can sound like an ocean roar.

He would probably reject the idea as absurd, but Mabern is a more rewarding and efficient pianist than Newborn. His technique, though ripe enough, never overwhelms his expressive power. He's achieved a secure alloy that marries McCoy Tyner's percussive modality with rippling asides that stem from Tatum and the nasty glisses of gospel-driven blues piano. If he lacks the poise of the older man's every-finger-a-bell-tone touch, he can convey an unembarrassed elation that evaded Newborn, and when he puts his mind to it, as on "It's a Lonesome Old Town," he is Newborn's match in the realm of blue ballads. That selection, inspired by the Sinatra record but in Mabern's interpretation more reminiscent of Kay Starr's earthy lament, is a highlight of *The Leading Man* (1995), a DIW album distributed by Columbia in its Legendary Pioneers series—yet another instance of a jazzman making the transition from who? to living legend without passing Go. Pianist and Blakey-groomed jazz activist James Williams, the most gifted Memphis-born musician in a generation, produced the session with gracious discernment.

Like Newborn, Mabern and his contemporaries apprenticed in Beale Street rhythm and blues bands, an experience they resented at the time but are now delighted to flaunt. Only five years younger than his mentor, Mabern, born in 1936, made a typically Memphian detour from blues when, after relocating to Chicago in 1954, he studied harmony with Ahmad Jamal. Drawn no less to the long eccentric winding phrases of lesser-known pianist Chris Anderson and the driving brilliance of Bud Powell, he developed a comprehensive modern style, though, as he told *Jazzis* editor Larry Blumenfeld, "I think of myself today as a blues pianist who understands jazz." His new album, *Mabern's Grooveyard*, co-produced

by Williams and Kazunori Sugiyama for DIW, is perhaps his most satisfying to date.

It opens with an informal trilogy of jazz standards that progress in
tempo and feeling from medium groove to hurtling groove. Carl
Perkins's "Grooveyard" is perfect for cerebration in a lyrical mood,
copiously sprinkled with blues glisses (a Mabern hallmark), the tension
sustained with dramatic tremolos and pleasingly dissonant block chords.
Tadd Dameron's "Lady Bird" begins deceptively as a faux blues with an
8-plus-4 introduction that flows into the 32-bar theme, rendered as bop
with a gospel edge. Two years back, Mabern recorded Duke Pearson's
"Jeannine" as a piano duet with Geoff Keezer on *For Phineas* (Sackville);
here he attacks it with pulsing, light-fingered percussiveness, from the
treble repeat in the head through a riff-laden and unusually fitting fade-
out. Of the pop tunes, "East of the Sun" gains nothing from a bossa nova
arrangement or a slipping-into-space fade, but "A Hundred Years
from Today" is a model of unpretentious, open-hearted melody playing,
paced and buttressed with forthright chords. The 1933 Victor Young
melody might have worked for Fats Waller, who never recorded it—
Mabern's rendition inspires such speculation until the harmonic onslaught
of his coda brings you back to the 1990s.

The album's success owes much to drummer Tony Reedus, whose plush
cymbal work has a fitting hominess, unlike the spare and angular attack
of Jack DeJohnette on Mabern's previous DIWs, including *Straight Street*,
which emphasizes the more progressive half of the Memphis equation.
Christian McBride's contribution is on par with Mabern's. Few bassists
can make the prospect of a bass solo on almost every selection palatable,
but McBride never bores. His arco solo on "It's a Lonesome Old Town"
and plucked accompaniment on the same album's "Moment's Notice"
show an affinity between him and Mabern that is fully realized here,
especially in his bowed choruses on Gigi Gryce's ebullient 16-bar
blues "Minority" (a retrospective of Gryce's crafty tunes is long overdue)
and an uncustomary version of Avery Parrish's "After Hours." Parrish's
seductive keyboard blues—memorably revived last year by David
Maxwell (*Maximum Blues Piano*) and the 84-year-old Pinetop Perkins
(*Born in the Delta*), who added lyrics—finds Mabern strumming his
second chorus with tremolos. Just as you begin to anticipate another
good idiomatic workout, he initiates a stop-time figure and hands it
to McBride for three beaming choruses. Mabern's return, backed by
McBride's pizzicato shuffle beat, is anticlimactic, but typical of the
Memphian penchant for turning the blues on its head.

[*Village Voice*, 20 January 1998]

60 ❖ Old Man Rivers
(Sam Rivers)

A funny thing happened to Sam Rivers on the way to his 68th birthday last Friday—he turned 75. Every reference book and liner note states his birth year as 1930. He professes not to understand why, cheerfully affirming the correct year as 1923, a change that holds more than actuarial interest. When Rivers first came to attention, in 1964, touring with Miles Davis and recording his sagacious Blue Note cult classic, *Fuchsia Swing Song*, he was considered a late bloomer, someone who, along with Jaki Byard—whose own 75th birthday, in 1997, was not celebrated nearly enough—had spent more than a decade in the fertile realm of Boston jazz.

Now we find he bloomed even later, quite possibly the only key figure in jazz to make his recorded debut past 40. The age differential helps explain the unusual nature of his originality, which was a long time fermenting, and makes him the poetically ideal representative for forty-somethings of the '90s, the first generation in jazz history to take a consistently more adventurous musical stance than players half its age. The celebration was mounted last week at Sweet Basil in grand manner, three nights of the Sam Rivers Trio followed by three nights of a star-studded big band, which trooped into the studios of BMG the following Monday to record.

Everything about Samuel Carthorne Rivers, who was born in El Reno, Oklahoma, raised in Little Rock and Chicago, and educated at the Boston Conservatory of Music, is distinctive, not least his looks and superhuman energy. Rail thin and tall, with a brow high enough to accommodate two standing volumes of the *OED* and a perpetually amiable mien, he plays and conducts with his entire body, punching rhythms in the air, dancing, shoulders rippling like a souped-up Nicholas Cage. Why so happy? His music is a better-kept secret than Kenneth Starr's sex life. Few of his major recordings have been available on CD, not even his groundbreaking Impulse albums of the '70s. In that decade, he and his wife Beatrice operated Studio Rivbea, a jewel of the loft era that encouraged new music capable of assimilating the lessons of previous eras. Which is what he did during those long years in Beantown, before etching a resume that includes T-Bone Walker, Cecil Taylor, and Dizzy Gillespie, in that order. By his own account, he mastered styles of great players and then dispensed with the specifics of those styles.

Most avant-garde players in the '60s invented or seized upon radical procedures that mandated a separation from the harmonic labyrinths, modal plains, and pedal-point ostinatos governing virtually all improvisation in modern jazz. But, like Jaki Byard, who could rumble the piano in or out of chord changes and access a panoply of techniques in and out of jazz, Rivers adhered to no musical religion but his own. His idea of free jazz meant the freedom to do whatever he wanted. Some of his most difficult and layered music is entirely notated—on *Colours* (Black Saint, 1983), he edited out the solos—though he is best known for prodigious feats of sustained improvisation (the 1973 Impulse album *Streams* is exemplary). But what exactly is his style? Leonard Feather's *Encyclopedia of Jazz in the 60s* suggests a compound of Coltrane, Parker, Webster, Young, Hawkins, and Rollins, with incipient interest in Ayler and Shepp, which certainly covers all bets, yet inadvertently underscores the distracting thing about Rivers: He isn't radically individual, yet he doesn't sound like anyone else. In weeding out the familiar, he has forged a fluid virtuoso style beyond style—an authoritative and emotionally resonant gloss on the modern idiom, almost diffident in its smooth, vibratoless glow. Or, as he says on the bandstand regarding his huge and rarely heard repertory: "something old, something new, nothing borrowed, and everything blue."

He further deepens the mystery of style by subdividing his prowess four ways—on tenor saxophone, soprano saxophone, flute, and piano. The idea that he is a tenor saxophonist who doubles sells him short: Rivers is a distinctive soprano saxophonist with a warm, mercurial, and well-tempered sound; a robust flutist capable of a rich timbre or Rahsaan vocalizations; and a delirious yet ironhanded pianist whose contrapuntal pouncing prefigures his orchestral arrangements. One of his meatiest piano raptures is on the 1976 duet "Deluge," with Dave Holland (one of two volumes on IAI, both in print, as is his much celebrated appearance on Holland's ECM classic *Conference of the Birds*), but he ought to record on the instrument more frequently. It brings out in him a nostalgic soulfulness, explored in ringing dynamics and melody—though he can also go the way of all Cecil.

For a musician who has been marginalized as noncommercial, Rivers is singularly jubilant. Ballads make him moody on his '60s Blue Note standards session, *A New Conception* (though his take on "Temptation" is ecstatically irreverent), but his own music is a rush of criss-crossing angles, stacked chords, and crashing clusters that collide and part like cells, often supported by a funk beat, a simmering ingredient in his music since the red hot 1976 Impulse date, *Sizzle*, which in its day was derided as fusion (right, with rock and rollers Dave Holland and Ted Dunbar). Clearly there are times when he wants to be on the one, courting not some chi-chi variation on funk, but the thing itself, the bomp-a-bomp-bomp of electric bass. He has found in Florida, where he lives with his wife of 50 years, empathic support in Anthony Cole, who plays drums, saxophone, and piano, and Doug Mathews, who plays acoustic bass, bass guitar, and reeds. On opening night of his Sweet Basil engagement, his comely "Ripples" had Rivers playing soprano, Cole tenor, and Mathews bass clarinet, blending and parsing melodies that almost burst at the seams. He phrased the inevitable "Beatrice" on tenor over a stop-time backbeat, ruminating sotto voce without a trace of nostalgic posturing, and on "Nightfall," showed how to run the changes without running banalities.

Rivers's writing for larger bands is slightly mythic. One hears of large quantities of music in multiple arrangements, ranging greatly in length, usually excerpted on the rare occasions when they are heard at all. You can follow his progress from *Dimensions and Extensions* (Blue Note, 1967), in which he mastered the ploy of setting solos against the ensemble like long balls falling into a glove; to the much-debated *Crystals* (Impulse, 1974), a case study in notated anarchy; to the drier and more contained 10-piece saxophones-and-flutes unit, "Winds of Manhattan," on *Colours* (one wonders if original tapes with the excised solos exist). But the records don't prepare you for the dense and clamorous enchantment of hearing his orchestral music on stage. The 14-piece ensemble at Sweet Basil was a long time coming, and if it short-changed Rivers as soloist, it offered a conception sure and seasoned, despite the music's evident difficulty, limited rehearsals, and dearth of public performances.

The repertoire, including an updated "Tranquility" (from *Crystals*), with layered dissonances and harmonies that mimic Rivers's vocal squalls (or vice versa); a sumptuous orchestration of "Beatrice," with handsome passages for the reed section; and the funky "Rejuvenation," which gave each band member 8 or 16 bars to sign his name. Two constants: The pieces are sewn from episodes that change precipitously; and the solos are very, very short, forcibly reprising the gift for brevity that flourished in the days of radio remotes and three-minute records, and then disappeared. The music often crashed against itself, with soloists suddenly popping above the fray to have their say before falling back, from rowdy Hamiet Bluiett (who played a baritone solo in a range higher than the preceding altoist) to contemplative Chico Freeman to brawny Gary Thomas to punctilious Greg Osby to silvery Steve Coleman, just to mention the bravura reed section. You felt you got to know something essential about each of them from those compressed volleys. Trombonists Ray Anderson and Joe Bowie have never played with more concentrated wit, and Anthony Cole modulated a funk passage into an elated second-line strut. After Rivers exulted in closing chordal squalls, the band played "Happy Birthday." Jazz was aging and not minding at all.

[*Village Voice*, 6 October 1998]

61 ❖ *Who's Gonna Throw That Minstrel Boy a Coin? (Bob Dylan)*

It was disconcerting to flip the channels in August 2003, and come upon the brusque, croaky "Love Sick" in an ad for Victoria's Secret. Bob Dylan's brain was wired: He walked the dead city, the clouds weeping amid thunderous silence, sick of love but ready to give everything for . . . frilly lingerie? The commercial was almost as surprising as his humble gratitude in accepting an Academy Award a few years back for "Things Have Changed." I don't fault him for taking easy paydays or succumbing to Hollywood's fantasia; nor would I suggest that either inclination signals decline—not after *Love and Theft*, my favorite Dylan album since *Highway 61 Revisited*. Yet I miss the conceit of the young, scruffy outsider who shuns the glitter, though I recognize it was never really his conceit. Dylan has always been a climber, dreaming of Liz Taylor, hungering for admittance to a motley of restricted organizations—the Folk Music and Protest Association, the Rock & Roll & Racquet Club, the Nashville Chamber of Commerce, not to mention high-lit, movies, Christianity, Judaism, and the mafia. He was so much older then; he's older now.

TV ads are only marginally lower on the devolutionary scale of capitalist compromise than indentured servitude to the record industry, and Dylan is nothing if not marketable. Still, a measure of his genius is the ability to sustain, withal, the promise of the eternal unrepentant underground man—a troubadour with an attitude, a Celine with a song in his heart. His originality continues unambiguously in the infinitely analyzed Torah of his collected lyrics, defining his role as a prophet, satirist, and social critic, and as a phrasemaker unrivaled since Johnny Mercer, if not Kipling. But Dylan's assault on musical conventions precedes his words and music; it begins with his delivery. His voice (or voices) and the way he uses it (them) generates the first visceral responses of attraction or revulsion.

In the '60s, his singing was often found so repellent that his admirers readily apologized for it. Forget the voice, they said, listen to the words

—an argument that found its logical outcome as well as box-office support in covers by Peter, Paul and Mary and the Byrds. Yet it was Dylan's unmistakable anti-stylish stylish singing that made him irresistible and unique to those very admirers. His singing was so original that they praised it chiefly for what it wasn't: smooth, which is to say commercial. Approbation, such as it was, centered on his rough-hewn timbre, Woody-like naturalness, road-tested coarseness, conversational ease. Detractors who claimed that he was unintelligible simply were not listening—Dylan's early elocution was crystal. They were too much put off by the snarling, chortling, demonic voice that implied "fuck you" even while insisting, "All I really want to do is, baby, be friends with you."

They never got far enough to worry about the things that roiled Dylan fans: his politics, women, rhythms, rhymes, melodies, drug use, hair, liner note jive, sallow color, and harmonica playing, let alone the relative merits of acoustic versus electric music. The voice was challenge enough: In song, the messenger precedes the message. The musical divide between coarse and smooth is far wider than that between acoustic and electric or between folk and pop. Early admirers of Louis Armstrong's singing frequently advised unsophisticated listeners to get beyond the grainy, guttural inflections to the notes, until it became evident that those inflections *are* the notes and, incidentally, attracted rubes by the millions. When Ornette Coleman first recorded, not a few pundits paid lip service to his talents as a composer while complaining that his saxophone sound was too raw to do justice to the melodies it produced.

The fact that Dylan emerged as one of the most dynamic singers in the 1960s is now beyond cavil. He was an American original—as distinctive and decisive as Guthrie or, for that matter, Al Jolson, Louis Armstrong, Bing Crosby, Jimmy Rushing, Jimmie Rodgers, Lead Belly, Blind Willie Johnson, Frank Sinatra, Hank Williams, Elvis Presley, and James Brown. Whatever he may have lacked in relative range, control, and interpretive diversity, he shared with the select few the ability to concoct a fresh attack that precisely suited his material. His vocal approach telegraphed his meaning, fixed his attitude, and sold his viewpoint. You could not ask for a better illustration of Dylan in full theatrical mode than his corrosive rendering of "Like a Rolling Stone"—especially as compared with the flat live version on *Self-Portrait*, performed without the sting of callow vengeance. Yet commentators continue to ignore his singing qua singing, preferring to invoke Rimbaud, Whitman, Blake, Milton, and Dante.

His singing is what made his first album worth hearing, and overcame the puerile excesses of the second. He never sounds like he's trying to be someone else, or paying homage to classic repertory, or instructing us in the wonders of old-time music. In a period when white blues singers were offering scrupulous carbons of black blues classics, memorializing cotton-picking or sentimentally growling the party songs of juke joints, *Bob Dylan* was too self-conscious and enthusiastic to bother with respectful imitation. Listening to his versions of "Fixin' to Die" and "In My Time of Dyin'," one can almost forget their origins and imagine them as Dylan tunes; he treats them as songs worth singing and not as artifacts for study. From the beginning, he was fishing for style. If the most acute changes in Dylan's vocal mask would unfold between the pugnacious hilarity of *Blonde on Blonde* (1966), the phlegmatic remoteness of *John Wesley Harding* (1967), and the strange hollow crooning of *Nashville Skyline* (1969), the chameleon was already evident on the 20-year-old's 1961 debut. He switches from the dark bluster of Delta blues to the hearty openness of "Man of Constant Sorrow," yet both approaches are certifiably Dylanesque.

And where was he fishing? Not solely in the approved texts of, say, Harry Smith's *Anthology of American Folk Music*, but also—as liner notes to *Bob Dylan* make clear—in the territory of Elvis and the Everlys. No one wanted to believe him, certainly not then. Adulators preferred Robert Shelton's *New York Times* assessment (also printed in the notes) of a Dylan who captured "the rude beauty of a Southern field hand musing in melody on his porch." The Elvis-thing was provisionally mooted with the arrival of the prophetic Dylan of "A Hard Rain's Gonna Fall," "The Times They Are A-Changin'," and other jeremiads, conveyed with a dauntless, saber-rattling authority unparalleled in America's secular music and intrinsically different from the parallels in black gospel and blues. Those songs are so definitively *sung* that, unlike numbers in his catalogue that inspire sundry covers (memorable jazz takes include Bob Dorough's "Don't Think Twice, It's All Right," Abbey Lincoln's "Mr. Tambourine Man," and Cassandra Wilson's "Shelter from the Storm"), they practically defy secondary interpretations, as numerous attempts— see dylancoveralbums.com for the farcical details—prove.

To the national vocal mask as it existed in 1963, Dylan added the divinatory insight (no mean accomplishment in itself), bitter retaliation, adolescent giggle, and generational sneer—songster poses as old as minstrelsy, but dormant so long they were all but forgotten. His emphatic nuances underscored the asymmetrical phrases and repetitions of his melodies and suffused his lyrics with a persona that might exude contempt but rarely sacrificed intonation. Rock and roll heightened his assurance. His fervor spiraled to a new plane, at once lighter and darker, in "Ballad of a Thin Man" and the matchless "Desolation Row." His appetite for the absurd hit full throttle on *Blonde on Blonde*.

But rock also required a greater obeisance to Tin Pan Alley formalism. As country blues singers of the 1920s learned when they joined urban jazz bands, you can stretch a blues chorus to thirteen and a half bars by yourself and hardly anyone will notice; a band needs to begin and end at the same time. The transitional LP was the undervalued *Another Side of Bob Dylan* (1964). "All I Really Want to Do" displayed Dylan's interior rhyming dictionary (a Tin Pan Alley necessity); "Black Crow Blues" and "Motorpsycho Nightmare" were rhythm and blues dry runs for the rock breakthrough of the next year's *Bringing It All Back Home* (the restored *g*, deleted from *Freewheelin'* and *Changin'*, seemed notable, a renouncement of the cosmetically folksy); "Spanish Harlem Incident" stretched his range while the more Espanolish "To Ramona" employed subtle chords and discreet melisma in a melody that might have served the 1940s hit parade; and the self-pitying cruelty of "Ballad in Plain D" prefigured the sniping rage of "Like a Rolling Stone."

After *Blonde on Blonde*, Dylan's voice proved more chameleonic than ever. His stylistic gambits ranged from deliberate unintelligibility to gentle articulation, offering something to disenchant everyone at one time or another. For me the breaking point was the high, arid whimper heard in *Nashville Skyline* entries like "Lay, Lady, Lay" and "Tonight I'll Be Staying Here with You." The anger, excesses, and rampaging id were gone, and *Self Portrait* affirmed where they'd gone to—the sea of Elvis, whose crooning influence found intermittent traction on "I Forget More Than You'll Ever Know" (a touch of Blind Willie McTell there, too), "Let It Be Me," "Take Me as I Am," and—in what suggested a deeper accord with traditions of mainstream songwriting—"Blue Moon," which his biographer Robert Shelton disdainfully and wrongly described as "a la Bing Crosby." It was, of course, Elvis who had recorded it and not Bing.

"Why had he recorded 'Blue Moon'?" Shelton asks Dylan in *No Direction Home*, clearly unsatisfied with his explanation that it "was an expression," part of a middle of the road jaunt in the mode of Presley and the Everly Brothers. He would have done better to ask him about the truly incomprehensible "All the Tired Horses" or "Wigwam." Because Lorenz Hart, with his ingenious internal rhymes and caustic outlook, was Dylan's kind of lyricist: The insistent consonants of "alone" and "own" and the quadruple rhyme and near-rhyme of "there for," "prayer for," "care for," and "appeared before" were right down his alley. How much Dylan admired Richard Rodgers's melody became clear when he sponged the song's main four-bar hook for "Bye and Bye" on *Love and Theft*, a gusher of Americana that subsumes minstrelsy, pop, folk, blues, rhythm and blues, rock and roll, and jazz.

By then the throaty rasp that had always been an element in his vocal makeup ("Watching the River Flow" trailed "Lay, Lady, Lay" by only two years) had taken over. It added weight, in 1978, to "Little Pony," on *Street*

Legal, a reminder of Dylan's country blues affinities; and grit, in 1983, to
Infidels ("Jokerman" has an intricate rhyming grid worthy of Hart); and
consumes *Oh Mercy*, in 1989, the sandpapery timbre eradicating the early
range and mannerisms while producing a colorblind gospel on "Ring Them
Bells." The idea that Dylan might tackle Tin Pan Alley was put to rest by
his disastrous rendering of "Tomorrow Night," on 1992's intrepid but
uneven solo stint, *Good As I Been to You*. But *Time Out of Mind*, in 1997, a
tour de force from "Love Sick" through the magisterial "Highlands," suggested his renewed comfort zone as a singer, his coming to grips with
the not-unpleasant huskiness that achieved greater satisfaction four
years on in *Love and Theft*, for which he proceeded to invent his own Tin
Pan Alley. He'll be hard-pressed to match it, though no more so than when
he traveled down *Highway 61* to *Blonde on Blonde*. Dylan's never really
had to compete with anyone but himself. In the meantime, there's
always black satin and lace.

[*Studio A: The Bob Dylan Reader*, edited by Ben Hedin, Norton, 2003]

62 ❖ *Fresh Flowers*
(Albert Ayler)

If art is news that stays news, avant-garde art is news that stays avant-
garde. Most radical innovations, however misprized at first, eventually
become as warming and familiar as Van Gogh's sunflowers. But not
all. Some achievements remain on the fringe, requiring total attention,
dedicated suspension of disbelief, and a willingness to be seduced by
alien powers again and again. To be sure: One person's avant-garde is
another's home on the range. Still, most people persist in finding Milton
and Schoenberg harder to "get" than Shakespeare and Stravinsky.
Teaching a jazz history course, I discovered that Charlie Parker's "Koko"
jolted students raised on heavy metal into a condition of glassy-eyed panic.
There is much to be said for art that retains its otherworldly edge in the
long haul.

American music would be a poorer thing without the lusty hysteria
and fastidious control of Albert Ayler (no contradiction here: He contained
multitudes). Having spent the last few weeks immersed in Revenant's
grand and, yes, truly revelatory *Holy Ghost*, I have no doubt that, 34
years after his death, Ayler continues to represent the highest degree of
aesthetic challenge. If you don't pay attention, you hear only the squalling

—the "energy" playing, as Ayler liked to call it. Yet, having converted everyone who inadvertently ventured into Ayler's tempest simply by inviting each potential admirer to sit down and listen to a track or two, I also know that he is hardly inaccessible. He is, in fact, irresistible.

Holy Ghost may be reviewer-proof. Ayler fans have been slavering for months and need only know that the initial release of 15,000 copies (a third more than Revenant pressed of its Charley Patton project) is priced at a reasonable $100 each. Neophytes might be advised to begin with such milestones as *Spiritual Unity, Spirits Rejoice, Lörrach/Paris 1966* or *Live in Greenwich Village.* Yet none of those well-known albums are better than some of the work uncovered here, and the assemblage in its entirety, including misfires, tells one of the most gripping and disturbing stories in jazz. Previously unheard except on sonically inferior bootlegs, this music traces his career from the beginnings in Europe to final performances in the United States and France. In the span of eight years, 1962 to 1970, Ayler went through several stylistic changes; Revenant's 10 discs—seven of music, two of interviews (including recollections by Don Cherry), plus an eight-minute bonus of two 1960 Army band numbers that will foil any blindfold test—cast retrospective light on every step.

Sadly, Ayler is shrouded in ludicrous falsehoods even now: that he played marathon solos; devoted himself exclusively to improvised firestorms; latched onto Coltrane's coattails; lacked technical competence. Ayler recorded a few longish works (he averaged six or seven minutes), but you won't find many solos exceeding three minutes—there is no "Chasin' the Trane" in his discography. From 1966, he focused as much on composition as on improvisation, at times practically eliminating the latter; indeed, some Ayler fans resent his preplanned performances. Coltrane, who asked him to play at his funeral (a performance included in *Holy Ghost,* and a more fitting way to acknowledge the passing of a great man is hard to imagine), stated that Ayler taught him as much as he learned, and the evidence is QED. As for technique: Good heavens, Ayler *owned* the tenor saxophone, reinventing it through a virtuosity of startling dimensions, from the unexampled weight of his sound to a studied control of timbre, intonation, and vibrato that allowed him not only to veer effortlessly between octaves but to invoke them all at the same time.

Disc one is a novella in its own right, beginning in Helsinki in 1962, as Ayler sits in with a dreary bop band. He offers an appealing theme statement and generic yet individual solo on "On Green Dolphin Street" and a "Sonnymoon for Two" that portends the young David Murray. Ayler is evidently stifled—stuck in the wrong room and worried about scratching the furniture. Five months later, in Copenhagen, he finds liberation in the furnace of Cecil Taylor's engine, stoked by Jimmy Lyons and Sunny Murray, and all four of them killing: Where have these marvelous 22 minutes been all our lives? Then on to New York in 1964, where the Ayler of *Spiritual Unity* emerges, accompanied by Gary Peacock and Sunny Murray: Here are the florid ululations, deep barking, yodeling cries, and melodic flourishes (check out his entrance after the bass solo on "Spirits" or his reveling at 3:15 into "Children"). Here is a vocalized animal passion that never loses focus or interest. On "Ghosts," Ayler smashes the furniture and flies out the window.

A 1966 Cleveland club date introduced Ayler's marching-band-with-strings period, which happens to be my favorite. He had just recruited violinist Michel Samson, who had to figure out his function during the course of the gig; by the time the quintet toured Europe in the fall, Samson had gone from being fifth wheel ("Spirits Rejoice") to plucky disciple (untitled waltz) to empathic collaborator ("Ghosts/Bells" in Berlin). The tunes are compact and diverse, notably Donald Ayler's tender "Our Prayer," and shoot off sparks of satisfaction as Ronald Shannon Jackson's rocking drums augment Ayler's intensity. The musician who merits most reconsideration from this boxed set is brother Don Ayler on trumpet. He fills out the ensemble, establishes key centers, complements Albert, and solos with enthusiasm and feeling.

One of the most captivating performances in *Holy Ghost* is the Berlin concert, which may be closer to classical music than to jazz, but by any standard is gorgeous. At times the tenor-violin-trumpet harmonies suggest Vivaldi for bagpipes; Samson, who is Ayler's match in the vibrato department, sounds like he's strumming a banjo at the beginning of "Truth Is Marching In." A performance in Holland the same week is dramatically different, especially in an untitled piece that suggests middle-period Joe Maneri and gives Beaver Harris a workout. Milford Graves brings another tactic to percussive interaction at Newport and the Coltrane service, though Bernard Purdie is a fish out of water at a studio rehearsal for what became the proto-fusion *New Grass* debacle. Yet the blues that begins that session is one of the collection's wonders.

In interviews, Ayler left no doubt about who was responsible for *New Grass*: "They told me to do this. Bob Thiele. You think I would do that? He said, 'Look Albert, you gotta get with the young generation now.'" Still, it was undoubtedly Ayler's idea to sing, to opt for electric bass and regressive rhythms, to rely on the meager abilities of pianist Call Cobbs and his personal and professional partner, singer-songwriter Mary Parks. Nonetheless, that preparatory blues shows what might have been; it is a fundamental ride through the basic 12, except that Ayler rings compound overtones and undertones while maintaining steady intonation at the center. The Ayler captured here—paradoxically, his longest solo in the box—might have won him the larger audience he coveted.

Subsequent selections are marred by bad sound, painful edits, and a diminished Ayler; his control declines and he retreats to the hidden frequencies, sacrificing contrast and clarity. More troubling is the portrait that emerges in nearly two hours of interviews. In 1964 he was unfailingly soft-spoken and hopeful. Six years later, he is uncontrollably manic, talking faster than he plays, determined to remain positive despite outbursts of anger and bizarre boasts. He is doing well, $10,000 a record, only later he concedes it was for two albums, and later that the label subtracted $3,000, and later that he doesn't know if he still has a contract. He rotates between certainty that America is now coming around (even Frank Sinatra is copying his stuff) and an obsession with America's neglect of Charles Ives. Recorded months before Ayler's body was dragged from the East River, an apparent suicide, these monologue/interviews are harrowing, as are two hidden tracks: an undated phone call from a booker at 3:55 of the last cut on disc eight, and an embarrassing argument at an airport at 15:30 of the last cut on disc nine.

Holy Ghost was surely a labor of love for Revenant's owners, Dean and Laurie Blackwood, and project supervisor Ben Young. In addition to the CDs and a 210-page book (especially good at documenting Ayler's work in Europe and his performing life, and rife with descriptive anecdotes and rare photos), the keepsake box includes a pressed forget-me-not; archival-quality replications of a snapshot, a scribbled note, a Slugs handout, and a booklet with three articles from Amiri Baraka's arts journal *Cricket*; a facsimile tape envelope with the two Army selections; and a Paul Haines poem prepared for the first edition of *Spiritual Unity*. The CDs are buried in a well at the bottom, witness to a tragic, glorious epic.

[*Jazz Times*, December 2004]

63 ❖ *Put Your Voice Where Your Mouth Is (Lip-syncing)*

Ashlee Simpson got caught with her microphone down on *Saturday Night Live* in October, and five weeks later, on December 5, *Good Morning America*, which had been especially gleeful in its post-mortem of the debacle, presented Lindsay Lohan in a "live singing debut"—lip-syncing just like Simpson. Good thing this was a slow news year so that the press could pay appropriate attention to a cultural issue that has dismayed many Americans over the age of 16. Forget the occupation of Iraq, the burgeoning debt, the war over values, and the passion of the Christ: This was the year we were obliged to face up to the fact that show business is show business.

Among many other performers accused of moving their lips while a machine does the labor are Britney Spears, Luciano Pavarotti, Shania Twain, Beyoncé, and Madonna. (One person who won't be accused of lip-syncing is Kevin Spacey, but everyone who has seen *Beyond the Sea* wishes he had.) As for performers who sing in tandem with prepared tapes or backup tracks, this page could no more contain their number than it could that of film actors with lasered body parts. It is a wonder anyone bothers to deny it. Back in February, it was reported that Britney fans prefer her to lip-sync—despite her denials of doing so (contradicted by her own director)—because they expect flawless digitalization when they pay serious money for a concert. Besides, as Simpson complained to Katie Couric on *Today*, it's not like she engaged in anorexia or wardrobe malfunction.

Indeed, the worse thing she did, beyond displaying an inability to ad-lib and the childish inclination to blame others (many others) for her mishap, was to reveal that behind the curtain of contemporary showbiz is a man with his finger on a button. The father of modern entertainment was not P. T. Barnum, but Thomas Edison. We have been living in an increasingly lip-synced world for some 75 years, and we have yet to reach the bottom of a slippery slope. No profitable advance in technology has ever vanished and this one is here to stay—along with mini-microphones on Broadway, fake laughter on television, computer-generated images in the movies, and Donald Trump. You want reality? Go to a ballgame. Oh, right: forgot.

Baby boomers who now shake their heads in alarm at what the world is coming to grew up with lip-syncing. On Dick Clark's *American Bandstand*, there was no band and no bandstand, only the fear that the record might skip while a grinning performer gyrated, his or her lips moving as mutely as those of Steve Reeves in *Hercules*. The old movies that were then a routine part of network television offered jokes and plotlines built on the deception of lip-syncing. In *Singin' in the Rain*, Jean Hagen is laughed out of the theater when the audience sees her mouthing Debbie Reynolds. In *Road to Morocco*, Bing Crosby, Bob Hope, and Dorothy Lamour reluctantly lip-sync one another.

Lip-syncing got its first and steadiest boost in Hollywood, shortly after the introduction of sound. In 1929, MGM prerecorded an intricate number, "The Wedding of the Painted Doll" for *The Broadway Melody*. Most sound engineers regarded dubbing as undignified; they argued that music ought to be live, especially given technological advances that allowed them to capture vocal nuance. They were overruled by three problems, all solved by lip-syncing.

First, singing is physically constraining—a singer cannot maintain pitch and vibrato while leaping around a stage—and movies depend on movement. An example of the dilemma can be seen in the first feature film by the Marx Brothers, *The Cocoanuts*, in which the romantic couple stops the film in its tracks in the seconds it takes them to draw a breath or summon the proper vocal mask.

The second problem was one of economics. By lip-syncing musical numbers, the production did not have to install an orchestra on the set or worry about repeated takes or the noise made by crane shots. In 1930, Universal was desperate to stop the hemorrhaging of money in completing its revue, *The King of Jazz*, featuring the bandleader Paul Whiteman. Whiteman suggested that the musical numbers be prerecorded; that way carpenters could hammer new sets while his musicians, singers, and dancers went through the motions on the ones already built.

The studios invented and resolved the third problem when they realized that audiences didn't notice lip-syncing, let alone mind it. Producers reasoned that if actors could lip-sync themselves, they could just as easily lip-sync others. You want Rita Hayworth and Ava Gardner but don't trust their singing? Bring in stunt-singers—like they do in *Singin' in the Rain*. During the same year Whiteman was filming *King of Jazz*, Duke Ellington introduced the song "Three Little Words" in the film *Check and Double Check*, but the three musicians he assigned the vocal part weren't very good. So Ellington asked the director to hire the Rhythm Boys (the trio, with Bing Crosby, that Whiteman made famous). Since the movie could not show a racially integrated ensemble—white singers in a black band—the Rhythm Boys stood behind a curtain with a microphone, while band members lip-synced them. How far a slide down the slope is it from Audrey Hepburn pretending to sing in *My Fair Lady* to Milli Vanilli pretending to sing on their Grammy winning 1990 album, *Girl You Know It's True?*

In 1946, Crosby revolutionized the entertainment world when he walked out on his NBC contract, which forbade him from prerecording his radio show. Crosby reasoned that taping a program would allow him to edit and perfect it; besides, he had prerecorded countless shows for the troops overseas and no one had complained. The networks argued that audiences would never accept a canned show in a live medium. The networks, of course, were wrong. On one occasion, Crosby's engineers realized that the program was a minute or so short; one of them found a piece of tape with applause and laughter and suggested editing it in to fill the time. How far a slide is it from borrowed laughter to fake laughter to fake audiences?

Crosby, paradoxically, was one of the few musical film stars who occasionally insisted on filming a song live. In Frank Capra's *Riding High* (1950), Crosby had a complicated number, "Sunshine Cake," involving Colleen Gray, Clarence Muse, and lots of physical business, including Crosby playing spoons and Muse playing guitar. When you see the film you are really seeing those performers singing and dancing. Or are you? It happened that Muse could not play guitar or convincingly fake it, so for the closeups they brought in studio guitarist Perry Botkin and blacked up his hands. (Why they didn't hire a black guitarist is another story.) How far a slide is it from fake hands to a fake Fred Astaire vacuuming in a commercial to a fake cast in *The Polar Express*?

We protest that live performance is different, the last bastion of reality. But we surrendered to illusion long ago, when we accepted electrical amplification as a substitute for natural acoustics. A series of Memorex ads boasted that we could no longer be certain if Ella Fitzgerald or a mechanical device was popping glassware with high notes. For that matter, we couldn't be certain if singing had anything to do with the shattering of the glass because, after all, it was a TV ad. On Broadway, singers are so over-miked that their disembodied voices suffuse the theater, coming at patrons from every direction except the singers' throats. If a modern-day Mary Martin were suffering from, say, acid reflux, and were to expertly lip-sync a performance one night, how many in the audience would know? Or care?

Recording devices, along with every technological development since the taming of electricity, frighten us. Like the aborigine who fears his soul will be stolen by a photograph, we are made suspicious by the dehumanizing potential of canned speech. Movies have long exploited that mistrust. In Fritz Lang's *The Testament of Dr. Mabuse*, made in 1933, the eponymous megalomaniac uses a recording device in order to pretend to be where he isn't. A decade later, Hitler did the same thing. In the middle 1940s, when Crosby was making headlines because of his insistence on prerecording his radio show, a series of films explored the nefarious side of deceptive recordings—to advance blackmail in *Nightmare Alley* and murder in *The Unsuspected* and *The Falcon's Alibi*.

By that time, Hollywood was dubbing more than vocals; feet-dubbers were also needed, to match dance steps to scenes in which the dancers were filmed without sound. One of the best, Miriam Nelson, has told of dubbing the tap routine of a musical-comedy star with notoriously bad timing. Nelson asked the director if she should duplicate the star's taps or follow the music. The director told her to follow the music, explaining that if the audience heard the correct taps it would buy the illusion that the star was on point.

We buy into worse illusions all the time. In the 1960s, it was a matter of pride for musicians as varied as Vladimir Horowitz and Dave Brubeck to refuse touch-ups on their live recordings. Does that kind of pride exist in a world of automatic pitch shifters that can adjust off-key singing, and digital fixes that eliminate human error and a bit of humanity itself? The world in which Al Jolson (who lip-synced songs in his film appearances in the 1930s and was himself lip-synced in *The Jolson Story*) had to reach the last row of the highest balcony on lung power alone is long gone. Ladies and gentlemen, Jolie has left the building. Cue Ashlee Simpson.

(The New York Times, 29 December 2004)

64 ❖ *On Her 90th Birthday (Billie Holiday)*

We live under the sway of artists who haunt our lives, who take hold at an early age and never let go; they inform us of our progress in the world as our perceptions of them change. Faulkner once said that *Don Quixote* had to be read three times, in childhood, adulthood, and old age, because it is really three books and aspects of it are available only in stages. Over time, we bring more connections to works of art—connections that belong to us, not necessarily to the work or the artist. In a world remade by Alfred Hitchcock, for example, it may be impossible to read Dickens's *Hard Times* without noting that the Sleary circus is a blueprint for the carnival in *Saboteur*; that Mrs. Sparsit is a template for Mrs. Danvers in *Rebecca*; that the Devil's creed, "a charming Italian motto. What will be, will be," was very differently interpreted by Doris Day in *The Man Who Knew Too Much*.

These juxtapositions are no less true of music. As long as we're alive to it, music is a living thing, changing and growing as we do. When I started writing, an established music critic told me he could not imagine ever running out of things to say about Mozart, because every time he listened he discerned something new. I feel that way about jazz in general and especially about certain artists. Sometimes the discernment turns out to be an illusion. I'll hear a recording, experience a eureka-moment, rush to write it down, and in time realize that I had had the same epiphany 15 years ago. But it is not all illusion: The epiphanic urgency is real the first or the hundredth time.

The jazz world has held few artists as close to its heart as Billie Holiday, the subject of at least 10 books and of chapters in many times that number. Her music has always been available, while time has changed its ramifications, much as her life changed over the mere 44 years of its span. Like *Don Quixote*, Holiday is three works in one, and the distinctions have as much to do with her stages as ours. First, there's the spirited Billie of the Columbia sessions, wailing a chorus with the boys in the band, buoyant with youthful glow and full-throated optimism. Then there's the middle-period Lady of white carnations, recording for Commodore and Decca, still effervescent but mannered, briefly politicized, and seeking respectability in string ensembles. Finally, there's the stark, vigilant, yet faded and sometimes fading Miss Holiday of the Verve sessions. I love all three periods and always have, but I find myself reverting from one to the other and reacting differently to each as time goes by.

I prefer the quality of her voice in the middle period, but grow impatient with the predictability of some of her improvisational gambits. I prefer the emotional reality of the later period, especially when pianist Jimmy Rowles clears the air around her, but at times the familiar tics undermine empathy. That's the Holiday paradox: We know what she is going to do, yet we fall for it anyway because she puts everything on the line —her heart, her technical limitations, her musical ingenuity, manifested not only in melodic finesse but also in huge open-hearted vowels (something Abbey Lincoln learned from her) that punctuate her songs with unbowed affirmation.

And what of the fabled early work, as much celebrated for her bandmates—most particularly Lester Young—as for her vocals? I played them to distraction growing up, infatuated with every aspect of the music, identifying with the singer to an unearthly degree. My emotional involvement was such that inevitably I stopped listening to them for stretches of time, during which I discovered that other singers moved me as much or, in the case of Sarah Vaughan, more. But I always go back, as one does with family, and I've found in recent years, to my great surprise, that what absorbs me more than the sound of her voice, more than the less-is-more improvisational brio, more than the legato swing, more than the wistful, plaintive, occasionally jejune sad-eyed lady of the lowlands intelligence, is the way she imbues lyrics, even—no, especially —the dumb ones, with credibility. She accepts them for what they are, and honors their sentiments by embracing them with both plump red-blooded arms. Just as the revulsion she makes palpable in "Strange

Fruit" is beyond the ken of other singers, so is the adoration she expresses in "A Sailboat in the Moonlight."

Recently I played a few of her early records for students who had never heard her. They were reminded of Norah Jones, and why not? If Dickens makes me think of Hitchcock, who was born 29 years after the novelist's death, why should not Holiday remind people of a singer born 20 years after her death, who is known for articulating lyrics and keeping a firm beat? We have no control over how generations perceive each other and it is lovely to think that Holiday may sustain her audience not because her life is a series of sociological or political metaphors, or because she is revered in the jazz hall of fame, but rather because her music—the way she sings songs—speaks to people who can scarcely imagine the life she led or the world in which she led it. That's an immortality worth having, an artist's immortality. Your Billie may not be my Billie, but let us drink to the good health and long life of both.

[*Jazz Times*, May 2005]

PART FOUR

Books

I talked to him of Forster's "Voyage to the South Seas," which pleased me; but I found he did not like it. "Sir, (said he,) there is a great affectation of fine writing in it." BOSWELL. "But he carries you along with him." JOHNSON. "No, Sir; he does not carry me along with him; he leaves me behind him: or rather, indeed, he sets me before him; for he makes me turn over many leaves at a time."
> —James Boswell, *Life of Johnson*

65 ❖ "Harsh as the sound of a man's snore was the name of Khufu" (Norman Mailer)

Ancient Evenings, Norman Mailer's windbreaking novel, is of less interest for the immensity of its failure—this was to be the book on which he would stake his legacy—than for the apparent firmness with which it squats midway up the best-seller list. True, prepublication excerpts in *Playboy* and the current full-page ads from Little, Brown emphasize the novel's sexual content. True, also, the press has disguised its disdain with garlands. Peter Prescott, the *Newsweek* critic, had to "push" his way through *Ancient Evenings*, "part of the way in four-wheel drive," but nonetheless found the book worthy of "perhaps our awe." (This is perhaps the literary equivalent of what *Newsweek* said about the Hitler diaries—they are important even if they are not important.) *Time* presented a four-page bacchanal by Paul Gray: a three-page profile and one-page review, even though he found the honored work to be of "utterly invisible significance."

The *New York Times Book Review* played a shell game with Benjamin DeMott's front-page notice, which declared—or appeared to declare—the book a masterpiece; you had to turn the page to discover that he really thought it a "disaster," a point that didn't deter the editors from citing the work in the following issue's list of staff favorites. In a weirdly vacillating essay in *The New York Review of Books*, Harold Bloom conceded that the quality of *Ancient Evenings* "is not durable and perhaps does not attempt to be." Yet despite his disinterest in posterity, "Mailer is desperately trying to save our souls." Souls of future readers can look out for themselves. The important thing, Bloom argues, is that we have "another warning that Mailer is at home on Emerson's stairway of surprise" (third floor: ladies' lingerie; fourth floor: ka and ra; fifth floor: don't ask). Duly warned, we are left to wonder how many readers are actually plowing through this long wallow in the feces of ancient Egypt.

Surprises are scarce in *Ancient Evenings*—Mailer's obsessions are as familiar as his hot flashes of linguistic virtuosity. Indeed, nothing is more surprising than that he followed a performance as controlled, resourceful, and readable as *The Executioner's Song* with one so bloated and sluggish. We would gladly forgive the nattering silliness of his ideas for a good time. But *Ancient Evenings* creaks along like an old pharaoh who has been out in the sun too long. It's an epic without epic thrust, a flagpole without a flag. Mailer has a plan, yes, but does he have a plot? Try this: A corpse comes to life, crawls out of a pyramid, and runs into another ambulatory corpse, Menenhetet I, who may or may not be his great-grandfather and who relates to him—after warning the younger shade that he is in for a long haul—episodes of his four previous incarnations as well as the story of Isis and Osiris. It's a saga of paranoia and exploitation, gods and monsters, warring and fucking—brutal, relentless, damp, limp.

Some time after he completed his Egyptian tetralogy, Thomas Mann explained that it was intended as comedy. There is plenty of evidence to support the contention that *Ancient Evenings* is comedy, too—private jokes that seem to refer to the plodding excess of the book, horrid puns, little comedies of errors. Yet as much as one would like to believe that Mailer had not abandoned his predilection for pugnacious irony, the quicksand of his prose and the deadly earnestness of his obsessions choke off all hope. If the novel's bawdiest set piece, an interminably detailed orgy called the Night of the Pig, is at times laughably gross—more DeMille than Griffith—the problem isn't that Mailer can't make his words do his bidding, but that they do it all too well. It is in its ideas and underlying motivations that *Ancient Evenings* blows itself apart.

Mailer may be the only major American novelist writing today who doesn't know anything about sex. He is certain that an erection is involved and that male pride is on the line with every hard-won orgasm; consequently, he regards sex as dangerous—something to be avoided by most people and taken lightly by none. He compensates for his prudery with gross literalism, but just as the best of his early books, *Advertisements for Myself*, established him as a tourist among the beats, a voyeur among the hip, his fearsome and fearful apotheosis of sex and his contempt for every expression of sexuality other than those sanctified by marriage and/or procreation lash him to the very Puritans he abhors. Bisexuality is the villain in *The Deer Park*; anal sex is a communion with the devil in *An American Dream*. In *The Prisoner of Sex*, orgasm shared by a man and a woman, represents communion with God. In *Pieces and Pontifications*, he takes his stand against masturbation. His rages against contraception are famous—in order truly to enjoy sex, he has said, a man ought to be able to fantasize, during lovemaking, the death of his partner in childbirth. Can I hear amen?

For a principled existentialist who demands that society and writers take risks ("Do you think I became Overseer of the Lord God Osiris by daring too little?"), Mailer wants it both ways. It may be necessary to kill (violence is purgation against cancer, that dread disease of repression), but sexual freedom weakens moral fiber. Mailer finds sex slurping over the ramparts of reason and swamping us all. With *Ancient Evenings*, however, we learn that sex isn't the only bodily function that gives him pause. Mark Twain is supposed to have said that Henry James wrote as if he'd never been to the toilet. No one will ever say that of Norman Mailer.

In *Ancient Evenings*, he has pitched his pyramid in the place of excrement. Human waste constipates the flow of his narrative so relentlessly that you begin to interpret every reference to a canal as intestinal. "Something came apart then in the long aisles of my pride, and I had a view into the fundament of pain, the view as beautiful as it was narrow." Parody is obviated. Shit is everywhere, sometimes neatly ("three large wet deposits were laid on the stone"), usually not. Anal sex is rampant, chiefly between men, and usually as a means of domination and humiliation. A colleague of mine thinks this is a book for gay men. I think it's more likely a book for people, like Mailer, who are disgusted but fascinated by gay men.

It's difficult to be sure, though. There is throughout an abiding weakness for regal members—"the stoutest longest friend any man ever carried," "so I continued to kiss and to lick, seeking to give pleasure to Him whose appetite was best satisfied by the body of a God." Nubians are especially given to backdoor work ("until they are rich enough to afford a wife"—go figure), but Menenhetet himself, a risk-taker for the ages, is not above buggering a lion. And when he lays hold of the Queen's royal buttocks, he is rewarded by this sermon from the mount:

"Oh," she said, "you are so wicked, you are in my sha. You are on My field, you are on My estate, oh, you swim in my swamp. Sesh and sesh. Write on Me, inscribe Me, sesh and sesh, You are My mud and My maher, My canal, My ooze, you are a devil of a man, sweet Kheru, My swamp, My robber, My enemy, oh, go deep into the rot, stick it deep, touch the dead, oh, khat, khat, khat, put it in My tomb, give it to My ancestors, fuck Them all, give it to My ass, My ass."

What ever happened to that nice German maid in *An American Dream*?

And what is the meaning of all this buggery and shit? Shit is the foundation of life, the glue that holds all life together—shit, ladies and gentlemen, is the better part of ourselves. Shit is that which "we cannot afford to take into ourselves—all that is too rich, too courageous, or too proud for our bearing." Think about that before flushing. Mailer has been thinking about it for a decade. He's come up with a horrific world in which all the forces in the universe are marshaled against the possibilities of a peaceful life; his ancients can't even get a little rest on the toilet.

It hardly needs to be said that there are extraordinarily fine passages in *Ancient Evenings*—vivid descriptions, calamitous battle scenes, engagingly rendered myths; yet none offer the emotional clarity and descriptive precision that makes *The Executioner's Song* a rare achievement in ficto-journalism and unique in Mailer's body of work (marred only by second-act shyness, as he and his packager enter the plot). These passages are far between if not necessarily few, and some of them should make it into the inevitable Norman Mailer reader. That's where they belong. Americans are suckers for extravagant if empty virtuosity, and Mailer in full throttle bellows like Horowitz hammering "Stars and Stripes Forever." We expect great writing from a great writer, and Mailer has periodically delivered. *Ancient Evenings*, however, belongs not with *Advertisements for Myself, Armies of the Night*, and *The Executioner's Song* but with *Barbary Shore, Of a Fire on the Moon*, and *Of Women and Their Elegance*; like them, it manages to be at once preposterous and banal. The final sentences—"We sail across dominions barely seen, washed by the swells of time. We plow through fields of magnetism. Past and future come together on thunderheads and our dead hearts live with lightning in the wounds of the Gods"—have summoned comparisons with Fitzgerald. I hear Arthur C. Clarke.

[*The Nation*, 25 June 1983]

66 ❖ *The Grove of Academe* (The New Grove Dictionary of American Music)

In the world of reference books, it promised to be one of the great publishing events of the decade. Weighing in with four volumes of more than 2,700 pages, bound in distasteful green buckram, the *New Grove Dictionary of American Music* (DAM), edited by H. Wiley Hitchcock and Stanley Sadie, is a stepchild of *The New Grove Dictionary of Music and Musicians*, the 20-volume landmark edited by Sadie and published in 1980. A necessity and luxury for music lovers, that far-reaching work is daunting in its sobriety and scholarship: More than that, it is immensely, often compulsively readable. In five years of frequent consultation, it has rarely let me down. But then I've never looked to it for insight into jazz or most other aspects of musical America. Perfunctory allusions to the new world abound, but *Music and Musicians*, as the editors of the DAM concede, "retains a firm base in European musical and cultural traditions" and fails to scrutinize "the essence of American music."

The DAM's stated purpose is to reflect that essence. It fails comprehensively. During the several weeks I've read it at leisure or grabbed it for information, the DAM has almost always let me down. The omissions immediately took on an unmistakable pattern. The DAM's agenda has little to do with a balanced and encyclopedic investigation of its subject. Once again, European concerns are given priority, but with a twist: Rock and contemporary pop styles are also treated in depth. More venerable pop styles are handled cursorily. Jazz, which one might argue is the essence of the essence of American music, is the orphan poking around the kitchen for leftovers. Failing to respect the past, the DAM mocks its mission. It works so hard at being au courant that it skewers history.

No reference work with as much information as the DAM could reasonably be called worthless. It will surely prove useful for the entries on academic composers, some of the meatier essays on general subjects, and as a record of birth and death dates. For my purposes, which the DAM seems by its own words intent on serving, the four volumes add up to a bust. I'll focus on three areas: jazz, pre-rock pop, and criticism. The editors pride themselves on being up-to-date. There are entries for Ruben Blades, Blondie, the Talking Heads, and the New York Dolls. Most of the major figures who have come into jazz during the past 15 years are omitted. I'm not talking about obscure instrumentalists who produce a vanity recording now and then. I'm talking about Henry Threadgill, David Murray, Julius Hemphill, Arthur Blythe, James Newton, Oliver Lake, Ronald Shannon Jackson, Chico Freeman, Hamiet Bluiett, Don Pullen, George Adams, Bobby McFerrin (who is not even mentioned in the entry for his father), and Branford Marsalis (ditto in the entry for his brother). Given the inclusion (minuscule though it is) of World Saxophone Quartet, you expect to find its members cross-referenced, especially after you come across an item as inane as "**Rabbit**. *See* HODGES, JOHNNY." But, no, a stranger standard obtains for contemporary jazz.

The one thing almost all the younger jazz players included have in common is an association with music in the educated European tradition: Wynton Marsalis and his concerti, Anthony Davis and his opera, Keith Jarrett and his "works from the classical piano repertory," and George Lewis, who "refuses to be categorized as a jazz musician." Major jazz composers and arrangers (the DAM virtually ignores the art of orchestration, which is about as essential to the American spirit as you can get) of every era are omitted. You won't find Edgar Sampson or Bill Holman or Frank Foster or Ernie Wilkins or Van Alexander. Perhaps the most shocking entry is the curt dismissal of Billy Strayhorn—19 lines, as opposed to two full pages on Frank Zappa. A ludicrously small entry for Muhal Richard Abrams is one of many indications of a white-oriented solipsism.

Consider some of the didoes in the A's and B's. You will not find Aeolian Hall, where *Rhapsody in Blue* debuted—out of sight, out of mind. Steve Allen, who gets twice the attention of Abrams or Strayhorn, is noted for many never to be forgotten or remembered songs, but not Fred Ahlert ("Mean to Me," "I'll Get By") or Harry Akst ("Dinah," "Am I Blue") or Gus Arnheim ("Sweet and Lovely," "I Cried for You") or Johnny Burke ("Pennies from Heaven," "Swinging on a Star"). As for early pop singers, you won't find the most prolific recording artists of the first 30 years of the 20th century: not Gene Austin, Chick Bullock, or the longtime sales champion Billy Murray. But you will find Blondie, Blue Oyster Cult, and Pat Boone, who, in the revisionist DAM, has been raised from a crooning minstrel to a singer "widely imitated in the 1950s"—more imitated, no doubt, than Big Maybelle, Ruth Brown, and La Vern Baker, who go unmentioned. Additional absences in jazz include Lovie Austen, Joe Albany, Rashid Ali, Lillian Armstrong, Sidney Arodin, Kenny Barron, Bill Barron, Ran Blake, Jaki Byard, Paul Bley, Dollar Bramd, Milt Buckner, Kenny Burrell, Billy Butterfield, Teddy Bunn, Joe Bushkin, Georg Brunis, Lawrence Brown, Wellman Braud, Jimmy Blythe, and Ruby Braff. Along with the once-celebrated Whiteman trumpet star Henry Busse, they've been displaced by Herb Alpert and Julie Andrews. Dancers? Fred Astaire is represented, poorly, but not John Bubbles (or Baby Laurence or Honi Coles or any other black dancer I have looked up other than Bill Robinson). Blues? Bruce Springsteen commands twice the space of Bessie Smith. Robert Johnson, Charlie Patton, and Muddy Waters *combined* do not receive the attention accorded Van Morrison. The development of the Butterfield Blues Band and the Byrds is detailed, but the influential saxophonist Don Byas is peremptorily noted as a "transitional figure" who made "many fine recordings." The entry on "avant-garde jazz" is 12 lines long; that on "art rock" 19 lines long; "heavy metal" gets 42.

The entry on Louis Armstrong (which one might reasonably expect to be among the largest in the entire work) ignores the last 35 years of his career because after 1936 "he became primarily a popular entertainer," a statement that, even if remotely true (it isn't), ought to guarantee him a far lengthier discussion than his jazz if the treatment of black artists was at all consistent with that of white artists. It is impossible to infer from Grove the impact of black vocal styles on American music. Barbra Streisand and Linda Ronstadt are discussed as major figures, as is the immortal James Taylor, who receives a whopping 44 lines ("his music is so smooth and understated as almost to belie the usually despairing lyrics"): Dinah Washington gets 18. Listen: Ivie Anderson, Johnny Hartman, Abbey Lincoln, Sheila Jordan, King Pleasure, Helen Forrest, Dick Haymes, Jeanne Lee, Annie Ross, and Helen Merrill didn't make it at all. Eddie Jefferson, interestingly enough, did, but get this: James Moody didn't.

The subsequent publication of Grove's two-volume *Dictionary of Jazz* can hardly excuse or explain the blatant segregation of jazz from a purportedly inclusive work on *American Music*, even if the editors of the latter had noted their deliberate intention to do so, which they did not. They are no better on jazz-era pop. Comments about Al Jolson, Eddie Cantor, Ethel Waters, Jimmy Durante, Bing Crosby, and pioneers in minstrelsy and vaudeville are so devoid of ideas and perspective that no one could glean from them an historical overview of the development of American popular music before Presley. Yet current moneymakers are treated scrupulously and sometimes defensively. Of Michael Jackson, we get this extraordinary hedge: "So phenomenal a success could not help but be psychologically disturbing, and like many other child stars Jackson seemed confused by adulthood." We learn nothing of the effects of success on more enduring prodigies, like the Nicholas Brothers, because they aren't included.

Scholarly appendages—bibliographies and discographies—are erratic and often untrustworthy. The biographies of composers in the European tradition have extensive if not complete worklists; composers in the American tradition—including Ellington!—do not. James Patrick's exemplary entry on Charlie Parker shows how jazz might have been handled throughout, but it's disconcerting to find at its conclusion less than half a column of recordings, followed by more than an entire column of bibliography, when the very next entry, for late 19th-century composer Horatio Parker, concludes with a worklist of two full pages followed by less than half a column of bibliography. How did DAM's priorities get reversed when it came to jazz? Gershwin's worklist is longer than the complete section on Ellington. Inconsistency extends to figures who surround the music. By what logic was Norman Granz included, but not George Wein or Moe Asch; why Jon Landau, but not Tommy Rockwell, Jack Kapp, Orrin Keepnews, Bob Thiele, and Bruce Lundvall? Les Paul gets inadequate attention as an inventor, but John Mullen, whose development of tape recording made Paul's dubbings and the entire modern recording industry possible, is omitted altogether.

Nowhere is the bizarre agenda of the DAM more apparent than in the area of criticism. Other than Robert Palmer and myself, none of the jazz critics who have come along in the past 20 years—and few of our predecessors—is included, while contemporaries in rock are celebrated with a solemnity bordering on religious avowal. Dave Marsh "grew disillusioned with the pretensions of the so-called psychedelic and collegiate soft- and folk-rock movements and became a champion of black music and ... working class rock"—despite his lack of "tolerance and intellectual refinement." You could look it up. John Rockwell has "a reasoned overview of cultural history," while the writings of Greil Marcus earned him "unparalleled respect both inside and outside the rock community."

As one of Marcus's admirers, I point out that that sentence appears in a 2,700-page reference work that found no room for Lafcadio Hearn, Gilbert Seldes, Theodore Adorno, Sidney Finkelstein, Otis Ferguson, Fred Ramsey, Charles Edward Smith, Wilder Hobson, Barry Ulanov, Marshall Stearns, Stanley Dance, Ira Gitler, George Simon, John Wilson, Peter Guralnick, and John Litweiler, just to mention some white writers who have written books that earned parallel respect. Black writers, scholars, and editors, with the exception of Olly Wilson and Eileen Southern, are omitted en masse—and, yes, that includes, W. E. B. Du Bois, Daniel Alexander Payne, E. Belfield Spriggins, Ralph Ellison, Albert Murray, Amiri Baraka, A. B. Spellman, Antoinette Handy, James Haskins, Bill Cole, and Stanley Crouch. Yet space was found for the likes of Donal Henahan (admittedly with the shortest squib in the book) and Peter G. Davis, whose high visibility seems to be their principal credential. Incidentally, both came through with reviews. Davis thought the work admirable, while Henahan complained of too much coverage of jazz. Typically, B. H. Haggin, whose career survived several generations of hacks, is criticized for displaying "little sympathy for most developments in music of the 20th century," rather than noted as one of the few classical critics to write enthusiastically and perceptively of early jazz. Grove has failed the mandate it set for itself, and no one else is likely to attempt it for years to come. I will wager my copy against a plate of rice and beans that when the job is properly done, however far down the road, Billy Strayhorn's reputation will be more secure than James Taylor's.

[*Village Voice*, 13 January 1987 / 1992, dedicated to Martin Williams,
whose brief DAM entry concludes, with no details,
"Williams has written several books."]

67 ❖ *Carrying a Torch*
(The Modern Library)

Somebody gave me this book for Christmas. It's a Giant Modern Library Book. Did you ever see one of those? It's less attractively bound than the Proceedings of the New York State Assembly and it weighs more.
—Helene Hanff, *84 Charing Cross Road*

Helene Hanff's harsh comment, in a book gushing with aromatic post-war cheer, came to mind at the news that the Modern Library had been redesigned and revamped by Random House on the occasion of its 75th anniversary. Hers is the only unkind remark I have ever encountered about the Modern Library. Many readers of my generation (born shortly after World War II) are likely to swoon when recalling the first volumes they purchased; they invariably credit those once ubiquitous, multicolored, myriad reprints as the latchkey that delivered them to literature and the bibliomania that is every bookworm's curse and solace.

Hanff goes on to make several pointed comments about a particular volume that paired Donne and Blake; many of the 750 or so titles that appeared under the Modern Library imprint are open to reproach. Yet, for most of us, the series itself, which had dwindled to fewer than 140 titles by the mid-70s, is very nearly hallowed. Random House deserves one cheer for giving it renewed life, and another for doing so with style: The starting lineup of 27 volumes is a conventional selection, from Aristotle and Austen to Welty and Wilde, with the promise of 90 more over the next two years. I'll reserve a third cheer for proof of a long-term commitment and a few improvements.

The Modern Library is the only imprint in American publishing that inaugurated two major houses. It began in 1917, when the bon vivant Horace Liveright, desperate for a get-rich-quick scheme, met an office clerk named Albert Boni, who told him of his idea to publish reprints of esteemed contemporary European writers. With a loan from Liveright's father-in-law they established the firm of Boni & Liveright, the most radical and adventurous publishing company of the 1920s. Beyond reprints, its list included Dreiser, Freud, Faulkner, Hemingway, O'Neill, Crane, Eliot, Pound, Jeffers and many other modernist perennials.

The outfit was built on the foundation of the hugely successful Modern Library, priced at 60 cents a volume and bound in navy lamb-skin (the first title was Oscar Wilde's *Picture of Dorian Gray*). In an era before high-quality paperbacks, the Modern Library was almost universally acclaimed for democratizing literature. Classic American writers and even modernists—led by Sherwood Anderson (*Winesburg, Ohio*)—were added to a rapidly growing catalogue that exemplified, in Liveright's words, "the sophisticated, the subversive and the avant-garde."

Yet the flamboyant, self-destructive Liveright was fated for a fall, one he hastened with his most disastrous decision as a publisher. After squandering a fortune on the stock market and theatrical ventures, and already in debt to his disapproving father-in-law, he agreed to sell the Modern Library, in 1925, to a striving young employee, Bennett Cerf, who had come to work for him two years earlier, after a spell on Wall Street.

According to Liveright's biographer, Walker Gilmore, he was known around the office as Jesus Junior, because "he was perpetually shocked at what was going on." He cannot have been as shocked as Liveright's associates were when they learned of their boss's determination to sell the company's most profitable asset for a mere $215,000.

In his autobiography, *At Random*, Cerf recalls, "Mr. Pell, the treasurer, was outraged, of course, when he heard of the deal." I should note that Arthur Pell, who eventually assumed control of the company that became known as Horace Liveright Inc., was my wife's great-uncle. I uphold Uncle Arthur's outrage. Still, Cerf and his partner, Donald Klopfer, superbly marketed the Modern Library. In two years, they made back their investment, added original titles to the catalogue, and changed the name of their company from the Modern Library Inc. to Random House.

At first Cerf preserved the series' look and style. He used a slightly more flexible version of the leathery lambskin cover, and continued Liveright's practice of prefacing each volume with an introduction by a prominent writer. Jesus Junior even sustained the company's penchant ("sophisticated . . . subversive") for books that could boast of banishment from Boston and other equally prudent locales; titles included *Jurgen, Painted Veils, God's Little Acre, Nana, The Sex Problem in Modern Society,* and an abridged version of *Casanova's Memoirs*. He did change the colophon and endpaper design, from the artist Horace Brodzky's muscular, naked workmen lifting huge blocks bearing the initials M and L to Lucian Bernhard's leaping and also naked (though definitely not muscular) torchbearer. The 75th-anniversary editions restore Bernhard's endpapers —a nice touch. By the 1930s, lambskin, which was better suited to prophylactics, had given way to a more orthodox cloth cover with a dust jacket.

Within two decades, the impact of the Modern Library on generations of readers had greatly exceeded that of a mere reprint company. As early as 1920, it had bolstered the rediscovery of Melville (Raymond Weaver, in his introduction to *Moby-Dick*, wrote, "Melville, no less than God, created great whales"). It also deleted—and continues to delete—the hyphen that appeared on Melville's title page (but not in his text). By the time Faulkner won the Nobel Prize, in 1950, his work was generally available only in Modern Library editions. Countless readers discovered *Ulysses* in the Modern Library, complete with the court decision that permitted its publication in the United States. Some of the new introductions became almost as widely known as the works they preceded, among them Aldous Huxley's to *Brave New World* ("You pays your money and you takes your choice") and Faulkner's to *Sanctuary* ("To me it is a cheap idea, because it was deliberately conceived to make money"). Only the prolific translator Constance Garnett did more than the Modern Library to introduce Dostoevsky to American readers.

Although the Modern Library flourished right through the Second World War, it is my contention that it had a peculiarly different appeal for the middle-class readers who came upon it in the '50s and '60s. By then, paperbacks could be found in every corner drugstore. Thus the attraction of the Modern Library was not merely cheap editions of famous books, but rather the specific tactile pleasure of hard covers; they were especially valued by adolescents who could wrest from the Modern Library an incipient library of their own. The degree to which those squat and alluring volumes (Hanff be damned) were fetishized is attested to by my informal poll of contemporaries, many of whom as young consumers stripped the Modern Library editions of their dust-jackets, the better to line them in uniform display. Such spines they had—a varying three tones (for example, a deep blue cloth with a maroon inset on which Dorothy Parker's name was writ in gold). Not that the jackets were necessarily discarded. One of the Modern Library's most ingenious marketing ideas was to print a complete catalogue on the inside jackets. "Which of these 403 outstanding books do you want to read?" one of them challenges. More pointedly, another asks, "Which of these outstanding books do you want to own?" They understood adolescent compulsions very well.

In retrospect, it seems clear that Random House was preparing my generation for a life of series servitude. First we were primed with the company's Landmark Books, an impressive collection of uniform, cloth-covered biographies and histories for children. Then, with such transitional offerings as Cooper, Poe, Irving, Dickens, Hawthorne, and Mark Twain, the company drew us to the Modern Library (trim-size editions and Giants). Just as we began producing our own 2.3 children, Random House's Jason Epstein helped launch, outside the company, an upscale coup de grace, the Library of America, which has enjoyed several triumphs—not least, the reinstatement of Francis Parkman and the reconstruction of Richard Wright, though it persists in ignoring Edmund Wilson who thought up the idea. For those unimpressed by the Library of America's $35 price for a pair of Sinclair Lewis novels, here comes the Modern Library all over again.

(Note that Knopf, a division of Random House, has revived the Everyman's Library, originally published in the United States by Dutton, but more widely celebrated in England, where it was launched by J. M. Dent & Sons in 1905. The selection and price are similar to the Modern Library's, but the superior bindings are fully sewn. Unhappily, the half dust jackets, covering only the front of the book, are a nuisance, and the type is often minute.)

So how does the new Modern Library stand up in the three areas by which it has always been judged—price, package, and content? The price is fair but hardly low, ranging from $12.50 to $21 a volume, falling in the mid-range between paperback and full dress. The Modern Library's two-volume Jane Austen, at $39, is a logical alternative to Oxford's illustrated six volumes ($85) and Penguin's one-volume paperback ($15). The $20 editions of Poe (which includes three poems inadvertently left out of the Library of America Poe) and Joyce (the 1961 reset *Ulysses*, with the court decision) occupy similar middle ground. But until recently, the Modern Library's Plutarch was a single volume ($20); now it's two ($38). Given recessionary pricing, it seems unlikely that today's Modern Library can have the demotic appeal it had 30 years ago.

The new covers partake of the Our Poets or Famous Authors School of design. The metallic olive jackets feature representations of the authors, and though the styling is handsome, the effect suggests duty rather than pleasure. A large percentage of faces fit Van Wyck Brooks's description of "kindly, gray-bearded or otherwise grizzled old men." The portraits are usually concurrent with the work, but is that sweet young thing adorning *Middlemarch* really George Eliot? Yes and no: It's the D'Albert Durade painting of Mary Ann Evans, long before she took a man's name and began publishing fiction, more than 20 years before she wrote *Middlemarch*. (A graybeard imposter disfigures Emerson's *Selected Writings*; corrected covers are on the way.) I much prefer the diverse covers of old—the blue sky and silhouetted carriage on *The Brothers Karamazov*; the raven and skull on Poe; the weird, genderless smoker on *Sanctuary*. Beneath the jackets, the cloth is uniformly gray, alas. On the other hand, the newly reset pages—fewer lines per page—befriend the eye and the bindings are tight. As more titles are added, the catalogue will presumably resume its rightful place on the inside of the dust jacket.

The first selection is typical, impressive, and safe—nothing remotely subversive or avant-garde. But there are a few surprises, including the debut of the first two volumes of yet another revision of C. K. Scott Moncrieff's translation of Proust's *Remembrance of*—sorry, *In Search of Lost Time*. The now preferred English title, which Random prevented Terence Kilmartin from adopting in 1981, when he originally revised Moncrieff, is official. D. J. Enright, who took over after Kilmartin's death last year, has made numberless small changes and at least one eye-popping deletion: The first chapter of *Swann's Way* is no longer Overture but is subsumed in the larger chapter called Combray. Enright's insufficient translator's note doesn't bother to explain why.

In fact, the series suffers from a chronic absence of vital introductory information, unlike Everyman's Library, which has commissioned new forewords. How many readers have a vita on Arthur Hugh Clough, whose edition of *Plutarch's Lives* was first published in 1864? The Modern Library identifies it as "the Dryden translation" (a less circumspect earlier Modern Library edition carried the credit "translated by John Dryden"), but there is no evidence that Dryden actually worked on the translation. An explanatory note would be helpful.

Absolutely indispensable is the Modern Library edition of *The Sound and the Fury*, the only one in print with the "Appendix" Faulkner added in 1946, and which Random unreasonably and inexplicably dropped from its revised text of 1984. The Modern Library employs the 1984 alterations but presents the work whole, as Faulkner intended. Another essential entry is the Francis Steegmuller translation of *Madame Bovary*; despite a movie tie-in edition published recently by Vintage, the best of the Bovarys has not been as widely available as other translations. Also welcome is Richard Aldington's irresistible translation of *Candide*, with its single-paragraph chapters and relentless deadpan tone—undoubtedly the funniest representation in English. The Voltaire volume is filled out with *Philosophical Letters* in a version that differs unaccountably from others—again, an explanatory note would help.

Basic Writings of Nietzsche, translated and edited by Walter Kaufmann, is more straightforward than its variously translated Modern Library predecessor, *The Philosophy of Nietzsche*, but it omits *Thus Spake Zarathustra*. I can understand why editors dropped Hervey Allen's introduction to Poe (concerned, as it is, with the damage inflicted on Poe's posthumous reputation by the envious Rufus W. Griswold), but Brooks Atkinson's unaffected introduction to his Emerson selection is missed: "Although he was a lovable man, he was shy, modest and deficient in animal spirits, and he felt that he was too cold for social intercourse." Ralph Ellison's 50th-anniversary preface to *Invisible Man* is now part of the Modern Library edition. *Moby-Dick* (or *Moby Dick*) includes the marvelous Rockwell Kent woodcuts; but the old, unattributed Modern Library pen and ink sketches have been dropped from *Madame Bovary*.

All such quibbles pale, of course, in light of the larger issue of how the catalogue is to be selected, developed and modified. One of the enduring pleasures of the Modern Library in its ever-mutable glory days was the appearance of books that briefly gained classic status by sole virtue of their inclusion. I recall with gratitude coming across books I might never have read if they hadn't received the Modern Library imprimatur, among them Arthur Morrison's *Tales of Mean Streets* and George R. Stewart's *Storm* and especially John A. Symonds's *Life of Michelangelo*. If the Modern Library is to flourish again, may it have the courage to look beyond the realm of Famous Authors and wave the torch again for some of those lost in the breach. By all means, give us Dostoevsky (and keep the Boardman Robinson watercolors when getting around to *The Idiot*), but bring back Romain Rolland's *Jean-Christophe* and Eugene Sue's *The Wandering Jew* and Edmund Wilson's invaluable *The Shock of Recognition* (three mammoth works that fully justified the weight of Modern Library Giants), and say yes to another turn by those forgotten decadents Pierre Louys and James Huneker, whose music criticism ought also to be revived, as well as Norman Douglas and Richard Hughes, and do please induct Constance Rourke, Bernard Wolfe, Andrew Lytle, Dorothy Baker, Chester Himes, Richard Yates, and . . . Oh, but of course they won't. The Modern Library is a business—and I am indulging my inner Jesus Junior.

[*New York Times Book Review*, 6 December 1992]

68 ❖ *Muddy Waters, I Presume (Alan Lomax)*

As a student in the 1960s, I occasionally postured at being Alan Lomax, not by trekking into the Deep South, but by approaching the touring Skip James, Mississippi John Hurt, Bukka White, and other fabled bluesmen with a tape recorder and a thousand questions. At one session, someone asked the often distracted but ingenious Skip James about the Delta blues singer Robert Johnson. James ruminated in his mournful, hesitant, high-pitched voice that now that we mentioned it, he hadn't seen his old friend in about 26 or 27 years, leaving us with the jaw-dropping implication that he didn't know Johnson had died—26 or 27 years before. He then told us he had taught the younger man how to play "32-20 Blues," and played it vigorously as if to confirm ownership.

Musicians like James, who spurred the country blues revival, seemed strangely foreign to many avidly credulous white Northerners, attracted chiefly to their music but also to the existentialist myths of the black troubadour. They were representatives of an America we could scarcely imagine. In 1980 Peter Guralnick wrote a keenly observed novel, *Nighthawk Blues*, about blues collectors of our generation who did travel south. But perhaps only one white man could tell what it was like combing the backwoods when Son House, David (Honeyboy) Edwards, and

Muddy Waters were robust young artists and not the patriarchal legends of a later day. Now he has.

Lomax is a nearly ubiquitous figure in American folklore and music. Born in Texas in 1915, he was a protégé of his father, the folklorist John A. Lomax, with whom he created the Archive of American Folk Song at the Library of Congress and brought to public attention the baronial giant of the 12-string guitar, Lead Belly. Generations have grown up with his Library of Congress recordings of Lead Belly, Woody Guthrie, and Jelly Roll Morton, as well as Lomax's 1950 book derived from the Morton sessions, *Mister Jelly Roll*—one of the most influential and widely quoted works ever written about jazz. That remarkably disparate trio does not figure in his lengthy and much-anticipated memoir, *The Land Where the Blues Began*, which is concerned almost exclusively with his trips through the Mississippi Delta in the 1940s.

Lomax is too serious a man to write autobiography and not serious enough to write history. History requires the collation of everyone's research, and Lomax prefers to mine his own, enlarging on his experiences, as documented on disk and tape, with vivid recollections that compellingly establish the time and place of every encounter. This book makes clear (as his several others did not) that he can be a stunningly evocative writer, conveying the excitement that fueled his wanderings through Coahoma County half a century ago.

Lomax notes that one of his associates, a black folklorist named Lewis Jones (one of the book's several elliptical heroes), characterized their research "in terms of the three main modes of transport" linking the Delta to the outside world: steamboats, railroads, and highways. He then goes on to describe the first:

Beating the brown belly of the mighty river to froth with their great paddles, filling the sky with black clouds from cathedral-like smokestacks, at night their furnaces breathing dragonlike flames across midnight waters, gliding through the semiwilderness of the Southwest like swift heavenly chariots, loaded down with well-dressed dudes, fancy women, double-jinted roustabouts and new cotton millionaires—these floating palaces roused the awe of the Delta songsters.

Inevitably, Lomax offers a couplet by way of an amen: "The big Kate Adams headin' down the stream / With her sidewheel knockin'—'Good God, I been redeemed.'" Always his recollections lead to and from the musical examples he preserved on 15-minute acetate disks. He captured the call and response of spirituals, whole sermons and conversations, and countless blues, play songs, and work songs. At one point, he requests the reader to listen to some blues records, any blues records, before returning to the text.

At times, Lomax's adventures in bluesland read like an American version of "Dr. Livingstone, I presume," as when he makes his way through the "broomweed pastures" of Senatobia, in "the hills" of Mississippi, and encounters Blind Sid Hemphill, a drum major with a fife-and-drum outfit whose style of long narrative ballads shows a direct African influence. Of course, he also encounters hostile natives—all white, law officers and plantation bosses, one of whom ominously warns Lomax, "We've been told to be on the lookout for Jap agents," and then threatens to lock him up for prefacing Son House's name with the honorific "Mr." The entire book veers between musical commemoration and outrage at racist barbarism.

But *The Land Where the Blues Began* is also a journey into the folklorist's own heart of darkness. For as disinclined as he is to write about himself, Lomax is forced to acknowledge his arrogance as a young government-sponsored missionary: He simply is not ready to handle racism and the submissiveness he finds in its victims. After a Delta church service, he notes, "My heart had struck a depth of sorrow and hurt such as I had never imagined." Lomax has always been a somewhat regressive defender of old ways and styles. He has mellowed enough to enjoy the accomplishments of such newfangled idioms as gospel music, yet he regrets the loss of the improvised spiritual harmonies it displaced. Surprisingly, he finds sexist villainy at the root: "The age-old female religious collective was being replaced by a male-dominated hierarchy."

Lomax's reluctance to place his own research in the context of the larger historical canvas is more problematic. He does not attempt to trace the origins of songs beyond his own discovery of them. Some were popular hits that he would have recognized had he spent more time in front of a radio, but Lomax disdains most commercial music. He perpetuates myths long since discounted by other researchers—including the recurring legend of Bessie Smith dying needlessly because she was refused admission to three hospitals, a story popularized in a play by Edward Albee that Lomax notes in his bibliography while omitting the scholarly writings on Smith that disprove it.

So *The Land Where the Blues Began* is not a comprehensive or reliable history, but it is something rare and valuable—the firsthand account of a sympathetic, capable, and committed Boswell (I'm thinking less of the biographer than the diarist of travel) determined to preserve for all time not only the innovators of the blues but also the vanishing communities that produced them. Lomax gives us Muddy Waters before and after he traveled to Chicago and became a star; and, though he muses perhaps sentimentally that blacks alone understand the secrets of life's pleasures, he gives us Big Bill Broonzy describing with articulate passion the economic and sociological privations of this loamy region that gave birth to the blues. In Alan Lomax's discerning reconstructions, such long-ago visits miraculously evade the blurring of time. They give life to a domain most of us can never know, one that summons us with an oddly familiar sensation of reverence and dread.

[*New York Times Book Review*, 4 July 1993]

69 ❖ *Soupspoon's Blues (Walter Mosley)*

The RL of Walter Mosley's novel, *RL's Dream*, is Robert Johnson, the Delta blues singer who died young and violently in 1938. (No one knows why Johnson called himself RL, and the author doesn't attempt an explanation.) Admired by blues connoisseurs in life, he was rediscovered by the largely white, middle-class folk and blues revival of the 1960s, and reborn in a big way 25 years later to a pop audience that adopted him as a dark-of-night, piney woods conjurer who prefigured everything from Chicago blues to hard rock—a tormented visionary who bartered his soul to the Devil. And what did he get in return—genius? women? recognition? Robert Johnson eludes material narrative as do many seminal artists who lived short, messy, and contrary lives of mythic resonance.

Although Mosley brings him to ground in a tangled vignette that arrives about midway in the book, allowing him to breathe hotly on the page, it is ultimately the mythic Robert Johnson who haunts this often startling, emphatic, but intermittently convincing modern-day fable. Mosley's RL is at once a blues virtuoso who makes dancers go wild, whose "blues would rip the skin right off yo' back," and a gloomy apparition of futility. One disciple who can't shake the dread is Atwater (Soupspoon) Wise, a black Mississippi orphan who briefly traveled with Johnson. Now dying in New York, he is obsessed with recounting and defining their association. Mosley first zooms in on him on the Lower East Side, hobbling in blind terror and befouled agony, with a busted hip and advanced cancer, hallucinating "a young man with short nappy hair and one dead eye."

Upon reaching his apartment, he is expelled for nonpayment of rent and left to die on the street.

Enter Kiki Waters, in pain herself after being stabbed that day by a 10-year-old black boy. One of the more unlikely saviors to enter American fiction in recent years, Kiki—who hails from Arkansas, where she was the victim of unspeakably savage sexual attacks from her father—is a white woman in her early thirties: She is alcoholic, ferociously independent, unpredictable, scary, and smart. A tenant in Soupspoon's building, though they have never met, she throws a tantrum regarding his eviction and insists that he move in with her. She quickly dispatches her sometime boyfriend (a Negro convinced by his mother that he isn't), the landlord, and others who stand in her way. Undeterred by Soupspoon's stench, she undresses him, carries him—despite the pull on her stitches—to the tub and bathes him. Soup thinks, in concert with the reader: "Maybe she was crazy. Drunk maybe, or insane." She cuts loose "the loneliness that had been his life for years."

RL's Dream is about Soup's last stand as a musician and how he and Kiki alternate roles of nurturer and invalid. Set in the north, this is nonetheless a story of a country left behind, the Deep South, which haunts their New York dreams. "While Soupspoon was counting dead bodies in his sleep, Kiki called out, 'No, daddy.' Her dream was Southern too." Yet their obsessive recollections have entirely different tenors. Atwater's are elegiac or at least verging on Faulknerian gothic—even his litanies of violence, murder, racism. "For all that it was barren, the Delta was a beautiful land too. It was a hard land but true. It had the whippoorwill and the hoot owl and crickets for music. It had pale dead trees that stood out in the moonlight like the hands of dead men reaching out of the ground." Kiki's past is so bad she drinks herself into a stupor for fear of remembering.

It may be useful, at this point, to assure his admirers that this is indeed the work of the Walter Mosley who has written four celebrated detective novels set in Los Angeles during the 15 years following World War II, and starring the serenely cool and competent Easy Rawlins. In *RL's Dream*, Mosley has risked a lyrical leap beyond genre fiction and landed on one foot, working for the first time in the third person and substituting an omniscient probing of damaged lives for the modulated fastidiousness of Rawlins. His practiced reportorial eye is fully focused on New York's street life as well as tarpaper bucket-of-blood juke joints of the Delta. Several episodes are as well tuned as anything he has written, including the violent conclusion, and particularly a tense and comic tour de force in which Kiki embezzles a million-dollar insurance policy from her company to pay for Soupspoon's chemotherapy. More impressive is the cast—excepting a few stock roles (villain, milquetoast), it is original and often credible.

Still, episodes congeal into gross sentimentality, underscored by gnomic utterances designed to render Soupspoon as a kind of cosmic bluesman. Sitting in the park, Soup meditates on ants and worms. As he begins his observation ("Everybody's doin' their business"), you suddenly recall that his name is Wise and wish it weren't. Wise sayings mount up all too quickly. On music: "It's all about gettin' so close to pain that it's like a friend, like somebody you love." On blues: "Blues is the Devil's music an' we his chirren. RL was Satan's favorite son." Yet when he considers RL's remark "They ain't no gettin' away from yo stank, Soup," he concludes, "The words just didn't make sense." They make a lot more sense than Soup's lyrics, most of which are self-consciously arty and foolish, confirming the reader's suspicion that Mosley knows little about the blues or the lives of bluesmen. Incidentally, it's inconceivable that those who listen to Soup using the names Robert Johnson and RL interchangeably would not ask why or register confusion.

Such moments of unreality, including an episode in which an 18-year-old beauty seduces Soupspoon, are jarring because Mosley's intonation is usually dead on. By the story's almost too perfect conclusion, you know Kiki—"this redheaded white girl, drunk and jagged, who thought slaps were kisses and whisky was milk"—well enough to recognize her on the street. The author's pleasure in her is confirmed in the crazily ripe future he gives her. Nor does Mosley miss a beat with Randy, her black friend who thinks he's Egyptian; or Mavis, Soup's former wife and once RL's lover, who inhabits an apartment decorated entirely in white and is still mourning her five-year-old son. The boy's accidental death half a century ago was indirectly related to a rowdy night Mavis spent dancing to RL and Soupspoon in a juke joint.

Mavis tells Kiki you can't plan your life no matter how you try, which is the apparent point of *RL's Dream*. Even as he regains his strength to put on an old-time suit for one last musical job in a back-alley gambling joint, Soupspoon Wise realizes his life was a mirage, a dream, and not entirely his own dream. "I never played the blues, not really," he says. "I run after it all these years. I scratched at its coattails and copied some notes. But the real blues is covered by mud and blood in the Mississippi Delta. The real blues is down that terrible passway where RL traveled, sufferin' an' singin' till he was dead. I followed him up to the gateway, but Satan scared me silly and left me back to cry." It never occurs to him that the blues might be a form of musical expression—12 measures, three chords—about good times as well as bad, and not an extended gig in hell.

[*New York Times Book Review*, 13 August 1995]

70 ❖ *Short and Acerbic*
(M. M. Liberman)

Maggot and Worm and Eight Other Stores initially appeared with silk-screen illustrations by Byron Burford in a fastidious edition of only 300 copies, published by Iowa's renowned Cummington Press. When a very few of those copies showed up in the Grinnell College bookstore in the academic year of 1969–70, those undergraduates who admired Mr. Liberman's writing took root at the table where they were displayed, gently thumbing the pages while contemplating the quite forbidding price of $25. We had heard of the stories, most of which originally appeared in the late 1950s, including an O. Henry prizewinner, but hadn't yet read them. (Two months later, "The Cross Country Runner" was featured on the cover of a one-shot student magazine called *Montage*.)

On the day I coughed up my $25, a copy of *Maggot and Worm* was stolen from the bookstore. Mr. Liberman soon let me know that he appreciated my interest, adding that he didn't know if he should be more flattered by my extravagance or by the thief's recklessness. I risked only money: the thief everything.

M. M. Liberman was the reputed curmudgeon of Grinnell College's English department in the 1960s. Most English majors were intimidated by him. Short and dour with a perpetual keep-away look that on sunny days promised caustic humor and on cloudy ones an implacable scowl, he was an uncompromising, devoted teacher and a scrupulous individualist—a rare bird who refused the Ph.D. route to academic success; a Jew turned Catholic; an Easterner mired in the Midwest. I understood why he unnerved sophomores when I took my first course with him. His class did not operate as a democracy, with a lot of raised hands and chitchat back and forth. He presented a lecture, then asked for comment. The lectures were riveting, often brilliant. But better not volunteer a comment without thinking it through. Ask a stupid question, and he might stare at you with uncomprehending sorrow. Ask a good one, and he would lean back and engage you in surprisingly amiable colloquy.

The main thing, of course, was the lecture. You had to have read the book and not a summary to know what he was talking about when he argued that *The Great Gatsby* did not live up to its author's intentions, or that *Ship of Fools* redefined the relationship between novel and short story. He had no patience for exegesis, and considered it insulting to "explain" the meaning of a work. After his gemlike book, *Katherine Anne Porter's*

Fiction, was published, I asked him what he thought of another work on the same subject. He shrugged and said, "Plot summaries." Liberman was pithy in everything. His essays, stories, and books are short. He says only what he wants and nothing more. What does a fiction writer do? "He transforms the materials of the everyday world—a world in which design or pattern or order is difficult to find—and imposes a discernible order on it."

As a would-be critic, I adopted him as a model and buried myself in the critical books he wrote with other members of the English department, Sheldon P. Zitner, James D. Kissane, and Edward E. Foster—*The Practice of Criticism, A Preface to Literary Analysis, A Modern Lexicon of Literary Terms.* To be sure, there was a juvenile avidity in my search for a model, one as near as the classroom, whose very presence made the possibility of criticism real. In the end, Liberman gave me far more than I anticipated.

The murders at Kent State led to Grinnell shutting down in May 1970. During those last weeks, a relaxation between faculty and the student body took place. Those of us graduating were told we would receive degrees in the mail, but there were academic odds and ends to attend to—including, for me, an oral comprehensive exam with Mr. Liberman. He suggested we meet in the student union over coffee, and asked about my subjects (Hemingway, Eliot, Edmund Wilson) as though he were inquiring after a relative's health. In a few minutes, he said, "You seem to know this stuff." We chatted for a while as I worked up my courage to broach a difficult subject. I had written a story for his fiction seminar and he had said nothing about it. He pinched his face as if pained by the memory and said there was nothing he could say—"it wasn't any good." I looked at him and swallowed, waiting for an antidote to the pain, and it came. He described my potential as a critic with remarkable generosity, especially from him, and told me to stick with it. I left campus suffused with optimism.

A few years later, after I had found my subject in jazz, Mr. Liberman wrote me a congratulatory letter, signed Mike (I thought I'd have to address him as Mr. for life) and revealing his own interest in jazz. This piece of information astounded me. On a couple of occasions, I visited Mike and his wife Mathilda, with whom I had also studied (freshman paper: animal similes in *The Iliad*). In 1977, I commissioned Mike to write an article for the *Village Voice*. His very short and funny piece, largely an excoriation of politically correct jazzcrit, begins, "What I know about music, very strictly speaking, you could put in your left eye and never feel it." Yet he observed, "If you just lay back and don't get too serious, you can hear in those horns the human voice (song) and human movement (dance) as they play out the romance that few of us confess to but all of us live by."

Eight years after that, while writing a series of pieces on forgotten books, I reread *Maggot and Worm*, and was pleased to find that it had lost nothing to time. Each of the stories fulfills Liberman's dictum that "the short story implies the universe that the novel describes" (*Katherine Anne Porter's Fiction*); taken together, they display a universe in which proud, misunderstood children are in perpetual conflict with the disaffected, disapproving adults they are likely to become. Sleep is always uneasy. What's to prevent one's son from turning into "another cool mindless cat like Blenn, his soul parted neatly on the side, his colon dozing, his voice perpetually at room temperature"? Or oneself from becoming an untethered middle-aged man who can never explain to anyone the futility of duty, so that the knowledge abides as "a dull blade scraping your heart as if it were an old potato." Guilt and loneliness are pervasive and even nostalgia can kill you. The best hope for one young man is to "enjoy a sense of alienation rather than be eaten by it." Beyond that there is the elusive dream of community realized in the exceptional title story, a painful parable of magnanimity.

As a collection, *Maggot and Worm* suggests a progression in three movements of three stories each. Childhood recollections are the substance of the first group. In each, an act of violence—a quarrel, an assault, a suicide—triggers apprehension. In the next three, the narrators are young men far from home, trying to sink roots into life, and the mode is sardonic comedy. The absurdist tone thickens in the final three stories, centered around men in their forties, feeling worn down and awed by the banality of the mess they've gotten themselves into. In all of Liberman's stories, the light of compassionate acceptance follows directly from his insistence on accurate reporting. The clarity of his observations, musical in their efficiency and bite, enlivens the diverse settings and offsets the doom-laden conventionality of his people and their trials.

After the review appeared, a major publisher contacted Mike about collecting his stories. He was very excited about the discussions, but in the end they offered the same bait-and-switch he had experienced for 30 years —write a novel first, then we'll issue the stories. Katherine Anne Porter's ardent defender was the last person to be persuaded by that kind of argument. He continued to publish stories in the little magazines (one of the last concerned a student obsessed with his socks), and perhaps someday they will find their champion. For now, I salute Grinnell College for restoring *Maggot and Worm* in a small printing, without the silk-screens but at an affordable price.

[*Maggot and Worm*, Grinnell College, 1996]

71 ❖ *Oxford Jazz*
(Sheldon Meyer)

Byron is said to have presented his publisher with a generously inscribed Bible that the recipient proudly exhibited for many years, until a visitor pointed out an alteration at John 18:40. Byron had edited the sentence "Now Barabbas was a robber," changing the last word to "publisher." If publishers are not universally admired by the writers they usher into print, neither can they be much exalted by a public inured to tales of conglomerate-owned houses that offer seven-figure book advances to celebrity girlfriends, talk show hosts, and dishonored or traumatized memoirists while eradicating professional midlist writers—midlist being an industry euphemism for those who fail to scale the best-seller lists.

Until the recent spate of articles about the woes of publishing, it never occurred to me that I was a "midlist author." For a writer of books about jazz, midlist sounds like a promotion. Yet, along with several colleagues, I have never felt professionally marginalized in the publishing world, and for that we have one man to thank. On the occasion of his semi-retirement at age 70 from Oxford University Press, Sheldon Meyer merits no less than a flourish of saxophones, a melody by Jerome Kern, and a high-kicking chorus-line salute. Over the past 40 years, Meyer turned the world's oldest and most staid publishing house into the leading chronicler of jazz, Broadway musicals, popular-song writers, broadcasting, and black cultural history. And he and his masters made money at it.

"I had some problems in the mid-60s," he recently told me. "The head of the press in England said he had begun to notice some odd books appearing in the Oxford list, and I said, well, I'm responsible for them. Since he was a papyrologist—a guy working with old documents, old rolls of paper—he didn't have much connection with this world, to say the least. So I said to him, 'Well, look, as long as these books are authoritative and make money, it seems to me they're appropriate for the press to publish.' Fortunately for the future of my career, that turned out to be correct."

The main part of Meyer's list to that point and after was American history, particularly black history and the Civil War. A few classics he edited in the former category include Lawrence W. Levine's *Black Culture and Black Consciousness*, Albert J. Raboteau's *Slave Religion*, John Blassingame's *Slave Community*, Robert C. Toll's *Blacking Up*, Nathan Irvin Huggins's *Harlem Renaissance*, A. Leon Higginbotham Jr.'s *In the Matter of Color*, Thomas Cripps's *Slow Fade to Black*, Richard C. Wade's *Slavery in the Cities,* and Louis R. Harlan's two-volume biography of Booker T. Washington. A Civil War book, however, brought him his most humbling experience—working with Edmund Wilson on *Patriotic Gore,* a sweeping appraisal of the period's literature that he inherited a few years after arriving at the company.

"Wilson was a hero of mine," Meyer recalls. "But as a human being he was pretty impossible, he really was. He only wanted to deal with the head of the house, and only if you had a bit of information that was valuable to him would he have a conversation with you. But he delivered the manuscript for *Patriotic Gore* to me, at the Princeton Club, naturally, looking very weary. He had been working on it for 15 years. He promptly downed two double manhattans and said to me: 'I'm just heartily sick of this book. I just know it's gotten too big. Can you help me? Can you make suggestions for cutting this book back?' Well, of course, I immediately confused myself with one of the great editors who was going to have my impact on American literature through this book. I went away with a huge manuscript, well over a thousand pages, and took about 200 pages out of it. I sent him a note saying what I had done, and waited for his call. The phone rang, and he said in his very high-pitched voice: 'Meyer, what are you trying to do, ruin me? Put it all back!' "

Another Civil War book helped to change Meyer's standing at Oxford. The tremendous success of James M. McPherson's *Battle Cry of Freedom* in 1988 (one of the company's rare best sellers) earned him a raise and the nearest thing Oxford provides to a personal imprint. "I had became head of what we call trade publishing for the firm in the late 60s," he says. "But in the 80s I was given my own publishing unit, called special editorial, and taken out of an administrative role, for which I was very grateful. The jazz list really accelerated, from 10 to 15 percent of the list to about a third, maybe even 40 percent."

Tall, soft-spoken, and donnish in appearance, Meyer created that rare domain where he could publish books he believed in on subjects he relished—a relatively low-profile world where advances hover in the middle four figures and sales follow suit. He has said the compliment he most cherishes is one that called him "the Goddard Lieberson of publishing"—a reference to the president of Columbia Records who, in the 1950s, helped pioneer synergy between the recording industry and Broadway, spurred John Hammond's talent scouting, and supported the signing of the blacklisted Pete Seeger, among other accomplishments. Significantly, Lieberson reigned when music lovers dominated the business, before the marketing wizards took over.

When Meyer came to Oxford as an assistant editor in 1956, after five years with Funk & Wagnalls, the company had just published Marshall

Stearns's seminal study *The Story of Jazz*, which indicated a receptivity at Oxford that was hardly fashionable. "The elements of what people call popular culture meant a lot to me, but didn't seem to mean a lot to intellectuals," he explains. "We went through that whole time in the 1950s, when German refugees were telling us that popular culture produced Hitler, so no one wanted to deal with it." In 1958, the year he became a full editor, he was invited by Stearns to sit on a panel at the Newport Jazz Festival. Among the participants was critic Martin Williams, who became a friend, adviser, and the author of many Oxford books, including what is often cited as the most distinguished critical work in the field, *The Jazz Tradition*. Through Williams, Meyer met Gunther Schuller, whose *Early Jazz* remains the most influential musicological statement on jazz's infancy.

Asked to name the books of which he is proudest, Meyer mentions those two and adds Erik Barnouw's three-volume *History of Broadcasting in the United States* and Alec Wilder's *American Popular Song*, written with James T. Maher. "I met Alec at a party for Gunther Schuller, who had just become president of the New England Conservatory. Alec had been talking about doing the book but didn't seem to be getting anywhere. But then I met Alec for lunch at the Algonquin, and he introduced me to Jim Maher. I soon realized that with Jim there, there was really going to be a book. But it was to stop in 1950. I said, 'Alec, why does it stop in 1950?' He reared up and said, 'Because that's when the amateurs took over.'"

Those four titles, among quite a few others—from Siegfried Kracauer's *Theory of Film* to Gerald Bordman's *American Musical Theater* to Whitney Balliett's *American Musicians* to Mark Tucker's *Duke Ellington Reader*—did quite a bit better than is average for midlist, and continue to sell. This season Meyer will close a circle by publishing Oxford's first concise jazz history (by Ted Gioia) since Stearns's long outdated work. With a two-year consultancy contract, he is also guiding to completion, among a dozen others, *The Biographical Encyclopedia of Jazz*, *The Oxford Companion to Jazz*, and biographies of Charles Mingus and Bill Evans.

In 1987, Oxford's jazz and pop music list won a Carey Thomas award for creative publishing, and Meyer gave a party for his writers at Sardi's. He notes: "I had an advantage in staying at one place for 40 years—I never could have done the jazz list if I was moving around to three or four publishers during this period. It is kind of an extreme irony that the greatest university press in the world, with these high standards, should become the major publisher of jazz, broadcasting, popular music, all these areas. But I was there at the right time and I had a group of people at the press who had enough flexibility and understanding to let it go forward. Now everybody is enormously proud of this whole thing. I couldn't ask for a better career."

[*New York Times Book Review*, 16 October 1997]

72 ❖ *A Public Burning*
(Ralph Ellison)

The one-novel career, while hardly unique to the United States (Europe offers Canetti, Rilke, and Lampedusa, among others), produced a peculiar frisson of suspense in this country in the postwar era. Not chiefly with those who died young, like James Agee, or consummated extended literary callings with one big fictional outburst, like Katherine Anne Porter, but through writers who made an indelible assault on the consciousness of several generations with a prodigiously incisive novel and left us loitering, season after season, in the vain hope of a second strike.

Four cases stand out. Henry Roth published *Call It Sleep* in the 1930s, but it belongs as much to the '60s, when it was read and celebrated. Breaking what may be the longest silence in publishing history, he persevered to write a memory-novel so long we are three volumes away from the finish and lingering in a zone of cautious endorsement (four of six planned volumes were published individually, under the collective title *Mercy of a Rude Stream*). J. D. Salinger would surely top best-seller lists with *The Pitcher in the Chaff*, but most of us have stopped caring; nor has Harper Lee's silence about the New South or anything else, since *To Kill a Mockingbird*, in 1960, caused sleepless nights. Ralph Ellison's death in 1994, however, was a blow—prayers unanswered once and for all.

A deconstruction of race and identity fixed on the most reverberant metaphor since the white whale, *Invisible Man* succeeded so well in addressing what Ellison called "human universals" that we recall with a sad jolt the admiring condescension with which it was greeted in 1952. At a time when not a few white intellectuals presumed that Negro novels were or ought to be proletarian protest fiction (and that Negro novelists were or ought to be limited in their reach by a species of intellectual ebonics), countless readers were encouraged to approach *Invisible Man* as a sociological inquiry into the Negro condition: Me Tarzan, you invisible. Not the least indication of Ellison's transfigurative powers is the chagrin engendered by that memory.

Invisible Man is a reverse *bildungsroman*, in which a coming of age is refracted through the prism of ripened—indeed, nearly fatal—experience. The hibernating protagonist speaks to us "on the lower frequencies," from a coal bin he has illuminated with 1369 lightbulbs and the grace of Louis Armstrong, all powered by pilfered electricity. Though the second novel Ellison worked on for decades never materialized, the excerpts he infrequently let fly, as well as his essays and interviews (a form he made artful), affirmed a comic aptitude for lighting up dark places with ungrudging lyricism that could not be subverted.

John F. Callahan, who assembled a volume of Ellison's nonfiction for the Modern Library in 1995, has been entrusted with collating the books Ellison shyly or modestly or stubbornly held back. The unfinished novel is a mammoth manuscript, so perhaps a visible magnum opus is still in the offing, though which of us isn't prepared to settle for a lesser Ellisonian clue to life after hibernation?[1] Ellison's early reviews, written for *The New Masses*, have never been collected; likewise, stories reworked or cut from his published and unpublished novels. We are promised a more prolific posthumous career for Ellison than most of us had expected.

Flying Home and Other Stories is a slim but shining installment, collecting 13 short fictions written between 1937 and 1954, six previously unpublished. Callahan, who commands a significant editorial clout (he effects "silent" emendations, omits a story he admits Ellison would have included, and invents titles for two stories Ellison left untitled), has sensibly organized the material to reflect sequential maturation that, with two notable exceptions, fuses the central characters as one: The stories spin outward, not only from early youth to early manhood, but from the South to the North and back, from horror to horror averted. They have a befitting unity, on the order of *In Our Time* or *Dubliners*, which Ellison himself could not have intended.

The least of these stories are distinctive, the best are gripping, and two are genuinely terrifying. Still, it is scarcely possible to read them without noting sundry apprenticeship connections to *Invisible Man* and to Ellison's most accomplished nonfiction, especially the disarmingly cheerful memoir, "An Extravagance of Laughter." Nor is it difficult to see why Ellison dawdled over publishing them. It would have been like

---

[1] But not *Juneteenth*, the 1999 novel-length excerpt that Callahan edited and presented as a novel in its own right. The motive was presumably to provide Random House with a handsome payday (it cannot have been to bolster Ellison's standing). The public's head was not so easily turned; a scholarly presentation of the entire text has been promised.

Beethoven making his name with his Ninth Symphony and, forty years later, offering his First. Some books, however admirable, are better dispensed by estates. Ellison excelled in relating old tales from the security of a hard-won ripeness—these tales are fresh, even raw. Many are candidly autobiographical, and even the most skillful and symbol-laden betray his search for a voice.

Surprisingly, Ellison, an unequivocal master of the first-person narrative, appears to have been intimidated by that mode in the 1940s. Five of the volume's six unpublished stories are in the first person (most of those persons are unnamed); six of the seven he did publish are in the third person and—excepting the three that appeared in 1944 and conclude the book—are conspicuously flatter. All are told from the perspective of a boy or a man, almost always linked through geographical and situational connections to Ellison. The exceptions are remarkable tours de force.

"A Party Down at the Square" vividly depicts a lynching and burning from the perspective of a visiting white boy whose body rejects the horrific episode ("the gutless wonder from Cincinnati," his uncle calls him), but whose mind works hard to accept it, finally coming to rest in a kind of hapless if Hemingwayesque admiration: "God, but that nigger was tough. That Bacote nigger was some nigger!" Ellison puts in the boy's mouth a few didactic asides in a futile attempt to explain or understand the inexplicable. But this is an important work, commanding a forbidden ringside view of barbarians at play, rivaled only by the best of Erskine Caldwell, especially his novel *Trouble in July* and a few of his short stories. Ellison's tale is also fascinating in the ways it augurs his novel. The frenzied confusion that ensues when a pilot, disconcerted by the fire, crashes his plane in the square is a foretaste of the meticulous episodes of disarrangement in *Invisible Man*, from the battle royale to the Harlem riot. No less predictive is the blank-slate narration, recalling the Invisible Man's early and equally unformed recollections. Obtuseness is a human condition, not a racial one.

The nattering violence in "King of the Bingo Game" occurs almost entirely in the head of the protagonist, a southern black man in Harlem, whom the Oklahoma-born Ellison takes pains to distinguish from fellow Southwesterners at the center of the other stories. This story is marked by a brief memory interlude as seamlessly inserted as that in a Mizoguchi film, and sneaks up on the reader like a cop with a blackjack. Overwrought and hysterical in its narrow focus on a man electrified by the machinations of a bingo wheel, it closes with the promise of fate affirmed, even as it borrows Hemingway's device of disguising one fixation with another.

Hemingway's influence is rife in early Ellison, and so, in the fastidious overlay of symbols, is T. S. Eliot's. Echoes of writers Ellison admired occasionally intrude with unmistakable clarity: Hemingway ("the swift rush of water in the irrigation canals and the fish panting in the mud where the canals were dry and rotting in the sun where the mud had dried"), Eudora Welty ("the horns were blasting brighter now . . . like somebody flipping bright handfuls of new small change against the sky"), and William Faulkner ("his whole life was determined by the bingo wheel; not only that which would happen now that he was at last before it, but all that had gone before, since his birth and his mother's birth and the birth of his father"). At times Ellison tests his technique like a pilot taking out a new plane—trying out a Faulkner-type flashback (and Hemingway-type dialogue) in "A Hard Time Keeping Up" or a "Snows of Kilimanjaro" flashback in "Flying Home." Other times you can track the transition from influence to assimilation—compare the Faulknerian repetition of "vomit" in "King of the Bingo Game" and the Ellisonian repetition of "humiliation" in "Flying Home."

Ellison's voice ultimately prevails, from personal metaphor ("they seem to feel just the place to kick you to make your backbone feel like it's going to fold up like the old cellophane drinking cups we used when we were kids") to ebullient non sequitur ("When we jam, sir, we're Jamocrats!"), to more specific indicators of what was soon to come: minute descriptions rendered with cool detachment, gently pointed satire, expressionistic waking scenes, a naked woman dancing, the surreality of a boy attempting to snatch a plane from the sky, a humanizing grandfather, the kind of emotional violence that substitutes a chimera for reality, and, perhaps most distinctive of all, the combination of terror and revelation that resolves itself in uncontrollable laughter.

The memoir-essay "An Extravagance of Laughter" concludes with a long-delayed punch line of Ellison erupting in ill-suited and unruly laughter during a performance of *Tobacco Road*, an outburst he associates with "my emotional and intellectual development." The first incident recounted by Invisible Man shows how violence was deflected when his own outrage turned to laughter. In Ellison, laughter is rarely unforced or natural, and nowhere is its violent yet emancipating power more warranted than in the story "Flying Home" ("blasts of hot, hysterical laughter tore from his chest, causing his eyes to pop"). A Tuskegee airman (named Todd, another precursor) is brought to earth by a buzzard in hellish Alabama and is caught between the possibility of a casual redneck murder in the person of a plantation owner, who assumes murder is his birthright, and the shame of abiding black acquiescence, in the person of a grandfather who is sharper than the airman initially wants to admit. It is a fearsome story, edgily confined to the wounded pilot's vision, and Ellison's conclusion is surprising, unsentimental, and moving.

Less successful are the Buster and Riley stories, a sequence of four pastoral dialogues that take place over a period of about two years; they are filled with word games and play acting, but are undermined in their banter by touches of vaudeville and authorial intrusions that hint none too subtly at what we ought to make of what we are invited to overhear. Yet they capture the value of imagination in quelling the insecurities of childhood. One of them, "Then I Had the Wings," tells of an incident Ellison related from his own past about the time he tied parachutes to chickens. In an interview with John Hersey in 1974, he was quick to point out that none of the chickens died; in the story, one bites the dust. In "A Couple of Scalped Indians," a sexual initiation story published four years after *Invisible Man*, Riley is an unnamed first-person narrator, in the manner of the novel.

Two slight but sharply told anecdotes about riding the rails address the narrators' suspicion regarding kindnesses proffered by whites, a theme given full-dress treatment in "In a Strange Country," the account of a serviceman in Wales, brutalized by racists in his own division but brought to communal harmony by the patriotic singing of his Welsh hosts. Music is too much the essence of life in Ellison ("a gut language") to serve merely symbolic ends, but rarely is he as ingenuous as here, bringing the dislocated American back from a reverie of forgetfulness ("I can remember no song of ours that's of love of the soil or of country") to a restored sense of identity when the Welsh band honors him by striking up "The Star Spangled Banner." It is usually Ellison's stubborn Americanism that his critics find so galling—they miss the piercing anger that gives it meaning.

A note of caution: In a long introduction that would have served the volume better as an afterword, Callahan writes, "Ellison's readers must earn the right to be interpreters." You may lose that right if you read Callahan's extended summaries and exegetical comments before encountering the stories.

[*New York Times Book Review*, 19 January 1997]

73 ❖ *Doin That Waitin*
(Albert French)

In the quarter century since *Gravity's Rainbow*, American novelists (along with homage-obsessed American musicians, choreographers, and theatrical producers) have increasingly fixed their boldest inventions in the past, usually their own early years or a time long before they were born—in contradistinction to postwar writers who vigorously peeled away World War II and the social fabric of the 1950s. Last year alone, Philip Roth returned to the '60s, Don DeLillo to the '50s, Thomas Pynchon to the 18th century, and Norman Mailer to Jesus Christ. Nowhere is the turnaround from troubled present to mythic past more manifest than in the work of black writers. We can scarcely imagine Richard Wright, Chester Himes, Ralph Ellison, or James Baldwin looking backward; we can scarcely imagine Albert Murray, Charles Johnson, or Walter Mosley—not to mention the Toni Morrison of *Beloved* and *Jazz*—doing much else.

Whether the past is elegiac, as in Murray, or horrific, as in Morrison, it creates a trusty platform from which we begin to put two and two together in adducing the present. In the work of Albert French, one of the more distinctive voices of the '90s, the past has the irremediable tragedy of folk songs, violent old ballads sung so often that we discern where the singer is taking us but gasp nonetheless at the outcome. Five years ago, he published his astonishing first novel, *Billy*, a vividly shocking tale of injustice in the South of the 1930s, crowded with fully realized characters and appalling images, particularly that of a 10-year-old black boy strapped into an electric chair, his legs too short to bend at the knees. French created a vanished community in such claustrophobic detail that it morphs into the geography of a universal past. (Anyone who thought the story's brutality was circumscribed by racism or unique to '30s Mississippi got a wake-up call last spring, when gun lobbyists advocated executing the 11- and 13-year-old white assailants in the Jonesboro shootings.) Yet what makes *Billy* an uncanny experience is in large part the breakneck pace, fueled by a folk-like diction that objectifies events even as it invades the hearts and minds of its characters, protagonists and walk-ons alike. Nothing is allowed to hamper the narrative's expeditious tempo.

In *Holly* (1995), French's story of a hopeless interracial romance, the setting is North Carolina in 1945, told from the perspective of a young white woman; the vernacular cadences and yarn-spinning urgency are muted and the story flaccid, but again French persuasively illuminates a faraway time and place. Last year he published his stinging memoir of the Vietnam War, *Patches of Fire*, his least stylized book (the only one in which gerunds have their *g*'s intact), yet built for speed—much dialogue, few adjectives.

With his third novel, *I Can't Wait on God*, the searing vision of *Billy* is all but blinkered in mannerisms. French is back in the more distant past of 1950 Pittsburgh and Wilmington, North Carolina, the eve of the Korean War. This part of Pittsburgh is a spirit-killing back-alley community where the preacher survives by cleaning office buildings on the midnight shift and the larger world is mere rumor carried in the whistling of trains. In French's fiction, community embodies a harsh provincialism, segregated in the fullest meaning of the word, and war is an unpromising way of escape—a vital memory of the last war is of two men who left training camp and were lynched.

Escape is the primary concern of *I Can't Wait on God*, and French focuses on parallel flights, cutting from one to the other. For Willet Mercer and Jeremiah Henderson, the goal is New York, and the means is the money they take off a pimp she has impulsively murdered. Willet, who animates just about all the action in the story, insists they drive to Wilmington to see the son she abandoned at birth. They are living on borrowed time and know it. For Mack Jack, a talented musician who retreated from the big city after a bandleader stole his music, the goal is to recover his inspiration and the means are drugs that will keep him spinning his wheels without tracking ground.

But French is intent on painting a far more comprehensive canvas, from which the principals emerge almost incidentally, as if he could as easily have chosen other characters and followed them, told their stories. His novel is populated with dozens of individuals, each named and invested with a thumbnail history; no one is permitted anonymity—not a gas jockey or a nosy prostitute or women on their porches or a turtle named Toby. This presents a problem, encouraging French to opt for an over-mannered style that takes vernacular omniscience to the edge of unintentional burlesque. Every object and action is modified by a "that" or "them," suggesting an alienation so extreme as to imply feebleness rather than dislocation. Everything is strangely new—children, the sun, ice cubes in a glass "makin them little clangin sounds." The narrative is laden with affectation. It begins in the past tense but almost imperceptibly shifts to the present, where it remains bogged down in numberless thats and thems: "He did that lookin up the road and that hopin he could drive up it soon. But he's sittin back in that cookin room now, doin that waitin."

More debilitating is the ennui of the protagonists, who are less dynamically drawn than some of the cameos. Jeremiah and Mack Jack spend most of their time staring, never saying anything, and we don't get to know or care much about them. Everyone jabbers at Mack Jack, wanting something from him—rent money, sex, music, companionship —but nobody seems to notice that he is not responding. An attempt to explain Willet, interpolated at the end, is unconvincing. Yet, in spite of itself, *I Can't Wait on God* has some of the wit, compassion, and acute observation we expect from Albert French, as well as a modicum of suspense; the walk Willet takes to her mother's house and the fears generated about the fate of her son are melodramatic but effective, and the disquieting recovery of a lost time and place remains impressive. This time out, though, setting is the author's most credible invention and cannot compensate for the tactless mirth of misjudged writing.

[*New York Times Book Review*, 20 September 1998]

74 ❖ *Closed Minds (Saul Bellow)*

Several short stories have been expanded into novels, but *Ravelstein* may be the first novel expanded from a eulogy. Almost every incident, every sentence, Saul Bellow delivered in memory of Allan Bloom at his funeral service in 1992, and published two years later in his essay collection, *It All Adds Up*, reappears in his portrait of Abe Ravelstein, a Chicago academic who writes an unlikely philosophical best seller (unnamed) and succumbs to AIDS. Bellow's idea of discretion is to change not only the names of friends, but of machines, too; Bloom's beloved Mercedes is Ravelstein's beloved BMW. In his last months, Ravelstein prevails on his close and much older friend Chick (no last name) to write his biography. Did Bloom make such a request of Bellow? Does it matter?

Bellow begins so offhandedly, so autobiographically, that you have every reason to fear a roman bound by its clef; but he keeps pulling aces out of his sleeves and by the time you have made the trip—a characteristically time-warped journey that juts one way and then another, with more talk than anecdote—you know you have been had as only Bellow can have you. Might as well forget Bloom's detestable book, *The Closing of the American Mind* (my favorite bit: Louis Armstrong betrayed Weimar culture), because Ravelstein's controversial book is ignored, notwithstanding occasional references to relativism and obligatory puffery of the most general sort.

Chick says repeatedly—he says many things repeatedly—that he is ill-equipped to discuss philosophy, and besides, his friend Abe did not expect him to explicate his book, but rather to portray him as a character. "I am not interested in presenting his ideas. More than anything else, just now, I want to avoid them." Me too. At Chick's suggestion, Ravelstein had turned his lecture notes into a book and become a millionaire. At Ravelstein's suggestion, Chick had attempted a biography of Keynes, and Abe's favorite part was a Bellow-like description of Lloyd George's Jew-baiting. Chick prefers the physical, for example Macauley's *Britannica* entry on Dr. Johnson: "Thanks to him I still see poor convulsive Johnson touching every lamppost on the street and eating spoiled meat and rancid puddings." Thanks to Chick, Ravelstein will be remembered as a strutting dandy and self-described "invert," who collects Lalique crystal and Mont Blanc pens and purchases in Paris—this is the punch line to the wildly discursive opening section—a $4,500 Lanvin sports jacket on which he promptly spills coffee and takes umbrage when Chick advises he might want to have it cleaned.

At 85, the most philosophical novelist in American letters has written, inevitably, an inquiry into memory, friendship, and death, also obligation and longing. "In my trade you have to make more allowances," Chick observes, "taking all sorts of ambiguities into account—to avoid hard-edged judgments." *Ravelstein* is Bellow's knottiest fiction in a decade (length-wise, it splits the difference between *Seize the Day* and *The Victim*), raveling enough threads from his earlier novels to imply a valedictory. "We have to keep life going, one way or another. Marriages must be made. In adultery men and women hope for a brief reprieve from the lifelong pain of privation." "The best we can hope for in modernity is not love but a sexual attachment—a bourgeois solution, in bohemian dress." Still, this time, Bellow's agnostics bet firmly on an afterlife.

Ravelstein is one of those outsize Bellow heroes whom V. S. Pritchett once described as moral figures who play the clown, an attitude buoyantly conveyed by his delightful name. Bellow makes a point of inventing names that are ambiguously Jewish or, at the very least, slightly askew from those you might find in the phone book: Citrine, Tamkin, Corde, Kreiggstein, Wulpy, Velde, Wustrin, Fonstein, Trellman, and the incomparable Rinaldo Cantabile, the *Humboldt's Gift* mafioso (what TV music *The Cantabiles* might have made). Putting aside symbolic niceties concerning the raveling and unraveling of biography; the result held in Ravel's musical stein, that master of 11th chords denoting the 11th hour; not to mention France, et cetera ad ridiculum, "Ravelstein" passes the Dickensian test of sounding good, twinkling with wit. His character is less persuasive, because Chick tells more of his search for love, his humor, his brilliance, than he shows. Ravelstein, like Humboldt, gets the show on the road, but the tale's soul is Chick.

Yet Chick is a cipher. What precisely is his trade? We hear of his attempts at nonfiction, his essays on subjects Bellow has himself explored, but nothing of fiction or his stature and fame. He is Bellow in every detail but the accomplishment. For a writer of fact, Chick (or Bellow, there is no way to know which) is surprisingly trusting of memory; he conflates Macauley's essay on Johnson with the one Macauley wrote about Boswell's biography; guesses Remagen as the scene of a famous Second World War incident that happened at Bastogne; and, unforgivably, misquotes a Mel Brooks routine, cited as an example of Abe's love of Jewish vaudeville humor, though since the bit derives from a 1981 movie, it hardly seems the stuff of prodigious nostalgia. In each instance, I'd wager that the error is Bellow's and not one of those unreliable-narrator ploys. No matter, or, as Chick says, "Not to worry" (he also says "shan't," twice). His brain and not Ravelstein's poses the quandaries, and his strangely hallucinogenic near-fatal illness—the result of food poisoning in the tropics—powers the narrative, enabling him to fulfill his promise to write about Abe, despite a comical, intervening obsession with cannibalism, reminiscent of *Humboldt*, though here with the inevitable hint of biography as self-fattening.

In an especially affecting passage, Chick discusses *The Death of Ivan Ilyich* with his wife, Rosamund, and spells out his concern with seizing, literally, the day—slowing it down to the cadences realized by children. "If only we could bring back the full days we knew as kids. But we become too familiar with the data of experience. . . . Art is one rescue from this chaotic acceleration. Meter in poetry, tempo in music, form and color in painting." Unlike Ilyich, who did not began to ask the big ones until cancer claimed him, Chick is a veteran questioner. (He may even have read *The Magic Mountain*, where that same point is stressed.)

If Chick's pensees fill a vacuum created by his amusingly modest refusal to explore Abe's, his vivid autobiographical fragments upstage the man as well. The novel's most startling image is of Chick's imperious European scientist ex-wife, Vela (imagine Minna of *The Dean's December* turned into Countess Dracula), pushing her pubic hair into his face, then walking off—her way of announcing her intention to obtain a divorce. Perhaps she was thinking of the pickpocket in *Mr. Sammler's Planet*. Other characters are etched in wonderfully detailed grotesquerie, as is the city of Chicago, ornamented with a nest of parrots. It has been said countless times, but say it again: No one since Dreiser has the urban pulse in his blood like Bellow. So when Chick reprises Ravelstein in his closing pages, he is something of an anticlimax. True, Ravelstein helped slow the day with his concentration on clothing, luxury, music, his students' mating habits, the political secrets harbored by graduates. But it is difficult to share Chick's pleasure in him. Chick is the one you would want at a dinner party. He evokes what the legendary con man Yellow Kid Weill once told Saul Bellow, "My purpose was invisible. When they looked at me they saw themselves. I only showed them their own purpose."

[*Village Voice*, 25 April 2000]

75 ❖ *Laughing Man*
(Moss Hart)

At the time of his death, in 1961, Moss Hart was one of Broadway's benevolent mandarins—admired, industrious, well liked, and known far beyond Times Square, thanks to his movie scripts and television appearances; a well-known marriage to the singer, actress, arts advocate, and game-show panelist Kitty Carlisle; and a best-selling memoir. As a playwright, director, producer, and play-doctor, he had been indispensable to the theater for 31 years, a tireless collaborator who reliably helped to mint the only currency Broadway trusts: hits. A showman above all, he was regarded by many as a comic genius—or half of one in tandem with George S. Kaufman, another writer who required accomplices. In 1942, the Modern Library collected six of the nine plays they had written together, enshrining them in a series that also offered Wilde, Chekhov, and O'Neill.[1] More recently, in 1956, Hart had shepherded the most celebrated musical success of the postwar era, *My Fair Lady*, and his 1959 account of his first 26 years, *Act One*, had crowned the *New York Times* best-seller list for an astonishing 22 weeks. He was much mourned, and soon forgotten.

Directorial brilliance in the theater is evanescent, and Hart's plays, despite frequent and occasionally cogent revivals, have been undermined by the very influence they exerted on subsequent writers for the stage, film, radio, and television. The cultural landscape is so thick with wisecracking

---

[1] In 2004 the Library of America collected three of these plays in a volume built around George S. Kaufman, called *Kaufman & Co: Once in a Lifetime, You Can't Take It With You,* and *The Man Who Came to Dinner.* The rest of the volume consists of plays Kaufman wrote in collaboration with Edna Ferber (*The Royal Family, Dinner at Eight,* and *Stage Door*), Morrie Ryskind (*Animal Crackers* and *Of Thee I Sing*), and Ring Lardner (*June Moon*), inadvertently underscoring his singular affinity with Hart.

dames, foppish egoists, idiot savants, batty relatives, and city slickers among the rubes that we are more inclined to pay homage to Kaufman and Hart for popularizing—indeed, practically inventing—those and other stock characters than to revisit the prototypes. *You Can't Take It With You, The Man Who Came to Dinner*, and *George Washington Slept Here* have achieved a churning immortality in amateur theatricals, but they have aged and are aging still.

Act One, always in print, although reading it is no longer the rite of passage it once was, exercised an emotional hold on a generation of would-be writers. Here was the eternal theme, rife in the 1950s, of the alienated special child who escapes poverty and small-town (well, Bronx) provincialism in favor of the grander provincialism of the arts. As Hart described it, the theater was a surrogate family of loving eccentrics; playwriting was not a lonely vigil, beyond a few necessary all-nighters (at the beach), but, rather, collaboration with other writers, actors, directors, producers, friends, kibitzers, and even critics. Today, *Act One* seems overlong, a bit lofty, and evasive about details, but its fledgling epiphanies continue to echo:

> A week after I had written "The Curtain Slowly Falls," I went into the bathroom, locked the door, and settling myself with a pillow behind me in the empty bathtub, I opened the closely written pages. The play's awfulness did not dawn on me slowly—the full impact of its hackneyed dreariness hit me by the sixth page. I was hard put to finish it without getting out of the bathtub and flushing it down the toilet, and it was difficult by the second act for me to believe that I had written it at all.

Surprisingly, for 40 years no one accepted the implicit cue in Hart's title to second-guess his recollections and add to them Acts Two and Three. This lapse was perhaps an indication of his diminished stature, though it is difficult to think of anyone more ideal for grounding a history of Broadway's golden epoch. In *Dazzler: The Life and Times of Moss Hart*, Stephen Bach narrows his sights—a shame because, fixed on the man, he falls prey to the biographer's curse of personal disenchantment. Bach himself discovered Hart through *Act One*, which brought "color and glow" to his "dreary" student days. He concludes his book with a paean to that memoir and its ability to capture "the yearning that theater can inspire, the sense of refuge from an otherwise inhospitable world it can provide." But he now knows that Hart was a troubled man, a revelation that inspires sarcasm where compassion would suffice; he is shocked to learn that Hart was occasionally a credit hog and probably bisexual. Yet he has marshaled most of the facts, and when his story avoids the tone of petty irritation, it is fascinating.

Hart was born in 1904, to transplanted English Jews, and raised in what he described as "shabby gentility." His unusual name probably derives from dropping the "e" in Moses. His father, a cigar-maker, and his mother, who took in laundry, were meek, reticent, and distant. Any show of passion in their rattling apartment was triggered by Moss's grandfather, a garrulous tyrant, and Aunt Kate, who escaped cares and responsibilities by going to the theater, often taking Moss with her. In *Act One*, he describes her as a Blanche Du Bois, a frivolous eccentric dependent on the kindness of her relatives. Bach reveals that she grew dangerously mad, scrawling obscenities on walls and setting fires in theaters, and died many years after Hart said she did. But Hart had great affection for her, which Bach discounts, ominously suggesting, without explanation, that she "appropriated" Moss "in some unsettling way." In any event, Hart followed Aunt Kate into make-believe, and by the age of 19 he had sold a play about Oscar Wilde to a movie producer, who died before he could produce it.

Two years later, working as an office boy, Hart persuaded his boss, the second-string vaudeville producer Augustus Pitou, to mount a play he credited to a nonexistent friend. *The Hold-Up Man*, retitled *The Beloved Bandit*, toured the provinces but folded before reaching Broadway. Bach reports that Hart worked on it with Edward Eliscu (later famed for his song lyrics), though he did not acknowledge him then or, to Eliscu's dismay, in his memoir. For the next few years, Moss mastered various elements of stagecraft at summer resorts and with amateur groups, directing, writing, and acting in ambitious productions, from musicals to *The Emperor Jones*. He idolized O'Neill, Chekhov, Ibsen, and Shaw, but conceded to Eliscu that *Merton of the Movies*, by George Kaufman and Marc Connelly "was more in their line." Then, in 1929, inspired by articles in *Variety*, he wrote *Once in a Lifetime*, a three-act satire of the turmoil in Hollywood over talking pictures. Sam H. Harris agreed to produce it on the condition that Hart work on a revision with Kaufman, who dominated 1920s comedy to the degree that Eugene O'Neill dominated 1920s drama.

Beaumont and Fletcher notwithstanding, the theater has usually been ruled by solitary writers who can and occasionally do decree absolute obeisance to every word and stage direction. But collaborations proliferated on Broadway as it developed its vaudeville pedigree into more sophisticated fare, and Kaufman favored teamwork to the point of compulsion. His idea of starting a play was to invite another writer over to exchange ideas. By the time the 26-year-old Hart nervously telephoned him, Kaufman, then 40, had scored at least one hit every year between 1921 and 1929 (except for 1926, when he collaborated with Herman Mankiewicz), in association with Marc Connelly, Edna Ferber, Ring Lardner, and Morrie Ryskind. *The Butter and Egg Man*, which premiered in 1925, was the only success he would ever have on his own. In addition, he scored as a director, giving *The Front Page* its racehorse verve.

Broadway was in clover. As Bach notes, 26 theaters opened in New York between 1924 and 1929, bringing the total to 90, which housed "an *average* of 225 new productions a year for the decade." Working with Kaufman, Hart soon realized that collaboration was a three-way street and that the key decisions were dictated by the third entity, the audience. The struggle of nurturing *Once in a Lifetime* to its victorious opening is the centerpiece of *Act One;* some of that book's most memorable scenes describe Kaufman and the emulating Hart madly pacing behind the orchestra seats during out-of-town tryouts, concentrating less on their play than on the frequency, duration, and nature of laughs it sparked or failed to spark. The audience's silence told them their third act was no good. Kaufman despaired of getting it right and decided to quit, but Hart won his confidence and salvaged the play by suggesting that they discard an elaborate, costly nightclub scene and add a touch of romance.

Hart learned to monitor the responses of his customers as closely as a political candidate does a focus group. The Hollywood practice of reediting movies to satisfy preview audiences has been thoroughly derided, yet Broadway's submission to human laugh meters in New Haven or Washington, D.C., has saved and undoubtedly improved countless comedies and musicals. The wisdom gleaned from audiences was not, however, cumulative. Playwriting "is not only the most difficult of literary forms to master," Hart augustly wrote, "but it is a craft one never seems to truly learn anything about from one's past mistakes." One thing he had to relearn frequently over three decades was the peril of employing flamboyant sets and stage gimmicks that dwarf the drama and inhibit laughs.

Kaufman, for all his experience, bowed to Hart's appetite for teeming spectacle. They reached the peak of immoderation with the 1939 flag-waver, *The American Way*, which required 60 speaking roles and nearly 200 townspeople, immigrants, children, soldiers, sailors, and policeman, as well as a Community Novelty Band. The immense scale did not strengthen the play's pious liberalism, which was conveyed more effectively and to more people that year by Earl Robinson's radio cantata, *Ballad for Americans*. Kaufman and Hart had been on firmer ground working within the constraints of their 1936 Pulitzer Prize-winning play, *You*

Can't Take It with You, though its sole set and 19 actors managed to accommodate two families, IRS and FBI men, a black servant and her beau, a White Russian dance teacher, and a depraved actress, not to mention fireworks, ballet, and xylophone solos. Grandpa Vanderhof and his eccentric family, which avows hobbies at the expense of humdrum work and has the resources to indulge them, struck a chord with Depression audiences. Josephine Hull, who played Mrs. Sycamore, a happily muddled playwright and painter, eventually cornered the market in blithe eccentricity, taking on *Arsenic and Old Lace* and *Harvey*, neither of which seems imaginable without the Kaufman and Hart precedent.

They did not invent sentimental nonconformity: Al Jolson had flaunted it in the movie *Hallelujah, I'm a Bum*, in 1933, and Frank Capra, who went on to leach most of the charm out of *You Can't Take It with You*, had already visited *Lost Horizon*. But they imbued it with a defining warmth and structure. Bach convincingly argues that, as a rule, Hart was responsible for the warmth and Kaufman for the structure. Hart had a generosity of spirit that complemented Kaufman's acerbic wit, much as Kaufman's zeal for economy balanced Hart's extravagance. Neither was particularly good at portraying women. "Tenderness and sentimentality weren't in Kaufman's inventory," Bach notes, "and frank sexual attraction wasn't in Moss's." Yet the two men, possibly inspired by Kaufman's friendship with Dorothy Parker or by Hart's recollections of Aunt Kate, gave birth to a type made emblematic by Eve Arden, whose voice one hears as early as *Once in a Lifetime*, when the caustic May, a lone beacon of sanity played by Jean Dixon, is faulted for not having rehearsed the ingénue in a certain scene:

JERRY: May, what about the church steps? Susan says you didn't rehearse here.

MAY: Susan, I know your memory isn't very good, but I want you to think way back to—Oh, pretty near five minutes ago. We were sitting in your dressing room—remember?—and we rehearsed that scene?

SUSAN: But that isn't the scene he means.

MAY: Outside the church, is that right?

SUSAN: Outside the church—Oh, yes, we did *that*! You said the church steps.

MAY: Susan—we feel that it's time you were told this. Outside the church and the church steps are really the same scene.

SUSAN: Are they?

MAY: Yes. In practically all churches now they put the steps on the outside.

In Kaufman and Hart's second play, *Merrily We Roll Along* (1934), the pungent May morphed into Julia, a once idealistic writer who becomes, in her own words, a drunk and a whore. But in *You Can't Take it with You* a word-association game Mrs. Sycamore imposes on the Kirbys, a puffed-up businessman and his wife, provides one of the funniest scenes in the play, and one of the few sympathetic insights into women in a body of work that aches with misogyny. Hart, who was addicted to psychiatry, almost certainly thought it up. Asked for one-word responses to "lust" and "sex," Mrs. Kirby says "human" (her husband says "unlawful") and "Wall Street" (her husband says "male"). More typical is the brief appearance of Gay Wellington, who is described in the stage directions as "an actress, a nymphomaniac, and a terrible souse." One suspects that Kaufman provided the few political jibes, notably Kirby's accusation that Grandpa's live-and-let-live philosophy is "un-American" and "downright Communistic."

Bach chides Hart for writing "dismayingly little that expressed any political viewpoint more profound or nuanced than Tin Pan Alley or Hallmark." He makes occasional cracks about Hart's failure to measure up to O'Neill and the rest of his early idols, which is a bit like attacking a chocolate soufflé for not being Chateaubriand. Yet Hart and Kaufman also worried, briefly, about whether comedy fully tested their mettle, and they dithered with certain candor on the subject in the perennially futile, flawed, difficult to produce (it calls for a cast of 95), and frequently riveting *Merrily We Roll Along*. This is the play that begins at an opening-night party with the playwright's star and lover being blinded by his wife, who was formerly his star and lover, a circumstance that had driven her first husband to suicide, as we learn in a progression of scenes that recede chronologically to show how the principals sacrificed their principles for fame and fortune. Best known for its time-reversal device, employed more effectively by Harold Pinter in *Betrayal* (1978), *Merrily We Roll Along* might have played more cogently in straight time, kicking off with a callow invocation of Polonius at a college graduation and ending with the stunning violence of the party.

Even so, the play is impossible. The antihero Richard Niles is berated for writing plays about which his most damning critic gripes, "I liked it. I laughed. And by the time I got to Broadway and Forty-fifth Street I'd forgotten all about it." Kaufman and Hart portray Niles as grasping, deceitful, and corrupt, yet go to great lengths to justify him, ultimately shifting the blame for his descent into prosperity to the loathsome women in his life. Still, the hand-wringing has an autobiographical bite. Amid much name-dropping and several thinly disguised portraits, they include a colloquy that barely disguises themselves:

RICHARD: Thank you, David. You'll have your own hits pretty soon.
DAVID: I hope so. But I'm never going to forget what I owe to Richard
Niles. I'd have given up after the first one if it hadn't been for you.
RICHARD: The first failure doesn't mean anything. You've got stuff.
Just go right ahead and don't listen to anybody. Not even me.
DAVID: Well, on *my* fortieth birthday, if I'm where you are, I'm going
to be a pretty happy man.

At 40, Hart was at least as far along in his career as Kaufman had been
in his when they first met, though according to Bach he was happy only
on the up-curve of a manic-depressive cycle. Hart was in thrall to his ther-
apists, whom Bach portrays as fame-seeking quacks. He writes that
"once or twice a day" Hart saw Dr. Lawrence Kubie, who believed in "cur-
ing" homosexuals. Kitty Carlisle, who declined to speak with Bach, has
told of asking Dr. Kubie for sedatives to counter Hart's insomnia and being
refused because pills would "mask his symptoms." In 1941, working with
composer Kurt Weill and lyricist Ira Gershwin, Hart brought analysis to
the stage for the first time, in the charmingly dated musical *Lady in the
Dark*, which made a star of Danny Kaye (Hart later wrote one of Kaye's
most successful movies, *Hans Christian Andersen*), whose electric scene-
stealing inspired the difficult and competitive Gertrude Lawrence to
outdo him and herself as she sashayed through "The Saga of Jenny." *Lady
in the Dark* remains one of only a handful of classic American musicals
not adapted from history or works in other idioms. In addition to the
uncanny standard, "My Ship," the comic novelty "Tschaikowsky" (Kaye
raced through the names of 49 Russian composers in well under a
minute), and an analytical cure by the final curtain, it offers an unmistakably modern structure, beginning without an overture, in a psychiatrist's office, and unfolding through four spectral dream sequences.

Hart went on to direct the light comedies *Junior Miss* and *Dear Ruth*
(a substantial wartime hit), and to write and direct the patriotic 1943
Air Force pageant, *Winged Victory*. Three years had passed since he last
worked with Kaufman; the collaboration was over. Bach writes, "Their
separation seemed to many on Broadway to spell the end of the era," which
is unlikely, as they had never arrived at a formal break. Kaufman went
on to work with Edna Ferber and Howard Teichmann, among others, yet
his great days were past, and so, at least as a playwright, were Hart's.
He wrote a few prominent movies—*Gentleman's Agreement* and the Judy
Garland remake of *A Star Is Born*—and took a fleeting turn on TV (an
episode Bach omits), emceeing a Sunday-evening quiz show, *Answer
Yes or No*, in 1950, and preparing a telecast that same year of *You Can't
Take It with You*, to inaugurate the *Pulitzer Prize Playhouse*. By then, he

had married Kitty Carlisle and they had two children. Meanwhile, his plays wrestled with the dilemma outlined in *Merrily We Roll Along* as he attempted to reconcile art with commerce, invariably compromising both. Only his backstage comedy, *Light Up the Sky* (1948), has enjoyed significant revivals.

In 1954, Hart suffered a heart attack, but bounced back as the initially reluctant director of Lerner and Loewe's musical version of *Pygmalion*, a project that Oscar Hammerstein had confidently told Alan Jay Lerner could not be done. The story of *My Fair Lady* and its far less exalted follow-up, *Camelot*, brings Bach to life as well. With Hart offstage for much of the tale, he puts aside the huffy tone ("He puffed on the pipe he had lately taken up, so much more writerly than a cigar"), the forced witticisms (a Hollywood populated with Broadway types is "Sardi's with bougainvillea"), the disparaging asides (Hart "dug himself into a foxhole in Bucks County"), and the puns ("This Hart's beat was Broadway"), to vividly recount the battle-scarred road from Mrs. Patrick Campbell's Eliza in 1914 to Julie Andrews's unexpected 1956 triumph, abetted by a private workout with Hart in the face of Rex Harrison's withering, foul-mouthed contempt. Hart saved more than Andrews's career; he forced Lerner to do numerous rewrites and recapitulated the lesson of his first hit, *Once in a Lifetime*, by removing a pointlessly spectacular sequence while underscoring romance and cutting 20 minutes.

Hart alone prevented the early close of *Camelot*, a disaster that was suffering "as many as two or three hundred walkouts in the course of a single performance." Illness had sidelined him before opening night, which Lerner insisted on directing, causing a permanent rent in his association with Frederick Loewe. Hart recovered from his sickbed and realized that they had one chance. *The Ed Sullivan Show* was preparing a tribute to Lerner and Loewe, including excerpts from *Camelot*. He rigorously rehearsed the cast for a week in preparation, and cut the running time of the production so that the horde of ticket buyers stimulated by Sullivan would see a far more trimly structured show than the critics had seen. It was a gallant display of editorial ruthlessness, and it confirmed his touch as a theatrical fix-it man who did not give up. Three months after Sullivan's March broadcast, Kaufman died at the age of 71. On December 20, Hart followed, dead of a third heart attack, at 57. Their work, Bach writes, is "honored by every television situation comedy that derives from it." But the 1983 revival of *You Can't Take It with You*, which Jason Robards and Colleen Dewhurst played with familial warmth rather than firecracker jokiness, suggested a worthier legacy. One way to honor Hart on his centenary, a few years down the road, would be to remount *Lady in the Dark*, with its shimmering score, magical dream sequences, and an

approach to analysis so quaint it seems eerily beyond time. The best of
Moss Hart may now be so old it's new.

[*The New Yorker*, 21 May 2001]

76 ❖ *He's Got No Kick Against*
Modern Jazz
(Robert Christgau)

The *Village Voice* had been publishing my jazz reviews for 18 months when
news came of a takeover, followed by meetings of grim determination
that could do nothing to halt the arrival of a new boss. Diane Fisher, the
music editor, had told me when we first met—with unmistakable asper-
ity—that I would have to pay *Voice* dues to earn the column I coveted.
Now, in the fall of 1974, she assured me that I had paid those dues and
could have my column were she allowed to continue in her job. She was
gone within days, replaced by Robert Christgau, and I fully anticipated
the boot. All I knew about the new editor was a "Secular Music" column
that ran in *Esquire* shortly before commencement of my junior year at college: in part, a trouncing of Miles Davis and Bill Evans. He called right
away and said he was killing several music columns then in place—beat,
beat—but wanted me to write one. He suggested we meet at an espresso
place near his apartment.

Espresso Bob.

Defensive and wary, I did not expect to like him, but Bob's gift for being
charming and intimidating at the same time proved irresistible. Still, I
crankily brought up the 1968 *Esquire* piece, which he conceded may have
been a little off (like his claiming Miles's music had not changed in the
past several years), while insisting it had lots of good stuff—he was right
on both counts. Undaunted, I then noted, with jazz missionary hauteur,
that rock and roll was for kids and not very smart. After patiently explaining the difference between rock and rock and roll, he said that that
could not possibly be true because he liked it and he was very smart.
I looked at him and thought, "Jesusfuckingchrist, he *is* very smart and
I don't know what the hell I'm talking about." Thus was I reborn. They
don't call him Christgau for nothing.

Twenty-eight years later, Bob was still my editor and had been for most
of the intervening period. When people asked me, as they sometimes did,

why I stayed at the *Voice*, my standard answer was (a) No one else has offered me a steady job, and (b) the *Voice* offers me the perquisite of being edited by Bob, the best line-editor I have ever known—although I've worked with several great ones (as well as several certifiable morons). Any good editor will help you clean up a slipshod sentence, untangle a mixed metaphor, point to questionable taste, and offer various other kinds of basic aid. Bob does all that and also offers solutions of stunning finesse. This talent partly reflects a personal generosity and unwavering, nearly scientific devotion to the art of sentence making. Chiefly, however, it manifests the fact that, unlike most editors, he is chiefly—duh—a writer.

Bob once pointed out to me a favorite sentence of his. I'm almost sure Sir Thomas Browne wrote it, but all I recall of the passage is that it began with orotund refinement and ended with the phrase, "piss on't." That mixture of the high-flown and vernacular is one of the most remarkable aspects of Bob's style, perfectly mirroring his terrific authority—the voice not only of a learned critic, but also of an appallingly poised writer who knows who he is, what he is about, and how the infinite options of style can best be employed. His command is apparent not least in his uncommon ability to be casually autobiographical. It is most evident in the way he conjoins a logician's clarity and streetcorner jive without seeming silly, pretentious, or secondhand. Try and find a cliché in his writing. Please try.

After 30-plus years of Consumer Guides, Christgau can pack a sentence like a steamer trunk; indeed, there are times I wish he would unpack a little. Given my ignorance of most rock, hip-hop, and other domestic and world products that come under his scrutiny, much of his writing is over my head. Yet every so often he writes about someone I love—Armstrong, Monk, Ellington, Dee Dee Bridgewater—and I'm invariably astonished as he hits bulls-eye after bulls-eye, getting to the core of a record with a handful of words and insights only he has. Sometimes, thanks to a spate of reissues, I'll explore an artist I had ignored—Stevie Wonder, Fela, Neil Young, Al Green—and after listening to half a dozen albums, look them up in the Guides and wonder anew at how he can encapsulate the general character of a work while homing in on specifics. More than 20 years ago, I remarked that his essay on the Clash would outlive the Clash, because I was certain that anyone who wanted to understand the late-1970s would have to read Bob's piece regardless of what one might think of the band. Rereading it in *Grown Up All Wrong*, I do not think I was mistaken.

Once, he asked me to edit a piece he wrote about Miles Davis. Reversing roles, he came to my place and sat on the sofa, earphones in place, while I tried to pretend he wasn't there and read the essay. I pointed out a couple of factual issues, which he happily revised, noting that this proved I was the right person to edit the piece. But all I could offer writing-wise was the suggestion that he change a semi into an em-dash or vice versa—a suggestion he accepted, to my great relief, as it made me feel not entirely unproductive. The next day I ran into Bob's regular editor and asked if his copy was always that clean. "Pretty much," he said. Damn, I thought.

As an editor, he cuts to the chase quickly and precisely. In the early years, we often ended up killing the first paragraph—the one I worked the hardest on and which frequently amounted to an overwritten tune-up. Before Bob began editing me, I had published about 200 pieces: film reviews in a Hollywood trade that were never edited, jazz magazine pieces that were edited mostly for space, liner notes that were never edited, and *Voice* riffs that were never edited. All that never-edited business convinced me I could write. So the first sessions with Bob, which took hours and ended with nearly every sentence rejiggered, gave me palpitations that soon gave way to the intoxication of learning a craft.

Voice music writers occasionally congregated informally at Bradley's, near the old 11th Street office, and Bob frequently came up in conversation. Disgruntled freelancers would complain that he tried to force them to say what he wanted, politically and musically. Not true. He tried to get you to make your argument clear and convincing, even if he thought it was rot. The longer we worked together the more rot I was able to publish. Eventually it became evident that on most important matters of aesthetics we pretty much agreed. But whether we did or not, our mutual respect had turned into a safety net and encouraged me to take risks, knowing full well he would catch me if I tried one somersault too many—or too few. He has a particular knack for approving a witticism and then helping to sharpen it. "This could be funnier," I've heard him say many times.

Reading my old columns recently in the course of collecting them for this book, I was reminded of a recording I once heard of a showbiz roast from the 1930s, in honor of Jack Benny, who spoke last, complaining that all the good words had already been taken. He told the crowd that should he happen to say something funny, he hoped that everyone wouldn't turn to the table where his writers sat and nod their heads knowingly. Perusing columns from 10 or 12 years ago, I recognize idioms, words, and conceits that evolved in the editing process—which is a long-winded way of saying that Bob offered more than the occasional turn-of-phrase. I have an image of readers sagely murmuring, "Christgau, yes, undoubtedly." So in the spirit of Enoch Soames, I want to be very clear about this now, to forestall any future archivist from promulgating the idea that I am nothing more than a pseudonym Bob invented to disguise his lifelong adoration of Art Tatum.

If I am reticent to talk about Bob as a friend, it's probably because I'm still a little intimidated by him—despite the countless discussions about diverse subjects and two-plus decades of editorial work (each session ending with a 10-minute headline and sub-head hunt); despite years observing his transformation from messy bohemian to king of his castle, exemplary family man, doting husband to wonderful Carola, and committed father to Nina, who, thank God, gives him the same guff the rest of us have to take from our children; despite evenings when our families got together to watch the Yankees; even despite warm reunions that follow periods when, because of my books or his, we haven't worked together and he tells me what a joy it is to work with me and I say back-atcha and leave—even now—feeling as though the prom queen had batted her lashes at me. Part of what I find daunting about him is the Dorian Gray thing (never mind that Dorian was Evil and Bob is Good): When will he begin to look and act his age? When will he grow up? Part of it is a dread of sentiment, and on that score let me tell you about the edit after September 11. I was especially nervous about that column, combining the events of the day with a consideration of singers. The edit was solid, even uplifting, and I thanked him, as I almost always do. The following week when the paper came out, I apprehensively read my piece in print and marveled at how, after one quick reading, he had known precisely where to turn the screws. So during our next edit, I said so. Bob said, "I remember you thanked me at the time and I was pleased. Don't overdo it." I haven't.

[*Don't Stop 'til You Get Enough: Essays in Honor of Robert Christgau*,
edited by Tom Carson, Kit Rachlis and Jeff Salamon,
Nortex Press, 2002]

77 ❖ *Mr. Ellington, Meet Mr. Matisse (Alfred Appel Jr.)*

The logroll is a two-step worth avoiding. It's OK to lead, but to follow is to invite public ridicule. As it is considered highly moral not to return the favor of a kind review, I have happily waved morality's flag to dodge the works of betters, rivals, and dolts alike. Last year, however, I champed at the bit when Alfred Appel Jr.'s eagerly anticipated *Jazz*

Modernism appeared, refraining even from mentioning it in my year-end wrap-up, though few who aren't related by blood were likely to know that in 1998 Appel gave a book of mine a kinder review than I'd have given it myself. I was so certain that his provocateuring originality would rouse the jazz press to impassioned debate that it seemed pointless to weigh in. The ensuing silence has been deafening. Worse, a couple of critics I expected to at least understand it, responded as if personally affronted.

So what do you have to do to get attention for a major work on jazz and culture? It helps to join the union. If Appel has an audience in mind beyond the general public (he prefers puns and anecdotes to lit'ry jargon every time), it is the academic world where he spent most of his life (he's professor emeritus of English at Northwestern University and the author of *The Annotated Lolita*), not "the insular, marginalized province of enthusiastic fans alone." His subversive intent is to sneak Louis Armstrong, Duke Ellington, Fats Waller, Benny Goodman, Billie Holiday, Jack Teagarden, Charlie Parker, and Thelonious Monk into the academic great-art canon. This doesn't sit well with jazz critics who prefer insularity. Nor does Appel's style: a contagious, orgasmic rush of mollybloomery that had me scrawling "no, no" as well as "yes, yes" in many a margin.

Historically, jazz criticism has shied away from lyrics, often patronizing them as necessary sops to pop. So maybe it takes an English teacher to point out that on "Just a Gigolo," Armstrong transforms the title phrase into "just another jig I know"; or that in "Star Dust," only Armstrong ("a daring liberty and act of intelligence") effaces the pompous closing line ("what exactly is 'love's refrain?'" Appel asks); or that Armstrong obliterates the word "shine" with scat before reprising key phrases in a rhythmic assault that reminds Appel of "grotesquely sprung eyeballs in some of Picasso's preliminary drawings for *Guernica* [1937]," as well as "flying body parts and vectors" in Tex Avery cartoons and *The Nightmare of the White Elephant* in Matisse's *Jazz*, all of which amounts to a typical stroll through Appel's open museum.

As lyrics are wed to music, Appel's record collection finds a stunning correlative (subjective, I think) in 127 illustrations taken mostly from Matisse, Mondrian, Miro, Calder, Picasso, Brancusi, album covers, phonography, baseball, and jazz photography. In his nonstop, garrulous, not-quite-stream-of-consciousness flow (the prose is controlled and well-timed; trapdoors noted on one page are sprung several pages later when you've forgotten to watch out for them), jazz interacts with visual and literary arts on so many levels that the music begins to echo from the paintings, all of modernism soaring in the same orbit—though I can think of no book that made me more impatient to get back to the music itself. The assumption that a jazz outsider must be a dilettante is laid to rest early, with diverse observations and two of the best jazz anecdotes I've ever read (I'll get to them), and completely buried in chapter two, which may be the shrewdest analysis of Waller's "way of making light of weight-lessness" ever written.

The jazz anecdotes alone should have had the jazz world chattering. Were Parker and Stravinsky ever in the same room? According to Appel, they were, and he provides details. Better still is the blow-by-blow account of an evening when Buddy Rich went up against Sid Catlett, the former playing everything he knew at supersonic speed, only to be undone by Catlett, rolling the beat with one hand and lighting a cigarette with the other, at which point Rich yelled, "Sid, you motherfucker!" and kissed him. I hear complaints that Appel's artistic references are too far ranging for most readers, but I don't buy it. The pictures he cites are right there in the book; the records you already own or can buy; and if you've never read Hemingway or Joyce, he will make you want to read Hemingway and Joyce—and also Nabokov and Albert Murray, who, in a radical break with jazzcrit, is commended as a novelist for his "syncopated prose." Appel is at his best locating the reality behind the metaphorical flights of Eudora Welty's riff on seeing Waller one night, the much-anthologized story, "Powerhouse."

The central metaphor in *Jazz Modernism* is the ragpicker, the collagist who picks and chooses from the leavings of the 19th century, the tech-nological wonders of the 20th, and anything else lying about high or low, to remake the world—the essence of modernism that Appel sees not as Pound's and Eliot's forbidding footnotes and idiograms, but as an exu-berant burst of affirmative actions. Convinced that only accessible art counts at the highest levels, he disputes the postmodernist assumption that modernism is arch and arcane. He concedes a problem here with Joyce, but bats it away: Skip the brief "Proteus" and the heftier but dated "Oxen of the Sun" episodes, Appel recommends, and *Ulysses* opens up like a candy store. The teacher in him cannot resist a few helpful hints—and cross-references, of course, though not to Malory, Carlyle, or even (especially) Homer, but rather to Rex Stewart's "Menelik (the Lion of Judah)." Calling a fart a fart, he connects the notorious opening episode of the Stewart recording, which initially kept RCA from releasing it, to Bloom's hard-earned "Pprrpffrrppfff," and goes on to argue that Ellington's (Stewart was nominal leader of the session) putative tribute to Haile Salassie actually mocks "a colonial pawn, a toothless lion."

Appel may be wrong about that—Ellington probably wouldn't have said even if asked (the fact that he wasn't is germane to Appel's impa-tience with cultural segregation)—but his interpretation is a convincing example of the insightful uses to which he puts old-fashioned close reading. In contrast, jazzcrit, invested as it is in Intentionality and Authenticity, has always been skeptical about textual analysis. Appel can prove that Mondrian loved and understood boogie-woogie, but not that Waller had in mind Varese and Gershwin when he employed the "aleatory" sirens in "The Joint Is Jumpin'," and he concedes that Armstrong's closing "yes, yes" in the 1934 "Honeysuckle Rose" is only an "unintentional echo" of Molly Bloom. All he can do is juxtapose textual facts, which you may or may not see his way. The refreshing thing is that Waller and the rest are presumed to be titanic artists soaking up the world outside the jazz sanctum, every bit as much virtuoso ragpickers as academically accepted white artists of the same era. He gives no racial passes; the only noble savage in this book is Brancusi's "King of Kings."

Appel has interesting things to say about race, not least regarding a photograph of Waller trying to jitterbug with a smiling if firmly planted English woman on a transatlantic liner. He shows how color was subverted on album covers—Armstrong turned terra cotta, Bix and Trumbauer red and green, boogie-woogie hands rendered as one black and one white. And if it seems a stretch to note that the Victory Red lipstick advertised by Elizabeth Arden is the same as that painted on the Ellington caricature used for his wartime bandstands, well, you figure it out. Why is Ellington wearing lipstick anyway? Several startling passages concern Teagarden, so widely accepted as an honorary Negro that no one thought twice about his singing "Black and Blue." Armstrong integrated his band with Teagarden one month after the Dodgers signed Jackie Robinson (and a year before Parker hired Red Rodney), but how to explain Louis's publicly addressing Teagarden as Homes, Brother Jackson, Boy, and Daddy, something he did not do with "the bona fide blacks in the first, best edition of the All Stars."

Appel also traces the evolution of Armstrong's public sexuality. Making race records, he was rambunctiously sexual. Moving upward and outward into Tin Pan Alley acceptance, he focused on melancholy and submissive love songs, though he soon reinvested them erotically by punctuating phrases with the epithet "Mama," a code designed to suggest a black woman, which made it all right. Appel captures Armstrong's plight in his description of "I Can't Give You Anything but Love": He sings the words "breathlessly, as though he were walking up a hill or is on the brink of hyperventilation," and then erupts with stop-time ejaculations of word fragments—a "vertical column in space," in Appel's description, and "a thrilling moment in Armstrong's life and art, the genesis of his great international career."

There is plenty to disagree with. The jazz avant-garde does too offer humor and joy. Waller's first take of "I Can't Give You Anything but Love" is not mediocre, though I'm glad Appel forced me to dig out the arguably superior alternate version. Monk ultimately proved most accessible and lots of people can hum "Criss Cross" and "Evidence." Appel underestimates resources involved in the Hot Fives and Sevens when he says they don't employ the strategies of ragpicking. Nat Cole could be a damned erotic singer, and I won't get started on Bing Crosby. Appel's biggest misstep politically is to state more than once that territory he explores has never been tackled before—hell, his take on the Armstrong-Mills Brothers sessions is in the book of mine he reviewed. But he vastly extends the territory, pushing buttons and framing arguments in ways that deserve an imaginative response. How many works of jazz criticism have done that? How many practitioners of jazz criticism are ready to extend the dialogue?

[*Village Voice*, 14 May 2003]

78 ❖ *Fighting for Freedom and Bad Taste (Sammy Davis Jr.)*

Is it possible for an entertainer who achieved the pinnacles of success— wealth, fame, power, a critical and collegial regard verging on awe, at least during the long climb to the top—to be remembered primarily as a cultural martyr? In the case of Sammy Davis Jr., a qualified yes seems reasonable. Unlike Frank Sinatra, whose music will ultimately obliterate the man's boorish qualities, Davis has virtually disappeared from the cultural landscape while his immense, long-lived celebrity clouds the minds of those who endured it. To many of us born in the 1940s and 1950s, he had become a joke: a bejeweled, Nehru jacket-wearing, women-and-stimulants pursuing, faux-hipster caricature who cackled at racially stupid jokes that were designed to show how progressively good-natured the tellers and their victim-buddy were.

Yet Davis had once been renowned as a performer of spectacular gifts who could do everything. Sadly, "everything" usually proves to be the most evanescent of talents. His early appearances were virtuoso displays of dancing, singing, and mimicry that defied indifference; he would stop at nothing until he brought the entire audience into his fold. There were not many holdouts in the '50s, beyond the kind of bigots who barraged

Eddie Cantor with hate mail because he mopped Davis's brow after presenting him on the *Colgate Comedy Hour* in 1952. Sammy was the dazzling kid (actually 26 years old) in a troupe called the Will Mastin Trio featuring Sammy Davis Jr. The unbilled partner was his father, Sammy Davis Sr. Mastin, 72 when he made his national debut, was purported to be an uncle, though he was unrelated.

It was a strange, unforgettable act. The two older men, natty and understated, offered precision soft-shoe with some winging and spins thrown in, before stepping back to give the spotlight to the prodigal man-boy whose energy and autonomy made you wonder why the elders were there at all. Sammy had performed with them since the age of four—he had never attended school, never knew any other life, never bonded with his mother, who had once appeared in a Mastin revue. Now he was carrying his mentors.

Yet when he died in 1990, the man who had been so generous, so profligate with his talent was largely derided or ignored. Where had he gone wrong? Two biographies—one florid and contemptuous, the other dry and admiring—agree on most of the bad turns while inadvertently making the case that Davis cackled for our sins, breaking down more racial barriers than many of the more dignified black luminaries of the era. The cost was a legacy in shreds, and the posthumous mockery of writers like Wil Haygood, whose *In Black and White: The Life of Sammy Davis Jr.* is a singularly nasty piece of work.

Jack Benny once got a big laugh on radio when he asked Bing Crosby, who had complained that a country club didn't admit actors, "Bing, how would you like to be an actor and a Jew?" Davis got many laughs by describing himself as an actor who was a Jew and a Negro and one-eyed. He might have added two more equally damning handicaps: an exploited childhood and a brief interlude with Richard Nixon. The stolen childhood evidently contributed to his unslakable thirst for love and its material proofs. The Nixon hug unleashed another kind of bigotry—a feeling of betrayal on the part of blacks to whom he had long been suspect as a performer for infiltrating white citadels, from the Friars to the bedroom, and of impulsive superiority on the part of white liberals. (Like me. I wrote a snide review of Davis's 1975 talk show—collected in Gerald Early's *The Sammy Davis Jr. Reader*, alas; I don't retreat from the specifics, but I regret the supercilious attitude.) Of course, race was always the decisive factor, the other impediments merely second bananas, good for a nightclub guffaw. Davis's besetting sin was not extravagance, philandering, imbibing, or reckless optimism concerning a president. It was trying to live life as though color did not matter. He was a naïf savant.

In *Gonna Do Great Things: The Life of Sammy Davis, Jr.*, Gary Fishgall notes that "the relatively few African Americans who had become national celebrities" in the mid-20th century "spoke carefully and acted with rectitude, as if they were walking on egg shells," while Davis "went about his business as if he didn't care about breaking eggs or setting a good example for anyone. That was his choice." That last sentence is a good example of writing on eggshells, but the point is valid. Davis is not remembered for being outspoken in the '50s about race or anything else. Neither biography recounts Davis's criticism of Louis Armstrong for protesting Eisenhower's dithering in Little Rock. But then, who remembers Armstrong's political courage? Both men were later scorned as Uncle Toms, though they had overturned numerous color bars. One has to conclude that they were assailed not for what they did or did not say, but for who they were, for images that did not comport with changing attitudes in America's ceaseless struggle to be cool.

This was a constant problem for Davis, whose entire show business orientation flirted with traditions that had grown passé and were now considered offensive. Having spent his childhood on the road and in the backwaters of the Negro theatrical circuit, he loved old-time comedians like Pigmeat Markham, whose career he recharged, and Tim Moore, whose indelible characterization of the Kingfish was endlessly imitated. Bad enough that his film career disappeared with the waning of the film musical, but when tap dancing fell afoul of cultural umpires who recoiled at the memory of all those leaping-and-mugging teams on Ed Sullivan, Davis had to rethink his greatest gift—a dance tradition to which he had added a spontaneous panache, blending the hat-and-cane elegance of John Bubbles with the jazzy virtuosity of Baby Laurence.

Haygood (whose narrative is festooned with factual errors, mind-reading, and flamboyantly bad writing) finds Davis irresponsible and clueless about race. He punctuates passages with a Vonnegut-like tag phrase, "Ha ha ha," to signify Davis's jovial indifference. "Sammy was happy. He had broken nightclub records. It mattered little to him that he had to slip through backdoors and side doors as he was playing those first-class clubs." How could it not have mattered? One has only to open Davis's autobiography, *Yes I Can* (1965) to almost any page or read Davis's interviews to see how deeply it mattered. Haygood argues repeatedly that Davis wanted to be white; he quotes a Davis employee who says, "He thought he *was* white." He apparently did think that he could live his life as though he had the same rights as anyone else, which meant that he could emulate white entertainers as well as black ones, and pursue women of any color. Prince Spencer of the Four Step Brothers tells

Haygood that he saw "Sammy 'Uncle Tomming' with white people, and I resented it. The Step Brothers, well, we knew our place was not to be in while people's company." Which is a more courageous attitude, knowing one's place or refusing placement?

Color was an issue from the beginning, and Davis could not have escaped knowing where he stood in the spectrum. His maternal grandmother was of Cuban ancestry and disdained dark-skinned people, including her son-in-law and grandson. The Davis family was no less vain concerning their hues. He escaped the squabbling at the age of three, when his father took him on the road, sharing parental responsibilities with Mastin. Haygood says Sammy's career began a year later when he "ambled" on stage and got laughs. In Fishgall's account, he imitated performers at a rooming house rehearsal and one of the dancers ran to tell Sammy Sr. and Mastin, who, "laughing and applauding," promised Davis an onstage role, whereupon his father picked him up and introduced him to "the players he'd been traveling with but had never met."

Having few friends his own age and nothing like standard playtime, Davis found escape in movies and comic books. He received a modicum of backstage schooling, and like other child vaudevillians would remain self-conscious about his limited reading and writing abilities. As vaudeville withered, Mastin stubbornly held to the road, though he did land Sammy in two 1933 shorts, the comedy "Seasoned Greetings" and the Ethel Waters vehicle, "Rufus Jones for President," the only production in which she came up short in scene-stealing. Although the film is racked with racist caricature (parodying some of the images D. W. Griffith had once offered as history), eight-year-old Sammy's Rufus is vibrant, confident, irrepressible—what a partner he would have made for five-year-old Shirley Temple, soon to be high-stepping with Sammy's idol, Bill Robinson.

Nothing came of it except that Mastin now featured Little Sammy in his billing. Davis had to wait until 1951—after two decades on the road—for his breakthrough. Janis Paige was opening at Ciro's, a much-publicized event and a good bet to be seen by Hollywood's power elite. Mastin's agent landed the trio the opening slot, but Mastin balked: the offer was 50 dollars short. Fishgall quotes Mastin as saying, "No point taking a cut just to work a place." Haygood, who portrays Mastin as a manipulative paranoiac, says that "in the recesses of his mind" Mastin believed the club owner "was quite possibly conjuring up a way to steal Sammy." The deal was finally closed, but as Paige had the only dressing room, the trio was consigned to a corner of the attic. It was still the most elegant place they had ever worked. Fishgall writes that Davis refused to rehearse at the club, not wanting to reveal the force of his performance and frighten the star. After one mock rehearsal, the owner said, "I still don't know what you boys do. I'll tell you what. You open the show, make it fast and take only one bow." Paige's contract forbade them from taking more than two bows. In the event, they took eight. A stunned Paige had the sense to reverse the order of the show; on the second night, she opened for the trio.

Davis won over the crowd with his impersonation of some of the stars present. This was a double victory. Mastin had long ago warned him, "No colored performer ever did white people in front of white people." A hardened professional who had pounded the black show-business circuit since the turn of the century and would live to 100, Mastin is the most stimulating supporting figure in both books. Fishgall treats him as paternalistic, out of sync with the times, and the beneficiary of Davis's insistence on a three-way split that obtained until 1969. Haygood's unforgiving portrait depicts Mastin controlling Davis through an ironclad contract he wielded through 1965, which, if it existed at all, would have violated prohibitions against indentured servitude. As neither biographer is big on sourcing, the truth is impossible to ascertain.

The Cantor show followed. Soon Davis was a recording star ("Hey There"); Broadway star (*Mr. Wonderful*); movie star (a dapper, slithering Sportin' Life in *Porgy and Bess*); and Rat Pack insider with Frank and Dean, enduring a relentless stream of race jokes in case anyone did not notice his complexion, and containing his impulses so as not to upstage the alternately munificent and petulant Sinatra. To top it all, he became a best-selling memoirist with the fanciful but still affecting *Yes I Can*. All this while engaging the nation with personal drama: America shuddered when he lost an eye in a car accident, marveled when he adopted Judaism, and grimaced, applauded, or sent bomb threats when he married the Swedish actress May Britt. It was a measure of his stature that the marriage did not choke his career. Nor did it stifle his philandering.

He triumphed again on Broadway (*Golden Boy*), but his gift for doing everything found few outlets beyond road shows. Like Jerry Lewis, whose haircut he copied, he was too much on TV, pontificating or falling down laughing. Sometimes he affected a broad English accent in the manner of ballad singer Al Hibbler, as if that weighted his insights. He also kissed Archie Bunker in 1972, which, the two biographers agree, represented a big step for race relations.

And he embraced Nixon, a story with a tricky dimension worth exploring. As vice-president, Nixon had attended the trio's show at the Copa in 1954, introducing himself afterward and making a big impression on Davis. In 1960, Davis worked diligently with the Sinatra gang to elect Kennedy, who treated him abominably. Fishgall says that Davis was disinvited from the inauguration so as not to upset the Dixiecrats; Haygood recycles Richard Reeves's account of Kennedy demanding May Britt be hidden at an unpublicized meeting of Negro leaders before the photographers saw her. When nearly a decade later, Nixon asked for his support, Davis felt honored.

The reaction among blacks especially was devastating, and Davis was horrified and confused by it. In Haygood's account, Jesse Jackson requested a $25,000 contribution "for my charity" in return for repatriating Davis at a convention of Jackson's organization, Operation PUSH. It didn't work. Insistent as he was, Jackson could not quell the relentless booing as Davis stood silently. Fishgall, who says nothing of the bribe, quotes Davis's response: "Nothing in my life ever hurt me that much" —not even, he said, the accident that cost him his eye. Davis never completely recovered. He divorced, remarried, neglected his children, discovered pornography and drugs, and worked unremittingly, scoring a couple of hit records but never rekindling the old magic and stature.

Yet he lived long enough to see the world turned on its ear. In 1979, he danced with Kim Novak at a party and none of the photographers thought it worth shooting. In the 1950s, the mob and Columbia Pictures had promised to shoot him for good to prevent his being seen with her. If the tap-dance revival, jewelry decked hip-hop moguls, interracial marriage, integrated nightclub acts, and black Republicans are now too commonplace to merit comment, credit must be paid to Davis's childlike refusal to mind his place. They also serve who only play.

[*New York Times Book Review*, 28 December 2003]

79 ❖ *Pops and Pops* (Louis Armstrong & Paul Whiteman: Two Kings of Jazz)

In 1988, I wrote a short book about Louis Armstrong in which I attempted to underscore the disparity between his achievement and his lack of formal education by drawing a comparison with the ongoing who-wrote-Shakespeare debate. I imagined a scholar in the distant future arguing "that the man who virtually invented jazz and swing, who put blues improvisation and the vernacular voice on the map, could not have been an untutored black kid from Jane Alley. It must have been somebody trained in the subtleties of phrasing, intonation, and harmony." I was being facetious: I never expected that claim to emerge at any time, let alone in my lifetime.

Moral: Never underestimate righteous condescension in defense of the disheartened white race.

In *Louis Armstrong & Paul Whiteman: Two Kings of Jazz*, a title that invites and defies parody, Joshua Berrett explains away modernist elements in Armstrong's epochal Hot Five recordings by crediting them to his second wife and occasional pianist, Lil Hardin Armstrong—who was educated at Fisk University. In his previous compilation of writings by and about Armstrong (*The Louis Armstrong Companion*, 1999), Berrett had argued that Armstrong assimilated every kind of music circulating in turn-of-the-century New Orleans, from blues to opera. Now he speculates that the famous major seventh in Armstrong's "Struttin' with Some Barbecue" must have been his wife's work because it reminds him of a passage in Satie's *Trois Gymnopédies*—"a 'white' sound by a white European." He hears in the four-measure theme of Armstrong's "Skid-Dat-De-Dat" a reference to Mozart's "Jupiter," helpfully described as "one of the staples of the European symphonic canon." In full Francis Bacon-must-be-the-guy mode, he concludes: "Knowing the extent of Lil Hardin's studies of classical music, the connection with Mozart or Satie is highly plausible."

Plausibility has nothing to do with it. Welcome to a revival of the white man's burden, jazz-style. It gets restaged every few years: Armstrong as noble savage or self-hating Negro or (in some ways most perniciously) as merely one creative figure among the many that represent all races at the dawn of jazz. Berrett all but swoons in his haste to remind us that Armstrong admired and befriended many white musicians, including Paul Whiteman. Every time you think we have gotten past these feckless attempts to explain Armstrong by diminishing him, another brick flies through the window.

This time the argument has the imprimatur of Yale Press, though it leans on two customary if creaky motives—one dormant since the 1930s, the other dormant since the House Un-American Activities Committee. Berrett wants Armstrong and Whiteman to lead us into the old melting pot of musical history, where we can simmer together, confident that Satchmo, great as he was, played a role of no greater consequence than Whiteman, the dance band leader and prophet of symphonic jazz— the school of music he apotheosized with his 1924 debut of George Gershwin's "Rhapsody in Blue." That splendid piece of music was touted as an antidote to the messier precincts of jazz, where improvisation ruled. As late as 1956, the World Book Encyclopedia included as its entire definition of jazz: "See Gershwin, George." As a Whiteman admirer, I have no intention of debunking him. (Indeed, I celebrate his achievement in my biography of Whiteman's vocalist, Bing Crosby.) But if debunkers are sharpening their knives, Berrett's hyperbole supplies a whetstone.

He begins his argument with reference to Plato's "noble lie"—in this instance, the lie of "jazz history as an African-American narrative of appropriation and exploitation by whites." Berrett goes on to highlight every aspect of European classicism he can attribute to Armstrong and every aspect of improvisation he can attribute to Whiteman in an attempt to buoy the willful fiction that there is parity between them, that jazz is as much a consequence of educated whites as it is of, oh, naturally gifted blacks. It's old-fashioned cultural snobbery, not without elements of truth (though a better case can be made for the interaction in New Orleans between self-taught blacks and musically trained Creoles of Color), but overstated and then gingered with a political twist manifest in Berrett's second motive.

Why has the "noble lie" enjoyed such traction for the better part of a century? Why has Whiteman slipped from favor? You've probably guessed: The Communists did it. "Whiteman," Berrett writes, "was a casualty of a socialist agenda coupled with the heightened black consciousness emerging during and directly after World War II. And it was a political process which effectively denied or ignored much of what he had achieved to foster the careers of such African-American musicians as Don Redman, Earl Hines, William Grant Still, Duke Ellington, and others." This observation leads him to compose a potted history of the Russian Revolution, the Comintern of 1928, the "agitprop journalism" of the *Daily Worker*, and the Scottsboro Boys, which, he concedes was an appalling miscarriage of justice, except that it advanced "the radicalization of the masses," also a bad thing and apparently ruinous for jazz.

The villain of the piece is producer, critic, talent scout, and Vanderbilt heir John Hammond, best known as the man who discovered and/or recorded Billie Holiday, Count Basie, Charlie Christian, Aretha Franklin, Bob Dylan, Bruce Springsteen, and other notables. As a young man, Hammond covered the Scottsboro case for *The Nation*. From then on, in Berrett's inimitable phrasing, he traveled a "downward mobility to champion *black music and related causes*." (Emphasis added.) On a 1933 London-bound ship, Hammond punched out Armstrong's crooked manager, Johnny Collins, for calling Armstrong "nigger." According to Berrett, "There was a special force behind that punch"—the force of Communism, which relegated Whiteman to history's sideline "even though Whiteman actually had both black and white talent on his payroll." Proof of iniquity came in 1938, when Hammond's mostly Negro Carnegie Hall concert, "From Spirituals to Swing," was widely praised, while Whiteman's mostly Caucasian "Eighth Experiment in Modern Music," two nights later in the same hall, was practically ignored.

Helpfully or ironically, depending on your perspective, in February of this year, that concert was at long last released in full on a double-CD set, *Paul Whiteman at Carnegie Hall* (Nostalgia Arts). Interested listeners can decide for themselves if a socialist conspiracy was required to suppress Bert Shelter's "The Farmer Leaves the Hay," Walter Gross's "Cowbell Serenade," or Duke Ellington's "Blue Belle of Harlem," the evening's one commission that survived on its own, though it hardly stands with Ellington's finest achievements.

What really seems to stick in Berrett's craw is that "the leading leftist monthly," *New Masses*, sponsored Hammond's event. He writes: "Somewhat skittish about the source of his dollars, Hammond insisted that there be no obvious involvement on the part of *New Masses* and its Communist activists. . . . For perhaps similar reasons, one can paren-thetically speculate that Joe Glaser was against having his most valuable property, Louis Armstrong, participate in this event." This simply is not true. If it were, one might have expected Berrett to applaud Hammond for keeping the focus on music and not politics; but, in fact, the *New Masses* is prominently mentioned on the cover of and throughout the program handed out at Carnegie Hall that evening in 1938. (The title in full reads: "The New Masses Presents an Evening of American Negro Music 'From Spirituals to Swing' [Dedicated to Bessie Smith]") As for the second point, the crafty use of *perhaps* and *parenthetically speculate* do not make this unsupportable nonsense any the less risible. Duke Ellington, Billie Holiday, Ella Fitzgerald, and dozens of other major black artists also did not participate, not because of political affiliations but because Hammond did not hire them. In any case, Armstrong was far too big an attraction to sign on for a cameo appearance, and he and Hammond had personally fallen out by 1938.

Berrett speculates a lot. One of the pivotal moments in jazz history is Armstrong's relocation from New Orleans to Chicago in answer to a tele-gram from his mentor, King Oliver. Berrett, reluctant to concede creative deliberation to a modestly schooled black artist, writes of Oliver's invi-tation: "It is likely that Joe Oliver now felt an acute need to have a sem-blance of stability in his professional life in the person of a highly gifted, supportive, eager, deferential young man who looked up to him as a father." He finds it "somewhat baffling, on purely musical grounds, to understand why Oliver called upon Armstrong to join him as second cornet, since this additional instrument was extremely rare in the New Orleans hot bands of the period." Baffling? On purely musical grounds, one can appreciate Oliver's reasoning by listening to Creole Jazz Band recordings or reading accounts of patrons who were blown out of their seats by the power of the Oliver-Armstrong cornets. Actually, the double-cornet lead was introduced by Buddy Bolden. Berrett cannot conceive of Oliver as capable of innovation. And he isn't done: "For Armstrong, Oliver 'was a Creator.' But *Creator* could also take on the more biological meaning of *procreator*"—but let's leave that to Dr. Phil.

Berrett's fundamental argument about Whiteman's importance, removed from his shroud of paranoia, has much truth. Whiteman was one of the most absorbing, successful, and influential bandleaders of the 1920s, and his most interesting jazz period, from 1927 to 1930, has never lacked for champions, though thoughtless dismissals are also abidingly persistent. The latter are less a consequence of resourceful socialists than of two concrete issues that shouldn't but do roil the waters: lingering embarrassment at Whiteman's publicity-driven crowning as King of Jazz (immortalized in a movie of that name, purporting to show the universality of music but limiting the Negro influence to a passage from "Old Black Joe" and dancer Jacques Cartier outfitted as an African chieftain) and his retreat from jazz because he found it insufficiently commercial. Whiteman's response to the Depression was to fire most of the musicians Berrett lists as evidence of his commitment to jazz. All that happened a long time ago, and only laziness can explain any reluctance on the part of today's listeners to get beyond it.

A good if sometimes misguided man, Whiteman hired black arrangers (as did his rival, Vincent Lopez) and would have hired black musicians as early as the 1920s if social conditions and his management had permitted. But Whiteman was an idealist and he believed in something antithetical to what Armstrong represented. Here is an important subject Berrett might have profitably explored: the battle for what the word *jazz* defined and for what kind of artist it would ultimately signify. Whiteman was the leading spokesman for those who thought jazz would evolve as homegrown concert music based on the folk resources of African Americans—notably, "Rhapsody in Blue," in 1924. That same year, with little fanfare beyond the elite of New York's black musicians, Armstrong was proving that those putative folk resources *were* the homegrown art.

When, in 1926, Whiteman realized that he was on the wrong side of the debate, he hired genuinely gifted jazz artists, most notably Bing Crosby, cornetist Bix Beiderbecke, and arranger Bill Challis. The jazz records he made over the following three years were and are deservedly admired. But by 1930, Ellington and Armstrong were spearheading a music that reversed Whiteman's old formula; for them, European classicism was a sometimes-useful resource for a music that did not need to borrow prestige. They were in the vanguard of an art that comprehensively revised standards of musical composition, performance, and presentation. When *Time* featured Armstrong on a 1949 cover, wearing a crown of trumpets, the symbolism wasn't intended, as Berrett argues, to oust Whiteman. The old man had deposed himself. The caravan had moved on, and the *New Masses* was a long way from the driver's seat.

Berrett is never more preposterous than when playing no-degrees-of-separation between Armstrong and Whiteman, each of them nicknamed Pops. They both liked Guy Lombardo: connection! They both had weight problems: connection! They both played in California: connection! They both played written music: connection! One instance of his logic goes like this: Whiteman wanted to hire the violinist Armond J. Piron. Piron and his partner, Clarence Williams, once stole a song from Armstrong that became a big hit. Yet Armstrong later recorded for Williams. Conclusion: "So it was that the worlds of Armand Piron, Clarence Williams, Louis Armstrong, and Paul Whiteman overlapped." The author outdoes himself in his windup, which centers on Wynton Marsalis, presented as a kind of love child of Armstrong and Whiteman for having jazz and classical interests. It would be amusing to hear Marsalis's response, especially as he presented Whiteman's music at the Rose Theater earlier this year. It isn't amusing to find racial politics (still) dogging music appreciation.

[*Brilliant Corners*, Summer 2005]

80 ❖ *Seduced* (Classics Illustrated)

1.

I have never seen any good effects from comic books that condense Classics. Classic books are a child's companion [sic], often for life. Comic-book versions deprive the child of these companions. They do active harm by blocking one of the child's avenues to one of the finer things in life.
— Fredric Wertham, M.D., *Seduction of the Innocent*

On Sundays in the middle and late 1950s, we often ate dinner at an Italian restaurant near our home on Long Island's south shore. While our parents lingered over coffee and cigarettes, my sister and I would scamper to the bar to vote for Miss Rheingold, stuffing the ballot box for our mom or my sister. Then the four of us would stroll to the corner candy store, where my father loaded up on Tootsie Rolls, Goldenberg's Peanut Chews, Spearmint Leaves, and Bonomo's Turkish Taffy, to be dispensed during the drive home, and I would wheedle—they never refused, but I always felt I was wheedling—two or maybe three *Classics Illustrated* comic books. I'd promise not to read them all that night, but, if necessary, I had a flashlight ready under the blanket. I wasn't big on patience, and the comics quelled apprehensions of the Monday morning ordeal, for which I was never prepared.

The *CI* bug had bitten me at age six at the local synagogue's annual bazaar, where neighbors unloaded curios relegated to attics and basements. Someone donated a pile of *Classics*, and the anomalous covers, combining historical costumes and gruesome violence, held my attention like a hypnotist's swinging watch-fob. I managed to acquire the pile. So by the time of our Sunday evening ritual, I was familiar with The List, an ever-changing guide to available *CI* titles printed on the back of each issue. Unlike other comic books, *Classics* were prominently numbered and irregularly reprinted and published—or so it seemed to those of us who read and collected them (one activity mandating the other). What did we know or care of the Gilberton Company's commercial considerations? All we knew was that the lists tweaked our curiosity about missing numbers, and that the earliest issues listed titles like *Mr. Midshipman Easy* and *The Black Tulip* that were practically impossible to find. One might search in vain for months, and then—oh, joy!—locate an obscure *CI* gathering dust in a Brooklyn store or in the home of a DC addict who was happy to trade it for a couple of tepid *Jimmy Olsen*s. Cultural considerations aside, comics inducted us into the art of laissez-faire trade. Eventually I found all 169 titles, many in multiple editions. I have them still, though until now I had not looked at them in 30 years, beyond an occasional peek, like driving by the old homestead.

William Gass has written, "Lists are juxtapositions, and exhibit many of the qualities of collage." They may, in fact, offer the primitive pleasures of serendipitous art. For example, a computerized list of popular songs published during the first half of the 20th century reveals an infinite treasury of found poems: Flip to any page, put your finger on any title, and track the first 10 songs upward or down, and voila, instant lit. Lists of art works are both serendipitous and canonical, too—not just the pompous-ass variety (Famous Authors Choose the 100 Best Novels of the Century by Dead Persons and Themselves), but also publisher's catalogues and individual work-lists. The most influential film book of the 1960s,

Andrew Sarris's *The American Cinema,* is little more than an annotated list. In subdividing by directors a comprehensive selection of movies, he offered a more sophisticated canon than those built around movie stars to a generation raised on *The Early Show, The Late Show, The Million Dollar Movie, Shock Theater, Saturday Night at the Movies,* and the rest of TV's cinematic windfall. My first jazz canon consisted of 10-best lists volunteered by critics for a middlebrow magazine called *Cue;* my first classical music canon was edited and boxed by *Reader's Digest.* Preliminary literary canons included the catalogues printed on the inside jackets of Landmark Books and the Modern Library and the roll of prize-winning books in the almanac. But in the beginning, there was the curious collage, *Classics Illustrated.*

The back cover of each issue included the Gilberton Company's yellow ordering form—matching the yellow *CI* cover logo—and advice: "Mail coupon below or a facsimile." (*CI* fans had "facsimile" in their vocabularies before reaching adolescence, though my recollection is that none of us knew how to pronounce it.) On two occasions I tried to outsmart Gilberton by making a facsimile of old coupons with deleted numbers; the company flouted my pleas by sending me whatever issues were at hand, always ones I already owned. I had an image of a mailroom clerk, an ancient twisted harridan as drawn by *CI*'s Henry Kiefer, a master of the woodenly grotesque, bellowing "Ha! Ha! Ha!" while sending off yet another copy of *Caesar's Conquests* when I had optimistically paid my 15 cents for *Two Years before the Mast.* My frustration wasn't merely that of a completist with missing numbers to fill, but of an avaricious reader (albeit mostly of comics) besotted with the very idea of *"Classics"* and the historical claims they represented. It was easy to figure out the reasoning behind a 19th-century ragbag such as could be found on any *CI* printed around 1958:

42. Swiss Family Robinson
46. Kidnapped
47. Twenty Thousand Leagues Under the Sea
48. David Copperfield
50. The Adventures of Tom Sawyer
51. The Spy
52. The House of the Seven Gables
55. Silas Marner
57. The Song of Hiawatha
58. The Prairie
62. Brett Harte's Western Stories

But what of those missing numbers? What were they and why were they deleted? Had certain *Classics* been demoted from the rank of classics, or vice versa? Obviously not, as a comparison of various *CI* lists made clear:

43. Great Expectations
44. Mysteries of Paris
45. Tom Brown's School Days
49. Alice in Wonderland
53. A Christmas Carol
54. The Man in the Iron Mask
56. The Toilers of the Sea
59. Wuthering Heights
60. Black Beauty
61. The Woman in White

In time one would hear a variety of explanations, including poor sales, imminent revised versions, and censorship by a kind of HUAC for kids, the House Un-American Accursed Comics tribunal stimulated by that wannabe Dr. Spock of mental hygiene—the former director of Bellevue Hospital, Dr. Fredric Wertham. To its great credit, the Gilberton Company refused to sign on to the Comics Code Authority. On the other hand, it did not want to press its luck. The opening graveyard sequence in Kiefer's 1947 *Great Expectations* was singled out as especially vile, though obviously influenced by the David Lean film of the year before. "You bring me a file and vittles," Magwitch threatens Pip. "Bring 'em both to me or I'll have your heart and liver out!" Today that reads like a droll moment from the Hannibal Lecter franchise, except for *CI*'s assumption that kids could make sense of "vittles"—just as it assumed that kids would buy adaptations of Shakespeare far more authentic than, say, the retellings of Charles and Mary Lamb.

2.

I have yet to see a child who was influenced to read "Classics" or "famous authors" in the original by reading them in comic-book versions. What happens instead is that the comic-book version cuts the children off from this source of pleasure, entertainment and education.

—Fredric Wertham, M.D., *Seduction of the Innocent*

Most issues of *CI* ended with the motto: "Now that you have read the *Classics Illustrated* edition, don't miss the added enjoyment of reading the original, obtainable at your school or public library." Always a sucker for added enjoyment, I did or tried to do just that, as did everyone I know who grew up with *CI*. When I mentioned to an editor of the *New York Times Book Review* that I was writing this essay, he broke into a smile and said, "I love *Classics Illustrated*. They introduced me to Dostoevsky" —or Dostoyevsky, as *CI* preferred. Me too. The only *CI* with a more urgent endnote than the one promising added enjoyment was *Crime and Punishment*: "Because of space limitations, we regretfully omitted some of the original characters and sub-plots [like Sonya and Svidrigailov] of this brilliantly written novel. Nevertheless we have retained its main theme and mood. We strongly urge you to read the original." Maybe artist Rudy Palais felt guilty, though he had no cause. Other *CIs* were far less faithful, and his rendering of the murder, and the mounting hysteria of Raskolnikov (drawn to resemble Peter Lorre), and Porfiry's inquisition were expertly done. Yet who could resist "strongly urge"?

The only thing harder to find than deleted *CIs* in small 1950s Long Island villages was a genuine bookstore. But it was not uncommon to find display cases of the Modern Library, Landmark or Signature Books (rival nonfiction series for young readers), and paperbacks in supermarkets, drug stores, and stationery stores. My dad drove me to the latter when I begged him for *Crime and Punishment*. We were standing before a counter taller than I while the storeowner looked through the Modern Library at his rear, only to report that he must have sold it. He did, however, have *The Brothers Karamazov* by the same guy. When my dad turned and asked if I wanted it, the storeowner, who hadn't noticed me, peered over the counter and said, "It's for *him*?" This inclined my dad to ask, sotto voce, if it was a dirty book. I carried it around for months, reading and rereading the first hundred or so pages until it dawned on me that Alyosha and Alexey were the same character, same for Dmitri and Mitya, whereupon I gave up, hoping in vain that *CI* would get to it. On another occasion, I searched everywhere for the "original" of Eugene Sue's *Mysteries of Paris* and reluctantly settled for *The Wandering Jew*, an even more horrific farrago of malignant plots and tortuous intrigue, set in motion by Jesuits who would have scared the pantaloons off Torquemada.

CI never tackled the 1350 pages of *The Wandering Jew*, but it did briefly risk accusations of anticlericalism with its 1947 edition of *Adventures of Cellini*, which had enjoyed a revival of interest the year before in a volume sexily illustrated by Dali. Cellini's rant against a succession of shortsighted and dim-witted popes is fully intact in the *CI* adaptation; though dull in stretches, August M. Froehlich's primal art emits a claustrophobic feeling for the Renaissance absent from the more briskly paced and vividly narrated 1961 version (artist unidentified). The popes are just as corrupt and avaricious in the toned-down remake, but less stupid. The narrative strategy is also different. The first version shows Cellini dictating his story to an apprentice (as, in fact, he did); the second recapitulates the memoir's actual first-person telling. All *Classics Illustrated* comics included page-long bios of the authors, and 1961's account forestalled criticism by describing Cellini as a liar and rogue.

One of those Eureka moments when I knew I'd be a writer occurred in fourth grade when I leaped from the *CI* version to the Hawthorne version of *The House of the Seven Gables*, a novel with which I remain obsessed. The *CI*, despite its splendidly horrific opening exposition, is better and more accurate than either of the two Hollywood travesties, and served as a stirring prelude to the real thing—the definitive American assessment of inherited guilt. Soon I was devouring "originals." After reading Verne's *From the Earth to the Moon*, I was moved to compose a short story and submit it to my teacher. It concerned a pack of scientists who launch themselves beyond Earth's gravity in a giant bulletlike projectile; the plot focused on the apparent murder of a passenger haunted by his ancestor's crimes. A detective who happens to be on board discovers that the fellow had accidentally killed himself by falling against a broken coathook. (It remains unpublished.) *CI* led me to Robert Louis Stevenson, Mark Twain (including *Pudd'nhead Wilson*, not often recommended to young readers), Doyle, Poe, Cooper, Wilkie Collins, *Jane Eyre*, *Frankenstein*, *Lord Jim*, the Bounty trilogy (when I matriculated at Grinnell College, I knew little of the place other than James N. Hall had been a student there, though that wasn't my motivation). Before long, I abandoned *CI*. But The List remained imprinted on my brain, an abiding source of curiosity and bemusement.

I continue to find myself grabbing at obscure *CI* source material when I come across it. Twenty years ago, while lecturing in Philadelphia, I found a 1902 edition of Edmund About's *The King of the Mountains*, and delighted in its brisk, funny narrative—a satirical, politically astute kidnapping story. It's probably safe to assume that no one beyond *CI* readers and French lit scholars know of it or About, which rhymes with Camus, since a web-search shows no American edition in the last 90 years. Honored in France as the equal of Hugo (himself represented with four *CI* titles, including *The Toilers of the Sea*, originally done in the stark, faded, newspaper style of August Froelich, and then updated in the more conventional and intimate manner of EC comics veteran Angelo Torres), About is one of the mysteries of the canon. So far as I can tell, *King of the Mountain* is the only one of his books to be translated and published here; its renown peaked between 1900 and 1910. I thank *CI* for the tip and heartily recommend it. A few years later, I finally found a UK import of *Mysteries of Paris*, and searched out the gory parts. More recently I've derived simpler satisfactions from *The Black Tulip* and the surprisingly mirthful—the *CI* version had revealed no such comedic spirit—*Mr. Midshipman Easy*. A fascination triggered by *CI*'s *The Oregon Trail* (not one dialogue balloon) and *The Conspiracy of Pontiac* inclined me to tackle the three volumes of Francis Parkman in the Library of America—another odd canon in the making.

Many of the 169 *CI* titles are now unread, including a good many copyrighted (20th century) titles. But the List abides as a fair and appropriately idiosyncratic reflection of the old-school literary canvas as inherited by American-born and immigrant readers in the early years of the bygone century. The series, which began in 1941 as *Classics Comics* and changed its name to the snootier *Classics Illustrated* in 1947, was largely a postwar phenomenon. Its canonical vision, however, was established before 1925. The personal and sometimes peculiar tastes of *CI* founder Albert Kanter and his staff embodied the reading habits of our grandparents, which proved readily accessible to children of the 1950s. Few of those books are as enthusiastically embraced today, beyond a small forest of evergreens like *The Three Musketeers* (issue #1), *Treasure Island*, *Tom Sawyer*, *A Tale of Two Cities*, *The Count of Monte Cristo*, and *Twenty Thousand Leagues Under the Sea*, and even some of them are shunned as creaky, remote, and pitilessly long. Besides, the thriving kiddie-lit industry knows better than to look to the public domain for big profits.

So the canon appeared far more settled in Kanter's day, with confirmations everywhere. One measure of stature was inclusion in Scribner Illustrated Classics (and similar series), now remembered mostly for N. C. Wyeth's paintings, introduced before the First World War and cheaply reprinted in the 1940s. In addition to the usual titles by Stevenson, Verne, and Cooper, *The Boy's King Arthur*, and *Arabian Nights*, Scribner and other catalogues offered minor works by the same writers (*The Black Arrow*, *Michael Strogoff*, *The Pilot*), and other volumes bound for obscurity, like *The Scottish Chiefs*, *The White Company*, and *Westward Ho!* *CI* did them all. Do kids still read *Men of Iron*? The last generation to seek out Howard Pyle's story may have been primed by *CI*. The same may be said for *The Last Days of Pompeii*, *The Cloister and the Hearth*, *Soldiers of Fortune*, *Waterloo*, *King—of the Khyber Rifles*, the collected works of hunter Frank Buck, *The Crisis* (by American novelist Winston Churchill, born three years before the PM)—erstwhile classics at best, given one last shot at a mass audience by *CI*. Ouida's ponderous *Under Two Flags* must have disappointed many who gasped at the comic's climax, in which raven-haired beauty

Cigarette gallops into view bearing a pardon and throws herself before a firing squad to save her lover:

CIGARETTE: Stop! In the name of France, STOP!
EVIL LEGIONNAIRE: Aim!
CIGARETTE: Do you not hear me? Stop!
EVIL LEGIONNAIRE: Fire!
CIGARETTE: Read! Read! AH-H-H-NNN . . .

Classics Illustrated extended the lifeline of the late-19th-century middle-brow canon much as early TV extended the life of old Hollywood. Indeed, hit movies sanctioned and influenced the List. Within a decade of *CI*'s start-up, the founder's son, Hal Kanter, succeeded as a Hollywood comedy writer (he eventually wrote for Bing Crosby and Bob Hope and directed Elvis Presley), and he would alert his old man when a public domain classic was in one of the studio pipelines. What a coincidence that the movie *Master of the World* was released the same year *CI* issued that title and its companion piece, *Robur the Conqueror* (*CI* turned to Jules Verne 10 times, more than to any other writer). Same thing with *The Red Badge of Courage, Knights of the Round Table, Rob Roy, Ben-Hur, The Cossack Chief* (*Taras Bulba*), and others. When *The Hunchback of Notre Dame* was filmed anew in 1957, *CI* outfitted its 1944 version with a new cover depicting a couple not unlike Gina Lollobrigida and Anthony Quinn; the comic itself showed its age with a caricature of Hitler in the Feast of Fools episode, and a semi-happy ending in which Esmeralda lives (as in the movies) while Quasimodo plummets to his death from the bell tower (an original touch from *Classics Illustrated*). Sometimes *CI* outpaced the pipeline, hitting the mark a couple of years before the movie, as happened with *Cleopatra, Lord Jim,* and a couple of H. G. Wells stories. Sometimes the series took cues from TV, as with Wild Bill Hickok and Davy Crockett (*CI* did several biographies, usually of western heroes, but also Lincoln and Joan of Arc). Only once did Hal Kanter broker a direct movie tie-in—unfortunately, it was for the lumbering 1959 remake of *The Buccaneer*.

In the early years, *CI* artists often relied on their memories of old movies for treatments as well as titles, producing an inconsistent fidelity to the books. *Frankenstein* is true to Shelley; Dr. Jekyll's girlfriend is pure Hollywood. Usually fidelity won out, even regarding the incomprehensible *The Last Days of Pompeii*, which has more characters than the phone books of small cities. Ah, but there were howlers, too. In the last panel of the 1942 edition of *A Tale of Two Cities*, Sydney Carton doesn't get the last line; no sooner does he ponder a far better rest than the executioner

adds, "Put your head on the block Evremonde!" A far, far better version
was prepared in 1956 by former EC regulars Joe Orlando and George Evans.
At the close of *Robinson Crusoe*, Friday waves at the reader with a big smile
and says, "Me like big city!" For *Cyrano de Bergerac*, the company's most
prolific and characteristic artist, Alex Blum, added a childhood scene you
don't find in Rostand. Blum also concluded *The Iliad* with a flash-forward
of Achilles' death from an arrow in the chest—the source of that familiar phrase, "He has an Achilles chest." To be fair, Homer didn't use the
heel business either.

3.

> *There is a high correlation between intelligence, vocabulary and*
> *reading. Comic-book readers are handicapped in vocabulary building*
> *because in comics all the emphasis is on the visual image and not on*
> *the proper word. These children often know all that they should not*
> *know about torture, but are unable to spell or read the word.*
> —Fredric Wertham, M.D., *Seduction of the Innocent*

Dr. W had a point, if you believe that the generation bred in the era of
silent movies could not speak and was forced to communicate in mime.
He was undoubtedly correct, however, about torture, primers in which
were offered by such issues as *Two Years before the Mast*, *Mysteries* ("The
Pit and the Pendulum"), *Mysteries of Paris*, *The Man in the Iron Mask*, *The
Man Who Laughs*, *The Last Days of Pompeii*, *Uncle Tom's Cabin*, *Pudd'nhead
Wilson*, and others, not least *The Spy*, in which English officers are shown
whipping bare-bottomed men strung up by their wrists, bleating, with
rather finicky punctuation, "Help, help!" while the limey bastard snarls,
"Ha, ha! Give it to 'em boys." The myth of *CI*'s high-mindedness tends
to obscure its place as the primeval modern horror comic. The great Swiss
playwright and novelist Friedrich Dürrenmatt, whose work would have
made splendid additions to the List, once referred to fright as "the modern form of empathy." Fright is also the eternal mode of empathy for young
people unafraid to admit the compatibility of curiosity and terror; most
middle-class children don't get the chance to experience many other
frissons.

Intensely conscious of its socially redeeming qualities, *Classics
Illustrated* was forever touting itself as an educational tool. The 1948 issue
of *Twenty Thousand Leagues Under the Sea* had the moxie to run a feature
called, "From Our Mail Sack": "We are brother and sister in High
School," one letter begins, "and we read many of your *CLASSICS
Illustrated* in our classes." This probably didn't play well with critics who

feared that students would use them as cheats, though it's hard to imagine anyone in the age of Cliff's Notes trying to fob off a book report based on a comic. The letter is illustrated with a Kiefer drawing of tousled-hair junior, pencil in hand, his sexy mom right behind him, her fingers proudly squeezing his shoulder, while his cross-eyed dad—a double for Alexander Woollcott (thick glasses, square face, mustache) holds up a copy of *Classics Illustrated*. But kids didn't buy *Twenty Thousand Leagues* to improve their marks; they bought it for the attack of the octopuses (the lonely giant squid exists only in Disney). The jokey villains in *Superman* and *Batman* were fruitcakes compared to *CI*'s monsters, human and otherwise, which prefigure the Iron Age of EC.

A very freely adapted *Dr. Jekyll and Mr. Hyde* (issue 13, 1943) started the *CI* horror line; it ends, presumably for moral instruction, by depicting a green devil with pointy ears, a white beard, and a steeple spouting from its head, carrying a triton. A calmer 1953 version, drawn by science-fiction specialist Lou Cameron, cagily evaded the censors and evidently stayed in print till *CI*'s demise. Not the case with the infamous *3 Famous Mysteries* (1944, wiped out by HUAC-for-kids in the '50s), which ends with a wondrously inept and scary riff on Maupassant's "The Flayed Hand." The hand is terrific: long bony fingers with knuckles you can almost feel. The Frenchmen are something else, with their narrow faces and uniform open-mouthed expressions, as if they had all sat on whoopee cushions. A good artist, like Robert Hayward Webb, could generate genuine fear, as in *Kidnapped*, when Balfour mounts the dark stairs and emerges from two mostly black panels onto the exposed parapet, illuminated by a triple-branch of lightning bolts. Too bad N. C. Wyeth didn't think of that.

My favorite *CI* artists were stylistically unmistakable: Henry C. Kiefer and Rudy Palais. Kiefer was pushing 60 when be began bringing his nightmares to *CI*. An old-fashioned hack trained in the age of woodcuts and profusely illustrated novels, he was a true primitive, his art often stiff and looming despite his eye for theater and pageantry. William B. Jones Jr., whose *Classics Illustrated: A Cultural History with Illustrations* (McFarland, 2002) is definitive, writes of Kiefer's "willful antiquity" and "an air of historical accuracy and almost metaphysical mystery not found in any other comic book line." Kiefer's heroes and heroines look disconcertingly alike, except that the men have facial hair and the women wear lipstick. (If you've ever defaced a portrait by adding a goatee, you qualify for the Kiefer School of Fine Art.) His villains, however, are inspired: lumpy morons, maniacal savages, and calculating hags—obvious predecessors of EC's Old Witch. He was not great at children: On the cover of *A Christmas Carol*, Tiny Tim looks slightly psychotic. Kiefer's backgrounds employ elaborate waves of smoke, rain, and fog that unite multiple panels. Yet it was also Kiefer who adapted "Hans Pfall" as a comically ribald jaunt, including a depiction of the universe with several ringed planets.

Kiefer did 24 titles in six years, including *Great Expectations, David Copperfield, Pudd'nhead Wilson, King Solomon's Mines, The Prisoner of Zenda, The Oregon Trail, Twenty Thousand Leagues Under the Sea, Around the World in 80 Days, Wuthering Heights, The Cloister and the Hearth, The Lady of the Lake, Western Stories,* and the ineffable *Mysteries of Paris.* In the last, we meet the deadly Schoolmaster, with his porcine nostrils, yellow hair, and acid-scarred face. The do-gooder hero straps him to a chair and orders his assistant to burn out the Schoolmaster's eyes, hoping that will reform him—fat chance. Then there's the one-eyed witch Screech-Owl, who tries to pull little Marie's tooth out with her fingers and threatens, "If the girl sings out for the police, I'll break my bottle of acid across her snout!" Nights are blue-black, days are saturated with reds and greens, and the many flashbacks are pale-blue pen sketches; varied frames, heavy dialogue, and a complicated plot suggest the density of a novel. One four-page section includes the following notices: "We leave Rudolph and go back several years"; "Getting back to the present"; "We leave Marie in the hands of her abductors for the present and return to No 25 Rue Du Temple." The *CI* biography of Sue says his books "have many technical faults" that are overlooked because of the good stuff. "He became imbued with the socialist doctrine that influenced his most important works" and, though "rambling and diffuse," he has "something of the narrative gift of Dumas and something of the ethical earnestness of Hugo." This was for nine-year-olds?

Rudy Palais didn't do horror per se, though the old pawnbroker in *Crime and Punishment* might disagree. Yet his characters are so intense, so wired, and so damned pissed off, that sequences another artist might pass off as tea-and-crumpets become in his hands cruelly volatile. His years at *CI* overlapped with Kiefer's, but he came from another world, having made his way through the Depression designing posters for Hollywood studios. His credo was action: Instead of stick figures, you find characters caught unawares, shot from weird angles, moving from frame to frame with sweaty resolve. His gnarly, livid faces are never merely misshapen; they are contorted by meanness and fury, often exemplified in distended Adam's apples. Palais did only eight *CI* titles—small potatoes compared to Kiefer, Blum, or the most prolific of the later artists, Norman Nodel— but they are among the most memorable, including the best of Cooper, *The Pioneers* (configured more as a mystery and revenge story than the novel, which gets bogged down in feats of pioneering) and *The Prairie*; the second and third parts of the Bounty trilogy, especially *Pitcairn's Island,* a tour de force of paranoid duplicity; and *David Balfour*, in which every minor character is distinctive.

Not surprisingly, when the censors buried EC, many of its writers and artists found work at CI, invariably in mainstream titles. Graham "Ghastly" Ingels bided his time with *Waterloo*, but *The First Men in the Moon* looks like what it is, a collaboration between *Mad*'s George Woodbridge and *Weird Fantasy*'s Al Williamson. George Evans became a regular, and one of the best pages he ever drew depicts with striking economy the death of Lord Jim. Racial horror was also on CI's agenda, despite stock natives found in many issues and a 1944 pass at *Huckleberry Finn* that depicts Jim as a simp; the 1956 version restores his and Huck's spunk, but misspells "sivilize" with a *c*. Topsy is more of a minstrel stereotype than was necessary in *Uncle Tom's Cabin*, yet CI's 1943 rendering was uncompromising and timely, with pointed references to the Constitution and Exodus and a line about religious persecution; the angel coming for Eva is a bit much (in Stowe's bio, we learn that she too was taken by "a force from beyond"), but Legree and the other slave traders are as nightmarish as anything in the horror genre, and the characterization of St. Clare's dreadful wife is no less merciless. In 1946, CI hired black artist Matt Baker, who died young after creating a gorgeous Lorna Doone that made Bettie Page look like a Chihuahua; Lorna rivaled Uncle Tom as an all-time best seller. CI closed shop in 1969, after issuing *Negro Americans—The Early Years*, stories of a dozen or so luminaries from Crispus Attucks to Matthew Henson. By then, *Classics Illustrated* had gone soft (Nodel's 1962 *Faust* excepted), returning over and over to animal adventures, Verne, and Dumas. Its day was over: What's the point of comics, classic or otherwise, if they're shorn of the sensational?

4.

Radio, movies and television are considered worthy of regular serious critiques in newspapers. Nothing like this exists for comic books. Nor is it even possible, for the few critics who have written about them find them subjects for toxicology rather than criticism.
       —Fredric Wertham, M.D., *Seduction of the Innocent*

When I headed for college, I knew my mother would visit retribution on the comics stacked in my closet, and I didn't much care, except for the *Classics*. So I wrapped them in my late grandfather's tallis and squeezed then into his tallis bag and hid them under cushions and in game boxes. Sure enough, they alone survived the comics holocaust. Now they are simply relics. In the course of writing this essay, I've come to admire again what they were and what they did for me but have lost the emotional attachment that had waxed in memory. They are, after all, childhood pulp, and one would not go home again even if one could. They will go back into storage and someday my daughter, who has no interest in comics, will deal with them as she sees fit. Maybe she'll get a lot of money for them, or donate them to a bazaar, where some young antiquarian will take them to heart and make the mistake of trying to read *The Cloister and the Hearth*. And maybe she will close the circle I prevented my mother from closing and throw them out. That's jake with me. I just don't want to be there when it happens.

[*Give Our Regards to the Atomsmashers*, edited by Sean Howe, Pantheon, 2003]

81 ❖ *Fear and Trembling (Friedrich Dürrenmatt)*

When *The Visit*, tailored for the Lunts, triumphed on Broadway in 1958 (two years after its European debut), Friedrich Dürrenmatt achieved international celebrity. Writing in German with a fashionably postwar mixture of dislocation, grotesquerie, and high moral purpose, the young Swiss writer was treated as an instant classic, compared with Brecht—the intricate stagecraft, politics, and distancing techniques of his early-'50s plays, *Romulus* and *The Marriage of Mr. Mississippi*, had underscored his debt— and also glibly, mistakenly conjoined with the absurdists. Translations of his plays, novels, and a widely anthologized essay, "Problems of the Theater," culminated in another Broadway coup, *The Physicists* (again, two years after its debut) in 1964. *The Visit* unwinds as an edge-of-the-seat thriller about the debasing and deadly effects of money; *The Physicists* dwells comically in the ironies of madness and murder as benign alternatives to the kind of knowledge that might blow us all up.

Dürrenmatt's subsequent plays enjoyed little global recognition, and much of his work remains unknown in English, including his radio plays—a literary form taken seriously in Europe that in the United States has never progressed beyond pre-television adaptations of famous novels. Still, his place in 20th-century drama appears secure. It is his fiction I wish to cheer, at least the seven novels that have been made available here; his short stories and last, posthumously published novel have yet to be translated.

In 1984, I wrote briefly of the first five novels, most of them then out of print in English. Those tales had haunted me for more than 20 years, their images of cinematic vividness—a deadly dwarf crawling through a transom; a crazed detective by the roadside, wretchedly fixated; murder on a scenic bridge, committed as a dare; a chance stag dinner morphing into judicial execution—periodically bringing me back to Dürrenmatt's brief, macabre meditations on evil. Recognizing that evil had been psychoanalyzed into oblivion, except in the precincts of genre fiction and films, he adapted generic conventions. I don't want to overstate; Dürrenmatt's novels are perhaps too schematic and clever, claustrophobic in their obsessions, stunted in their outrage, impatient of characterization. They are also gripping, unexpectedly comic, wasteless, and morally rigorous.

Dürrenmatt, born in 1921, the son of a Protestant minister, watched the war from "neutral" ground, attending university in Zurich and Bern, studying philosophy and theology and growing increasingly cynical of Switzerland's putative disengagement. By 1950, when he published what became his first novel, *The Judge and His Hangman*, as a magazine serial, he had come to reject logical explanations for the unspeakable as monotonous and possibly depraved. Extending Conrad's assertions that man requires no help from the supernatural to carry out every iniquity and that terrorism succeeds only in the absence of motive, he conjured a hellish nihilism. In *The Judge and His Hangman*, an insufferably pompous novelist lectures Commissioner Barlach about the villainous Gastmann as philosophical hero:

> If I've called him evil it is because for him to do good is merely a matter of caprice or accident. The same applies to the evil that I think he's capable of. Moral conviction, one way or another, doesn't enter into it. He'll never do evil in order to reach a certain goal, the way ordinary criminals do: to gain money, women, or power. He will do evil at a time when it serves no tangible purpose. For him there are always two possibilities—the good and the evil—and pure chance decides what course he will take.

Motive became more important to Dürrenmatt in his sixth and seventh novels, an obsession in its own right, motoring the plots into halls of mirrors in which truth recedes infinitely, like refracted light, ultimately impenetrable. But what motive can one ascribe to the Mengele figure in his second novel, *The Quarry*, who, having changed his identity, presides over a fortress sanitarium for the very rich? Here the Jewish giant Gulliver tells the failing Barlach, "We can help only in single instances, not in the whole. Therefore, we ought not to try to save the world but to get through it—the only true adventure that remains for us at this late hour."

I came across *The Quarry* by chance, a teenager drawn to a dramatic Grove Press cover (a Black Cat Book, 50 cents, high for such a slim volume), and soon found cheap paperbacks of *The Judge and His Hangman*, *Traps*, and *The Pledge*, as well as the newly published *Once a Greek . . .* and the plays. I was elated to see *The Physicists*, with its dynamic cast (Hume Cronyn, George Voskovec, and Robert Shaw as the scheming "physicists," Jessica Tandy as the despotic Fraulein Doktor) and its emblematic '60s righteousness and high dudgeon: This was also the Broadway year of Rolf Hochhuth's *The Deputy*, James Baldwin's *Blues for Mister Charlie*, and Arthur Miller's *After the Fall*. Dürrenmatt was in the groove, and I claimed him as only an adolescent can claim a writer, even seeking him out in Neuchâtel during an undergraduate jaunt from Grenoble to Switzerland, an ordeal he was spared by being or claiming to be out of town.

By the 1970s, though still prolific, he had fallen out of favor, along with most political theater. He had now, in his fifties, entered a period of international honors and appointments, including university positions in California. In 1981, on the occasion of his sixtieth birthday, the Zurich publishing house Diogenes brought out a uniform edition of his complete works, 29 volumes—several more were yet to come. Yet he had had nothing important in English after 1965. He continued to write plays for stage and radio, but the failure of his plays, especially the much-revised *Achterloo*, bitterly disappointed him and he abandoned the stage. He published at least one short story and several book length essays, including an argument for coexisting Israeli and Palestinian states that he described as the work closest to his heart, and he devoted much of his time to painting, including illustrations for a prose ballad, *Minotaurus*. None of this work has arrived in translation.

More surprisingly, given their expeditious pleasures, the five short novels written between 1950 and 1958 and translated between 1954 and 1965 vanished, though Maximilian Schell filmed *The Judge and His Hangman* in 1975, and a dramatization of *Traps* aired shortly after on HBO. For many years, only *The Judge and His Hangman* remained in print in the United States, secreted in a Dürrenmatt anthology called *Plays and Essays*; that novel was then paired with *The Quarry* (the other Barlach story) in an omnibus edition. And that was all: At a time when international *policiers* found immense popularity, the neglect of Dürrenmatt's haunted riddles was as inexplicable as his apparent retreat from fiction.

Then, in quick succession: two new novels from Random House. In keeping with the random order with which the first five had appeared in English, they were translated in reverse order. *The Assignment or On the Observing of the Observer of the Observers* was issued in 1988, two years after the Swiss edition. Its predecessor, *Justiz* (1985), Dürrenmatt's longest and most intricate work of fiction (though barely exceeding 200 pages), was published here as *The Execution of Justice*, in 1989. He died in 1990, in Neuchâtel, at 69, having completed a final novel, *Durcheinandertal* (meaning Disorder Valley), published in 1998. It concerns the gangland takeover of a nursing home, customary territory, and has been described by Dürrenmatt scholar Gerhard P. Knapp as "perhaps the most joyful" of his works. In 2001, Sean Penn directed a faithful, highly imaginative film of *The Pledge*, the setting convincingly transferred to Nevada as a vehicle for Jack Nicholson. Critically admired, it generated a paperback reprint that was largely ignored—at present none of the novels are available here, though University of Chicago has announced republication of *The Judge and His Hangman*.

So they continue to return, as I continue to return to them (the two 1980s novels casting retrospective insights on the first five), yet without achieving that mandarin seal of approval that lifts inimitable books beyond culthood. Twenty years after I first wrote about them, I continue to wonder at their elusiveness—these seven fierce stories, which could be contained in a single middleweight volume. They linger in limbo between, say, the low-art craftiness of James M. Cain and the high-art gloss of Albert Camus, sharing with each a distinctly insular vision. But they also belong to a more specialized literature of horror, of a fear and trembling in the face of historical as opposed to unnatural iniquities— among them such later novels as Sven Delblanc's *Speranza*, and Charles Johnson's *The Middle Passage*, which look unblinkingly at the slave trade; or Ian McEwen's *The Innocent* and *Black Dogs*, which echo Dürrenmatt's mapping of cold war undercurrents (from Communist bicycle clubs to a Polish concentration camp to the Berlin Wall) as filtered through un-requited romance and acrimonious marriage; or a tradition of Japanese crime novels, such as Seicho Matsumoto's *Inspector Imanishi Investigates* and *Zero Focus*, which trace corruption to the American occupation and forced accommodations to the West, and Natsuo Kirino's recent *Out*, in which four women sharing a Wal-Mart-like servitude confront oppression with bloody deeds, unleashing a full-bore psychopath. Dürrenmatt's *The Assignment* adumbrates the erotic surrender to death that *Out* amplifies.

Dürrenmatt's novels are dreams, fairy tales, hallucinations, in which the demarcation between good and evil is under siege by fate and caprice. They vibrate with magical numbers and topsy-turvy reversals, with shimmering discursive details. The world is out of whack and noth-ing quite scans—not even metaphor. At the sight of a child's raped and dismembered body, the townspeople stand silently, while "from the lashing trees great raindrops continued to fall, glittering like diamonds." Good men attempt to stem the tide of evil, ruminating ponderously on the human condition, but most of their talk is blather. Guilt lurks everywhere; honor and justice are up for grabs. What better modus operandi for Dürrenmatt's purposes than the detective novel, that spreadsheet of facts and assumptions? All of his novels other than *Once a Greek* . . . are thrillers, and even that satire on morals and cultural identity moves at a thriller's pace. They are set in European cities and villages cornered by three postwar temptations: the shameful and shameless Nazi past, the blandishments of American consumer goods, and the promises of revolution. Like his plays, Dürrenmatt's fiction asks big questions and hums mordantly over the answers.

The Judge and His Hangman (published here by Harper & Brothers in 1955) introduced Police Commissioner Barlach and his nemesis, a monstrously refined sociopath who can and does kill for a whim or to taunt justice. To snare the devil, Barlach will be the devil. In its grotesque companion *The Quarry* (1953, published by New York Graphic Society in 1961), Barlach submits to torture in his determination to find the war criminal who he believes is running a chic clinic. Barlach's aides are the giant Gulliver and a killer dwarf (initially the devil's creature, but finally Gulliver's— they had known each other in Stutthof, a fictional concentration camp). In *Once a Greek* . . . (1955, published by Knopf in 1965), his most flippant and least-known novel, Dürrenmatt recruits Cinderella as his paradigm for a fable about a dim middle-aged patriot-virgin who advertises for a bride, is promptly engaged to a fabulously wealthy, beautiful courtesan— a prototype for Claire in *The Visit*—and dispatched from one mythical land (bureaucratic Europe) to another (the Greece of Aphrodite and Chloe). In *Traps* (1956, published by Knopf in 1960), a novella with a Macbeth template, a ruthless and superstitious businessman is brought to justice by three witches in the garb of ancient, gluttonous, retired members of the bar.

Traps initially appeared as a radio play, a year before the novella, and much later (1979) resurfaced in Dürrenmatt's unsuccessful stage adaptation. Similarly, the last and perhaps the best of the 1950s novels, originated as a screenplay, filmed in Switzerland in 1958 by director Ladislao Vajda as *It Happened in Broad Daylight* and again in Germany in 1995 by director Rudolph Van Den Berg as *The Cold Light of Day*. Yet the novel, published in 1958 as *Das Versprechen: Requiem auf den Kriminalroman* and in 1959 as *The Pledge* (by Knopf), has a particularly literary edge, employing the second-person conversational style Camus used in *The Fall*. Another updated fairy tale, it probes the aftermath of a horrific tragedy: Little Red Riding Hood is brutally murdered on her way to grandmother's house. A serial child-killer is on the loose, but Dürrenmatt's requiem for detective fiction expends little interest in this particular M, whoever he is, and focuses instead on a tragically scrupulous police detective Matthai, who swears by his "soul's salvation" to find the fiend. Undone by his pledge, the detective is sucked into obsession, diligence turned on its head, scruples abandoned.

Dürrenmatt's fixations wax with cumulative power in these novels. Scenes and settings are painted in the broad strokes of folk literature; changes in weather work like musical accompaniment to the action. He does not digress, though some characters are given to windy preachments; his occasional literary flourishes gleam like silver in dark woods. Dürrenmatt's precise, unruffled prose (translated by Richard and Clara Winston and others) balances infrequent sentimentality with cold sarcasm. If his plots make little sense, they are not entirely of the waking world, and dreams have their own logic, especially when generated by ethical indignation.

When he returned to fiction, a quarter-century after *The Pledge*, the dreams had mutated into insomniac philippics, elusive justice into unachievable justice—though the images and fixations are familiar. I sympathize with those, including, I suspect, Dürrenmatt, who regard *The Execution of Justice*'s tortuous narrative as a brave (or not) failure. It lurches forward and backward, gathering a small phonebook of players, occasionally wilting into the prattle of an admittedly drunk narrator, a lawyer, who misdirects and is misdirected. For all the mayhem, gothic details, and deadly guile, the novel never quite achieves the patented Dürrenmatt chill. It requires effort. In a curious postscript, Dürrenmatt divulges that he began the novel in 1957 (parts one and two are set in the mid-'50s) and abandoned it until 1980, when he considered publishing it as the thirtieth volume of his collected works. "But I could get nowhere with the development of the plot," so he rewrote it, "probably in a different way from what I had originally planned."

Yet none of his other novels have quite so many memorable characters or ingenious detours. Digressions, for once, are indulged, fittingly as the plot and the form replicate a bank shot in billiards. Instead of A killing B, he kills C (ball hits cushion) as a way of destroying B (rebounding ball hits ball). He commits the murder in a crowded restaurant and, following a quick conviction, engages the narrator, Spat—a young attorney for whores who has never played billiards—to postulate, as an intellectual exercise, an alternative theory of the crime; to Spat's horror, his activities eventually succeed in winning A his freedom. How Dürrenmatt brings this off, amid a crushing cast of protagonists and cameos, provides narrative fascination, but the reader is constantly diverted from the keystroke of the cue by other bank shots. For one inconsequential example, an architect hears that a man has died, leaving a desirable widow. Spat asks, "And now you want to marry this splendid female?" "No young man, I don't want to marry the widow, but the wife of her lover. Another female deluxe. Got it? Quite simple: If the lover wants to marry the widow, he's got to get divorced first, and then I'll marry his wife." Got it?

The big surprise, commencing with part three, is that the novel itself is a bank shot. As Spat drives off to meet his destiny, Dürrenmatt enters with a long "Editor's Afterword," explaining how he came to know the story and critiquing Spat's telling: "The author, a lawyer, was no match for his material. The present kept interfering. He waited till the end to tell the most important part, and then all at once he ran out of time." Spat's incoherence doesn't undermine the clarity of his gargoyle portraits, however, including a hideously crippled dwarf and armaments heiress who hires a whore to indulge the sexual passions denied her (combined, they add up to yet another version of *The Visit*'s Claire); an apoplectic prosecutor named Jammerlin who is taunted to death by a detective; a walk-on named Schonbachler, who posits theories of symphonies as ambient noise and nationalism as a psychological disorder; two enigmatic beauties, Daphne and Helene; the rich, eminent, elderly murderer and games-player Dr. Kohler; and many others, not least Spat, who spins theories of Swiss duplicity ("prayers before battle and orgies after slaughter") and weapons as prostheses. "I am a test-tube human," he decides, "bred in a model laboratory, raised according to the principles of the pedagogues and psychiatrists that our nation had produced along with precision watches, psycho-pharmaceuticals, secret bank accounts, and eternal neutrality. I would have been a model product of this experimental institute, except that I lacked one thing: a billiard table."

The inchoate aspect of *The Execution of Justice*, deliberate or not (I think not), makes all the more remarkable the masterly feat that succeeded it. Until *Durcheinandertal* crosses the Atlantic, *The Assignment* may provisionally stand as Dürrenmatt's most mature work, technically and thematically. *Justice* requires the reader to hunt and feint alongside the shaky narrator. *The Assignment* is a turboprop, moving too quickly to permit backward glances. Not that its reversals and misperceptions are any the less confounding: The form itself inclines the reader to ride now and worry later. *The Assignment* consists of 24 chapters, corresponding to the 24 books of *The Iliad*, each a single lucid sentence. Despite characters named Achilles and Polypheme and other Homeric allusions, Dürrenmatt's compressed tour de force (129 pages, translated by Joel Agee) doesn't much mess with Joycean parallels, except for fun, though it is seriously concerned with the changing relationships between humans and their gods—indeed, Kierkegaard is also conscripted.

Or, as the long subtitle suggests, who's observing whom? In the "dispersing universe with billions of Milky Ways," a personal god "as world regent and father" is hardly feasible. Besides, as the photographer-journalist Polypheme reasons, "only if God were a pure observer could he remain unsullied by his creation." The photographer also strives to remain uninvolved, but he is nonetheless subject to observation; whereas, the thing that makes God God is his immunity from spying: "God's freedom consisted in being a concealed, hidden god, while man's bondage consisted of being observed," and the observers are in turn observed, as they must be in order to have any power. Like a mob hitman who leaves a mutilated corpse as a warning to other transgressors, politicians perpetrate occupations and skirmishes that serve no purpose except to advertise the wares of weapons-exporting countries. Thanks to the abiding threat of nuclear annihilation, "conventional wars had become quite acceptable, giving renewed impetus to the production of conventional weapons and justifying the war in the desert, a perfect cycle, brilliantly designed to keep the weapons industry and therefore the world economy productive and happy."

Dürrenmatt does offer a plot to animate the spy versus spy paranoia, and it's a good one. The stunning wife of a psychiatrist leaves him and is found raped and murdered in an Arab country used by industrial powers to test armaments and keep tabs on each other. The husband brings home the corpse, eaten away by jackals, and hires F., a filmmaker, to take her crew to the desert and find out what happened. Advised in part by D. (guest appearance by the author), she rejects her best instincts and accepts the assignment, entering into a nasty wonderland, which she (as D. observes) is lucky to survive. Among genuine filmmakers, perhaps only Fritz Lang could have parsed what happens to her, a mixture of apocalyptic science fiction, political intrigue, and mystery, some of it quite funny, all of it pure Dürrenmatt—including another dwarf (you tell me), this one a Danish traveler who, not unlike the innocent man driven to death by anxious police in *The Pledge*, is executed to promote the illusion of justice. F. watches as he civilly stubs out his last cigarette before bullets rip him apart, blood jetting from holes all over his stunted body.

Writing in an era of Mutually Assured Destruction, Dürrenmatt saw beyond the stratagems of superpowers toward the increasing threat of terrorists. Justice was impossible in the industrial nations because the worst criminals curried the most favor from the state or were, in truth, representatives of the state. "This was a danger bigger than Stalin and all other Joes taken together," Dürrenmatt concluded in *The Quarry*: "The game that should be hunted, the really big beasts, were under the protection of the state, like beasts in a zoological garden." But the state cannot control terrorists, whose capability depends on the godlike ability to elude observation while demanding recognition. In *The Assignment*, where man distrusts the state for invading his privacy and the state distrusts man for his distrust (hello, Patriot Act), Dürrenmatt reconsiders our siblings, the terrorists:

> their case was a bit more complex, their goal being not an observed but an unobserved child's paradise, but because they experienced the world in which they lived as a prison where they were not only unjustly locked up but were left unattended and unobserved in one of the dungeons, they desperately sought to force themselves on the attention of their guards and thus step out of their unobserved condition into the limelight of public notice, which, however, they could achieve only by, paradoxically, drawing back into unobserved obscurity again and again, from the dungeon into the dungeon, unable, ever, to come out and be free, in short, humanity was about to return to its swaddling clothes, fundamentalists, idealists, moralists, and political Christers were doing their utmost to saddle unobserved humanity with the blessing of being observed, and therefore with meaning, for man, in the final analysis, was a pedant who couldn't get by without meaning and was therefore willing to put up with anything except the freedom to not give a damn about meaning.

[2005]

82 ❖ *Kaddish for the Jews (Soma Morgenstern)*

1.

Soma Morgenstern's elusive career is one of the strangest and most frustrating in modern literature. Many who know his work venerate it, yet it remains little known and generally unavailable, especially in the United States—where he lived most of his adult life, though he wrote exclusively in German. The one nation where he is widely read and discussed, thanks to the recent publication there of his complete works[1] (11 volumes),

---

[1] This remarkable achievement is the work of Ingolf Schulte, who came across Morgenstern while researching Joseph Roth and, in the words of Morgenstern's son, Dan, has devoted himself to "salvaging, organizing, and preparing for publication every word he could uncover." The publisher is zu Klampen. See footnote 3 for details.

is Germany, the focus of his rage. Morgenstern's masterwork, *The Third Pillar*, a crushing, illuminating, indispensable novel of the Holocaust, has been adapted as German radio and stage plays. At least one of his four novels has appeared posthumously (he died in 1976), usually to a mixed reception, in Austria, Switzerland, Israel, and Holland, and his memoirs of two close friends, Alban Berg and Joseph Roth, have been translated into French, Spanish, and Italian. Since 2002, he has been the subject of diverse papers at two conferences at Auburn University, in Alabama: one on Morgenstern's "lost world," the other on "Four Great Galician Storytellers": Morgenstern, Roth, W. H. Katz, and Manes Sperber.

None of his work is presently available in English, a conspicuous absence in this, the fiftieth anniversary of *The Third Pillar*'s initial appearance. Indeed, it is almost that long since it all but disappeared from American letters, despite a double-barreled 1955 sendoff by Farrar, Straus and the Jewish Publication Society; a spellbinding translation by Ludwig Lewisohn (who ranked Morgenstern with Proust and Mann); and favorable reviews. Other than as an e-book, it has not been reprinted. Morgenstern's readers have kept elements of his work alive, albeit chiefly in the realm of Conservative Judaism. In the 1920s and 1930s, as Morgenstern established himself in Vienna as a critic and fledgling novelist, his younger fans included the future theologian, mystic, and social activist Abraham J. Heschel. Three decades later, in New York, Heschel introduced Morgenstern to Rabbi Wolfe Kelman, the Vienna-born vice-president of the Rabbinical Assembly. A man of vast energy, passion, and obstinacy, Kelman championed Morgenstern, futilely nominating him for a Nobel Prize and encouraging Rabbi Jules Harlow to adapt passages of *The Third Pillar* in the prayer books he edited for the Assembly's publication division. Harlow included one passage in the Yom Kippur service— thereby rendering an excerpt from the novel Morgenstern characterized as "a necrology, a kaddish for the Jews" as a prelude to the Yitgadal.[2]

Morgenstern lived 35 years in the United States, relying, like Milosz and Singer, on translators. (During an early period on the West Coast, he visited Arnold Schoenberg, who tried to convince him to write in

---

[2] Rabbi Kelman introduced me to Morgenstern's work (the novels, published in the United States between 1946 and 1955, were plentifully available at secondhand bookstores) and, eventually, to Soma himself—before I realized that he was the father of my mentor, editor, and friend, jazz critic Dan Morgenstern. Not long before his death, Soma, a striking man (tall, lean, with a full shock of white hair) and captivating storyteller, spent an afternoon at our home, dining on pierogi, prepared in the manner described in his "Lost Son" trilogy (now called *Sparks in the Abyss*). Wolfe claimed to shy away from meeting writers he admired because they often disappointed him as people. He loved Soma not least because he lived up to the image of the man he had perceived in his work. I am indebted to Dan Morgenstern, and his 2004 paper, "Soma Morgenstern in America," for much biographical and bibliographical information included here.

English, emphasizing Conrad as an example. As Morgenstern recounted to reporter Israel Shenker, he responded, " 'Mr. Schoenberg, suppose I am a violinist and I come to New York and you tell me I have to be a cellist from today.' This he understood.") Yet after *The Third Pillar*, he published nothing, though he continued to write. His neglect has been attributed to the language gap and to a presumption—rife in the years before the 1950s breakthroughs by Bellow and Malamud—that Jewish fiction interested only Jews. In the 1970s, Kelman and others argued that something more pernicious was at stake: that Morgenstern had fallen afoul of the movement, supported by Jewish assimilators then and now, to universalize Nazi barbarism with platitudes about shared guilt. Morgenstern had attempted a work of art: fiction grounded in unforgiving specificity, antithetical to internationalism or smart theories of culpability.

Before and during the war, Morgenstern wrote his trilogy, *Sparks in the Abyss* (*Funken im Abgrund*), in which his essentially urban intelligence documents with compassion and longing the vanished life of Eastern Europe. In a setting where community customs are inseparable from issues of continuity, faith, and assimilation, he chose an approach suggesting Tolstoyan thoroughness and detail. Qualities of those novels, including humor, parody, and pining nostalgia, recur in *The Third Pillar*, but here the debate over Jewish integration is supplanted by a reckoning of the cost of Jewish redemption. The style, radically altered, meshes parable, fable, and prophetic testimony.

In Morgenstern's fiction, Judaism is vital less in its theological tenets (important as they are) than in its branding matter-of-factness. Morgenstern had lost his birthplace, adopted country, freedom, career, and members of his family not because of a pervasive breakdown in civilization, but because he was a Jew. If Judaism could get him killed, it could also effect his salvation. Morgenstern did not feel guilty (a glib response, as W. G. Sebald argues); he felt justified. In comprehending a crime of unfathomable magnitude, he required a severe rhetoric and an insuperable metaphor. He found both in the Bible: prophetic diction and the third pillar—the pillar of blood, specifically that of 1,100,000 children, offered God as a warranty for the Torah. *The Third Pillar*, a short work intensified by oracular prose and a time-shifting narrative-within-narrative structure, is a record of deliverance: "The time of atonement is over and redemption is at hand."

2.

He was born Salomo Morgenstern, in 1890, the youngest of three brothers and two sisters, in a village in Galicia, a predominantly Jewish region bordering Poland and the Ukraine, ruled by Austria. His mother called him Soma, a diminutive he adopted professionally around the time he began publishing, in 1923. (A misreading or mistyping of that unusual name may have saved his life, according to his son, Dan. While a refugee in Marseilles, he was asked if he knew a Sonia Morgenstern, whom the Nazis were trying to find; he said that he did, but no longer knew where she was.) He grew up speaking Yiddish, Hebrew, Polish, and Ukrainian, adding German on his father's advice that without it he would not be an educated person; this made it possible for him to attend high school and university, where he studied law. When Russian troops invaded Galicia at the outset of the war, in September 1914, Morgenstern, his sisters, and mother (his father had died a few years earlier) moved to Vienna. He served in the Austro-Hungarian army for the duration, and then earned his law doctorate in 1921. Morgenstern spent a few years in Berlin, publishing his first articles, including a study of Kafka, before returning to Vienna in 1928, where he married and worked as a journalist, writing mostly musical and theatrical criticism. He lived there nearly 20 years, seven of them as a cultural critic for *Frankfurter Zeitung*. His close ties to a community of artists that included Berg (he first met his wife in Berg's home), Roth, Robert Musil, Otto Klemperer, Theodor Adorno, Stefan Zweig, and others, inclined early commentators to mischaracterize him as an Austrian rather than as a Galician (his own preference) writer.

The rise of Chancellor Dollfus and his Christian Socialist Party scattered Morgenstern's circle. Dollfus inherited an impossible position: He was a Fascist who suspended Parliament and used the military to repress socialist resistance, but was also anti-German and determined to keep Austria independent. During his brief reign, Morgenstern fled to Paris (as did Roth), where he completed his first novel, *The Son of the Prodigal Son*, in 1934. That year, Hitler ordered the assassination of Dollfus in an unsuccessful attempt at a coup, and Morgenstern returned to Vienna. The novel was published in Berlin, in 1935, but non-Jews were prohibited from buying it and the printing ended up in one of Goebbels's bonfires. The Anschluss ended Morgenstern's ties to Austria: On the day the Germans entered, he took the last train back to Paris, where Roth had remained (he had published his masterpiece, *The Radetzky March*, in 1932). Urged on by Roth, Morgenstern completed a draft of the second novel in his trilogy, *In My Father's Pasture*, and began the concluding volume, *The Testimony of the Lost Son*. Roth died in 1939.

A year later, Morgenstern was declared an enemy alien and interned in two French concentration camps, at Montargis and Audierne, from which he escaped. He then traveled the exile's route to Marseilles, Casablanca, Lisbon, and New York, arriving in 1941. Only later did he learn that his eldest brother, a sister, and his mother had died, respectively, in Buchenwald, Auschwitz, and Theresienstadt. His wife, who was part Danish, and son were permitted to leave for Denmark, and did not see him again until they came to New York in 1947 (Morgenstern and his wife had grown apart and did not live together again until the last decade of his life). Morgenstern had spent most of his first two years in the United States in Beverly Hills, having driven cross-country with a friend, before settling in a New York hotel.

As in Vienna, Morgenstern's New York circle of friends included several prominent figures in the arts and journalism, among them the German-born actress Dolly Haas and her husband, caricaturist Al Hirschfeld, theater critic Brooks Atkinson, theater designer Boris Aaronson, film editor Paul Falkenberg (*M, Diary of a Lost Girl*), and two boyhood friends, conductor Jascha Horenstein and composer Karol Rathaus, as well as his frequent confidante Alma Mahler. With the support of Ludwig Lewisohn, Maurice Samuel, and other admirers, *The Son of the Lost Son* appeared in an English translation (by Joseph Leftwich and Peter Gross), in 1946, published simultaneously by Rinehart and the Jewish Publication Society. During the next few years, the JPS brought out *In My Father's Pasture* (translated by Lewisohn) and *The Testament of the Lost Son* (translated by Jacob Sloan and Samuel)—novels that would not be published in their original language, German, until the 1990s, when Ingolf Schulte prepared an edition of the complete works, most of which had never been published at all.[3] Morgenstern began *The Third Pillar* in 1946 and finished in 1952; after its publication, three years later (the first German edition appeared in Vienna in 1964), he worked on his autobiography and an unfinished novel but published nothing else of importance before his death, at 86.

Morgenstern's trilogy of Eastern Europe is a philosophical yet lyrical epic, admirable for its meticulous evocation of rural life and traditions, especially as detailed in the second volume. It begins in 1929, at a conference of Orthodox Jews in Vienna, and tracks the education of Alfred Mohylewski, the son of a Jew who had converted to Greek Orthodox Christianity. Alfred has known only the cosmopolitan community of assimilated Jews, but through the intervention of his uncle, he discovers

---

[3] The 11 volumes, with English translations of the German titles by Dan Morgenstern, are (1) *Joseph Roth's Escape and End: Memoirs*, (2) *Alban Berg and His Idols: Memoirs and Letters*, (3) *In Another Time: Youthful Years in Galicia* (reminiscences assembled by Schulte), (4–6) the three novels that make up *Sparks in the Abyss*, (7) *The Third Pillar*, (8) *Flight in France* (a novelistic work based on Morgenstern's internment and escape), (9) *Death Is a Flop* (an unfinished novel), (10) short stories, sketches, early plays, (11) the largest volume, containing his work for *Frankfurter Zeitung*, including music, theater, film, and literary criticism, sports and travel writing, and a brief diary kept during the period of the postwar Holocaust revelations. Only 4–7 have been published in English.

a liberating, alternative life in the seemingly idyllic province of Galicia. Yet that region's apparently settled ways mask political bickering, corrosive suspicion, and an environment of Christian distrust that culminates in the savage killing of a child. Kafkan deliberateness (as opposed to the clichés of Kafkaesque paranoia) marks Alfred's quest and Morgenstern's mapping of city and country, oppressor and victim, lost and found. It's there, too, in Morgenstern's representation of the lure of hard, communal, nonintellectual work. Like Kafka himself, Alfred ultimately longs to settle in Palestine. The three novels that comprise *Sparks in the Abyss* prefigure themes compressed into the crystalline density of *The Third Pillar*.

After the war, writing in New York, Morgenstern abandoned the epical manner of an essentially 19th-century form, along with the voice of a cultured European. Recognizing that he belonged to Judaism rather than to Europe, he wrote *The Third Pillar* as if by a man uninformed by literature, a man who had never read anything other than the Bible and is steeped in its parables, reveries, and horror. Acknowledging and defying Adorno's assertion that it is barbaric to write poetry after Auschwitz, Morgenstern devised an implacable voice, leavened with humor, parody, and nostalgia—with mundane detail and Judaic incantation. Wedding realism and fantasy, he reconfigured paradigms from Cain to the Golem, invoking them with visionary clarity while steering clear of psychology, self-pity, and moral ambiguity.

3.

The Third Pillar is set in March 1944, in a border town by the River Seret, which connects Poland and Ukraine, on the day the Soviets advance and Germans retreat. Before "the cleansing process," 26,000 Jews had lived here; now there are not enough for a minyan. Three publicans, foraging through ruins like three blind mice, find a box with an inscription they cannot understand; thinking it may contain food, they take it to an abandoned synagogue, where their attempts to pry it open fail. A miracle of sorts has taken place in this old shul. Crude drawings of crucified Jews appeared on a wall after the S.S. invaded, and though the Germans removed them more than once, the drawings reappeared unchanged. Set down near the drawings, the box assumes the world's weight and can no longer be budged. The publicans sniff at it: Two of them—a Christian who has secretly aided Jews to a hiding place along the Seret, and a Jew who pretends to be Christian—find it aromatic; the third, a German collaborator, is sickened.

The collaborator eventually leads a small band of fleeing Nazis and two priests to the synagogue. Even in flight, the S.S. soldiers want to execute the remaining Jews who escaped to the river through a tunnel in the shul's basement. Lured here by an unknown force, they soon discover that they are no more in control of events than they are of the box—which an officer recognizes as a gift that had been awarded his division the previous Christmas. A messenger appears, who instructs the S.S. that the box is to be regarded as a shrine. At the same time, survivors who escaped via the tunnel now return through it and set up a tribunal. This sequence of events is the setup for the trial that frames the rest of the narrative.

The next section, related by the Torah scribe Zacharia Hahoken, tells another miraculous story, which begins (like *The Son of the Lost Son*) in 1929, and details the birth and raising of two sets of twins: the sons, Nehemiah, destined to console his own people, and Jochanan, destined to console the whole world, and the daughters, Esther and Rachel, to whom they are betrothed. They come of age in a world where miracles are the bread of life—literally, in the instance of a bread loaf that lasts, like Maccabee's oil, for the nine months the boys are carried to term. Every character, every action is ordained to carry out this story: A local water carrier who saves the boys from drowning will turn up again as one of the publicans; a game of hide and seek becomes a paradigm of responsibility.

Most remarkable, for the reader, are the abrupt changes in tone, from Old Testament fury to paternal gentleness to political burlesque. As in the trilogy, Morgenstern pauses to explore the secular value of religious ritual, in this instance, the baking of matzoh and a comic travesty of nuptials—in effect, a story within the story within the story. The boys prepare for their bar mitzvahs with Socratic dialogues, amid prophecies of exile and devastation. Flee to the East, the families are warned: What "comes from the West no man, who is worthy of being a man, will survive." Survival is the Jews' primary weapon. "Did not the angel say to Ezra, 'The survivors are far more blessed than those who have died'?" This is a singular Jewish tenet, obviously at odds with Christianity and Islam.

A dreamlike night presages the invasion: "The night was cold and clear by the gleam of the new moon and the stars. In a sharp wind the icicles under the eaves tinkled. The slender sickle of the moon and the stars seemed gray and cold as though made of ice." And then: "The S.S. were upon us." The massacre begins when the S.S. invades the synagogue on the eve of Yom Kippur. At first, they merely demand the repeat of a prayer, reducing the worshippers to performing monkeys. Soon, thousands are driven into the forest and forced to dig their own graves. Others are butchered in the synagogue. During a cease-fire ("The mortally wounded had no place to fall. They bled to death in the arms of those who had not yet been wounded"), an S.S. officer incarnates the Kafkan bureaucrat: "We will teach the Jews to respect the regulations of the German army. This is a battle territory. Political assemblies are forbidden. These Jewish cheats, however, act as though they are praying and hold political meetings in all synagogues."

Then the slaughter of the children begins. In the turmoil, a mother has been separated from one of the twins, Rachel, who is betrothed to Jochanan. She asks an officer to let her fetch her child. He offers, in his "comfortable South German dialect," to "fetch the lassie for you!" In a scene that exemplifies Morgenstern's power and method, a tribunal witness recalls what happened next.

> With broad, tranquil tread, as though he were walking across a freshly mowed meadow, his rifle with fixed bayonet in his great peasant's fist, he traversed the breadth of the middle passage in the direction where the girl Rachel stood, petrified by terror and grief, over the body of her father. One or two paces from the child the S.S. man wound his other fist over the butt of his rifle. He gave a brief thrust, ran the bayonet through the bosom of the child, lifted her up and with that same slow, comfortable tread he returned across the passage, his gun with the bayoneted child bleeding high in the air.
>
> Everyone, the light of whose eyes was not extinguished by this sight, remembered the tread of that S.S. man. His comrades looked on with grins. But the mustering out process was interrupted. When he had reached the spot where the mother of the victim had fallen in a faint, the S.S. man lowered his gun above her and let the dead child slide with precision onto the lap of the mother. Then he said, "Now the whole *mishpoche* is nicely united."
>
> "You . . . murderer . . . German! The lightning will slay you!" Jochanan cried into the creature's face. The S.S. man, as though hardly trusting his own ears, listened with astonished eyes to the boy's voice. Then he swung the butt of his gun high.
>
> And now the thing happened. Someone—and to this day one knows not who—spat into the murderer's face in a precise arc. The spittle hit the man between the eyes. The swinging rifle fell from his fists. With a cry: "My face is burning up!" the assassin crashed on the floor. Three S.S. men hastened forward and tried to lift him up. But when they saw his face, which had been burned crisply to the very bone, they too took fright and let him lie.
>
> After a brief consolation one of them went to the commander, who stood on the top of the stair and in the twilight of the evening could

not clearly oversee the bloody goings on. Another S.S. man who had been near the dead culprit recognized Jochanan and going near him ran the bayonet through him. Jochanan fell down next to Rachel. He had been standing above her. A game of childhood had betrothed them; death wedded them forever.

These sentences begin with long, scrupulously composed phrases, and wind down into short declarative statements, as though the narrator had lost his wind. They restrain the mounting hysteria of the event with measured words like *precise* and *extinguish*, while combining the mark of Cain, a grisly Yiddish joke, and the miraculous. They prepare the reader for worse to come, as the Germans burn the Torahs and attempt to turn the synagogue into a brothel. The S.S. is ordered to additionally dehumanize the mounting dead by calling them Figures.

At which point, as if defeated by realism, even of a magical sort, Morgenstern switches to heavy-handed satire and a Grosz-like burlesque set in the inner precincts of the "highest triumvirate of murder," where The Screamer (given to "convulsive ranting") and his battling deputies, Marshal Fat-Belly and Club-Foot, the chief weaver of lies, discuss the pros and cons of genocide—the mistake of creating martyrs and the conclusion that the dead must be defiled. They arrive at the idea of turning their flesh into soap and their hair into mattresses: "We have made a shameful thing of their lives; we must desecrate their deaths." They turn to science: "When you have a cynical notion, the best thing to do is to submit it to the scientists. It is surprising how many clever answers our professors had, when this problem was brought before them." They snicker at the capitulation of the Vatican. But what of the Second Coming? "Is it not possible that the Redeemer will be born again somewhere as a Jewish child? Will you take it upon yourself to make soap of the body of the Redeemer?" The Screamer "relished" the question: "I have not seceded from the Church, because I have always avoided giving a warning to powerful enemies. The Church is still a powerful enemy. But once the Jews are exterminated, the very root will be gone and the whole of Christianity will drop like a rotten tooth out of the pus-filled jaw of Europe. I secede from the Church? I will force the Church to secede from Europe! History asks no questions."

The next chapter switches, no less abruptly, to statistics of the genocide and a commentary on those who ignored cattle cars passing through their towns and farms—a theme Claude Lanzmann pursued decades later in his monumental film, *Shoah*. Germany begins to manufacture Warranted Genuine Figure Soap, and the first box is addressed to the S.S. division at the Seret ("With the gratitude of the leader. Christmas, 1943).

Now that box may be opened: It contains a soap statue of Jochanan. Even a messenger from Satan, who attends the tribunal, is appalled: "What the Germans call devilish, the devil calls German." The messenger observes, "It cannot be unknown to this court that once upon a time my Master had six pairs of wings and bore the title: Malackh shel rahamin, the angel of compassion." He concludes, "Satan stands, as we all do, in tears."

The twin Nehemiah delivers the final sentence, which involves a riposte to God and the Zionist determination to leave Europe for Jerusalem. "Like the pillar of fire by night, like the pillar of cloud by day, thus will this our third pillar, the pillar of blood lead us through all the wildernesses into the Holy Land." This is the beginning of redemption, the 1,100,000 slain children a pledge that can be achieved only by the living, through a physical and spiritual transformation. "There is no vicarious suffering, even as there is no vicarious remorse and expiation."

Morgenstern does not blink at the difficulty. As the tribunal comes to a close, the Soviet army arrives, its general a Jew pretending to be otherwise. The worshippers bow before the Russian liberators much as they had to the Nazis, weighing passivity and generosity against defiance and recrimination. A comedy of reasoning follows in the face of yet another miracle: The crucifixion graffiti fades from the synagogue wall. The Soviet leader boasts, "We have fixed this matter of redemption. We don't need miracles." Russia is beginning a new book in history and the surviving Jews may write their own chapter, but if they fail to cooperate "the wheel of history will crush you as it rolls over you."

Not one to let a metaphor go unamplified, the tribunal judge responds: "Many wheels of history have rolled over us into the abysses of the night and plunged with broken axles into the darkness of oblivion, the while we have arisen again, we, who are the perpetual witnesses of the Creator, we, who are the companions of Eternity." Meanwhile, the priests decide to report the miracle of the vanished drawings to Rome: "Then Rome will decide whether it was a miracle." And the Russian Commissar will report it to Moscow: "Moscow will decide whether a miracle has taken place." The Jews, with a minyan assembled, thanks to the presence of the Russian general, recite the kaddish for the dead, which "says rather than sings: I know how difficult, how dangerous, how piteous it is to be a human being. I know, too, how fair and great and glorious it is to be a human being."

4.

Morgenstern's ending is too shrewd to be conclusive or contented. The Yitgadal, with its affirmation of the creator and the creation, provides a temporary relief from the terror. But it is just a prayer, solemnization, ritual—a token in the struggle for renewal. *The Third Pillar* concludes with a Joycean/Jewish series of yeses, yet the context is one of foreboding. Describing the Yom Kippur massacre, Morgenstern writes, "This was a species of soldiery such as the history of the world has not seen; such as the history of the world will never see again—unless, in truth, humanity in blasphemous self-forgetfulness ever again permits that people to raise its blood-drenched head." But it isn't Germany's blood-drenched head he fears. At the moment of liberation, he recognizes the potential for another juggernaut, this one coming from the East. He could not foresee that "species of soldier" arising in Cambodia, Uganda, Bosnia, Rwanda, Iraq, and elsewhere, but he had no illusions about the fixed evil of genocide. In this regard the Old Testament wrath of Morgenstern's kaddish is profoundly universal, even as he nails the crime against the Jews as a crime against the Jews.

[2005]

Index

Note: The titles of books, plays, record albums, and other major works are credited, parenthetically, to their authors. Feature films, television show, radio shows, and comics are identified, parenthetically, as such. Titles in quotes, rather than italics, refer to songs, short films, and short stories.